Ericksonian Psychotherapy
Volume I: Structures

Editorial Review Board

Ericksonian Psychotherapy

Volume I: Structures

edited by

Jeffrey K. Zeig, Ph.D.

BRUNNER/MAZEL, *Publishers* • New York

Library of Congress Cataloging in Publication Data
Main entry under title:

Ericksonian psychotherapy.

   Proceedings of the Second International Congress on Ericksonian Approaches to Hypnosis and Psychotherapy, held in Dec. 1983, in Phoenix, Ariz.
   Contents: v. 1. Structures—v. 2. Clinical applications.
   1. Erickson, Milton H.—Congresses. 2. Hypnotism—Therapeutic use—Congresses. 3. Psychotherapy—Congresses. I. Zeig, Jeffrey K., 1947-   .
II. International Congress on Ericksonian Approaches to Hypnosis and Psychotherapy (2nd; 1983; Phoenix, Ariz,)

[DNLM: 1. Erickson, Milton H. 2. Hypnosis—congresses. 3. Psychotherapy—congresses. WM 415 E6854 1983]
RC490.5.E75E76 1985   616.89'162   84-24331
ISBN 0-87630-380-7 (v. 1)
ISBN 0-87630-381-5 (v. 2)

Published by
BRUNNER/MAZEL, INC.
19 Union Square
New York, New York 10003

To Sherron S. Peters and Nicole Rachel Zeig

"Don't you think the Congresses should have their rewards?"

" Each person is a unique individual. Hence, psychotherapy should be formulated to meet the uniqueness of the individual's needs, rather than tailoring the person to fit the Procrustean bed of a hypothetical theory of human behavior. **"**

Milton H. Erickson, M.D.

Contents

Introduction

The two volumes entitled *Ericksonian Psychotherapy* present the proceedings of the Second International Congress on Ericksonian Psychotherapy held in Phoenix, Arizona, December 1983. Volume I on *Structures* includes theoretical issues and descriptions of technique. Volume II on *Clinical Application* presents case materials and information relevant to immediate application.

The First International Congress on Ericksonian Approaches to Hypnosis and Psychotherapy was held December 4-8, 1980, in Phoenix. Erickson was a member of the organizing committee of that Congress and one of the purposes of the meeting was to give him the opportunity to see the impact of his work. Unfortunately, he died eight and a half months prior to the Congress. The proceedings of the first Congress were published in *Ericksonian Approaches to Hypnosis and Psychotherapy* (Brunner/Mazel, 1982).

Whereas the first Congress was organized to honor Erickson, the second Congress was intended to broaden and advance Ericksonian methodology, and it had a different tone.

CONGRESS FORMAT

The program was academic, experiential, and interactive. The academic program consisted of keynote addresses, invited presentations, accepted papers, and panels. In total, 100 speeches were made. The faculty was composed of 125 members (including moderators and co-presenters).

It is the academic portion of the Congress that is reported in these proceedings. Most of the 100 presentations were submitted for publication. Of those papers, 76 are included in the present text. A discussion by Haley and Weakland that was part of the Congress media program is also included.

The experiential component of the Congress consisted of three-hour workshops that were held each day. In total, 75 workshops were offered. A unique feature added to the workshop was small group practicums.

Each three-hour practicum consisted of no more than 12 students and was led by a faculty member. Topics included utilization of hypnotic phenomena, pain control, confusion technique, habit problems, metaphor, and family therapy.

On the third day of the Congress, the format changed to allow for interactive events; no workshops were conducted and no papers were presented. Rather, that day consisted of demonstrations, conversation hours, group inductions, discussions of videotapes of Milton Erickson, and special topical panels. Also presented was a special keynote address on Erickson's child-rearing techniques, featuring a panel composed of six of Erickson's eight children.

The evening programs of the Congress included an authors' hour, media events, a hospitality reception, and a banquet.

The Second International Congress was even larger than the 1980 Congress, probably making it the largest professional meeting held on the topic of hypnosis. More than 2,000 attendees came from 19 countries, a striking indication of the continuing influence and growth of the therapeutic legacy of Milton H. Erickson.

ACKNOWLEDGMENTS

The assistance of a great many individuals was instrumental in the success of the meeting. I would like to take this opportunity to thank them.

The following professionals reviewed abstracts of papers submitted for presentation at the Congress: Joseph Barber, Ph.D., Stephen Gilligan, Ph.D., Melvin Hector, M.D., and Bill O'Hanlon, M.S.

The Editorial Review Board is listed in the front of the book. The editors made an important contribution in reviewing papers for publication in these volumes. Each paper was read by a minimum of two editors and a maximum of seven.

On behalf of the Board of Directors of the Erickson Foundation, I want to take this additional opportunity to thank the distinguished Faculty of the meeting. It was their theoretical and clinical contributions that made the Congress a successful training event.

The staff of the Erickson Foundation worked endless hours in handling the registrations, meeting arrangements, and administrative tasks. The following people had the temerity to work on both the first and second Congresses: Sherron Peters, the Administrative Director of the Foundation, Mildred Pardee, Bookkeeper, and Barbara Bellamy, Administrative Assistant. Barbara deserves special recognition for the excellent job she did compiling the Congress syllabus. Other Foundation staff who were instrumental included Lori Weiers, Secretary and Coordinator of Volunteers, Curtis Stone, Tracy McVey, and Ranee Tran.

A number of volunteers helped both prior to and at the Congress, including Charles and Jean Achtenberg, Hazel Arnett, Alfred Cox, Ed Hancock, Philip McAvoy, Will Weiers, Martin Zeig, Ruth Zeig, and Edythe Zeig. In addition, there were 79 student volunteers who served as monitors, and photographers, and who staffed the registration and continuing education desks.

Deserving special recognition are Mrs. Elizabeth Erickson and Kristina Erickson, M.D., who gave generously of their time and energy to make many executive decisions about the Congress. They have worked tirelessly on behalf of the Erickson Foundation.

Jeffrey K. Zeig, Ph.D.
Director
The Milton H. Erickson Foundation

The Milton H. Erickson
Foundation, Inc.

The Milton H. Erickson Foundation, Inc. is a federal nonprofit corporation. It was formed to promote and advance the contributions made to the health sciences by the late Milton H. Erickson, M.D., during his long and distinguished career. The Foundation is dedicated to training health and mental health professionals. Strict eligibility requirements are maintained for attendance at our training events or to receive our educational materials. The Milton H. Erickson Foundation, Inc. does not discriminate on the basis of race, color, national, or ethnic origin. Directors of the Milton H. Erickson Foundation, Inc. are: Jeffrey K. Zeig, Ph.D., Sherron S. Peters, Elizabeth M. Erickson, and Kristina K. Erickson, M.D.

ERICKSON ARCHIVES

In December 1980, the Foundation began collecting audiotapes, videotapes, and historical material on Dr. Erickson for the Erickson Archives. Our goal is to have a central repository of historical material on Erickson. More than 300 hours of videotape and audiotape have already been donated to the Foundation.

The Erickson Archives are available to interested and qualified professionals who wish to come to Phoenix to independently study the audiotapes and videotapes that are housed at the Foundation. There is a nominal charge for use of the Archives. Please write if you are interested in details.

PUBLICATIONS OF THE ERICKSON FOUNDATION

Books

The following books, in addition to the present volumes, are published by Brunner/Mazel, Publishers:

A Teaching Seminar with Milton Erickson (J. Zeig, Ed. & Commentary) is a transcript, with commentary, of a one-week teaching seminar held for professionals by Dr. Erickson in his home in August, 1979.

Ericksonian Approaches to Hypnosis and Psychotherapy (J. Zeig, Ed.) contains the edited proceedings of the First International Erickson Congress.

Newsletter

The Milton H. Erickson Foundation publishes a newsletter for professionals three times a year to inform its readers of the activities of the Foundation. Articles and notices that relate to Ericksonian approaches to hypnosis and psychotherapy are included.

The Ericksonian Monographs

The Foundation has initiated the publication of *The Ericksonian Monographs*, which will appear on an irregular basis, up to three issues per year. Edited by Stephen Lankton, M.S.W., the *Monographs* will publish only the highest quality articles on Ericksonian hypnosis and psychotherapy, including technique, theory, and research. Manuscripts should be sent to Stephen Lankton, P.O. Box 958, Gulf Breeze, Florida 32561. For subscription information, contact Brunner/Mazel, Publishers.

Audio and Video Training Tapes

The Milton H. Erickson Foundation has available for purchase professionally recorded audiotapes from its meetings. Professionally produced video cassettes of one-hour clinical demonstrations by members of the faculty of the 1981, 1982, and 1984 Erickson Foundation Seminars and the 1983 Erickson Congress can also be purchased from the Foundation.

Audiotapes of Milton H. Erickson

The Erickson Foundation distributes tapes of lectures by Milton Erickson from the 1950s and 1960s when his voice was strong. Releases in our audiotape series are announced in the *Newsletter*.

Training Videotapes Featuring Hypnotic Inductions Conducted by Milton H. Erickson

The Process of Hypnotic Induction: A Training Videotape Featuring Inductions Conducted by Milton H. Erickson in 1964. Jeffrey K. Zeig, Ph.D., discusses the process of hypnotic induction and describes the micro-dynamics of technique that Erickson used in this 1964 induction. Length: 2 hours.

Symbolic Hypnotherapy. Jeffrey K. Zeig, Ph.D., presents information on using symbols in psychotherapy and hypnosis. Segments of hypno-therapy conducted by Milton Erickson with the same subject on two consecutive days in 1978 are shown. Zeig discusses the microdynamics of Erickson's symbolic technique.

Length: 2 hours, 40 minutes.

Videotapes are available in all U.S. formats, as well as in the European standard.

TRAINING OPPORTUNITIES

The Erickson Foundation organizes the International Congress on Ericksonian Approaches to Hypnosis and Psychotherapy. These meet-ings are held triennially; the first two meetings were held in 1980 and 1983. Each was attended by over 2,000 professionals. The next Inter-national Congress is scheduled for December 3-7, 1986, in Phoenix, Arizona.

In the intervening years, the Foundation organizes national seminars. The seminars are limited to approximately 450 attendees and they em-phasize skill development in hypnotherapy. The 1981, 1982 and 1984 seminars were held in San Francisco, Dallas and Los Angeles respec-tively.

Regional workshops are held regularly in various locations.

Programs held at the Foundation include beginning and advanced ongoing training in hypnotherapy and strategic family therapy.

All training programs are announced in the Foundation's *Newsletter*.

ELIGIBILITY

Training programs, the newsletter, audiotapes, and videotapes are available to professionals in health-related fields, including physicians, doctoral level psychologists, and dentists who are qualified for mem-bership in or are members of their respective professional organizations (AMA, APA, ADA). They are also available to professionals with grad-uate degrees in areas related to mental health (M.S.W., M.S.N., M.A., or M.S.) from accredited institutions. Full-time graduate students in accredited programs in the above fields must supply a letter from their department certifying their student status if they wish to attend training events, subscribe to the newsletter, or purchase tapes.

Faculty of the 1983 International Congress on Ericksonian Approaches to Hypnosis and Psychotherapy

FACULTY

Leo Alexander, M.D.
West Newton, MA
Nachman Alon, M.A.
Yaffo, Israel
*Lonnie Barbach, Ph.D.
Mill Valley, CA
*Joseph Barber, Ph.D.
Los Angeles, CA
*John O. Beahrs, M.D.
Portland, OR
*Patrick J. Brady
Quincy, MA
*David L. Calof
Seattle, WA
Chong Tong Mun, M.D.
Singapore, Singapore
*James C. Coyne, Ph.D.
Berkeley, CA
*O. Spurgeon English, M.D.
Narberth, PA
Allan Erickson, M.S.
Columbia, MD
Elizabeth M. Erickson, B.A.
Phoenix, AZ

Kristina K. Erickson, M.D.
Columbia, MO
Lance Erickson, Ph.D.
Ann Arbor, MI
Robert Erickson, M.A.
Phoenix, AZ
Betty Alice Erickson Elliott, B.A.
Dallas, TX
John H. Frykman, M.Div.
San Francisco, CA
Anthony Gaito, A.C.S.W.
Syosset, NY
Stephen G. Gilligan, Ph.D.
Newton Highlands, MA
*David Gordon, M.A.
Lancaster, CA
*Harold Greenwald, Ph.D.
San Diego, CA
Jay Haley, M.A.
Rockville, MD
F. William Hanley, M.D.
Vancouver, BC, Canada
*Norman W. Katz, Ph.D.
Albuquerque, NM

*Indicates faculty who also presented invited workshops.

Roxanna Erickson Klein, M.S.
  Dallas, TX
Moris Kleinhauz, M.D.
  Ramat-Chen, Israel
*Alfred Lange, Ph.D.
  Amsterdam, Netherlands
*Carol H. Lankton, M.A.
  Gulf Breeze, FL
*Stephen R. Lankton, A.C.S.W.
  Gulf Breeze, FL
*Jean Lassner, M.D.
  Paris, France
*Marc Lehrer, Ph.D.
  Santa Cruz, CA
Alan F. Leveton, M.D.
  San Francisco, CA
Camillo Loriedo, M.D.
  Rome, Italy
*Herbert S. Lustig, M.D.
  Ardmore, PA
*Cloe Madanes
  Rockville, MD
Judith Mazza, Ph.D.
  Takoma Park, MD
Jesse S. Miller, Ph.D.
  Berkeley, CA
*Bill O'Hanlon, M.S.
  Blair, NE
*Robert E. Pearson, M.D.
  Houston, TX
*Martin Reiser, Ed.D.
  Los Angeles, CA

Madeleine Richeport, Ph.D.
  Santurce, Puerto Rico
*Michele Ritterman, Ph.D.
  Oakland, CA
*Sidney Rosen, M.D.
  New York, NY
*Deborah Ross, Ph.D.
  Santa Cruz, CA
*Ernest L. Rossi, Ph.D.
  Los Angeles, CA
Hans-Ulrich Schachtner,
  Dipl Psych
  Munich, West Germany
*Irving I. Secter, D.D.S., M.A.
  Lauderdale Lakes, FL
*Lynn Segal, L.C.S.W.
  Palo Alto, CA
*Margaret T. Singer, Ph.D.
  Berkeley, CA
*Charles R. Stern, Ph.D.
  Detroit, MI
Sandra M. Sylvester, Ph.D.
  Tucson, AZ
*Kay F. Thompson, D.D.S.
  Carnegie, PA
*Richard Van Dyck, M.D.
  Oegstgeest, Netherlands
*Paul Watzlawick, Ph.D.
  Palo Alto, CA
*Jeffrey K. Zeig, Ph.D.
  Phoenix, AZ

FACULTY PRESENTING WORKSHOPS ONLY

Norma Barretta, Ph.D.
  San Pedro, CA
Philip Barretta, M.A.
  San Pedro, CA

Richard Fisch, M.D.
  Palo Alto, CA
Edward Goodman, Ph.D.
  Dallas, TX

---

*Indicates faculty who also presented invited workshops.

Alan Griffin, Ph.D.
  Richardson, TX
Marion R. Moore, M.D.
  Memphis, TN

Lars-Eric Unestahl, Ph.D.
  Orebro, Sweden
John H. Weakland
  Palo Alto, CA

FACULTY SERVING ON PANELS ONLY

Carrell Dammann, Ph.D.
  Atlanta, GA

Carl Hammerschlag, M.D.
  Phoenix, AZ

ACCEPTED PAPERS

James R. Allen, M.D.
  Tulsa, OK
Brian M. Alman, Ph.D.
  San Diego, CA
Daniel L. Araoz, Ed.D.
  Mineola, NY
Christopher J. Beletsis, M.A.
  La Jolla, CA
Ronald R. Brown, Ph.D.
  Knoxville, TN
John D. Buksbazen, M.A. cand.
  Los Angeles, CA
Robert A. Burnham, Ph.D. cand.
  Cambridge, MA
Lisa Chiara, M.A.
  La Jolla, CA
Henry T. Close, Th.M.
  Coral Gables, FL
Klaus G. Deissler, Dipl Psych
  Marburg, West Germany
Richard E. Dimond, Ph.D.
  Springfield, IL
Yvonne M. Dolan, M.A.
  Denver, CO
John Edgette, M.S.
  Philadelphia, PA
Jeffrey B. Feldman, Ph.D.
  New York, NY
Steven H. Feldman, M.A.
  Seattle, WA

Julian D. Ford, Ph.D.
  Burbank, CA
Michael E. Forgy, A.C.S.W.
  Le Claire, IA
William B. Freeman, Jr.
  Burlington, VT
Wilhelm Gerl, Dipl Psych
  Munich, West Germany
Peter W. Gester, Dipl Psych
  Marburg, West Germany
Lawrence R. Gindhart, M.A.
  Indianapolis, IN
Eric Greenleaf, Ph.D.
  Berkeley, CA
D. Corydon Hammond, Ph.D.
  Salt Lake City, UT
Ronald A. Havens, Ph.D.
  Springfield, IL
C.A.L. Hoogduin, M.D.
  Delft, Netherlands
Lynn D. Johnson, Ph.D.
  Salt Lake City, UT
Marc Z. Kessler, Ph.D.
  Burlington, VT
Sung C. Kim, Ph.D.
  San Francisco, CA
Dee Krauss, Ph.D.
  Seal Beach, CA
Dennis Leri, M.A.
  San Francisco, CA

John D. Lovern, Ph.D.
  Marina del Rey, CA
Don W. Malon, Ph.D.
  Clayton, MO
Dan C. Overlade, Ph.D.
  Pensacola, FL
Burkhard Peter, Dipl Psych
  Munich, West Germany
Noelle M. Poncelet, M.S.W.
  Menlo Park, CA
Mark Reese, M.A.
  San Diego, CA
Helmut Relinger, Ph.D.
  Berkeley, CA
David Rigler, Ph.D.
  Santa Cruz, CA
George A. Sargent, Ph.D.
  Vista, CA
Gunther Schmidt, M.D.
  Heidelberg, West Germany
John C. Simpson, Ph.D.
  Charlotte, NC
Donna M. Spencer, Ph.D.
  St. Louis, MO

Harry E. Stanton, Ph.D.
  Hobart, Tasmania
George Stone, M.S.W.
  Morrill, NE
Bruce L.M. Tanenbaum, M.D.
  Reno, NV
Bernhard Trenkle, Dipl Psych
  Heidelberg, West Germany
James E. Waun, M.D.
  Ludington, MI
Dawn M. White, Ph.D.
  Whiteriver, AZ
James W. Whiteside, Ph.D. cand.
  Charlotte, NC
James Wilk, M.A. (Oxon.), M.Sc.
  Milwaukee, WI
J. Adrian Williams, Ph.D.
  Charleston, IL
R. Reid Wilson, Ph.D.
  Cambridge, MA
Michael D. Yapko, Ph.D.
  San Diego, CA
Hillel Zeitlin, M.S.W.
  Berkeley, CA

MODERATORS

James R. Allen, M.D.
  Tulsa, OK
Neil Di Capua, D.D.S.
  Woodland Hills, CA
Michael J. Diamond, Ph.D.
  Los Angeles, CA
Richard E. Dimond, Ph.D.
  Springfield, IL
Bengt Essler, D.D.S.
  Stockholm, Sweden
Jeffrey B. Feldman, Ph.D.
  New York, NY
Lawrence R. Gindhart, M.A.
  Indianapolis, IN

David Henderson, Ed.D.
  Mequon, WI
C.A.L. Hoogduin, M.D.
  Delft, Netherlands
Lynn D. Johnson, Ph.D.
  Salt Lake City, UT
David Northway, M.A.
  Eugene, OR
Jane A. Parsons, C.S.W.
  New York, NY
Helmut Relinger, Ph.D.
  Berkeley, CA
Donna M. Spencer, Ph.D.
  St. Louis, MO

Eric C. Steese, Ph.D.
  Olympia, WA
Michael D. Yapko, Ph.D.
  San Diego, CA

Lenora M. Yuen, Ph.D.
  Palo Alto, CA

Ericksonian Psychotherapy
Volume I: Structures

PART I

Keynote Addresses

Paul Watzlawick and Ernest Rossi are clinical psychologists with Jungian backgrounds who have interests in investigating philosophical issues related to human consciousness.

Paul Watzlawick, Ph.D., has been a research associate and principal investigator at the Mental Research Institute in Palo Alto since 1960. Watzlawick is a clinical professor in the Department of Psychiatry and Behavioral Sciences at Stanford University Medical Center. He serves on a number of editorial boards and has received a number of awards, including the Distinguished Achievement Award from the American Family Therapy Association (1981).

The international impact of Watzlawick's work is substantial. His writings have probably been translated into more languages than those of any other strategic practitioner. At the time of the Erickson Congress, he had authored and coauthored nine books published in 46 editions. Familiarity with his work is essential for all serious students of psychotherapy.

In his chapter, Watzlawick notes that strategic and Ericksonian methods are based on doing rather than understanding. Communication is both indicative and injunctive. It is the injunctive characteristics of language that induce change.

Ernest L. Rossi, Ph.D., is a clinical psychologist based in the Los Angeles area. He is on the faculty of the C. G. Jung Institute in southern California and is a member of the Editorial Board of the American Journal of Clinical Hypnosis.

Irvington, Inc., has published his books on Erickson. There are three volumes coauthored with Milton Erickson: Hypnotic

Realities, Hypnotherapy: An Exploratory Casebook, *and* Experiencing Hypnosis: Therapeutic Approaches to Altered States. *He has edited* The Collected Papers of Milton H. Erickson *(4 volumes); and he is currently coediting volumes on Erickson's lectures in the 1950s and 1960s. Rossi has been tireless in making material on Erickson available to practitioners.*

As far as his own areas of investigation are concerned, Rossi has written extensively about dreams and authored a volume entitled Dreams and the Growth of Personality: Expanding Awareness of Psychotherapy *(Pergamon Press). Recently, he has been conducting theoretical inquiries into neurophysiological manifestations that can be of interest to psychotherapists.*

Rossi reviews, elucidates, and extends some of the contributions made by other faculty members at the Congress. He presents previously unpublished anecdotes about his relationship with Erickson and points to the importance of observing minimal cues in the naturalistic (nonformal) use of hypnotherapy. Also, he notes that it is important for clinicians to extend investigations into the realms of physiology.

Chapter 1

Hypnotherapy Without Trance

Paul Watzlawick

My thesis is the obvious fact that many aspects of psychotherapy are unclear, debated, esoteric and contradictory, and that especially its main vehicle—language—is insufficiently understood.

What I would like to show is that some properties of language can be called therapeutic in and of themselves; they can help change human behavior not because of their *content*, but because of their *structure*. Curiously, these effects of language have found little attention in general psychotherapy, while in hypnosis they have been used for a long time.

Before going into detail I want to stress that nothing of what follows should be construed as implying a monadic view of human behavior (i.e., the traditional view that people live as isolated individuals and therefore can be treated as monads), which ignores the basic tenets of the interactional, systemic viewpoint. As everybody knows, different as the traditional schools of therapy may be, they are all based on a view of language as the vehicle of explanation, confrontation and interpretation; hence, in most cases, as the vehicle of insight.

But language has a far greater potential. Take the example of the famous thirteenth century experiment, carried out by Emperor Frederick II and reported by his chronicler Fra Salimbene di Parma (1926). The emperor wanted to know whether infants who were isolated since birth from exposure to human language would spontaneously begin to speak Greek, Latin or Hebrew. Unfortunately, the experimental subjects all died. Seven centuries later René Spitz (1945, pp. 53–74) provided the explanation of this lethal outcome through his studies of hospitalism and marasmus.

That language can influence people has, of course, been the object of study for much longer—at least since the fifth century B.C. when the science of rhetoric as a way of convincing people (and thus changing

5

their outlook on reality) was developed by the early Greek philosophers.

It is this use of language to which my title, "Hypnotherapy Without Trance," refers. In general terms, my topic has to do with linguistic structures—or language-games, as Wittgenstein would have called them—that have a virtually hypnotic effect, although no formal trance induction precedes them. Especially in the second half of his professional life, Milton Erickson used such structures with increasing frequency, and this use of language has become an essential part of our work at the Mental Research Institute. (I am, of course, aware of the fact that Erickson was a master not only of the use of verbal language, but also of nonverbal communication.)

Hypnotherapy without trance, then, is meant to include those language-games which have their origin (or are at least used predominantly) in hypnosis, but can be taken over and applied to the larger context of general psychotherapy. The following list of techniques and/or interventions immediately comes to mind, but is not meant to be all-inclusive:

1) Learning and using the client's "language";
2) Avoidance of "n"-words (negations) and, in general, of negative formulations;
3) Puns, condensations, innuendos, etc.;
4) Preempting;
5) Unresolved remnants;
6) Utilization of resistance (and even its deliberate creation for the purpose of subsequent utilization);
7) Storytelling and the use of other metaphors;
8) The confusion technique;
9) The "worst fantasy" technique.

Using the terminology of cerebral asymmetry theory in a sloppy way, one may consider most of these interventions "right-hemispheric"—if only in the sense that they utilize some of the properties attributed to the functioning of the right half of the brain, but also in the sense that they depart from the previously mentioned traditional language of psychotherapy. The difference between these two "languages" was once stated succinctly by Galen (1974):

> Parts of the experience of attending a symphony concert are not readily expressed in words, and the concept "democracy requires informed participation" is hard to convey in images.

The language of description and explanation is called *indicative*, and for a long time it was considered the only conceivable language of science. For instance, in his book, *La Morale et la Science*, the French mathematician and philosopher, Henri Poincaré (1913) wrote:

> The principles of science, the postulates of geometry are, and can only be, in the indicative mood; [. . .] and on the basis of science there is not, and there cannot be, anything else. [. . .] Therefore, even the most subtle dialectician may juggle these principles as he wishes, [. . .] whatever he will get from this will be in the indicative. He will never obtain a proposition that says: do this, or don't do that. (p. 22)

About 60 years later, especially this last sentence had lost its dogmatic character. In his book, *Laws of Form*, the British logician George Spencer Brown (1973) mentions, almost in passing, that even the language of science is more an *injunctive* than a descriptive one; one that says precisely, "Do this!":

> Even natural science appears to be more dependent upon injunctions than we are usually prepared to admit. The professional initiation of the man of science consists not so much in reading the proper textbooks, as in obeying injunctions such as "look down that microscope." But it is not out of order for men of science, having looked down the microscope, now to describe to each other, and to discuss amongst themselves, what they have seen, and to write papers and textbooks describing it. (p. 78)

And further:

> It may be helpful at this stage to realize that the primary form of mathematical communication is not description, but injunction. In this respect it is comparable with practical art forms like cookery, in which the taste of a cake, although literally indescribable can be conveyed to a reader in the form of a set of injunctions called the recipe. Music is a similar art form, the composer does not even attempt to describe the set of sounds he has in mind, much less the set of feelings occasioned through them, but writes down a set of commands which, if they are obeyed by the reader, can result in a reproduction, to the reader, of the composer's original experience. (p. 77)

One can hardly fail to grasp the importance of Brown's remarks for our field. All therapy is concerned with conveying to the client the essence of experiences that are difficult or even impossible to communicate in descriptive language. It is obvious that the main difference between hypnosis and other forms of therapy is that the former always has employed injunctive language.

In this connection it is useful to point to yet another important lesson that hypnosis can teach general therapy. Those of us who work with injunctions—simple or paradoxical behavior prescriptions, homework assignments, rituals and the like—know that they must be given in virtually posthypnotic language. In fact, the mistake most likely committed by the novice is the tendency to cram the prescription into one or two brief sentences, and then to be disappointed if clients completely forgot about it, misunderstood it, or were otherwise unmotivated to carry it out.

But how, our clients sometimes ask, can "mere" talk change "facts"? It is at this juncture that the undeniable results of hypnosis force us into rethinking some of our seemingly most "obvious" views of reality. If, in December 1983, one were to point out that the vast majority of all our decisions and actions are based on communicated information, few people would find this as novel and remarkable as it might have sounded in the mid-fifties, when the Bateson group began to study the behavioral effects of communication. And yet, we rarely are aware of this fact in our everyday lives; we treat communicated information and information that is provided by our immediate perception as being virtually the same. Those present at the Erickson Congress who never have been to Phoenix before obviously believed, without a shred of certainty or any direct proof whatsoever, that the city really existed, that there would be hotels, this conference and hundreds of other similar "facts." They relied on hearsay, maps, the information supplied by airlines and travel agents, and even Jeffrey Zeig's program. In other words, they behaved *as if* Phoenix existed and eventually found that their fiction led to a concrete result. But even this certainty is evanescent: If you close your eyes and ears, the conference, and with it Phoenix, would be nothing more than a figment of your imagination. There are bound to be many people who will reject especially this last proposition as utterly ludicrous. But it originated in greater minds than mine. Take Ludwig Wittgenstein, who in his late work, *On Certainty* (1969), wrote:

> What reason have I, now, when I cannot see my toes, to assume that I have five toes on each foot?

Is it right to say that my reason is that previous experience has always taught me so? Am I more certain of previous experience than that I have ten toes?

That previous experience may very well be the *cause* of my present certitude; but is it its ground? (Sect. 429)

I meet someone from Mars and he asks me, "How many toes have human beings got?" I say, "Ten. I'll show you," and take my shoes off. Suppose that he was surprised that I knew with such certainty, although I had not looked at my toes—ought I then to say: "We humans know how many toes we have whether we can see them or not?" (Sect. 430)

In the same work Wittgenstein further states:

I want to say: it is not that on some points men know the truth with perfect certainty. Rather, perfect certainty only relates to their attitude. (Sect. 404)

And again:

"A is a physical object" is a piece of instruction which we give only to someone who does not yet understand either what "A" means, or what "physical object" means. Thus it is instruction about the use of words, and "physical object" is a logical concept. (Like colour, quantity, . . .) And that is why no such proposition as: "There are physical objects" can be formulated.

Yet we encounter such unsuccessful shots at every turn. (Sect. 36)

For Wittgenstein, then, the supposed existence of a real reality is but a language-game and, therefore, fiction.

This is also where the profound difference between member and class comes into play—and plays havoc. A class is not only the totality of all objects that have certain essential properties in common, but it is also none of these. It is an abstraction and thus a fiction, albeit a necessary fiction. Still, "The class of all cats," Gregory Bateson used to say, "is not itself a cat; it has neither fur nor claws." In his double-bind theory he pointed to the weird dilemmas arising out of the paradoxical attempt to treat a class as if it were a member of itself, and also to the potential inherent in the therapeutic use of paradox.

Let us behave *as if* all of this were so. What happens, then, is that our idea of an objectively existing reality breaks down and with it the seemingly so simple criterion of reality adaptation as a measure of mental health or illness. Not much would be lost: The idea has been untenable since the days of Locke, Hume and Kant; it has remained dogma only in our field, and probably only because therapists are not usually also philosophers of science. Rather, we go on talking about "schizophrenia," "borderline syndrome," and the lack of reality adaptation of the "psychiatric patient."

Elsewhere the idea of a reality, existing independently of our *idea* of reality, has been replaced by the realization that of this reality we can at best know what it is *not*; never what it *is*. In other words, the only concrete experience of its existence comes at the point where our image of reality breaks down and thereby proves to be incorrect. As long as our reality construction does not shipwreck by running up against some submerged cliff, we are like people who crossed an unknown, pitch-dark room without bumping into a piece of furniture. All that we know by the time we get to the opposite wall is that we did not collide with anything, but we have no idea what the room is "really" like.

This is one of the basic ideas of modern constructivism; the study of how our individual, social, scientific and ideological "realities" are constructed by us and are then believed to be "really" existing out there. It is succinctly expressed by von Glasersfeld (1984) in his essay on Radical Constructivism:

> The real world manifests itself exclusively there where our constructions break down. But since we can describe and explain these breakdowns only in the very concepts that we have used to build the failing structures, this process can never yield a picture of the world that we could hold responsible for their failure. (p. 39)

Thus, we are prisoners in a world of our own fictions or, if you prefer, our own facts—as long as it is remembered that *factum* comes from *facere* (to make, to produce) and therefore means something *made*, not *found*. At first blush it seems utterly amazing that we should not only be able to survive in a totally fictional world, but that, like the people who safely crossed the dark, unknown room, we do arrive at concrete results.

Yet even this is nothing new. The German philosopher Hans Vaihinger (1924) used 800 pages to explain how even the "hard" sciences arrive at concrete results by introducing fictional or imaginary concepts and elements into their pursuits; elements that are discarded when the practical result is reached. One example, taken from geometry, is to treat the circle *as if* it were a multicornered plane. This fiction permits the application of straight-line geometry to any part of a circle's curve and enables the geometer to arrive at practical results, after which the fiction can be ignored. Another of his numerous examples, vastly more important and far-reaching than the one just mentioned, is the totally unproven and unprovable fiction that human beings are endowed with free will. In other words, we all behave and see the world *as if* people were free. The result, by and large, is and always has been a tolerable degree of order in human affairs. In pursuing this idea, Vaihinger pointed out that judges who base themselves on this fiction of freedom and, therefore, responsibility in order to arrive at a verdict, do not examine the fiction of freedom. Judges act *as if* it were the case, for without laws there can be no social order: It is to this practical end that the fiction of freedom was invented.

What this procedure amounts to is that: 1) a situation exists that requires a practical solution; 2) a fictional, *as-if* assumption is made; 3) the fiction is introduced into the situation as if it were a concrete fact, and produces a nonfictional, practical solution; and 4) after this the fiction can be discarded, or has become unnecessary, precisely because it led to a concrete solution. At one point, Vaihinger summarized this procedure succinctly: The illogical is a necessary step towards the logical.

From our school days we remember the strange properties of the imaginary number i, that is, the square root of minus one. Here a mathematical procedure, root extraction, is applied *as if* it were applicable, when it clearly is not. But while volumes have been written by now about the havoc that the equivalent of i, namely, paradox, causes in philosophy and—closer to home for us—in human interaction, mathematicians, physicists and engineers remained unimpressed by it and found i eminently useful for the purpose of achieving practical results. Yet, for our everyday thinking, i remains a mystery, a mystery that is well expressed by the Austrian novelist Robert Musil (1958) in his book *Young Törless*. The young man finds himself for the first time confronted with these almost magical properties of the imaginary number:

> I don't quite know how to put it. Look, think of it like this: in a calculation like that you begin with ordinary solid numbers, representing measures of length or weight or something else that's quite tangible—at any rate, they're real numbers. And at the end you have real numbers. But these two lots of real numbers are connected by something that simply doesn't exist. Isn't that like a bridge where the piles are there only at the beginning and at the

end, with none in the middle, and yet one crosses it just as surely
and safely as if the whole of it were there? That sort of operation
makes me feel a bit giddy, as if it led part of the way God knows
where. But what I really feel is so uncanny is the force that lies in
a problem like that, which keeps such a firm hold on you that in
the end you land safely on the other side. (p. 106 f)

But the funniest and probably most immediately convincing example
of the essence of this strange procedure is the oriental story of the father
who leaves his earthly belongings, consisting of 17 camels, to his three
sons with the instruction that the eldest son is to receive ½, the second
⅓, and the youngest ⅑. No matter how they try to divide the camels,
they find it impossible—and so will you, if you care to try for yourselves.
Eventually a mullah comes along on his camel, and they ask him for his
help. "There is nothing to it," he says. "Here, I add my camel to yours,
which makes eighteen. Now you, the eldest, receive ½, which is nine.
You, the middle son, are entitled to ⅓, which is six; here they are. You,
the youngest, get ⅑, that is two camels. This leaves one camel, namely,
my own." And having said this, he mounts it and rides off.

It would probably be difficult to find a better illustration of this technology of fiction or, for that matter, of the usefulness of storytelling as
a therapeutic tool.

However, what I have not made clear yet is where these clever remarks
are supposed to lead. The answer is that they make hypnosis appear in
a new light. It is generally assumed that hypnosis operates by somehow
providing a temporary element of unreality or irrationality to the subject's view of a given situation (and here the hypotheses range from
compliant role playing to cortical inhibition). But in view of the foregoing, this is the rule and not some sort of exception as far as our
experience of reality is concerned. In other words, we always live in an
as-if world, a world of pretenses (as long as this term is not understood
to have the negative connotation of insincerity or deception usually
associated with it). Not only hypnotherapy, but therapy in general,
attempts to change one as-if pretense to another, less pain-producing
one. This is the essence of *reframing*. When Cloe Madanes asks her
patients to pretend that things are a certain way and not the way they
thought that things were, she masterfully utilizes the as-if nature of our
world and, I can imagine from my own experience, is promptly criticized
for her "insincere manipulations" by that strange breed of therapists
whose fiction is the conviction that what wells up from within their
innermost being is, of course, the ultimate truth.

I would even go so far as to claim that we are always in a trance, that, as Calderón de la Barca so masterfully showed in one of his plays, life is a dream and dream is life, or—as Indian philosophy has it—we live in a *maya* world, a world of appearances.

Nowhere does the as-if nature of our world become more starkly obvious than in the mechanism of self-fulfilling prophecies, whose clinical importance we barely have begun to appreciate. By behaving as if something were, or will be, the case, a truly reality-transforming fiction is introduced or, in other words, creates its own reality. What seem to be the basic laws of our reality are turned upside down: Imagined effect produces concrete cause; the future determines the present; the prophecy of the event leads to the event of the prophecy. The truly mind-shaking potential of self-fulfilling prophecies reveals itself in a case reported by Gordon Allport (1964):

> In a provincial Austrian hospital, a man lay gravely ill—in fact, at death's door. The medical staff had told him frankly that they could not diagnose his disease, but if they knew the diagnosis they could probably cure him. They told him further that a famous diagnostician was soon to visit the hospital and that perhaps he could spot the trouble.
>
> Within a few days the diagnostician arrived and proceeded to make the rounds. Coming to this man's bed, he merely glanced at the patient, murmured "moribundus," and went on.
>
> Some years later the patient called on the diagnostician and said, "I've been wanting to thank you for your diagnosis. They told me that if you could diagnose me I'd get well, and so the minute you said 'moribundus' I knew I'd recover. (p. 7)

REFERENCES

Allport, G. W. (1964). Mental health: A generic attitude. *Journal of Religion and Health, 4*, 7-21.

Brown, G. S. (1973). *Laws of form.* New York: Bantam Books.

Galen, D. (1974). Implications for psychiatry of left and right cerebral specialization: A neurophysiological context for unconscious processes. *Archives of General Psychiatry, 31*, 572-83.

Glasersfeld, E. von (1984). Introduction to radical constructivism. In P. Watzlawick (Ed.), *The invented reality: How do we know what we believe we know?* New York, London: Norton.

Musil, R. (1958). *Young Törless* (E. Wilkins & E. Kaiser, Trans.). New York: Noonday Press.

Poincaré, H. (1913). *La morale et la science* (p. 22). Paris: Flammarion.

Salimbene di Parma, Fra (1926). *La bizarra cronaca di Frate Salimbene.* Lanciano: Carabba.

Spitz, R. A. (1945). Hospitalism. In *The psychoanalytic study of the child* (Vol. 1, pp. 53-74).

New York: International Universities Press.

Vaihinger, H. (1924). *The philosophy of "as if": A system of the theoretical, practical and religious fictions of mankind* (C. K. Ogden, Trans.). New York: Harcourt Brace.

Wittgenstein, L. (1969). *On certainty* (D. Paul & G. E. M. Anscombe, Trans.). Oxford: Basil Blackwell.

Chapter 2

Unity and Diversity in Ericksonian Approaches: Now and in the Future

Ernest L. Rossi

During the opening convocation we gained an impression of the rich diversity of interests that have become unified around the method and approaches pioneered by Milton H. Erickson. A central theme for this Congress, therefore, seems to revolve around the concept of *unity in diversity*. During both the pre-Congress Training Institute and the Congress, I made an effort to attend as many different types of workshops and presentations as possible. I wanted to answer the question, "Who are we?" I soon recognized that there were two major groups within our midst: the group primarily interested in hypnosis and hypnotherapy, and the group primarily interested in the use of strategic psychotherapy and strategic family therapy. This second area of interest was essentially new to me—I have not had any formal training in family therapy or the strategic approach. I looked forward to learning about it.

ERICKSON AND STRATEGIC INJUNCTION

As I sat in the audience listening to Cloe Madanes and her husband Jay Haley, I was prepared to hear that strategic therapy was a particular variety of family therapy—which was itself but one variety among many forms of psychotherapy. As their presentations proceeded I was unprepared for the revolution that took place in my thinking. I suddenly recognized that strategic therapy is not just another variety of therapy. It is distinctly different, and the difference involves a profound paradigmatic shift—whose direction was explained in a superb presentation given by Paul Watzlawick.

In a highly theoretical presentation, Watzlawick delineated the differences between the *injunctive* and the *descriptive* modes of experience. He asserted that all descriptive knowledge is really a metaphorical "as if" fiction designed to give us rules that direct action-injunctions for *doing* things. The implication of this concept is that *all the different schools of psychotherapy are myths*: they are all descriptive approaches (metaphors) designed to help us *do something* with our clients so that they can *do something* with themselves. Strategic therapy, however, goes directly to the essence of this matter: it is the process of getting down to "what does the therapist actually *do*?" While all the descriptive schools of psychotherapy and hypnotherapy have their values, nonetheless *they are metaphors that tend to give the idea of what to do with clients.*

Watzlawick's address contains a profound implication that, I believe, goes right to the essence of the Ericksonian approach. An epigraph that appeared in one of Watzlawick's books (1976) featured Albert Einstein's comment that "it is the theory which decides what we can observe." It seems that Watzlawick has taken this idea an essential step further to say that it is the injunctions contained in metaphoric descriptions that decide what we can do. We can now understand that Erickson's brilliance in refusing to write yet another descriptive theory of psychotherapy was the basis of his individualized approach. He gave us what he called *techniques* which are the *injunctions* Watzlawick has proposed as the essence of all forms of psychotherapy. Erickson did not wish to create a new mythology or another descriptive science. *He just wanted to tell us what to do*—and it was this genius that helps us to find what is *best to do in each individual situation.*

This, then, is the central connection between family therapy, the strategic approach, and Milton Erickson, which I had not previously understood. I expect that future studies in this area may be of significance in facilitating the great paradigmatic shift in psychotherapy that we are currently initiating: the shift from a *descriptive metaphor-for-all-situations approach* to an *injunctive doing-what's-best-in-each-individual-situation approach.*

THE EVOLUTION OF THE MICRODYNAMIC ANALYSIS OF HYPNOTHERAPY

It was in 1944 that Erickson wrote the paper, "The Method Employed to Formulate a Complex Story for the Induction of an Experimental

Neurosis in a Hypnotic Subject." For the first time Erickson reproduced the words that he was saying to the client on one side of the paper and then explained the significance of the words on the other side. He made this a "micro-analysis" by explaining the significance of each word.

Fifteen years later Haley and Weakland visited Erickson and together they published a paper entitled "A Transcript of a Trance Induction with Commentary" (Erickson, Haley, & Weakland, 1959), which once again utilized this type of micro-analysis. Haley and Weakland were able to add another dimension to the analysis: namely, the double bind. While working on that manuscript they discovered that Erickson was using a therapeutic *double bind*. Erickson had simply called his method a *bind*, and he had been using it all his life.

It was an additional 17 years before "Two-Level Communication and the Microdynamics of Trance and Suggestion" (Erickson & Rossi, 1976) and *Hypnotic Realities* (Erickson, Rossi, & Rossi, 1976) were published. In these works Erickson and I added another dimension to microdynamic analysis by naming and illustrating all the different forms of indirect hypnotic suggestion.

Now, in 1983, we have people coming along and doing even better analyses—and there has been only a seven-year gap. It is evident that knowledge and discovery in this area are beginning to accelerate. I fully expect this area to reveal some of the most exciting and fruitful developments of our work in the future. What we now need are empirical studies on the parameters of the factors we are uncovering with our microdynamic analyses. Recently, while on the doctoral dissertation committee for the Simpkins' work on "An Experimental Study of the Indirect Method of Hypnotherapy" (1983), I learned once again how this type of necessary experimental study is the heart and hard work of any science. The Simpkins' study and others like it (Angelos, 1978; White, 1979) will be an important wave of the future that we all need to support.

ERICKSONIAN APPROACHES AND CREATIVE LEADERSHIP

In his presentation, "The 'Uncommon Therapy' of Mohandas K. Gandhi" (Chapter 34), James Allen proposed that Gandhi, one of the most creative social leaders of our time, was using multilevel communication, metaphor, etc.—the same approaches Erickson was using—for achieving change on a social and political level. As I listened to Allen, suddenly my mind expanded again: Have we moved from working with individuals, to families, to the social leaders of a culture? Is there anything we need more desperately than creative leadership?

Many years ago I read Jay Haley's *The Power Tactics of Jesus Christ* (1969). I remember the exact mood I was in when I finished reading it. I was lying on my bed looking out at the trees, and I tossed the book (a paperback) aside on the floor. With a grin I said to myself, "The gall of this guy. This obviously was written tongue-in-cheek—he really wasn't serious!" I consider myself a transpersonal psychologist. For me Jesus Christ, Buddha, and religious leaders in general were people of higher consciousness—they did not deal with *power*.

When James Allen began talking about the relationship between his work on Gandhi and Haley's *The Power Tactics of Jesus Christ*, my dogmatic slumbers were disturbed once again. I saw that Haley had formed a revolutionary concept, that is, it took James Allen's paper to help me see this. These concepts may provide the foundations of a profound approach to disarming the social-political-cultural bind that we are in today. Suddenly I was in a turmoil of excitement, feeling that the next Congress should include presentations on Ericksonian approaches to sociocultural issues.

ERICKSON AND ANTHROPOLOGY

These sociocultural issues involve whole new understandings of who we are and what our potentials are, and they have tremendous implications for clinical practice. I discovered some of this when I attended Madeleine Richeport's presentation on the use of Ericksonian concepts in her anthropological field studies on ritual trance. Erickson was instrumental in Richeport's decision to go into anthropology. A number of other presenters also touched upon the anthropological theme, so I gather that this is another area that has been facilitated by Ericksonian approaches.

Speaking of anthropology reminds me of one of my most disconcerting experiences with Erickson. It took place in the early years of our work on an extremely hot afternoon—the temperature was over 100 degrees. He was talking about Margaret Mead and Gregory Bateson's anthropological work. I was beginning to wonder what all this had to do with hypnotherapy when Erickson suddenly became so enthusiastic about his anthropological themes that he almost leapt out of his chair. He said, "Go call so-and-so." So-and-so, a teenaged American Indian hired by the Ericksons to help with the yard work, was out in the back yard.

Once this youth was seated in the office with us, Erickson explained that he wanted to illustrate a few points about Native Americans to me. So Erickson began talking to me about Native Americans. He spoke about their neuropsychophysiological differences—primarily about their psychophysiological superiorities—and about how clearly the Indians had a superior behavioral or intellectual quality because of this or that feature. I thought the man was mad! But the madman kept motioning his chin toward the youth, as if to say, "You damn fool, stop looking at me—look at him!" Finally I did and found that he was staring blankly with a slight grin on his face. As Erickson continued talking, the young man began nodding his head; then sure enough, his eyes closed and remained closed for another ten minutes while Erickson continued explaining how the psychophysiological qualities of American Indians were developing in a process of cultural evolution. Then Erickson said, "Thank you," and the lad's eyes opened. Obviously rejuvenated and filled with strength, he stood up, grinned sheepishly, said, "Thank you," and walked out. I don't think he even knew that he had been in a trance. The words *hypnosis* and *relaxation* were never mentioned.

Meanwhile, I was simply irritated with the entire episode. I felt I had wasted an hour and almost erased the tape. This is what poor material—me—Erickson was working with when I began! I was the worst of all possible students. I was the last one to get it—to understand the vast scope of his vision. Now I understand that the entire social-cultural-anthropological view is an essential part of the Ericksonian approach. I expect we will have more papers and workshops on the important relationship between Ericksonian approaches and anthropology in the future.

ERICKSON AND NEUROPSYCHOPHYSIOLOGY

Another important area is the neuropsychophysiological approach. I have recently written two papers on the ultradian rhythms (Rossi, 1982, 1984). Ultradian rhythms are natural psychophysiological rhythms that occur every hour and a half to two hours throughout the day. It is when we come into the rest phase of the parasympathetic cycle that we need to take a break. It is at this time that we tend to become a little more right-hemispheric, so to speak, a little more prone to fantasy, etc.

When Erickson began teaching me to recognize minimal cues, I began writing down the observable behavioral features characterizing a person's readiness to go into trance: patterns of eyeball behavior, eyelid behavior, body immobility, retardation in the sensory-perceptual reflexes, etc. Between 1972 and 1978 I noted about two dozen behavioral characteristics that I had learned to identify in my patients. I wanted to develop the sensory-perceptual skills that Erickson used in order to utilize the spontaneous alterations of consciousness and tendencies toward trance that people manifest naturally, in everyday life as well as in hypnosis and psychotherapy.

It was during 1978 that I accidentally discovered the research literature on ultradian rhythms. What a revelation! All the psychophysiological behaviors that were being studied by the ultradian research people (and these were all researchers in the medical sciences, the psychophysiological sciences, and experimental psychology) appeared on my list of behavioral signs that indicated trance readiness—indicators of what Erickson called the common everyday trance (Erickson & Rossi, 1979). Much ultradian research is funded by the U.S. government in an effort to learn more about levels of performance in radar operators, computer operators, etc.

Excited by the coincidence, I began to explore a hypothesis that the common everyday trance and the behavioral correlates of hypnotic trance are actually due to rhythmical variations in our normal neuropsychophysiological processing (Rossi, 1982). These psychobiological rhythms are malleable and subject to psychological factors such as stress and motivation. Perhaps this accounts for why we can be successful in inducing trance no matter what stage of the ultradian rhythms a subject is in. However, the stage the subject is in can indicate some things about the subject's state of consciousness and how to facilitate the development of trance.

Investigators in both human and animal research have found evidence that when the rest phase of the ultradian cycle is continually interrupted, psychosomatic reactions develop. Experimental animals were found to develop ulcers, neurodermatitis, and a variety of neurotic behaviors, while human subjects manifested all the classic signs of various forms of psychosomatic disorders.

Hypnosis has been used traditionally as an effective approach with psychosomatic disorders; the naturalistic approach to hypnosis, in particular, may simply give patients permission to reduce stress and allow themselves to go into that resting phase of the ultradian rhythms where they can correct themselves. Thus, hypnosis may reach to the psychophysiological foundation—to the very psychophysiological sources—of psychosomatic symptomatology. I feel that the continued study of this relation between ultradian rhythms, hypnosis, and psychosomatic problems may reveal the basis of the neuropsychophysiological foundation of hypnosis. This certainly is important work for the future.

THE NASAL CYCLE AND CEREBRAL HEMISPHERIC ULTRADIAN RHYTHMS

One of the most recent ultradian rhythms to be thoroughly investigated is the nasal cycle. Did you know that every hour and a half or so, one of your nostrils is more open in letting in air? Then an hour and a half later that nostril closes and the other nostril opens? This nasal cycle has been recognized for about 100 years. I have documented 50 years of research involving all the different approaches to measuring it (Rossi, 1984). Why is this important? Because of one incredibly seminal piece of research conducted by a young woman named Deborah Werntz in 1980 at the University of California at San Diego in conjunction with researchers at the Salk Institute (Werntz, 1981). In essence they found that an open right nostril is correlated with a dominance of the left hemisphere, and an open left nostril is correlated with a dominance of the right hemisphere. Previously, this natural alteration in hemispheric dominance (which is itself an ultradian cycle) had only been demonstrated during the transition from REM to non-REM sleep. Within the past five years it was demonstrated in relation to cognitive tasks in which an hour-and-a-half shift was found to occur: For one hour and a half, we tend to be better at linear tasks; the next hour and a half we tend to be better at sensory-perceptual tasks (Klein & Armitage, 1979).

In their next experiment, Werntz et al. (1981, 1982) found that they could change hemispheric dominance by forced breathing. If my right nostril were closed, for example, I could block my left nostril and force air through my right nostril—which in turn would change my hemispheric dominance. Why is this important? Because the alternation in hemispheric dominance is also correlated with a contralateral parasympathetic-sympathetic dominance that alternates between the left and right sides of the body. Many of you know that for thousands of years the ancient science of altering states of consciousness and psychophysiology has been the science of *pranayama* taught by the yogis. For thousands of years they have written ecstatic books on this subject—books that seem so strange to our Western consciousness because of their unusual admixture of poetry, instructions and mythologies. (See Iyengar, 1981, for an excellent summary of this esoteric material.) Reading these old books can be very irritating. There are strange instructions such as, "Breathe through the left nostril five times; rest; breathe through the right nostril three times"; and this given with the assurance that a particular part of the body will be positively affected. In other words, the ancient yogis were using the nasal cycle to achieve changes in various parts of their physiology, to alter their consciousness, and to achieve enlightenment. The body changes they achieved are now recognized as autonomic nervous system changes whereby the balance between the sympathetic and the parasympathetic systems in various parts of the body is altered.

HYPOTHESES ABOUT READING FACIAL CUES FOR CEREBRAL HEMISPHERIC DOMINANCE

Since learning about the nasal cycle, cerebral hemispheric dominance, and their relation to autonomic-system dominance on the left and right sides of the body, I have been training myself to study the two sides of the face. The theory suggests that one side of the face actually has more sympathetic activity when the other side has more parasympathetic activity. Could we see the alternations in these cycles by just looking at facial characteristics? In Figure 1, I list 15 characteristics I have isolated for study.

I am never too anxious to tell my clients about my observations regarding their facial laterality. I would rather use my observations as minimal cues regarding their psychodynamics. I am exploring a number of interesting avenues for utilizing these minimal cues in psychotherapy and hypnosis. For example, if I look at the side of the client's face—particularly the eye that is dominant (lifted)—will I be attracting the attention of this cerebral hemisphere that is more active and receptive at that moment? Will whatever I say be received more acutely if I beam it to the active hemisphere? Suppose I focus my attention on the less dominant side of the face: Will what I say tend to be received on a more unconscious level, where it can continue to remain active even though the client tends to be amnesic for it? Erickson loved to sway from side to side when he was using suggestion. He believed he could beam the suggestions in a conditioned manner to the patient's conscious and unconscious minds in this way. Can our facial cues from facial laterality be a means of helping us decide which side is more unconscious in order to facilitate this approach?

In inducing hypnosis, which side of the face should I look at? Should I first focus on the active side to get the subject's attention initially, and then turn off this active side by shifting my engaging focus away from it to the less dominant side? This certainly would be an interesting research project. I've noticed that when some subjects begin to go into trance slowly, they tend to let one eyelid droop a little bit more than the

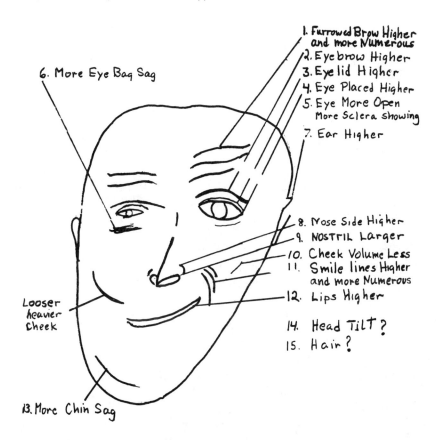

6. More Eye Bag Sag

1. Furrowed Brow Higher and more Numerous
2. Eyebrow Higher
3. Eyelid Higher
4. Eye Placed Higher
5. Eye More Open More Sclera showing

7. Ear Higher

8. Nose Side Higher
9. Nostril Larger
10. Cheek Volume Less
11. Smile lines Higher and more Numerous
12. Lips Higher

14. Head Tilt?
15. Hair?

Looser heavier Cheek

13. More Chin Sag

Figure 1. Face laterality: Left lifted face and smile suggesting right hemispheric dominance at this moment in time?

other. Does this mean that the contralateral cerebral hemisphere is turning off or going into rest more quickly than the other? This is another research question that could easily be answered by some standard EEG monitoring during hypnotic induction.

People with a well-balanced face and no obvious laterality often show rapid shifting patterns of lateral facial lift. In one moment, for example, the right side of the face will be higher; then as that drops back to normal the left side will take on a few uplifted features. More rarely there will be a complex facial profile with perhaps a prominently uplifted right eyebrow seemingly opposed by an uplifted left side of the mouth. Such mixed patterns indicate that in these features, humans are vastly more complex than described by our linear schemes of behavioral classification. Thus, no simplistic, one-to-one correspondence between lateral facial profiles and mental or personality characteristics is likely to emerge from these observations.

ERICKSON AND MINIMAL CUES

We study minimal cues because they are the signs of those spontaneous alterations of consciousness that Erickson called the common everyday trance. The *naturalistic hypnotherapist* needs only to observe when a spontaneous trance is becoming manifest and to suggest, by various means, that the patient enjoy the relaxed parasympathetic state that has begun. The common everyday experiences that most people call "taking a break," "spacing out," "a rest," or "a little nap" can be developed into a trance with suggestions for any of the classical hypnotic phenomena. Thus, it is *this skill in observing and reinforcing the commonplace alterations in consciousness* (Rossi, 1984) *that is the cornerstone of Erickson's naturalistic approach to hypnotherapy*. Naturalistic techniques have begun to supplant the authoritarian techniques of the past, wherein power over and manipulation of the gullible were the cornerstones. I will emphasize the importance of minimal cues in the next few sections.

I would submit that one of the most fundamental contributions of Erickson to the process of training in hypnotherapy was in teaching us to read our clients' minimal cues. Erickson always attended to his clients' minimal behavioral responses and interpreted them as critical feedback on how they were responding to his suggestions. The clients' responses guided Erickson in his explorations of what they next needed to hear to achieve their therapeutic goals. The basic idea here is that clients have problems because they are not appropriately responding to their own minimal bodily, emotional, and cognitive cues. They have *learned limitations* that prevent them from recognizing and utilizing their own best perceptions and responses to changing life circumstances. By reading minimal cues back to his clients in the form of hypnotic suggestions Erickson was actually retraining them to recognize and to use their own potential and bypass or reevaluate learned limitations.

Erickson often opened his discussions of minimal cues by pointing out that a good fortune teller can read faces. A good fortune teller can read the cues that express aspects of people's lives and of which they are usually unaware. A fortune teller can, therefore, know more about what is going on in a person's experience than the person is consciously aware of.

It is this kind of sensitivity and responsiveness to minimal cues that Erickson developed over a lifetime of compensating for his congenital sensory-perceptual handicaps and the poliomyelitis that left him partially paralyzed. To understand the way people saw the world, Erickson studied people carefully and thought a lot about their behavior (Erickson & Rossi, 1977).

ERICKSON AND HYPNOTHERAPEUTIC SKILL

If we want to advance in our hypnotherapeutic skill, we need to develop this kind of sensitivity to minimal cues. We need to learn to discover our abilities and develop our skills of observation. The beginner in hypnosis usually has only a rote, verbal patter that is applied to all subjects, regardless of their responses. The intermediate student begins to adjust suggestions to the obvious behaviors the client is manifesting by commenting on such behaviors and utilizing them. This skill of making adjustments enhances rapport and makes trance available to a larger number of clients. The advanced student has a greatly expanded sensitivity to the minimal cues of clients—to those minimal behavioral responses that clients do not even know they are demonstrating. Advanced practitioners are sensitive to clients' minimal cues to such an extent that they are more attuned to what the client is experiencing than the client is. Although advanced practitioners may use ideomotor finger signaling set up in a formal way to help some clients ratify their own hypnotic state, they typically depend more on clients' unique, spontaneous ideomotor signals.

Erickson seldom used obvious forms of ideomotor responses such as finger signaling or head nodding because clients could be conscious of them. He preferred to use the unique, subtle, spontaneous responses that his clients could show, but that they would not know they were showing. However, Erickson frequently did make an effective show of ideomotor signaling to ratify trance for clients skeptical about the presence of an altered state.

ERICKSON AND EXTRASENSORY PERCEPTION

Erickson believed that minimal cues were the basis of all so-called extrasensory perception: mind reading, palm reading, crystal-ball reading, and so forth. He believed that skilled practitioners of these psychic arts are simply good readers of minimal cues. It was not necessarily a matter of insincerity; sometimes these practitioners hallucinated images in crystal balls that reflected something about their clients. But the images do not really come from crystal balls. The wise fortune tellers do not even know that they are actually picking up minimal cues from their clients' behavior, processing the information through their own unconscious and projecting their understanding, in a hallucinated form, into the crystal ball. This is a rational-empirical-scientific explanation of the occult.

A NOBEL PRIZE IN HYPNOSIS: THE MIND-GENE CONNECTION

How could one earn a Nobel Prize in hypnosis? While this category of honor does not exist, it certainly would be created for those who were able to unequivocally demonstrate a reciprocal pathway between gene action and mind action. Is this really preposterous? Figure 2 depicts a schematic outline of what we already know about the interrelationship of neuropsychophysiological and genetic processes.

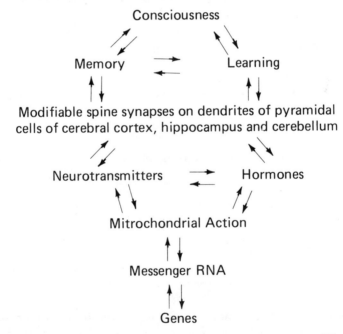

Figure 2. A broad schematic outline of the gene-mind connection. Who will be the first to demonstrate that hypnosis, as a special focusing of conscious and unconscious processes, can utilize the neuropsychophysiological processes of memory and learning that interact with and influence gene activity?

Most biochemical events are reversible. Therein exists a key to how hypnotic suggestions will eventually be used to influence biochemical processes, and perhaps even genetic processes. Whoever first demonstrates the mind's effect on genetics, in a form that can be validated by generalizing it to the effects of hypnotic suggestion on gene activity, will surely deserve a Nobel Prize in hypnosis. Man's mind will at last be able to operate non-invasively on its own sources in its physical genes.

One day Watson and Crick decided to do the impossible and crack the genetic code—they decided to discover the molecular structure of DNA—and they eventually did, despite the fact that neither of them was a specialist in genetics! The knowledge and technology to solve the problem already existed. Watson and Crick had the boldness to ask the questions and the persistence to pursue the answers—like a pair of Furies—and they used many people's data in the process!

I would submit that we are in an analogous position with regard to the mind and an elucidation of its effects on genetic processes. I believe that our knowledge of neurophysiology (McGeer, Eccles, & McGeer, 1978), psychoneuroimmunology (Locke & Hornig-Rohan, 1983) and gene action (Schmitt, Bird, & Bloom, 1982) is advanced enough on the one hand, and our understanding of the microdynamics of hypnotic suggestion is sufficiently in place on the other, to pursue an investigation of the possible interrelatedness of mind and matter. The commonplaces that we take so for granted today, were inconceivable impossibilities in a not-too-distant past.

Neuropsychophysiology can have profound implications for our hypnotic work in the future. I believe that the neuropsychophysiology of hypnosis will become a critical dimension of our diversity in future Erickson Congresses. In this next year I am going to be studying psychoneuroimmunology—I believe this is an important research foundation for modern hypnosis. I am going to be studying the actions of neurotransmitters and the process by which genes send out messenger RNA into the cell. The RNA gives messages to the mitochondria and other cell structures that produce the neurotransmitters and the hormones that give rise to the spine synapses on the dendrites and nerve cells in the cerebral cortex, cerebellum, and hippocampus—where certain physiological alterations coincide with new learning. These neurophysiological alterations are presumed to be the basis of memory. These factors, combined together, give rise to the self and to consciousness. Since we can trace a biochemical route from genes to consciousness, and since most biochemical reactions are reversible, why not utilize the conscious and unconscious processes of memory and learning via hypnotic suggestion to reverse the direction of untoward biochemical reactions? I hope this psychophysiological route will be familiar and well-traveled by the practitioners of naturalistic hypnotherapy in the future.

Most of you are probably familiar with the clock depicted in *The Bulletin of Atomic Scientists*. Scientists have been advancing this clock from time zero to 12 o'clock; they have established 12 o'clock as the time of global nuclear destruction and they have the clock set at about three minutes to 12 now. Instead of advancing the minutes to human destruction, I propose a time line of advancing human evolution: *the mind-gene clock*. I would like to start the mind-gene clock right now. Since my announcement of the possible interrelatedness of the mind and of genetic processes, I am going to advance the mind-gene clock one hour—so it is now one o'clock. With the publication of every paper in this area I am going to advance this clock one hour—until it gets to six o'clock. Then I am going to become more stringent. Each excellent paper will advance the clock by only one-half hour. By the time it is 12 o'clock we will have "cracked the mind-gene code" and it will appear in the textbooks with which we train physicians, psychologists, and marriage, child and family counselors. We will be giving unprecedented instructions on how to increase the positive influences of minds on genes, on physiology, and on behavior. The impossible or inconceivable of today can be commonplace and taken for granted in a not-too-distant tomorrow. It is now one o'clock and I am counting. . . .

REFERENCES

Angelos, J. (1978). *A comparison of the effectiveness of direct and indirect hypnotic induction techniques for the control of cold-pressor pain*. Unpublished doctoral dissertation, California School of Professional Psychology, Los Angeles.

Erickson, M. (1944). The method employed to formulate a complex story for the induction of an experimental neurosis in a hypnotic subject. *The Journal of General Psychology, 31*, 67-84. Also in E. Rossi (Ed.). (1980). *The collected papers of Milton H. Erickson on hypnosis* (Vol. 3, pp. 336-355). New York: Irvington.

Erickson, M., Haley, J., & Weakland, J. (1959). A transcript of a trance induction with commentary. *The American Journal of Clinical Hypnosis, 2*, 49-84. Also in E. Rossi (Ed.). (1980). *The collected papers of Milton H. Erickson on hypnosis* (Vol. 1, pp. 206-257). New York: Irvington.

Erickson, M., & Rossi, E. (1976). Two-level communication and the microdynamics of trance and suggestion. *The American Journal of Clinical Hypnosis, 18*, 153-171. Also in E. Rossi (Ed.). (1980). *The collected papers of Milton H. Erickson on hypnosis* (Vol. 1, pp. 430-451). New York: Irvington.

Erickson, M., & Rossi, E. (1977). Autohypnotic experiences of Milton H. Erickson. *The American Journal of Clinical Hypnosis, 20*, 36-54. Also in E. Rossi (Ed.). (1980). *The collected papers of Milton H. Erickson on hypnosis* (Vol. 1, pp. 108-132). New York: Irvington.

Erickson, M., & Rossi, E. (1979). *Hypnotherapy: An exploratory casebook*. New York: Irvington.

Erickson, M., & Rossi, E. (1981). *Experiencing hypnosis: Therapeutic approaches to altered states.* New York: Irvington.

Erickson, M., Rossi, E., & Rossi, S. (1976). *Hypnotic realities.* New York: Irvington.

Haley, J. (1969). *The power tactics of Jesus Christ and other essays.* New York: Discus Books/Avon.

Iyengar, B. (1981). *Light on pranayama: The yogic art of breathing.* New York: Crossroads.

Klein, R., & Armitage, R. (1979). Rhythms in human performance: 1½ hours oscillations in cognitive style. *Science, 204,* 1326-1328.

Locke, S., & Hornig-Rohan, M. (1983). *Mind and immunity: Behavioral immunology: An annotated bibliography, 1976-1982.* New York: Institute for the Advancement of Health.

McGeer, P., Eccles, J., & McGeer, E. (1978). *Molecular neurobiology of the mammalian brain.* New York & London: Plenum Press.

Rossi, E. (1982). Hypnosis and ultradian cycles: A new state(s) theory of hypnosis? *The American Journal of Clinical Hypnosis, 1,* 21-32.

Rossi, E. (1984). Altered states of consciousness in everyday life: The ultradian rhythms. In B. Wolman (Ed.), *Handbook of altered states of consciousness.* New York: Van Nostrand.

Schmitt, F., Bird, S., & Bloom, F. (Eds.). (1982). *Molecular genetic neurosicience.* New York: Raven Press.

Simpkins, C., & Simpkins, A. (1983). *An experimental study of the indirect method of hypnotherapy.* Unpublished doctoral dissertation, United States International University, San Diego.

Watzlawick, P. (1976). *How real is real? Confusion, disinformation, communication.* New York: Random House.

Werntz, D. (1981). *Cerebral hemispheric activity and autonomic nervous function.* Doctoral dissertation, University of California, San Diego.

Werntz, D., Bickford, R., Bloom, F., & Singh-Khalsa, S. (1981, February). *Selective cortical activation by alternating autonomic function.* Paper presented at the meeting of the Western EEG Society.

Werntz, D., Bickford, R., Bloom, F., & Singh-Khalsa, S. (1982). Alternating cerebral hemispheric activity and lateralization of autonomic nervous function. *Neurobiology, 4,* 225-229.

White, D. (1979). *Ericksonian hypnotherapeutic approaches: A case study of the treatment of obesity using indirect forms of suggestion.* Unpublished doctoral dissertation, United States International University, San Diego.

PART II

Overviews

This section provides an orientation to the Ericksonian approach. It parents multiple models of Ericksonian methodology, along with underlying assumptions to the Ericksonian approach.

Bill O'Hanlon, M.S., conducts his practice in Omaha, Nebraska. He earned his degree in the family studies program at Arizona State University. In addition to his work as a therapist, O'Hanlon travels internationally to provide training to professionals interested in learning Ericksonian techniques. He serves on the Editorial Board of the Journal of Strategic and Systemic Therapies *and has coauthored with James Wilk a book entitled* Shifting Contexts: Clinical Epistemology and The Generation of Effective Psychotherapy *to be published by Guilford Press.*

A dedicated supporter of the Erickson Foundation, O'Hanlon is the editor of the Foundation's Newsletter; *the organizer of the five-day Pre-Congress Institute held prior to the Second International Congress; and coorganizer of the 1984 annual Seminar on Ericksonian Approaches to Hypnosis and Psychotherapy.*

O'Hanlon presents a study guide of published frameworks on Ericksonian hypnosis and psychotherapy. His guide provides an overview of the territory, explains the basic positions of the experts, and allows for easy comparison between points of view.

Ronald A. Havens, Ph.D., is an associate professor of psychology at Sangamon State University who earned his degree in clinical psychology from West Virginia University. He has authored and/or coauthored more than 20 publications, mostly in the areas of hypnosis and the training of psychologists. He edited a volume

31

entitled The Wisdom of Milton H. Erickson *which is in press
with Irvington Publishers.*

*Havens provides a piercing analysis of the difference between
Ericksonian and traditional methods, showing how the Ericksonian
approach reflects a revolutionary departure in phenomenology.
Flexibility is preferred to dogmatic adherence to theory.*

*David Gordon, M.A., earned his degree at Lone Mountain
College. He is an extraordinarily effective trainer of hypnosis and
Neuro-Linguistic Programming.*

*Gordon has authored two books which are mainly on Erickson's
work, both published through Meta Publications:* Therapeutic
Metaphors: Helping Others Through the Looking Glass *and*
Phoenix: The Therapeutic Patterns of Milton H. Erickson,
*coauthored with Maribeth Anderson. In his presentation, he shows
that there are five basic presuppositions inherent in Erickson's frame
of reference. These presuppositions influenced the directions that
Erickson took as a practitioner.*

*Charles R. Stern, Ph.D., has earned both an M.S.W. (Wayne
State University) and a Ph.D. in clinical psychology (The Fielding
Institute). He conducts a private practice in psychotherapy in Detroit
and provides training and supervision to students. In addition to his
interest in Ericksonian approaches, he has published on the topics of
Transactional Analysis and multiple personality.*

*Stern's chapter dovetails nicely with the chapter by Gordon. Stern
examines additional presuppositions in Erickson's work: Theoretical
formulations and explicit definitions are limiting; the conscious mind
is important in the change process; not everyone can be successfully
treated; and the therapy should not always be brief.*

Chapter 3

A Study Guide of Frameworks of Milton Erickson's Hypnosis and Therapy

Bill O'Hanlon

Various students of Erickson have attempted to systematize his approaches and techniques into coherent frameworks to make the work more accessible. In this chapter, the major frameworks of Erickson's work that have been published will be summarized. The chapter is limited to those frameworks that deal with Erickson's hypnosis and/or therapy as a whole. While each framework has many more details and aspects than those included here, a distillation of the essential elements from each is listed. Where the name of the element is not self-explanatory, an explanation or definition is provided.

The frameworks are covered chronologically for the most part, with the earliest models summarized first, except in the case of one person having two or more frameworks from different time periods.

The types of elements included in the various frameworks are of two types: 1) descriptive categories: those that just name and describe the elements in Erickson's work; and 2) presuppositional categories: those that seek to elucidate the premises underlying all the elements.

HALEY'S FRAMEWORKS

Haley proposed several different frameworks for Erickson's work at several different times.

First Analysis (1963)

In 1963, Haley characterized Erickson's work as directive: therapists were to get their patients to do something, often by directing them to behave in the symptomatic way with some addition. Therapists used positive redefinition and accepted patients' behavior to ensure cooperation and to facilitate therapy. The directives utilized the patients' assets and personality factors. Implication was often used indirectly to elicit behavior from patients. The goal of therapy was arranging or changing the environment for symptomatic behavior.

Second Analysis (1967)

In 1967, in the afterword to his collection of Erickson's papers, Haley offered additional Ericksonian elements:

1) The therapeutic posture—therapists must incorporate and modify techniques to express their individual personalities; therapists must modify techniques to deal with unique, individual patients.
2) Expectation of change—therapists expect that change is not only possible, but inevitable.
3) Emphasis on the positive—normal behavior and growth are the process of living and psychopathology is an interference with that process. The unconscious is a positive aspect of humans, not a cauldron of repressed, primal urges and conflicts. The patient's deficits can become assets.
4) Accepting what the patient offers—this includes symptoms, pessimism, resistance, rigid ideas and delusions.
5) Emphasis on the range of possibilities—for the therapist in approaching the patient, for the patient behaving and viewing things differently.
6) Willingness to take responsibility—therapists must be willing to take responsibility and make decisions for people if it is necessary; each case is handled individually as to how much responsibility the therapist needs to take.
7) Blocking off symptomatic behavior—therapists are not concerned with the "roots" of symptomatic behavior; symptoms are malfunctions to be corrected. To this end, they might block the symptomatic behavior either by relabeling the behavior, by taking it over and changing it under direction, or by providing an ordeal which makes it difficult to continue symptomatic behavior.

8) Change occurs in relation to therapists—therapists create an intense relationship and then use that relationship to get the client to co-operate or therapeutically rebel to prove the therapist wrong.
9) Use of anecdotes—analogies, stories, anecdotes or jokes are used to peg ideas or to make a previously unacceptable possibility acceptable.
10) Willingness to release patients—once the particular symptom is resolved, the patient is released from treatment. No attempt is made to resolve all present or future difficulties.
11) Erickson's approach has five premises:
    (a) The focus is on the present;
    (b) The focus is on interactions;
    (c) Symptoms are communications;
    (d) Awareness/insight is unnecessary for change;
    (e) The cause of change (and the persistence of that change) is the rearranging of the patient's situation.

Third Analysis (1973)

In 1973 Haley offered yet another framework. He examined Erickson's work through the framework of the family life cycle and characterized it as strategic. He also listed the elements of Erickson's work as follows:

1) Encouraging resistance;
2) Encouraging a response by frustrating it;
3) Encouraging a relapse;
4) Providing a worse alternative;
5) Amplifying a deviation;
6) Using "hypnotic" skills and communication devices in nonhypnotic therapy, including:
    (a) Amnesia and the control of information;
    (b) Seeding ideas;
    (c) The use of space and position;
    (d) Awakening and disengagement;
7) Causing change by communicating in metaphor.

According to Haley, Erickson rarely strived for insight on the part of the patient about unconscious processes, interpersonal difficulties, transference or motivations. His therapy was based upon the interpersonal impact of the therapist outside the patient's awareness. Carrying out directives causes changes of behavior.

BEAHRS' FRAMEWORK

Beahrs (1971) provided a framework which includes basic orientations, hypnotic techniques, and therapeutic techniques.

Basic Orientations

The basic orientations in Erickson's work according to Beahrs are:

1) Present or future time orientation;
2) The recognition of, acceptance of and participation by the therapist on all levels of the patient's behavior and communication;
3) Indirectness;
4) Manipulation (for the patient's benefit, not for the therapist's pleasure);
5) Versatility.

Hypnotic Techniques

There are three types of inductions: standard inductions, interspersal techniques, and the surprise technique.

Standard inductions

Erickson's standard inductions are indirect and characterized by an experiential orientation, i.e., they elicit and utilize the patient's internal experience as the induction content. The approach is designed to elicit unconscious responses. Erickson would increase expectancy by inhibiting responses and by pauses and hesitations. He would validate the subject's response (however minimal) by offering thanks for it.

Interspersal techniques

Beahrs includes several items in this category:

1) Standard induction interspersed with small talk, which is used when no specific problems are in evidence;
2) Utilization techniques, in which the resistances which present obstacles to both hypnosis and therapy are encouraged;
3) The confusion technique, in which the patient is given a set of overwhelmingly illogical statements until he or she gives up trying to

follow and goes into trance. This technique is used for resistant obsessive-compulsive intellectualizers;

4) The interspersal technique proper, as Erickson defined it, is when suggestions are interspersed in the midst of discussions, dictation, etc.

Surprise technique

The surprise technique is effected by the therapist's offering rapid and unexpected communication or behavior followed by or incorporating a suggestion.

Psychotherapy—General Principles

Beahrs listed several general principles that characterized Erickson's therapeutic approaches:

1) Therapists attend to patient communication at all levels;
2) Therapists meet the patient at his or her level;
3) Therapists modify the patient's behavior, thereby achieving control;
4) Therapists manipulate the patient so behavior will change from within to be more acceptable to self or others;
5) New mental patterns should exclude or displace earlier undesirable ones, and must be compatible with the patient's basic personality structure;
6) Therapists must work with the unconscious, which is viewed as a positive resource rather than a negative cauldron of suppressed impulses and conflicts;
7) The chief goal of therapy is not abreaction or uncovering, but coordination between conscious and unconscious functioning.

Therapeutic Techniques

Behavioral techniques. Erickson gave task assignments in order to effect conditioning and provide desensitization.

Deep or uncovering therapy. The techniques of automatic writing and drawing are typical of this aspect of Erickson's work. Indirectness in the uncovering is used, as well as controlled amnesia to limit the rate of insight.

Displacement of cathexis. Beahrs considers this approach to be the most significant of Erickson's contributions. The patient is guided to transfer psychic energy from the original symptom or conflict to other areas. Sometimes just developing rapport or training the patient in hypnosis will effect such a displacement, as the conflictual energy will divert into the healthy therapeutic relationship and then generalize to other relationships (or, in the case of hypnosis, the energy will transfer to the newly developed hypnotic skills).

The innovative techniques that Erickson used to effect displacement of cathexis are:

1) Symptom substitution in which a new symptom that is easier to change or to live with is installed in place of the old;
2) Symptom transformation is the redirecting of the underlying anxiety or conflict to a new object;
3) Time falsification, either of the past (in which the cathexis is displaced to a newly constructed relationship or experience in the past) or of the future (in which patients construct a personal fantasy of how their cure will be obtained and the energy is displaced onto this projection).

BANDLER AND GRINDER'S FRAMEWORKS

In their first published work on Erickson's hypnotic patterns and techniques, Bandler and Grinder (1975a) delineated a mainly linguistic model for inducing a trance. In contrast to this early linguistic model assisting therapists to challenge missing or distorted aspects of patients' world views or verbal reports in therapy (the "Meta Model"), they have called their later model the "Milton Model" (Bandler & Grinder, 1975b).

The Milton Model

The overall pattern of Erickson's hypnotic work, according to this framework, is pacing (matching, accepting, and utilizing the client's experiences and behavior) and leading (assisting the client to gain access to personal resources to build other experiences or to experience things in a way different from usual). Verbal pacing initially consists of describing to clients their ongoing observable behavior, being careful to stay within sensory-based descriptions. Next the hypnotist starts to describe the client's ongoing, nonobservable experience, using the linguistic categories provided below.

The broad categories for organizing the patterns in the linguistic model are: 1) linguistic causal modeling processes; 2) transderivational phenomena; 3) ambiguity; 4) lesser included structures; and 5) derived meanings.

Linguistic causal modeling processes

Causal linkage is used to tie sensory-based descriptions to other statements, requests and suggestions of the hypnotist. There are three levels of linguistic causal linkage:

1) Conjunction—the use of the connectives "and," "but," etc.;
2) Implied causatives—the use of the connectives "as," "while," "during," "before," "after," etc.;
3) Cause-effect—the use of predicates which claim a necessary connection between portions of experience; e.g., "make," "cause," "require," etc.

These categories claim or imply a linkage between the present (observed) behavior and the desired experience. Each level implies progressively more linkage and causality.

Transderivational phenomena

Transderivatonal search is the name Bandler and Grinder give to the internal search that clients must conduct in order to make sense of utterances by their therapist that have various meanings. In Erickson's hypnotic work, language forms that maximize this process are used to facilitate the induction of trance, the accessing of resources and the client's active involvement in the hypnotic procedure. Categories included are:

1) Generalized referential index—using nouns that do not refer to any specific person, place, thing or time; e.g., ". . . some interesting ideas from someone from another time. . . ."
2) Selectional restriction—using language that syntactically makes sense, but which violates basic cultural/personal understandings; e.g., "The rock yelled at me."
3) Deletion—leaving out the subject (actor) or object (acted upon) in a sentence or phrase; e.g., ". . . and learning . . . and really beginning to wonder. . . ."
4) Nominalization—using a process (action) word as a noun (thing). This includes elements of deletion and generalized referential index;

e.g., ". . . the comforts and understandings . . ."
5) Unspecified verbs—using a verb that does not specify the action to be performed; e.g., ". . . I'm going to ask you to do something."

Ambiguity

There are various types of ambiguity in Erickson's work:

1) Phonological ambiguity—puns and homonyms; e.g., "Hand levitation can be a disarming phenomenon."
2) Syntactic ambiguity—using a word in such a way as to produce two possible meanings; e.g., "Hypnotizing hypnotists can be tricky."
3) Scope ambiguity—creating confusion about where the previous reference ends; e.g., "I can see that you are sitting in a chair and going into a trance . . . can be an interesting experience. . . ."
4) Punctuation ambiguity—creating confusion about where one sentence ends and the other begins; e.g., "I see you are wearing a watch very carefully that arm and hand."

Lesser included structures

This category includes:

1) Embedded questions—asking a question without really asking; e.g., "I'm wondering if you can really begin to sense the changes."
2) Embedded commands—indirectly telling the person to do something without making it an obvious order or demand; e.g., "I think it would be very interesting for you to just relax and go into trance."
3) Quotes—this entails reporting what was said in another setting in order to give the person in front of you the same message; e.g., "Then I told her, 'Just relax and go into a trance.' "
4) Analogical marking—the technique in which certain parts of a communication are emphasized or marked off analogically (extraverbally) to give a separate message than that which is included in the larger message.

Derived meanings

Derived meanings are those that are not stated directly but implied by what the hypnotist says:

1) Presuppositions—the structure of the verbalization presumes that something is the case; e.g., "I wonder whether you are aware just how deeply you are in trance."
2) Conversational postulates—"polite commands" used by most people in daily life to ask for something indirectly. Instead of ordering, "Close the door," one could say, "Can you close the door?" "Is the door open?" or "You can close the door," etc.

Other Conceptions

In various writings, Bandler and Grinder have applied their own model (called Neuro-Linguistic Programming) to hypnosis, but considered here will be only those aspects of their work that attempt to describe Erickson's methods.

The notion that experience is made up of sensory-based elements of current external, or past internal, perceptions and representations is the cornerstone of much of the further conceptions offered. At any given time, a person is experiencing some aspect of what is called a 4-tuple, made up of four sensory elements (visual, auditory, kinesthetic, and gustatory/olfactory). These may be sense data attended to in the present or represented from the past. What the person attends to is called his or her representational system. All other aspects of the experience are out of awareness ("unconscious"), and accessing those into consciousness is one way to bring about an altered state of consciousness. The sensory process that is used to access experience or memories into consciousness is called the lead system. By utilizing or bypassing these elements, therapeutic and hypnotic goals can be accomplished.

The other main concept of relevance here is the notion of anchoring. Anchoring is the verbal or nonverbal cue or association of some particular experience. It is used to evoke and alter the client's experience to facilitate therapeutic goals.

Finally, Grinder, Delozier and Bandler (1977) offer sequencing of Erickson's hypnotic work:

1) Accessing and anchoring of experiences;
2) Polarity pacing;
3) Dissociation;
4) Metaphor/meta-instructions;
5) Creation of a reference experience;
6) Testing effectiveness of the work.

ROSSI'S FRAMEWORK

Rossi, in three books co-authored with Erickson (Erickson, Rossi, & Rossi, 1976; Erickson & Rossi, 1979; Erickson & Rossi, 1981), offered his analyses and models of Erickson's work. He stated that two major aspects of Erickson's work are indirect forms of suggestion and the utilization approach.

Indirect Suggestion

The interspersal approach

This approach includes the following three techniques:

1) Indirect associative focusing—mentioning topics (without specifically directing them towards the patient) to initiate associational processes related to those topics;
2) Indirect ideodynamic focusing—providing examples of responses to prime the patient to respond in the same way;
3) Interspersal technique—emphasizing certain words or phrases within a conversation or sentence.

Truisms utilizing ideodynamic processes

This includes eliciting responses in the motor, sensory-perceptual, affective and cognitive realms by making a simple statement about that particular experience or behavior.

Truisms utilizing time

The therapist states the fact that the desired experience or behavior will occur at some time in the future.

Not knowing, not doing

This involves the use of suggestions for allowing, rather than making things happen.

Open-ended suggestions

The therapist offers a variety of possible responses and validates all as hypnotic.

Covering all possibilities of a class of responses

The therapist restricts the range of possible responses, but accepts and validates all possibilities within that range.

Questions that facilitate new response possibilities

1) Questions to focus associations;
2) Questions for trance induction by association;
3) Questions facilitating therapeutic responsiveness.

Compound suggestions

Here a truism and a suggestion are usually connected by a conjunction, e.g., "and":

1) The yes set—asking a patient various questions to which the answer is yes or making observations with which the patient would agree sets up a positive response tendency;
2) Contingent suggestions—linking the suggested response to some already occurring or upcoming behavior or experience;
3) Apposition of opposites—juxtaposing opposite concepts or experiences;
4) The negative—juxtaposing the positive with the negative;
5) Shock and surprise—saying something shocking, provocative or surprising; pausing; then defusing the situation by completing the sentence to modify the meaning.

Implication

The therapist structures and directs the patient's associative processes by voice dynamics and language. The implied directive has three parts:

1) A time-binding introduction;
2) The implied (or assumed) suggestion;
3) A behavioral response to signal when the implied suggestion has been carried out.

Binds

The therapist offers a free, conscious choice of two or more alternatives and whichever choice is made leads behavior in the desired direction.

Double binds

The therapist offers possibilities of behavior that are outside the patient's usual range of conscious choice and control:

1) Time double bind;
2) Conscious-unconscious double bind;
3) Double dissociation double bind;
4) Reverse set double bind;
5) Nonsequitur double bind.

Multiple-level communication

1) Stories
2) Puns
3) Jokes
4) Riddles
5) Folk language
6) Analogies
7) Symbols

The Utilization Approach

The utilization approach is defined as accepting responses, behaviors and ideas as valid and using them to further therapeutic goals. This approach includes:

1) Accepting and utilizing the patient's manifest behavior;
2) Utilizing the patient's inner realities;
3) Utilizing the patient's resistances, including displacing and discharging resistance by eliciting the resistance and diverting it away from the therapy situation;
4) Utilizing the patient's negative affect and confusion;
5) Utilizing the patient's symptoms.

GORDON AND MYERS-ANDERSON'S FRAMEWORK

In their book, David Gordon and Maribeth Myers-Anderson (1981) offer several algorithms (explicit step-by-step instructions) for describing and reproducing Erickson's therapeutic, rather than strictly hypnotic, work.

They break up the major types of interventions into:

1) Reference frame interventions;
2) Behavioral interventions.

They offer three generalizations about Erickson's basic orientation in therapy:

1) The importance of flexibility of both the client and the therapist;
2) The importance of humor;
3) The future orientation.

They give the three types of "pacing" which are important for the therapist to use in order to gain rapport: "content," "behavioral," and "cultural." The therapist matches the client's model of the world in each of these areas to develop and maintain rapport.

Reference Frame Interventions

Under the rubric of reference frame interventions (which might also be called reframing), there are three categories with their corresponding algorithms:

Sorting for assets

This is used when an individual has some behavior or characteristic that is personally undesirable, but which would be difficult or impossible to change. The formula for this intervention is as follows:

1) Identify the cause-effect relationship between the undesired behavior/characteristic and the client's goal;
2) Identify some highly valued desired state or criterion to which the unwanted behavior/characteristic is (or could be) connected;
3) Pace the client's experience by explicitly stating your understanding of what he or she identifies as the cause and effect of the problem situation;
4) Get the individual to commit to defending the present perspective;
5) Make explicit the cause-effect relationship between the client's presently unwanted behavior/characteristic and the highly valued desired state identified as being within his or her model of the world.

Sorting for big liabilities

This is used when it is possible and desirable for clients to change behavior, but their frame of reference provides a rationale to make such inappropriate behavior acceptable. In such a case the algorithm provided is:

1) Identify the pattern of behavior to be changed, making sure that it can be changed *and* that it is useful to do so;
2) Identify within the client's model of the world some *highly valued* criterion, behavior, circumstance or outcome that is or could be described as being jeopardized by the inappropriate behavior;
3) Pace and enhance the client's security in his or her accepting the present perspective in relation to the inappropriate behavior;
4) Make "explicit" to the client the cause-effect relationship between his or her present behavior and the jeopardy it creates for what has been identified as being of great importance to him or her.

Sorting for relevance

In this pattern, the therapist arranges an experience that naturally generates the desired change in perspective that would lead to the new behavior, rather than explicitly providing that new perspective. The formula for this pattern is:

1) Identify what change in perspective would be most useful for the client (either seeing a former liability as an asset, or seeing a former acceptable behavior as undesirable);
2) Generate an experience that would *naturally* lead to the acquisition of that perspective;
3) Maintaining rapport at all times, assist the client in accessing that experience either through external behavior in the real world or vicariously through the utilization of internal representations.

Behavioral Interventions

This type of intervention begins with the distinction between the content and patterns of behavior. The content includes the specific aspects of behavior involved. The pattern is a sequence of behaviors characteristic to some particular context. There are several premises upon which Erickson's behavioral interventions are based:

1) Because people's behaviors are patterned, any change in that pattern will result in new interactions and experiences;
2) Patterns of behavior are perpetuated by the corresponding chains of environmental feedback created by those new behaviors;
3) It is unnecessary to delve into the ontogeny of a problem in order to effect a profound and lasting change;
4) There is a correspondence between one's model of the world and behavior such that altering one's behavior has a direct impact on the individual's experience and generalizations.

Three formulas are given for behavioral interventions. The first is to effect changes in inappropriate behavior through behavioral interventions:

1) Explicitly identify the outcome for the client in terms of what behavior and/or interactions are needed within the problem context;
2) Identify a situation which *naturally* (normally) results in anyone engaging in such behavior or interactions;
3) Utilize rapport and, if necessary, changes in frames of reference in order to inject the client into that situation.

Altering limiting frames

1) Specify what would constitute appropriate behavior within the problem context and what change in perspective would naturally produce that behavior;
2) Identify what real world experience would naturally install in almost any individual the belief or perspective you want the client to have;
3) Identify what behavior you could engage the client in that would naturally foment the previously identified experience *and*, if possible, utilize as a catalyst that characteristic or behavior that the client identifies as being the "cause" of the problem;
4) Utilize rapport and any necessary reference frame shifts to motivate the client to engage in the behavior.

Extinguishing an unwanted habitual behavior

1) Accept the client's unwanted behavior;
2) Attach as a contingent to it some additional piece of behavior that will eventually prove decisively burdensome.

OMER'S FRAMEWORK

In an article, Haim Omer (1982) offered a model of Erickson's therapeutic techniques. He divides the strategic functions in Erickson's therapy into three categories:

1) Mobilization of change-promoting forces;
2) Creation of boundaries facilitating change;
3) Symptom modification and decontextualization.

Mobilization of Change-Promoting Forces

1) Capitalizing on misery—Erickson allowed or encouraged the patient's pessimism to reach low ebb and then started treatment;
2) The pressure-cooker technique—the therapist builds naturally growing urges to change and then blocks the patient's normal outlets;
3) The Hitchcock ploy—Erickson enticed the patient's curiosity on a vital issue and then delayed the satisfaction of that curiosity.

Creation of Boundaries Facilitating Change

This category allows for breaking time into distinct phases by providing a "change" milestone as a rite of passage does. This category includes:

1) The dramatic overture—Erickson begins treatment with exaggerated flourish and fanfare;
2) Precommitment—the patient agrees to abide by the therapist's order, no matter what;
3) Achieving closure—dramatic or clear indications for the termination of the therapy are provided;
4) The therapeutic ordeal—a rite of passage, with a clear break from the previous situation, an extreme intensification of therapeutic pressure leading to an ordeal, and a gradual assumption of the new normal life roles.

Symptom Modification and Decontextualization

Symptom modification is encouraging the symptom with immediate modifications of the symptom itself. It usually proceeds by minimal changes. Decontextualization (which involves far-reaching modifications of the symptom's context) is accompanied by great leaps or reversals. Included in these categories are:

1) Gradual symptom modification—slight changes in the symptom are gradually introduced;
2) The divide and rule technique—a symptom is broken into successive stages and the therapist either blocks the progression from one stage to another or mixes up their normal order;
3) Modifying the spatial context—changing the location in which the symptom occurs;
4) Modifying the interpersonal context—reversing or altering the interactions surrounding and supporting the symptom;
5) Modifying the affective context—reversing or altering the feelings associated with the symptom;
6) Modifying the cognitive context—reframing, reconnoting or redefining the symptom.

LANKTONS' FRAMEWORK

Steve and Carol Lankton (1983) offered a model that describes Erickson's work and offers further concepts developed by them. Presented here are only those aspects of their framework that describe Erickson's work.

The Erickson Approach

Three features that typify an Ericksonian approach:

1) Indirection—the use of indirect suggestion, binds, metaphor and resource retrieval;
2) Conscious/unconscious dissociation—multiple-level communication, interspersal, double binds and multiple-embedded metaphors;
3) Utilization of the client's behavior—paradox, behavioral matching, naturalistic induction, symptom prescription and strategic use of trance phenomena.

Principles Underlying Erickson's Work

Eleven basic principles are said to underlie Erickson's work:

1) People operate out of their internal maps and not out of sensory experience;
2) People make the best choice for themselves at any given moment;
3) The explanation, theory, or metaphor used to relate facts about a person is not the person;
4) Respect all messages from the client;
5) Teach choice—never attempt to take choice away;
6) The resources clients need lie within their personal history;
7) Meet the client at his or her model of the world;
8) The person with the most flexibility or choice will be the controlling element in the system;
9) A person can't not communicate;
10) If it's hard work, reduce it down;
11) Outcomes are determined at the psychological level.

The flow of induction is delineated by the following seven steps:

1) Orient to trance;
2) Fixate attention and rapport;
3) Create conscious/unconscious dissociation;
4) Confirm and deepen the trance state;
5) Establish a learning frame or learning set;
6) Utilize trance state and phenomena for clinical goals;
7) Reorient to waking state.

Trance phenomena are used strategically to retrieve resources. There are four ways given to elicit trance phenomena:

1) Direct suggestions
2) Indirect suggestions
3) Anecdotes and metaphors
4) Structured amnesia

The model of metaphor given by the Lanktons includes several elements and is structured to elicit amnesia for the direct work that is done within the session. The phases of this model, called "multiple-embedded metaphor" are:

1) Induction;
2) Matching metaphor;
3) Metaphor to retrieve resources;

4) Direct work on core issue;
5) Linking resources to the social network;
6) End-matching metaphor;
7) Reorient to waking state.

REFERENCES

Bandler, R., & Grinder, J. (1975a). *Patterns of the hypnotic techniques of Milton H. Erickson, M.D.* (Vol. 1). Cupertino, CA: Meta Publications.
Bandler, R., & Grinder, J. (1975b). *The structure of magic: A book about language and therapy* (Vol. I). Palo Alto, CA: Science & Behavior Books.
Beahrs, O. (1971, October). The hypnotic psychotherapy of Milton H. Erickson. *The American Journal of Clinical Hypnosis, 14*(2), 73-90.
Erickson, M. H., & Rossi, E. L. (1979). *Hypnotherapy.* New York: Irvington.
Erickson, M. H., & Rossi, E. L. (1981). *Experiencing hypnosis.* New York: Irvington.
Erickson, M. H., Rossi, E. L., & Rossi, I. (1976). *Hypnotic realities.* New York: Irvington.
Gordon, D., & Myers-Anderson, M. (1981). *Phoenix: Therapeutic patterns of Milton Erickson.* Cupertino, CA: Meta Publications.
Grinder, J., Delozier, J., & Bandler, R. (1977). *Patterns of the hypnotic techniques of Milton H. Erickson, M.D.* (Vol. 2). Cupertino, CA: Meta Publications.
Haley, J. (1963). *Strategies of psychotherapy.* New York: Grune & Stratton.
Haley, J. (1967). *Advanced techniques of hypnosis and therapy.* New York: Grune & Stratton.
Haley, J. (1973). *Uncommon therapy: The psychiatric techniques of Milton H. Erickson, M.D.* New York: Norton.
Lankton, S., & Lankton, C. (1983). *The answer within: Clinical frameworks of Ericksonian hypnotherapy.* New York: Brunner/Mazel.
Omer, H. (1982). The macrodynamics of Ericksonian therapy. *The Journal of Strategic and Systemic Therapies, 1*(4), 34-44.

Chapter 4

Erickson vs. the Establishment: Which Won?

Ronald A. Havens

The title of this chapter was derived from a comment made at the First International Congress on Ericksonian Approaches to Hypnosis and Psychotherapy by Robert Pearson M.D., one of Erickson's earliest and most ardent admirers. Pearson said, "Erickson took on the establishment single-handedly, and he won. They don't know it yet. . . ." (Rosen, 1982, p. 18). The Second Congress would seem to be an auspicious occasion to once again raise the issue of Erickson's battles with the establishment, not simply to celebrate his victories but, more importantly, to examine what we can do to protect them.

Actually, it could be argued that it is still too early to determine which one won, because "which one won" is an issue that can be decided only after everyone knows what the fundamental differences are between Erickson and the establishment and then chooses which direction they will follow. Thus far, however, the truly revolutionary assumptions which formed the basis for Erickson's perspective and which placed him in direct conflict with the establishment have been too easy for us to ignore or overlook. In fact, the present trend seems to be to minimize conflicts and to focus instead upon seeming similarities or compatibilities between Erickson's approach and the approaches used by various members of the psychiatric, psychotherapeutic and hypnotherapeutic mainstreams. If such minimization of the basic dichotomies between Erickson and the establishment continues, it is quite possible that the members of the establishment never will know that he won because he will have been absorbed into and usurped by them.

The primary purpose of the present chapter, therefore, is to identify several features of Erickson's perspective which seem to set it apart from those currently in vogue. My intention is to amplify conflicts rather than to minimize them. It also is my intention to describe the natural forces at work throughout the field and within each one of us which, if left unchecked, may obscure conflicts and thus undermine the impact of Erickson's hard fought victories. Finally, I would like to suggest that hypnosis may be the ultimate weapon in our struggle to become effective clinicians, not merely as a technique to be used for working with our patients, but also as a strategy for helping us understand what Erickson had to offer.

Erickson's war with the establishment consisted of more than an effort to promote a few innovative techniques and concepts. Erickson was a maverick who proposed a major revolution in the fundamental paradigms employed by hypnotists and psychotherapists alike. He challenged the essential underlying processes used by his colleagues to formulate their understandings or opinions and, naturally enough, he rejected the resulting understandings and opinions. He argued not only that there is a better way to do psychotherapy and hypnosis, but also that there is a better way to think about them as well.

In general, most members of Western civilization operate on the unspoken assumption that correct or enlightened action stems from access to correct or enlightened thought. Plato apparently originated this notion with his proposition that philosophically derived Universal Truths provide the only legitimate basis for decisions regarding correct behavior (cf. Rorty, 1982). Since that time religious insight and scientific theory have been added as acceptable alternative sources of guidance, but the underlying assumption has remained the same, that is, that correct or appropriate responses emerge only after contact has been made with some universal secret or special source of ultimate knowledge.

The fields of psychotherapy and hypnosis were constructed within this framework. It pervades our thinking and is a fundamental axiom of the establishment. As members of the establishment, we assume that it is possible and even necessary to acquire an intellectual insight into the nature of human functioning. This intellectual insight is sought because it supposedly allows us to explain the behavior of others, to understand the source of their problems, to prescribe a desirable goal state and hence to decide how to behave toward patients in a curative manner. Psychoanalysts, for example, use a complex set of assumptions regarding the nature of people, the causes of psychopathology, and the structure of personality to explain events and to guide their behavior. Humanists, behaviorists, social-learning theorists and eclectics all employ different sets of hypotheses and assumptions to accomplish these same ends, but they likewise remain firmly committed to the premise that what they do with any given patient should be based upon general understandings or insights derived from a specific theoretical orientation. The unifying paradigm of the establishment, therefore, is the belief that the use of a procrustean bed of hypothetical constructs, theoretical propositions or philosophical assumptions is feasible and desirable.

Erickson, on the other hand, argued that thought and action should be based purely upon the information and learnings acquired through careful observation of the realities we experience directly. He did not believe it was possible or productive to go beyond the raw data provided by his patients. He rejected efforts to draw speculative conclusions on the basis of theoretical generalizations, and limited his understandings solely to the information he obtained from his patients by careful observation. Unfortunately, he had learned how to gain information or communications from such remarkably subtle and usually overlooked sources that it often seemed to others as if he must be relying upon special theories, insights or intuitions. He vehemently denied such misconceptions whenever they occurred, however, and constantly reiterated that he based what he did *solely* upon the information he acquired via careful observation.

Erickson's suggestion that we use observation as the basis for our knowledge and action bears a striking resemblance to the "pragmatic" orientation recently described by Rorty (1982) as a reaction against the philosophical establishment. Pragmatism is a movement within philosophy which also challenges the validity of the Platonic assumption that Universal Truths are knowable, much less usable, as the basis for correct action. Pragmatists argue that the best possible responses in everyday life stem not from access to Universal Truths, but from a direct and detailed awareness of what *is* at any point in time. Observationally based experiential learning is their preferred source of guidance, not philosophically derived assumptions. As we have noted, Erickson preferred the same and he used direct experience both as the basic element within his therapeutic interventions and as the basis for his knowledge about the goals and processes of therapy and hypnosis.

This dichotomy of paradigms between Erickson and the establishment also bears a striking resemblance to a dichotomy which exists among the practitioners of psychic reading. According to Hyman (1981), psychic readers can be divided into two groups. One group assumes that mind reading and fortune telling actually are possible if the psychic can obtain special intuitive powers, special knowledge or contact with a supernatural source of information. The other group rejects such notions as nonsense, but maintains that it is possible to acquire a tremendous amount of information surreptitiously from a careful observation of the various verbal and nonverbal cues unintentionally and unwittingly provided by the client. Although Hyman found that both groups depended upon such unintentional cues, as well as upon vague Barnum statements, to create the illusion of mind reading, only members of the disbeliever group were consciously aware of what they were doing. True believers remained firmly convinced that their "insights" must have been derived from the supernatural or mystical sources of knowledge that they thought they were using at the time.

The psychotherapeutic and hypnotherapeutic establishments suffer from delusions remarkably similar to those of the true-believer psychics. As indicated previously, it generally is believed within these fields that it is possible and even necessary to utilize theories of human behavior as the basis for understanding others and for deciding what to do to them. From Erickson's perspective, this assumption is comparable to the assumption that mind reading is possible. The only difference is that the true-believer mind readers assume they need a mystical source of insight whereas the true-believer psychotherapists assume they need a theoretical one.

Although Erickson made this point on numerous occasions, perhaps his strongest statement in this regard was originally published in 1966 when he said that he did not know of ". . . anybody who has ever really understood the variety and purposes of any one patient's multiple symptoms despite the tendency of many psychiatrists to hypothecate, to their own satisfaction, towering structures of explanation often as elaborate and bizarre as the patient's symptomatology (Rossi, 1980, p. 202). Not only does this hypothecation result in an enormous waste of time and energy in the pursuit of something that Erickson maintained was not possible, it also prevents practitioners from objectively perceiving the information that is continually provided to them by their patients. Instead, they are encouraged to interpret everything from within a rigid and restricting conceptual framework and, hence, become unable to perceive what is actually there.

Furthermore, the idea that there must be a right way of thinking about things almost necessarily leads to the assumption that there must be a right way of doing things. By assuming that somewhere there is an as yet undiscovered, theoretical basis for therapy or hypnosis, the establishment implicitly has assumed that somewhere there are derivative universally effective techniques for doing these things.

The resulting frantic search for the specific rituals which are inherently universally therapeutic or hypnotic, in turn, has contributed to the wide-spread assumption that therapists should be taught *the* right way to do therapy *to* patients or that hypnotists should be taught *the* right way to do therapy *to* patients or that hypnotists should be taught *the* right way to do hypnosis *to* subjects. Erickson specifically stated that there can be no single best technique for enabling hypnosis or therapy to occur and encouraged his students instead to continually devise unique ways of doing things with each patient. He also maintained that patients, not therapists, do therapy and that subjects, not hypnotists, do hypnosis. From within Erickson's perspective, therapists and hypnotists play the same role in these processes as do parents running along holding up bicycles while their children learn how to ride. The children do the learning, whereas the parents merely provide the opportunity to ex-perience the learning process more easily or safely.

In summary, therefore, the wars Erickson fought with the establish-ment were neither battles over which techniques were more useful than others nor were they minor theoretical or philosopical debates. Erickson fought for an entirely new way of looking at things and thinking about things. The underlying attitudes of the establishment promote a search for universally applicable theoretical explanations of human behavior; encourage logical deduction within specific theoretical frameworks as a means of obtaining insights into the causes of a particular patient's problems; and foster the ritualistic use of specific patterns of behavior to do a form of therapy or hypnosis to others that is deemed to be inherently therapeutic or hypnotic. Erickson, in contrast, was obsessed both by the task of learning via observation of the conditions under which people do therapy and hypnosis to themselves, and with learning how to help others create those conditions for their own benefit. He suggested that an accurate description of the underlying causes of hu-man behavior cannot be deduced on the basis of theory but can be obtained only by learning how to understand what patients are com-municating in their own unique ways.

WHICH WON?

If the Second International Congress on Ericksonian Approaches to Hypnosis and Psychotherapy were to stimulate a widespread adoption of Erickson's fundamental perspective, it would send shock waves throughout the psychiatric, psychotherapeutic and hypnotherapeutic communities. On the other hand, unless we are careful, the Congress could contribute to the ongoing trivialization and usurpation of his basic paradigm by the very cognitive processes he opposed and endeavored to overthrow.

Consider, for example, the almost irresistible temptation to try to explain Erickson's work from within one or another of the traditional theoretical frameworks or to suggest that his approaches can be understood more easily by comparing them to those used by gestalt therapists, Rogerians, behaviorists, cognitive therapists or some combination thereof. Such conceptual exercises may be appealing or comforting, but they are inherently antithetical to the promotion or adoption of an Ericksonian perspective. After all, it would seem to be logically impossible to enter into a perspective which has rejection of theoretical speculation as its cornerstone by engaging in theoretical speculation.

An equally counterproductive approach to the study of Erickson's strategies is to focus exclusively upon the mechanics of one or more of his techniques and to assume that becoming an Ericksonian means learning how to utilize those particular techniques. This tendency to reify the specifics of a technique and to apply that technique ritualistically to every individual as if it possessed universal curative powers is another example of the establishment mentality at work. As indicated previously, Erickson promoted a specific conceptual perspective from which to view the processes of hypnosis and psychotherapy, not the universal application of specific techniques. He did not tell us what to do, he taught us how to use our own resources to recognize the nature of the situation and to respond to it in an appropriate way for our patients and ourselves. Therapists or hypnotists who emphasize one Ericksonian technique or another instead of an Ericksonian perspective merely perpetuate the mentality Erickson fought against.

In spite of Erickson's increasing popularity, therefore, the essential ingredients of his underlying perspective tend to be undermined and contradicted continually by our own ongoing, well-intentioned efforts to translate his words and to make his techniques more easily comprehensible and more widely imitatable. As he so frequently noted, we attempt to interpret what he said and did from within our previous orientations instead of using what he said and did as a way of entering into his orientation. Consequently, we perpetuate the very attitudes and behaviors he strove to overcome.

If Erickson's victories are to be translated into a major revolution and if his effectiveness is to become a standard for the profession, then each one of us must make an attempt to reject our underlying biases and prejudices and to transcend the limitations placed upon us by our previous immersion in the modes of thought of the establishment. We must reject our lazy tendency to explain events, including Erickson's work, from within theoretical frameworks. We must resist the seductive notion that we can become effective professionals merely by memorizing concepts or imitating techniques. We must challenge those who would have us believe that we can approximate Erickson's wisdom and effectiveness in any manner that does not involve a total commitment to his way of seeing things and to his way of learning about others.

Essentially, we must refuse to be led astray by those who claim to be Ericksonian but who remain committed underneath to old beliefs, constructs and unwarranted assumptions. Becoming an Ericksonian does not mean absorbing his wisdom and techniques into our old perspectives nor interpreting his wisdom from within our previous frameworks. It means having the courage to relinquish our commitments to the establishment and to enter into new ways of thinking and acting as professionals. Therefore, it probably also means creating a new profession, one that bears no more loyalty or relationship to the traditional approaches of the establishment than astronomy does to astrology.

Within this revolutionary new profession, individuals would no longer refer to themselves as behaviorists, gestaltists, analysts, eclectics or any other term reflecting commitments to specific theoretical explanations or to particular techniques. Even Ericksonians might no longer exist as such. All that would remain would be professionals who provide therapeutic services based upon the universal recognition that all people, including hypnotists and psychotherapists, run into problems whenever they subscribe to rigid, restricted or arbitrary concepts of what is or should be instead of to objective observations.

At that point Erickson will have won, although there will be few, if any, members of the establishment left to acknowledge it. By refusing to provide pat answers or theoretical rationalizations and by instead encouraging us to utilize the perspective offered by our own experiential realities, Erickson set the stage for his ultimate feat. That psychotherapeutic wizard and master hypnotist created the conditions necessary for the eventual disappearance of the professional establishment as we now know it. When we stop believing in the myths and assumptions upon which the establishment is based, it will vanish just as miraculously as did the emperor's new clothes.

PROMOTING THE REVOLUTION

Unfortunately, recognizing that a new, more objective and more pragmatic perspective is necessary as the basis for the development of

Ericksonian understandings and approaches is easier than actually adopting such a perspective. Professionals are just as immersed in their biased mental sets as patients are in theirs, and intentionally entering into Erickson's way of seeing things is just as difficult and confusing for therapists set in their traditionally based patterns of thought as it is for neurotics to intentionally become more rational.

In this respect, it is worth noting that Erickson did not rely exclusively upon rational discourse nor intellectual analyses when dealing with either his patients or his students. In both instances, he frequently used hypnosis as a means of stimulating an increased objectivity and receptivity with regard to new ideas, unconscious capacities, and transformational learning experiences.

It might even be argued that Erickson used trance as a means of enabling his students to enter into a state or perspective compatible with his own, a state within which they could actually personally experience the validity of his observations and the impact of his interventions. The qualities or basic features of the trance state, after all, are similar to the basic ingredients of the perspectives or qualities underlying Erickson's work. Each involves focused awareness, openness or receptivity, flexibility, literalness, a lack of assumptions and access to unconscious understandings or abilities. The hypnotic view of reality, in fact, may be the one view of reality from within which an Ericksonian perspective can be learned and utilized.

Beahrs (1977) was one of the first to suspect that Erickson's observations and responses stemmed, at least partially, from an almost continual immersion in trance. This suspicion is given additional credence by Erickson's admission that "when there is a crucial issue with a patient and I don't want to miss any of the clues, I go into trance" (Erickson & Rossi, 1977, p. 42).

This is not meant to imply that all anyone needs to do to learn how to think or act in a manner comparable to Erickson's is to go into a trance state. Rather, it is meant to imply that learning how to enter a trance and how to experience events in that state of mind may be one of the most efficient and effective strategies for undergoing the shift out of a traditional mode of thought into an Ericksonian one. What better way to let go of conscious biases and rigidities that otherwise might obscure perceptions and understandings than to enter into a state of mind designed to do exactly that? What better way to learn about the unconscious or about the impact of puns, metaphors and confusion techniques than to experience them directly during trance?

This may seem to be a rather bizarre or frightening proposition to some people. We are used to learning how to think and act by reading books, attending lectures and watching demonstrations. We are not used to the notion that effective professional training might consist, instead, of learning how to enter a trance state, of being given the opportunity to experience the effects of different interventions upon ourselves while in that trance state, and even of learning how to do therapy while in a trance, with the full confidence that our trained and perceptive unconscious will know the right thing to do at the right time.

These may seem like strange propositions, yet they are exactly the intervention strategies that Ericksonians promote for their patients. If they are appropriate and useful for our patients, certainly they could be equally appropriate and useful for ourselves. The old dictum, "Physician heal thyself," would seem to be especially applicable in this instance, only it probably should be altered to read, "Ericksonian hypnotize thyself."

CONCLUSION

Much as his followers might admire or respect Erickson's approach and aspire to adopt it as their own, the establishment mentality they carry within them threatens to turn his accomplishments into just another fad which the traditional schools can simply ignore or eventually absorb. What is needed in order to prevent such an outcome seems to be a dramatic and widespread shift in perspective among his followers, a shift that is unlikely to be initiated by logical analysis of his work, careful descriptions of his techniques or comparisons of his approaches to those with which people are more familiar and more comfortable. Intellectual rationalizations and conscious intentions are not the most productive basis for such global shifts into a pragmatic perspective and do not promise creation of the new profession Erickson pioneered.

Hypnosis, Erickson's primary therapeutic tool, does seem to offer an appropriate and potent stimulus for such conceptual transformations. Rather than reserving this tool for our patients' use alone, we might do well to begin using it upon ourselves. The hard sciences came of age when they stopped relying upon pure speculation and began using instruments of various sorts to more closely observe the realities they were attempting to understand. Hypnosis very well may be the instrument needed by the helping professions to observe the realities of therapy.

REFERENCES

Beahrs, J.O. (1977). Integrating Erickson's approach. *American Journal of Clinical Hypnosis,* *20,* 55-68.

Erickson, M.H., & Rossi, E.L. (1977). Autohypnotic experiences of Milton H. Erickson. *American Journal of Clinical Hypnosis, 20,* 36-54.

Hyman, R. (1981). The psychic reading. In T.A. Sebeok & R. Rosenthal (Eds.), *The Clever Hans phenomenon: Communication with horses, whales, apes, and people.* New York: New York Academy of Sciences.

Rorty, R. (1982). *Consequences of pragmatism.* Minneapolis: University of Minnesota Press.

Rosen, S. (1982). *My voice will go with you: The teaching tales of Milton H. Erickson, M.D.* New York: Norton.

Rossi, E.L. (Ed.). (1980). *The collected papers of Milton H. Erickson on hypnosis* (Vol. 4). *Innovative hypnotherapy.* New York: Irvington.

Chapter 5

The Role of Presuppositions in Ericksonian Psychotherapy

David Gordon

Explanations of Milton Erickson's work usually take the form of extractions of patterns of his therapeutic interactions. These patterns often are codified and standardized as *techniques*. For example, in *Uncommon Therapy*, Jay Haley (1973) described many of Erickson's techniques, such as encouraging a client to respond more fully by intentionally frustrating the client's expression of behavior. Bandler and Grinder (1975) presented a number of hypnotic techniques in Erickson's verbal patterns, such as embedding direct commands within an otherwise non-suggestive sentence. In *Phoenix*, Meribeth Anderson and I (1981) discussed several ways Erickson led his clients to new beliefs and behaviors, such as changing a client's perspective regarding a defect by associating that defect with some higher order, highly valued outcome or criterion. Other books, articles and the Ericksonian conferences have provided more examples of his techniques. And, of course, there are articles in which Erickson described in his own words techniques such as his interspersal technique (Haley, 1967).

As technical descriptions of Erickson's work proliferate it must be remembered that he did not create most of those techniques. They are the creations of those who described his work, and did so from their own (biased) perspectives. Erickson just behaved as himself. Despite distortions in descriptions that investigators might introduce, techniques are classified as "Ericksonian" by virtue of the therapeutic orientations the technique fulfills (or at least *intends* to fulfill).

Of course, work Erickson himself described as techniques are definitely "Ericksonian." The interspersal technique, for example, is immediately identifiable as being congruent with Erickson's closely held beliefs about the responsiveness of the unconscious mind, the presence in every person of the necessary reference experiences, the responsibility of the therapist as guide, and so on.

This is not to say that the psychotherapeutic and hypnotic techniques Erickson developed had to wait for him to be discovered. There have been individuals unfamiliar with Erickson's work who nevertheless developed some of the same techniques. An explanation that can be provided for how it is that people have "on occasion" done what Erickson did (Erickson *always* used Ericksonian approaches) is that such approaches are the natural consequence of someone having had compelling life experiences that were similar to those that Erickson had learned from (as opposed to occurring as the result of an "accidental" set of circumstances, a moment of inspiration, or genetics).

As much as people might like to reproduce the kind of work that Erickson did, it is impossible to step into his personal history or be able to *be* him. We are left with the choice of trying to emulate his behaviors in the form of techniques with the hope that this will reproduce the same outcomes Erickson himself achieved. One also can hope that techniques can be described in a form that makes it possible for almost anyone to use them successfully. A "good" technique might be measured both by how homologous it is with the work of its originator and by the extent to which it is consistently effective.

The value of a "good" technique is that it allows one to get the same outcomes as did the person from whom it was gleaned *without* having to be that person. A limitation of even a good technique, however, is that it is usually little more than a description of behavior(s) to be performed within a (hopefully) specified context.

What is generally left out of technical descriptions are the *presuppositions* out of which the technique evolved. By presupposition I am referring to those beliefs/assumptions/biases (whether conscious or not) that a person takes for granted as being true; that is, the standards with which an individual perceives and judges the world. Like looking at the world through a piece of colored cellophane, presuppositions act as filters of experience, promoting to significance those perceptual and cognitive experiences that fit the bias of the presupposition and deleting or distorting those experiences that do not fit. Erickson demonstrated this point while lecturing a group of students:

> In teaching medical students I'd give long lectures to the effect that they should do some outside reading, and I'd point to a certain bookcase. I would tell them, "There is a book there on Human

Laterality," and I would ask one of the students to go and find that book in that bookcase, and his frame: "It has the title Human Laterality printed on it very plainly and there's no mistaking the book—it's a hardcover book, a brilliant red in color." And then I'd let him go to the bookcase to find the book while the class watched him. And some of the students whose vision was good enough could locate that title and would be surprised when their classmate went right past the book. After he had searched the bookcase repeatedly, hoping he would find that bright red, hardcover book, titled Human Laterality, I would tell him, "Begin in the upper left-hand corner of the bookcase, upper left-hand corner of the top shelf and read the titles one by one until you've found the book, that bright red book, titled Human Laterality." And he would read each title, including Human Laterality, and go on to the next book. The class was always startled when he read, "Human Laterality" without attaching any meaning to it and then when he had read the titles twice and declared emphatically that book was not there, then I would tell another student, "Go and pick out from the bookcase a book called Human Laterality—it's blue." And he'd find the book easily because it *was* a hardcovered, blue-colored book. Now his classmate had searched for that book with a certain frame of reference, and that frame of reference included a hard cover, a bright red color and two words—"Human Laterality." Those are distinctive words, but they were only a mere *part* of a frame of reference in which he was searching. Just reading the two words was not sufficient. And we do that all the time. And you are blind to things, fail to hear things, fail to feel things, we fail to smell things, we fail to taste things, we fail to recognize kinesthetic sensations, proprioceptive sensations . . . and that's part of living, because in your conscious living you tend to select certain parts and remain unaware of other things. (Gordon & Anderson, 1981, p. 183)

The significance of Erickson's demonstration is that by having a preset representation (perceptual template) of what he should see (set by Erickson's instruction), the student became response-blind to that which did not meet the perceptual template. It was not that the student did not see the correct book, but that since it was not congruent with what he was looking for, it had no significance for him. Undoubtedly everyone can find in their own personal history a similar example. Each of us also has many closely held presuppositions about the world which will compel experience in just the same way as does looking for a red book that is actually blue.

The direction that internal response and external behavior take is greatly influenced by the presuppositions under which one operates. All things being equal, two people with two different presuppositions about a certain context will respond differently within that context. Since our concern here is to understand the nature of Erickson's approach to psychotherapy and because presuppositions influence the effectiveness of technique, it is important to specify the presuppositions that combined to create the perceptual and cognitive filters that he used (however unconsciously) in developing approaches. Five presuppositions are especially relevant:

EACH PERSON HAS A UNIQUE MODEL OF THE WORLD

And remember this. That all of us have our individual language, and that when you listen to a patient, you should listen knowing that he is speaking an alien language and that you should not try to understand in terms of your language. Understand the patient in *his* language. (Rosen, 1982, p. 116)

This first presupposition—that every one of us has a unique model of the world—is one that is frequently noted when Erickson's work is described. Most of his work was structured to take into account and pace (match) the model of the individual with whom he was working. Even techniques Erickson developed that were intended to be used with almost anyone, such as the handshake induction or interspersal technique, were structured to be inherently flexible and responsive. Using the handshake induction or interspersal technique without the benefit of this presupposition of individual uniqueness results in only fortuitous success. A pat routine of handshake interruption and pressure changes often fails because the technique demands that those pattern interruptions and pressure changes occur in relation to the responses of the subject. Similarly, a routinized interspersal induction often fails since the technique demands embedded suggestions which are in accord with the *subject's* timing, ability to detect the suggestions, momentary needs, etc.

An example of Erickson's recognition of, and respect for, the uniqueness of each individual's model of the world can be found in his treatment of a psychiatric inmate who believed himself to be Jesus Christ:

I told him how desirable it was for the doctors to play tennis in the recreation hour. They were using muscles and skills and abilities that God had endowed them with. And it was very imperative that the tennis grounds be kept in good shape . . . dirt court. And we wandered down to the tennis court. We made a lot of comments about the trees that God had made, the beautiful grass, the creation of the earth itself, and then I noticed that there were some rough spots on that dirt court and I told him I was sure that God didn't want those rough spots there and could he in some way succeed in having the tennis grounds leveled carefully and smoothed out? He said he would try, he was there to serve Mankind. So I left him. He was an excellent tennis court grounds keeper. As for the Psychology Laboratory, they wanted some bookcases built. I happened to mention Jesus was a carpenter. So he built the bookcases. He became a handyman around the Psychology Laboratory. (Gordon & Anderson, 1981, p. 43)

That Erickson *utilized* his client's model of the world (rather than merely appreciating it) led to his becoming *flexible* in his judgments and interactions with clients, since the presupposition of uniqueness precludes assuming that any one approach can be applied to more than one client without at least some revision.

When you listen to people talk, listen to all the possibilities. Be comprehensive and unrestrictive in your thinking and don't just try to apply the third line, the fourth page of Carl Rogers' book to *any* patient. (Rosen, 1982, p. 182)

Once a therapist perceives each individual as representing a unique model of the world, it becomes appropriate (and perhaps necessary) to develop flexibility of judgment and response, since no prepackaged interactions will be effective in all cases. This is true not only of therapeutic interactions, but of all interactions. Accordingly, Erickson often oriented his clients toward flexibility in thinking about their problems and life in general.

MANIPULATION IS INHERENT IN INTERACTIONS

I've been accused of manipulating patients—to which I reply: Every mother manipulates her baby—if she wants it to live. And every time you go to the store you manipulate the clerk to do your bidding. And when you go to a restaurant, you manipulate the waiter. And the teacher in school manipulates you into learning to read and write. In fact, life is one big manipulation. (Rosen, 1982, p. 213)

Although the notion of "manipulation" is immediately offensive to many individuals, the sense in which Erickson used it was "to handle or influence with artful skill." Erickson's presupposition was that manipulation is inherent in interactions. Since it is inherent, the only questions left to be decided are the form, quality, and direction of the manipulation.

In general, Erickson artfully and skillfully influenced his clients so as to provide them with the opportunity to utilize their own resources to achieve their desired outcomes. Rosen (1982) recorded a revealing example of the functioning of this presupposition. Erickson instructed a client to climb Squaw Peak. After some resistance to the request, she finally did it. When asked why he had her make the climb, Erickson replied: "So she would obey me." Erickson often pointed out that it was important that the therapist direct the treatment. If he could not obtain obedience in at least one specific area, he would feel that there was no point in continuing treatment (Rosen, 1982, p. 235).

It is also important to understand that Erickson's presupposition about manipulation was tempered by his presupposition about the uniqueness of each individual. Without the assumption of individuality, manipulation can take the form of a mold into which all individuals are squeezed. With the presupposition of uniqueness, however, Erickson's manipulations took the form of a dance in which the movements of his client had to be taken into consideration, responded to, and used if the work together was to be successful.

THERE IS AN ACCESSIBLE UNCONSCIOUS MIND

Therapy is primarily a motivation of the unconscious to make use of all its many and varied learnings. (Rosen, 1982, p. 163)

In this quote, Erickson expresses two important aspects of this presupposition: There is an unconscious mind, and it can be used. Erickson defined the unconscious mind as being "made up of all your learnings over a lifetime, many of which you have completely forgotten, but which serve you in your automatic functioning" (Zeig, 1980, p. 33). To Erickson the overall task of psychotherapy was to assist the client in accessing the unconscious learnings he or she needed to achieve the desired outcome. Erickson's notion of what constituted unconscious learnings was broad, encompassing not only unconscious processes but the wealth of actual perceptions and experiences (or "reference experiences") that each person has stored over a lifetime. One of the consequences of this broad definition of the unconscious was that it expanded the scope of utilization from the context of formal trance to any interaction in which reference experiences are accessed. Consider the following short piece of therapy from Zeig's *A Teaching Seminar With Milton H. Erickson*. Jane, the client, has asked for help with Raynaud's disease. Erickson tells her about another Raynaud's patient of his that he instructed to set "little fires" in his fingertips:

Jane: The only thing is, I'm toes.
E: So set a fire there every now and then, mentally.
Jane: Now?
E: If you could think *right now* of what I could think, it would make your face turn red. (laughter) Now, you know that you have capillary control in the face?
Jane: (nods her head)
E: In your arms? You have had goosebumps there before. (Jane looks at her arms.) When you go from warm weather to zero weather, you get goosebumps there and all over your body. I hope that you've had the experience of stepping into the bathtub when the water was too hot and discovering that you had a lot of goosebumps on your legs because there is an overflow from the heat receptors to the cold receptors.

  Now you can blush with your feet as well as your face. (Erickson chuckles.) You have found out that you can set a fire in your face. (Erickson laughs.) And thanks for the demonstration. (Everybody laughs.)
Jane: It is very hot in here. (laughter) (Zeig, 1980, p. 190)

In this excerpt Erickson was assisting Jane in accessing previously unconscious learnings without resorting to a trance induction. The listing of case studies in the references for this chapter provides numerous examples of tranceless utilization of stored unconscious reference experiences. In fact, *most* of the cases described in those references do not include formal trance.

This presupposition has a great deal to do with determining Erickson's approach to therapy. Without the presupposition of an accessible unconscious, his skillful, individualized therapeutic manipulations would be directed toward simply modifying the client's behavior and/or toward reorganizing the client's conscious understandings. The addition of the presupposition about the unconscious changes the tenor of those manipulations dramatically, leading Erickson to discover ways of recognizing, communicating with, accessing, and using each client's unconscious processes.

EXPERIENCE AND BEHAVIOR ARE PATTERNED

Human beings being human tend to react in *patterns* and we are all governed by patterns of behavior. And when you start a pattern of behavior they tend to follow it. You don't realize how very rigidly patterned all of us are. (Gordon & Anderson, 1981, p. 104)

Although everyone possesses a unique model of the world, there are patterns of experience and behavior which are characteristic of individuals and of people in general. By "pattern" I refer to sequences of internal and external responses which almost invariably occur within a specified context. For example, ask people, "How are you?" (context) and they will respond automatically with some variation of "fine"—whether they really are fine or not. Such everyday patterns as exchanging greetings, apologizing for bumping into someone, and shaking hands, are so ingrained as sequences that interrupting them usually results in profound confusion and inability to proceed to the next response. Similarly, individuals have characteristic patterns. The person who acquiesces to every request and the person who responds to requests as demands and refuses to accede to them are both demonstrating unique patterns of characteristic behavior which are in response to the same context.

The impact of Erickson's presupposition regarding behavioral and experiential patterns is evident throughout his work. The way in which this presupposition often was manifested in his work was in the fact that he typically made *small* changes—changes that he was confident would lead to the desired outcome because of the patterns of experience and behavior of which that change was a natural precursor. For instance, Erickson's work with a pianist with stage fright consisted of instructing him to lay out a row of different colored towels leading from the wings to the piano, and to then decide as he went down the row which of the towels he should faint on. In this way the pianist's attention was so absorbed in something other than being frightened that he ended up sitting at the piano, playing comfortably (Gordon & Anderson, 1981, p.

139). In another case, a woman called Erickson about her college-age son who suffered from a "vicious case of acne":

> I said, "Well at Christmas time you can probably afford to take him to some ski resort, a long distance from Massachusetts." She took him to Aspen, Colorado. And upon my instructions she rented a cabin and disposed of all mirrors. And in two weeks time his acne cleared up. He got in a lot of skiing. He never had a chance to look in a mirror, he never had a chance to pick at his face . . . And acne is very much perpetuated by mirrors. (Gordon & Anderson, 1981, p. 127)

Erickson needed only to suggest a small change, and everything else necessarily changed. This is the basis of the "snowball effect" to which Erickson often referred. Since experience and behavior are based on patterns, the therapist's task is to assist clients in establishing new patterns of behavior by engaging them in contexts which will lead naturally to new patterns.

CHANGE COMES ABOUT AS THE RESULT OF EXPERIENCE

> Learning by experience is much more educational than learning consciously. You can learn all the movements of swimming while you're lying on your belly on a piano stool. You can establish your rhythms, breathing, head movement, arm movements, feet movements, and so on. When you get in the water, you only know how to dog-paddle. You have to learn to *swim* in the *water*. And when you have learned that, you have got a learning. Learning experientially is the most important thing. (Rosen, 1982, p. 163)

One of the most important and (I believe) undervalued presuppositions influencing Erickson's therapeutic interventions was his belief in change through direct experience (rather than through insight and understanding). Most examples of Erickson's therapeutic work are built around the notion that it is experience which changes people. The most obvious examples are his task-oriented interventions, in which he directed clients to engage in certain real-life experiences. This could have taken the form of an unhappy couple climbing Squaw Peak (Gordon & Anderson, 1981, p. 93), an exasperated mother sitting on her destructive and abusive 8-year-old son (Haley, 1973, p. 213), a female-fearing young man enduring an embarrassing dinner with a divorcee (Haley,

1973, p. 68), etc. In the following example, Erickson works with a "horribly depressed," reclusive woman. He could have explored her reasons for being depressed, or encouraged her to get involved with others, but instead:

> I . . . asked to be taken on a tour of the house. In looking around I could see she was a very wealthy woman living alone, idle, attending church but keeping to herself, and I went through the house room after room . . .and I saw three African violets and a potting pot with a leaf in it being sprouted as a new plant. So I knew what to do for her in the way of therapy. I told her, "I want you to buy every African violet plant in view for yourself . . . those are yours. I want you to buy a couple hundred potting pots for you to sprout new African violets, and you buy a couple hundred gift pots. As soon as the sprouts are well rooted, for every birth announcement you send an African violet, for every Christening, for every engagement, for every wedding, for every sickness, for every death, every church bazaar." And one time she had two hundred African violets . . . and if you take care of two hundred African violets you've got a day's work cut out. And she became the African Violet Queen of Milwaukee with an endless number of friends. (Gordon & Anderson, 1981, p. 124)

Perhaps less obvious examples of Erickson's experiential orientation toward learning and change were his metaphorical and hypnotherapeutic interventions. Metaphors usually are *vicarious* experiences; however, they subtly engage the listener's representational processes in such a way as to give that person at least some of the sensory experience that they would have if they actually were living the story being told.

Moreover, Erickson made extensive use of hypnosis to provide his clients with experiences, rather than simply as an opportunity to convey directive suggestions. These experiences took the form of either (or both) accessed reference experiences from the client's past, or created experiences which he generated for a specific purpose. For example, Erickson hypnotized a suicidal woman and took her on a hallucinated trip to the arboretum to see everything growing there, to the zoo to see the baby animals, and to the beach to "*marvel* at the vastness of the ocean . . . all the *mysteries* of the ocean" (Gordon & Anderson, 1981, p. 102). Instead of committing suicide, the woman joined the Navy, traveled, married, and had children. Rather than using the trance to explore the reasons for her wish to kill herself, or to instruct her *not* to kill herself, or even to explain to her that growth, children, and the mysteries of life made life worth living, Erickson chose to lead her through *experiences* which presupposed those learnings.

A natural corollary of Erickson's presupposition regarding the primacy of experience is that *it is the client who does the work*:

> I dislike authoritative techniques and much prefer the permissive techniques as a result of my own experience. What your patient does and what he learns must be learned from within himself. There is not anything you can force into that patient. (Haley, 1967, p. 535)

It is the job of the therapist to create an opportunity for change, to get the ball rolling, and perhaps to offer some guidance as the client progresses, but it is the client who must sieze the opportunity and expend whatever effort is required in utilizing it for personal benefit.

Erickson's belief in experience as the source of change and that it is the client who does the work naturally led him to develop such intervention formats as metaphor, tasking, and reference-experience–based trance work. Two additional consequences of this orientation should be mentioned. The first is that Erickson had little use for insight. Since it will be the experiences that a person has which will (or will not) lead to change, insight takes on value only when it forms the necessary basis for some learning experience:

> I didn't talk to him about his fear of women. I showed an interest in his physique and worked with him on what sort of apartment a man with his musculature and strength and brains should have . . . As his body image improved, he changed his ways. Why should I ever tell him he was afraid of women? He isn't anymore. He's married. (Haley, 1973, p. 67)

A second consequence of Erickson's experience-based orientation is that he was patient when it came to therapy. Much is said about Erickson's seemingly miraculous ability to bring about change in a session or two. This speed should not overshadow the fact that Erickson often worked with clients over periods of months and years. Erickson's premium was not placed on being fast and precipitous, nor was it placed on being slow and deliberate. Rather, it was on providing his client with the opportunity to experience what needed to be learned—and that could take a moment or it could take years.

DISCUSSION

Certainly, Erickson was guided by more presuppositions than the five listed here, but most of those other presuppositions were more highly contextualized (that is, relevant to specific contexts, such as "depressions" or "resistance") than the ones just described, which address the relatively broader context of human experience and interactions. The presuppositions that

- Each Person Has a Unique Model of the World
- Manipulation is Inherent in Interactions
- There is an Accessible Unconscious Mind
- Experience and Behavior are Patterned
- Change Comes About as the Result of Experiences

are pervasive throughout Erickson's work. These presuppositions are reflected in Erickson's approach and interventions in *every* case study in this chapter. They comprise the essential set of perceptual and cognitive filters through which clients were viewed and interventions designed. It is important to consider, then, to what extent and in what ways these underlying presuppositions continue to be of importance to the successful use of techniques that have evolved out of those experiential filters.

First, since people with differing presuppositions will perceive the same situation differently, one should consider how the presuppositions of individuals describing Ericksonian techniques affect the homologousness and effectiveness of those techniques. It seems appropriate and essential that any technical descriptions of Erickson's (and anyone else's) work be evaluated by that technique's in-use *application* of presuppositions of the person from whom the technique was drawn. Any technique derived from Erickson's work should incorporate Erickson's presuppositions. Referring back to the homologousness and effectiveness criteria for a "good" technique, this evaluation of in-use presuppositions is important because (1) any approach which violates Erickson's presuppositions will, of course, not in fact be an Ericksonian approach, and (2) techniques derived from Erickson's work which violate his presuppositions are not likely to achieve the intended outcomes with any consistency.

Furthermore, assuming that a technique—or even *all* techniques —derived from Erickson's work is homologous with his model of the world, can we therefore hope that those techniques will make it possible for therapists to reproduce in their own practices something approaching Erickson's effectiveness and creativity? I doubt it. The very notion of "a technique" seems fundamentally opposed to "creativity." Furthermore, it seems that a case can be made, at least within the realm of Ericksonian psychotherapy, that ongoing "effectiveness" is largely due to ongoing creativity. And the particular ways in which Erickson was creative in interacting with, and intervening for, his clients was a direct function of the perceptual and cognitive filters under which he operated. That is, the sense he made out of his clients' situations and the interventions that occurred to him were the direct result of the presuppositions he had about what was significant to pay attention to, how people learn, what was the nature of interactions, how people change, and so on. The importance of underlying presuppositions to the effective use of a technique, then, is that *it is the presuppositions which provide the perceptual filters that make available the information and perspectives which the technique is designed to address and utilize.*

If you take a moment to search through your personal history, you can probably discover an instance in which another person's responses to a particular situation seemed to be wrong, foolish, or senseless, but that you later found out something about *their* perceptions of the world that immediately made their previous responses seem completely appropriate (within their model of the world). Thus, temporarily assuming another person's presuppositions will, more than in any other way, make it possible for you to comprehend how that person makes judgments and responds in the way that he or she does. If your aspirations go beyond an appreciation of another person's reality, such that you intend to *emulate* in your own ongoing behavior the behavior of another person, then being able to adopt (*when appropriate*) that person's presuppositions will be essential (in both senses of the word). This is, of course, the very situation addressed here, that is, the effective and appropriate emulation of Erickson's unique brand of psychotherapy.

If we are to gain an understanding of Erickson's work, it must be remembered that his psychotherapy was the natural development of a certain man who had a certain model of the world. Knowing the man, knowing his work, we may want to know more about (and perhaps emulate) his model of the world. Of course, no amount of study and effort will ever (or should ever) allow anyone to become Milton Erickson. But does that mean that his brand of hypnosis, his brand of therapy, his brand of humanity, will therefore be lost? Certainly he survives in the lives of those that he interacted with personally. Whether or not Ericksonian psychotherapy survives will depend on whether his work is distilled as a set of techniques to be applied to people and situations, and whether that distillation is sweetened by the perceptual and cognitive responsiveness that comes from the practitioner's ability to step into the world of presuppositions from which those techniques were originally derived.

A NOTE ON IMPLEMENTATION

Given the thesis of this chapter, it seems appropriate to include some means of actually operating out of the presuppositions described above. It is not enough just to say, "Oh, yes . . . everybody is unique." That "everybody is unique" must be a part of one's experiential integrity (at least in the context of therapy) if it is to have any perceptual and behavioral impact. Erickson's integrity (which included the presuppositions described above) was the natural outcome of his personal history, which, of course, is not your personal history. But you do have a personal history that is rich in reference experiences—richer, perhaps, than you now suspect.

The first step in making available any of the presuppositions described above is to review your own personal history for experiences that exemplify the presupposition in which you are interested. Taking the first presupposition, for instance, you might recall an experience in which you discovered that something you assumed everyone perceived the same was in fact dependent upon individual subjectivity. Continue ferreting out such experiences, "stacking" the subjective impact of each additional one upon the others (that is, use each one to reinforce the presupposition) until the validity of the presupposition seems to you to be well-founded.

The next step is to identify a past experience that seems to be contradictory to the presupposition you want to acquire. Reorient your perceptions with regard to that incident so that you can now perceive how it in fact does *not* contradict the presupposition (or better yet, proves it). Do this to other apparently contradictory past experiences until the perceptual reorienting you need to do in order to bring the example into accord with the presupposition becomes almost automatic and immediate.

The final step is to imagine several situations you expect to find yourself in sometime in the near future *and which are contexts in which you want to use the presupposition*. In your imagination, "step into" each of those contexts, noticing how your understanding of, and responses to, what is going on are different from those they might otherwise have been. This last step is called future pacing and is intended to provide continuity between your new learnings and those contexts in which those learnings will be relevant.

Whether or not that presupposition becomes a characteristic and automatic element of your work as a psychotherapist will be determined by the ongoing feedback it engenders as you operate out of it. As you use that presupposition in your work (or whatever contexts you have specified) either you will discard it as it will have proved itself ineffective and/or fundamentally incompatible with presuppositions that are closely held by you, *or* it will become a pervasive influence within your model of the world.

REFERENCES

Bandler, R., & Grinder, J. (1975). *Patterns of the hypnotic techniques of Milton H. Erickson* (Vol. 1). Cupertino, CA: Meta Publications.
Gordon, D., & Anderson, M. (1981). *Phoenix: Therapeutic patterns of Milton H. Erickson.* Cupertino, CA: Meta Publications.
Haley, J. (Ed.). (1967). *Advanced techniques of hypnosis and therapy.* New York: Grune & Stratton.
Haley, J. (1973). *Uncommon therapy.* New York: Norton.
Rosen, S. (1982). *My voice will go with you.* New York: Norton.
Zeig, J.K. (Ed.). (1980). *A teaching seminar with Milton H. Erickson.* New York: Brunner/Mazel.

Chapter 6

There's No Theory Like No-Theory: The Ericksonian Approach in Perspective

Charles R. Stern

My first encounter with Milton Erickson (1975) was the most profound on the one hand and the least memorable on the other. I spent an average of five hours a day for two weeks alone with him. When I returned home, I could not recall most of the experience. I had nearly total amnesia! Strangely, however, I knew that somehow I had learned a great deal, but I was uncertain about just what that was. I remembered that I began each day asking questions—I had quite a list—but he answered with stories I could not remember. On a subsequent visit he inscribed one of his books for me, "To experience is (to) learn often without knowing that one has learned."

When I resumed my practice, a strange thing occurred during a therapy session with a 30-year-old Latin American man who had dark smooth skin and black hair. While he was telling a fairly lengthy story about himself I began to feel a little "bored" even though his story was rather interesting. I looked at him again and "saw" a gray-haired older man with sad sunken eyes and a wrinkled, worried face! I realized that I had gone into a trance spontaneously to "see" that this man felt old, tired, sad, and worried.

In addition to this hallucination, stories came to mind which I began telling to my client (stories I had known before meeting Erickson). I realized that they all had something to do with the feelings I had perceived in him. When the session was over, he checked his watch in puzzlement and protested that he had just arrived.

I was amazed that I had been able to do these things spontaneously.

Before I went to Phoenix I had read everything I could by or about Erickson. I had attended presentations by some of his students, and I was doing therapy in the Ericksonian style, but it had been a great conscious effort to do so. But after my first visit with Erickson, I was spontaneously saying things which proved to be more therapeutic, and I discovered that, without realizing it, I was inducing trances in my clients. Later Erickson signed another of his books for me, "To learn what you already know is one of the hazards of education."

Erickson was delighted when he could assist others to experience themselves and the world in new ways. He taught me to experience myself and those around me differently and, more importantly, to trust my own unconscious processes.

EXPERIENCE

Experience was the key. Erickson knew that learning required students to experience something outside of their frame of reference. He believed that people had positive experiences in their lives which could be called forth and utilized as resources for change. He believed that one could utilize these past experiences to facilitate a change (Erickson & Rossi, 1979) or one could create a new experience through the therapeutic relationship that would lead to a change (Rossi, 1980, Vol. 4).

NO-THEORY

Erickson's approach was nontheoretical. He knew that once a theory is developed, it tends to become a framework against which further information is measured. Theory often becomes a learned limitation—the very thing from which therapists try to free their clients. Therapists tend to reject, ignore, distort, or in some way maintain their theory in the face of contradictory data.

Another problem with espousing a theory is that others, who believe in their own theories, tend to resist those of others. When this occurs, both sides seem to work harder to "prove" the superiority of their own viewpoint. They therefore step further from the real world and the task of helping clients to change and move further into the abstract limitations of their own frame of reference.

The fact that Erickson had no rigid theoretical position made it possible for him to deal more effectively with those who tried to oppose him through an emotional attachment to their own views. There are several stories of Erickson's being challenged by colleagues whereby he simply utilized the challenge to induce trances in those who opposed him (Haley, 1967; Rossi, 1980, Vols. 1 & 4). He preferred to teach them through the induction of a new experience rather than to struggle with them.

I have heard some Ericksonian therapists say that Erickson really had a theory, but that he was secretive about it or that it was implied (Haley, 1982). They seem to believe that this theory could be gleaned from observing his work. I think that the confusion lies in the way the word "theory" is conceptualized. If Erickson had theories, they were not theories in the sense of a single view of personality, behavior or therapy. Instead, his "theories" were simply possibilities, hypotheses to be considered, empirically tested and modified moment by moment for each situation. As he explained, each patient is unique and no single theory will fit everyone. That is why, he said, he developed a new theory for each person (personal communication, 1977). He spoke many theoretical languages and many therapists ended up believing he agreed with theirs (Haley, 1982).

I remember that when one person gave Erickson some books on transactional analysis, he smiled, graciously accepted them and said, "How did you know I have a special interest in the work of Eric Berne?" But Erickson told me on a previous occasion that such theoreticians were limiting in their views and mentioned Berne in a list of those with whom he disagreed. He had not lied, but perhaps his "special interest" was a negative one.

Having freed himself from the pitfalls of rigid notions, Erickson had no need to fit his patients into a theoretical frame. I think Erickson's being a successful agent of change while having no theory demonstrates that theories are not of primary importance. Theories are merely arbitrary rationalizations which make theoreticians feel better; they are unnecessary in producing change.

Erickson's view of theories was like his view of interpretations. They are absurd reductions of the complexities of human experience (Haley, 1982). This is why he relied primarily upon case examples and metaphors to explain his ideas. If he had a theory, it would have to be considered a "no-theory," i.e., a theory which fit only a particular situation and the people in it, and which evaporated when elements of the situation changed.

Erickson knew that the procrustean myth not only referred to someone with a rigid view, but that the result of that rigidity was Procrustes' own demise. Erickson was a modern-day Theseus who took great pleasure in slaying theories in their own procrustean beds.

ERICKSON'S APPROACH IN PERSPECTIVE

Certain aspects of Erickson's approach have been emphasized by many who advocate his ideas. This leaves a somewhat skewed interpretation. Among these suppositions are: unconscious changes and the relegation of conscious aspects of the individual to an unimportant position in the change process, the view that he could successfully treat most anyone, and that therapy should always be brief. While these ideas are important, there is a wider view and more balanced perspective.

A Working Definition of Hypnosis

In order to understand more fully Erickson's opinions it is important to examine his view of hypnosis. Despite his nontheoretical approach, he often defined hypnosis, although he did not present a rigid framework. On the contrary, in exploring this with him personally and through his writings, I discovered that he defined hypnosis in various ways. These definitions ranged from, "nothing more than a special state of conscious awareness in which certain chosen behavior of everyday life is manifested in a direct manner" (Rossi, 1980, Vol. 4, p. 54), to "a relationship between two people" (Rossi, 1980, Vol. 3, p. 6), and "an artificially enhanced state of suggestibility resembling sleep wherein there appears to be a normal, time-limited, and stimulus-limited dissociation of the 'conscious' from the 'subconscious' elements of the psyche" (Rossi, 1980, Vol. 3, p. 8).

I once asked Erickson (personal communication, 1977) about Ernest Hilgard's (1977) theory of a "divided consciousness" in relationship to hypnosis and especially Hilgard's notion of the "hidden observer." Erickson said that Hilgard was experimentally validating what he, Erickson, had said for many years. I asked if hypnosis is a kind of divided consciousness in which the "conscious" elements of the mind or awareness become focused on one thing and the "unconscious" elements focused on a different set of stimuli. I wondered whether the narrowing of attention takes place on the conscious level while the unconscious becomes more responsive to the hypnotist. He seemed to agree, so I asked if this narrowing of consciousness could be the key to trance depth. That is, the narrower the focus of conscious attention on one thing or idea, the deeper the trance until the focus was so narrowed (and the trance so deep) that conscious awareness, for practical purposes, ceased to function at all. He agreed that this was a reasonable assumption. He told me that it is important to have a working definition of hypnosis, but cautioned against rigidifying it. He said that it was his practice to emphasize a certain aspect of a definition for his subjects or students depending upon their frames of reference. He indicated that, instead of defining it, he preferred to help them experience hypnosis. In a later discussion (personal communication, 1977) he said that no definition of hypnosis is adequate because it cannot be precise enough to have real meaning when examined closely. He pointed out that one would have to further define the words in any definition of hypnosis. For example, how would one define awareness or consciousness?

He said that my ideas were correct as far as they went, but no matter how hard I tried to define hypnosis, experiencing it was the only way anyone would truly understand it.

Erickson believed it useful to have a flexible working definition of hypnosis. I have combined the elements of Erickson's various definitions along with the above views to construct my own working definition hoping that the reader will consider it a rule-of-thumb more than an inflexible theory:

> Hypnosis can be defined as a special but normal state of aware-
> ness or consciousness and a special state of responsiveness which
> draws upon and utilizes the subject's own experiential learnings,
> memories, and patterns of behavior. This special state is generally
> elicited through an interpersonal relationship. This relationship is
> based upon cooperation and multilevel communication in such a
> way that the individual (subject) develops a dual awareness (or
> divided consciousness). The conscious attention narrows while the
> unconscious becomes more focused upon and receptive to the ideas
> presented by the hypnotist.

In other words, the hypnotist communicates on at least two levels of awareness: on the level of consciously known meanings and under-standings and on the level of behaviors and understandings which are, at that moment, outside of the individual's conscious field of awareness or control. The conscious field of attention is narrowly focused (at times so narrowly that it is temporarily inoperative) in such a way that the unconscious processes can operate more freely. This enables the indi-vidual to exhibit "unusual but normal behavior" in the sense that certain experiences and actions of everyday life are elicited directly in a more focused or controlled way during the hypnotic state ("trance") than at other times. During this state, ideas ("suggestions") are presented to the individual which tend to be more readily accepted for consideration than they might be otherwise.

Conscious-Unconscious Integration

> This brings us to another important point regarding the use of hypnosis. Because you are dealing with a person who has both a conscious mind and an unconscious mind achieving good results with a patient in a deep trance does not mean that the patient will benefit from it in the ordinary waking state. There has to be an integration of unconscious learnings with conscious learnings. (Erickson & Rossi, 1981, p. 6)

If change is to evidence, it is essential that unconscious processes be integrated with the conscious processes. This does not mean that clients must gain insight into their problems nor does it mean that they must be conscious of how or why changes occurred. What is necessary is that unconsciously generated changes are accepted as real (ego syntonic) and that those processes which led to the changes are trusted. This may be manifested in the form of surprise and delight upon realizing a desired change has occurred. There might be a realization about the problem which resembles insight, but this often occurs after the changes have taken place—as a kind of hindsight. Although this hindsight is one possible indicator of the conscious acceptance of change, it is neither essential nor does it occur in every case. Another indicator of the conscious acceptance of such changes is an apparent nonchalance whereby the client just seems to lose interest in the problem once the changes are complete.

Occasionally some clients seem to struggle in a conscious way to regain their symptom as a way of testing the permanence of their changes, but they eventually give up and accept their new experience. This became apparent to me when I tested the durability of the loss of my congenital back pain after Erickson worked with me on it. I tested it for a week (bending and moving in ways that used to hurt). I was pleased and convinced that I could not bring about the return of the pain.

This, however, must be contrasted with individuals who are not merely testing their changes, but who are unwilling to accept the loss of their symptoms/problems. For example, I once worked with a woman to resolve her sexual dysfunction. She went into a profound trance and my work with her seemed to resolve the problem. I suggested amnesia for the work she did while in the trance. Two weeks later she reported that for a week and a half she had enjoyed a satisfactory sex life for the first time in her life, but it bothered her that she could not remember what had occurred in hypnosis. She concentrated on it (thus inducing autohypnosis) and eventually remembered what had transpired. From that moment her problem returned in full force.

Erickson was an excellent example of an individual who trusted his own unconscious resources. He once told me of a time when, while sitting in his backyard at the picnic table, he wondered what his unconscious would teach him. He looked around and saw nothing in any direction. The house, the tree, even the picnic table and the ground were gone. He reached out in all directions and felt nothing. He was nowhere (personal communication, 1976). Many people would have been frightened by such an experience, but Erickson was delighted! He considered it an important experience. As Erickson himself stated in another context, "In the formal trance situation the successful utilization of unconscious processes leads to an autonomous response; the ego is surprised to find itself confronted with new datum or behavior" (Rossi, 1980, Vol. 1, p. 450).

The Unchangeables

Given Erickson's view of human nature, therapeutic relationships, and the nature of change, it is not surprising that many people believe that he could successfully treat anyone. It was therefore quite surprising to hear him tell me, during one of our meetings, that there were some individuals who would never change regardless of what the therapist did. I had difficulty believing this and my subsequent realization that he would send certain people away or tell them not to come to see him when they called or wrote made me think that he realized his own limitations. I, however, thought that everyone could change if approached properly.

A serendipitous occurrence changed my beliefs. Another therapist referred a woman to me. She told me that he had done so, but I had as yet no contact with him. During her first session I was impressed by her willingness to travel some distance to see me, and by her claim that she was highly motivated to change. However, I soon found that she was negative on every issue, and I had great difficulty "getting a word in edgewise." She had seen several other therapists, but none had ever helped her. I had seen clients who had sought help from other therapists, or who had difficulty letting me talk, or who were negative, but I never experienced all of these combined with such intensity. I began to wonder if she was one of those unchangeable clients about whom Erickson warned me. She came only one more time and terminated with no explanation.

I finally reached the referring therapist who told me that this woman was referred to him by Richard Bandler when she requested his help. Bandler said that this woman had previously petitioned Erickson to be his patient and that Erickson refused to treat her. Erickson had considered her untreatable!

Erickson knew that therapeutic change takes place within a relationship. My client's way of interacting did not allow for a relationship that would lend itself to cooperation. He also knew that some individuals refuse to give up their problems/symptoms. On one occasion (personal communication, 1977) he told me of a case in which an extremely obese man requested that Erickson hypnotize him to lose weight. However, he demanded that Erickson do nothing to interfere with his daily consumption of several loaves of bread, a bag of which he had brought with him to the office. Erickson summarily dismissed the man and refused to treat him. There was also a case in which Erickson treated a man for gagging. The treatment was successful for months until the patient inexplicably reverted to his old behavior and was totally unconcerned about it. Even Erickson was at a loss to explain this "Successful Hypnotherapy that Failed" (Rossi, 1980, Vol. 4, pp. 139-143), despite the fact that the patient appeared to have no sign of severe pathology.

Doing Brief Therapy

I have encountered professionals who believe that Erickson's therapy was always brief and that being brief was his goal and should therefore be theirs. This has always seemed to me to be an unfortunate view. It is true that Erickson sought to treat his patients in such a way that they could change as quickly as they were able, but his goal was to guide them at *their own pace*, not his. I do not believe that he would sacrifice a client's needs for the sake of speed. Rather, I think of Erickson's method as a way of doing brief therapy by proceeding slowly. That is, he allowed his patients to change at their own pace.

According to Haley, Erickson would say, "If you get a one-second change in a symptom that exists 24 hours a day, you have made a major change. . . ." As Erickson put it, "If you want a large change you should ask for a small one" (Haley, 1982, p. 23). Haley also claimed that, "When he [Erickson] did long-term therapy, it was when he could not solve the problem more briefly" (Haley, 1982, p. 23).

Erickson did therapy as briefly as possible, but there were times when he saw a patient over a long period of time. This was not just because he could not solve the problem briefly, but also because he recognized the need for a long-term development of certain kinds of experiences, e.g., the "February Man" case (Rossi, 1980, Vol. 4). Granted Erickson did not generally see patients weekly, but at times he saw people for three to five hours each day for a week or two. This certainly was intensive, irregular, and brief, but he sometimes saw the same individual intermittently for years.

It must be realized that the important thing that Erickson tried to teach us was that the focus is on the clients and their needs and not on speed. One should do therapy as briefly as possible given one's own level of skill combined with the quickest pace the client can achieve. If that means that it takes a longer time, so be it.

Erickson took many years to learn to do therapy briefly. Not everyone has his skill and experience and he often admonished his students not to try to be another Milton Erickson. He encouraged others to learn what they found useful from him, but to integrate it into their own styles.

> He [Erickson] recommended that a therapist use techniques which worked and discard those which did not, independent of tradition. He did not suggest you look to a prominent person to lend support to your practices but rather that you defend your work by its results. (Haley, 1982, p. 18)

CONCLUSION

Once there was an Asian teacher who was well respected in his community. One day some people passed by his home and saw him with his followers dancing, singing, and making merry on the lawn. The witnesses were divided in their opinions of this scene. Some said, "What a pity that this man cannot take his practice seriously." Others said, "Isn't it wonderful how happy they are! There's too much seriousness in the world."

Some time later a group of people passed by the teacher's residence and saw him sitting with his followers quietly in meditation. "Ah," said some among them, "he has finally come to his senses and is practicing his beliefs in earnest." But others said, "Oh what a pity. There's too much seriousness and he has abandoned the enjoyment of life."

And so it was that many conflicting stories were circulated about the teacher. Some said he was a wonderful teacher, others said he was not, while some changed their minds back and forth in confusion and more dared not venture an opinion.

One individual who had witnessed both scenes visited the teacher and reminded him of the two seemingly conflicting scenes. He asked the teacher to explain.

The teacher smiled and said, "What you saw the first time was a group of students who were much too serious when they came to me. The second group was made up of people who were much too undisciplined. I was merely instructing them in the opposite of their normal experience in order to teach them balance."

It has been my intention in this chapter to present some points which seem to be overlooked, and to expand our understanding of a great teacher. When I once asked him which author he thought best explained his views, he told me that Haley had one view, Bandler and Grinder had another, and Rossi a third, but that no one had a complete view. It is my hope that this chapter has made a contribution to a more balanced perspective of Erickson's work.

REFERENCES

Erickson, M. H., & Rossi, E. L. (1979). *Hypnotherapy: An exploratory casebook*. New York: Irvington.
Erickson, M. H., & Rossi, E. L. (1981). *Experiencing hypnosis: Therapeutic approaches to altered states*. New York: Irvington.
Haley, J. (Ed.). (1967). *Advanced techniques of hypnosis and therapy: Selected papers of Milton H. Erickson, M.D.* New York: Grune & Stratton.
Haley, J. (1982). The contribution to therapy of Milton H. Erickson, M.D. In J.K. Zeig (Ed.), *Ericksonian approaches to hypnosis and psychotherapy* (pp. 5-25). New York: Brunner/Mazel.
Hilgard, E. R. (1977). *Divided consciousness: Multiple controls in human thought and action*. New York: John Wiley & Sons.
Rossi, E. L. (Ed.). (1980). *The collected papers of Milton H. Erickson on hypnosis* (Vols. 1-4). New York: Irvington.

PART III

Reflections on the Ericksonian Approach

This section consists of personal reflections on the Ericksonian approach. The authors present new insights that should be of value to all clinicians using Ericksonian methodology.

Kay F. Thompson, D.D.S., is in private practice of general dentistry and teaches at the University of Pittsburgh in the Departments of Community Dentistry and Psychiatry. She earned her degrees at the same university. A close associate of Milton Erickson for 30 years, she has received awards for her work in hypnosis from the American Society of Clinical Hypnosis, the Society for Clinical and Experimental Hypnosis, and the Netherlands Society of Clinical Hypnosis.

Thompson is an internationally renowned practitioner and teacher of hypnosis and has served on the faculty of meetings organized by the Erickson Foundation each year from 1980 through 1984. Her presentations are always highly rated by participants. In fact, the address that comprises this chapter received the highest rating of any invited address presented at the Congress.

There are two facets of Erickson's approach that Thompson demonstrates masterfully: She freely uses hypnotic language to make her points, and she is able to step outside of familiar frameworks to present revealing insights.

In describing Erickson's approach, Thompson addresses the use of direct versus indirect techniques. Milton Erickson did not limit himself to the use of indirection. It may be that Erickson seemed indirect to the observer; to the respondent he was being direct because he was speaking the patient's experiential language.

Erickson was not "fuzzy" in his approach. He was strong-willed and had exacting standards for training and practice.

Richard E. Dimond, Ph.D., is a psychologist in private practice in Springfield, Illinois, whose clinical psychology degree was earned at Kent State University. He has extensive experience teaching on the college level and has published papers and coauthored an introductory psychology textbook.

Dimond's presentation on the trials and tribulations of becoming an Ericksonian therapist is witty and perceptive. He addresses the importance of observing patients and of finding a way to use Ericksonian methods that is compatible with one's own style.

Lawrence R. Gindhart, M.A., practices individual and family therapy in Indianapolis, Indiana. He is one of the principal promoters of Ericksonian therapy in the Midwest, and has organized numerous workshops and has presented his own training seminars.

An award was presented for the most scholarly submitted paper at the 1983 Erickson Congress. Gindhart was co-recipient for his paper on "Hypnotic Psychotherapy."

Gindhart describes an orientation to Ericksonian methodology that can help practitioners reach inside themselves to find enhanced sensitivity to therapeutic processes. Similar to Dimond, Gindhart presents perspectives on his own orientation to therapy. Similar to Stern, he speaks to the fact that Ericksonian approaches are "theory inconsistent."

Chapter 7

Almost 1984

Kay F. Thompson

Time does pass. Milton Erickson has been dead for only four short years, but the changes that have taken place in the way his work has been interpreted and imitated make me wonder whether 1984 and beyond will be an Orwellian nightmare in which history, experience, individual thought, and just plain hard work are replaced by the facile allure of Newspeak and Doublethink. As Orwell knew, it is all too tempting for people to take the easy way out, to rely on slogans, to speak in preset formulas, and to cover our lack of knowledge and understanding with a veneer of jargon which the unsuspecting accept as truth. I see this happening to Milton Erickson's work, and it frightens me.

The horror of Orwell's 1984 was the way the past was sanitized, condensed, and edited until it was reduced to a series of maxims so simple, and so simpleminded, that they could be readily remembered but never understood. The complexity was lost. What was lost in quality was made up for in quantity. That which was left was repeated over and over so that it became "true" through the simple process of constant repetition. I'm sad and worried to say that I see much the same thing happening to Erickson's work in the past few years. The work that Milton Erickson did day in and day out as a practicing therapist has been largely pushed aside. The range, complexity, and variety of therapeutic approaches that he worked a lifetime to develop and apply have been supplanted by a narrow, simplified view of his work as interpolated from the teaching seminars he conducted in his last few years. This substitution has narrowed and distorted his work and, more importantly, narrows and distorts the work that those who try to follow him are now able to do.

In most cases, but not all, this distortion has not been a deliberate attempt to destroy the record, but, more simply, the result of ignorance. Erickson worked as a teacher and therapist for more than forty years, but most of the people who claim to be his followers knew him only in the last few years when his strength was declining and when he presented his techniques to students in ways that were least taxing to him. Students who had never observed him working as a therapist assumed that the teacher and the therapist worked in identical ways. Erickson's work thus has been simplified and narrowed to the point that I am quite sure he would not recognize it as his own.

The problem that I see is not simply one of setting the record straight. The past is not important in and of itself. Erickson would be the last to want us to carve his ''fe in stone and proclaim it as the new truth, the one and only truth. The past is important, however, as a source of knowledge and information. If we are to invest our time and efforts in developing successful therapeutic techniques, we need to understand the base from which we are starting. For that reason, I think it's important to examine what has happened in the past few years, to take stock of our stock, to examine our bonds, and to wonder about our options for future investments.

One thing that has clearly happened is that Erickson's name and some parts of his work have become widely recognized. Erickson would, I'm sure, be pleased and amused to see that Ericksonianism has changed from an endemic state to an epidemic one. He would not, however, be pleased to see the way his ideas have been formulized and promoted so that he has become a kind of Big Brother whose name and slogans are invoked to lend credence and authenticity to ideas that he himself would not have supported. When we use Erickson in this way, we dehumanize him, and, in the process, dehumanize ourselves as well.

I guess I am forced to acknowledge that I found the endemic state much pleasanter, but I am also pleased to see how widespread recognition of Erickson has become. It _nay well be that those many people who have come to know Erickson's name, in whatever way, will become interested enough in the man and his work to delve, to inquire, to learn more about him and his techniques. If that happens, the confusion of the last few years may be worth the price. If it does not, we will find ourselves deluged with pseudo-Ericksonian ideas which will do little harm to him but may do much harm to the practice of hypnotherapy in the future.

The deluge has already begun, and it is damaging to both those who promote it and those who come eager to learn. All of the people who have never known the person that Milton Erickson was as a therapist can now watch videotapes, motion pictures which capture a two-dimensional quality and a tiny bit of what he did. By freezing and repeating the same images over and over, these tapes foster the false belief that they represent all of Erickson's work and all of his therapeutic techniques. This view oversimplifies and edits reality in much the same way that the TV news editor leaves all but a few selected segments of film on the cutting room floor. You have only to think of the difference in perception and learning that occurs when you witness an event yourself, when you read about it in detail in the newspaper, and when you watch it summarized in 30 seconds on the 11:00 P.M. news, to see how little one film or tape, no matter how good or accurate in itself, can teach us about a lifetime of work and ideas.

The videotapes are not, of course, the whole story. Those who seek to know something about Erickson can listen to audio tapes, read volumes of voluminous books, and take copious crash courses in how to understand and interpret Milton Erickson from the people who affirm that they know the essence of the man and his work. It would be really convenient if we could put the essence of Erickson in a bottle to be taken as needed. Like hypnosis, marketing is a fine art. The imitators take apart the real heart of the fragrance, and they put it together in different formulas and different quantities, and so the quality just isn't quite the same. Then they tell us how to wear it, or at least how THEY wear it, but it does not make sense for them to sentence us to make sense of the essence of the essential scent that we sent for, since that one was not the scent sent for us, and the sensitivity of the particular scent changes with the wearer.

The people who came to study with Erickson in his last few years don't even understand that they missed the beginning, so they don't recognize that they were too late to learn it all the way, all ways, because they were shortchanged by Erickson's weakness and his frailty and his illness and his age. They changed and shortened the rules of learning so that they could go out and teach what they thought they learned. But what they saw was not Erickson the therapist; they saw Erickson the teacher showing them only how to begin to know what to look for. He was the teacher lecturing his class, not the therapist working in a therapist-patient relationship. Because they never saw the therapist, they can imitate and teach only that which they learned as students.

The teaching seminars late in his life were made a lot more dramatic and effective by his use of tales and word pictures. This smorgasbord of stories was to be remembered for its fascination, as the diners were spoon-fed much of the main course in an effort to avoid upsetting their digestion. They had their appetizers before they ever got to the restaurant to dine, and it really would have been difficult for the chef, at his age, to select a new menu for each person; it was much simpler to offer a variety of choices and then let the guests dine on their own. When they did that, they were impressed by the variety and the significance of what they could see in each course, and they attributed all of that to the chef and his creativity. The praise of the chef really came from each diner's interpretation of what he liked best; the meal could be totally satisfying, but it could also be digested for future growth and sustenance, and could be recalled and reinterpreted as the diner wished.

The use of word pictures was an effective teaching device, but Erickson's reliance on it in those teaching seminars perpetuated the myth that he always used permissive and indirect suggestion and that his therapy was always done by metaphor and analogy. It is important to remember that the stories were used as illustrative teaching techniques. Those people who came were fulfilling their own needs and their own expectations when they chose to hear a special message for them in the significance of each story. I'm sure that each of us has been through that particular kind of enlightening experience and has benefited from it. I think we neglect, however, the premise that was the basis of Erickson's work and his style, and that is the fact that there is no set formula for working with any one individual, let alone for working with any group of individuals. It's ironic that many of us learn in our own individual ways but then turn around and try to impose only one way, the "right" way, on our patients. When we do this, we shortchange both them and ourselves.

We also shortchange our patients when we accept other myths about Erickson's work. There is, for example, the myth that if we will only trust our unconscious, our therapy will just roll out of our brain, onto our tongue, and out of our mouth, and the behavior of our patient will be quickly changed in this completely spontaneous fashion. This is nonsense of the highest order. It attempts to replace years of study, practice, learning, and experience with a set of magic formulas. While it is true that some of us may have more innate talent for certain skills than others, it is equally true that talent alone cannot produce and sustain success in the therapist-patient relationship. Erickson's life is, in fact, an excellent example of how talent must be maintained and fed with constant experience and growth.

Erickson's success was based on his own innate genius used in conjunction with a large number of basically self-taught skills. One of these skills was his phenomenal ability to observe the most minute cues his patients brought to him. There are few who can begin to emulate that particular skill, because we haven't had nearly enough practice. Another important self-taught skill was his ability to "get to where the patient was," and to speak the language of the patient, be he farmer or statistician. Sometimes that led to confusion, but *not* on the part of the patient. To so many people who were unable to "go" to where the patient was, some of Erickson's very direct approaches seemed to be confusing and nondirective as Erickson conversed with the patient in the patient's language. The patient was not confused, but the people listening, who could not speak that language, felt that it was very confusing and therefore must be an indirect approach.

I guess we could almost say that his indirect therapy was successful principally because of his extensive work with direct therapy. Erickson worked with variety and apparent spontaneity which anyone who had spent a lifetime practicing ought to be able to do. He worked with spontaneity, but he was not spontaneous. Because of his experience and his ability to observe, he could take things that people gave him and utilize those, and it appeared that he worked instant magic. But the instant magic was the result of long, hard years of working and learning and formulating and going back and trying various techniques over and over again. His vast repertoire permitted him to draft what would appear to be an appropriate approach to a patient and, at any given time, to modify that approach by using any of the multitude of modifications he had ready when it was apparent that they were needed. It was this smoothness in transition that I think misled so many. As people missed the transition, they settled for the idea that it had to have been a metaphor.

Erickson's technique of using word pictures has caused problems for those who would follow his techniques but do not have a lifetime of experience to draw on when doing so. We are all fascinated by the tales, and we all aspire to work the kind of magic we attribute to Erickson, but I think we must recognize that, in this instance, imitation is *not* the sincerest form of flattery. We can only do what he did if we do it in our own way. This is difficult because it requires us to put aside the myths about how Erickson worked and replace them with hard analysis followed up by years of rigorous practice. When, instead, we fall back on the myths as the easy way out, we lead ourselves astray.

There is a myth abroad that Erickson was able to come up with a new story for every patient, and many of his more recent followers strive to imitate him in this and often become bogged down in looking for stories when they should be working with the patient. I firmly believe that there are limits to the ability to come up with a *new* story for every patient and, indeed, limits to the therapist's ability to individualize the approach to each patient. I also believe that there are no limits to the ability to individualize each story for the patient, or to the patient's ability to individualize and adapt the story to his own needs. When we recognize this ability in our patients, we free ourselves from the constant need to individualize therapy. Since the same story can have a different meaning, a multitude of meanings, or sometimes even no particular meaning, why not use the same story with appropriate modifications. Consider, if you will, that every once in a while, Erickson told a story that had no meaning of any special sort. All that the story was told for was to give the patient time for the learning that was going on. It just distracted the conscious mind so that the unconscious could do its own thinking and feeling and organizing.

One aspect of individualization that the therapist must take responsibility for is the ability to determine whether or not the direct or the indirect approach is necessary. There were many patients who came to see Erickson who certainly did not need indirect therapy. They were ready and able to enter trance, and they were probably in the trance before they entered. They were ready to believe, and therefore receive, the strong help that they knew was appropriate. Sometimes they needed the excuse of being ordered to get well so that they could. Erickson was capable of complying with that need in a more authoritarian fashion than anyone I have ever known. Certainly, Erickson's manner of speaking was part of his style, his approach to people, but that was not where his expertise came in. His expertise was his ability to read the individual and determine whether the direct or indirect approach would be more appropriate. Whatever the method that was used, however, the foundation of the change was in the directive therapy, not in the direct or indirect way in which it was presented. Telling people what to do, and having them do it, is all very well and good, but we need to recognize that the telling can be either direct or indirect, but the directive therapy is the thing that brings about the change.

Erickson recognized that some patients needed the indirect approach, but others required a more direct, often confrontational approach. Many people who try to learn from Erickson have a difficult time with direct approaches which can be emotionally draining for the therapist. As intellectuals who are more accustomed to manipulating ideas than people, therapists often prefer to discuss resistance and hostility rather than trying to provoke them so that they can be brought into play as active participants in the therapy. These theoretical discussions satisfy the intellectual needs of the therapist in a nice, neat way but do little to help the patient who needs to have these needs met directly. Provoking patients to exhibit resistance and hostility takes more of a risk than many therapists are willing to chance.

Because the direct approach is so difficult, some therapists emphasize the effectiveness of the indirect approach. They work diligently at understanding how to be confusing, how to use metaphor, how to be nondirective. I must confess that I sometimes fall into this trap myself. I suspect that the root cause is simply that we do not believe in ourselves enough. Maybe we don't believe we have the *power* that we saw in Erickson to make the direct approach work. We chicken out and we justify our behavior by saying that we are utilizing his indirect approach. We state our intention to follow "Ericksonian principles," but what this really means is that we lack the belief and skills necessary to make the direct approach work.

Some therapists justify the exclusive use of the indirect approach by asserting that Erickson used only the direct approach in his younger years and abandoned it as he became more skilled in the indirect approach. To those who make that assertion, let me say this: Nonsense. I knew and worked with Erickson over a period of 30 years. He was still comparatively young when he was using both indirect and direct approaches. Furthermore, he continued using direct therapy when he was a lot older than I am now. I think that he continued using it all through his life when he worked as a therapist with patients who needed that approach.

Patients were one thing, but those people who came to observe and to learn as present or future therapists were another. For them, indirect therapy and indirect teaching were not only appropriate, they were easier. Considering the number of people he dealt with and the ways he had to deal with them, it was good that he could take the easy way for the people who were ready to accept this.

While we are on the subject of Erickson's age and how it might have changed his approach to teaching and therapy, I think it is safe to say that Milton Erickson had some strongly held convictions that he kept all of his life. One of his strongest beliefs was that all therapists must work to earn the necessary credentials of their field and must then continue to learn and to upgrade their skills and capabilities throughout their working careers. As a younger and extremely conscientious and powerful therapist, Erickson frequently objected to anyone who lacked appropriate training.

I'm sorry to say that we don't hear much about appropriate training anymore. We hear that therapists need "all kinds" of training, but the appropriateness of the training is extremely important. Those people who don't take the time to learn, to try, to make mistakes, to correct those mistakes, and then go on cannot be adequate therapists. We don't cure by magic or by offhand wise pronouncements. As therapists, we must have a plan in mind to present to the patient and be ready to alter that plan on the basis of the data that they give us. To do this, we need constant practice, constant assessment, constant learning. This requires mellowing and seasoning and can only come with hard work and experience over a long period. Erickson maintained that patients need a wealth of neuropsychophysiological reorientation in order to be as good as they know they have the potential to be. I think as therapists we need a wealth of experience to be as innovative and perceptive as we would each like to be. I hope that learning is an ongoing process for each of us, and that those therapists who are beginning their explorations in hypnosis, gifted though they may be, will pay their dues in time.

Erickson believed that experience counts, no matter how smooth the words, no matter how brilliant the hypotheses learned and put forth. It's ridiculous to even suggest that we can follow our spontaneous unconscious before the "spontaneous" unconscious has enough in it to be spontaneous. It's nice to teach about change outside of conscious awareness, but there has to *be* an unconscious awareness before that can happen, so one needs, as Erickson stressed, an abundant "experiential life." Rigorously trained professionals develop their awareness of these broadened interests through a symphony of movement. Moving back and forth easily between conscious and unconscious, between trance and nontrance states, is not easy. It requires discipline and hard work, but what you get when you finally play the music is well worth the practicing.

What do I see now instead of rigorously trained professionals? I see many watered-down, nondirective, metaphor-oriented therapists, afraid to take the risk of being authoritarian and direct, and justifying this action, or lack of action, in terms of confusion. This all sounds very much like Doublethink to me. Confusion should not accompany instructions that you want patients to comprehend and follow unless you know that their unconscious is not confused. I think that we need to spend more time understanding the principles that Erickson worked with and also go a little further. I think it's time for us to enact some standards, or guidelines, for the benefit of those unsuspecting individuals who don't have the background knowledge to be able to properly evaluate the plethora of workshops professing to teach Ericksonian hypnosis.

There are many who claim in their workshop brochures to have "studied with Erickson," or "trained with Erickson." What do all these phrases mean? Did the claimant spend three hours with Erickson? Thirty hours? Three years? The brochures never say. The magic now is in the assertion that the claimant spent time with the Master, but there are many unanswered questions: What kind of time? Where? With whom? At what point in Erickson's life? Did the claimant go for therapy? Did he or she go to study? Or just to have lunch?

The questions become more important and more relevant because the people who "use" the magical Erickson name should identify the circumstances under which they are entitled to connect that name with their own teaching. Why is it important? From my bias, it is important so that Erickson, unlike Big Brother, won't be accused of being on every corner and underwriting all the therapists who have ever sat with him for a few hours. Erickson deserves credit, not discredit, and tribute, not blame. There are those who would wipe out his name, as in 1984, and claim his ideas as their own, as in Newspeak. There are also those who would use his name to promote their own ideas, as in Doublethink. I think we need the courage and the integrity to acknowledge him as a major contributor in our work and our lives, and then move on to build our own work. We need to be originals because that is all we can be. That is what he expected of us.

At the same time, we need to agree to this credentialing so that there can be a mutual understanding of what the Doublethink language means in Newspeak. Everybody who teaches pretends to know the true meaning of the language he communicates so that he can show that his way is *the* way to speak the new language, even if he uses Doublethink to rewrite the language of Newspeak. However, learning any language takes time, no matter how it is taught. Unlearning an old one and replacing it with a new one takes even more effort, and we need to be patient and recognize the inspiration of the magical successes, but keep working when the successes are not magical, as often happens. Maybe if we are fortunate enough and we work long enough, hard enough, we may come to the perceptive perspective that there is no one way; there is only the way that works, whatever that may be.

As I look back over my own years of experience and learning, I wonder what I've learned outside of trance. Among other things, I've learned to be tolerant, but sometimes to be judgmental for my patients, to evaluate their state of readiness, and to give them time when they need it. More than anything else, I've learned to respect patients as individuals who have integrity which can be utilized for themselves and their benefit. I've learned that each individual has a particular history and sensibility, and that I cannot cast him or her into a mold or apply a ready-made formula and expect predictable results. In Orwell's world, there was the illusion that this molding and predicting was possible, but in the real world of 1984, we cannot deceive ourselves that it can be so.

Just talking in Newspeak metaphor doesn't magically produce results. I wish it did, sometimes, but I know that more than that is needed. The therapist must take a strong position in support of change. Insight may appeal to the therapist's need for orderly thought, but it doesn't help the patient unless the patient really wants to change, and that's where the skill, rather than the words, comes in. There are times for all patients when they need to know that someone is there for them. The someone needed will vary as the need varies, and the therapist must be capable of being all the someones needed at whatever times they are needed. But each time, the growth that's going on comes closer to the satisfaction of knowing that it is becoming, and gradually that becomes enough for the moment. Gradually, too, change becomes easier, although there is never an easy time for change or acceptance. The winds of change continue to be elusive. It's difficult from one's bulwark of being buffeted by the bluster of all these changing seasons, and reasons, and winds, to sense a very slight constancy in one direction and gradually develop a leaning in that way. When we look back, we can observe the direction of that growth and know that it grows as it should to get to where it knows that it wants to go.

In the transition phase that we are now experiencing, we must learn from the past while remaining open about our future, because nostalgia may be comfortable, but it's not progressive. Nostalgia is like a grammar lesson: We find the present tense and the past perfect. We must look, however, to the past not through the rose-colored lenses of nostalgia, but through the clear, well-focused lenses of our present knowledge and experience. The past must be preserved, not slavishly, but certainly accurately. When we know how Milton Erickson worked, we can choose to accept, reject, or modify his methods. What we must not do is distort, simplify, or reconstruct them in the image we would like them to have.

As we look back and see the sparkle of the diamond I have always considered Erickson to be, we must also see the sparks that come from his many facets. As we examine these facets, we must distinguish the fact and the reality from the myth. We cannot, however, look only to the past, because if we do, we are going to stumble over the unknown up ahead. What we can do is to use the memory from the past to enlighten our progress. I think we must expend the time to learn to expand our expectations and our horizons. I'd like to see us use Rethink, not Doublethink, and to keep Newspeak from becoming our language by going back to Erickson's ideas for individual development.

Since it is now 1984, this is a good time to experience the passage of a good time, to speak anew about accepting the risks and the challenges of change, to acknowledge our debt to the past, but to move on to a future of careful work, rigorous analysis, and hard-won experience. Milton Erickson lived that kind of life.

Chapter 8

Trials and Tribulations of Becoming an Ericksonian Psychotherapist

Richard E. Dimond

This chapter focuses on a phenomenon created by the recent popularity of Milton Erickson and his approach to hypnosis and psychotherapy. I first noted this phenomenon in myself and developed a deeper interest in it when I observed it in others. I am referring to the process of becoming an Ericksonian psychotherapist—the experience of therapists as they make the transition from their present orientation to an Ericksonian orientation.

I have come to realize that the adoption and use of Ericksonian method can be a process of *becoming* for the therapist (Dimond & Havens, 1980). Therapists who pay attention to adopting an Ericksonian *perspective* on people will experience a change in themselves. This change is both part of, and essential to, conducting therapy in an Ericksonian manner. In turn, adopting an Ericksonian perspective rests upon some basic principles. This chapter is about how I came to appreciate these principles.

MILTON ERICKSON: A MAN I WOULD GO TO WITH A PROBLEM

I discovered Milton Erickson when I was in Canada. In the summer of 1976 I was visiting Dr. Marvin Kaplan, an old friend and former professor. The conversation was going as usual as we compared notes on psychotherapy, on our most recent thinking, and on our newest ideas. For Marv, that meant gestalt therapy, systems theory, and family work. I was explaining prescriptive eclecticism and how my colleague,

100

Ron Havens, and I were close to developing a framework for the practice of an eclectic psychotherapy (Dimond, Havens, & Jones, 1978).

At some point in our conversation, Marv smiled in an impish way, opened a book and read. "That hurts awful, Robert. That hurts terrible" (Haley, 1973, pp. 189-192). He continued to present to me the account of Erickson's use of "hypnosis" with his injured son.

I remember that the grin was still on Marv's face as he closed the book and looked at me sitting across his study. After a while he said, "What does that mean?"

His question was lost on me. I was dazed. I was dazzled. I was in a trance. I had no idea what "it" meant, but I can clearly remember "knowing" that "it" was "right." There was something in those few lines which transcended everything we had been discussing, everything I had learned and had ever thought about the process of psychotherapy.

When I returned to Springfield I ordered this "strange" book. I read it; I enjoyed it; and, when I was through, I was a small step closer to being able to verbalize "it." About as close as I could come was, "Here is a man I would go to with a personal problem."

Certainly, Milton Erickson did some unusual things in his therapy. But somehow, what he did made sense. In fact, what he did in therapy was *less* unusual than many other things I had read about therapy. Erickson's patients did not engage in primal screams or analyze birth trauma. Neither did they attempt to resolve their death anxieties nor grieve the loss of idealized parent figures.

More than knowing what to do with patients, it seemed to me Milton Erickson knew something I did not know. Thinking about it now, what Erickson knew seems to have been captured nicely by Walker Percy (1983). Percy first posed a question concerning shyness and whether or not one should seek psychotherapy for such a "condition." He also provided a number of answers, one of which seems particularly Ericksonian:

It is better to seek help from a psychotherapist if the psychotherapist knows what not many psychotherapists know, namely, that the shy person may know something that the nonshy person does not know, that your self is indeed unformulable to yourself, that, indeed, varying degrees of idiocy are required not to be shy, that the very unformulability of your self is the only clue you have to the uniqueness of yourself, that otherwise one will become yet another Ralph among a thousand Ralphs, or worse still, become an imitation of the psychotherapist. (Percy, 1983, p. 35)

I knew I wanted to be able to do what Erickson did. I was on my way to becoming involved in an approach to learning and therapy which, paradoxically, was incredibly simple and most complex.

STIMULUS OVERLOAD

After reading *Uncommon Therapy* (Haley, 1973), I forged ahead, in my best obsessional style, reading everything I could find about Erickson. It was wonderful to have all this information available. I became aware that there were linguistic analyses of Erickson's work (Bandler & Grinder, 1975) and there were philosophical analyses of Erickson's work (Watzlawick, Weakland, & Fisch, 1974). There were neurological analyses of Erickson's work (Watzlawick, 1978); there were algorithmic analyses of Erickson's work (Gordon & Meyers-Anderson, 1981); there were experiential analyses of Erickson's work (Erickson & Rossi, 1981). Finally, there was the teaching seminar (Zeig, 1980) and a collection of teaching tales (Rosen, 1982).

I persevered. My obsession knew no bounds. I made varied attempts to contact my unconscious mind and to let it lead the way. I depotentiated my conscious sets so that I went for days in total confusion. I reframed all of my experiences so that I no longer recognized that my final frame was my original experience. I conversed with people at a meta-level so far removed from their comments that they politely removed themselves from my comments. I embedded metaphors so deeply that I spent hours trying to remember what I was trying to say originally. I created so many anchors for my own experience I became afraid to move for fear of collapsing like a white dwarfstar. I spent days not doing and not knowing. I began to *understand* Stephen Gilligan!

That scared me! My own obsessional state began to dawn on me. My children were helpful. They no longer wanted *my* opinion on things. "No, no, Dad," they would say, "what would *Milton Erickson* say about this situation?" Something had to give!

OBSERVING THE LEARNERS

As I slowly regained consciousness, I realized that, even though I had benefited from my experimentation, something was missing. For example, I really was not certain *why* I was doing all of this. I *knew* I had developed some new skills, but I was uncertain what to *do* with them. So, I took a break from the books and the techniques and I began to *observe*; I made my own learning of Ericksonian method into a phenomenon to be observed in myself and in others.

What I learned can be summarized briefly. First, I observed myself and others using Ericksonian technique without an appreciation for what they were attempting to accomplish—without a sense of *perspective*. Second, I observed myself and others attempting to use Ericksonian method while maintaining an allegiance to a particular theory—an allegiance to a set of beliefs. Finally, I observed a reluctance, a hesitation, to get people to change their behavior. Several examples can clarify these points.

I listened to a therapist describe his interaction with a patient. He spoke of his ability to recognize the patient's "game," or style, and described the manner in which he "defeated" this patient and sent him on his way. I was curious about this and inquired as to the goal of this interaction. The therapist responded with an elaboration on the importance of being "one up" and "in charge" and of breaking patient response sets. I wondered how this would be helpful to the patient; I wondered about the therapist's perspective, his level of understanding.

I listened to a particularly well-read therapist present a case for my input. I thought aloud until he objected, "That kind of thinking violates the assumptions of systems theory. You are putting the problem inside the patient." My response to him was not particularly Ericksonian. "Oh", I said, "I didn't realize you wanted a solution to this problem which *also* stays within the assumptions of a particular belief system." I made a note of his interesting orientation.

Finally, I helped a young therapist work out a solution to a patient's problem. As I finished elaborating a plan designed to change the problem behavior, I realized she was looking at me with horror on her face. It turned out she wanted me to speculate as to the "why" of her patient's behavior. The therapist had confidence in her own ability to discover "why." However, she was aghast at the thought of trying to get the patient to *change*!

INTEGRATING OBSERVATIONS

I began to realize there is more to becoming Ericksonian than meets the eye. I began to realize I was not alone in my frustration. Most importantly, I realized what I wanted from my study of Milton Erickson: I wanted his *perspective* on people. Erickson's perspective determined his techniques. If I wanted to do what he did, I would have to *begin to learn what he knew!**

From this vantage point came a new appreciation of Milton Erickson's wisdom. Basically, I could now appreciate the immense *differences* between Erickson's approach to people and other approaches. Up to this point in my learning I had sought clarification of Erickson's methods by resorting to my past education, by comparing Erickson to what I had learned previously about the theory of therapy (e.g., Beahrs, 1971). Suddenly, I knew that this kind of thinking was a liability in my desire to "become" Ericksonian. Erickson did not theorize and my impression of him was that he knew what he was about. Therefore, his lack of theorizing must have been for good reason. My task was to develop an Ericksonian perspective without having the comfort of a theory to refer to and without having Milton Erickson himself to guide me.

While I did not have Milton Erickson, thanks to Ernest Rossi (1980) I did have Erickson's writings. I went back to the original source to see what I could discover for myself. This time, however, I was looking for something different than I had in the past. Instead of looking for techniques, I was looking for what he knew about people, his attitude toward people, and his approach to them.

What emerged for me were several simple ideas: First, Erickson was interested in *changing behavior*; second, Erickson worked in a fashion which he had discovered was most *helpful* in changing behavior; third, Erickson possessed a broad understanding and *acceptance* of people, including knowledge of the unconscious mind (Dimond, 1981); fourth, Erickson worked within and through people's *experiences*; finally, Erickson's *perspective* was embedded in his behavior. He may not have written a theory, but he did *live* one! His "techniques"—what he did with people—reflected his knowledge of people (Dimond, 1980). In other words, *Milton Erickson knew more than I did!*

SIMPLE PRINCIPLE; SIMPLE MODEL

Naturally, I panicked. My past emphasis on technique was of limited value. My reading of what others said *about* Erickson's work was of limited value. I simply had a lot to learn about people. I had a lot to

---

* I believe it is this issue of perspective which is debated in a series of articles in *The Psychotherapy Newsletter* (Andreas & Andreas, 1983; Schoen, 1983a, 1983b) which I highly recommend. See also a "Letter to the Editor" (Holmes, 1982) in *The Family Therapy Networker*.

learn about helping people to change their behavior and their experience. How would I ever manage to learn all of this?

But, I remembered an Erickson comment. Erickson learned what he knew through observation of his patients (Zeig, 1980). *I had patients!* Perhaps I could begin to learn what Erickson knew by observing my own patients.

The idea sounded plausible. I knew *something* about behavior. I also knew I needed to keep my conscious biases out of the way and "start over" so to speak. I also knew I needed a framework for practice.

The model I derived is adapted from a colleague, Sol Rosenberg (personal communication, October 12, 1980), and is similar to the information-gathering model of the Mental Research Institute. When I encounter a new patient, I ask a series of questions which I use to structure the therapy relationship, to keep myself on track, and to permit me to observe without thinking too much. These questions are: 1) What do you want? 2) What is getting in the way? 3) What have you already tried to resolve the difficulty? and 4) Are you willing to experiment with something new?

Of course, while I ask my patient these questions, I am able to accumulate a great deal of useful information. In general, I can get to know my patients: who they are, what they are like, how they live, what kinds of ideas they find acceptable, and what they are already doing which may be helpful.

ADVANTAGES OF A SIMPLE MODEL

Now, I realize that this model is simple. Nevertheless, there are ways in which this approach has been important in my transition to becoming Ericksonian.

The Model Permits Learning

The model permits me to *learn*—to learn *from the inside out* (Dimond, 1981) and to learn *in my own way and in my own time*. My learning of Ericksonian method cannot come solely from reading what he wrote or from what others say about him. My learning must come from my own experience and I must learn in a way that is comfortable for *me*.

This realization led me to change my behavior. I suppose one could say I "backed up" and spent some time practicing as I did in the past. The difference was that I modified the techniques I was comfortable with so that I could use them to *observe* rather than to *intervene*. I used situations I was comfortable with as a way of experimenting with Ericksonian forms of communication and influence.

For a while, this meant I *stopped* using hypnosis and instead began experimenting with gestalt double-chair technique with which I was more comfortable. At first, I just observed and provided little structure or direction. Then, I began to intervene and influence the course of my patient's experience. In the process I learned about the use of words, voice tone, and expectancy sets. I also learned to be more sensitive to the needs of my patient.

Next, I experimented with providing sentences for my patients to say (Dimond, 1981). These sentences were formulated by observing unconscious, nonverbal behaviors in my patients. I asked my patients to say these sentences, to focus upon their bodies, and to let me know if, somehow, these sentences seemed "true" or "accurate." I enjoyed the reactions of my patients when they repeated these often "nonsensical" statements and agreed that, yes, they seemed "true." In this way I sharpened my observational skills, provided an intervention, and received information concerning my own accuracy.

From this experiential base, I found I could use effectively what I call "mini trances." I would ask patients to close their eyes and listen to me for a few minutes. This gave me experience with recognizing when and how patients were listening and experiencing and led me back into working hypnotically. However, now I had greater confidence and knew more about what I was doing.

The Model Permits Learning From Patients

My model permits me to approach my patients with fewer conscious biases. I am able to observe and to learn from my patients because *I do not know* how a particular, unique individual will answer my structuring questions.

It is good for me not to know. "Knowing" was getting in the way of my learning. A great deal of what I knew derived from my educational background: I "knew" about DSM I, II, and III; I "knew" about pathology; and I "knew" about behavioral deficits. In brief, my education taught me to believe I knew. The problem was pointed out by R. D. Laing (1970, p. 55): "If I don't know I don't know, I think I know."

So what happens when I know I don't know? I find myself behaving in ways that I recognize as Ericksonian. For example, I am able to *accept all of my patients' behavior*. After all, if you don't know, everything becomes of equal importance. In turn, this acceptance leads me to *get to know my patients* and to learn from them in a new way. All aspects of them are of importance, what they say is important and I do not "lop off" parts of them as I did when I thought I knew. Since my patients are really giving me an opportunity to learn, I find myself treating them with more *respect*.

But something else happens when I permit myself to "know I don't know." I discover the meaning behind the rest of Laing's comment: "If I don't know I know, I think I don't know" (Laing, 1970, p. 55). I begin to realize and appreciate what I do know and to let this knowledge guide me.

For example, I know that experience is the best teacher and that this realization is important for both my patient *and* myself. Consequently, my goal in therapy is to create helpful, therapeutic experiences for my patient as opposed to discussing issues at a conscious level. This process is new for me *and* for my patient. But I can apply Erickson's dictum that it is best to make use of, and build upon, past experience—what you are already doing and already know.

The Model Permits An Understanding of Milton Erickson

Finally, this simple model allows me to understand the meaning behind what Erickson wrote. When I am oriented toward learning, as the model facilitates, I am constantly observing and then "hearing" Erickson's words. Obviously, this is a different process than trying to remember what Erickson said and letting this "memory" guide the therapy. It focuses my attention upon aspects of Erickson's work which have received little emphasis elsewhere.

For example, I now notice that when I am working with "difficult" clients therapy seems to occur in two stages. In the first stage I am most "Ericksonian" and my goal is to *accept* and work *with* this "difficult" behavior. This involves such approaches as *encouraging* a woman referred by vocational rehabilitation as an untreatable "complainer" to continue her complaining. I listened carefully and began to "understand" her, which, in turn, permitted some major reframing to occur.

After some time, a change occurred in this woman. She complained less and began to evaluate her life more objectively. In this, the second stage, she was ready for more conventional therapy. Subsequently I was less "Ericksonian" and did not work so hard. As a result, I *believe* she has learned how to learn. But then again, I do not *know*.

CONCLUSION

I sometimes smile to myself when I pause to enjoy the subtleties, paradoxes, and ironies of what I have learned from my experience with Milton Erickson's work. I now have a simple way of structuring a therapeutic relationship. On the face of it, this model would seem to *limit* the extent of the interaction between therapist and patient. After all, my clients and I are not likely to get into a long discussion of their history.

Yet, the adoption of this simple framework has taught me to appreciate people in a way which heretofore was "beyond my experience." When I am able to accept all of my patient's behavior with respect, we are each experiencing an important kind of human contact which can be deeply moving.

Personally, these moments are most rewarding to me, and I also have a new respect for my own learning. For example, when working with an intelligent woman around the issue of her weight and physical well-being, I noted that she used the phrase, "Pretty is as pretty does." Later, I asked her to close her eyes and listen as I repeated a phrase three times: "Playing football builds character, but plenty of people with good character did not play football." She began to cry and I was quiet. When she spoke, we both knew something important had happened and I was secretly thankful of myself.

Obviously, there is more to be learned, and I am aware that "becoming Ericksonian" requires *me* to change, for becoming an Ericksonian psychotherapist requires me to expand my own behavior. It requires me to be external when I prefer to be internal; to take risks when I prefer safety; to be flexible when I am rigid; to be positive when I frequently feel negative; to take responsibility for making things happen with people when I prefer to shirk this responsibility; to be tolerant when I feel critical; to be confident and in charge when I frequently feel inadequate and one-down; to be creative when I prefer the beaten path; to recognize and accept ambiguity when I prefer the concrete; to be a positive, useful "parent" to myself when I am frequently discouraged.

The whole enterprise is a most satisfying and rewarding challenge. In the process I have learned how to learn and how I learn, and that is most important. The model is simple; the aspects of Erickson's method which it focuses me upon are simple. It is all very Ericksonian!

REFERENCES

Andreas, C., & Andreas, S. (1983). NLP: A reply to Stephen Schoen. *The Psychotherapy Newsletter, 1*(2), 19-24.

Bandler, R., & Grinder, J. (1975). *Patterns of the hypnotic techniques of Milton H. Erickson, M.D.* (Vol. 1). Cupertino, CA: Meta Publications.

Beahrs, J. O. (1971). The hypnotic psychotherapy of Milton H. Erickson. *American Journal of Clinical Hypnosis, 2,* 73-90.

Dimond, R.E. (1980). The wisdom of paradox: A new perspective on contralogical methods of problem formation and resolution. *Psychology, 17*(2), 29-41.

Dimond, R.E. (1981). Personal reflections upon hypnosis and psychotherapy. *Voices: The art and science of psychotherapy, 17*(1), 12-18.

Dimond, R.E., & Havens, R.A. (1980). The process of psychotherapy from the perspective of prescriptive eclecticism. In W. DeMoor & H.R. Wijngaarden (Eds.), *Psychotherapy: Research and training* (pp. 95-99). Amsterdam, Holland: Elsevier/North-Holland Press.

Dimond, R.E., Havens, R.A., & Jones, A.C. (1978). A conceptual framework for the practice of prescriptive eclecticism in psychotherapy. *American Psychologist, 33*(3), 239-248.

Erickson, M.H., & Rossi, E.L. (1981). *Experiencing hypnosis: Therapeutic approaches to altered states.* New York: Irvington.

Gordon, D., & Meyers-Anderson, M. (1981). *Phoenix: Therapeutic patterns of Milton H. Erickson.* Cupertino, CA: Meta.

Haley, J. (Ed.). (1967). *Advanced techniques of hypnosis and therapy: Selected papers of Milton H. Erickson, M.D.* New York: Grune & Stratton.

Haley, J. (1973). *Uncommon therapy: The psychiatric techniques of Milton H. Erickson.* New York: Norton.

Holmes, L. (1982). Losing "it." *The Family Therapy Networker, 6*(5), 8.

Laing, R.D. (1970). *Knots.* New York: Vintage Books.

Percy, W. (1983). *Lost in the cosmos: The last self-help book.* New York: Farrar, Straus & Giroux.

Rosen, S. (1982). *My voice will go with you: The teaching tales of Milton H. Erickson.* New York: Norton.

Rossi, E.L. (Ed.). (1980). *The collected papers of Milton H. Erickson on hypnosis* (Vols. 1-4). New York: Irvington.

Schoen, S. (1983a). NLP: An overview with commentaries. *The Psychotherapy Newsletter, 1*(1), 16-26.

Schoen, S. (1983b). Stephen Schoen's reply to Connirae Andreas and Steve Andreas. *The Psychotherapy Newsletter, 1*(2), 24-25.

Watzlawick, P. (1978). *The language of change: Elements of therapeutic communication.* New York: Basic Books.

Watzlawick, P., Weakland, J., & Fisch, R. (1974). *Change: Principles of problem formation and problem resolution.* New York: Norton.

Zeig, J.K. (Ed.). (1980). *A teaching seminar with Milton H. Erickson.* New York: Brunner/Mazel.

Chapter 9

Hypnotic Psychotherapy

Lawrence R. Gindhart

Prologue: Model for Orientation, Canon in D Flat

Model for Orientation

This is a model for orientation to Ericksonian methodology in the practice of psychotherapy. It is not a model of methodology.

Canon

In music, a canon, or canonic form, is said to exist when copies of a single theme are played against the original theme. The theme and its copies are played by various participating voices. Copies of the theme are variations created by alterations in time, pitch and speed. Copies also can be made by inversing or reversing the original theme, yet each copy precisely preserves the information of the original (Hofstadter, 1979).

In D Flat

Copies of this model are presented as four two-dimensional viewpoints, enumerated here, A through D. Hence "D Flat."

A. The viewpoint of being oriented according to the model itself.

B. The act of viewing the model as an abstract, relativistic, phenomenological structure. (As in the recursions of Part Three.)

C. The viewpoint of a clinician creating meaning-provoking contexts.

D. The viewpoint of a person interacting with a meaning-provoking context.

Three-Part Invention

Information of this model is written in loose-canonic form initially, and in recursive forms later. The model is initially presented in the introduction, and thematically established, albeit in a thinly disguised way, in Part One. In Part Two, thematic development continues, but it is couched in concepts of theory construction. In Part Three, full thematic

110

development occurs as the original model is presented in recursive form. *And Acknowledgment*

My chapter's design is unusual. The design emerged, as if from some germinal origin, and I watched as it grew and developed. Then, before my bewildered, curious eyes, it began to unfold. And I wrote, never knowing what the design's unfolding would eventually reveal. I am in debt to Douglas Hofstadter and his Eternal Golden Braid; an unfailing source of inspiration and amazement.

INTRODUCTION

What is hypnotic psychotherapy? Just as elusive and probably as exotic as the conversion of a DNA molecule into a physical organism, I think the answer resides in each one of us, in each of our patients (including those who don't know they are going to be our patients), and in the complex cycles of interaction between people. All of us favor certain ideas over others because we have unique backgrounds and we have had particular opportunities and training experiences. We do our best with what we know, and with what we understand. But, we can do even better with what we don't know that we know.

Concerning teaching, hypnosis, and psychotherapy, Jeffrey Zeig (personal communication, July 30, 1983) commented that it is often difficult to determine when Erickson was teaching, when he was doing hypnosis, or when he was doing psychotherapy. His manner of practice blurred their apparent differences considerably.

Part One

ORIENTATION IN THE PRACTICE OF HYPNOTIC PSYCHOTHERAPY

First I would like to describe my orientation to the use of hypnosis in psychotherapy. As I describe it, I invite you to discover something about yours that you would enjoy.

My orientation to the use of hypnosis in psychotherapy is simple in principle but complex in meaning, because it is not an orientation to hypnosis at all. Rather, it is an orientation to myself as I learn, and as I communicate with another human being. My orientation is important only in that my communication is meant to have an effect. The effect of my communication is related to my orientation to myself, oriented to the person with whom I am communicating.

Because I realize I know little about the person I am communicating with, I also realize I know little about the person I am oriented to—I know little of what they have experienced. The fact that people are capable of much more than I can know is an interesting part of my orientation; an enjoyable part of my orientation.

And practicing hypnotic psychotherapy does not necessarily involve any formal invitation to have some satisfying experience of trance. In practicing hypnotic psychotherapy, just as there is no need to formally induce going into a trance, neither is there any need to formally elicit or ratify classical trance phenomena, because they can occur easily, naturally, without the subject's conscious awareness. And trance phenomena can be experienced with or without a formally induced trance, just as trance can be experienced with or without a formal induction.

This orientation to using hypnosis in psychotherapy emphasizes *effect*, rather than any particular method of going about achieving that effect. It is the actual effect of the therapy, of the communication, that is more important than method, what is theoretically correct, or what the effect should have been.

In terms of effect, what is of value is: Whatever can make the task of reorientation and change easier; whatever can make needed personal resources more readily available; whatever can make the emergence of new associations, responses, and behaviors in relevant contexts automatic and effortless; whatever can help suit a communication to the unique qualities of the subject's conscious and unconscious mind; whatever can be provided to protect the integrity of the individual personality; whatever can help in forming my orientation to accomplishing these things.

Therapy is over when people are using their own resources to solve problems. And one of the resources they learn to use is to trust their unconscious mind. I frequently tell my patients, "Your unconscious mind knows all that you know, and much more that you don't know that you know. It is a vast storehouse of forgotten memories, of learnings that you take for granted." Erickson said, "It is a very delightful way of living, a very delightful way of accomplishing things" (Gordon & Anderson, 1981, p. 17).

Now, the promise of hypnotic psychotherapy is not logical relief from perplexity and distress, but experiential relief. When patients come into psychotherapy, they have attained whatever relief their logic, and their understanding will allow. Patients do not know what they are really capable of. Their presence in therapy is ample evidence of that. Their presence is an adequate indication that they have tried to solve their problem the best they think they know how, and any story they present is merely a description of that kind of knowledge. They cannot discover that they are capable and can do without help, and they need to discover that. Similarly, psychotherapists do not know what they, themselves, are capable of because they put their reliance on what they know they understand. People need to learn that they can put their reliance on what they do not know they know.

Psychotherapists know they can consistently use their particular theoretical orientation and have a beneficial effect with some people. However, in so doing they will not discover that they can help more people than they could otherwise. Erickson said,

> I think we all should know that every individual is unique. There are no duplicates. In the three and one-half million years that man has lived on earth, I think I am quite safe in saying there are no duplicate fingerprints, no duplicate individuals. Fraternal twins are very different in their fingerprints, their resistance to disease, their psychological structure and personality. And I do wish that . . . therapists . . . of various theories would recognize that not one of them really recognizes that psychotherapy for person number one is not psychotherapy for person number two. I've treated many conditions, and I always invent a new treatment in accord with the individual personality. (Zeig, 1980, p. 104)

When patients come into psychotherapy, they present their personal epistemology—their understandings, beliefs, perceptions, logic, reasoning, truth—they reveal their pathways of rigidity. Assisting patients along these same unyielding paths (e.g., attempting to better their understanding of what they understand, or attempting to answer their unanswerable question, "Why?") simply perpetuates their problem, and their inability to resolve it. No matter how good a theory of psychotherapy and personality may be, it cannot preclude the possibility of error, nor can it provide the certainty patients may believe necessary to have relief.

The promise of hypnotic psychotherapy is to produce experiential relief. Give patients a foundation of reassociations of their experience and they will alter their personal epistemology themselves, in accord with their distinct requirements as individuals, rather than the requirements of a theory of personality.

When asked, "Just what is psychotherapy?" or "What is hypnosis?" Erickson's elusiveness was no greater than the elusiveness of the phenomena themselves. Often he would reply with an interesting story, a case report, or quip with something like, "Two people go into a room together. One tries to figure out just what it is that the other one wants" (Gilligan, 1980).

I believe that a relationship exists between Dr. Erickson's persistent indefiniteness, and meaningfully ambiguous responses to defining hypnosis and psychotherapy, and the almost infinite variation in his methods of practice. Case materials show that Erickson's methods, applications and orientations to practicing hypnosis and psychotherapy were readily revisable. Yet, he was definite in his assertion that therapists should be oriented by their patients instead of their theories (Erickson, 1980). Erickson's orientation seemed to consistently consider what people can do, and how they can do it readily, naturally and beneficially. Therapy should be oriented towards the patient, because it is the patient who is creating and articulating change. Erickson consistently would consider particular patients as they were involved in their interpersonal and sociocultural context, and would "expedite the currents of change already seething within the person" (Watzlawick, Weakland, & Fisch, 1974, p. ix). And with consistent—and perhaps consequent variety—he would seek to attain that goal.

Psychotherapists shift their way of being oriented from a theory to the patient. In being oriented by their patients, psychotherapists can discover that they don't know their patients, or what their problems are. Patients don't know exactly what their problems are. They can tell only what they understand they know. Erickson said,

> In psychotherapy, you listen to your patient, knowing that you don't understand the personal meanings of his vocabulary . . . you listen to your patient, knowing that he has personal meanings for his words, and you don't know his personal meanings. . . . And he doesn't know your personal meaning. You try to understand the patient's words as he understands them. (Zeig, 1980, p. 158)

The author of a particular theory of personality or psychotherapy does not know the details of the histories, experiences, or problems of all patients. Erickson believed, "any theoretically based psychotherapy is mistaken because each person is different. Now, when you consider the psychotherapy, consider the patient" (Zeig, 1980, p. 131). It is against the landscape of each patient's life experiences that the processes of change must be fostered—to fit the lay of that particular landscape, with its unique features, its inhabitants, culture, wildlife, foliage, coloration, climate, and all the seasonal variations that it can have. Hypnotic psychotherapists know that they don't know how to fill in this landscape in the most satisfying way, because they understand that their patients have to do that for themselves. Patients know what they need, but they don't necessarily know that they know. Therapists provide them with experiences in which they can discover that kind of knowledge—that is the essence of experiential relief.

As psychotherapists develop their own orientation to using hypnosis in psychotherapy, they begin to realize that they always have a choice in the placing of importance. That is, one can place importance on a theory, or on understandable techniques. Granted, they will feel considerable certainty in what they know, as well as a sense of familiarity in what they understand and can explain. Or, they can place importance on their patients' unconscious knowledge of what their problems really are, on what their patients' experiential learnings are, and on what their patients' needs are. Psychotherapists feel a fortune of uncertainty and unfamiliarity, simply because these are things we don't know about, that we cannot gain direct access to. In practicing hypnotic psychotherapy, Erickson said, "You ought to learn that it's not what you do, it's not what you say, but what the patient does, what the patient understands" (Rosen, 1982, p. 154). And concerning what a patient understands, the "unconscious mind is made up of all . . . your learnings over a lifetime, many of which you have completely forgotten, but which serve you in your automatic functioning. Now, a great deal of your behavior is the automatic functioning of these forgotten memories" (Zeig, 1980, p. 33).

It is interesting to discover that people can enjoy learning; that they can do things they don't understand today, so that they can understand better tomorrow; and that they learn in an unusual way and it is a way that people do not know about.

SUMMARY

The form of a psychotherapist's therapeutic orientation is critically important. By orientation I mean the general attitude with which psychotherapists approach their patients, define presenting problems, intervene and evaluate progress, especially as this attitude concerns certainty and knowledge. Such an attitude includes an understanding or conviction towards several beliefs:

1) I will be learning as I do therapy with this individual.

2) I will have to rely on certain aspects of myself that I may be unfamiliar with, or that I may know relatively little about, in order to help my patient.
3) I will have to rely on certain aspects of my patient that may be unfamiliar or little known to him or her—that are indeed, little known to me—in order to help my patient.
4) My patient is a living, developing human being, and my communication is meant to have a meaningful effect in his or her experience.
5) My patient has an abundance of resources, knowledge and capabilities—far greater than I know he or she has.
6) For me to recognize and enjoy knowing these aspects exist in therapy is desirable and beneficial to my client, and to myself.

Fundamentally, Ericksonian methodology relies upon an autonomous, unconscious intelligence, inherent in every individual, for the orchestration and conduct of psychotherapy. It is the orientation to this intelligence, and to its knowledge, that necessarily individualizes the therapy to each particular patient.

There is a great deal about a patient that we can come to know, but in therapy we are able to discover a very small amount. Nevertheless, we can, in fact we must, proceed with an attitude of confidence and expectancy toward our patients' unknown capabilities. We must proceed with a sense of certainty that much of value is concealed in unknown aspects of our patients' experience. In this, we can each discover our own orientation to the mysteries of Mind, and a knowledge that, as Albert Einstein said, "The most beautiful experience we can have is the mysterious. It is the fundamental emotion which stands at the cradle of true art and true science. Whoever does not know it and can no longer wonder, no longer marvel, is as good as dead, and his eyes are dimmed. The experience of mystery—even if mixed with fear—[is] a knowledge of the existence of something we cannot penetrate, our perceptions of the profoundest reason and the most radiant beauty, which only in their most primitive forms are accessible to our minds" (1931, p. 11).

Part Two

ERICKSONIAN PSYCHOTHEORY: TO BE, OR NOT TO BE?

In the continuing era of our universe, at but a momentary intersection in the dimensions of space and time, we stand at our epoch in the advancement of humanity. Born to such opportunity, we contribute our very lives to advance advancement. It is understandable that we want to be certain of what we do, and certain of what we know; however, as Albert Einstein noted, "One has been endowed with just enough intelligence to be able to see clearly how utterly inadequate that intelligence is, when confronted with what exists" (1931, p. 41).

And we are confronted—with an incomprehensible universe, its mysteries, and its secrets waiting to be discovered, and with our agonies, and our accomplishments—with huge question marks that extend beyond our most daring imaginings.

Despite our tendency to avoid it, we turn our gaze toward the unknown in search of solutions. Confronted by the insignificance of what we know, we reach into the security of all that we have learned, to reach out toward all that we don't know, with hope for discovery and new learning.

The darkness of our uncertain search is shattered when ideas explode onto our hope-filled horizon, that can be so illuminating that they resolve many fundamental problems at once. It is by our courageous endurance of the unexplored, and the unknown, in search of solutions—searches necessitated by seemingly irresolvable problems—that we discover new learning vital to the advancement of humanity.

Between rare flashes of brilliant ideas, we mark mere candlelit paths with descriptions, and we draft charts of explanation to order our observations and guide future exploration. With our descriptions of what things are, of how they change, and with our explanations of why things are, of why they change—we firmly set a course. Descriptions and explanations: rudimentary elements in the construction of theory. Their value lies in the extent to which they can give us a thorough understanding, and the extent to which they can correctly predict the future.

Modern science is no longer interested in the absolute truth, rather, its interest is merely to create correspondences for what we observe in the world (Batten, 1971), but we cling to our theories for orientation and hope. For example, during one of the theoretical upheavals that occurred in physics, Einstein wrote, "It was as if the ground had been pulled out from under one, with no firm foundation to be seen anywhere, upon which one could have built" (1949, p. 45). Similarly, a few months before Heisenberg's paper on matrix mechanics pointed the way to a new quantum theory, Wolfgang Pauli wrote, "At the moment physics is again terribly confused. In any case, it is too difficult for me and I wish I had been a movie comedian or something of that sort, and had never heard of physics" (Kronig, 1960, p. 22). In contrast, five months later he wrote, "Heisenberg's type of mechanics has again given me hope and joy in life. To be sure it does not supply the solution to the riddle, but I believe it is again possible to march forward" (Kronig, 1960, pp. 25-26). Perhaps theoretical upheaval is a necessary precondition to discovery.

As these illustrations show, theories are important. The problem is, they can become all-important. For example, anyone who inadvertently criticized the theoretical view of another, has had the experience of being accused of an act tantamount to blasphemy of the ultimate truth. Thomas Kuhn has suggested that an apparently outrageous theory may cease to be outrageous providing the difficulties it promises to remove are enormous and worth nearly any price to get rid of (1970). I believe that this concept can be applied equally to the view of a scientist, as it can to the delusion of a psychiatric patient.

A danger exists in becoming so enchanted with developing a theory around some flash of brilliance that people lose sight of what was observed and, blinded by the illusion that they possess a future vision so clear in detail that it promises to obliterate the possibility of uncertainty and error, they lose sight of their purposes. Einstein warned us, "It is the theory which decides what we can observe." Theory gives form and substance to perceptual reality, and thus, dictates what we perceive, and how we proceed.

I believe human beings have developed some remarkable tendencies. As one writer put it, we have developed a "natural predisposition not to see anything we don't want to, weren't expecting or can't explain" (Adams, 1982, p. 36-37). It is as if we will either ignore altogether, or generate any explanation, in order to account for whatever we do not immediately understand.

How do people react when startled by an unfamiliar sound? Are they comfortable? Is it enough when they say, "What was that?" and answer, "I don't know?" If not, how do they get relief? I think there is more distress in seeking the sound's source, than in explaining its occurrence. A suspenseful search can stimulate one's imagination, while an explanation gives a sense of knowing. And we all know, "It must have been the wind!" Of course, if all else fails, one can mark it off as absolutely inexplicable, and proceed as if it never had happened.

Concerning psychotherapy, virtually all approaches have a foundation in a theory of personality (Corsini, 1979). In the development of theories of psychotherapy, some were preceded by a theory of personality, while with others, the theory of personality was derived from the practice of psychotherapy (Hall & Lindzey, 1970). The more axiomatic a theory, the better it is at accounting for any phenomenon. But, it is often an account by theoretical explanation, rather than by seeking a phenomenon's source. Discrepancies between a theoretically correct course of therapy, for example, and a patient's response to it, are easily accounted for as some inability, deficiency, or incompetence in the patient (Gindhart, 1983). That a theory can explicitly describe the true nature of people, or that it can know the requirements for healthy adjustment, is a dangerous illusion. From within a self-referential theoretical view, is it possible to know whether the requirements of a theory bear even a remote resemblance to a particular patient's requirements?

Whether practice is derived from theory, or theory is developed from practice, psychotherapies appear to have a Platonic practicality to their nature. That is, as practice becomes wedded to theory, the therapeutic orientation becomes cast in theoretical certainty. Constrained by this orientation, psychotherapists must attempt to deal with the highly developed, ambiguous, and highly personalized views from which patients seek relief.

While an alternative does exist, the choice is essentially between an orientation that is person-inconsistent or an orientation that is theory-inconsistent, a choice between attempting to alter a person to fit theoretic preconceptions, or creating a new theory to fit each person.

Theoretic psychotherapy generalizes that which is known, onto that which is unknown—the patient. For example, a young New York stock investment counselor who believed he was an anorectic, was starving himself and suffering from severe weight loss. He spent several years going from psychotherapist to psychotherapist, all of whom spent their efforts trying to convince him that he couldn't possibly be anorectic, because only young women have anorexia nervosa. None of them did anything to get him to change some habits and gain weight. Fortunately, he ran across a doctor who would agree with his diagnosis, and would treat his problem. Now the young man has his weight back and is well-adjusted.

Ericksonian approaches to hypnosis and psychotherapy are essentially theory-inconsistent. The reliance of these approaches on general principles (Lankton & Lankton, 1983) serves to avoid what I call the illusion of advanced knowledge—an attempt to anticipate in detail all possible eventualities. I believe that the abundant variety of methods and techniques in Ericksonian approaches is due to the corresponding absence of theoretical constraints on its practice, a result of Erickson's persistent unwillingness to engage in psychotheory construction. Erickson said,

> Too many psychotherapists try to plan what thinking they will do instead of waiting to see what the stimulus they receive is and

then letting their unconscious mind respond to that stimulus. I don't attempt to structure my psychotherapy except in a vague, general way. And in that vague, general way the patient structures it. He structures it in accordance with his own needs. And the loose structure allows him to discover, bit, by bit, some of the things he . . . doesn't know about himself. There are a lot of things we know, that we don't know we know, but we need to know that we know it. (Gordon & Anderson, 1981, p. 17)

In an Ericksonian approach to hypnotic psychotherapy, psychotherapists learn to operate from a general position in which no single concept can stand firm. They learn to ignore the familiar so that they can attend to the unique and unfamiliar. They learn to sense a pleasing feeling of self-trust in themselves, amid the uncertainties of being "on the right track." In fact, the patient must define what the right track is.

Jeffrey Zeig once asked Dr. Erickson if he ever got bored telling the same teaching stories. "Bored!" The tone of Erickson's reply was incredulous, "I am purely interested in what I can learn" (J.K. Zeig, personal communication, June 12, 1983). In practicing this hypnotic psychotherapy, psychotherapists are interested in learning something special and in discovering something unique about each patient. Ideas develop progressively, from an inquiry with the patient. This is a subtle method of cooperating with the patient to gain the patient's cooperation in accomplishing the therapy. These ideas underscore Jay Haley's description of hypnotic interaction as "an example of the powerful influence one person may have upon another if both cooperate fully" (1976, p. 101).

In an Ericksonian hypnotic approach to psychotherapy, therapists attempt not to prove they are right in what they think they know and understand about their patient. Instead, they attempt to proliferate a course that proves right to the needs of the patient.

SUMMARY

I believe that the information of sensory experience is a paradise lost to the processes by which we create meaningful order out of what would otherwise be an incomprehensible labyrinth of multidimensional sense impressions. One such process is the construction of theories. It is the interaction of a theoretical structure, and its concepts, with sensory experience that reveals information as a meaningfully perceptible figure, while concealing other information as an unmeaningful or imperceptible ground (Gindhart, 1983).

A theory is simply a product of human thought, independent of experience, developed to account for some pattern of events or phenomena discovered in experience: a rule-bound body of conceptual elements that not only describes and explains the occurrence of such patterns, but also predicts their recurrence. The fewer and simpler its elements, the more universal its applications, and the more predictive its concepts, the better the theory (Gindhart, 1983). It is by imposing such theoretical preconceptions on the widely diverse information of sensory experience that we obtain a systematic, orderly view. But it is a view of dangerous clarity, a view that is open to an illusion of certainty and confidence in a perceptual reality that is itself created by habitually using theory to distinguish reality.

What of the existence of information rendered imperceptible to create such a clear view? Addressing a similar question, Einstein said, "In my opinion the answer to this question is, briefly, this: As far as . . . [theories] . . . refer to reality, they are not certain; and as far as they are certain, they do not refer to reality" (1921, p. 233).

In psychotherapy, the paradise lost to theoretic preconception is the information of how one person distinctly differs from all other people, and how each patient's experience, history and problem are unique. In relation to its subject, theoretical psychotherapy is in a state of inherent error, precisely because each individual, and every family is unique.

Part Three

AN EPIGENETIC EPILOGUE

For the more than 2,000 from around the world in attendance at the Second Ericksonian Congress, the Congress was a collective commitment to establish meaningful understandings of Ericksonian approaches to the use of hypnosis in psychotherapy. It is known that much of value exists in Erickson's methodology, and while we are beginning to understand many of its elements, we have yet to comprehend its meaning.

At first glance, the language of Ericksonian methodology appears deceptively similar to the prevailing therapeutic languages. Viewing it to discover how it is similar to what we already know is to lose sight of how it is distinct and vastly different.

I shall paraphrase a Douglas Hofstadter (1979) metaphor, to outline the task that I believe is ahead of us. It is a task that is comparable to cracking a complex alien language. In deciphering Ericksonian methodology, we now stand at a point where we know the sounds of the letters of the alphabet. We are beginning to understand a little of the syntax and grammar, but we do not know the meanings of the words. Interestingly, this is about where we stand in our current understanding of genetics; we can translate short strands of DNA into various amino acids (the alphabet), but we do not know what they mean. We have learned, however, that all of their meaning resides in the entirety of DNA itself! Genetics provides useful metaphors for interactional experience.

Genetic information, or the instructions for the bit-at-a-time evolution of a physical organism, is said to reside all at once in the double helix of a DNA molecule. By a very complex process (epigenesis), involving the manufacture of proteins, the replication of DNA, the differentiation of cell types, etc., a DNA molecule is converted into a physical organism. Epigenesis is a process of conversion, or transformation, that is guided by enormously complex cycles of chemical reactions and feedback loops. It is these complex cycles of interaction that evoke specific genetic codes for when, and under what conditions, various developmental transformations will occur. The DNA's structure contains all of the information of the resulting organism's structure. This means that the two are isomorphic. But, the isomorphism is exotic because there is no structural correspondence between a DNA molecule, and its resulting organism. (Prosaic isomorphisms have structural correspondence: parts of one structure are similar to parts of another).

The processes of epigenesis are not in DNA. Instead, a chemical context is required to evoke, or to pull out the information residing in DNA that guides organismic development. To reveal genetic information, DNA is entirely dependent upon the existence of, and its interaction with the specific chemical contexts required to pull such information out.

Nor does DNA create these contexts. Rather, it simply awaits their existence and only then will DNA reveal its meaning, i.e., epigenesis will give rise to a living organism, the structure of which was exotically preserved in the genetic information of the DNA from which it emerged. In other words, DNA is meaningless out of its chemical context, and to become meaningful, a relevant context is necessary (Hofstadter, 1979).

Although many will agree that epigenesis is a wondrous, and magnificently orchestrated phenomenon, it could be asked, "What does it have to do with human experience, and with Ericksonian methodology?" In reply, I present one recursion of epigenesis for human cognitive processes and another for the phenomenon of unconscious knowledge.

Please keep two things in mind. First, recursion is a representation of the same thing occurring in several events or classes of events at once, wherein that which is the same does not vary from event to event, despite many differences in the events themselves (Hofstadter, 1979). For example, the blood circulatory system, a water-displaying fountain on a public square, and the Freon-carrying system in an air conditioner or refrigerator are very different from one another. They are recursive, however, in that invariant features of information are contained in each of the examples. By contrast, canonic form (introduced in the Prologue) exists when information of one event is precisely duplicated in a variation of that event.

Consider one's face as information. This information on a mirror is a copy with variations of location (right is left), and size (depending on the distance of the subject from the mirror), and possibly proportion (depending on the surface plane of the mirror; convex, concave, etc.). The information on a recent photograph is a copy with variations of size, color, time, and resolution. Recursive form presents sameness-in-differentness, while canonic form presents variations-of-sameness. Information of the same individual's face, preserved on each of 20 photographs taken at two-year intervals, is simultaneously canonic and recursive.

Second, I am not a geneticist. The subject matter of genetics is new and unfamiliar to me, and I expect that discrepancies exist between my conception and a sophisticated comprehension of epigenetic processes. This epigenetic metaphor merely supplies a framework, without which I could not convey meaningfully certain ideas and relationships. Compromises in sophistication belie my comprehension of an enormously complex subject that I simplified for the sake of clarity.

Although the information that I will present as recursions of epigenetic processes exists in the model for orientation presented in Part One of this paper, I have added the dimension of relativistic, generative relationships. I maintain that these relationships are fundamental parameters of orientation in Ericksonian methodology.

ADVANCED CODED POTENTIALS

The genetic information residing in the double helix of a DNA molecule gives rise, not only to the structure of a human being and of its central nervous system, but also to its potentials for various sorts of information processing and mental capabilities. Because of this, one's behavior is ultimately under genetic control, albeit very indirectly (Dawkins, 1976). Dawkins notes that genes work by controlling protein synthesis, a powerful but very slow means of control (e.g., it takes months of pulling protein strings to build an embryo). Protein synthesis is far too slow a means for dealing with the environment directly—that is, too slow for an organism to survive. By contrast, behavior and various mental processes can occur in seconds, and fractions of a second. Genes therefore can only do their best work in advance. That is, genes build the central nervous system as an extremely fast biocomputer, complete with pre-programmed codes and developmental potentials, designed to develop and cope with many possible eventualities that will be encountered in living. Life, though, offers far too many possibilities for all of them to be anticipated exactly. Accordingly, these advanced codes and potentials exist in general form rather than as explicit strategies.

Advanced coded potentials exist all at once, at any time in a human, and yet they evolve gradually into explicit, multidimensional cognitive structures and perceptual strategies over the course of a lifetime. The process of converting coded potentials into established cognitive structures is guided by infinitely complex interactions of the human in environmental contexts. The process of interacting in specific contexts selects, and then transforms particular potentials into functioning cognitive structures that: 1) regulate information processing phenomena such as attention, comparison, abstraction, generalization, etc.; and 2) sensory-perceptual processes such as dissociation, anesthesia, amnesia, and pseudo-orientation in time.

Since advanced codes exist in the form of general potentials, they must be accessed and refined in order to become functional. The elicitation of a specific potential for explicit development, depends entirely upon encountering a sufficiently evocative environmental context. The codes to evoke and refine various potentials appear to rely only on the fact that the required enviromental contexts will eventually be encountered. The value of a general form of coded potentials lies in the idea that all possible occurrences in living cannot be exactly anticipated—they exist as advanced preparation for the vagaries of life.

Without appropriately evocative contexts, however, these preparations are meaningless. In order for these potentials to become meaningfully developed, specific contexts are necessary. A natural verbal language system, for example, is the necessary context for pulling out language acquisition strategies. Genetically, it is unimportant which natural language is initially encountered, or even that natural languages differ considerably from one another. General potentials for acquiring language do not have to know any of that in advance. Instead, they rely on systematically recurring, context-specific patterns and sequences of sound, to evoke the potentials which make the context explicit and meaningful.

UNCONSCIOUS KNOWLEDGE

Now, if humans can have a barely comprehensible intelligence which guides our genetic life, can we not have a corresponding intelligence which guides our unconscious life? Extending the recursion to unconscious knowledge (a frequent reference in Erickson's teaching and therapy) becomes equivalent with DNA (as the concept of advanced coded potential was equivalent with DNA in the preceding section).

Unconscious knowledge includes all of an individual's past experiences, and all of his information and sensory-perceptual processes, sensory and symbolic representations of information in simple and multidimensional, cognitive and psychophysiologic structures, the processes by which one makes meaning out of his or her world.

Unconscious life is interaction with context. Context is a discontinuous heartbeat of life. The variety of contexts that humans can encounter are as infinite as the interactions they can experience are complex. Unconscious knowledge exists as the principle means for processing, and competently participating in this critical aspect of human existence.

In its entirety, unconscious knowledge is continually brought forward through time, and even though it exists all at once, its meaning is revealed only gradually. This knowledge is organized in accord with specific requirements for the growth, development, and integrity of the individual, and is organized in general, and in well-developed forms. But this knowledge is not inherently meaningful. Meaning is revealed through interaction in context. The emergent meaning of unconscious knowledge, especially the extent to which this meaning is in accord with the health and integrity of the individual, is entirely dependent upon the existence of, and the eventual interaction with, contexts that are capable of evoking appropriate configurations of unconscious knowledge. It is the relationship between unconscious knowledge and context that creates the configurations of information which eventually become meaningfully developed abilities for coping with and enjoying life.

ORIENTATION AND CONTEXT

The idea of a general form of unconscious knowledge—a form that can generate definite structures in response to specific contexts—is evident in Erickson's orientation to hypnotic psychotherapy. I will again

present Erickson's description of his orientation because of its perti-
nence. He said,

> Too many psychotherapists try to plan what thinking they will do
> instead of waiting to see what the stimulus they receive is, and
> then letting their unconscious mind respond to that stimulus.
> (Gordon & Anderson, 1981, p. 17)

Fundamentally, Erickson's methodology relies upon an autonomous
intelligence that is inherent in every individual. It is an intelligence that
neither the individual, nor psychotherapist can directly access. Nonetheless it possesses: 1) intimate knowledge of the experiences, the learnings, and the idiosyncratic needs of the self; 2) refined capacities for
discriminating configurations of information that are contained in contexts; and 3) extraordinary capabilities for creating contexts that contain
meaning-provoking patterns of information.

When interruptions in integral developmental processes are signaled
by the emergence of psychological distress, or psychophysiologic symptoms, it is this intelligence which is relied upon to reestablish momentum
in the processes of growth and development as well as integrity in the
individual. But, in psychotherapy, it is the interaction of this intelligence
in context that creates meaning (e.g., change, symptom resolution, re-
sumption of developmental processes), the psychotherapist's orientation
to this intelligence that evokes the particular configurations of information from which meaning is made; and the psychotherapist's orientation that creates the therapeutic context.

An important dimension of this context is linguistic. The psychotherapist's orientation determines the formal properties of communication
in the therapeutic context.

In this section, the referent of the psychotherapist's orientation has
been ambiguous. The purpose of such ambiguity is to meaningfully
emphasize the importance of being oriented to, and relying upon the
unconscious intelligence and knowledge of one's self, and of one's patient, as an essential element in the process of creating a therapeutic
context.

ISOMORPHISM AND FORM

If there are some qualities of communication that are capable of evoking richer forms of unconscious knowledge than others and some interactional contexts capable of creating deeper meaning than others,

these capabilities are of particular relevance to the development of a psychotherapeutic orientation.

Not only do I believe that such semantic–interactive contexts exist, I believe they exist in Ericksonian methodology as isomorphisms of the structures and functions in unconscious intelligence that generate meaning. And according to Hofstadter (1979), meaning is created from the perception of isomorphisms.

I am interested in the concept of emergent meaning as a function of form, and I am especially interested in the isomorphisms between experiential learnings and the structure of semantic–interactive contexts that provoke these learnings.

While reviewing virtually any of Erickson's case transcripts, consider the idea that a relationship exists between the properties of form and the processes by which we make meaning of the world. Such a review will reveal a predominance of ambiguous, multilevel communication forms, including interspersals, binds, indirect suggestions, anecdotes and metaphors. Together, these communication forms affect levels of confusion and disorientation, shock and surprise, sufficient to disrupt established patterns of understanding and stimulate a search for new meaning. But how is this search directed?

Form itself can be thought of as having either syntactic or semantic qualities. The information of syntactic form is unambiguous, close to the surface, and contained almost completely within the communication under consideration (Hofstadter, 1979). Conceptually, syntactic form resembles the properties of first-order change (Watzlawick et al., 1974), in that it reduplicates, or yields itself. While environmental contexts and verbal and extraverbal communications all can have semantic or syntactic form, for now let us consider solely verbal communications.

I can illustrate with an example of a simple chain of causal logic. "You are sitting there now, and sensing yourself sitting will cause you to feel the support of your weight." Thus, the information of syntactic form is immediately available and self-evident.

By contrast, hiddenness and ambiguity characterize semantic form. Semantic form evokes open-ended searches for meaning because the information of the communication is not localized in the event or in the communication under consideration. Rather, correspondences and relationships are possible with potentially infinite classes of information (Hofstadter, 1979).

I can illustrate semantic form in the following: "Is there not something of importance you may like to discover, before or after you next leave this room, concerning that vague matter, bearing its weight on you?

And cannot the light of discovery, passing through a doorway, cause you relief of that weight?" Since the information necessary to make this communication meaningful is not contained in either the communication, or the immediate context, additional information must be obtained before meaning can be created. This nonlocalization of information initiates a search for additional information and thus establishes the potential to proliferate meaning.

Now, if meaning is not necessarily localized within a communication, or in a communication's context, then where is it, or how is it created? A model describing meaning-making processes necessarily would include the capacity for communication forms to stimulate searches for sameness-in-differentness throughout the information available in a communication, in a context, and in the subjective experience of the listener since, by definition, it is the perception of isomorphisms that creates meaning.

Consider that our minds can accept certain communication forms that inherently create multidimensional cognitive structures of information, far too complex to be described. Our minds attempt to integrate these structures with preexistent information in order to establish meaning. On this, our minds commence an open-ended search for links, or correspondences of sameness, with other multidimensional cognitive structures that have encoded our previous experiences. The extent of this search is determined by the extent of semantic qualities that characterize the communication form. As this process takes place, meaning can gradually unfold. In fact, it may take years before a person feels he or she has achieved the full meaning of something (Hofstadter, 1979). It is interesting to note that some of Erickson's former patients and students report dramatic changes occurring years after their last contact with him, which they attribute directly to that prior contact.

The creation of meaning is a process that establishes isomorphic connections between one multidimensional structure and any number of a variety of others. Semantic form is an essential element in the creation of meaning because it necessitates a deep penetration into the vast, rich domains of unconscious knowledge. In my view, communication forms capable of provoking these meaning-making processes lie at the heart of both Ericksonian methodology and the reassociation of experiential life.

CONTEXT, CODING AND THE AVAILABILITY OF EXPERIENCE

Presently, we are in the unforeseeable future of some distant past. Which experiential learning from that time, which has been unavailable until now, if it became available now, would contribute value to our current capacities and capabilities? How does one gain access to experiential resources of the past? To attempt to do so within the current structure of experience might be like using the key of one's present home, to unlock the door of one's childhood home. The ways in which we store, encode, access, and associate experience change across time, in accord with our learning and development. We have the experiential resources of our personal history, an unconscious knowledge, but how do we make that knowledge meaningful? If people can have access to experiential learnings of the past that they wish they didn't have, and if they can desire experiential learnings of the past that seem inaccessible in the present, then psychotherapists need to learn methods that can reassociate experience in satisfying ways.

SEMANTIC FORM, ISOMORPHISM, AND REASSOCIATION

Structures of unconscious knowledge that are revealed by the semantic form of Ericksonian methodology and the structure of therapeutic communications themselves contain isomorphisms whose meaning is a reassociation of experiential life. In an illustrative example, Erickson and Rossi (1979), reported on the case of a young woman with a circumscribed amnesia for giving birth to her first child. The woman bore this child with a caudal, rather than a general anesthesia, because she wanted to participate in giving birth as consciously and actively as possible. Despite the fact that she had a caudal anesthesia, she remembered little, and she felt that she had somehow missed out on participating in this important moment in her life. It was for this reason that she sought therapy.

Factors which contributed to the production of the amnesia were these: Moments before delivery, the patient's pleasant anticipations of childbirth were suddenly shattered by the painful cries of a woman in the next room who had a stillbirth. The patient had not expected that. Neither had she expected her hands to be tied down during the delivery, nor to hear the "snip" of doctors instruments cutting her flesh during the episiotomy. Her pleasant anticipations became a feeling of indignation because of what she felt were "unnatural procedures," and being treated as if she were "a wild animal without any sense."

This woman had expected childbirth to give her many pleasures. Instead, she received a series of shocks. The amnesia protected her from becoming aware of the memory, and of the unpleasant emotions associated with it.

In the therapy, Erickson created a communication, the meaning of which was a sensory-perceptual reorganization of the patient's memory of childbirth. Although it is not evident in the case material, I feel safe in saying that the patient's problem may not have been limited to her childbirth experience. Rather, it may have been a general pattern of structure in her subjective experience. The point of my speculation is this: The similarities between the patient's presenting problem and her presumed tendency establish the potential for generalization of the benefits of therapy. The therapy of a circumscribed problem can have a pervasive impact on the nature of a patient's experiential life, and I believe that the pervasiveness of the impact is due to the extent to which the presenting matter is isomorphic with other matters as well as the extent to which the patient must engage in a search for meaning. The latter is determined by the semantic qualities of the therapeutic communication.

In the following brief excerpt from the therapy, a communication is examined because of its semantic qualities. The information of the communication is not localized in the communication. The patient must therefore initiate an open-ended search through preexisting, multidimensional cognitive structures, in order to localize relevant information. In this search, it is the process of perceiving isomorphisms between the patient's representation of Erickson's communication, her representations of previous experiences containing information of the meaning of his communication, and her representation of experiencing childbirth that creates meaning.

The communication was presented to the patient while she was in a trance: "Now your unconscious mind can eliminate the intrusion of the other woman's sounds. And let them become the dim sounds, the dimmed memories. Your memories have that pleasant and beautiful vividness that belongs to you. And you need to realize in each first experience, not knowing prevents us from noticing, even though we do record."

In response to the therapy, the patient said, "The first experience! Because you've never experienced it before, you don't know. It's unknown even though your mind records things, its still unknown to you. And it unfolds to you. And that's how a certain mild shock of a first unknown experience . . . now that's dimmed, all that turmoil. That's what it was—turmoil and noises—and I don't know what was going on over next door. That's sort of dimmed. That's sort of taken second place. The awareness of what was happening to me is heightened."

Concerning this therapy, Erickson and Rossi commented that "psychotherapy would be much easier if everybody realized a major function of psychotherapy is to let unimportant things fade into the background, and only the relevant things come into the foreground" (Erickson & Rossi, 1979, pp. 309-310).

Erickson was a master creator of communications that created the kind of complex cognitive structures which converted implicit unconscious knowledge into meaningful forms—a creative process wherein the patients perceived correspondences between their representations of the therapeutic communication and representations of any of the learnings, experiences, and sensory-perceptual processes that constitute unconscious knowledge. This process, which is the basis of reassociating experience, is a process that works in accord with the distinct experiential history and the unique requirements of every individual.

Rather than a formal summary, I wish to conclude this section with a personal one. I learned a great deal as I wrote this paper, not only about psychotherapy but about myself. I can summarize one of the more important of these new ideas in the following way: The learnings of a lifetime can reveal a gradual, unfolding trust in yourself—it is your trust—in what you don't know that you know. It is a delightful way of living and it is a delightful way of learning. It is your way. You let your patients discover theirs—for they are master creators of psychotherapy.

COMMENT

This chapter represents my effort to emphasize the critical importance of the psychotherapist's orientation in the practice of hypnosis and psychotherapy. It is a way of being oriented that is not like a schooled captain, who is oriented by the standard displays on a ship's navigational equipment and by forecasted weather reports, but like wind, motion, and currents of the sea orient courageous sea explorers, in well-provisioned ships, to their voyages on unfamiliar waters. The orientation is an outlook that is not like that of the captain who once again plots a course he knows he has taken so many times before, but like that of the explorer who knows that every voyage is a unique encounter, and that even a look into crystal waters does not reveal all undersea life.

I have attempted to describe and demonstrate a psychotherapeutic orientation that is consistent with certain principles of Ericksonian methodology and then duplicate this orientation, in loose-canonic and recursive forms, to create thin contrasts between isomorphic structures. (By loose-canonic I mean that my use of symbolic language to reproduce meaningful variations of a theme is not as precise as it is in a canon in musical notation.) I have hoped that such a structure would help to create a meaningful view of this orientation.

I have been concerned with specific techniques of Ericksonian methodology only to the extent that an orientation to creative, unconscious processes is the principal basis upon which techniques are proliferated and individualistically applied—a condition that depends largely upon the express absence of a theory of psychotherapy.

To conclude, I will mention a fundamental concept that recurs throughout this orientation. It is the necessity of losing in order to win. One loses the familiar to gain the unfamiliar, or loses certainty to gain uncertainty. These are simply different ways for me to say you lose what you know to gain what you don't know that you know. It is a paradoxical orientation where losing one's self means winning one's self and a unity of self within the order of nature.

REFERENCES

Adams, D. (1982). *Life, the universe and everything*. New York: Harmony.

Batten, T. (1971). *Reasoning and research*. Boston: Little, Brown.

Corsini, R. (1979). *Current psychotherapies* (2nd ed.). Itasca, IL: Peacock.

Dawkins, R. (1976). *The selfish gene*. Oxford, England: Oxford University Press.

Dukas, H., & Hoffmann, B. (1979). *Albert Einstein: The human side* (p. 41). Princeton, NJ: Princeton University Press.

Einstein, A. (1921). Geometry and experience. In A. Einstein (1954), *Ideas and opinions* (S. Bargmann, Trans.). New York: Bonanza.

Einstein, A. (1931). The world as I see it. In A. Einstein (1954), *Ideas and opinions* (S. Bargmann, Trans.). New York: Bonanza.

Einstein, A. (1949). Autobiographical note. In P. Schlipp (Ed.), *Albert Einstein: Philosopher-scientist*. Evanston, IL: Library of Living Philosophers.

Erickson, M. (1980). *The collected papers of Milton H. Erickson* (Vols. 1-4). E. Rossi (Ed.). New York: Irvington.

Erickson, M., & Rossi, E. (1979). *Hypnotherapy: An exploratory casebook*. New York: Irvington.

Gilligan, S. (Speaker). (1980, December). *Matching type of induction strategy with type of subject* (Cassette Recording). Presented at the First International Congress on Ericksonian Approaches to Hypnosis and Psychotherapy. Phoenix, AZ.

Gindhart, L. (1983). *Resistance or cooperation in hypnosis and psychotherapy: The hypothesis of linguistic relativity*. Unpublished manuscript.

Gordon. D., & Anderson, M. (1981). *Phoenix: Therapeutic patterns of Milton H. Erickson*. Cupertino, CA: Meta Publications.

Haley, J. (1976). Development of a theory: A history of a research project. In C. Sluzki & D. Ransom (Eds.), *Double bind: The foundation of the communicational approach to the family*. New York: Grune & Stratton.

Hall, C., & Lindzey, G. (1970). *Theories of personality* (2nd ed.). New York: John Wiley & Sons.

Hofstadter, D. (1979). *Gödel, Escher, Bach: An eternal golden braid*. New York: Vintage Books.

Kidder, T. (1983). Science as a contact sport. *Science 83/American Association for the Advancement of Science, 4*(7), 58-66.

Kronig, R. (1960). The turning point. In M. Fierz & V. Weisskopf (Eds.), *Theoretical physics in the twentieth century: A memorial volume to Wolfgang Pauli*. New York: Interscience.

Kuhn, T. (1970). *The structure of scientific revolutions* (2nd ed.). Chicago: University of Chicago Press.

Lankton, S., & Lankton, C. (1983). *The answer within: A clinical framework of Ericksonian hypnotherapy*. New York: Brunner/Mazel.

Rosen, S. (1982). *My voice will go with you: The teaching tales of Milton H. Erickson*. New York: Norton.

Watzlawick, P., Weakland, J., & Fisch, R. (1974). *Change: Principles of problem formation and problem resolution*. New York: Norton.

Zeig, J. (1980). *A teaching seminar with Milton H. Erickson*. New York: Brunner/Mazel.

PART IV

Therapeutic Methodologies

This section consists of descriptions of therapeutic methodology. Rather than discussing specific techniques, these authors present basic aspects of their clinical approach.

Carol H. Lankton, M.A. (University of West Florida), is a marriage and family therapist in Gulf Breeze, Florida. She is internationally known for providing training in Ericksonian hypnosis and psychotherapy. With her husband, Stephen, she coauthored an important volume, The Answer Within: A Clinical Framework of Ericksonian Hypnotherapy *(Brunner/Mazel, 1983), which is the first comprehensive model of an Ericksonian approach written by some of Erickson's students. The* Answer Within *does not only provide a model, it presents important advances such as the Lankton's multiple-embedded metaphor technique.*

Carol Lankton describes the "snowballing effect"—changing one aspect of a symptom changes the system. She provides information on treatment planning and presents a successful case of treating hypertension.

Stephen R. Lankton, A.C.S.W., earned his M.S.W. at the University of Michigan. He is an extraordinarily talented practitioner and teacher of Ericksonian methods and he has served as a faculty member at all of the yearly meetings sponsored by the Erickson Foundation. In recognition of his excellent work, he was recently appointed the founding editor of The Ericksonian Monographs, *a new periodical of the Milton Erickson Foundation which will be published by Brunner/Mazel, Inc., and which will include articles on Ericksonian hypnosis and psychotherapy, including technique, theory, and research.*

Stephen Lankton travels internationally to provide training in Ericksonian psychotherapy. In addition to The Answer Within, *he authored* Practical Magic: A Translation of Basic Neuro-Linguistic Programming into Clinical Psychotherapy *(Meta Publications), and he has a number of notable chapters and articles to his credit.*

In his chapter, Lankton presents the essence of his multiple-embedded metaphor technique. Important diagnostic parameters and intended therapeutic outcomes are delineated.

Stephen G. Gilligan, Ph.D., currently conducts his private practice in Boston, Massachusetts, but is soon to move to San Diego, California. Gilligan is an internationally recognized authority on Ericksonian approaches and is popular on the lecture circuit. He has served on the faculty of all the Congresses and Seminars organized by the Erickson Foundation to date. His Ph.D. is from Stanford University and he has a number of publications on learning theory.

Gilligan presents important aspects of the Ericksonian epistemology. He describes a case of treating a patient with a "bashful bladder" to illustrate his approach to helping clients generate autonomous change.

Chapter 10

Generative Change: Beyond Symptomatic Relief

Carol H. Lankton

This last decade has witnessed a new emphasis on holistic health. Less frequently do patients approach their physicians expecting isolated treatment for a specific symptom. There is a new awareness that symptoms are only a means by which the body communicates something about the workings of the system as a whole. More and more, treatment involves the total system. Boundaries between purely "physical" difficulties and problems that are "all in the mind" are becoming indistinct as a new epistemology emerges. And yet, both physicians and psychotherapists still see those clients who, perhaps as a result of previous conditioning, naively request that a specific symptom be cured or that a habit be "removed" with no expressed regard for the broader context in which it developed. Hypnotherapists, as a special group, are perhaps more frequently approached by clients searching for "short cuts" to weight control, smoking, migraines, hypertension, and other well-defined symptoms. When the professional believes that "symptoms cannot be cured without producing a basic change in the person's social situation which frees him to grow and develop" (Haley, 1973), difficulties may arise as a result of discrepancies between the client's expectations and the actual direction treatment will take. These discrepancies need not, however, be resolved by educating the client to become well-versed in theories of psychotherapy or family systems, at least not in the Ericksonian approach.

This is not to say that focusing on and curing the symptom are misguided efforts because the "real" problems are ignored or because another symptom will simply arise to take the place of the one that has been removed. Indeed, I am in accord with Erickson's view that symp-

137

toms can and should be cured, ameliorated, or altered, albeit in a way that may differ greatly from the client's expectations. Haley quoted Erickson as saying that "the symptom is like the handle of a pot; if you have a good grip on that handle, you can do a lot with the pot" (1982, p. 19).

This chapter will refer primarily to Erickson's hypnotherapy as practiced in his later years. Traditional hypnotherapy, in contrast to an Ericksonian approach, became associated with techniques of progressive relaxation and direct suggestions primarily aimed at symptom removal or habit control. Freud denounced that type of hypnosis in his early writings. He did so based on his belief that symptoms suppressed in such a manner would recur. On the other hand, this chapter details an Ericksonian method of treatment planning that addresses interpersonal elements of a client's life even when the relationship of such aspects to the symptom may not be immediately apparent. In this way, symptom resolution is facilitated by dealing not only with specific techniques for symptom containment, reduction, alteration, etc., but also with personal factors such as the client's attitudes, self-image, behavioral and emotional flexibility, and family structure which are important to the larger process of generative change. Though certainly it is desirable in most cases for the symptom to be removed as soon as possible, we must thoughtfully consider when to pronounce therapy complete and the problem resolved. It is the question of resolution that Erickson seemed to be referring to when he wrote:

> The idea of simple "symptom removal" is a gross oversimplification of what sound hypnotherapy can be. The hypnotherapist is more appropriately involved in the broader program of facilitating a creative reorganization of the patient's inner psychodynamics so that life experience is enhanced and symptom formation is no longer necessary. (1979a, p. 147)

An increase in family therapy is another outcome of the trend toward a holistic view of the person. Early family therapists worked against prevailing theory to establish the notion that not only were symptoms often indicative of more pervasive malfunction somewhere in the client's personal system but that "psychopathic distortion and symptom formation are late products of the process of internalization of persistent and pathogenic forms of family conflict" (Ackerman, 1966, p. 75). Though Erickson emphasized the patient's inner psychodynamics, he did so with a keen appreciation and understanding of how these dynamics occur in relationship to significant others who form the individual's social network. In this regard, he was a family therapist, even on those occasions when he was only seeing an individual. But Erickson deemphasized psychodynamic conflict as the basis for symptom formation in order to favor the notion that symptoms develop due to deficits in social and experiential learning or as "important signs of developmental problems that are in the process of becoming conscious. What patients cannot yet clearly express in the form of a cognitive or emotional insight will find somatic expression as a body symptom" (1979a, p. 143). Though lack of such conscious dealing may result in symptom formation, once symptoms have developed, insight for the dynamics will not usually cause a cure.

Ackerman defined a symptom as "a unit of relational adaptation that is irrational, inappropriate, automatized and repetitive" (1966, p. 90). This definition is consistent with Erickson's learning model in that the symptom restricts the learning of new levels of interpersonal adaptation and/or results from difficulties in doing so. Ackerman believed the goal of family therapy was to "shake up pre-existing pathogenic relationships and alignments to open the way for healthier family bonds to form" (1972, p. 440). Strategic family therapists such as Jackson agreed that the therapist's first goal is to disturb the existing system. Erickson seemed to concur but went on to stress the goal of eliciting from the client, often at an unconscious level, options of experience, perception, and behavior that would facilitate formation of the desired "healthier family bonds." He expressed it this way:

> Symptoms may be resolved by working with a patient's psychodynamics in such a manner that consciousness does not know why the body symptom disappears. Moreover, the developmental problem that was expressed in the symptom is also resolved in an apparently spontaneous manner. (1979a, p. 143)

Whether symptoms and associated developmental problems are resolved in an unconscious "apparently spontaneous" manner or in a more direct fashion, the crucial distinction concerns the matter of first- or second-order change. Watzlawick, Weakland, and Fisch (1974) defined first-order change as change within a system which itself remains unchanged. Symptoms *removed* in this way are less likely to be *resolved*. Second-order change, or change in the system itself, is the emphasis of the therapeutic approach described in this paper. Though not fully developed in this chapter, we might consider true generative change to be third-order change in that it not only results in change in the current system, but shapes resources and perception to generate and prepare the client to create and notice in future systems, continuing outcomes of changes begun at an earlier time. As Watzlawick pointed out, second-order change may be initiated with only "a small, peripheral change in a system's functioning (that) produces large repercussions throughout its entire structure" (1982, p. 151). This is in line with Erickson's admonition paraphrased by Haley: "If you want a large change, you should ask for a small one" (1982, p. 23).

Erickson frequently directed clients to plant a tree, and in so doing, symbolically encouraged them to begin an ongoing process of generative change. Planting a tree may seem to be one simple act but in fact presupposes having a place to plant it and care for it. The person caring for a tree becomes "rooted" to some extent in order to facilitate and appreciate the tree taking root and growing. And too, as the tree grows and changes, so does the person. It is a process analogous to becoming pregnant. That one "simple" act sets in motion a staggering array of changes that will shape and influence at least three lives in an ongoing manner, changing both current and future family systems. And yet the changes proceed so gradually and in such a logical, subtle, time-released manner that they can (for the most part) be comfortably absorbed by the changing system.

RATIONALE AND IMPORTANCE OF SEEKING GENERATIVE CHANGE

Generative change can be simply defined as change which stimulates and encourages, inspires and brings forth additional changes. It is second-order change that produces many changes of first-order nature and it is often third-order change from which the client learns to make additional second-order changes during subsequent life development. A metaphorical analogy is the process of throwing a snowball off of a hillside into a snowbank in such a way that it continues to roll down the mountain, collecting more snow and momentum as it goes.

As therapists, we see clients who have realized and stated a need for some degree of change in their lives though they often have not considered how this change may be incompatible with their current learnings, lifestyle or social sanctions. Assuming that symptoms or habits were formed for some good reason, as the best choice available at the time for meeting a need, therapy ought to assist the client beyond taking a problem away. It must teach new options for satisfying needs or solving developmental tasks. Since any presenting problem exists in a social or family context, the therapist must assess interface points between the client and others in which the symptom and any therapeutic changes function. Therefore, changes in the individual client's self-imagery, feelings, attitudes, and behaviors can be expected to constitute a change in "personality," or a change in how the client establishes and uses social interfaces. Change at that level will generate additional change beyond removal of the symptom or habit. Additional changes often take the overt form of changes within the family structure. As developmental tasks occur and specific stages of family development are encountered, still more novel behaviors and experiences may be produced. As such, treatment with an individual for a seemingly specific symptom often can (and should) become "family system therapy," even though other members may have never actually been seen in the therapy sessions.

Using the term "personality" presents a special opportunity to clarify an epistemological framework for doing Ericksonian therapy. Likewise, it presents a special challenge. The challenge comes from the difficulty that social science, and especially psychology/psychotherapy, face as they attempt to share current understandings and observations with a vocabulary that is oftentimes centuries old. The case in point is the term "personality." The word, from the Latin "personalitas," refers to the state of being that is more than an abstraction, an animal, or a thing. But, both common usage and professional usage disregard this "spiritual" aspect and instead use the word to refer to "qualities" possessed by a person independent of environment or social milieu.

The common understanding that an individual's organized character traits developed independent of setting emanated from the historical world view of the seventeenth century and the subsequent enlightenment of the eighteenth century. Most literate people still hold the notion that nouns are things and that things are composed of solid particles. This is the age when common understanding conceives of the world according to Isaac Newton. This digression is based on the observation that social science, although constantly evolving and reformulating its ideas in response to changing conceptions in physics and chemistry, usually lags behind the changing world views brought on by discoveries in these hard sciences. The term "personality" may be a good example. It is a convenient term but it must be taken to mean an "interconnectedness" and not a thing. Better still, it ought to be considered a probability of interconnectedness. For example, consider that in physics, since the turn of the century, the changing conception of the atom has made an anachronism of the model previously purported by Newton via Descartes, Bacon, and others. The concept of the atom and its indivisible particles once taught in secondary and undergraduate school is obsolete. Atoms were once considered things, as were electrons and protons. As physical sciences gradually come to accept quantum physics, there has been a change in the understanding of the "reality" of the atom that reveals the paradoxical nature of these previously irreducible "things." They exist only as things because of our manner of observation. One might say subatomic particles are only interconnections between larger things and those things in turn are only interconnections between larger things, and so on. Electrons are only a probability of a measurable occurrence. So, the solidness of matter exists only in relation to other relations. As common understanding accommodates to this understanding and thus formulates a newer world view, eventually social science will adjust basic understandings accordingly (Capra, 1982). The term "personality" should be one of the first targets for such change.

If something as seemingly finite and unchanging as a hydrogen atom is only a sort of changing field of energy relationships, how can we hold the view that a personality exists independently of the social context? Personality is not a thing but rather an interconnection between larger things such as families. And families are not things but interconnections between still larger things. The personality is a locus of minds influencing other minds. It represents an interface. It is this interface and the phenomena of interconnecting that Erickson seemed to take into account, and which I take into account in order to replicate and understand Erickson's scheme of treatment. I will use the term "personality" but I use it in this hybrid manner referring to an interface phenomena and not a thing possessed by a person.

ASSESSING THE INDIVIDUAL'S REQUEST

Most therapists are familiar with various ploys clients use, both consciously and unconsciously, to open the process of more extensive therapy. "Often, the presenting problem is a smoke screen for underlying issues or an unrecognized rationalization that provides an acceptable reason for seeking out treatment" (Zeig, 1982, p. 257). Erickson stressed to his students the importance of listening (at the social and psychological level) to everything patients have to say and treating them accordingly. In a teaching seminar (1979b) he presented an example of patients who subtly ask for more extensive treatment, by discussing the case of a 52-year-old woman who called him for hypnosis to quit smoking. She asked for more extensive treatment by giving information unnecessary and unrelated to her problem with smoking. She volunteered, for instance, that she had a daughter 20 years old and a son 19 years old; that she worked at a mental health clinic; that her husband was a professor at Arizona State University; and that she made as much money as he did. Erickson cautioned his students against trying to treat clients only for their initial complaint instead of recognizing the real purpose behind it.

Respecting all the messages from the client involves responding in some way to the initial complaint but it also requires responding to its deeper aspects. In this case, Erickson responded to the presenting problem while he simultaneously expressed his doubt that hypnosis for smoking control was the primary issue, by challenging the woman about her sincerity. He said to her: "People your age who call up and ask for hypnosis to quit smoking are usually not sincere. To demonstrate your sincerity, I'd like to have you climb Squaw Peak at sunrise every morning for the next week and call me next Saturday" (Erickson, 1979b). With this communication, the process of second-order generative change was initiated by directing the woman to begin a line of action that was symbolic of self-discipline, control, strength, and perseverance in areas of her life unrelated to smoking.

Erickson addressed the matter of habit control the following Saturday when she came in, having "passed" her sincerity test. He confiscated her cigarettes and matches, and told her that she could reclaim them in three weeks if she wished, otherwise, they would be thrown in the compost. She volunteered that she should go home and get the rest of her cigarettes as well. Erickson complimented her own idea, remarking that it sounded good to him. When she returned, the additional cigarettes were likewise confiscated and the woman was then asked whether she wanted to pay by cash or check as her hour had expired. She was given an appointment for the next Saturday and Erickson suggested at this point in his seminar that the students should have been able to guess accurately what she would say at that next appointment.

While at the social level all communications addressed her smoking, at the psychological level of communication Erickson invited her to participate in a more extensive therapy by challenging her to initiate a new action-oriented approach to life, whether it involved only smoking or whether it involved family relations. This challenge was given in the sincerity test before she was even seen and also modeled by Erickson as he matter-of-factly asserted himself in the first interview, confiscating the cigarettes, stating the terms of their return, reinforcing her own ideas, and then abruptly closing with a bind of comparable alternatives (whether she would pay by cash or check) that presupposed she must comply with his legitimate demand to pay fully and immediately in some manner. Therefore, Erickson was not surprised (and even expected that his students should be able to predict) that at her next appointment the woman used her entire hour relating an incident in which she assertively demanded new cooperative action from her husband and how she persevered in a confident manner until he complied.

In the incident, she asked her husband to type a letter for her, emphasizing that he had published a book and was an excellent stenographer whereas she could not type. She related how he first put her off saying it wasn't a good time for it and that he would do it tomorrow. She insisted that she wanted it that night, to which he suggested that she act her age and come to bed. She persevered to the point that she "grabbed the covers, pulled them off, grabbed him by the ankles, hauled him out of bed and said, 'I want that letter typed tonight.' " He complied in a typical passive-aggressive way by typing a letter with "more mistakes than it's humanly possible to make in a simple letter." The wife persevered again until a satisfactory letter was produced. Having shared her response to Erickson's invitation to take new action, she went on to explain more fully how "there's something strange about our marriage." She recounted how her family ate every evening meal together at home and that before they were married, her husband liked gourmet cooking and insisted that she learn to cook in that manner. He also promised at that time that he would do the cooking every other week. She then remarked that even though the daughter was 20 and the son 19, her husband's turn to cook next week had not yet come.

Erickson's strategic assignment to the woman was to go home and announce to her husband that his week to cook finally had arrived. She predicted that he would boil potatoes and fry hamburgers and hotdogs in retaliation. This was to be accepted, but the wife, son and daughter were instructed to bring home for their evening meal a take-out dinner from a gourmet restaurant. At her next appointment, she described how he had said nothing but glared at them as they ate their gourmet dinners. And now what was she to do since it was her turn again? Erickson suggested that since her husband had spent a careful week teaching her the kind of gourmet cooking he liked, she was to prepare the same for him during her week while she and the son and daughter continued to bring home their gourmet dinners. The following week she announced that, without encouragement, her husband had made the necessary preparation for doing gourmet cooking during his next turn. She added that he also allowed the children to bring friends home and play their phonograph records, whereas previously they had to socialize at the homes of their friends. She made a summary statement that her husband realized the four of them had a home and it wasn't his kingdom; they all had a share in it. She added that she was happily married but would see Erickson again if her husband didn't mend his ways.

Certainly many presenting symptoms are more than just a means to get into more extensive therapy for real purposes. Many symptoms or obsessional habits constitute serious and intense difficulties for the client and the request for help in alleviating them should be considered directly and pursued earnestly. Part of taking them seriously is assessing the problem thoroughly, including its interface with significant others or with developmental tasks represented or obstructed by the presenting problem. This includes an assessment of how the individual interfaces with others and in the case of avoidance, how the individual ought to be interfacing (taking into account unique cultural idiosyncracies). The treatment to alleviate the symptom or control the habit often must go beyond work directed specifically at the symptom or habit.

A 29-year-old single woman presented the long-term (16 years duration) problem of bulimia and related hopelessness and was consciously convinced that her real problem was primarily a lack of self-control which resulted in ongoing cyclical binges of eating and vomiting. She regarded related problems such as her poor self-concept and impoverished social skills as insignificant by comparison. The patient may even have expected that these were not worth mentioning since, from her frame of reference, if the bulimia could be controlled, these other difficulties would simply disappear spontaneously.

In fact, helping the client develop a sense of self-control over the initial impulses to binge was a result of a relatively brief and effective set of interventions during the first treatment session. These interventions immediately provided her mastery over her bulimic habit. And yet, had treatment been terminated at this point, it is quite possible that she would have become bulimic again (or even suicidal), as no interventions addressed the social maladjustments which encouraged indulging the habit as a dependable means of immediate gratification. Although the client had not overtly requested therapy to accomplish anything other than control of the bulimia, she communicated other needs at the psychological level by her physical appearance (much like a 13-year-old boy), interpersonal manner (timid and hesitant), and by her responsiveness to interventions which contained information relevant to her unspoken needs. On the basis of these messages and our belief, like Haley's (1973, p. 44), that "symptoms cannot be cured without producing a basic change in the person's social situation which frees him to grow and develop," this client was seen in co-therapy with my husband, Stephen, for four additional sessions in which we intervened to help her resolve developmental tasks (such as the self-assertion a teenager normally learns), learn new emotional and behavioral options necessary to find gratification in social situations (such as a young adult usually learns), and develop attitudes and new self-imagery to support these changes. These sessions relied extensively on the use of hypnotic trance, metaphors, and indirect suggestions and therapeutic binds to apply the learnings to herself in whatever ways her unconscious mind knew to be relevant for her.

When we followed up with this client some months later, she enthusiastically described her new social life, respect for herself, and the fact that she looked more like a woman. Then, she added, almost incidentally, that she also had controlled the bulimia very successfully and was eating nutritiously in order to maintain a more appropriate weight for her new lifestyle. These social aspects of her life were not overtly discussed with her conscious mind during the additional therapy sessions. In other words, the treatment that resulted in alleviating her bulimia apparently was successful primarily as a result of going beyond work directed only at habit control. It was a fringe benefit that her conscious mind was able to save face and allow her unconscious mind to learn a great deal without admitting how impoverished she had been.

INTERVENING TO FACILITATE GENERATIVE CHANGE

In planning treatment designed to facilitate generative or second-order change, it is important to consider several variables. Initially, the parameters of the symptom are best assessed from a systems point of view. As Fisch observed, Erickson spent a "considerable effort in obtaining a rather detailed picture of the symptom, problem, or complaint and how it was performed, as well as how it was performed in conjunction with others involved in the problem" (1982, p. 158). The following questions might be asked: When does the problem occur? With whom? What conditions influence its becoming better or worse? What is being done about it? Who would be affected, either negatively or positively, by modification or alleviation of the problem?

When family is conceptualized as a system of interactive behaviors, communications, feelings, experiences, and perceptions, it becomes an interlocking system where each member is a subsystem that influences all other subsystems (Jackson, 1967). This concept was noted by Whitaker (1982) when he suggested that "changing the family as a symptom context is like changing the alcoholic spouse. It's more useful than any effort to change the identified patient" (p. 495). The moments of influence occur in the social interface. Therefore, therapeutic change in behaviors, communications, experiences, and perceptions of an individual presenting a habit or symptom may also stimulate further change in the structure or nature of the network of significant others with whom the individual interacts if the structure and nature of the social interface changes. This ripple or snowball effect will, of course, be dramatic to the extent that pervasive personality factors are also affected and the dynamics or operation of the presented symptoms take on new meaning.

In addition to the initial assessment of how and when the dysfunction is manifested, the client's current and next logical stage of social or family development must be considered. Also, an assessment of the client's mastery of those particular skills necessary for comfortable functioning at each stage must be made. Haley's framework of the family's life cycle (1973) is useful as a basic outline from which to roughly conceptualize stages and skills. His outline of the typical "crisis stages" in middle-class American families include: the courtship period, marriage and its consequences, childbirth and dealing with the young, middle marriage years, weaning parents from children, and retirement/old age/death. Haley emphasized that these stages provide only a rudimentary foundation for determining needed skills since our current knowledge about family cycles is constantly being updated as the culture changes. What does not change is the postulate that "symptoms appear when there is a dislocation or interruption in the unfolding life cycle of a family or other natural group. The symptom is a signal that a family has difficulty in getting past a stage in the life cycle" (Haley, 1973, p. 42). The therapist will need to conduct a thoughtful evaluation of the client's unique unfolding life cycle in order to determine which skills and experiences are needed. Generative change is facilitated by addressing both current (or recent past) needs and those potentially needed to move more gracefully through the transition to the next logical stage.

An awareness of typical abilities (skills, experiences, behaviors, and attitudes) required at each developmental stage can assist us in treatment planning for therapeutic outcome goals. In the expanded list that appears in the appendix, additional stages, as well as typical corresponding demands, are included. Early stages such as biological security, basic trust, early socialization, initiative and identity are included to emphasize that developmental retardation in these stages influences psychological age and thus ability to meet the demands of a later stage. In these cases, tangential education regarding the abilities involved or some form of "re-parenting" may need to precede therapy designed to teach and retrieve abilities required in the current or next logical stage of development. These early stages are also important to consider when a child is the symptom carrier.

Haley summarized Erickson's therapeutic strategy as "focusing sharply on symptoms . . . (while having) . . . as its larger goal the resolution of the problems of the family to get the life cycle moving again" (1973, p. 42). What is typically involved is accepting the family or individual at their model of the world, agreeing with them, redefining the symptom and perhaps even encouraging its continuation (under therapeutic control) while simultaneously introducing and elaborating new ideas, new behaviors, novel experiences, and attitudes that will stimulate ongoing, pervasive change within the family system or social network. The system then will learn to expand at future developmental change points as well. The ideal situation is not to be a problem-free system but for the system to deal effectively with problems as they arise.

This line of reasoning leads to questions on which specific therapeutic outcome goals to set and how the client and therapist set those goals. A strategic therapist takes responsibility for actively initiating and directing interventions in order to effect change in the client system. The first step in such an active intervention is to identify goals, based on all the information received from the client at verbal and nonverbal levels. This step may or may not be discussed with the client but it is safe to assume that the client is ultimately responsible for changing in desirable ways and that clients will make the best choice for themselves once viable new options are presented. Conversely, they can be expected to disregard interventions or options that are undesirable or inappropriate for their particular lifestyles. With this in mind, concerns about manipulating the client to fit the therapist's values subside.

There are at least six areas in which therapeutic options can be taught and noticed. These include: 1) changes in family structure; 2) attitudes that support development and continuation of the symptom; 3) emotional flexibility; 4) age-appropriate behaviors related to achieving intimacy or accomplishing developmental tasks; 5) self-imagery to reinforce and direct new attitudes, emotions, roles, and specific behaviors; and 6) changes in clients' ability to discipline as well as enjoy themselves. Basically self-explanatory, these terms are discussed elsewhere in detail in regard to general use, rationale and specific protocol for creating each with metaphor (Lankton, 1985; Lankton & Lankton, 1983, 1984). They are the components of a complete treatment plan and serve as indicators of how effective the therapy has been in accomplishing a personality change that will generate additional, ongoing change beyond symptom removal. In addition to these interventions, techniques directly involved in altering the symptom itself will now be discussed.

SPECIFIC TECHNIQUES DIRECTED AT THE SYMPTOM

The fact that symptom removal (containment, confusion, amelioration, etc.) is rarely sufficient (or even possible), without creating more pervasive change in the client's personality and functioning within the social system, does not diminish the importance of systematically designing and directing specific interventions toward the goal of confusing, removing, redefining or utilizing the symptom so as to change it. One of the therapist's primary functions is effecting change in the interactional sequence that precipitates and/or maintains symptoms or undesirable habits. Discussion here will be focused on methods that facilitate changes in transactions: 1) redefining or utilizing the symptom with paradoxical prescription and reframing; 2) offering a worse alternative; 3) removing the symptom with associational inhibition; and 4) confusing the symptom with "scrambling." These techniques are to be used in conjunction with other interventions designed to teach or retrieve new options so that the occurrence of the symptom will not only be confused or inhibited but also no longer necessary. Following this section on specific techniques is an explanation of a complete treatment plan to incorporate and integrate interventions that promote new options.

Redefining or Utilizing the Symptom with Paradoxical Prescription and Reframing

This set of techniques is useful for helping clients accept, take responsibility for, or otherwise appreciate aspects of their symptom that they previously considered only problematic. A segue to generative change is often created as alternative means for accomplishing what the symptom "accomplishes" for the client are taught. This is exemplified in paradoxical symptom prescription. The first step usually involves communications to the client that clearly establish the assumption that there is some good or logical reason for having the symptom (reframing) and even for doing it more intensely (paradoxical prescription).

With reframing, the next step may involve learning new ways to accomplish the intention without relying on the symptom. With para doxical prescription, the symptom either is redefined as something therapeutic which is then encouraged as an available means to a desired end, or is prescribed with some minor alteration added by the therapist, such that the typical sequence (and meaning) of the problem is disrupted and the client inadvertently learns either something about an unknown ability to change and control the problem or new therapeutic options.

Offering a Worse Alternative

This intervention can be considered a special version of paradoxical prescription in that the symptom is disrupted by asking the client to continue it but in some elaborately inconvenient way. For example, Erickson saw a man who suffered from insomnia (Zeig, 1980, p. 193) and he secured the man's agreement that he would follow the advice given no matter how unwelcome or cumbersome it proved to be. Subsequently, the man was instructed to get out of bed and scrub floors when experiencing insomnia. The insomnia soon disappeared spontaneously. Similarly, with a boy who had developed a worrisome thumbsucking habit (Rossi, Ryan, & Sharp, 1983, p. 117), Erickson enjoined him to continue to suck his thumb for the satisfaction it involved, but insisted that he should suck his fingers in a more democratic manner rather than just sucking the left thumb and neglecting the right thumb and other fingers. He wasn't just to suck randomly but to systematically suck each finger a specified number of minutes per regularly scheduled "session." And with the woman who smoked too much (Zeig, 1980, p. 185), he encouraged her to continue to smoke all she liked but in the manner he directed which only changed the placement of her cigarettes: cigarettes in the attic, matches in the basement. In each case, following the agreed-upon prescription became so tedious that the entire habit or symptom was abandoned.

This type of intervention is particularly useful to resolve rapidly symptoms detrimental to the well-being of a client, such as eating or sleeping disorders, and is most effective with those clients who are overly compliant since they will be more likely to follow rather than challenge the directive. Obviously, therapists will be most effective when they are congruent and earnest in the delivery of such interventions. A logical or at least seemingly logical rationale for following the directive also should be given to offset chances of the client's ignoring it. This technique is least effective with those clients who are particularly challenging or resistive.

Removing the Symptom with Associational Inhibition

This technique involves first retrieving one or several resource experiences incompatible with the typical occurrence of the symptom or habit and then directing it (them) to occur simultaneously at the first indication of the symptom. It may be necessary to direct such a pairing several times before the first signal of the symptom automatically triggers an association to the incompatible resource experience(s). Relaxation is a resource experience which typically is used in systematic desensitization but other resource experiences are often more powerful and specifically effective for disrupting a particular symptom or habit and provide stronger associational inhibition.

It is useful to help the client associate the resource experience(s) to the first identifiable signal. It is also helpful to reinforce overall associational inhibition to facilitate simple reciprocal inhibition to "edit" specific portions of imagery which contribute to or support the problem. For instance, attitudes, supporting memories, or other thoughts about the problem (represented in an auditory or visual manner) which the therapist identifies in the interview or actual therapy can be systematically confused and depotentiated by first retrieving an incompatible (or just different) set of imagery which is then directed to occur simultaneously just as the client is asked to imagine the former (Cameron-Bandler, 1978; Lankton & Lankton, 1983; Wolpe, 1948).

"Scramble"

"Scramble" refers to sequence confusion. It resembles associational inhibition that involves building an association between the incompatible resource experience(s) and any aspect of the symptom (as opposed to just the first signal). Scramble is a technique designed to confuse the conscious mind about how to have the symptom, while building an unconscious association to resources previously unavailable in the context of symptom occurrence. It was patterned after Erickson's confusion technique, but in a manner that could systematically "scramble" and thereby disrupt the normal sequence of a wide variety of symptoms, most particularly those of a psychosomatic nature.

The process involves having clients subdivide the experience of their symptom into (at least) five specific phases (phase 1—beginning, phase 2—midpoint between beginning and middle, phase 3—middle, phase 4—midpoint between middle and end, and phase 5—end); review those phases in a series of "scrambled" sequences (beginning with 1, 2, 3, 4, 5 but eventually covering a broad range of random sequences); and finally forget about the cumbersome burden of following such tedious directives and just enjoy the comforts of trance and any relevant resource experiences that are retrieved. This technique is described in greater detail elsewhere (Lankton & Lankton, 1983).

TREATMENT PLANNING

There are several issues to address regarding treatment planning: 1) order of interventions and integration of interventions directed specifically at the symptom and at the broader context; 2) length of treatment; 3) utilization and integration of various modalities, especially hypnotherapy and family therapy; and 4) whether communication will be primarily metaphorical or direct. There is, of course, no one correct way for treatment to proceed. A complete treatment plan can range from one comprehensive session to multiple sessions over a period of months or even years and can include various treatment modalities such as hypnosis, family therapy, strategic intervention, gestalt, some combination of these and more. In the case discussion to be presented, hypnosis utilizing multiple-embedded metaphors with an individual client was the primary modality, though an emphasis on changing family and/or social network relationships is evident. A complete treatment plan for symptom removal or habit control does not necessarily include interventions especially designed for each of the six therapeutic outcome goals mentioned earlier but will usually address at least four of these goals in addition to the symptom. Questions about how to coordinate various interventions, how to bridge from one to the other, how many sessions to plan for, which interventions will be delivered first, when other members of the client's family and/or social network should be involved, and what combination of therapeutic modalities should be employed are answered by considering the unique individual, his or her lifestyle, stage of family development, function of the presenting problem, availability of resources, psychological age, and so forth. There are, however, several useful guidelines with regard to these issues. Let's look at the order of interventions first.

Order of Interventions

Interventions directed specifically at the symptom often are used at the onset of therapy through symptom prescriptions and redefinitions but are more thoroughly addressed in the central portion of the total treatment. In the case to follow, symptom-directed interventions are the central portion of a multiple-embedded metaphor structure. Placing these interventions in the center of other therapeutic interventions ensures that attitudes supportive of the problem have been addressed and experiential resources have been retrieved. These may be experiences incompatible with the symptom, to be used in associational inhibition, or may simply be experiences (such as dissociation) to help the client examine the problem from a different (more comfortable, relaxed, or positive) framework. In this regard, Ericksonian trance induction often contains paradoxical directives to help the client begin to suspend the normal frame of reference and respond to subsequent interventions from a different, more receptive frame.

The steps or phases of treatment can be summarized as follows: 1) suspend normal framework; 2) retrieve resources; 3) alter client's experience of the symptom; and 4) intervene to help clients anticipate themselves in the future continuing and expanding changes (beyond simple symptom removal) in the context of the particular family or social network. The specific demands of the client's current and next logical developmental stage are taken into account in order to facilitate generative change. The therapist should demonstrate flexible willingness to consider other interventions in cases where immediate symptom resolution is crucial to the client's well-being, as when the client may be so discouraged over the symptom's presence as to be suicidal. However, it might be useful to take a brief tangent to retrieve experiential resources before concentrating on interventions to abate the symptom. For example, the bulimic client mentioned earlier was seen for a total of four sessions and it was the first session that contained interventions to disrupt her symptom and provide her with a new sense of hopefulness. Though the bulk of the session directly addressed altering her experience of the symptom, the initial interventions designed to retrieve experiential resources (confidence, self-worth, and self-control) created a therapeutic atmosphere which facilitated the creation of an associational inhibition for various stimuli that had previously initiated or prolonged the bulimic behavior. Subsequent sessions concentrated more intensely on retrieving other resource experiences, developing social skills and generating the newfound sense of self-worth into interpersonal and future areas of her life. Again, therapy was initiated through interventions directed specifically at her symptom.

Length of Treatment

In my own practice, I typically see clients from one to eight sessions, making exceptions for longer term therapy when necessary. In determining the total number of sessions complete treatment will require, I concur with Richard Fisch who said about brief therapy: "Therapy should be measured not by its brevity or length, but whether it is efficient and effective in aiding people with their complaints or whether it wastes time" (1982, p. 157). With this criterion, treatment is completed when the client has been (effectively) helped. Though some estimate is possible at the beginning about how many sessions a given problem is likely to require, I more typically evaluate how helpful each session has been and then decide whether another is necessary in order to accomplish goals previously outlined with the client.

Though criticized by some for his brief therapy, Erickson shared with Eric Berne the goal that therapy should result in as immediate a cure as possible. Berne used the analogy of strategically "removing the splinter" (1971, p. 12); Erickson (1980) referred to a reassociation of the client's "experiential life" (p. 38) and intervened in such a way as to "break up the logjam in a bend in the river" (Dammann, 1982, p. 198). Erickson often managed to accomplish this outcome very quickly with one strategic intervention or assignment. As an example, he worked with a married couple whose conflictual attempts to co-manage their restaurant were threatening their marital relationship (Haley, 1982). The wife was overly responsible and felt resentful that her husband wasn't showing more initiative. He was resentful of his wife's interference and bossiness. Though this conflict appeared to center around managing the restaurant, it was symbolic of a crisis in their marriage, representing role difficulties neither expressed directly. Erickson strategically assigned the husband to go to the restaurant half an hour earlier than the wife in the mornings, which resulted in immediate symptom resolution, and more importantly, resolved the developmental crisis in their marriage as each learned important new behaviors and associations in response to the original stimuli. In this case, the couple's complete treatment was set in motion in only one session which contained the intake interview and strategic assignment. Within the more typical time frame of one to eight sessions, hypnosis with metaphoric communication is frequently utilized, and other family members often participate in the therapy.

Utilization and Integration of Therapeutic Modalities

Hypnosis often facilitates briefer treatment, due in part to concentrated mental involvement, use of imagery, and the establishment of nonusual frames of associations. When family members or other persons close to the client are seen in the session, there is increased opportunity to have the client vividly associate new experiences and learnings to the stimulus of significant others and to facilitate supportive attitudes and perceptions on the part of significant others for changes the client is making. This kind of rapport and therapeutic association is more likely when significant others actually participate in the therapy whether or not hypnosis is used. When family members or significant others in the client's social network are unavailable for the therapy (or when their presence would be disruptive to the therapy), hypnosis allows clients to associate therapy learnings more vividly to images of the people with whom they will need to use them, rather than with images of the therapist and his or her office.

Metaphoric and Direct Communication

Finally, there is the question of when to communicate directly and when to communicate metaphorically. Using metaphor as a communication device offers several advantages. It is a face-saving way for the client to entertain novel experiences, learn new behaviors, and respond (or not) to directives contained or implied in the story. It is also a fail-safe way for the therapist to instruct the client indirectly in a way that avoids arousing the client's resistance because the client is ultimately the judge of what the story means, how it is interpreted, and what kind of response will be forthcoming. If material in the metaphor is not relevant to the client's needs, it will most likely be discarded and if the material is so relevant as to be stressful for the client, it can be consciously dismissed as "just a story" while the unconscious is free to respond in a meaningful way. More detailed rationale for and elaboration of metaphor as a technique can be found elsewhere (Gordon, 1978; Lankton, 1985; Lankton & Lankton, 1983), but it is presented here as an especially effective component of interventions designed both for disrupting specific symptoms as well as for stimulating or modeling generative change. Metaphor, however, rarely constitutes the entire treatment. There is usually a portion of the work in which direct communication is involved, especially in the intake and assessment phase as well as feedback phases following a primarily metaphorical session. Sessions involving other techniques such as gestalt, conventional family therapy, and strategic interventions may also be interspersed or combined with hypnosis and metaphor in order to accomplish specific results.

In the following case, metaphor was extensively used in the one session during which the client was in trance. No other family members were seen but assessment included much information on both his current family and family of origin. Interventions were designed to facilitate therapeutic outcomes related to both families.

HYPERTENSION CASE

Background and Presenting Problem

The client, Bob, requested therapy for labile hypertension which he had been experiencing for at least ten years. The following information about his current family, professional situation, and family of origin was taken to understand how his particular difficulty with hypertension began and was sustained, and what new options would be useful to disrupt his symptom and simultaneously stimulate generative change. This information, as will be seen, underlies the treatment goals that were developed.

Bob was a 37-year-old man in his second marriage. He and his current wife lived with their two-year-old daughter and on alternate weeks with an adolescent daughter from his first marriage. He described both of these situations as involving stressful demands but emphasized his difficulty meeting the demanding responsibility of fathering the two-year-old. He felt that he needed to achieve a more effective balance between family and career. A university professor, Bob reported enjoying his work, though he described anxiety related to performance and evaluation.

Bob exhibited a constellation of characteristics that could be regarded as representative of a hypertensive lifestyle. These included taking too much responsibility for others in his current family and also giving them too much responsibility for his own feelings. He emphasized a strong need to appear competent and productive, and approval from others was important. He measured his blood pressure daily and attempted to avoid conflict at all costs.

With regard to family of origin, he claimed a strong identification with his father who had a history of congestive heart failure and a personality orientation toward "suffering in silence," withholding feelings, worrying, being a perfectionist, and alternating periods of temper outbursts and indirect expression of anger. The father died of a heart attack two weeks before the therapy session. Bob described his mother as controlling, anxious, and loving only on a conditional basis. Bob was the older of two children and as such learned to be "in charge." This was a primary role for him.

Goals and Plan for Treatment

With this client, stimulating generative change would involve more than helping him retrieve and utilize mechanisms to lower blood pressure. He requested hypnotherapy since his customary attempts at symptom relief were only marginally successful. He probably assumed that hypnosis would help him get rid of hypertension more effectively even though he reported that meditation, biofeedback and other relaxation techniques provided only temporary reduction in blood pressure which would rise again as he became involved in his typical workday activities. In order to create generative change the therapist must take into account the function of the symptom or the language it speaks. In this case, in addition to interventions designed to disrupt the process by which Bob accumulated tension, treatment was planned to help him build new associations, emotions, and behavioral options to be generated instead in response to stimuli that previously resulted in hypertension. It was expected that change in this way would stimulate and facilitate additional, ongoing changes in areas of family relationships and career development. These treatment goals can be categorized according to the following areas of therapeutic outcome.

Attitude restructuring. Several attitudes expressed by this client directly supported the continuation of his symptom, including his fear and expectation that he was culturally and genetically predisposed to hypertensive disorder (due to his strong psychological identification with his father), his role expectations about being in control and taking charge of others (while ignoring his needs), and his beliefs about the importance of striving for perfection and concealing vulnerability, incompetence or imperfection.

Goals for restructuring involved discrediting the above attitudes and simultaneously suggesting opposite ones such as: it is possible to be different from father, you can take care of others by taking care of yourself, you don't have to be perfect—approaching perfection requires accepting imperfection.

Affective flexibility. Emotional states involving relaxation, satisfaction and comfortable vulnerability should be available in situations in which they previously seemed unavailable. He was familiar with these emotions and able to create them for himself but had not built associations to situations in which he most needed them.

Age-appropriate intimacy and role behavior. There were several specific behaviors that Bob had not learned in his normal socialization process, e.g., expressing anger, taking risks, revealing vulnerability, and allowing others to be in charge. These behaviors would be illustrated in the therapy to provide an opportunity for Bob to evaluate them differently and adopt them into his own lifestyle.

Family structure change. Attainment of goals in the preceding three areas should create change in family structure and roles. Specifically, he would become responsible about expressing feelings, letting others take care of him, playing one-down roles sometimes, etc.

Self-image. All of the above changes would be more immediately useful to Bob if his therapy included opportunities for him to accept and consolidate the changes and imagine gaining from their use in his everyday life. Self-image thinking goals, therefore, were to help Bob systematically form a visual image of himself interacting in such a way as to personally reflect having achieved goals in a way he valued.

Metaphors were constructed to address indirectly each identified goal (cf. S. Lankton, this volume). Trance was then induced and metaphors were delivered in multiple-embedded fashion (Lankton & Lankton, 1983). Since client and therapist reside in different cities, one long session (two hours) was arranged with a contingency for follow-up appointments if necessary.

Summary of Session

Prior to the session, assessment was accomplished through letters. Treatment was initiated with a trance induction containing paradoxical directives to focus awareness on and evaluate his performance. In this case "performance" concerned whether or not he was correct in accomplishing trance. As an orientation-to-trance statement, he was reminded that it is advantageous for a person to "let go" when going into trance and that he should therefore take charge and control his relaxation to the degree necessary to really let go in the way that was needed. In this way, the process of disrupting the normal sequence of symptom formation was begun because he seldom evaluated himself critically from an intentional position. If he did not follow this instruction and responded spontaneously in a situation that could involve evaluation and resulting anxiety, then his normal sequence would also be disrupted. Thus, he was immediately placed in a "win-win" paradoxical bind. Induction was continued and trance maintained using various anecdotes, conscious-unconscious dissociation statements and indirect suggestions to reinforce his various responses as "correct," including signs of difficulty such as tension in his brow, irregular breathing, etc. Hypnotherapy for his symptom was then initiated by elaborating the therapeutic outcomes one at a time.

The first metaphor was designed to address change in attitude regarding his assumption that he was "destined" to have difficulties similar to those fatal to his father. It focused on two previous clients who thought they suffered from genetic difficulties that couldn't be cured. The metaphor contained an obvious parallel to Bob's belief in his own genetic predisposition. However, it was also one step removed since it was "only a metaphor" to discuss other clients who were troubled with different afflictions—one with "sun" allergy and the other with skin cancer. It contained a tangent to discuss how personality and expectations were involved in development of a problem and not just genetics. Aspects of a "cancer personality" (Friedman & Rosenman, 1974; Greer, 1979; Rassidakis, 1978), e.g., reluctance to express anger and unwillingness to let someone else take charge, were briefly mentioned (seeded) to prepare for later elaboration about how to develop these behaviors. In a manner characteristic of multiple-embedded metaphor structure (Lankton & Lankton, 1983) this story was suspended and interrupted by beginning the second story.

The primary goal of the second story was to retrieve affective resources and secondarily to cast additional doubt on this matter of genetic predisposition. This second goal was accomplished by introducing two "identical" twins who were nonetheless quite different. Their activities aboard a scuba diving boat in Australia were described. One twin admittedly was anxious about his dive, hesitant and unsure about correct procedure. He was certain no one would want him as a dive partner because he failed to recognize that others could perceive his hesitancy as valuable caution in a life or death situation such as diving can be. The other twin wrongly thought he knew everything about diving and with his insolent, demanding manner alienated the other divers and didn't learn anything. In detailing and contrasting these differences, the story modeled the attitude that the willingness to show vulnerability is oftentimes interpreted by others as an admirable strength. A discussion about how I would have proceeded had this foolish "know it all" twin been my client provided a safe context to elaborate examples of affective resources such as comfortable dependency, satisfaction, relaxation, and appropriate vulnerability. For example, tangents were taken to discuss how a child can enjoy getting a free ride in the front of a canoe while his or her partner in the back does the work, or how comforting it is for a boy to know that his parent has a firm grip on the back fender as he wobbles about learning how to balance his bicycle.

The client was expected to consciously and unconsciously retrieve from his own personal history both somatic and psychological components of these experiences. These affective resources would be incompatible with elevated blood pressure and facilitate aspects of generative change as Bob utilized these experiences in responding to family, social and professional stimuli.

Since a general goal was to intervene to disrupt the sequence whereby Bob produced tension (instead of helping him try harder to simply release it more effectively), a set of interventions was designed to redefine and utilize his symptom. The work directed at the symptom itself was initiated after the second story. Interventions were presented directly and also contained in metaphorical sketches involving reframing and paradoxical prescription.

"Fear" was reframed as positive and several metaphors followed to illustrate how it could be used. This occurred systematically in several stages. First, the hypertension was redefined as "fear." Help was promised as possible only if Bob were willing to learn to *really* be very afraid. Ideomotor signaling was established. His willingness to continue was secured. He was directed to notice his fear in great detail and to "make it a friend." The rationale presented to Bob emphasized that it was not impossible to handle his fear and that it was, in fact, good to be able to notice it so he could use it to know what he needed from others. Since he was especially fearful of conflict, he was paradoxically encouraged to *use* his ability to avoid conflict to avoid getting stressed. He was to do this by plunging directly into the heart of the conflict and resolving it, perhaps by expressing himself, persevering, or even getting mad. In this regard, a metaphor was related about a client with psoriasis who only resolved his symptom when he learned to get mad and "break out" of limitations and restraints literally rather than symbolically with his skin.

The treatment plan now provided an opportunity for Bob to experience emotional release while noticing and accepting that area of fearfulness involving his emotional vulnerability in relationships. The metaphor designed for this purpose discussed a client presenting problems with authority who had learned to avoid fear by pretending not to have it. He had learned this habit through an overidentification with a rigidly constricted father. Via a complex structure, the learning that he could be emotionally vulnerable was conveyed. In this story, the client was told about a tough sheep farmer who thought he needed to find a balance between a man's role on the job and his role with his family, but what he really needed was to experience a father who knew that mistakes were a part of life, tears were acceptable, and who was willing to say "I love you" and hold his son affectionately. Emotional impact of the story on the client can be understood when the proximity of his father's death is recalled. The story provided an opportunity for him to experience an emotional closeness with his father and to create resolution. Also beneficial was his learning that he could have those interactions that he didn't get from his father when he was a boy *after* his father's death by creating the experiences for himself in trance and associating them to memories of his father. This completed the "fear" sequence in the center of the multiple-embedded metaphor structure.

The treatment plan next called for a context in which to illustrate and model specific behaviors such as expressing anger, taking risks, revealing vulnerability, and allowing others to be in charge. This context was created by resuming the previously suspended story of the "identical twins." Closure for the original drama was accomplished by returning to this story. The earlier attitude about genetic inheritance was further debunked by mentioning that one of the "identical" twins actually grew to be a full five inches taller than his brother. This metaphor accomplished its primary therapeutic purpose by detailing specific behaviors that the taller twin learned and utilized in his individuation process. It incorporated his experiences when he immigrated to America and "had to learn how to have the freedom that Americans have." He had to take responsibility for feelings by expressing them, protect his feelings by improving on insults, and watch others to model being the kind of American he wanted to be, etc. "Punch lines" such as "the more you show your ignorance, the more you approach perfection" and "only the fool knows it all" were included to reinforce earlier emphasis on attitudes supportive of the detailed behaviors.

The treatment plan also addressed the goal of self-image modification. I wanted to stimulate the client to create a personal map to guide his own ideosyncratic use of relevant new behavioral options. This was tangentially accomplished in the general context of the "twins" metaphor with indirect suggestions to imagine himself interacting (visually and with related "soundtrack") with new behavioral options in situations that were previously anxiety producing. This segment was designed to facilitate image modification by intensifying experiential associations and cognitive elaborations to the metaphors presented.

Finally, the multiple-embedded metaphor structure was given closure by returning to the first story about the clients with the skin conditions.

The goal at this point in the treatment was to facilitate generative change by creating associative links between trance experiences and specific demands of his current and next logical stages of family development. In order to accomplish this, an intervention was designed to appeal to his need to be responsible while simultaneously redefining "responsibility" as a healthy amount of selfishness as he takes care of himself by expressing feelings, giving over control to others at times, facing rather than avoiding life's conflicts, taking risks to be intimate with his wife, and being spontaneous in other aspects of his life such as career demands.

As a toddler's parent who was feeling overstressed by responsibility and deprived of time for himself, it was therapeutic to facilitate a situation whereby his daughter would serve as a stimulus for these new associations instead of reminding him of stress and unavoidable burden in his life. Therefore, his original attitude about responsibility was challenged with a paradoxical reminder that "everyone knows the best way to take care of children is to show them how to take care of themselves." This was part of the metaphor content as something that had been learned by the client troubled with skin cancer. It was pointed out that, as a leader in his community, he actually was doing others an injustice by taking care of them all the time in the same way that it would be a shame if a father failed to model for his child how a person should take care of him- or herself.

A final intervention was included during reorientation to offset possible "despair" if Bob's first blood pressure check failed to produce desired proof of change. This intervention emphasized the matter of when to notice change and served as permission to create and notice change either gradually or immediately. It also accomplished a conclusion to the sun allergy story. That client was said to be confused about when to start leaving the allergic reaction behind. It was mentioned that others knew he was cured because they saw him in the sun the first afternoon after his hypnosis but he had to test it and relax in the sun gradually, exposing more and more skin so that he could really trust changes he had apparently learned to make in his "metabolism."

Immediate Feedback and Follow-up Results

Specific feedback after the trance was limited as the client reported almost complete amnesia for the two-hour trance. He responded throughout in expected ways, giving ideomotor feedback both spontaneously and when specifically requested. He did recall having a vivid image of climbing into his father's lap and having a close emotional experience. Ideosensory feedback during that portion of metaphor which was designed to invite such an experience included several tears rolling over his cheeks.

In a three-month follow-up to the single session, the client reported even more amnesia for the trance but enthusiastically reported that his blood pressure consistently had been in the normal range since the session. He went on to add that he had noticed an increased motivation to engage in relaxed forms of therapeutic exercise like swimming, which he described as like "dropping into a trance." Another change he could not directly relate to the resolution of his symptom but which reportedly occurred simultaneously was a new spontaneity in his professional endeavors that he contrasted with a previous constriction. This spontaneity evidenced in professional areas would seem to be symbolic of similar changes in other aspects of his life as well, since work was previously the situation he had labored over and experienced anxiety about in the most intense manner. This assumption was verified in a six-month follow-up when the client wrote to report that he was finding himself to be more expressive of angry and sad feelings, that his relationship with his daughters had improved, and that he had become comfortable acknowledging his imperfections. He remained amnesic with regard to metaphor content but was pleased to learn when he read the discussion of his case that the changes he was noticing in his life were related to specific goals of the treatment plan. The point in presenting this case was not to focus on the stories told but to emphasize that they were presented as interventions designed to further his accomplishing his life goals even though therapy had been initiated simply to control a symptom.

CONCLUSION

I would like to propose a possible distinction between the terms "hypnosis" and "hypnotherapy." *Hypnosis* is often thought of as a device to remove a symptom with few or no suggestions to foster social development. The literature is replete with research in which hypnosis has been both successful and unsuccessful in this regard. Erickson's *hypnotherapy*, however, dealt with factors of social adjustment—typically using the symptom rather than providing suggestions to remove the symptom in exclusion of suggestions to foster personal and social development. In emphasizing interpersonal needs, relatively less time is spent removing the symptom.

Erickson did not operate from a fixed theory of personality but rather from a theory of intervention based on an assessment of the individual's social and developmental needs. This supports the contention that symptoms are the result of mismanagement of experiences intended to meet those needs. Hypnotherapy (and therapy in general) according to Erickson overwhelmingly favors a retrieval and association of experiences to help get the person moving within the developmental continuum, with an understanding that the symptom will fade when more appropriate adjustment is made. It has been my intention to familiarize the reader with these ideas and present a working concept of generative change, illustrated with a case example. A categorized list of typical developmental needs has been included as an aid in treatment planning and to stimulate further and more detailed elaboration of them in clinical settings. As research investigates this more pervasive treatment approach, it is hoped that hypnotherapy can begin to be appreciated for what Erickson hoped it would become.

REFERENCES

Ackerman, N. (1966). *Treating the troubled family.* New York: Basic Books.
Ackerman, N. (1972). The growing edge of family therapy. In C. Sager & H. Kaplan (Eds.), *Progress in group and family therapy.* New York: Brunner/Mazel.
Berne, E. (1971). Away from a theory of the impact of interpersonal interaction on nonverbal participation. *Transactional Analysis Journal, 1* (1), 6-13.
Cameron-Bandler, L. (1978). *They lived happily ever after.* Cupertino, CA: Meta Publications.
Capra, F. (1982). *The turning point.* New York: Bantam Books.
Dammann, C. (1982). Family therapy: Erickson's contribution. In J. Zeig (Ed.), *Ericksonian approaches to hypnosis and psychotherapy.* New York: Brunner/Mazel.
Erickson, M. (1979a). *Hypnotherapy.* New York: Irvington.
Erickson, M. (1979b). Taped seminar. The Milton H. Erickson Foundation, Phoenix, Arizona.
Erickson, M. (1980). Hypnotic psychotherapy. In E. Rossi (Ed.), *The collected papers of Milton H. Erickson* (Vol. 4). New York: Irvington.
Fisch, R. (1982). Erickson's impact on brief psychotherapy. In J. Zeig (Ed.), *Ericksonian approaches to hypnosis and psychotherapy.* New York: Brunner/Mazel.
Friedman, M., & Rosenman, R. (1974). *Type A behavior and your heart.* Greenwich, CT: Fawcett Press.
Gordon, D. (1978). *Therapeutic metaphors.* Cupertino, CA: Meta Publications.
Greer, S. (1979). Psychological enquiry: A contribution to cancer research. *Psychological Medicine, 9* (1), 81-89.
Haley, J. (1973). *Uncommon therapy.* New York: Norton.
Haley, J. (1982). The contribution to therapy of Milton H. Erickson, M.D. In J. Zeig (Ed.), *Ericksonian approaches to hypnosis and psychotherapy.* New York: Brunner/Mazel.
Jackson, D. (1967). Play, paradox, and people: Power and education. *Medical Opinion Review, 3,* 41-47.
Lankton, S. (1985). Multiple-embedded metaphor and diagnosis. In J. Zeig (Ed.), *Ericksonian psychotherapy, Vol. 1.* New York: Brunner/Mazel.
Lankton, S., & Lankton, C. (1983). *The answer within: A clinical framework of Ericksonian hypnotherapy.* New York: Brunner/Mazel.

Lankton, S., & Lankton, C. (1984, in press). Ericksonian styles of paradoxical treatment. In G. Weeks (Ed.), *Promoting change through paradoxical therapy*. Homewood, IL: Dow Jones-Irwin.

Rassidakis, N.C. (1978). A contribution to the study of the personality of cancer patients: A preliminary report. *Transactional Mental Health Research Newsletter*, Vol. 20 (1), 10-12.

Rossi, E., Ryan, M., & Sharp, F. (Eds.). (1983). *Healing and hypnosis*. New York: Irvington.

Watzlawick, P. (1982). Erickson's contribution to the interactional view of psychotherapy. In J. Zeig (Ed.), *Ericksonian approaches to hypnosis and psychotherapy*. New York: Brunner/Mazel.

Watzlawick, P., Weakland, J., & Fisch, R. (1974). *Change: Principles of problem formation and problem resolution*. New York: Norton.

Whitaker, C. (1982). Hypnosis and family depth therapy. In J. Zeig (Ed.), *Ericksonian approaches to hypnosis and psychotherapy*. New York: Brunner/Mazel.

Wolpe, J. (1948). *Psychotherapy by reciprocal inhibition*. Palo Alto: Stanford University Press.

Zeig, J. (Ed.). (1980). *A teaching seminar with Milton H. Erickson*. New York: Brunner/Mazel.

Zeig, J. (1982). Ericksonian approaches to promote abstinence from cigarette smoking. In J. Zeig (Ed.), *Ericksonian approaches to hypnosis and psychotherapy*. New York: Brunner/Mazel.

APPENDIX

Developmental Stages and Related Abilities

Biological security and basic trust

From 0-2 years old, the child's task is to establish symbiosis with the mother; to get food and physical attention; and to learn to make an impact on its environment. He or she must learn to test and oppose things and eventually learn self-feeding and break the symbiosis.

Early socialization

The child 2-7 years old should learn to consider feelings of others, to recognize when it is appropriate to speak up and ask questions. He or she needs to learn that it's all right to disagree. He or she develops feelings of tenderness toward others and learns to share possessions and affection with them.

Peer relations

The child 7-12 years old learns more sophisticated interactions, expanding on earlier feelings of comfort in the presence of others. He or she becomes more adept at arguing, competing, achieving, negotiating, joining, and interpreting nonverbal emotional responses from others.

Initiative and identity

At this stage (12-16) the person must learn how to be part child and part adult. He or she needs to develop a comfortable sexual identity and a self-image which includes and accepts an ability to initiate activities with others and to deal with selfishness and sharing. He or she needs to hold the attitude that he or she can, should and will grow up. Assertive behaviors begin to be developed within an environmental and social space. An attitude that curiosity and interest in the changing body is healthy should be developed, both for self and peers.

Courtship

At this stage, the young adult needs to have acquired a feeling of self-worth, an ability to fantasize, take risks, ask for time, and comfortably deny time to others. He or she should have the ability to express self honestly and to separate honesty from imagination. An attitude that an enjoyable relationship can be sustained is important. The ability for adequate sexual excitation must be developed.

Commitment and intimacy

At this stage, the individual must recognize personal self-worth and have an understanding that one enhances the life of another. Behaviors for time passing with another person must be developed. The person must be able to experience relaxation in the presence of the other person. He or she must be able to fantasize the continuation of the relationship into the future. Attitudes must be developed that disagreements, temporary "rifts" and disappointment in the loved one are not unusual or dangerous to the commitment.

Entering marriage

The person must first have the ability to expand previous abilities involved in commitment and then decide to do so. Choosing to remain single should be an ability as well and is often a viable option provided it is based on resource experiences which would enable the person to freely choose (as opposed to a "forced choice" based on deficits). All abilities listed in this section refer as well to various forms of "nonofficial" marriage (homosexual, cohabitation, etc.). To a large extent, remarriage after divorce is included though additional abilities to dissociate and benefit from previous mistakes are especially needed in that situation.

In this stage, the partners must successfully separate from families of origin and develop new ways of transacting with them and with in-laws. They must be able to choose among various options, sorting between external and internal pressures. They must have the ability to identify and express values as they go about the process of making decisions about where to live, power, friends, etc. They must have the ability to nurture one another, to ask for and receive nurturance. They must have the ability to problem solve independently and cooperatively. They must be able to play, be spontaneous, and enjoy each other. They must be able to delay gratification, to modify their behavior and suggest modification for the other's behavior. Each needs to be able to recognize the difference between blame and reason. They need an ability to realistically evaluate the severity of problems and to prioritize their urgency for resolution. Above all, an attitude of emotional openness and risk taking must be brought to the marriage or quickly learned.

Bearing children

Initially, potential parents should be able to separate from external pressures of parents or in-laws their desire to create and enhance the life of another and expand their own fulfillment before having any children. The first child demands that the parents have or develop the ability to deal with the dominant psychobiological needs of the child while still finding ways to meet personal needs. Later children only increase the pressure.

"Inheriting" stepchildren brings special demands of the parents, including the ability to dissociate from possible resentments of the child(ren). They must also have the ability to extend love in a broad way, separate from narcissistic needs to love only a child biologically their own.

The point at which children enter the home, whether by birth or otherwise, intensifies the need of the parent to be able to delay personal gratification. The parents must be able to nurture, direct, and manage the child from a dominant but friendly position. Behaviors involved in demonstrating love verbally and nonverbally are required as well as appropriate behaviors of firmness. The parents should be able to sustain transactions related to meeting the needs of the child and to suspend judgment regarding the meaning of the child's nonverbal behavior. The parent should be able to distinguish between their own projected fantasies of unresolved needs from their past and the honest ones expressed by the child.

Rearing children

Parents must have a variety of behaviors which are stimulated as the age of the child changes. The parents of a child 0-2 years of age must be able to try different, random behaviors to soothe the child, to continue giving unconditional positive regard despite the child's self-centered behavior, and to maintain a feeling of security and hope despite difficulties the child may manifest. They should be able to evaluate the baby's progress realistically.

Parents of a child 2-7 years of age must be able to install discipline, to encourage independence in the child by dissociating from compelling feelings to help and control. They must be able to make exploration available and communicate the attitude that it is good and proper. They must be able to maintain patience in responding to endless questions. The parents must simultaneously care for the child's needs while also teaching the child to care for his or her own needs by appropriate modeling. Thus, the parent must have and demonstrate the ability to care for himself and the attitude to support this healthy "selfishness."

Parents of 7-12-aged children must demonstrate more and more tolerance for differentiation and increased independence on the part of the children. They must be willing and able to discuss values rather than simply and firmly state held values. They need an ability to listen to the child's reasons and allow them to make an impact. They need an ability to be comfortable while the child moves about without immediate supervision from the parent. They need the attitude that the child will learn from the mistakes he or she makes.

Parents of teenagers face a special challenge requiring the ability to manage issues of control, conflict, definition of purpose, and influence of significant others outside the family. They must increasingly foster independence while continuing to offer protection. They will benefit from perceiving signs of success as evidenced by the child's hundreds of habits (such as grooming, word selection, socializing, etc.) to a greater extent than they notice deficits. They must be informed about drugs, sex, political, and significant cultural changes so as to realistically communicate with the child. They must be able to allow the child privacy.

As a single parent these skills are required as well as the ability to proceed with the above behaviors without the benefit of support from another parent. Parent partners, of course, must be able to amicably agree on methods of discipline, lenience, allowances, etc. They must be able to share success as well as responsibility for difficulties.

Marriage and financial enrichment: "sticking it out" vs. "bailing out"
Partners at this stage who "stick it out" will have developed the attitude that neither partner need be perfect. They can ask for help and receive it. They can listen to one another. They can recognize that temporary setbacks, either emotional or financial, are not signs of personal failure. They should have a feeling of ambition. During possible difficult times, they may need to relinquish pride involved in asking for outside

help or learn simple menial jobs such as sewing or auto repair. They may need an ability to aggressively stand up to outside injustice.

Letting children leave

This stage requires behaviors involved in withholding advice, being cheerful rather than emotionally manipulative as children make their own decisions which may be incompatible with parents' preferences or values. They need the attitude that the child's behavior doesn't have to reflect on them. They need to be able to confront the child in a casual, friendly manner. They must be able to support the child's own problem solving, independent behaviors.

Renewing partnership

Marital partners must find a new balance for getting personal needs met and problems solved. They must rekindle their ability to relate sexually and emotionally, expressing needs and asking for help. They must find a way to continue future plans despite any divergence in values. They should be able to allow and even encourage differentiation and separateness as each develops personal interests, perhaps a new vocation, hobby, or friends.

Sharing adulthood with adult offspring

This may require that parents behave in ways which were not modeled for them by their own parents. They need to be proud of the child's accomplishments rather than anxious, competitive, etc. They need the ability to overlook judgments or bias and accept the spouse and in-laws of the child. They must have the flexibility to accept and respect the child's new role(s) as parent, professional, etc. They may need to accept new roles themselves, perhaps that of grandparents. They may need to learn new behaviors to support their children as the type of support required will have changed.

Social evolvement and personal fulfillment

At this stage of possible retirement and leisure, the person needs to maintain an attitude that life is not over, simply because one role or roles have ended. They should be able to enjoy themselves, feeling that leisure is a privilege they are entitled to. They may need behaviors involved in reaching out, joining new clubs or groups or initiating new hobbies and projects. A feeling of fulfillment when reflecting back on one's life is a valuable experience at this stage as is the ability to call up memories of the past and accept them as valuable from a position of comfortable objectivity. They need an ability to relinquish unfulfilled dreams in favor of a realistic assessment of what is possible to accomplish now. Coping with impending death may require that the person reevaluate the meaning of his or her life. The person may have to deal with loss of physical abilities long before death and will therefore need to say goodbye and grieve appropriately while accepting the self as still vital and useful. They may also need to modify the self-image to include and accept being dependent in new ways, asking for help from children or grandchildren. Also, at this stage, it may be useful for the person to seize the opportunity to behave in a way consistent with his or her own needs and thoughts, despite the possibility that the behavior will be interpreted as eccentric by others.

Chapter 11

Multiple-Embedded Metaphor and Diagnosis

Stephen R. Lankton

Autogenic training is a variation of hypnosis that concentrates on the use of imagery and relaxation (as opposed to the Ericksonian approach which emphasizes the use of dissociation between conscious and unconscious experience). Autogenic training is designed to teach clients to experience a variety of psychotherapeutic responses, such as heaviness and warmth in the limbs, regulation of heart and respiration activity, abdominal warmth, and cooling of the forehead. In response, the subject is likely to experience slowing of heart rate, reduction of blood pressure and increased cortical discharges in the brainstem (Carruthers, 1981). To the extent that AT does not specify how and when to employ newly learned responses, clients are free to make these determinations according to their unique needs and circumstances. Of course, such freedom will not appeal to certain clients and, as an overall approach to treatment, AT fails to utilize the unique behavior, needs and personality requirements of some clients. Hypnosis combined with related autogenic training, however, has been found useful in migraines, hypertension, cardiovascular disorders (Carruthers, 1981), and gagging (Gerschman, Burrows, & Fitzgerald, 1981).

The point of this review is that hypnosis as a treatment modality would be more successful if clients were dealt with as more than "a symptom-carrying body." The most beneficial treatment, even when the presenting problem is defined as "only" a symptom, involves addressing the entire personality adjustment. This view is supported by evidence suggesting that purely symptomatic treatment of so-called neurotic clients may not forestall the eventual reemergence of symptoms because such treatment does not adequately take into account particular factors

171

of personality (Eysenck, 1969). Accordingly, this chapter deals with the controlled elaboration of hypnotherapeutic interventions that, because they are developed from a thoughtful diagnostic assessment of the individual personality and family social network, effect long-term relief from and alternatives to a symptomatic means of adjustment. Similarly, thoughtfully subdividing specific goals in sex therapy can reveal improvements in self-confidence, behavior acquisition, symptom removal, and resolutions of "neurotic" conflict (Brown & Chaves, 1980). This chapter traces a logical development from a diagnosis of the personality-in-a-social-continuum, to a treatment plan with therapeutic goals, to the design and delivery of multiple metaphors to reach those goals.

Individuals with symptoms are usually unaware of the conflicts and deficits that combined to create the symptom. Insight therapy assumes that understanding the dynamic cause will help release the inhibited feeling and impulses that lead to the tension. Unfortunately, insight into the meaning of the symptom, in itself, does not alter the person's or family's ability to cope effectively with the many roles, expectations, and tasks that represent a variety of parental, familial, and societal demands. To stimulate the experiential resources needed by a client to cope effectively with so many demands, much Ericksonian work is conducted in metaphor. Although metaphoric therapy reduces the opportunity for insight, it does increase unconscious involvement (Lankton & Lankton, 1983), a consequence that is tantamount to pervasive change of a symptom, personality, and a family's developmental course.

DIAGNOSTIC CONSIDERATIONS

Historically, the concepts and terminology of neurosis evolved from psychoanalytic theory. Since Erickson was not known to subscribe to this theory, my use of the term "neurosis" may need some explanation. I use the term to refer to personal difficulties deemed unacceptable by individuals who have a generally well-established sense of reality testing (i.e., ego-dystonic). I do not use the term to categorize these difficulties as situational or transitory, but to indicate that (a) functioning may be more or less grossly impaired, (b) that awareness that the difficulty ought to be remedied tends to create a situation where the individual is a relatively willing partner in the therapeutic process, and c) the family, if aware of the problem, usually expresses a consensus that the problem exists.

As relatively willing partners in the therapy, clients (and possibly their immediate families) are most likely to display few communication difficulties with their therapists and little conscious resistance to therapeutic aid. Under these circumstances, hypnosis can be used in a straightforward manner. Communication difficulties within the clients' families or social network often are, however, the root of the problem for the neurotic personality, because "mental disease is the breakdown of communication between people" (Erickson, 1980, p. 75). Erickson placed certain requirements on the assessment of clients' difficulties and on the scope of treatment. I will begin my examination of the treatment scope with an analysis of clients and family members' orientation to the problem.

CHARACTER OF THE INDIVIDUAL

People coming to therapy have a symptom which is dystonic to them and their families, and which causes discomfort they seek to alleviate. Although clients are able to express this desire relatively clearly, each will have an idiosyncratic manner of expression and will manifest personal adjustments that may be viewed as a characteristic interpersonal stance. The first assessment involves determining how to communicate with each person.

Erickson was respected for his ability to relate to the entire person and create a remarkable sense of understanding or rapport. He genuinely related to people on their own ground. Many who experienced Erickson personally contend that he seemed to "look into them" in a manner that they had not previously experienced. I personally find that being still, and briefly ceasing my usual conscious activity by going into a trance, facilitates noticing nuances in the client's ideomotor behavior. This state of observation helps me gain a deeper understanding and respect for the person. Ultimately, speaking to the person's real condition as sincerely as possible and doing so with realistic concern provides me with a guide to achieve some of the empathy conveyed by Erickson.

Assessing a client's characteristic interpersonal stance depends, to a significant degree, upon the personal depth and experience of the therapist. However, some useful guidelines for refining this ability can be shared. Assessment is based on two dimensions: interpersonal dominance and interpersonal affiliation. Individuals make a unique adjustment to their families and the world that becomes their practiced method of coping in interpersonal situations. Their interpersonal stance determines their public posture ("in control," "one up," "helpful," "needy," etc.). I have found it most helpful to organize diagnostically interpersonal behavior on a continuum from relatively dominant-to-submissive

and from relatively friendly-to-hostile (Leary, 1957). People who frequently or regularly present a "needy" persona, then, characteristically
would be friendly-submissive. As such, their behavior is predictable and
I can assume that the person provokes complementary roles and associates with those who are characteristically friendly-dominant. This person will be most comfortable if the therapist takes the complementary
role. Similarly, a person characterized as "one up," "smug," or "aloof"
will present a relatively hostile-dominant posture. Such behavior typically provokes self-doubt or rebellion (hostile-submission) from others
and the therapist should be aware of the rapport that can be achieved
when, depending on the degree of either dominance or hostility displayed, the therapist is self-doubting or challenging.

Carrying this initial assessment further, clients who appear "in control" and "sociable" will display a customary interpersonal posture of
friendly-dominance. In these cases the therapist will put the client most
at ease when appeals are made to the client's leadership or responsible
behavior. This is done by being flexible enough as a therapist to display
friendly-submissive behavior. Finally, the fourth logical category is for
clients who appear rebellious or full of self-doubt: the hostile-submissive
stance. This orientation tends to provoke relatively hostile-dominant
behavior in others, either in the form of narcissistic and competitive
behavior or overtly aggressive behavior. The therapist ought to consider
initially joining the client with behavior that will be felt as familiar by
being confident, directive and even somewhat distant.

From this initial assessment, several important factors related to the
symptom may be revealed. For instance, the person with certain somatic
complaints (hypertension, for example) will often display relatively high
friendly-dominant behavior. The preceding discussion suggests that the
therapist will put the client most at ease by relative friendly-submission:
asking questions, admiring, provoking leadership qualities, etc. One
may extrapolate that, in addition to the obvious need for learning to
relax, several interpersonal aspects of coping will be essential for the
person to learn. For example, can the person induce leadership rather
than merely be a leader? Can the person play a complementary role of
friendly-submission when a leader is present? In a more psychodynamic
vein, can the person identify and express dependency needs, tenderness
and erotic feelings (all a part of friendly-submission)? Also, if the person
is firmly entrenched in friendly-dominant behavior, what attitudes and
self-image barriers are presented that might prevent use of existing
friendly-submissive behaviors and perceptions also acquired? All of the

information from this assessment can be formulated into a treatment plan in accord with the acknowledged therapeutic contract.

Further, how can the family structure be altered to accommodate the use of new behaviors? If the spouse of this client has been cast into the complementary role of follower, does he or she know the necessary behaviors, feelings, etc., to play the friendly-dominant role from time to time? How can this enhance the family? What circumstances will encourage this reorganizing?

It can be seen, then, that the initial assessment of the client will reveal: (a) guidelines for immediate interpersonal management; (b) potential goals; and (c) interventions designed with each member's whole personality or family development in mind. The interpersonal style of the client is a significant clue to the behavior that the client customarily uses to cope with demands, and to the deficits in behavior that need to be faced and developed so the client can cope more effectively with these demands.

A complete assessment of personality, then, justifiably includes information of intra- and interpersonal, and social-historical dynamics: the family stage of development, family structure, and the developmental or psychological age of all family members who become clients.

To determine the stage of development of the family, the pressures on the family must be discovered. Since each family is unique, the range of possible difficulties is broad. Factors such as economic and sociometric variables determine, in large part, the expectations and needs of the family. In addition, the impact of each member's personal history and even such frequently overlooked aspects as local weather, chemical pollutants, chemical dependencies, and historically current trends will shape the unique character of each family. With the increasing diversity of lifestyles, such as nonmarriage, single-parent families, homosexual couples, group marriages, reconstituted families, remarriages, and divorces, reconsideration of "normal" trends in family development ought to be undertaken. However important, such a task is beyond the current scope.

It is possible to estimate some of the logical steps of family development and to create a list that can be lengthy, depending upon the degree of detail in which one wishes to engage. It is, in fact, the inclusion of considerable detail that facilitates the list's usefulness in evaluating a particular family. For the sake of discussion, I have a typical list of the changes involved in various stages of family development. Consider, for example, the following series of changes as points of departure for examining any particular client-systems: educational decisions, court-ship, initial employment decisions, commitment, marriage decisions (in the heterosexual person), child-bearing decisions, adjustment to the years of marriage stabilization or childrearing, adjustments to children leaving home for school, possible adjustments to relocation and change in employment, coping with possible separation and divorce or child custody concerns, possible domestic violence, alcoholism and other drug abuse, acceptance of life planning consequence, adjustment to children's becoming parents and creating families of their own, retirement, use of leisure, adjustment to community involvement, religious life, eventually coping with the death of loved ones, wills, allocation of property, and finally, adjustment to the imminence of one's own death.

An assessment of the client's stage of family development provides information that is critical in constructing interventions, especially met-aphors, which address current as well as future sources of stress. That is, the immediate future stage of development is as important as the present stage. Helping the client move successfully into courtship will be enhanced by teaching aspects of the final stages of courtship that lead, ultimately, to commitment and marriage. When the goals of the treatment are translated into actual metaphors designed to help the client create a reassociation of experience, a portion of those metaphors should deal with the behaviors, feelings, perceptions, etc. that influence abilities the client needs to cope with the sanctions and pressures of current as well as imminent development.

To accomplish this, the therapist must, as methodically as possible, consider the skills, perceptions, and the variety of resources that the client will need to adjust creatively to role demands at the current and the next logical stage of the family's development. In a similar fashion, the resources necessary to adjust and respond to an appropriate family structure must be elaborated. The variety of dynamics that constitute family structure can be discussed in logical segments and, indeed, ther-apy can address each element systematically, just as most learnings can be reduced to their component elements.

Some of the factors to consider in assessing family structure include: who talks to whom; what do they talk about; what is avoided; what is the typical affect; what is the usual role assumed; does anyone play a complementary role; is the complementary role supportive and healthy; how is the role parallel to the family of origin; does it represent scape-goating or protective loyalties; and does it embody myths or disagree-ments regarding values, identities, or actions? These factors are included in the diagnostic parameters that follow.

DIAGNOSTIC PARAMETERS

Marital Status . . .
Chronological Age . . .
Number and Ages of Children . . .

The marital status, age, number and ages of children are self-evident sources of diagnostic information. These areas are important guideposts to a thorough assessment of the predictable pressures that influence crisis and adjustment. Chronological age, for example, gives a rough indicator of the client's life experiences. One would expect a person of 20 to know how to maintain a balanced checking account but this would not be readily expected of a child of 11. Likewise, marital status and age roughly indicate the expectations being placed on the individual by others (both current external and past internal expectations of others).

Cultural Background or Identification . . .
Stage of Family Development . . .
Next Logical Stage of Development . . .

Cultural background tempers our understanding of pressures with which a person operates. A gypsy may not need to know how to read but a middle-income Caucasian child is expected to read. Concerning family development, Haley attempted to clarify Erickson's thinking around logical stages of family development (Haley, 1973). In so doing, he explicated important factors of diagnostic assessment. But the requirements and pressures of family development are elusive. It is difficult to categorize comprehensively the stages of "normal" family development.

Needs of courtship differ from the needs of commitment and marriage. In courtship one needs to recognize a variety of abilities, including a sense of self-worth and an understanding that one enhances the life of another. The individual needs to be able to engage in "small talk," to be verbally vague, to say "no," to laugh, to smile, to dance, etc. During courtship, a person needs to relax while in the proximity of the preferred sex, to be able to fantasize, to have a cognitive framework that explains mild social rejection and *faux pas* as natural and necessary occurrences, etc. The subtleties are staggering when they are articulated. But as clients gain a few related skills, they begin to generate other learnings that are closely related. Many clients learn to learn with an ever-increasing efficiency in the present developmental context.

The needs of marriage require a modification of the abilities and skills that lead to success in the courtship stage. The modifications are an ability to keep ever more complex commitments, to value the enhancement one provides for another and to reciprocate the experience of being valued. Simple fantasizing about being together ought to become goal-directed planning and problem-solving. Small talk must become straight-talk, and eroticism must become emotional openness and intimacy built upon risk-taking and trust. The immediate gratifications of courtship must be replaced with the delayed gratifications that are part of a successful marriage. The elements of each stage are nearly endless in number when broken down into all of the experiences and transactions that comprise them.

The task of isolating and describing all of the experiences and transactions needed at each stage of family development may seem monumental. But in therapy, one needs only to identify the current developmental stage and then assess the experiences and transactions needed for all clients to most effectively evolve to the next stage. This assessment can become the basis for metaphor content and the object of the therapeutic goals developed with metaphor. Other stages of development in marriage include child bearing, child rearing, financial enrichment, etc., as mentioned. To use these stages effectively in diagnosis and therapy, one ought to develop detailed accounts and explanations of the experiences and transactions typically involved in each stage. An assessment of the stage of development and its particular components is necessary if one is to understand how symptomatic behavior occurs and persists during a particular stage in a family system.

Psychological Age

Determining "psychological age" involves assessing the client's developmental orientation of thought and emotion. Psychological age can be judged by style of manipulating the therapist, vocabulary, rate of speech, values, self vs. other orientation, muscle fluidity vs. rigidity, role-played expressions, naivete, etc. For example, a man was seen for obesity and marital difficulties. The therapist was struck by the man's emotional immaturity and infantile behaviors: His fluid face muscle expressions editorialized everything he heard or saw; his vocabulary for the word "no" consisted of the sound "ehhn," and "inh"; he was extremely self-oriented with complaints, excuses, etc.; and his general demeanor seemed to convey a demand that the therapist "do something" to relieve his discomfort. There was little to indicate that he took personal responsibility for his own experience or life course. By judging emotional age the therapist can create metaphors which more likely would appeal to and hold the attention of the ego state that will be listening in therapy.

Family Structure

The structure of the social network is a vital part of the diagnosis. This information reveals which adjustments to current social pressures are occurring, which needed adjustments are not being realized, and how this situation is being maintained. An Ericksonian approach sensitizes clients and families to resources they have, and engages potentials for coping. Such an approach includes relabeling perceptions, retraining perceptions, reframing cognitions, and challenging attitudes held about any number of things (aggression, sexuality, discipline, fate, anxiety, specific behaviors in a spouse, etc.). The following questions are useful in determining the family structure:

(a) Who talks to whom within the system?
(b) Are the topics of interchange rigid and predictable? What are they?
(c) How involved with one another are the members? Is the involvement over- or underinvolvement? Is it a conflictual or overaccepting involvement?
(d) What is avoided in the relationship?
(e) What is the typifying affect in the interchanges? Is there a way to characterize the usual roles taken by the client(s)? What role(s) is the therapist expected to fulfill?
(f) Are family members needed to play compatible roles of support or criticism or does the client take the typical roles despite "reality?"
(g) How is the current social system a copy of the family of origin of the client(s)? What dynamic interplaying is explainable by seeing the complaints as attempts to recast (or avoid recasting) each spouse's family of origin?
(h) Are there observable transactions that reflect a disagreement on values, identities, or actions of family members?
(i) Are there loyalties, scapegoating, myths, or other means of overtly shifting the responsibility and deficiencies of one or more members?
(j) Is there a function of the symptom expressible in terms of how it secures immediate gratification or manufactures an avoidance of

some anxiety-producing behavior for all family members? Can the symptom or its consequences be seen as metaphoric to a current coping pattern in the family?

(k) What are the available and potentially needed resources of the clients? How might the resources be engaged to propel the clients toward their goals? What will be required to get the family to support healthy roles and reorganize accordingly?

(l) What does the client present as the problem and what is the treatment contract that has been negotiated?

Following a thoughtful assessment of the client system, therapeutic goals can be logically formulated.

THERAPEUTIC OUTCOMES WITH METAPHORS

Multiple-embedded metaphor is a vital tool used to achieve therapeutic goals. The method involves interspersing one metaphor within another, or a number of others, in the course of a single session in order to address certain aspects of three to five therapeutic goals. Goals that can be addressed with dramatic therapeutic metaphors include: family structure or development change, age-appropriate intimacy or task behaviors, affect and emotional flexibility, attitude restructuring, enhancing self-image thinking, and intensifying discipline and enjoyment.

I intend for these categories to represent a comprehensive and mutually exclusive set of therapeutic goals, but because I have stated the goals in general terms, my intention will not be met in a rigorous sense. These six categories do, however, provide a practical method of satisfying the primary aim of several established therapies: e.g., gestalt (emotional flexibility); family therapy (family structure or development change); cognitive and rational-emotive therapies (attitude restructuring); psychodrama, behavioral therapies, and assertiveness training (behavioral change); supportive and parental therapies (discipline and enjoyment changes); transactional analysis and gestalt, encounter, and psychoanalysis (age-appropriate intimacy).

A helpful approach for formulating therapeutic goals is to imagine being a therapist of a specific discipline and answering the question, "What would therapy hope to accomplish?" This method results in estimates of the adjustments that could be achieved in successful treatment for each discipline and for each category of therapeutic goals. For example, what about a case of a workaholic lawyer? As an operant behaviorist or as a psychodramatist, what behaviors does the client need to acquire to make more adequate use of the resources in his or her social arena(s)? For instance, does the lawyer need to ask for help, to praise others, to accept advice, to listen calmly, to learn to agree with others? If so, which of these behaviors will become the behavioral goal for which treatment sessions? This line of reasoning can be conducted for each category of therapeutic goals. It must be remembered that outcomes affect one another and are reached best by interventions that affect all levels of family and personal organization.

The same approach, when applied to areas of family structure, feelings, attitudes, behaviors, discipline, enjoyment, and self-image thinking, yields distinct sets of therapeutic goals—goals that will become the heart of therapy sessions. Each session, while dealing with the presented concerns of the client, will provide opportunities to convey one or more goals from several of the categories, and also can lay the foundations for more complex learnings to be conveyed in the next session. For example, in the treatment of a sexual problem, the first session may deal with the client's emotional connection to his or her parents. The second session may develop that foundation into emotions and feelings of likes and dislikes, and a subsequent session may make actual arousal available in the developing foundation of emotional resources. The learning tasks, such as sexual feelings, can begin with mundane but prerequisite experiences to be built upon in subsequent sessions. Likewise, in the first session simple attachment behaviors (relaxation, smiling, touching) can be developed into social skills (eye contact, small talk, direct confrontation, etc.) and eventually into sexual skill (sensate focusing, kissing, fondling, coitus, etc.). Thus the emotional goals and the behavioral goals would be built hand-in-hand during the sessions. Likewise, attitudes and self-image goals would be identified and offered in support of the emotional and behavioral changes that are accomplished at each step of the way.

Two major points concerning the relationship of metaphor to therapeutic goals remain. First, discipline-enjoyment changes involve the use of metaphor to convey some particular focus on where to find pleasure in the course of disciplined personal conduct. This can be encouraged with suggestions regarding the use of personal resources within a thought-provoking story, so that a depressed father of six-and-seven-year-old daughters might, for example, be presented with a reframing suggestion to "give up the joys of childhood so you can take pleasure in finding the joys of manhood." The potential to carry out such suggestions can be reinforced by delineating certain manly joys. The discipline-enjoyment metaphor, more than the other five types mentioned, is employed to deliver indirect suggestions in embedded quotes within the story, thus allowing the client to grasp it or reject it without resistance.

The final point concerns the following two-step sequence: First, there is more to be gained through thoughtfully wording the goal in "nonmetaphoric" terms; and, second, proceeding to a metaphoric counterpart. In other words, one ought to avoid the temptation of hearing aspects of the client's difficulty and thinking, "Oh, this is like the story of. . . ." Professionalism requires one to devise goals first, and be able to justify the use of particular interventions. The Ericksonian approach is more cohesive when treatment goals are thought out at the onset, as nonmetaphorically as possible. Once the goals are determined, the therapist can state them in metaphoric terms, for it is the structure of metaphor that stimulates the client's thinking along clinically relevant lines (family changes, etc.). Actual learning is a joint effort between the client's conscious need to frame the learning and the client's unconscious thought process—an interplay that is facilitated by metaphoric communication—in which clients rely on their own identifications, their own interpretations, and their own conclusions. Therefore, manipulation by the therapist is not coercive in any way, at any time. In a metaphoric approach, compliance and resistance are markedly reduced and freedom of choice for the client is maintained.

The following protocols are meant to provide a convenient and dependable structure for designing dramatic metaphors. The protocols are not meant to constrain but rather to guide and add certainty to the therapeutic process. By way of analogy, consider how a diagram of dance steps assists the learner become familiar with complex movements. In the execution of the dance, however, one's memory of the diagram is only a background aid and a small and intermittent part of the experience of the dance. The learned diagrams are not meant to inhibit creative execution or enjoyment but rather to give license as well as form to an otherwise limitless variety of opportunities.

The protocols are the result of countless hours of categorizing, analyzing, and re-creating elements of Erickson's therapeutic metaphors. I will present a succinct three-step version of each protocol. From one angle, they can be considered as recipes in a cookbook. From another, they can be viewed as procedures in a manual. Manuals are meant to be references that users become familiar with and then consult from time to time, especially when difficulties or anomalies occur or when errors need correcting. Manuals are most helpful when complex or unfamiliar tasks are being carried out and success is imperative.

I begin with a therapeutic goal that has been restated metaphorically for each category. Only then should the three-step protocols be applied to design procedures or to develop metaphoric detail. Once the steps have become familiar, they can be used quickly just as the steps involved in speaking a language and selecting words properly have become largely unconscious. For a period of time, I recommend mentally adjusting each selected metaphor to the three steps. This procedure will add to the therapist's confidence as he or she tells the metaphors while conducting therapy. As one becomes more advanced in the use of these protocols, one discovers an occasional, but remarkable "syncronicity" between the images, symbols, and themes of the metaphor, and aspects of the client's life which previously had not been explicitly revealed. The protocols are simple diagrams of most complex structures. They are meant to allow maximum freedom for creative thought for the client while providing a dependable therapeutic structure and direction for the therapist.

1. Attitude Restructuring: The Metaphor Protocol

1) Examine the behavior(s) in question from the protagonist's perceptions.
2) Examine the same behavior(s) from the perceptions of significant others.
3) Relate the consequence(s) of the behavior(s) to the perceptions held by both the protagonist and the observing others.

To exemplify the use of this protocol in the selection and design of a metaphor to restructure an attitude, consider the case of a young man of 30, whose attitude toward marriage was expressed in the following remarks: "Marriage is a trap," and "If you come from a bad home life you can't have a happy married life." This outlook caused conflict with his live-in woman friend who increasingly pressed for marriage and children. He hoped that therapy would help him to continue the relationship and to overcome his fear that marriage would spoil the relationship. He had not considered that his attitude was, in fact, a primary mechanism creating a fear that he used to express his long-held beliefs based on only a few reinforcing observations.

The metaphor used to address this aspect of the young man's difficulty concerned the unfortunate life of Brenda (not her real name, of course) from my hometown, and the life of her counterpart, Kathy. The characters' lives present a metaphoric counterexample to the client as illustrated in the following:

1) Examine the world through the eyes of Brenda: fine home, sociable parents, good marriage, goals of college, family, children . . . smooth sailing.

2) Examine the world through the eyes of Kathy: poor marriage between parents, (some) domestic violence, sad for portion of childhood, lived in foster home for a time. She rather naively hoped but doubted that she could have a college education, a good marriage, children, and happiness.

3) In the dramatic story line Brenda (who was, in fact, modeled after a young woman from my high school) was shot and killed by her husband only a week before our ten-year class reunion, but Kathy had a lovely family and was finishing her master's degree in public health. The story hints that Brenda never learned to work for what she wanted, but Kathy, because of her difficult life, learned many ways to approach and to solve problems.

Delivering a metaphor requires a variety of skills (examined in detail in Lankton & Lankton, 1983) that include attention to the client's ideomotor behavior, to the use of pause, inflection, speed of speech, to the use of interspersal of indirect suggestions and binds, sincerity, and to the use of drama. An important consideration is the matter of dramatic interest. The story began with, "Even knowing how life turns out, it was a surprise that my classmate had been shot and killed by her husband only a week before our class reunion." From this shocking beginning, the story flashed back to the home life and perspectives of both girls when I knew them in high school.

The element of drama is added to gain the interest and attention of my client, and to call upon his ability to judge the outcome of these girls' lives. To do so he must call his attitude into play—but, it is not clear that his attitude is being challenged and he is not defensive or offended. To the client, the metaphor has all the right reasons but it gets the wrong answer. Thinking through the story he must conclude that his attitude is incorrect. Otherwise, he is left with the options of (a) requestioning his memory of what he just heard from me, (b) doubting his skill at predicting in this sort of situation (how marriages turn out), or (c) disregarding the entire incident. Actually, he would resort to the third option only after ruling out the other two, but the process of checking his memory and examining his reasoning possibly will be an overload to consciousness especially since the session continues. His attitude, therefore, becomes more confusing than helpful. Information intended to help resolve the confusion will be provided later in the session in another metaphor, but even this metaphor hinted that the ability to solve problems in marriage was due to having problems before marriage, and had been the most important variable in Kathy's successful marriage.

2. Affect and Emotional Flexiblity: The Metaphor Protocol

1) Establish a relationship between the protagonist and a person, place or thing which involves affect (e.g., tenderness, anxiety, confusion, love, longing, etc.).
2) Detail *movement* in the relationship (e.g., moving with, moving toward, moving away, orbiting, etc.).
3) Detail the internal physiological changes that coincide with the building emotion.

The metaphor for affect need have only one goal: to sensitize the client to, or elicit, the therapeutic feeling. There is no need for this metaphor to connect the feeling to a world that is parallel to the client's world. In fact, if the story can elicit the experience without sounding like the client's life, the client will be less defensive and resistance will not be aroused.

The affect metaphor should parallel real life situations that naturally wake emotions. The metaphor should establish and change a relationship, and then comment on the bodily response to the changes. By way of illustration, consider that sadness commonly represents the loss of an important relationship. A metaphor constructed to elicit sadness would sufficiently depict a positive relationship, followed by an account of the protagonists' moving apart, and concluding with an emphasis on their bodily reactions (to incorporate some of the client's actual experience). This could be a story of two friends (or a child and pet, etc.) who, in the course of the story, become separated. The client, properly engaged in the story, will respond unconsciously by generating various component experiences for sadness. The subsequent focus on bodily reactions helps crystalize that unconscious response and brings it out of the background of experience for use in the overall treatment session.

To elicit the feeling of anger, for instance, use of the protocol is quite the same but the direction of movement is modified: for example, the story might detail a relationship with teenage children who persist in throwing garbage over your fence into your yard to be irritating; the movement must involve the protagonists and antagonists moving even closer. The physiology of adrenalin flow in the body ought to be detailed around points of confrontation.

Joy can be elicited by detailing a relationship between two dear friends separated except for jovial phone calls. The relationship changes to move the protagonists closer together rapidly when the friends rendezvous at a bus station. Their feelings of longing and mild pleasure naturally turn into joy. The physiology of blood flow to the tender organs of the body, smiles, etc., in the two friends, again, are to be related to whatever minute changes the client exhibits.

Finally, I will give a slightly more complex illustration. Confidence and its physiological component can be facilitated when the relationship includes a series of mild anxiety-producing moments (say, the protagonist's relationship with an undependable auto on cold winter days) and when the change leaves the protagonist with a series of pleasant experiences in place of the anxious ones (his or her first few days with a new automobile which is dependable—heater works, it starts, tires have rubber, windows seal tightly, radio plays, etc.). The protagonist's increased awareness of bodily changes ought to be correlated as much as possible to the client's responses to the story (relaxation of various muscles, sitting more erect, increased ease of perceptions, raised sternum, etc.). Detailing physiological responses, even when they are not apparent in the client, has the effect of perceptual training, and teaches the client to notice aspects of pleasant bodily sensations.

Sometimes several trainings are needed to perform a response well (e.g., confidence, joy, anger, or any other complex learning). In these cases each session may contain an affect metaphor until the client no longer needs it.

3. Age-Appropriate Intimacy or Task Behavior: The Metaphor Protocol

1) Emphasize goals and not motives while detailing the protagonist's observable behavior related to the desired behavioral role to be acquired by the client.
2) Detail the protagonist's internal attention and nonobservable behavior used to support the actions he or she displays.
3) Extend the metaphoric context in order to repeat the explanation of the desired behavior.

With this protocol, the therapist attempts to convey a heightened sense of the actual, observable behaviors that provide relevant feedback to a person who is learning the behaviors, and attempts to instruct the client in appropriate and successful behaviors by means of the metaphor. The client will need to know some internal behaviors as guides for any new learning. Some clients rely on self-talk, others upon the visual image of the goal, etc. A metaphor that poses a protagonist in a situation where analysis or education about behavior is taking place serves nicely. If the therapist wishes to instruct a husband on ways to praise his wife, or to instruct a depressed single person about how to make friends, etc., the metaphor needs only to be about someone learning new behaviors (preferably in a situation different from that facing the client, in order to allow him or her to consider the metaphor without consciously censoring it) *and* without naming or discussing the motive of the protagonist.

For the husband the story might be about *what* I explained to the new business manager about *how* to give praise (what I told him in trance, later what I expected him to do with employees, and finally, what I noticed him doing). The focus is on both the external behaviors (words, gestures, voice tone, breathing, etc.) and on the internal experience that supports such behaviors (self-talk, memories of praise received, etc.). The focus is not about *why* he needs to learn, or how difficult it is to learn, or about how rewarding it is to learn . . . just how it is done! For the depressed person to learn social behaviors, the context of a child in a new neighborhood could be employed. The metaphor can give instructions for several greeting behaviors (smiling, giving name, asking names, listening, etc.), and it can repeat several of the learning and some internal supporting experiences but not the tension or motives. The goal is to sensitize the client to the behaviors and *not* to emphasize the importance of learning the behaviors in order to "get somewhere" or "get something." That connection is exactly what is not wanted; the story ought not be "you need to learn this and here's why." Rather, the learning about the behaviors should be presented as a clue, or an aside. As such, clients get to make the connections for themselves and earn credit in the process.

4. Self-Image Thinking Enhancement: The Metaphor Protocol

1) Detail the protagonist's appearance to create a central self-image with visual imagery that emphasizes the appearance of the person *as* he or she experiences a set of desired experiential (emotional, attitudinal, behavioral) resources previously retrieved.
2) Detail rehearsal of the central self-image through successive scenarios involving increasing difficulty or potential anxiety.
3) Culminate with the use of an experience of actually being a part of

an image of a successful future that resulted from reliance on the acts rehearsed in the scenarios. Have the client (from the orientation of the future) "think back" through the events (good and bad, etc.) that led to the success.

The protagonist's experience, of course, ought to overlap with the experience of the client to increase the client's involvement in the learning. A metaphor involving mirrorlike reflection is useful with self-image thinking enhancement. For example, the following is a story that I have used often: One of my clients left an evening session to catch an airplane home. His reflection in the plane window that night was his own image altered by the feelings, attitudes, and behaviors gained in the session. The story progresses through different scenarios as the reflection changes and appears to involve other forms and other persons. The reflection must be described in sufficient detail for the client to understand the possibility of looking, feeling, and acting realistically with the new resources. Since self-image thinking requires a good imagination, leaving proper details up to the client is often a poor use of therapy time. If the client could imagine how to better use personal resources to succeed, he or she might not be a client. Self-image building metaphors ought to follow the metaphors that build affect, behavior, and attitude so that the imagining done by the client in the trance facilitates creating models of success. Clients' thinking about any particular new set of conduct will be richer and more fertile than if they are left to unaided speculation. That is, the child abuser can better imagine himself being relaxed and tender about his children after tenderness is evoked (affect protocol) and he is sensitized to tender behaviors (behavior protocol). Even though each metaphor was about some life different from his, the association he will make to tenderness and tender behavior during the self-image metaphor will be more elaborate than if he used his previously unresponsive and unprepared imagination to construct the new roles for himself around his children.

5. Family Structure Change: The Metaphor Protocol

1) Illustrate how the protagonist's discomfort is related to his or her family structure.
2) Illustrate how the protagonist changed his or her relationship within that family.
3) Show how the discomfort was resolved by change in the family.

The general theme of this type of metaphor is that a problem with a symptom disappears when a change occurs in the family. There is no need to make logical the relationship between the symptom and behavior change in the story. All that matters is that the client is invited to wonder about the possibility of effecting the symptom by adjusting the family's structure toward one that is more adaptive. It is advisable for the symptom to be entirely different from the client's. It is often helpful, however, to illustrate a similar behavior in the metaphoric family as the one(s) needed by the client. (These should be changes he or she has not considered.)

6. Enjoyment and Discipline in Living and Changing: The Metaphor Protocol

Finally, this protocol employs an isomorphic construction strategy for metaphors. Metaphors so constructed lend themselves quite well to rather thinly disguised embedded "quotes," commands of psychological implication, direct suggestion, or authoritative advice. Once the decision to act briefly "in loco parentis" has been made, supportive or parenting statements can be delivered to the client. The following protocol provides a useful means for doing so.

1) Create a metaphoric situation that is isomorphic or matches the client's difficulty.
2) Focus awareness on how pleasure is to be found in the situation.
3) Deliver instructions, advice, or commands within the metaphor as with embedded quotes while the pleasure is experienced.

This procedure creates a situation where the client hears direct advice only after he or she has been made experientially ready. It is like telling the protagonist in the metaphor to "make up your mind" after focusing on some pleasant experience such as smiling. The result is that a pleasantly smiling client hears, "Use that experience as you make up your mind about what you're going to do." Consequently, the client can learn a way to develop a more enjoyable way of deciding.

MULTIPLE-EMBEDDED METAPHOR DELIVERY

The final stage involves constructing a vehicle to deliver metaphors to be used in the session to accomplish the therapeutic goals. Placing one story within another is a practice conducted by Erickson that we call multiple-embedded metaphor (Lankton & Lankton, 1983). It can be used to accomplish a number of results including interview management, trance maintenance, and a structure for the several therapeutic goals.

The general structure is shown below:

a)   Induction   Reorientation
b)   Story 1 begins . . .   . . . Story 1 ends.
c)   Story 2 begins . . .   . . . Story 2 ends.
d)   Story 3 complete.

MULTIPLE-EMBEDDED METAPHOR STORY STRUCTURE

The metaphors in sections b, c, and d, above, do not need to be lengthy for the format to result in the multiple-embedded structure. In fact, normal conversation and numerous literary and motion picture examples have conformed to this structure. "Normal" conversation might consist of a discourse such as this: "I went to the theater this weekend . . . , by the way I sat next to an engineer and he said the same thing we heard on TV . . . , remember, the Mazda 626 is the car of the year and a very good buy, . . . and he worked for years in the field—so he ought to know what he's talking about, . . . anyway, the play at the theater was *Master Harold and the Boys*. Have you seen it?"

This type of digression probably is familiar to the reader. Such a communication can manage and convey lots of information, much of it out of context. That is, the information about the Mazda belonged in a context of discussing "best buys in automobiles" and not in the context of discussing the theater. But, the conversation also indicates that the speaker has a deeper and broader relationship to the listener by pre-supposing several other contexts in addition to the theater. A similar result comes from telling longer therapeutic stories within the frame-work. The client is not sure what the context of the comments in b, c and d really was meant to be. The client is free to assume no threat from the possible inference that he or she needs to take the information therein personally. In fact, the information at the vortex (part d) is often lost from consciousness. With the help of confusion or amnesia suggestions bracketing the material at point d, the material delivered there is cus-tomarily able to be forgotten by the client's conscious mind. To some degree amnesia is created by the contextual shifts in the framework, which interrupt conscious associating mechanisms, and by the relief of closure brought about when story 2 (part c) and story 1 (part b) are completed. Moreover, because of the "recency and primacy" effect, there is a tendency to lose conscious access to material that is delivered in the middle of a series.

The crux of the therapy does not take place in any one part of the multiple-embedded structure; it takes place throughout. The need to attend sensitively to the client's ideomotor behavior is of utmost importance because there are times when the treatment plan must be abandoned or temporarily postponed so therapy can deal with unique and unpredicted responses that clients can show. When, on the other hand, treatment is progressing according to plan, it is most efficacious to begin with a metaphor (story 1) that most closely approximates the client's conscious concerns and treatment contract (if he or she came with family concerns, the metaphors might begin with the family metaphor protocol, etc.).

The second metaphor position is well-suited for the retrieval of most or all of the resources that will be used in the session. This is the point for using the affect metaphor protocol or for retrieving trance phenomena (age regression, dissociation, etc.) that will be directly called upon later in the session to reassociate experiences and effect therapeutic goals. The use of indirect suggestions, binds, and short anecdotes while telling the metaphors can increase the client's understanding and involvement in the retrieval of resources. Without the proper engagement of the client in the process of resource development, reassociations or relinkings of experience may be weak, constituting less effective learnings.

Material placed in the vortex (part d), is most protected from the client's conscious mind. It is a fine place to deal with that portion of the problem with which the client is likely to be most defensive or threatened. This is the place in the multiple-embedded structure to work toward resolving unconscious emotional conflict with reframing, reciprocal inhibition, catharsis, reliving and redecision, or other "techniques." In addition, this is the place where therapists can be the most direct or instructive. For instance, the therapist working with a pain control case might direct the dissociation (elicited in part c), from the client's levitated arm to the exact location of a pain experience, thus instructing the client to directly deal with the symptom. In the case of a volatile child abuser the vortex was used to assist the client to do that which would be too threatening otherwise, namely, to be relaxed and tender around his daughter! The rule of thumb: Use the most embedded portion for the protocol that is likely to deal with material that is most threatening to the client's conscious framework.

Story 2, the metaphor introduced to retrieve resources, may be de-signed according to the affect protocol in the first half of the session. In the second phase it should end after utilizing the benefits of the embed-ded framework. The chart below illustrates which protocols may be used in which parts of the multiple-embedded structure and still maximize the logical effect. The column called "Linking" (includes "behavior," "self-image," and "family" protocols) is the most useful for associating the client's new learnings and resources to appropriate contexts, and for maximizing the thoughts of the entire embedded-metaphor structure.

Two protocols can be used to design a single metaphor. Continuity and coherency in the story line can be achieved simply by retaining the same characters and the same locations. For example, in the beginning of story 2 the protagonist is in a relationship that changes and produces bodily-emotional responses (the affect protocol). This story is sus-pended, and a different story with another protocol, and therefore a different goal, is completed at the vortex. When story 2 picks up, again it may employ the behavior protocol. Thus, we might find the protag-onist in the process of learning behaviors that satisfy the treatment plan. The situation in which the protagonist uses the behaviors may be entirely different from that established in the beginning of this story. In this process, the story conforms to one protocol, fulfills that purpose, and then the same story line conforms to another protocol and fulfills that purpose.

This aspect of one metaphor combining two protocols in a single story line can be used twice in the multiple structure. Part b of story 1, for example, can be used to suggest that changes in the client's current development will continue in his or her future development; that is, to associate the gains of the therapy to those occasions when the client will be confronted with new or unexpected life-demands. The child abuser who has learned to be tender to his teenage daughter ought to think a

Protocol	Begin Story 1: *Matching*	Begin Story 2: *Retrieving*	Story 3: *Directing*	End Story 2: *Linking*	End Story 1: *Future*
Attitude	X		X		
Affect		X	(X)		
Behavior	X	X		X	
Self-Image	X			X	X
Family	X			X	X
Discipline	X		X		
other interventions:					
Trance Phenomena		X	X		
Catharsis/Reliving			X		
Conflict Resolution			X		

bit about tenderly, proudly, holding his yet unborn grandchild. When his teenage daughter eventually produces his grandchild, the prearranged associations produce a feeling of success, rather than one of failure because of ruling with an iron hand. The self-image thinking and the family-structure change protocols fill this requirement very well.

It is important to note that the use of three metaphors and five protocols can be too much to plan and present in a single session (the first session, especially). The structure should be modified when this is the case. For example, the extension of therapeutic gains into the future can be postponed until the next session. Nonetheless, a multiple-metaphor structure containing several metaphors and several protocols can be employed in general clinical practice to accomplish therapeutic goals by addressing family members' entire range of personal experience, rather than merely addressing a symptom. Once learned, this approach adds more certainty than difficulty to the conduct of psychotherapy.

The process of formulating therapeutic goals from the assessment may require very little time to several days, but once conceived, the protocols guide the therapist in creating predictable structures to achieve these goals. Once learned and regarded as aids to thoughtful planning, predictable structures can be created in a matter of a few minutes. Such efficiency is one result of this explicit method of formulating Ericksonian interventions.

SUMMARY AND CONCLUSION

What I have outlined is the form of intervention used most frequently in my approach to Ericksonian hypnotherapy. It is not necessarily a single session approach, but an approach that I sometimes extend across several sessions. Although there are instances when I do plan and produce the entire structure in a several-hour session, far more frequently, however, a few sessions spanning two or more months are required. In some cases therapy can continue for more than a year depending on the client's resources, our ability to communicate, and which adjustments of living are being addressed. Most sessions in which I use multiple-embedded metaphor take from one to one and a half hours depending upon how much discussion and feedback of progress precede or follow the treatment.

The thrust of this chapter has been to illustrate one logical structure that underlies diagnosis and treatment planning. It is a structure designed to have an impact on the total person and his or her total life situation rather than on a symptom (C. Lankton, Chapter 10). Thoughtful treatment planning helps therapists organize their attempts to stimulate clients to use their resources to create a holistic change—a change that complements all aspects of their clients' experiential and interpersonal lives. This ambitious aim is undertaken almost regardless of the apparent simplicity of a client's symptoms or problems. Integrating change into all areas of a client's experience is a matter of clinical efficacy that can reinforce, strengthen, and even accelerate the course of therapy. (Brown & Chaves, 1980).

Regardless of the intrigue or the promise that the embedded-metaphor structure can prevail on a clinician's good intentions, it is the general attitude towards a client, as a unique and whole person, that prevails upon a client's well-being. Little has been done to view the benefits of hypnosis within a larger diagnostic framework as in this explication of an Ericksonian approach. Research on successful hypnotherapeutic treatment aimed only at symptom removal is nearsighted. It is necessary to focus on the larger perspective that Ericksonian methodology provides and the extent of improvement that can be realized by considering the whole person.

REFERENCES

Balson, P. M., & Dempster, C. (1980). Treatment of war neurosis from Vietnam. *Comprehensive Psychiatry, 21*(2), 167-175.

Benson, H. (1978). Treatment of anxiety: A comparison of the usefulness of self-hypnosis and meditational relaxation technique: An overview. *Psychotherapy and Psychosomatics, 30*(3-4), 229-242.

Brown, J., & Chaves, J. (1980). Hypnosis in the treatment of sexual dysfunction. *Journal of Sex and Marital Therapy, 6*(1), 63-74.

Carruthers, M. (1981). Voluntary nervous system: Comparison of autogenic training and siddha meditation. *Experimental and Clinical Psychiatry, 6,* 171-181.

Erickson, M. H. (1980). Hypnosis: Its renascence as a treatment modality. In E.L. Rossi (Ed.), *Innovative hypnotherapy: The collected papers of Milton H. Erickson on hypnosis* (Vol. 4, pp. 52-75). NY: Irvington Publishers.

Eysenck, H. J. (1969). Relapse and symptom substitution after different types of psychotherapy. *Behavior Research and Therapy, 7*(3), 283-287.

Gerschman, J., Burrows, G., & Fitzgerald, P. (1981). Hypnosis in the control of gagging. *Australian Journal of Clinical and Experimental Hypnosis, 9*(2), 53-59.

Greenberg, I. (1977). *Group hypnotherapy and hypnodrama.* Chicago, IL: Nelson-Hall.

Haley, J. (1973). *Uncommon therapy: The psychiatric techniques of Milton H. Erickson.* NY: Norton.

Horowitz, S. L. (1970). Strategies within hypnosis for reducing phobic behavior. *Journal of Abnormal Psychology, 75*(1), 104-112.

Howard, W. L. (1979). The modification of self-concept, anxiety and neuro-muscular performance through rational stage directed hypnotherapy: A cognitive experiential perspective using cognitive restructuring and hypnosis. *Dissertation Abstracts International, 40*(4-A), 1962.

Klug, B. (1980). Hypnosis as a treatment modality in psychiatric practice. *Australian Journal of Clinical and Experimental Hypnosis, 8*(1), 37-40.

Lankton, C. (This volume). Generative change: Beyond symptom control.

Lankton, S., & Lankton, C. (1983). *The answer within: A clinical framework of Ericksonian hypnotherapy.* NY: Brunner/Mazel.

Lankton, S., & Lankton, C. (1984). Ericksonian styles of paradoxical treatment. In G. Weeks (Ed.), *Promoting change through paradoxical treatment.* NY: Dow Jones-Erwin.

Leary, T. (1957). *Interpersonal diagnosis of personality.* NY: Ronald.

Marks, I. (1971). Phobic disorders four years after treatment: A prospective follow-up. *British Journal of Psychiatry, 118*(547), 683-688.

Van Pelt, S. J. (1975). The role of hypnotic suggestion in the aetiology and treatment of the psychoneurotic. *Journal of the American Institute of Hypnosis, 16*(6), 27-33.

Waxman, D. (1975). Hypnosis in the psychotherapy of neurotic illness. *British Journal of Medical Psychology, 48*(4), 339-348.

Chapter 12

Generative Autonomy: Principles for an Ericksonian Hypnotherapy

Stephen G. Gilligan

INTRODUCTION

I do not know much about gods; but I think that the river
Is a strong brown god—sullen, untamed, and intractable,
Patient to some degree, at first recognised as a frontier;
Useful, untrustworthy, as a conveyor of commerce;
Then only a problem confronting the builder of bridges.
The problem once solved, the brown god is almost forgotten
By the dwellers in cities—ever, however, implacable.
Keeping his seasons and rages, destroyer, reminder
Of what men choose to forget. Unhonoured, unpropitiated
By worshippers of the machine, but waiting, watching and waiting.
His rhythm was present in the nursery bedroom,
In the rank ailanthus of the April dooryard,
In the smell of grapes of the autumn table,
And the evening circle in winter gaslight.

The river is within us, the sea is all about us.

(From *Four Quartets*, by T.S. Eliot)

I think the "strong brown god" flowed through Milton Erickson. He moved with the life rhythms that most of us have forgotten but can never escape from. His words and his expressions washed away the dust of our everyday living and freed many feet entrenched in the dried mud of frozen positions. Like water, Erickson adapted his form of expression to the ruts, grooves, and patterns of the ever-changing, unfolding terrain.

Sadly, Milton Erickson is no longer with us. Yet he was around long enough to inspire many people to realize that the river *is* within each of us and that the sea *does* surround us all. What do we do with this realization? We can sink or swim; we can dam or build bridges that lead us to forget; we can continue to explore these waters on our own.

Generations pass and pass on their "living ideas" to the next generation. Now that a new season is upon us, how shall we as a "common-unity" of individuals inspired by Milton Erickson respond? Milton Erickson was one of a kind, especially in his special ability to experientially convey that *each of us is one of a kind*, though we all share a deep common-unity. Thus, a shared set of values, ideas, and principles will be expressed in different ways by different individuals.

Realizing this "autonomy in common-unity" was easier when Erickson was the unitary *embodiment* of "Ericksonian approaches." Now, I believe the challenge is to cooperate, rather than compete—to further develop some extraordinary ideas.

This chapter is offered as a possible contribution to this process.* It presents the view that the "reality" we experience is self-generated by processes circular (and thus usually unconscious) in nature. A further assumption is that these self-reflexive processes can culminate in either expanding circles of autonomy or "vicious" circles (cycles) of unchanging patterns, depending on whether experience is valued or devalued. The problem processes also are seen to be the solution processes; this is the fundamental Ericksonian principle of utilization. Thus, the structure of therapy is determined by the structure of the client's "reality," *not* by some *a priori* frame held by the therapist. The hypnotherapist joins a client's "circle" of recursive looping to expand a self-devaluing "intrapersonal trance" to a self-valuing "interpersonal trance" state. Hypnotherapeutic skills of 1) context valuing, 2) balancing complementary relationships, and 3) generating multiple associative pathways are utilized in "re-sourcing" a client's "circle of autonomy." This "circle" ac-

---

*Among those to whom I owe debts of intellectual and personal gratitude are Milton Erickson, Gregory Bateson, T.S. Eliot, Gordon Bower, Buckminster Fuller, John Lilly, G. Spencer Brown and Francisco Varela. Also, my deepest acknowledgment goes to Denise Ross, who inspired and supported my explorations with her irreplaceable love and partnership.

cesses the "generative unconscious" which is a source of transformational change.

To develop these themes, the first section overviews key ideas regarding how a reality comes into being via acts of distinction. The second section applies these ideas to seven representative areas of Ericksonian hypnotherapy: 1) problems as double binds; 2) the hypnotherapy relationship; 3) the hypnotherapist's personal absorption in the hypnotic interaction; 4) generating interpersonal trance loops; 5) the circular structuring of ideas in the hypnotic loop; 6) "circuit breaking" loops as diagnostic cues; and 7) a general hypnotherapy procedure for reuniting organizational structures within their circle of autonomy.

DRAWING DISTINCTIONS

A major tenet of this chapter is that we actively participate in generating our experience. The Ericksonian therapist thus seeks to identify *how* a client is generating painful realities, and then utilizes these very processes to enable their transformation. This approach assumes that no "objective reality" exists independent of observers, and that all experience and behavior emerges from, and indicates values of, relationships. Accordingly, self-referential paradoxes are unavoidable, i.e., *all relationships are circular in nature*. This applies not only to a client's interactions in "problem" situations, but to the therapist's interactions with clients. All expressions—internal experience, diagnoses, techniques, etc.—simultaneously indicate the "reality" of *both* "subject" *and* "object" (and thus are neither "subjective" nor "objective"). In this "both/and" view, the therapist is a "co-operator" in an "inter*personal*" relationship, *not* a "programmer" or impersonal (i.e., depersonalized) operator. This relationship, like any other, can be either a "vicious cycle" in which the client's experience continues to be devalued or a "common-unity context" enabling autonomous and self-valuing change processes.

In this view, the distinctions one makes are fundamental to the reality one experiences. This section briefly overviews key ideas underlying this orientation.

Distinctions as Purposive Acts

Any reality is the result of self-generated distinctions. This view is expressed most cogently by the work of G. Spencer Brown (1979), who observed:

A universe comes into being when a space is severed or taken apart. The skin of a living organism cuts off an outside from an inside. So does the circumference of a circle in a plane. By tracing the way we represent such a severance, we can begin to reconstruct, with an accuracy and coverage that appear almost uncanny, the basic forms underlying linguistic, mathematical, physical, and biological science, and can begin to see how the familiar laws of our own experience follow inexorably from the original act of severance. The act is itself already remembered, even if unconsciously, as our first attempt to distinguish different things in a world where, in the first place, the boundaries can be drawn anywhere we please. At this stage the universe cannot be distinguished from how we act upon it, and the world may seem like shifting sand beneath our feet. (p. xxix)

Thus, a reality—individual or collective—arises and is maintained by self-distinguished relationships. A primary distinction is an act or *injunction* that *crosses* the boundary of a unified space and cleaves it into "inner" and "outer" states, thereby calling into existence a complementary correlation within a common-unity space.*

As can be seen in the simple illustration of Figure 1, *distinction is a form of closure, an act of generating boundaries.* A distinction is a correlation, a distinguished relationship, an indication of "this and not that."

A distinction expresses the values and intentions of the distinguisher, indicating a "difference which makes a difference" (Bateson, 1979). As Brown (1979, p. 1) notes, "There can be no distinction without motive, and there can be no motive unless contents are seen to differ in value." Thus, one side of a distinction is "marked" (i.e., exhibited, emphasized, "pointed to," identified) as having some particular value; the

---

*As will be elaborated throughout the paper, the view is not one of causality but rather "co-relation"; that is, a phenomenological reality "e-merges" to express relationship values. We can choose how to cooperate with these self-distinguished relationships (and thereby determine the quality of our experience), but we can never unilaterally control them, since all relationships have the paradoxical quality of being "a part of and apart from" the observer-participant.

This view differs radically ("from the root or center") from the rational ("ratio-making" or "dividing") doctrine which most of us have learned to accept without question. It does not reject the "either/or" logic of the rational approach, but emphasizes it within the deeper and more inclusive context of "both/and" logic. A major foundation for this new epistemology is modern physics (e.g., see Zukav, 1979). In this regard, it is ironic that psychology developed its structural foundations according to those of 19th century physics, but has virtually ignored the revolutionary developments in physics in this century that have shown these foundations to be markedly inadequate.

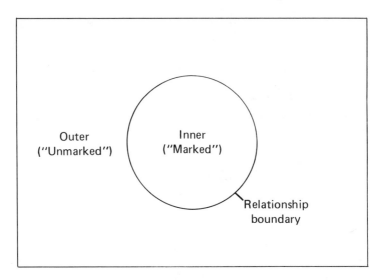

Figure 1. The act of distinction

other is "unmarked" (i.e., inhibited). The marked state is a figure within the "ground" or "field" of the unmarked state. Both states are united in a deeper common-unity, although this is not evident phenomenologically ("in appearances"). Thus, every distinction contains 1) a marked state, 2) a complementary unmarked state, 3) a correlational boundary (i.e., a mutually specifying relationship), and 4) a deeper common-unity. Also, *every distinction is self-referential*; i.e., it refers back to its maker.

In this regard, *the most primitive distinction we make is the self-definition of our respective identities as autonomous (self-regulating) persons within a "common-unity."* This self-identity is fundamental to our existence, serving as the constant context filter which generates (i.e., determines) what we experience (and don't experience), what we do (and don't do), what we value (and don't value), etc.

Precisely because it is a primitive distinction (i.e., a fundamental *context*), self-identity is not directly observable. It can, however, be inferred from invariances and regularities in its structural interactions (behavioral, cognitive, imaginal, etc.). Some parameters we will consider in this regard include: 1) *where the primary boundaries are drawn* (e.g., individual, family, group); 2) *the criteria of a distinction* (e.g., What "outside" state(s) mutually define the distinguished boundaries? How are the complementary states seen to differ in content and value? Are these differences valued or devalued?); 3) *the flexibility (or rigidity) of relationship boundaries* (e.g., Do they contract and expand rhythmically according to organismic needs?); and 4) *any devaluing and dissociated "loops"* (i.e., recurrent patterns of self-devaluation).

Depths of Self-Distinctions

An individual operates in domains of experience in patterned fashions. These patterns are essential for stability and for growth but, like all artifacts, they have equal potential to limit or liberate. To appreciate how they are used in Self-expression, four levels of Self-distinction may be distinguished: 1) Self-common-unity as the life essence; 2) Self-autonomy as organizational unity; 3) Self as complementary correlator; and 4) Self as varying correlations of interactional content.

The illustration shown in Figure 2 may be considered from an inner-

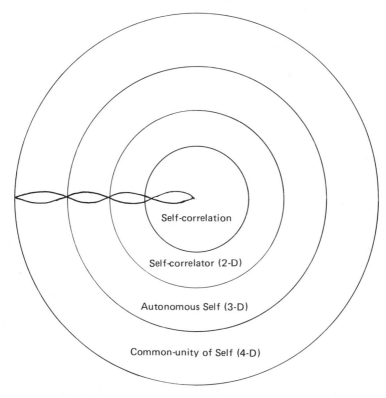

Figure 2. Depths of self-distinction: One possible set of boundaries

outer or outer-inner viewpoint. That is, movement can and does occur in both directions: outwards (towards more awareness) and inwards (towards less awareness and more reference). From this view, an experiential reality is a phenomenological "standing wave" or "interference pattern" generated from the interaction of outwards- and inward-directed signals.

1) Self as common-unity

This primary distinction may be considered as the source of generativity referred to by Erickson (1980b, p. 345) as "that vital sense of the beingness of the self (that) is often overlooked." It is usually overlooked precisely because it is not phenomenologically apparent. In fact, it cannot be controlled or represented in any way other than metaphor. It is the un-nameable, the Tao, the essence of common-unity, the Deep Self, the collective unconscious. It is, to use the words of T.S. Eliot (1963), "a condition of complete simplicity costing not less than everything."

We might imagine the Deep Self as a four-dimensional hypersphere enfolded in the topological form of a torus. The torus ("Möbius sphere" or "doughnut sphere") has been used by Einstein and Eddington as a model of the universe (Davis & Hersh, 1981; Young, 1972; Zukav, 1979). Among its fascinating properties is that every point in the sphere is a center point, being described by the same Fourier transform mathematics used to generate holograms (Davis & Hersh, 1981). Thus, the whole is contained in each of the points (as in holograms). In this view, each person is a unique representation of the same "seed."

A dynamic representation of the torus is a tornado, whose complementary actions are illustrated in Figure 3.

2) Self as organizational autonomy

This next level is the spherical domain of phenomenological experience and of systemic organization. It is the domain of the "personal unconscious" that distinguishes "self" (as individual, family, culture, etc.) from "other." Critical at this level is the notion of autonomy ("self-regulation"). Autonomy reflects the wonder of a unique life (within the common-unity of Life), a distinct form within (the universe of) Form. Autonomy does not separate but distinguishes a being as "a part of and apart from" the common-unity. This complementary relationship implies complementary goals: (a) preserve the circle of organizational identity and (b) regenerate and expand autonomy (i.e., grow).

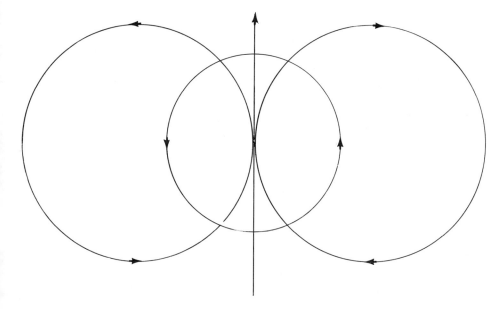

Figure 3. Separate motions of the torus vortex

The concept of autonomy is central in Ericksonian therapy. Erickson (1952) distinguished the "core personality" of the patient from the expressed personality patterns, and suggested that even though the client was unaware of this "core," it was that which the therapist needed to align with and stimulate for therapeutic change.

A system's sphere of autonomy is the organizational identity through which it can interact with integrity ("wholeness") in the common-unity. The sphere of autonomy expands through developmental cycles ("circles") of transformation which expand its domain. A transformational cycle is like a quantum (whole unit) leap to a next wave orbit; learnings from previous cycles remain along with fundamental relationships, but their values and expressions are modified by the additional "response-abilities," capacities, and challenges of the next autonomous context. For example, one's parents will always be one's parents and the biological and social patterns inherited from them are non-negatable; but growth in autonomy achieves increased "response-ability" for individual ("individuating") modifications of these patterns, thereby enabling (though not assuring) the continued growth of individual and common-unity.

3) *Self as complementary correlator*

To express autonomy within common-unity, a system requires relationship ("correlational") structures. Thus, this two-dimensional level
is the domain of the "conscious mind," the correlator and intentional
actor, the symbolic ("re-presenting") self. It might be represented to-
pologically as "hemi-spheres," triangles, or circles. It is the domain of
roles, sensory-motor cybernetic loops, goal-achieving programs, analysis, rationality ("ratio-making"). Distinctions may be organized at this
level in terms of triadic unities such as those shown in Figure 4.

4) *Self as correlational content*

From the correlation of complementary structures, the content of experience emerges. The transitory content of experience (behavior,
thoughts, feelings, images, cognitions, etc.) "e-merges" from relationship. The content is the form resulting from ongoing interference patterns (e.g., correlations).

Concluding Notes

To conclude this overview of the centrality of distinction in generating
experience, a few additional points might be made.

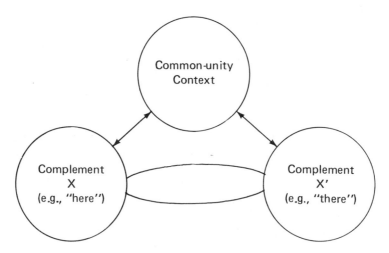

Figure 4. The triadic unity of complements in common-unity

1) We cannot NOT participate!

We can never operate "outside" of the universe. We actively participate in constructing our reality. No observation (description, relationship, perception, etc.) occurs independently from the actions (i.e.,
distinctions) of an observer. Reality is not "out there" in an "object"
sense; "reality" is the constellation of experiential correlations expressing
distinctions that *we* draw (mostly unconsciously). Thus, we are responsible for (and thus able to respond to) our experience.

*2) The principles of unity, complementarity, and multiplicity are
extremely generative for Ericksonian hypnotherapy*

Organizational unity is assumed to underlie all correlations and distinctions. Unity forms a common-unity context in which all complementary structures interact—e.g., "inner/outer," "observer/observed,"
"friend/enemy," "sound/silence," "self/other," "thinker/thought," etc.
This common-unity is often not realized. Complements become framed
in an either/or relationship of opposition ("standing in the way of") or
dissociation, thereby prompting attempts to develop (or identify with)
one complement and control ("defeat," "overcome," "get rid of," etc.)
the other. Since complements are inseparable (though distinguishable)
and negation is impossible, such control strategies usually create increasingly "vicious" cycles (i.e., circles) of dissociational functioning. As
we will see, a major therapeutic value of trance is its "both/and" quality
("a part of and apart from," as in "my hand is lifting but I'm not lifting
it") which allows integration of common-unity complements.

3) Distinctions are arbitrary, but their consequences are not

The integrity ("wholeness") of our distinctions is reflected in the consequences of our actions. Any representation (e.g., image, theory, description, interpretation) is a biased "suggestion" regarding *what* to
observe and *where* to observe it from. A representation is a time-frozen,
fixed-position "pointer" to a pattern which it is not. Thus, multiple
instances of complementary ("double") descriptions are generally needed.

4) We are the territory, but only perceive the maps

Korzybski's (1933) dictum that the map is not the territory is often
used to claim that we don't have direct access to "the world of experi-

ence." This proposal does not jibe well with the view that we create our world of experience. While our phenomenological experience is limited to three-dimensional transformations, our Self is undeniably part of the unitary, four-dimensional universe. We can only talk about or conceptualize maps, but primary knowing (such as in deep trance) can be made of the territory from which such maps are derived. Stated in another way, we can know the territory but not know we know the territory.

5) A distinction may be called ("indicated" or "named") in many ways: commands, instructions, names, descriptions, expressions, etc.

This indication may be recalled also in many ways: posthypnotic cues, images, internal dialogue, posture, names. Calls may differ in appearance, but are identical in indicating the underlying motive and marked value of a distinction. This equivalency allows condensation or reducibility of a number of calls to the value of the primary distinction. The value of a call made again (and again, however many times one wishes) is thus simply the value of one call (Brown, 1979).

This equivalency of different names of a distinction may help or hamper change. For example, individuals seeking therapy are typically dominated by "re-calls" of some self-devaluing state. That is, they repeatedly call forth some undesirable and threatening state which they (erroneously) perceive as being "caused" by "non-self" actions—i.e., by uncontrollable "outside" influences such as harassing thoughts, "the past," family members or other persons, etc. In such cases, individuals are generally not aware that the problem states are self-generated, for straightforward reasons to be addressed later.

A somewhat less obvious example concerns the theoretical frames of the therapist. A therapist using models specifying *a priori* content values (e.g., diagnostic categories) will generally perceive only the values and distinctions projected by that model (e.g., Rosenhan, 1984). Many argue that no viable alternatives exist, that some biased structure is needed. Erickson demonstrated otherwise in his emphasis on creating a "new theory" for every client. He emphasized the need for the therapist to "degenerate" his or her description frames and tune to (and utilize) those unavoidably expressed by the client. Tuning to how the client recalls an undesirable state, the hypnotherapist can then apply the Ericksonian cornerstone principle of utilization by acting in accord with the client's distinctions. This synchronization makes the "external" experience of the client equivalent in value to his or her "internal" experience. This enhances trust and cooperation, allowing for the dissipation of rigid frameworks and the autonomous development of generative trance processes.

With these distinctions in mind, let us turn to consideration of their clinical applications.

GENERATIVE AUTONOMY IN THE HYPNOTHERAPEUTIC RELATIONSHIP

To give a flavor of how ideas of generative autonomy can be applied in Ericksonian hypnotherapy, seven representative topics are overviewed in this section: 1) problems as double binds; 2) the hypnotherapy relationship; 3) the hypnotherapist's personal absorption in the hypnotic interaction; 4) generating interpersonal trance loops; 5) the circular structuring of ideas in the hypnotic loop; 6) "circuit-breaking" loops as diagnostic cues; and 7) a general hypnotherapy procedure for reuniting organizational structures within their circle of autonomy.

Problems as Double Binds

Autonomy ("self-regulation") is essential to the existence of any organizational unity, and therefore will always be the dominant intention underlying expressions. Autonomy does not separate but distinguishes a being as "a part of and apart from" the community. This complementary relationship implies complementary goals: 1) preserve the circle of organizational identity, and 2) regenerate and expand autonomy (i.e., grow). When these complementary goals are not achieved, contradictory expressions and recurrent problems are the result.

In other words, problems develop when a correlational complement is devalued, forbidden, dissociated, etc. The result is that the system is split into oppositional camps, with the autonomy of the common-unity thus lost to both complements. To understand how this might occur, imagine a person cycling through dynamic complement loops within the circle of autonomy. At some point in this sequence, the person might interrupt participation in the dynamic loop. Rest might be needed, or threat to the integrity of the circle of autonomy may be encountered. In the latter case, the immediate priority of the system will be to desist from complementary interaction, "freeze" the circular loop in its present state (i.e., time-bind it, as in making an image), and withdraw into the circle of autonomy to protect and be protected. This withdrawal is natural, common, and essential, and will be evidenced by autonomic "fight or flee" cues such as restriction of breathing and motoric movements in general, disruption of natural rhythm in expression, increased tension, etc. These responses are necessary and vital messages reminding the person that as a precious and unique autonomous being, he or she is vulnerable (i.e., sensitive, alive) and therefore needs to balance contact and withdrawal in common-unity interactions.

The defensive state of tension, conscious monitoring, and physical rigidity will *not* dissipate until it is acknowledged and valued. While such a state is active, the person cannot participate directly (i.e., spontaneously) in the Natural domain; his or her actions will be regulated by computations made in the Imaginal and Symbolic domains. If this restriction persists, the tension ("holding pattern") will become "condensed" into symbolic and imaginal (i.e., time-frozen) distinctions, thereby giving rise to derived (mis)identification states such as "ego," "anxiety," and "conscious mind." The circle of autonomy will become dissociated from the dynamic expressions of its complements, though the underlying common-unity will always remain. (An individual is "indivisible," regardless of his or her experience or conceptions. Thus, you can't go anywhere without "your" Self or can't "find" your Self anywhere but where it always is—right where you are.)

At some point, however, the person will need to reconnect with and complete the *relationship* in the dynamic loop from which he or she "exited." (The alternative is to have the dissociated structure dominate your experience with absolute, life-denying certainty.) Reuniting Self with self-distinction (e.g., organizational identity) requires a sense of security and autonomy; *a person will never attempt to recross "time-frozen" boundaries if their integrity is in jeopardy.* The needed security can often be gained from a rest period or a recentering (e.g., trance), but sometimes one must develop greater integrity (i.e., increased autonomy) before reuniting the severed states. An example of this is traumatic incidents (e.g., rape or war victims), where the violation of integrity that prompted the dissociative withdrawal is so severe ("severing") that reuniting Self and expressions is often only possible after autonomous growth has been achieved.

It is important to realize that dissociation is not from a place or thing or object, but from an *experiential correlation* (i.e., a relationship pattern). These correlations are not time/space structures but patterns or forms of severing a unified space (Brown, 1979). (As T.S. Eliot [1963] remarked, "History is a pattern of timeless moments.") Paradoxically, dissociation affirms association at a deeper level. (As Freud noted about repression, the denial always affirms.) One cannot negate or escape self-correlations, because they never "go" anywhere; they are "time-frozen" states which can be transformed only by reentry and revaluation.

In this view, there is no "past" to "go back into"; problems are expressions of self-devaluing, time-frozen (i.e., nonrhythmic) oscillation patterns that are "a part of and apart from" a person's organizational identity. These time-frozen patterns act as screens to separate a person from others. Because all transactions will be conducted through these screens, problems are always in the "present tense," staring a person right in the face (so to speak). The transitory content of the problem—e.g., where it first started—is quite irrelevant. The "pattern which disconnects"—to subvert Bateson's (1979) distinction—is "the thing."

In life, the patterns which connect are always deeper (and thus less apparent) than those which disconnect. Thus, while a person may be dissociated at functional levels, he or she is always unitary ("indivisible") at the deeper (autonomy in common-unity) level of Self. Consequently, *a person's "unconscious" autonomy will always be generating that which is needed for integration and growth.* In other words, solutions are always present, awaiting discovery. They will become apparent (i.e., phenomenologically realized) only when dissociated experience (i.e., devalued relationships) is valued; they become more obscure when experience is devalued, as when a person identifies with one complement and attempts to dissociate from the other. In this sense, the solution is always contained in the problem, while the attempted solution contains (i.e., constrains) the problem from resolution.

This paradoxical relationship will be evidenced by a person "spinning" reiteratively through the same problem loop sequence—i.e., through structural invariance in interaction processes. In hypnotherapy, trance is used as an opportunity to allow a person to stop "spinning his wheels," and return to the Self center in the circle of autonomy in order to rebalance the system and allow generative autonomy to develop new expressions more suitable for the present needs.

Problems become chronic when a person (mis)identifies with one complement (X or X') and disidentifies with the other complement. Such a Self-(mis)identification initiates a vicious cycle of devaluation which cannot be changed through any consciously attempted solutions. (Mis)identifying with one complement, a person (mis)perceives the other complement as a threat to his or her identity and therefore devalues it as the "opposition" (i.e., the position of acting against). This self-generated devaluation is misattributed to the "reality" of the "world out there," thereby again severing "inner" and "outer" (self/other) complements. Severation becomes perseveration, and the individual becomes "locked" in the "cells" of his or her time-frozen pattern, barred from spontaneously participating or directly experiencing the natural domain.

Thus develops a reiterative cycle of self-defeating, dysfunctional dissociation. The paradoxical complements of self-expression become devalued, and a both/and complementarity degenerates into a neither/nor "no win" situation masquerading as "either/or" logic with "we shall conquer" rationality ("ratio" meaning dividing x/x'). Instead of the two hands of indivisible common-unity self-referentially drawing each other (as in the famous Escher prints), they viciously attack each other, oblivious of their interdependence.

This situation is never self-reflectively (i.e., "consciously") apparent, precisely because of the (mis)identification with the complements. Not only will the person be oblivious to their essential contributions in generating and maintaining a recurrent ("re-circling") problem, investigation will reveal that what the person thinks he or she is expressing in a problem situation is exactly the opposite of the actual expressions.

The more the person tries to overcome the problem, the more he or she creates and strengthens it. Oppositional splits between complements deepen and mutual devaluation increases, thereby intensifying the dissociation from the common-unity circle of autonomy which is the sole source of generativity for any integral solution. In other words, individuals become increasingly dissociated from their "unconscious mind" and more and more (mis)identified with the regulation of the "conscious mind." The generative autonomy they desperately seek is the generative autonomy they continually deny. This double bind creates "symptoms" which ingeniously express the nature of the devalued unconscious autonomy characterizing the system. This is the position the person is typically inhabiting when entering the therapy office. Let us move to examine some ways in which this state of affairs might be utilized and transformed.

The Paradoxical Nature of the Hypnotherapy Relationship

First and foremost, hypnotherapy is a cooperative correlation between autonomous individuals in a common-unity context. Therapist and client are *equals* at the most fundamental level; both are unique, incomparable individuals sharing a common ground of being. Realization of this fact is the basis for generative autonomy. The client is first and foremost a person to be valued and respected, not a depersonalized category or object to be manipulated.

Within this context of mutual autonomy, the therapist assumes the problem is also the solution. (This is the basis of Erickson's utilization principle.) The therapist experientially joins the client's system to expand its intrapersonal loops to an interpersonal circle. As a complementary co-operator both "inside" and "outside" the system, the therapist stimulates transformation by valuing its context, balancing its complements, and eliciting new modes of expression.

The therapist becomes "a part of" the system by *absorbing* the client's patterns, but operates "apart from" the devaluing correlations which disallow generative autonomy. This paradoxical "both/and" process is best accomplished through hypnotic processes, since a distinguishing characteristic of trance is this experience of operating as "a part of yet apart from" (e.g., Erickson & Rossi, 1981; Gilligan, 1981).

To the extent that the therapist matches client patterns while protecting client autonomy, therapeutic communications are "irresistible." The form (i.e., patterns) of the client's "inner" and "outer" world becomes indistinguishable, thereby voiding the "wall" between these states. *Trance emerges spontaneously as a result.* Thus, trance isn't induced by one person "doing something" to another (e.g., "putting them under"); it unfolds from experiential co-operation.

This trance is interpersonal in nature. The client feels "a part of but apart from" both his or her experience and from the hypnotherapist. It is a paradoxical "trinity" relationship in which therapist, client, and the therapist/client relationship are autonomous systems co-operating in common-unity.*

This experiential relationship may be viewed as a mutual trance developed from a mutual induction. The client serves up the structural induction (i.e., the patterns of his or her "reality"); the therapist counters with the context induction which values the presented patterns. The therapist does not identify with the binds or devaluing processes of the client's induction, but rather remains centered in an autonomous, externally directed state of experiential absorption in which his or her primary commitment is to protect and support the client's autonomy. (This relationship is not unlike the nondominating supervision an adult provides a child playing in a playground.) The therapist does not directly challenge the problem "trance" but rather seeks to expand its scope, enhance its attentional flexibility, balance its complementary relationships, and diversify the ways in which it is expressed.

The Hypnotherapist's Personal Absorption in Hypnotic Processes

Many difficulties arise from the time-frozen view that a therapist can or should be impersonally involved with clients. Many therapists believe

---

*It might be noted that this same "trinity" obtains in other mutually valuing relationships of intimacy. There is "me" plus "you" plus "us"; $1 + 1 = 3$. The illusions of control or separateness dissipate in such interactions, making possible the generative autonomy of creative expression.

that "one cannot not communicate" (Watzlawick, Beavin, & Jackson, 1967), but ignore or deny that an important correlate is "one cannot not experience." Consequently, false dichotomies between "objective" behavioral observations and "subjective" feeling processes are often constructed. This forces a "choice" between whether the therapist should deny feelings or indulgently focus on them. Both roads empty into the same ditch: feelings becoming dissociated and condensed with images and cognitions into "e-motions" ("away from motion"). To reiterate, feelings express ongoing correlations in physical domains (rhythm, resonance, shifts), while emotions are condensed feeling/cognition/image units symbolizing personal values (Gilligan, 1982; Gilligan & Bower, 1984). In other words, feelings are properties of natural *environment*, while emotions express values of constructed *systems*.

Feelings are essential to establishing any rhythmic and continuous expression. They are a major channel for tuning and remaining sensitive to the client's processes, and are fundamental to effective hypnotic communications and therapeutic observations. Feelings are analogical (continuous), not digital (discrete) communications. Thus, prolonged *discussion* of feeling often leads to a reified conceptual exchange where attempts are made to be "warm, empathetic and genuine." Thus, the hypnotherapist doesn't really talk about or categorize the content of feelings too much, but rather feels them like a continuous vibration (as in listening/feeling music) to modulate experiential involvement.

The hypnotherapist invites personal involvement in trance processes through experiential feelings. In this regard, I find the following principle tremendously valuable as an ethical and practical guide:

> Do not ask, direct, or expect the client to do or experience anything hypnotically until you (the hypnotherapist) have experientially demonstrated to yourself and to the client your own willingness and ability to do the same.

In other words, respond to your own suggestions before asking the client to do so. Generate the general state within yourself, and then invite the client to participate in it in their own fashion. As Erickson noted:

> It is your attitude toward the patient that determines the results you achieve. . . . Whenever you want any hypnotic results with your patients, you had better mean what you say. All you need to do (in order to convince yourself) is to look back through your

own personal history as a functioning human being. Look back to when you've had an anesthesia, when you've had analgesia. Recognize that you've had amnesia . . . on innumerable occasions. You really don't differ from other, normal human beings. Your total experience should teach that you are not asking anything of your patients that is beyond their abilities. When you give a suggestion to a patient, you'd better keep in mind, "I *know* this patient can develop an analgesia—I *know* this patient can develop an anesthesia—I *know* this patient can develop amnesia. (In Rossi, Ryan, & Sharp, 1983, p. 125)

Generating the Interpersonal Trance Loop

To generate an "interpersonal trance" with a client, the therapist must first "degenerate" his or her frames of correlation (i.e., "conscious mind"). Having emptied his or her own "tea cups," the therapist can absorb the client's "cup of tea." This is achieved by developing a trance-like state characterized by enhanced sensory awareness, balanced tonicity, experiential absorption, rhythmic continuity, effortlessness, non-linear thinking, and *complete orientation to the client*. Erickson commented on the therapeutic value of operating from such a state (Erickson & Rossi, 1977):

> If I have any doubts about my capacity to see the important things I go into a trance. When there is a crucial issue with a patient and I don't want to miss any of the clues I go into trance . . . I start keeping close track of every movement, sign, or behavioral manifestation that could be important. And as I began speaking to you just now my vision becomes tunnel-like and I saw only you and your chair. It happened automatically, that terrible intensity, as I was looking at you. The word "terrible" is wrong; it's pleasurable. (p. 42)

I suggest that these "working trances" may be essential to understanding and practicing Ericksonian hypnotherapy. Their paradoxes and complementarities—and especially their emphasis on a generative "unconscious mind"—seem to lie outside the boundaries (i.e., limitations) of a "normal" waking state.

Generating and utilizing this "both/and" state of generative autonomy is a clinical skill that needs to be learned and refined. The autonomy of both therapist and client need to be maintained while the deeper common-unity between the two is realized. This generally requires a warm-up period in which participants "feel each other out." The connection will unfold differently on each occasion.

There are many ways this process might be developed. I will note here in a general way some aspects of what I commonly experience in this regard. I usually begin by engaging the client in addressing general, open-ended issues. I'll initiate a transition process by fixating "over there" on the client. This allows me to enter trance while fully absorbed in the client's processes, not my own. Eyes may be softened or diverted if the connection between participants seems too intense for either participant, but the maintenance of an absorbed gaze is one of the quickest ways to develop trance in both self and other. (People need to shift their eyes to stay in an analytical state!) Tunnel vision usually develops within several minutes, and things get a little hazy momentarily as this dissociative state develops. I find it essential to remain fixated externally on the subject while also monitoring my physical comfort (e.g., breathing, distributed tension) during this time of boundary remarking.

Posture, muscle tension, breathing, and physical distance are all important factors. I find it important to adjust to a balanced symmetry in postural orientation (with slight forward tilting), with both feet flat on the floor. I begin to "suspend" my rhythms and "feel out" for the underlying rhythm of the client. (Breathing, pulse rate, and motor movements can be used as indicators, but these are not sufficient.) Everybody has a unique rhythm! At some point, a very distinct sense of a flowing feeling loop begins to develop.* Both parties usually soften, and I usually shift to an innocuous topic to allow time to adjust to this interpersonal trance. Muscle tonus takes on the balanced tonicity characteristic of ideo-dynamic (i.e., generative autonomy) expression (Erickson & Rossi, 1981), and an effortless sense of interpersonal connection develops.

While hypnotically synchronizing with a person, I find it essential to periodically veer away from attending to any specific aspect of the client's communications (especially their verbalizations), and work instead to develop a state of equi-potential attentional distribution, such that no "figures" exist (i.e., stand out) from the perceptual "ground." In this unusual attentional state, sensory modalities begin to merge together and perceptual blurring often occurs temporarily. It is at this point that synchronized hypnotic responses with the client develop, along with a heightened sense of autonomy (in both parties typically). This correlation

---

*For reviews of the extensive research on rhythmic synchronization ("entrainment"), see Leonard (1978) and Hall (1983).

is partly the result of the therapist having developed the trance by absorbing the client's patterns. To reiterate, such "interpersonal trances" can be developed only at a rate and pace suitable to both parties. If either party pulls away at any point, this indicates the need to slow down and perhaps take a break.

As the "interpersonal trance" loop unfolds, the therapist will often discover various images, feelings, or minute details (e.g., a particular emphasis given to a word) "popping out" into awareness. That is, attention is drawn to some idiosyncratic pattern. These are often spontaneous unconscious indicators of "where the action is." Thus, the hypnotherapist might puzzle over the possible significance of such cues even while continuing the general loop of the interpersonal trance.

These descriptions may seem rather bizarre, or too complex, or otherwise disconcerting to the reader. Again, it should be noted that the processes of hypnotherapy are naturalistic and therefore represented in other situational interactions as well. The "far-out" experiences one can have in reading science fiction, watching an engaging drama, listening to favorite music, playing competitive sports, making love, or daydreaming may be relevant reference structures. A major difference may be that the processes just described involve personal and professional responsibilities with another person. I believe that the exceedingly complex task of hypnotherapy requires both systematic, sincere, and careful planning and creative, nonlinear, and hypnotic interaction. To master this complementary balance, rigorous training is required.

The Balance Principle in Hypnotic Communications

The principle can be stated as follows:

> Generative autonomy is generated, maintained, and expanded by a co-operative expression of complementary forms.

The balance principle assumes that the mutually inclusive logic of "both/and" is a deeper and more generative relationship structure than the mutually exclusive logic of "either/or." "Either/or" relationships represent symmetrical complements (x, x') as $\{x \text{ and not } x'\}$, and are therefore useful in indicating preference, bias, sequence, intention, and so on. If the complements are expressed in a *rhythmic* and balanced (i.e., oscillating) fashion over time, such biasing is valuable. If an imbalance develops, the autonomy of the system will be threatened and behavior will become rigid and defensive.

The balance principle assumes that *generative autonomy* is expressed by "both/and" relationships. For example, the miracle of life emerges from the complementarity of biological complements. A key requirement for generativity is that the autonomous context of Self common-unity is valued (and not "e-valued"). This circle of autonomy always exists. It isn't created from a Hegelian "synthesis" of thesis and antithesis; it is the unitary common-unity context from which complements are distinguished.

However, generative autonomy is actualized only through a "both/and" relationship of interacting complements. An example is the "runner's high" achieved in jogging. Here the runner goes through a series of cycles (right foot/left foot, inhale/exhale, etc.) until at some indeterminate point an altered state of effortless expression may develop.

Another example is learning to walk. Milton Erickson described this process in recollecting how as an adolescent crippled by polio he learned to walk again:

> I learned to stand up by watching baby sister learn to stand up: use two hands for a base, uncross your legs, use the knees for a wide base, and then put more pressure on one arm and hand to get up. Sway back and forth to get balance. Practice knee bends and keep balance. Move head after the body balances. Move hand and shoulder after the body balances. Put one foot in front of the other with balance. Fall. Try again. (Rossi, Ryan, & Sharp, 1983, pp. 13-14)

This beautiful description can be applied to virtually any learning process.

A final example of the balance principle is in the process of hypnotic induction. One of the dynamic complements characterizing trance development is holding on and letting go. For example, you may begin to relax some, then orient externally a bit, wander a little more into trance before wondering, "Is it happening? Will it happen? Can it happen?" You might then discover yourself letting go a little bit more, holding on for security, and so on. At some point, "it" happens: you discover yourself experiencing the effortlessness, the autonomy, the hypnotic quality of trance.

In applying the balance principle in hypnotherapy, it is useful to keep in mind Erickson's description of hypnosis as a process of communicating ideas in an experiential fashion. To develop generative autonomy, these ideas may be expressed in a number of different complementary structures. One simple yet effective structure involves triplet statements indicating complements in autonomy. For example:

> (I don't know) and (you don't know) exactly how you'll go into trance, but what a nice thing to know that (your unconscious knows) how and when to respond in a manner appropriate for you as an individual.

> You can (consciously wonder) about trance and (experientially wander) into trance, and (autonomously operate in co-operative security) as you do so.

> Now you should (hold on) to your need for security and only (let go) now of any unnecessary tension, (holding on) to doubts and (letting go) of any need to actively attend here, all the while (discovering a secure balance of unconscious development).

> And you have had some (past experiences) you didn't like, and there are some (potential future) experiences you'd like to develop, and here we are in the gifts and presents of (the present presence of undeniable actuality) of unconscious expression.

A related loop structure is the following six-statement sequence:

1) A *general statement* of a universal skill, experience, response, etc.
2) A *general statement* indicating that 1) can occur in many ways.
3) A *specific possibility* x (of how "it" might occur).
4) A *specific possibility* y.
5) A *specific possibility* z.
6) A *general statement* concluding that subject will respond in some way.

For example:

1) Everybody has the ability to experience absorption.
2) And we all can develop absorption in different ways, at different rates, at different times. . . .
3) Some people become absorbed in feelings of security.
4) Some people become absorbed listening to a voice.
5) Some people become absorbed by allowing themselves to visually become immersed.
6) So I don't know how exactly which way you will discover that security

of internal absorption developing . . . .

This structure can be modified by adding complements to each specific possibility [(x, x'), (y, y'), (z, z')]:

1) We all experience many different kinds of sensations. . . .
2) And those sensations develop in so many different ways. . . .
3) So I don't know whether your hand will get cool or warm.
4) Or whether your left or right earlobe will feel that lack of sensation.
5) Or whether your shoulders will feel light or heavy. . . .
6) But I do know that you really can enjoy those autonomous developments and then some.

These simple examples indicate how various idea loops might be used to experientially develop autonomous unity, complementary balance, and multiple possibilities.

The simplicity of such "chunking structures" makes them extremely valuable tools for unfolding a trance process in a systematic yet unpredictable fashion. To appreciate this fact, an excellent training exercise is to write out (and/or tape) inductions consisting solely of such structures. This will demonstrate how such forms can provide structure and assure complementary balance for both hypnotherapist and client, thereby enabling the hypnotherapist to generate a circular flow of hypnotic communications.

These simple patterns are especially useful in the absorption and orientation of attentional processes. Thus they can be utilized to develop experiential absorption, disperse focus, displace symptoms, distract analysis, destabilize rigid patterns, and develop generative autonomy (i.e., therapeutic dissociation) in hypnotic explorations. They can enhance receptivity (by reducing dominant conscious loops); enable suggestions to be seeded; and encourage trust, spontaneity, and self-appreciation.

Virtually any distinction—i.e., therapeutic idea—can be looped in such structures, and multiple distinctions—e.g., regarding unconscious generativity, the client's ongoing patterns, client resources, client problems—can be interwoven to form new tapestries of expressions. This "weaving" style reflects, I believe, Erickson's emphasis on therapeutic hypnosis as the communication of *simple ideas* in experientially absorbing fashions. (In addressing problems, a degeneration of the problem description into many simple components is first required.)

It should be recognized that the balance principle applies in many other ways. For example, complementary *styles of communication* should be balanced within and across hypnotherapy sessions. Examples of complementary styles include:

associational/dissociational	cryptic/straightforward
direct/indirect	predictable/unpredictable
general/specific	focusing/distracting
serious/humorous	permissive/directive
pacing/leading	global/detailed
agreeing/disagreeing	self-referential/other-referential

Thus, the Ericksonian hypnotherapist will complement indirect methods with direct approaches, a humorous style with a serious side, pacing with leading, etc. The particular complements used should reflect what is natural for the hypnotherapist and what is appropriate for the client. I usually spend time identifying the cognitive style a client is most dependent upon (e.g., global). After some rapport has been achieved, I then take on the complementary style (e.g., detailed). By oscillating rhythmically between these complements during hypnotherapeutic interaction, the client is led away from rigid identification with any one way of being and toward a balanced and generative expression of complementary styles.

Diagnostic Cues: Exits from the Circle of Autonomy

Problems may be viewed as time-frozen double binds reflecting self-devaluing acts of e-valuation ("value pushed away") of a complementary co-relation. The intra- or inter-personal "co-relators" consequently shift from mutually inclusive double bonds to mutually exclusive double binds caught in a "vicious cycle" of painful violence. Thus, a major diagnostic task in therapy is to identify "split" correlational complements. This requires orientation to, and interaction with, the unique processes of each client. The hypnotherapist "deframes" by setting aside personal and theoretical biases, experientially "tunes" to the client's self-essence (via processes described above), and through circular and complementary probing identifies where and how the client dissociates.

A major assumption here is that form-specified diagnostic categories are unnecessary and probably counterproductive, since the client's experience is already formed in a unique yet discernible organizational pattern. Thus, the hypnotherapist develops an experiential state of ignorance and becomes the "hypnotic subject" of the client, "allowing" the latter to "draw" their distinctions onto the therapist's "blank slate." In this way, diagnostic information unfolds naturally through intense interpersonal absorption. Invariant patterns of self-devaluation manifest through observed repetitions, constancies, confusions, shifts, client metaphors, emotion, evaluations, and other processes.

In this process, inductive and abductive procedures are favored over the deductive logics characterizing traditional nomothetic frameworks. The diagnostic experience resembles a Sherlock Holmes mystery or a jigsaw or crossword puzzle; the operator *knows* that solutions exist and becomes absorbed in cooperating with the client to discover them. Trance processes play a central role for both therapist and client, especially in maintaining "autonomy in common-unity."

The diagnostic process operates during the entire therapy. Multiple modalities are utilized—e.g., written descriptions (family history, problem history, goals, etc.); casual conversation; hypnotic explorations; direct questioning; experiential "identification" with the client, etc. The goal is to identify "patterns which disconnect"—i.e., dominant "split co-relations." They are often not immediately obvious, being obscured (and protected) by the well-developed "distraction techniques" of the client. I usually find hypnotic orientation allows me to develop a general "feel" for underlying patterns, since such an orientation allows undistracted absorption. To bypass possible defenses and insecurities, I then "hone in" on the pattern via gentle and indirect probing.

Many verbal and nonverbal cues may serve as "red flags" indicating possible "correlational splits." The ones listed below are especially simple and useful, and should give a flavor of the idiosyncratic yet structured nature of such cues.

1) "Control" intentions

Power and control are painful illusions. We are controlled by what we try to control. We are dominated by what we try to dominate. We become what we attempt to violently oppose. Thus, attempts to unilaterally "control" any "co-relation" (i.e., any inter- or intrapersonal relationship) generally lead to vicious and "sense-less" loops of escalating violence. Simple examples of "control" statements:

(a) I try to control my eating, because I hate my fat body . . . I binge mostly when I feel depressed.

(b) I try to give myself suggestions to feel good, but I can't stop my internal dialogue from filling me with doubts.

(c) Over the past few months, I keep "catching" myself trying to withdraw and not go out and meet (a prospective wife). . . . I have to fight off the depression and make sure to keep going out, because I'll never meet anybody if I don't try. . . .

(d) I force myself to exercise two hours a day . . . but often get injured.

(e) Control is paramount in my life. . . . I was and still am controlled by my ma. I like to control my environment, who's in it, and what they do.

In each example, one "part" tries to "control" or "overcome" or "get rid of" its "subversionary" complement. (This implies that the "controller" is "out of control.") The result: Heads you lose, tails you don't win.

2) Evaluative terms

Values are unitary, unconditional, and refer to *being* states; e-valuations are dualistic ("good" vs. "bad"), conditional (e.g., only "good" is acceptable), and refer to *becoming* (i.e., performance) processes. Identification with a "positive" co-relation (state, experience, person, way of being, concept, etc.) necessarily also entails an identity bind to its "negative" co-relation complement: they are two sides of the same coin. Because one cannot exist without the other, one ("good") supports the other ("bad"). The unitary distinction is complementary in form! Thus, I keep lists of a client's "positive" and "negative" evaluations, finding them excellent pointers to key structures underlying a problem process.

The therapist must set aside his own evaluations in order to recognize those of the client. Typically, the "clearing out" process described above will need to be periodically regenerated.

3) Implied causatives

Underlying many problem loops is the belief that a given behavior *causes* a particular (undesired) state of being, and that the opposite behavior (therefore) will cause the desired state. A few examples:

(a) If I don't force myself to exercise, I'll die of a heart attack (like my father).

(b) If I don't hold on tightly to someone, they'll go away.

(c) If I can get rid of my mother's voice (inside of me), I'll be able to listen to what's happening inside.

Figure 5 illustrates how such statements generate double-bind loops. (Extended examples of such binds can be found in Ronald Laing's *Knots* [1971].) As with any double bind, dealing with *either* one *or* the other complement is futile. Neither is "true" or "false"; they are "partner" co-relations engaged in a dissociational cycle. The hypnotherapist must accept both complements in working to return them to their circle of autonomy.

4) Flip-flops

Double-bind loops can also be detected by recurrent flip-flops between self-contradicting states. For example:

(a) My father is a lovely generous man who is a bossy and controlling alcoholic . . . my way was never right in his eyes.
(b) I must exercise and diet to avoid premature death . . . but when I'm not dieting I'll exercise and when I'm not exercising I'll diet although sometimes I'll not do either although never both.

Flip-flop loops occur in many other ways, of course. A client may promise to carry out a homework assignment and then "forget" or otherwise fail to do so, or a couple may loop between two opposing states. Oscillations (i.e., temporal rhythms) are the basis of all living processes. Problems develop when the content processed in an oscillatory loop becomes fixed in self-contradicting, arhythmic, and disruptive loops.

5) Hedges and qualifiers

Such statements often suggest "split co-operators" arranged in a "front/back" position in which the "out front" actor is "puppeted" by a disbelieving and distrusting monitor. The "front" usually placates while the "back" monitors from its withdrawn "control tower" position. (This pattern is often labeled "passive/aggressive." Whatever the label, remember that the "parts" are one and the same structure.) Examples:

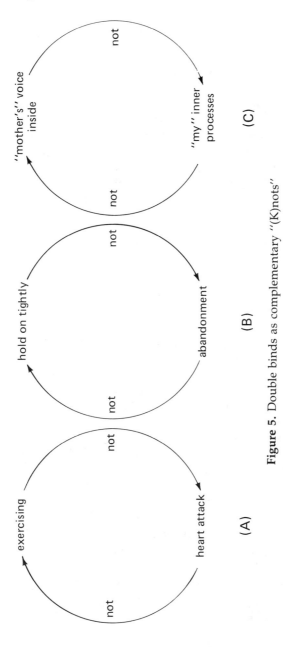

Figure 5. Double binds as complementary "(K)nots"

(a) The family story is that I. . . .
(b) I was mother's favorite, though I didn't consciously understand that while growing up.
(c) I'll try as much as possible to follow your suggestions.

Clients distinguishing themselves with such statements are often highly skilled in inducing the therapist to accuse them of "resistance" or a related unilateral co-relation. The therapist can bypass any such sense-less co-operational struggles by fully appreciating and encouraging the client's ability to maintain control and to not fully believe or respond to therapeutic communications. In other words, loop with the pattern.

6) Constants

Assuming that the unity of any distinction is expressed (e.g., actual-ized) in complementarity of form, the *fixed and invariant* presence of a belief, behavior, attitude, experience, etc., suggests that its complement, if not also clearly presented, is unconsciously dominant. Thus, the in-timidating person typically feels insecure; the forever cheerful person with a constant (usually frozen) smile is sunk in underlying sadness; the person who accepts everything accepts nothing. These fixed positions are usually maintained by induction (or reduction or seduction) of oth-ers—spouse, friend, enemy, therapist, client, etc.—into the comple-mentary role. Therapists' observations of their own fixed patterns with a client may be useful diagnostic cues in this regard. For example, in a recent session with a seemingly fragile middle-aged woman, I discovered my facial muscles sore from smiling so reassuredly (as was she). This "quick detection" of a "minimal cue" revealed a mutual induction ef-fective in distracting our attention from a painful experience.

Constancies are sometimes difficult to recognize, since *that which is constant becomes unconscious*! As Bateson (1979) and others have empha-sized, we perceive differences. Thus, that which never changes in a person's expressions often goes consciously unnoticed. I find hypnotic perception extremely useful in this regard, as it "draws" me to invari-ances in a person's expressions. These invariances may seem irrelevant or trivial, yet they often prove important.

7) Absolute quantifiers

This class of expressions is well-known to most therapists. Examples:

(a) I *never* would think of leaving a relationship.
(b) I *should* stop telling myself what I *should* be doing.
(c) I'm *always* the one that everybody can count on.
(d) I *must* succeed or I'll *always* be unhappy.

Such quantifiers indicate "time-frozen" correlations that forbid risking participation in the probabilistic world of temporal interactions. Thus, the events marked by "time-frozen" quantifiers will be experienced in a self-devaluing, dissociated fashion.

8) Emotions

To reiterate, emotions ("away from motion") may be considered as image/cognition/feeling condensations which symbolize an event's relevance to self-identified goals, beliefs, values, etc. (Gilligan & Bower, 1984). (For example, anger might translate generally as a perceived violation of one's integrity.) Emotion is evidenced by multiple cues which can be seen, felt, and heard: rhythmic shift, pupillary dilation, temporary motoric inhibition, increase in arousal, etc.

Tuning to emotional processes is essential to recognizing the personal values of the client in response to ongoing hypnotherapeutic communications. As Erickson emphasized:

> Keeping well and clearly in mind his actual wishes the author casually and permissively (or apparently permissively) presents a wealth of seemingly related ideas in a manner carefully calculated to hold or to fixate the subject's attention rather than the subject's eyes or to induce a special muscle state. Instead, every effort is made to direct the subject's attention to processes within himself, to his own body sensations, his memories, emotions, thoughts, feelings, ideas, past learnings, past experiences, and past conditions, as well as to elicit current conditionings, understandings, and ideas.
>
> . . . in the therapeutic use of hypnosis, one primarily meets the patient's needs on the terms he himself proposes; and then fixates the patient's attention, through adequate respect for and utilization of his method of presenting his problem, to his own inner processes of mental functioning. (Haley, 1967, pp. 498-499)

The client's emotional cues instruct the hypnotherapist how to maneuver in this way—when to stop or start or continue, when to lighten or intensify, focus or disperse, etc. A seemingly innocuous word or topic in an extended hypnotic discourse may stimulate happiness, sadness, anger, etc. The hypnotherapist makes note of the correlation and may immediately or later circle back to investigate it more fully. As a general rule, the hypnotherapist seeks to have clients absorbed in emotional processes without indulging or consciously focusing on them. (This may be described as the essence of a therapeutic trance.)

Breathing pattern is an important variable in emotional expression. If the client's breathing is rhythmic, I generally have complete confidence in his or her ability to autonomously explore and value the experience. On the other hand, inhibited or irregular breathing invariably has self-devaluing (dissociational) consequences. In such cases, the hypnotherapist's responsibility is to absorb the client into an interpersonal loop where self-valuing processes can be achieved.

9) Confusions or discontinuities

Experiential shifts of any kind in either therapist or client may be diagnostically meaningful. For example, the therapist might discover in acknowledging his or her own confusion the deft inductions a client successively uses to disorient self and other; the same skill can then be used as the basis for transformational processes.

Relatedly, idiosyncratic cues may signal the onset of a client's dissociational pattern. One client would twirl his thumbs when he started to withdraw into an intrapersonal loop. Dissociational markers for other clients have included neck muscles becoming extremely tight, scratching the arm of the chair, slight tilting of the head, increasing tempo of speech. (All constrict their breathing.) These are naturalistic ideomotor responses and hence minimal and repetitive rather than gross and voluntary in nature. They indicate how and when a client unconsciously withdraws into self-devaluing loops, and are thus of primary importance to the Ericksonian hypnotherapist.

Other common shifts of potential diagnostic value include sudden changes in topic; spontaneous and rapid development of, or emergence from, trance; a series of questions by the client; shifts in rhythm, tempo, attention, or posture.

10) Hypnotic observations

In hypnotically tuning to the client, the hypnotherapist may be surprised to find idiosyncratic and seemingly irrelevant cues "pop into" awareness. Experiential observation often reveals some significant pattern to which one's unconscious has drawn attention. This was discussed earlier, so it will not be elaborated further here.

In summary, these are a few of the patterns that can be used in unfolding awareness of a client's unique organizational tapestry. Many other patterns can be observed (idiosyncratic habits, emphasized words, stories the client tells, any repetition, etc.). Again, the key idea is that diagnostic information is best obtained from orienting fully and non-evaluatively to the client rather than to some predetermined constructs. Clinical training and professional skill is essential; so is allowing the client to determine how one's therapy skills will be applied.

It may be wondered whether these patterns are too general or vague or elemental. I find this to be their strength, i.e., they indicate where and when a client's constraints are but don't specify their content. The Ericksonian approach assumes that the client can do this much better than any model. Although many would disagree, diagnostic ("knowing through") models seem to be used more as shields protecting (and thereby deepening) a therapist's insecurity than as processes for serving the unique needs of the client. (As Brown [1979] observed, expansion of reference generally correlates with contraction of awareness.) I believe that *it is absolutely essential for the therapist to feel secure and autonomous in the therapeutic correlation.* As in any inter*personal* relationship, this need cannot be satisfied by denying (i.e., dissociating from) personal "response-ability."

The patterns described above enable the therapist to satisfy the dual "response-abilities" of 1) experientially absorbing *as a person* in a context of *being,* and 2) actively operating *as a therapist* utilizing sophisticated skills and techniques. Thus, the described diagnostic patterns assume a hypnotherapeutic context distinguished by Ericksonian principles and processes. It is difficult to imagine their value being realized in non-experiential contexts.

A General Procedure for Hypnotherapy

The Ericksonian hypnotherapist generates the structure of a therapy from the structure of a client's processes. The client's "theory" of how the world works becomes the therapist's "theory" of how to work both "inside" ("a part of") and "outside" ("apart from") the client's world. Many strategies can be used to guide this paradoxical process. Outlined below is one such procedure I developed for therapy and teaching purposes. Space considerations necessitate a selective presentation that is suggestive rather than complete. The model is illustrated with one of my therapy cases, a psychiatrist who could not urinate in public restrooms. I trust the reader to elaborate with his or her own content.

1) Develop process description of time-frozen relationship problem

To reiterate, this can be done in many ways. Preliminary information I find especially important to secure includes family history; present living situation; description of problem (when it started, where and how and with whom it occurs, where and how and with whom it does not occur, why it is a problem, etc.); previous solution attempts; assets, strengths, positive associations; boundary definitions; etc.

In the case of the psychiatrist* (whom we'll call Phil) with the "bashful bladder," inquiry disclosed:

- He was 37, married for 8 years with no children; very successful professionally; excellent writing skills; good extemporaneous speaker.
- Phil and his wife lived 200 miles apart, ostensibly because of professional commitments; immediately after marriage, Phil lost sexual attraction to his wife, though they seemed genuinely good friends (like brother and sister); Phil could urinate around Eileen "even more comfortably" than when by himself; he had periodic affairs with women (none of them clients) who admired his professional talents.
- The urination problem apparently had persisted over 30 years; mother would bring young Phil to Hollywood studios for screen tests, and when he was amidst other auditioning children she would loudly ask if he had to urinate; many different psychotherapies (including hypnotherapy) had failed; Phil claimed to be very responsive to hypnosis, and proved to be overly so (i.e., he would rush into trance and withdraw from any interpersonal connection).
- His parents were both Jewish immigrants from Russia; father described as a writer, trusting, lazy, uncommitted, out frequently with cronies; mother described as misunderstood, untrusting, unliked (except by Phil); family had unspoken rule that bathroom was never a private space; father would spend hours at a stretch on the toilet reading the newspaper.

---

*I have altered some incidental details in my description to protect the privacy of the client.

- Unacceptable experiences (self-disidentifications) included: expressing anger at anybody (except himself and his father); being lazy; failing; unreliable (e.g., not honoring commitments); abandoning his mother (or wife).
- Problem process included constant worrying about someone hearing him urinate; clamping down on abdominal muscles when trying to urinate (facial expressions as in constipation); eyes darting around; self-berating internal dialogue; occasional success via distracting attention by reading.

2) Ensure that description contains no pejorative expressions or clinical diagnostic terms

All processes are equally valid and thus "value-able" in their essence; they assume different functional values when contextualized in some action frame. Thus, "deframing" descriptions is essential to the Ericksonian cornerstone principle of utilization, which assumes that *everything* the person is doing is exactly what they should be doing. A "deframed" description is one holding no evaluative connotations (either "positive" or "negative") for either therapist or client. The potential of a process to be evaluatively positive is equivalent to its potential to be evaluatively negative. Thus, you will know you have a nonevaluative description if "positive" (i.e., acceptable) instances of its expression can be generated as easily as so-called "negative" (unacceptable) instances.

3) Identify "split" complements in description

That is, list all oppositional relationships indicated by the client. Some that were salient for Phil:

(a) mother vs. father
(b) mother vs. wife
(c) failure vs. success
(d) public performance vs. private performance
(e) not getting angry at others (except father) vs. berating self
(f) commitment to being with wife vs. not being with wife
(g) sexuality with wife vs. sexuality with admiring women
(h) urinating around wife vs. not urinating around anybody else
(i) declared identification with mother vs. declared disidentification with father

4) Generate deep structure pattern that seems central

Once multiple "splits" have been listed, I usually spend time contemplating what co-relational patterns seem centrally thematic. (Stated in another way, these themes are the structurally invariant patterns whose expression is essential for maintaining the organizational identity of a system.) Not surprisingly, I typically find correlations clustered in complementary or triangulated patterns. In Phil's case, the interrelated ideas of private/public expression, child/adult "con-fusions," and failure/success outcomes seemed pervasive.

Once identified, central patterns can be degenerated into their components and transformed into a general deep structure representation. For example:

> *PERSON(s)* (child, mother, father, illicit lover) *PERFORMING* (successfully, unsuccessfully) {BIOLOGICAL} *FUNCTION* (sexual, urination, parenting) in *SITUATION* (private, public) with *ATTENTIONAL STRATEGY* (images, sensations, motor patterns, internal dialogue, perception, memories, cognitions).

Figure 6 illustrates how the general frames can be represented by closed loops, with a frame's members also clustered in "k(nots)." This sort of representation can illustrate undifferentiated correlations bound such that all members of a frame are accessed when one of them is addressed. Thus, the "person" performing the (urinating) function may be conceptualized as a "boy/mother/father" family constellation. All of these "family members" should be addressed if hypnotherapeutic communications are to be effective. This can be accomplished in physical or imaginal (hypnotic) actuality; *the "pattern which disconnects" is equally present in the intrapersonal and interpersonal systems.*

Note that each member of a deep structure category can be expressed in many ways. Different linguistic tokens emphasize different perspectives of a multidimensional idea, pattern, or being. (The "maps" are not the territory.) Thus, "child" could be replaced in the person frame with "boy," "baby," "son," "brother," "son of a child's grandparent," etc. *Each token shades the meaning of its context in a slightly different manner.* By gradually substituting different tokens for an expression in the interweave of hypnotic communication, the pattern (and hence the meaning) of the overall tapestry of the representational structure can be unconsciously altered.

The deep structure loops also can suggest attentional patterns that are

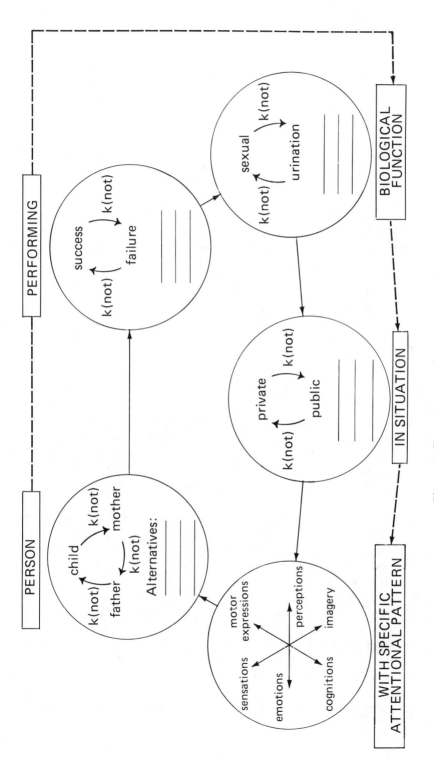

Figure 6. Deep structure loop representation

problem-relevant. For example, the experience of physical sensation and whether it was generated by external or internal references seemed relevant to Phil's situation and thus a potentially good entry point for indirect hypnotic interventions, as is noted below.

5) Generate for various correlational loops examples of a correlational process with equivalent potential to be useful or not useful

Again, the point here is to "deframe" descriptions so they are nonevaluative context-independent expressions. This can be accomplished by first translating a "negatively" framed problem process (e.g., "failing at urinating in public") into a "deframed" expression which is nonevaluative and context-general (e.g., "the value of not succeeding in expressing a biological function in public"). The therapist can then generate examples of when expressing this general process may be self-valuing and when it may be self-devaluing. The "symptom" is thus revealed as an essential skill that should be appreciated and actually amplified (e.g., differentiated) rather than rejected. *Its actual value derives from its actualized context; thus, shifting its context transforms its value.*

The nonevaluative description also constitutes a "re-source" description from which multiple hypnotherapy strategies can be generated. I think it is this fundamental level of pattern which Erickson had in mind when emphasizing hypnotherapeutic communication as a process of communicating simple ideas in a variety of different fashions.

6) Identify idiosyncratic client patterns (conscious processes, concerns, styles) that need to be included in any hypnotherapeutic strategy

For example, what might interfere with trance development? With carrying out homework assignments? With cooperating straightforwardly? Each person will have different patterns that will thwart straightforward strategies (e.g., a standardized hypnotic induction). The Ericksonian hypnotherapist gladly accepts such patterns as the changing topological ground on which all therapeutic communications are molded. A few of the issues I had to keep in mind in Phil's case were:

(a) *He needed privacy.* He needed to experientially participate in public (i.e., with me) while maintaining autonomy. Initially, the slightest attempts to focus on his personal experience triggered a "self-dissociating trance withdrawal." This suggested that a central hypnotherapy strategy should be dissociational processes. (To distinguish therapeutic dissociational processes from those already experienced by a client, full absorption in the "interpersonal trance"—e.g., client entranced with eyes open—should be ensured before intrapersonal trance is encouraged.)

(b) *He needed intellectual absorption.* Phil was a highly intelligent man who enjoyed unusual ideas. Hypnotherapeutic ideas were most effective when "seeded" among hypnotic communications that were highly complex, shifting frequently among many esoteric "far-out" topics, referring to childhood experiences periodically, and paradoxical in nature.

(c) *He needed interpersonal contact.* It seemed essential that some or all members of the "family system" (mother, father, wife) be included to connect Phil's private and public worlds. His parents lived 3000 miles away, with his father in a rest home. His wife lived 200 miles away and was more available, so I included her in some of the sessions.

These few examples emphasize the complete *acceptance* of idiosyncratic patterns. Once a pattern is absorbed into the *interpersonal* loop, hypnotherapeutic strategy shifts to expanding and unbinding the constraint. Thus, hypnotic communications with Phil initially were interspersed among "far-out" intellectual concepts; later, "close-in" experiential processes became the focus. Thus, the absorption of a process is used to gradually develop its complement.

7) Generate stories which emphasize multiple possibilities for balancing correlations in self-valuing fashions

The general idea description (step 4) can be used along with other processes in this regard. Strategies for constructing and delivering stories vary widely. For example, Lankton and Lankton (1983) and Gordon (1978) present highly structured formats for Ericksonian story-telling. My preference is to operate in a much less predetermined fashion. I think of stories as vehicles for interpersonally conveying general ideas and developing general processes through unconscious experiential channels. I generally do this best by holding in mind some simple generative ideas that can be hypnotically interwoven in elaborate and repetitious ways with the ever-changing ongoing processes of the client. I use free-form structures such as the 6-statement balance loops (outlined earlier) to chunk and return to basic themes.

I usually jot down before a session some stories from my personal experience that are likely to (a) absorb the client's general interests, (b) map without conscious mediation onto some aspect of the problem, and (c) function as a trance induction (or deepener) as well. The following are a few story themes I noted before a session with Phil. They suggest how any learning or idea can be organized and reorganized in an infinite number of fashions:

- Learning the elemental units of the alphabet and learning to combine and recombine these elemental units to spell out new and different meanings (e.g., one's name, a nickname, a city, a favorite sandwich, "relief").
- Learning elementary muscular relationships in learning to write without undue tension; learning to combine words into sentences into paragraphs into stories into books, and learning to "rewrite the right rite right without any lefts right except for the middle third"; my experience as a martial arts instructor and learning differentiation of sensations and muscular orientations; spending time at my word processor to form new meanings in private; a writer's block and the circle around it.
- The embarrassment and self-consciousness I felt at my first prom; wondering what others would think; where did the (pin) hole "open up"; remembering my parents' stern warning; having to learn "undercover" about "under the covers; learning to withdraw into an altered state; listening to angry voices (on rock music)"; always maintaining a hold on what was important; etc.

8) List hypnotic phenomena, processes, and strategies that can absorb the problem process and then expand and balance its structure

To do this, you might imagine the client as already in a "deep trance" induced and maintained by their intrapersonal and interpersonal patterns. That is, the symptom may be regarded as self-devaluing, spontaneously generated trance phenomena. Using this frame, one can ask: Which hypnotic phenomena are salient? Which are not? (Amnesia, ideomotoric responses, age regression, age progression, automatic talking, etc.) How does the person withdraw when threatened or under stress? How does he or she enjoy himself or herself? What sorts of processes does he or she absorb in? (Reading, sports, business, music, etc.) Identifying how a person naturalistically generates his or her "reality" (i.e., dominant constraints) will indicate what hypnotic processes will be effective. The following are a few of the hypnotic processes developed with Phil:

(a) *Ideo-dynamic processes*. I especially focused in great detail on ideo-sensory processes (sensation dispersion, constriction, displacement, etc.); ideo-imaginal processes (e.g., letting images come and go autonomously while maintaining security); and ideo-cognitive processes (e.g., internal dialogue). In training clients in such processes, it is usually best to orient away from the problem content until experiential learnings have been realized.

(b) *A "Trance-parent" (transparent) Self providing "SuperVision" and guidance*. This was a modified version of Erickson's "February-man" technique used to fill developmental gaps in a client's experience (Erickson & Rossi, 1979).

(c) *The pleasurable "void state" of the Middle of Nowhere*. This technique was suggested by his common reference to urination as "voiding." The state was initially described as a relatively neutral yet intensely absorbing universe of "empty space." Details added gradually included "that absolutely amazing and puzzling discovery" of little holes and passages which could "open and close before a blinking eye could wink twice" and oscillate "so successfully that one could not fail to be proud to be engaged in that "trance-mission" from those "United States of Consciousness" in which each state had its own governor. Thus, the hypnotic "void" state served multiple purposes, including (1) the establishment of a general context for autonomous and secure self-exploration and (2) a specific form in which indirect suggestions regarding the urination process were embedded.

(d) *Hypnotic dreams*.

(e) *Trance with eyes open and focused*. Phil learned to develop hypnotic tunnel vision in various ways, including complete fixation on his hands. Posthypnotic suggestions emphasized that he could "focus fully on the task at hand," i.e., attentionally absorb when in a public "stall." In a related process, Phil learned to "image" his (actual) hands with a "steadfast gaze" so that he would "only vaguely" feel the "private secretions of sensation" in "peripheral regions." This process was instrumental in solving the urination problem; the tunnel vision disenabled the access of panic-triggering images and related disruptive processes.

9) Generate homework assignments which satisfy requirements of step 8

I find it especially important to identify and "prescribe" processes the client habitually engages in that might "undo" therapeutic progress. Phil was given many homework assignments, a majority of them in the form of posthypnotic suggestions (since he was most responsive to dissociational trance processes). A few of them were:

(a) *Privacy*. Among many related prescriptions, Phil was instructed both in trance and waking states that he should withhold at least one secret each week.
(b) *"Be-rating processes."* Phil reported constantly "berating" himself for failing to urinate. I chided him at length for failing to "be rating" himself in more diverse fashions. His natural confusion to this paradoxical expression was utilized to secure his cooperation in developing a "multiple-modality system" so that he could "be rating" how well he *"succeeded in failing* to adequately be-rate himself as well as how well he *failed* at *succeeding* in finding ever new ways to critically orient to himself *and then some."*
(c) *Self-hypnosis*. Practicing self-hypnotic processes was deemed an important aspect of therapy, as Phil desperately needed an experiential context for enjoying secure privacy. I made some trance tapes for him, taught him several self-hypnotic processes, and assigned a variety of specific tasks (e.g., practicing tunnel vision).

10) Review all generated material to ensure intention is to experientially cooperate with a human being rather than to operate on a category or concept

It is easy to deeply absorb in generating and using patterns, sometimes forgetting that the living being is the only real source of change. For ethical and practical purposes, it is therefore useful to periodically check that orientation to the *person* of the client is paramount.

11) Reiterate loop if needed

The general procedure outlined here is really a rough framework for multiple session therapy. Thus, it can be reiteratively used as long as the problem(s) remains.

CONCLUSION

I have chosen in this chapter to paint in broad strokes some primitive distinctions for a generative autonomy approach in Ericksonian hypnotherapy. This work was motivated significantly by an increasing conviction that traditional models are hopelessly inadequate for representing Erickson's contributions. This chapter is an initial attempt to elucidate the bare bones of an alternative paradigm emphasizing generative principles of common-unity, complementarity, and multiplicity. The ideas are fleshed out and extended in other works (in progress). I invite the reader to respond with such an understanding, and look forward to common-unity participation in refining and modifying the views advanced above. In doing so, I would like to bring closure to this writing with the following beautiful passage from T.S. Eliot's *Four Quartets*:

> We shall not cease from exploration
> And the end of all our exploring
> Will be to arrive where we started
> And know the place for the first time.
> Through the unknown, remembered gate
> When the last of earth left to discover
> Is that which was the beginning;
> At the source of the longest river
> The voice of the hidden waterfall
> And the children in the apple-tree
> Now known, because not looked for
> But heard, half-heard, in stillness
> Between two waves of the sea.
> Quick now, here, now, always—
> A condition of complete simplicity
> (Costing not less than everything)
> And all shall be well and
> All manner of things shall be well
> When the tongues of flames are in-folded
> Into the crowned knot of fire
> And the fire and the rose are one.

REFERENCES

Bateson, G. (1979). *Mind and nature: A necessary unity*. New York: Dutton.
Bohm, D. (1957). *Causality and chance in modern physics*. Philadelphia: University of Pennsylvania Press.

Brown, G.S. (1979). *Laws of form*. New York: E.P. Dutton.

Capra, F. (1975). *The Tao of physics*. Boulder: Shambhala Publishers.

Davis, P.J., & Hersh, R. (1981). *The mathematical experience*. Boston: Houghton Mifflin.

Eliot, T.S. (1963). Four quartets. In T.S. Eliot, *Collected poems: 1909-1962*. London: Faber & Faber Ltd.

Erickson, M.H. (1943). Hypnotic investigation of psychosomatic phenomena: Psychosomatic interrelations studied by experimental hypnosis. *Psychosomatic Medicine, 5*, 51-58. Reprinted in E.L. Rossi (Ed.), *The collected papers of Milton H. Erickson on hypnosis* (Vol. 2). New York: Irvington, 1980.

Erickson, M.H. (1952). Deep hypnosis and its induction. In L.M. LeCron (Ed.), *Experimental hypnosis*. New York: Macmillan. Reprinted in E.L. Rossi (Ed.), *The collected papers of Milton H. Erickson on hypnosis* (Vol. 1). New York: Irvington, 1980.

Erickson, M.H. (1980a). Respiratory rhythm in trance induction: The role of minimal sensory cues in normal and trance behavior. In E.L. Rossi (Ed.), *The collected papers of Milton H. Erickson on hypnosis* (Vol. 1). New York: Irvington.

Erickson, M.H. (1980b). Basic psychological problems in hypnotic research. In E.L. Rossi (Ed.), *The collected papers of Milton H. Erickson on hypnosis* (Vol. 2). New York: Irvington.

Erickson, M.H., & Rossi, E.L. (1977). Autohypnotic experiences of Milton H. Erickson, M.D. *American Journal of Clinical Hypnosis, 20*, 36-54.

Erickson, M.H., & Rossi, E.L. (1979). *Hypnotherapy: An exploratory casebook*. New York: Irvington.

Erickson, M.H., & Rossi, E.L. (1981). *Experiencing hypnosis*. New York: Irvington.

Gilligan, S.G. (1981). Ericksonian approaches to clinical hypnosis. In J.K. Zeig (Ed.), *Ericksonian approaches to hypnosis and psychotherapy*. New York: Brunner/Mazel.

Gilligan, S.G. (1982). *Effects of emotional intensity on learning*. Unpublished doctoral dissertation, Stanford University.

Gilligan, S.G., & Bower, G.H. (1984). Cognitive consequences of emotional arousal. In C.E. Izard, J. Kagan, & R. Zajonc (Eds.), *Emotions, cognitions, and behavior*. Cambridge, MA: Cambridge Press.

Gordon, D. (1978). *Therapeutic metaphors: Helping others through the looking glass*. Cupertino, CA: Meta Publications.

Haley, J. (1967). *Advanced techniques of hypnosis and therapy: Selected papers of Milton H. Erickson, M.D.* New York: Grune & Stratton.

Hall, E.T. (1983). *The dance of life*. New York: Anchor Press/Doubleday.

Korzybski, A. (1933). *Science and sanity: An introduction to non-Aristotelian systems and general semantics*. Lakeville, CT: The International Non-Aristotelian Library Publishing Company.

Laing, R.D. (1971). *Knots*. New York: Pantheon Books.

Lankton, S.R., & Lankton, C.H. (1983). *The answer within: A clinical framework for Ericksonian hypnotherapy*. New York: Brunner/Mazel.

Leonard, G. (1978). *The silent pulse*. New York: E.P. Dutton.

Maturana, H.R., & Varela, F.J. (1980). *Autopoesis and cognition: The realization of the living*. Dordrecht, Holland: D. Reidel.

Pribram, K.H. (1971). *Languages of the brain*. Englewood Cliffs, NJ: Prentice-Hall.

Rosenhan, D.L. (1984). On being sane in insane places. In P. Watzlawick (Ed.), *The invented reality: How do we know what we believe we know?* New York: Norton.

Rossi, E.L., Ryan, M.O., & Sharp, F.A. (Eds.). (1983). *Healing in hypnosis: The seminars, workshops, and lectures of Milton H. Erickson*. New York: Irvington.

Varela, F.J. (1979). *Principles of biological autonomy*. New York: Elsevier North Holland.

Watzlawick, P., Beavin, J.H., & Jackson, D.D. (1967). *Pragmatics of human communication: A study of interactional patterns, pathologies and paradoxes*. New York: Norton.

Watzlawick, P., Weakland, J.H., & Fisch, R. (1974). *Change: Principles of problem formation and problem resolution*. New York: Norton.

von Forester, H. (1984). On constructing a reality. In P. Watzlawick (Ed.), *The invented reality: How do we know what we believe we know?* New York: Norton.

Young, A.M. (1972). Consciousness and cosmology. In C. Muse & A.M. Young (Eds.), *Consciousness and reality: The human pivotal point.* New York: Avon Books.

Zukav, G. (1979). *The dancing Wu Li masters.* New York: Bantam Books.

PART V

Perspectives on Therapy

These authors discuss particular aspects of the psychotherapeutic relationship that have special prominence in their practice. Included in this section are the use of awareness, indirect technique, and patient values.

Joseph Barber, Ph.D., is a clinical psychologist in private practice in Los Angeles, California. He has more than 20 publications to his credit, many in the area of hypnotic pain control. With his wife, Cheri Adrian, he coedited a highly valuable book entitled Psychological Approaches to the Management of Pain *(Brunner/Mazel, 1982).*

Barber earned his degree in psychology from the University of Southern California. He has held a number of academic appointments and is currently an assistant clinical professor in the Department of Psychiatry at the UCLA Neuropsychiatric Institute. He travels often to teach hypnosis and has served on the teaching faculty for the American Society of Clinical Hypnosis and the Society for Clinical and Experimental Hypnosis.

Not only is Barber a notable teacher and author, he is also an exceptional practitioner of hypnosis and psychotherapy. Barber's clinical demonstration at the 1983 Erickson Congress received the highest rating by attendees of any of the demonstrations. He has been invited to serve on the faculty of Erickson Foundation meetings each year since their inception.

Barber's approach to psychotherapy is eclectic. He received considerable training in gestalt therapy from Erv and Miriam Polster. In this chapter, he demonstrates how the gestalt concept of awareness of immediate experience can be used and enhanced in the

241

hypnotic situation. Case studies illustrate the depth of his creative technique.

   Daniel L. Araoz, Ed.D., earned his degree in marriage and family counseling from Columbia University. He conducts a private practice in psychotherapy and he is a professor at the C. W. Post Center of Long Island University. He is the founding editor of both the Journal of Family Counseling *and the* American Journal of Family Therapy.
   There are a number of areas in which Araoz has publications including marital and family therapy, and sexual therapy using hypnosis. His volume Hypnosis and Sex Therapy *(Brunner/Mazel, 1982) has been well reviewed and presents new methods for applying hypnosis in treating sexual dysfunctions.*
   His expertise as a teacher is well-known. Araoz is director of clinical education of the Milton H. Erickson Institute of Hypnosis of New York, which is located in Hempstead, and he is a faculty member of the American Institute for Psychotherapy and of the American Institute for Psychotherapy and Psychoanalysis.
   Araoz discusses his approach, The New Hypnosis, and emphasizes the similarities between his Ericksonian-based approach and Rogerian methods. His work dovetails with Barber's; Araoz describes how The New Hypnosis can be used to heighten the awareness of inner associations.

   Michael D. Yapko, Ph.D., is a psychologist in private practice in San Diego, California who is becoming nationally known in the field of hypnosis. Yapko is the main organizer of the Milton H. Erickson Institute of San Diego and recently authored a text on hypnosis entitled Trancework *(Irvington, in press).*
   Like Gordon and Stern, Yapko speaks to some of the underlying values inherent in Erickson's approach. He presents information about diagnosing and utilizing the patient's values to facilitate effective treatment.

   Dan C. Overlade, Ph.D., conducts a private practice of psychology in Pensacola, Florida. He has experience in forensic psychology and has held a number of academic appointments. Overlade has served as president of both the Florida Psychological Association and the Florida State Board of Examiners of Psychology.
   Where Yapko presented a general orientation to patient values,

Overlade develops a specific value, namely, the "resolution-seeking set." He defines this set and demonstrates its importance in human functioning. Clinical examples show how the resolution-seeking set can be applied in psychotherapy.

Harry E. Stanton, a Ph.D. psychologist who earned his degree from Flinders University of South Australia, resides in Hobart, Tasmania, Australia, where he teaches at the university and conducts a private practice. He has authored books on education and on positive approaches to health and living, and has written more than 150 articles on hypnosis, psychology, and education.

Stanton discusses the differences between hypnosis used in the experimental situation and hypnosis used in clinical practice. He presents four guiding principles of the permissive approach and describes how these principles and related techniques can be applied.

Norman W. Katz, Ph.D. (clinical psychology from Washington University, St. Louis), is an acknowledged expert on Ericksonian techniques. He is one of the directors of the Milton Erickson Institute for Clinical Hypnosis and Behavioral Science of New Mexico which is located in Albuquerque. In addition to a private practice in clinical psychology, he conducts training seminars for professionals and is active in professional organizations.

Katz has served as an assistant professor in the Department of Psychology at the University of New Mexico and is currently an adjunct clinical assistant professor at the University of New Mexico Medical School, in the Department of Family, Community, and Emergency Medicine.

Similar to Stanton, Katz develops differences between hypnosis as it is used in the laboratory and hypnosis as it is used in the clinical setting. Also addressed is the modification of hypnotic susceptibility. Patients can be taught to increase their hypnotic skills in a way that is clinically applicable. Skill development is not merely used to ameliorate symptoms; it can have generative effects.

Chapter 13

Hypnosis and Awareness

Joseph Barber

A psychotherapist who uses hypnosis is often known as a "hypnotherapist," and the therapeutic approach he or she uses seems to spring solely from the use of hypnotic techniques. This term creates an illusory sense of homogeneity. Actually, techniques are used in different ways at different times to achieve different ends depending on the therapist's theoretical orientation. For example, a psychodynamically oriented psychotherapist might use hypnosis primarily for uncovering early childhood memories or for generating hypnotic dreams. A cognitive-behavioral therapist may, on the other hand, see hypnosis as a technique for teaching a patient how to alter behavior and/or as a cognitive strategy for helping the patient cope with symptoms.

The value of hypnosis in psychotherapy has been well established within the context of many different psychotherapeutic approaches to psychotherapy (Araoz, 1982; Edelstien, 1981; Erickson [in Haley, 1967]; Fromm, 1965; Sacerdote, 1967, among others). Hypnosis is a facilitator of the therapeutic process, generally, and, more specifically, can be important in achieving particular therapeutic goals such as uncovering unconsciously repressed material; manifesting that material in forms that are meaningful for the individual (e.g., through hypnotically inspired dreams); and promoting behavior change (e.g., through suggestions for symptom alteration or through posthypnotic suggestions for behavior change).

An interesting question arises for the psychotherapist beginning to use hypnotic techniques: "How can I integrate hypnotic principles and techniques into *my* understanding of how to do psychotherapy?" This chapter focuses on that question, using the example of Gestalt therapy to demonstrate one way of integrating hypnotic principles and techniques into a psychotherapeutic approach.

A basic premise of Gestalt therapy is that the individual's awareness of his or her own experience is essential to good function. As Erving and Miriam Polster write in *Gestalt Therapy Integrated* (1973), "Before he can alter his behavior in any way the individual must first encompass the sensations and feelings which go along with it. Recovery of the acceptability of awareness—no matter what it may reveal—is a crucial step on the road to the development of new behavior" (p. 210). Insight is of less importance for the Gestalt therapist and is to be distinguished from awareness. *Insight* is the understanding of the meaning, the origin, and/or the mechanism of feelings or beliefs or behaviors. For the Gestalt therapist, insight is only one aspect of *awareness*, which simply entails the recognition of a feeling, thought, mental image, or behavior—without necessarily understanding the origin or meaning of what is being recognized. Awareness of present experience is, for the Gestalt therapist, a fundamental therapeutic component of subsequent change and growth.

Some psychotherapists who use hypnosis might argue that hypnosis is a technique that reduces awareness, rather than enhances it. This is a natural conclusion given the way hypnosis can be and often is used. For example, when an individual is hypnotized and responds to suggestions which result in diminished pain perception, that individual experiences a reduction of awareness, not an enhancement of it. Similarly, suggestions which result in amnesia constitute another example of reducing awareness, not enhancing it.

However, these are not the only ways hypnosis can be used. How can hypnosis be used to *enhance* awareness? The following example of a therapeutic posthypnotic suggestion is illustrative:

The patient, Daniel, was a 24-year-old man with severe congenital physical problems which left him with a battered and scarred body that was always a source of pain and anguish. Consequently, he treated himself badly (as if to punish his offending body), taking insufficient care of himself and ignoring his body's needs. While Daniel was in a hypnotic state, the following suggestion was offered:

> In a little while, when you're awake and beginning to leave my office, even though you may very well feel alert and strong and refreshed, you might also quite naturally feel dry and thirsty, as if you'd been working outside all morning in the hot sun. It's only natural that your throat and mouth will feel dry and parched from the hard work you've been doing out here in the heat. But that's alright. . . . You know you can get a drink of very good, cool water

out in the waiting room. And, at the moment you first feel the cool wetness of the water as it touches your lips and tongue and mouth, at that moment you'll have the opportunity to suddenly notice how nice it is to be able to take care of yourself in this way. To just suddenly appreciate how nice it is that you can quench your own thirst in this very natural and effortless way. And, of course, it isn't at all necessary for you to remember that I've mentioned anything about this at all. What I've been talking about really doesn't have anything to do with your very natural ability to be aware of your needs and to take care of them.

Other suggestions, some related, some not, were given and after a while it was suggested to Daniel that he awaken feeling alert and re-freshed and eager to begin to leave the office. He did so, and stopped in the waiting room to get a cup of water. After satisfying his thirst, he left.

The point of the suggestion was not to develop a compulsive behavior outside the patient's conscious awareness. Rather, the intention was to develop in the patient and experience of "spontaneous" awareness of his own bodily need, and of successfully and effortlessly taking care of it.

A number of other experiences contributed to Daniel's progress, par-ticularly to the development of his ability to take better care of his body, but this experience, repeated with variations in subsequent weeks, must have been significant to his increasing awareness of his needs and of his capacity to fulfill them. In this case, hypnosis was used to promote Daniel's fulfillment. It was also used to highlight the sensations of quenching Daniel's thirst—facilitating the working-through of his re-sistance to taking care of himself and the working-through of his disgust and unacceptance of his body.

The recovery of old experiences is more obviously related to the use of hypnosis, and this particular use of hypnosis is well-known. How-ever, the question arises again about awareness: If the patient recovers the memory while in the hypnotic state, will he or she be aware of it (remember it) later? This, of course, is a question of therapeutic strategy.

For example, Ellen was a 39-year-old woman whose presenting com-plaint was severe depression. Her depression seemed reactive to some painful and difficult problems experienced presently in her life. How-ever, during a therapeutic session in which hypnosis was used to in-vestigate a possible underlying process which could explain repeated bouts of significant depression, Ellen recounted that, as a child, she was frequently and repeatedly the object of sexual abuse by a brother. This information, expressed as a memory developed while age-regressed, was frightening and painful. It seemed in Ellen's interest to achieve a conscious working-through of this experience in order to find an adult way of coping with this memory and the associated feelings. However, I also believed it was too painful and frightening for her to consciously integrate all at once. Consequently, I suggested the following:

> The feelings you have been remembering and the feelings you have been feeling are your feelings. But you are more than these feelings. These feelings are just a part of you. And they've been with you for years, and your unconscious has kept them safe and undisturbed for you for the time when you will need them. So you can rely on your unconscious to keep them safe and undisturbed, and you don't need to remember them when you leave my office. In fact, you can really enjoy a kind of daydream memory of being here, a daydream that helps you to feel a renewal of energy, an increased awareness of your own inner strength, and a greater confidence that you have what it takes to live and to live well. If it becomes interesting and useful to you to begin gradually remembering these memories, you can be confident that the memories will come to you gradually and in a form that you can comfortably use. Until then, it is as if they don't even exist. Instead, when you open your eyes, it can seem that we have been talking and you have been really enjoying these feelings of inner calm and peace, and an increase in your feelings of strength and mental clarity.

These suggestions were intended to provide a means for Ellen to forget—to decrease her conscious awareness of these feelings. It was my judgment that she should ultimately increase her awareness of them and remember these feelings in degrees that would be manageable for her. And, happily, that is what she was eventually able to do. When Ellen left my office that day, she was evidently consciously unaware of what she had been experiencing. She seemed clearly undisturbed and made no mention of the events she had been so tearfully, so fearfully, relating to me. She was, however, inspired to feel greater awareness of her own ego strength, and of a greater confidence in her mental powers.

The following week she reported that she had had a dream the previous night that was disturbing to her. She had dreamt, she said, that her brother and she had done some "bad things" when she was a child.

I asked her if she would like to explore the dream to discover what meaning it might have for her, and she was interested. Using the hypnotic state both as a means of vivifying the dream and as a means of dissociating her from the possible affective pain, she relived the dream of the previous night and began to be aware of seemingly endless guilt over her role in this childhood episode. Although she was again experiencing fear and pain, she seemed also to have a greater capacity for managing these feelings, and I suggested that when she awoke from the hypnotic state, she would be able to remember whatever of these experiences she wanted. She then awoke and we discussed her feelings of guilt—and her total lack of awareness of any anger she may have toward her brother for his role in what was clearly a coercive experience on his part.

This, then, is an example of how hypnosis can be used, in effect, to *titrate* the enhancement of awareness of feelings and memories that might otherwise remain totally out of awareness due to their painful nature. While hypnosis was used initially to reduce awareness, ultimately it allowed the enhancement of that awareness to occur in a manageable way. (Later, Ellen was able to become aware of more and more details from her memory which served to help her become more aware of feelings of anger for her brother's behavior toward her. Her awareness of this anger played a significant role in the subsequent relief of her depression.)

Hypnosis is a technique for enhancing and facilitating the therapeutic process. In the foregoing example, the same result might have been obtained without the use of hypnosis, but it is unlikely that it would have occurred as quickly. Another example of the facilitative nature of hypnosis is provided by the following case:

> James was a pleasant, bright, ambitious, 24-year-old man whose presenting complaint was erectile dysfunction. His history revealed very limited sexual experience and severe ignorance of his inner life. He presented the image of a usually placid, eager young man with just one problem—no other conflicts, no other confusions, no other disappointments, nothing really bothering him but this one isolated problem which he could probably overcome on his own, but maybe, he thought, I could help him do it faster. He was extremely reluctant to come into therapy, and his doing so was a testament to his level of desperation. He required extensive reassurance of my commitment to confidentiality and he attempted to obtain my promise that the entire therapeutic process could be

dealt with within two to four sessions. He consistently denied, despite every opportunity for him to admit, the possibility of any other confusion or difficulty. To occupy his conscious motivations (and, besides, I thought the education would be helpful), I suggested that during the week he obtain and study certain sexual literature that I recommended. (He had never read a book about sex. In fact, he wasn't clearly aware of the appearance of female genitalia.) In the next session I suggested that hypnosis might be helpful for treating this problem and he eagerly agreed, since he had a magical belief in the power of hypnosis to cure his problem.

James responded quickly and fully to suggestions for development of a hypnotic state but simultaneously began to experience increasing anxiety as he felt less and less in control. The more well-developed his hypnotic state, the greater his symptoms of anxiety became, until he seemed about to experience a panic attack. I gave no suggestions for palliating these symptoms, judging rather that he needed to experience them as a means of discovering the nature of his difficulties. I suggested that he could remain in the hypnotic state undisturbed by my questions, and that he could speak to me. I then asked him what he was seeing in his mind's eye. Our conversation continued as follows:

James: (breathing is shallow and rapid) A cave. I'm looking at a cave.

Therapist: What are you feeling right now?

J: I'm scared.

T: What are you scared is going to happen?

J: I don't know. . . . I'm just scared. I want to go in the cave, but I can't. . . . I'm too scared.

T: That's right, you'd like to go into the cave. There must be something very interesting in that cave . . . but you're too scared. There might be something really, really scary there.

J: (panic rising) Yeah . . . Oh, God! . . . I'm too scared.

T: In a moment, when you're ready, you can look behind you and then you'll see what is *really* scary.

J: Oh, no!

T: What do you see?

J: My dad.

T: What's he doing?

J: He's just staring at me, like he's really, really mad at me.

T: You know why he's mad, don't you?

J: Yeah.

T: Is anyone else there?

J: My mom is, but she won't look at me.

T: Won't look at you?

J: She's ashamed of me (begins to cry).

T: Just let them come, let the tears come . . . and breathe. . . . No matter how terrible it is, you can still breathe . . . and just breathe and let the tears come. . . . No matter what they think, they can't stop you from breathing, can they?

J: Oh, God, it's so terrible!

T: Yes, it is so terrible . . . but right now, there's nothing you can do but cry and breathe . . . and breathe and cry.

J: Please help me.

T: What would you like me to do for you? How can I help you?

J: I don't know (still crying).

T: Tell your mom, or dad.

J: I can't.

T: You have no choice now. They know, and you can't change that. But you can talk with them. Tell them. . . .

J: Please don't be mad. . . . Please don't be mad. I'm sorry, I won't do it again.

T: Won't do what again?

J: My mom won't even look at me.

T: Tell her how it feels for her to turn away from you.

J: I can't . . . I have no right. . . . (crying slightly less now).

T: You have the right to talk with her . . . she's your mom. You can't help the way you are, but you can talk with her. She's your mom.

J: Mom . . . I'm sorry . . . please look at me. I won't do it again.

T: What's she doing?

J: She just looks so ashamed.

T: What have you done?

J: . . .

T: What is she ashamed of?

J: . . . of me (almost not crying now).

T: For what? What did you do?

J: I was . . . I was . . . I was . . . I can't talk about it . . . they're still here.

T: They can't hear you talk with me; you can tell me anything you want, and no one will hear but me.

J: Really?

T: Yep.

J: Oh! They're gone.

T: How do you feel right now?

J: Embarrassed.

T: What did you do?

J: When?

T: What did you do that your parents were upset about?

J: I was touching myself . . . I was, you know . . . I was playing with myself.

T: Where were you?

J: I was in my room.

T: And your parents came in the room?

J: I don't know . . . I guess so.

T: Do you think it's wrong to play with yourself?

J: I guess so . . . isn't it?

T: James, I don't know of anything wrong with learning to explore your body and your body's pleasure.

J: Really?

T: James, I want you to take a very deep, comforting breath now, and begin letting yourself relax a little more fully . . . and as you continue, I want you to begin letting yourself have a very, very pleasant image . . . maybe this image is from your memory, or maybe it is from your imagination about something you'd like to experience in the future. In any case, let yourself really, really enjoy this experience of pleasure and peaceful calm. And, in a few minutes, when I ask you to, I want you to open your eyes and begin to fully reorient yourself to my office, and enjoy how fully alert and awake and refreshed you feel, remembering clearly this very pleasant daydream experience. Nothing else needs to be remembered now about your meeting with me here today, only this very comfortable, pleasant daydream experience. When you awaken you can really enjoy how well you feel, how clear your mind is, knowing that there is nothing to bother you, and nothing to disturb you.

(When James opened his eyes, it was clear to me that he was still in a very deep hypnotic state.)

T: How are you feeling?

J: (with some difficulty speaking) weird . . . God . . . that's weird . . . wow.

T: Close your eyes and let yourself really relax back to that very pleasant place. Now . . . is there some reason you know of that it is hard for you to waken?

J: I feel like you have something of mine . . . that you took something of mine . . . took something away from me . . . I don't feel complete.

T: I haven't taken anything from you, James. I want you to keep your memory very safely tucked into your unconscious mind, and to keep it quietly there until it is needed in the future. I don't have it; you do. But you don't need to use it yet. Is that OK?

J: OK.

T: Fine. . . . Now, when you're ready, take a couple of very refreshing, energizing breaths and find yourself sitting alert, awake, feeling really good, really eager to go out and enjoy your day.

James now awoke quite fully, with no evident disturbance. He indicated no memory of the experience. When asked, he remembered a pleasant daydream experience of floating like a cloud.

This example is intended to illustrate the usefulness of hypnosis to facilitate the uncovering of memory, the clarifying and enlivening power of hypnosis to stimulate affect, and the usefulness of hypnosis to create temporary amnesia for the memories that have been uncovered. In subsequent sessions, James' memory for that experience (as well as for other painful memories relating to early sexual experiences) was gradually integrated into his conscious awareness in order to provide the opportunity for working-through of the conflict. Again, however, hypnosis was used to titrate that increase in awareness, in quantities and at a rate that James could reasonably manage.

The following illustrates how the hypnotic work with James was integrated with subsequent therapeutic work, both hypnotic and non-hypnotic:

At the next therapeutic session, James reported that he had experienced a feeling of great energy and freedom for three or four days following our session. He indicated that he felt more interested in and occupied with his own thoughts and feelings, and noticed with some amusement that he really was not interested in the opinions of those around him. Then, he found himself becoming gradually more oriented to the perceptions of others. He asked why that happened. I responded by asking him about Annie (a woman he'd recently become interested in). He described an evening they had spent together and indicated that his fear of dysfunction had lessened, though he had not experienced full and uninhibited erection. I asked him how his father would feel if he knew that James was experiencing such pleasure with a woman. He was startled, but he replied that his father would probably be proud of him. When I asked the same question regarding his mother, he became agitated and replied that she would not believe it possible for him to please a woman. We then discussed his parents' view of him as a boy and as a man, and his own view of himself. He began revealing his fears about his own inadequacy as a sexual being, and of his mother's characteristic criticism of him and of his accomplishments.

The hypnotic work was used to create a context within which James was able to consider and explore issues which he might not otherwise have been willing to consider or discuss. His visual fantasy about his parents' disapproval of "entering the cave" was evidence of conflict between his natural desires and his beliefs about their worthiness. It is unlikely that he would have been interested in a discussion about his feelings of worthiness or of his parents' attitude toward his own sexuality in the absence of the affective power of this hypnotic experience. In subsequent therapeutic sessions, hypnosis was used to heighten the focus of James' attention toward his inner processes and served the working-through process. As a result, not only was James able to learn about and manage awareness of his sexual fears and guilt, but he became more and more respectful of the fact that he had a vast unconscious awareness that could be a source of fascinating and powerful self-exploration. This enhanced appreciation of himself as a biological and psychological creature with a richness of inner experience was a significant contributor to his gradual increase in self-acceptance and to the resolution of his problem.

This exploration of the integration of hypnosis and psychotherapy has emphasized using hypnosis primarily as a modifier of awareness. There are many other uses of hypnosis in psychotherapy, of course. Within the context of Gestalt therapy, as we have seen, hypnosis can be a means of profoundly enhancing the vividness of fantasy exercises, of stimulating the association of particular ideas to particular sensations, and of catalyzing the occurrence of meaningful dreams.

It is apparent from the foregoing examples, however, that although hypnosis is a valuable facilitator of the therapeutic process, it is only one technique. It is not, in itself, a therapy, and its practitioners will inevitably—by default if not by intention—be using hypnosis within the context of a broad psychotherapeutic approach. Examining one's therapeutic assumptions and goals with an eye toward exploring how hypnosis might be used more fully to advance those goals is an important step in integrating hypnotic techniques into therapeutic practice.

REFERENCES

Araoz, D. (1982). *Hypnosis and sex therapy*. New York: Brunner/Mazel.
Edelstien, M. (1981). *Trauma, trance, and transformation*. New York: Brunner/Mazel.
Fromm, E. (1965). Hypnoanalysis: Theory and two case excerpts. *Psychotherapy: Theory, Research, and Practice, 2*, 127-133.
Haley, J. (Ed.). (1967). *Advanced techniques of hypnosis and therapy*. New York: Grune & Stratton.
Polster, E., & Polster, M. (1973). *Gestalt therapy integrated*. New York: Brunner/Mazel.
Sacerdote, P. (1967). *Induced dreams*. New York: Vantage.

Chapter 14

The New Hypnosis: The Quintessence of Client-Centeredness

Daniel L. Araoz

Those who see me demonstrate my approach, the New Hypnosis (Araoz, 1982), at workshops frequently remark that it is completely centered on the client. It could be said that the New Hypnosis is the quintessence of client-centered therapy, as developed by Carl Rogers. Without realizing it, Erickson was a real Rogerian and Rogers, to some extent, an Ericksonian. There are a number of points of comparison: Both were concerned with the uniqueness of individual needs; both showed a genuine sensitivity to people's existential, here-and-now perceptions, feelings and experience; and both started from an optimistic position based on the adaptive forces of human nature. As far as contrasts are concerned, Rogers uses more traditional techniques while Erickson's therapy was truly uncommon. Rather than comparing Erickson and Rogers, I intend to draw from both in order to explain how the New Hypnosis facilitates the existential meeting with the client.

EXISTENTIAL MEETING

An existential meeting entails my becoming as involved as possible with the current awareness of my clients. My involvement does not intrude; it is a sharing and a respectful way of being with the other as much as the other wants me. My involvement is an availability, a presence making the other's self-experience easier. I am a facilitator for the other's existential awareness. My presence facilitates here-and-now experience and awareness of self.

256

Rogers' basic hypothesis fits well with this view (Meador & Rogers, 1979; Rogers, 1961). It can be simply stated: When certain conditions are met, a person experiences growthful change. These conditions are congruence, positive regard for, and empathic understanding of another human being. This is true in all human relations. In the therapeutic relationship, as long as the therapist embodies these three qualities, the client will grow as a person. These are necessary for, and essential to, growthful change.

Human growth involves learning new actions and reactions, the expansion of one's perception and interpretation of the world, the trying of new reasonable risks to one's familiar security, the active challenge to one's old habits. Human growth means not to be blocked in the course of development.

A THREEFOLD ATTITUDE

The three conditions for human growth need to be explained. Before doing so, it is helpful to remember that these are not arbitrary concepts. Rather, they are derived from extensive research (Hart & Tomlinson, 1970; Rogers, 1959; Rogers et al., 1967; Truax & Carkhuff, 1967). One of Rogers' great distinctions has been his concern for scientifically studying how growthful change takes place. Thanks to his influence, some of the first scientific investigations of psychotherapy were undertaken (Barrett-Lennard, 1962; Halkides, 1958). Beyond the fields of counseling and psychotherapy, many studies in developmental psychology, from Piaget (Flavell, 1963) to Rosenthal and Jacobson (1968) and beyond (Levi-Strauss, 1963; Sullivan, 1953) justify the three conditions for human growth.

The first condition in the existential encounter is *genuineness or congruence*. This attitude of connectedness establishes a meeting at the human level, not at the level of roles (therapist-client), and not at the level of intellectual understanding but at that of experiencing. The therapist is fully there with the client, trying to experience what the client is experiencing.

This quality on the part of the therapist makes it possible for clients to bring into congruence their current experiences of self with their self-concept. They can include in the self-concept the current awareness, and thereby own, as being part of the self, whatever is being experienced in the here-and-now.

Positive regard is unconditional acceptance without judgment. It is an effort to trust the other person's subconscious wisdom and strength. By means of this attitude patients increase self-acceptance and discover that many old defenses against parts of self are no longer needed.

Empathic understanding attempts to describe what is needed for clients to feel understood. When we feel understood by another person, we are not talking about a merely intellectual, analytical understanding. It is a more total acceptance that we experience, a sense of respect from the other person which does not judge or attempt to change, correct or restructure our being.

A Clinical Example

Since the three conditions overlap and become fused, a brief clinical vignette may help clarify this threefold attitude. A 32-year-old man who had presented anxiety with a general emotional acceleration as his problem, and who had no medical conditions, was asked to pay attention to his body. (What part of your body are you especially aware of?) His response was a frightened stare and active fidgeting in the chair. He said, "That's the problem, I'm afraid I can't breathe." Trying not to reinforce this fear, I asked him to pay attention to his arms and hands and whatever sensations were there. He quieted down and looked at his hands, now together on his lap. I started to breathe loudly but slowly while he looked at his hands. I was trying to make my breathing coincide with his. Several times he looked up to me but I responded with a gentle smile indicating that he could continue to look at his hands: "You may become curious about the sensations you might be feeling now in your hands. What about their weight on your lap? Are both hands equally warm? Does one hand notice a slight breeze in the air? Just pay attention to your hands." When he blinked, I said, "It feels good to blink, a brief rest for your eyes. They may want to stay closed for a bit longer . . ." His breathing slowed down and became deeper. I mentioned it to him while he inhaled, "Breathing good feelings of inner peace; breathing out unnecessary tensions [while he exhaled], starting to feel much better than before. Your hands still resting comfortably; no rush, lots of time."

This brief vignette illustrates the threefold attitude so basic to Roger's therapy. I tuned into his current experience without judging it and accepting it fully. In so doing, I was being truthful and real. My attitude made it possible for the patient to tune into his own reality, expanding it, owning it more completely.

My client-centered attitude came across from my paying close attention to his behavior, from my true concern for his initial restlessness, from my pacing. This made it easier *for him* to be genuine and congruent. He could have become distracted with his psychogenic breathing difficulty but I helped him focus on his hands, another aspect—also real—of his awareness. By so doing, I expanded his inner awareness, from his breathing to his hands, from his hands to his blinking. Only then did I return to his breathing. By now, his own inner corrective mechanism had remedied the breathing difficulty and he was breathing with greater ease. When he started, his self-perception was overinvolved in his breathing *difficulty*. In a few minutes, his self-concept had absorbed another perception previously ignored, namely, that of his hands, his blinking and, yes, his easier breathing. He became more at ease, more centered on the positive realities of his current existence.

My attitude combined the three qualities: it would be artificial to decide at what point genuineness was at work and at what other moment, empathic understanding or unconditional positive regard were evident. The qualities are components of a particular attitude towards another human being which permeates every technique or intervention in the counseling session.

Rogers teaches the importance of considering psychotherapy as the opportunity *to start* a new effective life. It is not to produce an optimally adjusted person but "to start the development of a new pattern of adjustment" (Ford & Urban, 1965, p. 423). The ultimate goal for therapy is the realization of the conditions necessary for an actualized life. By actualizing new awareness, perceptions and evaluations, therapy starts *the process* of self-actualization which is then concretely translated into different behavior patterns. The therapist, therefore, is committed to the healthy growth of the individual, not to the concrete forms this growth will take.

Attitudinally, the therapist cannot compromise; growth and self-actualization must take place. Behaviorally, however, the therapist is not committed to any particular form. To give an example, to have different interests in life is part of self-fulfillment, but what these interests may be is up to the individual and will be decided when new perceptions and evaluations of his or her world start to change in therapy. In this sense, it may be said that the therapist is nonjudgmental at the behavioral level, but has unbending values when it comes to the basic attitude of self-actualization and growth.

THE PROCESS OF THE NEW HYPNOSIS

The threefold growth-producing Rogerian attitude does not emphasize enough what the client is experiencing in the present. The techniques used by Rogerians, e.g., reflection, clarification, summarization (Boy & Pine, 1982), are too intellectual; they are verbal (left hemispheric) maneuvers directed at helping the client be more in touch with feelings and inner perceptions.

The New Hypnosis, following in the footsteps of Milton H. Erickson, is eminently Rogerian. And Rogers would be a devout Ericksonian had he taken that extra step into the actual experience of the client. The New Hypnosis is Rogerian but enriched with the directiveness of the Ericksonian attitude. Here is the difference. Clients are not encouraged to verbalize but to experience. They are encouraged to stay with whatever is happening to them at the moment. Only after they have had the opportunity to experience fully should verbalization take place. Rogerian therapy transcripts often look like conversations between two sensitive people. In the New Hypnosis there is very little "conversation" as such. Clients are instructed *to focus* on some inner realities, to experience them with greater self-awareness; clients do not talk about problems.

In outline form, I follow this basic sequence: Observe, Lead, Discuss and Check—OLD C for short:

1) Carefully *observe* the client's:
   Language
   Significant statements
   Somatics (gestures, body posture, facial expressions).
2) Choose one of the above and *lead* the client to "stay with it, to get into experiencing it fully."
3) When the experience is completed *discuss* it with the client if he or she wants to discuss it.
4) *Check* the genuineness of the above by repeating Step 2 and monitoring how the body reacts to the process. This will either confirm what just happened or necessitate further work.

It is easy to realize that this process is client-centered. It starts with the client, and it stays with him or her as far as the experience continues. The therapist checks the whole process by the way the client feels about it and reacts to it bodily. This process usually does not take long and once people learn it, they tend to use it by themselves. In this way, it has similarities with what Gendlin (1978) calls *focusing*, a self-awareness process with many Rogerian overtones. It should also be remembered that, as a process, the four steps outlined above interplay with each other and overlap. The outline and explanation are pedagogical devices, convenient for understanding the process of the New Hypnosis.

The most important activity of the therapist in the beginning of the process is to be actively in touch with the client's experience. The three areas the therapist has to observe carefully, discussed below, are not primarily the content of what the person is saying. Most therapists are trained exactly in the opposite manner; they pay close attention to the content of the client's conversation.

Language

The first area to observe is the *structure of language*, not what the language expresses. By structure I mean the choice of words, figures of speech, sensory modality, etc. At some inner level people choose the expressions they use in language. We have five main sensory receptors with which we relate to the world, and it is interesting to observe which inner senses are used most frequently by a person (c.f. Bandler & Grinder, 1975). Expressions may be *kinesthetic*: such as "I can't stand it"; "it makes me sick"; "I'm stuck." They may be *visual*: "I see it clearly"; "I'm in the dark"; "let me throw some light on the subject." They may be *auditory*: "It sounds great"; "blasted out loud"; "it's music to my ears." These three senses are the most common in our culture, though we also have manifestations of *taste* and *smell* in our language: "It stinks"; "he came out smelling like a rose"; "my mouth is watering"; "it was a delicious experience."

The therapist should pay close attention to this element of language. When the person uses an expression that reflects an inner sense, the therapist can invite the client to stay with it, to experience what it feels like to have something sound great, or see something clearly, or feel stuck.

Another aspect of language is that of mental images. If a person says he or she feels "light as a kite," rather than asking for further explication, I would invite him or her to experience being light as a kite, to really get into this image and to go with it as far as possible.

For example, a patient wanted to focus on her relationship with men. She had been divorced for about seven years and had had more or less satisfying relationships with men since the divorce, one lasting two years. She told me, "Ever since I was eight, I remember thinking of a string that went from my vagina to my heart to my head." I invited her to relax a little and to try to get this image as clearly as possible, to try to see this string in her mind's eye. In less than a minute she reported that she was capturing the image. She saw the "string" as a gold braid but somehow she did not like it. (After clients capture an inner experience, I ask them to check it in their body—Step 4, above.) I requested her "to check what happens in your body when you focus on that gold braid." After a moment of concentration, she said she felt a line of tension going from her neck to her vagina. I suggested that she direct her breathing to that line of tension in order to either change the image or reduce the discomfort. She was to stay with the line of tension for a while. With a mild smile she reported then that the original string had changed. It was now soft and beautiful like a rainbow. I encouraged her to stay with this new image and to enjoy its beauty and any other good feelings that it generated. She took a few moments to do this, looking relaxed and happy. I asked again to check that line of tension. It was gone and she was still enjoying the rainbow. In fact, she was dancing or swimming in and out of the rainbow, but somehow the rainbow now connected her vagina and her head, bypassing her heart. When I asked her what happened she answered that her heart was to one side. I directed her once more to linger in the rainbow image and in all the good feelings that it generated.

The process continued for several more minutes. When she finally opened her eyes and discussed her experience, she had realized several important things: Good orgasms did not mean that she was in love with the man or that she had to love him. She could bypass the heart. Her head could allow her to have pleasure as something good in itself. The final step of her therapy session was to go back to the experiential process and to confirm her new perceptions with her body sensations, i.e., to feel good about her new learning.

Statements

The second item to observe carefully is important phrases or statements. I saw a young man who was in the process of deciding whether or not to continue a relationship with a woman. At the beginning of one session he said, "I know I have to end with Melissa." I asked him to repeat that to himself while he was relaxed and with his eyes closed. While he was doing that, I suggested that he check how his body reacted to this statement. He felt some tension in his chest. I asked him to "stay with that tension and to get into it." His breathing was to be directed to that area of his body so he could experience that area more fully. He did this and the tension was gone. He spontaneously saw himself in a bright, beautiful meadow, feeling happy, relaxed and at peace with himself. I encouraged him to enjoy that mental vision and all the feelings accompanying it. The therapy session continued by following what came spontaneously to his mind, until he said firmly and without hesitation that, yes, he had to end the relationship with Melissa and that he was going to do it that very week. I invited him to check once more how this decision affected his body. He felt positive about it and ended the session.

Somatics

The third area to observe is that of gestures, posture and facial expressions, what may be called *somatics*. Often by asking a person to repeat a gesture or to exaggerate it, important subconscious material is triggered. While talking about her current annoyance at her job a middle-aged woman made a gesture that looked like swimming the dog-paddle. She did this several times. I asked her to continue this gesture and to get into any feelings, memories, or sensations that became apparent. She soon started breathing heavily. I encouraged her to fully realize whatever she was experiencing. She uttered a few words, very faintly, "Small, beach, Arab." Again I prompted her to stay with her experience and to involve as many senses as possible. "You are there, really," I said, "living fully whatever is happening."

Her anxiety seemed to mount and I kept saying that it was all right, that whatever came up from her subconscious was important for her to relive now. That she had the inner resources to handle this experience and to benefit from it. At this point, she said a few words in a foreign language. Later she explained that it was Hebrew, the only language she used when she was six and lived in Israel.

After about 30 minutes she returned from reverie and discussed the experience with me. She had started by swimming in her mind. This had led her to the Mediterranean and to her early years. Then she saw herself on a beach in Israel where there was an older boy whom she liked; he was Arab. He was at a distance and seemed to be doing something like masturbating, though, as a little girl, she was not fully sure of what it was. She felt some sexual feelings, curiosity, and anxiety. But the anxiety slowly diminished and she was able to enjoy the beach again, to go swimming once more and to return home happy and feeling secure. Somehow this inner experience, obviously not related to her job, was connected with it and she felt much better about her job when the experience was over. She had such a thorough age regression that she spoke in the language she knew at the time.

Notice that in this case, this woman's subconscious was ready to cooperate. Had I allowed her to talk about her job, her dissatisfaction in it, etc., she probably would have left as unresolved as when she started the session. What resulted was the outcome of my respectful cooperation with her inner self. She did the work she needed at the time. I just made this possible.

For most of the session, I was not sure of what was going on—a position that many traditional therapists cannot tolerate. They have to know exactly what is happening, they have to ask questions, request explanations. Erickson repeated frequently through the years that we have to learn to trust the subconscious. To trust the subconscious leads to growthful change. This woman somehow used the voyage into her past to reassure herself about her current job, *to change* her attitude about her job. In a subsequent session, she confirmed that the experience had been beneficial; she was more relaxed at work, less open to the negative influence of a boss that previously triggered her own negativism.

SUMMARY

The totality of the client's experience in the here-and-now is used to make change possible. Verbalization is not necessarily the main means to work therapeutically. Rather than verbal free association, the New Hypnosis works with free association of inner experiences. However, these "free associations" are carefully directed by the therapist who is unreservedly receptive to whatever the client's subconscious brings up. The therapist then utilizes that material to allow the subconscious mind to find its own meaning, not to analyze it, connect it with previous material or interpret it. This approach is based on the Ericksonian faith in the subconscious which Rogers understood as "the inherent tendency of the organism to develop all its capacities in ways which serve to maintain or enhance the organism" (Rogers, 1959).

REFERENCES

Araoz, D. L. (1982). *Hypnosis and sex therapy.* New York: Brunner/Mazel.
Bandler, R., & Grinder, J. (1975). *The structure of magic, I.* Palo Alto, CA: Science & Behavior Books.
Barrett-Lennard, G. (1962). Dimensions of therapist response as causal factors in therapeutic change. *Psychological Monographs, 76*(562).

Boy, A. V., & Pine, G. J. (1982). *Client-centered counseling: A renewal*. Boston: Allyn & Bacon.

Flavell, J. H. (1963). *The developmental psychology of Jean Piaget*. New York: Van Nostrand.

Ford, D. H., & Urban, B. H. (1965). *Systems of psychotherapy*. New York: Wiley.

Gendlin, E. T. (1978). *Focusing*. New York: Everest House.

Halkides, G. (1958). *An experimental study of four conditions necessary for therapeutic personality change*. Unpublished doctoral dissertation, University of Chicago.

Hart, J. T. & Tomlinson, T. M. (Eds.). (1970). *New directions in client-centered therapy*. Boston: Houghton Mifflin.

Levi-Strauss, C. (1963). *Structural anthropology*. New York: Basic Books.

Meador, B. D., & Rogers, C. R. (1979). Person-centered therapy. In R.J. Corsini (Ed.), *Current psychotherapies* (2nd ed.). Itasca, IL: F. E. Peacock.

Rogers, C. R. (1959). A theory of therapy, personality and interpersonal relationships as developed in the client-centered framework. In S. Koch (Ed.), *Psychology: A study of a science, Vol. 3: Formulations of the person and the social context*. New York: McGraw-Hill.

Rogers, C. R. (1961). *On becoming a person*. Boston: Houghton Mifflin.

Rogers, C. R., Gendlin, E. T., Kiesler, D. J., & Louax, C. (Eds.). (1967). *The therapeutic relationship and its impact: A study of psychotherapy with schizophrenics*. Madison, WI: University of Wisconsin Press.

Rosenthal, R., & Jacobson, L. (1968). *Pygmalion in the classroom: Teacher expectation and pupils' intellectual ability*. New York: Holt, Rinehart & Winston.

Sullivan, H. S. (1953). *The interpersonal theory of psychiatry*. New York: Norton.

Truax, C. B., & Carkhuff, R. R. (1967). *Towards effective counseling and psychotherapy: Training and practice*. Chicago: Aldine.

Chapter 15

The Erickson Hook: Values in Ericksonian Approaches

Michael D. Yapko

I believe it was Milton Erickson who said that "anyone who can be socialized can be hypnotized." Like much of Erickson's communication, this quote demonstrates the ease with which he could make a complex issue seem elementary to the casual listener, while simultaneously retaining depth of meaning and complexity for the more profound thinker. Readers can discover that there is much information in the above seemingly simple quote, an approach Erickson commonly used in sharing his knowledge. In commenting on the relationship between socialization and hypnotic responsiveness, Erickson obviously was aware of the profound impact of the socialization process on all people throughout their lives. It is impossible to escape the influence of others as one daily attempts to balance personal needs against those of others in order to maintain a sense of individuality while enjoying the benefits of belonging to a group.

Perhaps the single most important dimension of the socialization process is the development of personal values, because it is a personal value system more than any other human dimension that determines what is and is not possible to do. The literature on values is surprisingly meager, perhaps because it is often suggested that while values are interesting and worth knowing about, they are "locked-in" at a relatively young age and are not likely to change significantly over time. It seems evident in Erickson's work, however, that *values can change, or, at least, that the specific way a value is expressed can change.*

A value is thought to change only when a profound enough stimulus, called a Significant Emotional Event, or SEE, is experienced (Massey, 1979). In some instances, psychotherapy can be viewed as the artificial or deliberate creation of a SEE in order to *alter* the patient's value system in a more adaptive direction. In other instances, psychotherapy may involve the *use* of a patient's values as a "hook" (Zeig, 1982) to facilitate desired changes.

The purpose of this chapter is threefold: 1) to delineate the relationship between personal values and the quality of existence; 2) to describe how to identify a patient's value system in order to attain rapport and discover where therapy may be aimed ("hooked") in order to facilitate change; and 3) to show how specific values may be either the catalyst or the target of a given therapeutic intervention.

THE ORIGIN AND ROLE OF PERSONAL VALUES

Humans are not born with values; they are acquired during the socialization process. The ongoing process of learning to make sense out of a chaotic world necessitates internalizing thoughts and feelings about what is right or wrong, normal or abnormal, acceptable or unacceptable, etc. Values are defined as subjective reactions to the world based on personal appraisal of the relative worth of the object or event under consideration. This definition includes judgments, internal reactions, and observable (external) reactions to experience. Through the socialization process, individuals develop a subjective world view that dictates the patterns of their judgments, and, of special importance to the clinician, what they can and cannot do. Values help define the limits of experience. The nature of the value operating in a person at a given moment is the filter through which experience is perceived. If, for example, one holds the value of "leading an exciting life," then it is predictable that such a person will take risks throughout life that others may consider dangerous, be in fairly constant motion, appear unsettled and noncommitted to observers who don't share the same value, and will generally demonstrate a variety of behaviors that are related to that single value.

Morris Massey (1979) described the acquisition and role of values from his "Value Programming" model. Massey pointed out that while individuals each have a unique personal history, they are also affected by the social milieu. Thus, many people are exposed to, and influenced by, the same societal events at the "critical" time at which values are forming, creating a commonality among them. Massey described the forces acting on the development of a value system by considering which cultural values were evident at the time the person was approximately ten years of age, plus or minus two years. In this four-year period,

Massey estimated 90% of one's values are internalized. Massey also pointed out that what one grows up *with* becomes routine and viewed as "normal." Unlike their grandparents, space travel and computers do not awe children of today. However, what one grows up *without* becomes very important to the person throughout life. The evidence for this point is abundant in clinical literature: families that are unstable produce human beings who crave security, just as homes that are emotionally sterile produce human beings who crave affection.

The role of values in the formation of one's world view cannot be overstated. Erickson understood this point and consistently made direct or indirect use of it in his work. Repeated so often whenever Erickson's work is discussed is his point that each person is an individual, with a perspective and personal history unlike that of anyone else's. Erickson's ability consistently to attain a workable rapport with his patients is described in numerous places (Bandler & Grinder, 1975; Zeig, 1982). Much of Erickson's ability to attain rapport originated in his ability to identify, accept, and utilize patients' values.

The things that are personally important to patients can easily be overlooked if the clinician is preoccupied with other factors less central to their current state and overall personality. It is all too easy to focus on things like Erickson's breathing rate or his use of peripheral vision at the expense of appreciating the intensity of the relationship he had with his patients, which microscopic analysis cannot define any more than one can analyze and define "love." The values of *the man Erickson* underlie *the psychiatrist Erickson*. Erickson's values of "accepting others" and "amplifying the positive" have many behaviors, thoughts, and feelings attached to them that have been analyzed and described in detail elsewhere (Watzlawick et al., 1974; Zeig, 1980b).

Erickson's ability to discover what was important to his patient, i.e., what his patient valued, allowed Erickson the opportunity to accept the person while finding the value(s) on which the maladaptive thoughts, feelings and behaviors were based. Thus, he could tailor the intervention to the patient's individual needs by either altering the limiting value or utilizing it as a catalyst for the desired change he would "hook" onto it.

IDENTIFYING VALUES

Having described personal value systems as the framework for interpreting the ongoing events of life (which, in turn, dictates courses of action), it becomes apparent that in order to truly understand individuals, their value systems must be identified. This is a diagnostic phase of the clinical interaction, a phase in which the values are determined either directly or indirectly. In this phase, the clinician has several goals: 1) to gather information about current and past experience relative to the presenting problem; 2) to form a rapport with the patient by developing an empathic understanding of the nature of the problem; 3) to formulate an impression of the problem's dynamics and where the therapy should be directed. How this diagnostic phase progresses will determine to a large extent the probable outcomes of treatment. Misdiagnosis of a problem's dynamics or the patient's values can prevent or inhibit positive treatment results.

Erickson's diagnostic criteria differed appreciably from that of more traditional clinicians. Attaching a specific label of pathology to a patient was not his diagnostic method. Rather, Erickson valued the nature of the patient's subjective experience. Zeig (1983, personal communication) described a series of "Ericksonian" diagnostic criteria including evaluating the patient's thinking style (e.g., linear vs. mosaic), response style (e.g., compliant vs. independent), and attention style (e.g., focused vs. diffuse). In terms of assessing the patient's value system, Erickson thought it important to consider such things as the patient's family size (specifically where the patient fit in) and early socialization environment (specifically where geographically one was raised and whether in an urban or rural environment) (Zeig, 1980b). Such factors are critical in determining values. For example, Erickson's rural upbringing cultivated in him a value of patience that few urbanites seem to develop. Farmers know the seeds they plant today will not yield anything for a long time, and so "time" takes on a different meaning for them, in contrast to the urbanite's fast-paced perspective of time (cf. Zeig, 1980b). Likewise, considering the value of time across generations as one might from the "Values Programming" perspective, today's older generation has a different perspective of history and the amount of time it takes to accomplish difficult things than do the young people of today who want and expect it all to happen "right now."

Assessing the patient's values is a necessary step in formulating an intervention. Utilizing the above example of the "time" value, how likely are young people to commit themselves to long-term treatment? In contrast, how are older people likely to view "brief therapy?" The difference between the two as to what is acceptable may hinge solely on the subjective value of time. On the basis of that single value, a person may commit to long-term therapy needlessly, never even considering a briefer approach. Values play an important part in determining the range of one's choices.

In attempting to identify patients' values, specifically what they believe to be correct, normal, and right, Erickson employed a number of different patterns that can be easily integrated into clinical practice. Before identifying and utilizing these patterns, it is important to note that Erickson attained rapport and thus gained the capacity for influence by assuming that the patient's values were right for the patient. It seemed that the issue for Erickson concerned the impact the values had in the patient's life, not the "correctness" of those values. The clinician need not agree with the values in order to be therapeutically effective. The clinician only need know how the particular value under consideration is helping or hurting the patient's everyday living. Erickson's acceptance of what was important to his client allowed his therapies to reach a much broader range of people than can those clinicians who directly or indirectly impose their own personal values on their patients. Contradicting, rejecting, or lightly dismissing something in the patient's value system as unimportant or invalid that *is* important or valid to the patient can only result in resistance at least and failure at most. Erickson's general strategy of "accept and utilize" was effective because it worked within the realm of what was important to the patient.

One pattern for identifying patients' value systems is to consider, as Massey (1979) did, their age and social background. Specifically, what was ongoing in society at the time the person was approximately ten years old? What values were operating in society in general and in that person's particular subculture in the formative years? Erickson did not have Massey's descriptive model to guide his thinking, yet Erickson's use of gender and ethnic stereotypes, his considerations of age-appropriate behavior, (Haley, 1973; Rosen, 1982a) and his insight into the forces shaping the patient as the patient was growing up, show an intuitive understanding and utilization of principles Massey considered relevant. An example of the age and socialization factors can clarify this point: Consider the person around age 60 who grew up in America during the Great Depression. With money scarce and times difficult for most, the uncertainty of the future created a great deal of insecurity. The result of such difficult times for many people in this age group is a strongly held value for financial security. This value can be expressed in a variety of ways from person to person: an intense desire to accumulate the material comforts lacking in childhood, the inability to "waste" food by leaving some left over on a plate even though physically full, the inability to spend money on "trivial" things like recreation or personal comfort, and the refusal to make purchases with credit cards. On a statistical basis, people around age 60 who are sent credit cards in the mail are likely to destroy them (Massey, 1979). In contrast, people in their twenties who are sent credit cards are likely to charge to the limit. How can such diverse reactions to a single stimulus—a credit card—be accounted for? People in their twenties did not experience the Depression and so *cannot* experientially relate to their elders' value of financial security. Younger people, on average, know only that they have been able to get the things they want. To them, if money is scarce, the object of desire can be charged, put on lay-away, or financed, so "why wait?" (Massey, 1979).

Massey (1979) studied the generational differences in particular values by asking such questions as: Is the person a "team player" or an individualist? A leader or follower? Obedient or questioning of authority? A puritan or sensualist? Desirous of a fixed social order or of social equality? A believer in work for work's sake or for personal fulfillment? A seeker of stability or an experimenter seeking change? A gatherer of material objects or meaningful experiences? Each of these values is or has been encouraged in society at some point in time, influencing the development of a personal value system by engendering conformity or nonconformity as an individual response to the standard.

The patient's age, family background, geographic point of origin and other such factors reveal a great deal of information about the nature of his or her value system. To diagnose how these factors reveal values, it is useful as Massey did to review events ongoing in society from decade to decade in order to discover the influences shaping the young at the time. Doing so can give one the "mind reading" ability Erickson appeared to have. In fact, one does not have to be a mind reader to know that the odds are in favor of a 60-year-old being conscious of financial security and against the "live now" philosophy of "irresponsible" younger people. Looking for evidence to support or refute the existence of an expected value in a given individual can speed up to a remarkable degree the attainment of rapport and the opportunity to use that value in one's therapies. In a sense, one doesn't have to "start from scratch" when one considers the values likely to be associated with a given age and background. Erickson often appeared to be a "mind reader" while simply making use of age-specific and culture-specific stereotypes.

A second pattern for identifying patients' value systems involves the identification of generalizations in patients' verbal and nonverbal communication patterns. When patients describe what a man "should" do, what a woman "always" thinks important, how a child must "never" do that, or when they behave in a consistent way in a certain context, they communicate their values in those areas. Observing how consistently patients act on their stated generalizations is the path most likely to lead to the underlying value. Patients may overtly (consciously) state that they are "always willing to try new things," but then balk at being given a homework assignment that calls for them to do something outside of their ordinary routine. Many clinicians interpret this correctly as "resistance," but attribute it to a source other than a value system. Likewise, values can be inferred quite reliably from behavior. For example, one need not ask readers of this chapter whether they value education and the ongoing development of clinical skill. It can be reasonably inferred from observing readers taking time to voluntarily read it.

Identifying the values underlying the generalizations that patients hold allows the clinician the opportunity to bypass an argument about the "truth" of the generalization. Contradicting patients' generalizations will only lead to a loss of rapport, not a change of belief. Leon Festinger's concept of "cognitive dissonance" (1957) holds true in the vast majority of cases: A person will tenaciously hold onto a belief, whether objectively "true" or not, and reject conflicting input in order to avoid the unpleasant internal dissonance such a contradiction would create. An exception occurs when the conflicting input is too great to be defended against through rationalization, denial, or the other defense mechanisms. At such moments the person experiences a Significant Emotional Event, the precursor of a change in values.

Generalizations can exist on multiple structural levels, including affective, cognitive, and behavioral levels. For the individual, generalizations encompass the various subgroup (age, gender, etc.) value generalizations. Repetitive patterns of thought, emotion, and behavior reflect underlying values, expressing values in a way that are consistent, though potentially maladaptive. For example, if a woman complains about being physically abused by her spouse yet is highly resistant to the clinician's suggestions to leave the man (a common pattern among women experiencing the "battered wife syndrome") it may have little to do with her "ego boundaries" as many clinicians assume. Rather, her repetitive emotional expression that she loves him, her repetitive thought that he is "basically a good man," and her repetitive behavior of defending him and going back to him and risking further abuse possibly can hinge on one deeply seated value: "A marriage is forever, for better or worse, and divorce is simply not an alternative." This key value may not even be in the woman's awareness.

A third pattern for identifying patients' value systems is simply observing the patient's lifestyle. In interviewing patients and taking a history, the clinician has ample opportunity to observe them and listen to their descriptions of lifestyle. What type (i.e., style, quality) of clothes are worn? Do they wear jewelry? What kind of job do they have and how do their job and personality relate? How much education do they have? Are they loners or are they involved with others, and if so, to what degree? What are their hobbies and favorite things to do? Do the people see themselves as masters or victims of their fate? Lifestyles that evolve are obviously directly related to value systems. The advertising industry in particular makes extensive use of this fact in "hooking" consumers into buying products by playing on their values. If a man values his masculinity he will "have to" buy a certain brand of beer, and if a woman values her femininity she will "have to" buy a certain brand of cosmetics. If one values safety, one will "have to" buy a certain brand of smoke alarm. Advertising as the biggest (i.e., most dollars spent) industry in our culture works on the principle of finding the consumer's relevant value and "hooking" the product's purchase to it. A similar structure is the essence of the Erickson "Hook." The task for the clinician is to find the relevant value in the patient's world and to hook the therapy to it.

A fourth approach to the identification of patients' values is a highly structured approach called "Value Clarification." Value clarification involves a series of structured experiential exercises designed to draw out a person's values. These exercises are often fun and can amplify awareness of personal values and even awareness of internal value conflicts. The exercises can vary in intensity from superficial to profound, and can aid in the identification and resolution of patient ambivalences. Such exercises are available in a number of works on the subject (Simon et al., 1972; Smith, 1977).

UTILIZING VALUES IN THERAPEUTIC INTERACTION

Values have been described as an enduring filter through which subjective experience is created, interpreted, and reacted to. In describing values as "enduring," the primary issue for the clinician is to determine in what manner patients' value systems will be utilized in the therapy. Utilization of patients' value systems may be accomplished on two distinct but overlapping levels: either by using values as a catalyst for facilitating changes on the behavioral, cognitive and affective levels, or by using a value as the primary target for a therapeutic intervention.

Values as Catalysts

In using a value as a catalyst, unique characteristics of the patient can be discovered and used. In this approach, altering the patient's values is *not* the goal of the clinician. Rather the clinician attempts to discover what is important to the patient, and then "hooks" the desired change directly or indirectly to that value. For example, consider a patient who maintains only casual relationships with others but wants a more intimate committed relationship "if only my partner could allow me the freedom I need." In such a case the therapy might involve hooking the value of "freedom" to the reframing of a committed relationship as "an *open-ended* sharing with virtually *no limits* of how much freedom you can build into your lives together any way you care to." Such reframing of "commitment" involves hooking the value of freedom to the experience of building an intimate relationship.

Using the "value programming" approach described earlier, the clinician can develop an awareness for individual differences in socialization factors and thus be more sensitive to the ways values can be used. For example, if patients value the role of the doctor as the unquestioned authority, as patients in Erickson's era were considerably more likely to do than are today's patients who are more likely to say "Thank you for your input and now I would like to get a second opinion," the doctor can be more direct and demanding. If patients value participation in the treatment on a more equal and personally responsible level, following blindly what appears to be an irrational homework assignment is not a likely response. Clinicians who have overlooked patients' value of participation is then likely to find their patients "resistant," i.e., not obedient. In such instances, clinicians are responsible for an impasse by not accepting and utilizing their patients' value systems.

Erickson's approaches to psychotherapy made abundant use of the things that were important to his patient, a clear reflection of his interest in and respect for those with whom he worked.

Values as Targets

In the values field, it is generally recognized that a value does *not* change until necessity dictates. "Necessity" takes the form of a Significant Emotional Event, an experience that is so emotionally powerful that the previously held value is overwhelmed and abandoned in favor of adopting a more relevant, adaptive value. Significant Emotional Events may occur naturally in life, such as when one experiences a trauma or has a profoundly moving or insightful experience. Creating a Significant Emotional Event artificially and deliberately is the essence of psychotherapy in general and Ericksonian approaches in particular. Evident in Erickson's work is the ability to rattle a patient's world view, unsettling basic beliefs so the patient may "find" a more useful, functional approach to life. Erickson was a master at finding the "hook"—the value on which to base the therapy.

Erickson's main objective was to bring the old value into direct conflict with the new, letting the more powerful (i.e., adaptive) one win out. Erickson had a number of approaches to accomplish this, three of which are discussed in this chapter, including homework assignments, hypnotically created pseudorealities, and the use of shock, surprise, confusion, and other such dissonance-causing methods.

Once the targeted value that the therapy is to be hooked to has been identified, any or all of the above approaches can be employed. The factor that makes the therapeutically created Significant Emotional Event important enough to alter an established value is the powerful *experience* of discovering the inadequacy of previously held values in effectively managing the current situation. The more personally meaningful a value is, the more significant the emotional event will be when it is discovered experientially that what is believed to be true is untrue. The general Ericksonian strategy, then, is to deliberately and artificially create a situation in which patients can experience directly how their current values are unnecessarily limiting. Simultaneously, patients are offered the opportunity to discover another value (or another, more useful means for expressing the original value) that is more adaptive. Unless a new possibility is created in the Significant Emotional Event, patients will only experience the frustration of discovering that what they value as meaningful is actually maladaptive, a prospect so potentially threatening that many would resist such a recognition and tenaciously hold on to the original, albeit dysfunctional, value. Evident throughout Erickson's work was the element of patient choice; whenever he blocked the symptom's destructive path, it was with an explicit or implicit offer of an opportunity to discover a healthier path to follow in order to meet one's needs.

Homework assignments: Case examples

Patients may be given homework assignments that bring limiting values into conflict with more adaptive ones, facilitating change through experiential integration of more functional values. Erickson described an intervention utilizing this principle with an out-of-state couple seeking marital therapy (Zeig, 1980b). The husband was a psychiatrist in practice for about 30 years, yet because of neglect he had not yet attained a satisfactory professional practice. His wife of six years had a job she did not enjoy, but she felt the need to work in order to support herself and her husband. Both were in analysis over many years but with little success. After a brief interview, Erickson assigned each to visit independently a different place of interest in Phoenix; he was to visit Squaw Peak, and she the Botanical Gardens. On reporting to Erickson the next day, the husband proclaimed his enthusiasm for Squaw Peak while the wife proclaimed her distaste for the Gardens. Erickson instructed them to switch and visit where the other had been the previous day. On reporting to Erickson the following day, the husband shared his pleasure in visiting the Gardens, while the wife complained bitterly about Squaw Peak. Erickson gave one last assignment, that they each visit a spot of their own choosing. The husband returned to the Gardens, the wife to Squaw Peak. The next day Erickson listened to the couple's differing reports and abruptly dismissed them, stating they had completed treatment. A few days later Erickson was called by the couple and told that the wife had fired her analyst and filed for divorce. Erickson viewed the resolution as arising from the wife's being "tired of climbing that mountain of marital distress day after day" (Zeig, 1980b, p. 147). Erickson accepted the value of the need to "save the marriage," but "hooked" the assignment to the greater value of "preserving individual identity," amplifying their individual differences through the homework assignments he gave them in order to create the Significant Emotional Event that allowed the marriage to end on a realistic note.

A second case example is derived from the author's clinical practice. A 31-year-old woman requested help to stop smoking. Her husband of two months was a tobacco company sales representative who smoked heavily. The couple had lived together amiably for three years prior to marriage, but since the marriage she thought her husband had become more demanding and controlling, "as if I became his property." In fact, she had become demanding as well, having many unrealistic expectations. The patient was depressed about the amount of tension so early in the marriage, and stated she smoked as an outlet for her anxiety and for her husband's "company image."

In a general discussion she agreed that a healthy marriage should have two strong equal partners, and the discussion soon turned to the importance of each person doing what is best for a personal sense of well-being without necessarily needing to ask for permission from anyone. She felt strongly that a woman should be independent and not controlled by a man—a positive belief but one that was contributing to the power struggle in her marriage.

Therefore, in the therapy, maintaining a sense of independence within the marriage was "hooked" to her desire to stop smoking. Her homework assignment given in the first session was to politely ask her husband for permission each and every time before smoking a cigarette. She found the assignment distasteful; her husband, however, thought her therapist obviously had a good grasp of the situation. Through this therapeutic maneuver, her values of "dependence" and "controlling others" through power plays were brought into conflict with the greater value of "independence," which ultimately dominated. By framing stopping smoking as symbolic of her not needing her husband's permission to do as she pleased, while simultaneously demonstrating she was internally strong enough to stop smoking, she could feel good about herself, make choices in her own behalf, and assert herself as an unquestioned equal. She stopped smoking within one week, and was seen a second time for reinforcement and formal instruction in self-hypnosis. As of a three-month follow-up, she had not resumed smoking and was pleased that she could stop a habit that her husband apparently could not.

Hypnotically created pseudorealities: Case examples

Through hypnosis, clinicians can create a subjective reality for patients that brings the dysfunctional value into conflict with the stronger, more adaptive one. In a case reported by Erickson (Zeig, 1980b), he was invited to speak about hypnosis at a national meeting of psychiatrists. In observing possible candidates to be subjects for a demonstration, Erickson chose a nurse whom he was later told was depressed and suicidal. Erickson elected to do covert psychotherapy on her while demonstrating hypnotic patterns to his audience. He created a pseudoreality for her, having her fantasize being in an arboretum and seeing the leaves of trees and bushes changing colors and dying, preparing for winter and the renewed growth of spring. Next, he had her experience herself at the zoo, where she could see the animals and their young living out different phases of their life cycle. Subsequently, he "took" her to an aviary to see the birds, commenting on their natural migratory instincts from season to season. He then guided her back to the hospital where she worked, then to a local beach to "watch" the huge storm waves quiet down, then back to the hospital again. Each place to which he guided her helped her rediscover the beauty and order of nature.

When she did not come back to work the next day, all who knew her assumed she had committed suicide. Although it was unknown until years later, actually she had joined the Navy, where she served two enlistments, married, had five children, and continued to work in a hospital! Erickson facilitated through hypnosis the experience of being in places where it was easy to appreciate many beauties of life, places that help make life worth living. In doing so, he hooked the value of life to being in all those places, amplifying its value and allowing it to dominate over the value of "doing what one should, not what one wants to" which was evident in her depressed lifestyle.

In another example, derived from the author's practice, a 32-year-old male presented the complaint of secondary impotence, having had successful but unsatisfactory intercourse only two or three times in a brief marriage originally designed to help him "get out of my mother's house." His former wife divorced him because of his impotence, and he soon returned home to live with, and take care of, his mother. His father had died when he was in his mid-teens and his mother had suffered a mild stroke during the time of his divorce and was demanding of his attention. He was casually dating a woman he liked who was interested in a sexual relationship with him, which he avoided. He felt guilty seeing her, a feeling compounded by his mother's overt jealousy and needling of the girl whenever she was with her son. Two sessions were spent in talking about a number of issues including his commitment to his mother, his feelings toward her, the effect of her manipulative ways on both his self-esteem and relationships with other women, and the type of intimate relationship he would like to have.

In the third session, hypnosis was used to facilitate the pseudoreality of being in his sixties looking back on his life. During trance he experienced the exaggerated effects of living solely for his mother's approval at the expense of forming a healthy, intimate relationship with a woman. As he experienced the loneliness, the self-loathing, and the fear of being totally controlled by women forever, he reacted emotionally and released resentment about his mother in particular and women in general. In reorienting to his current age and lifestyle, he firmly resolved to establish some limits in his relationship with his mother and relate to women as equals without having to capitulate to manipulation or unreasonable demands. In the week following that session, he redefined his relationship with his mother, was able to have intercourse with partial success, and felt very encouraged. By the fifth session he had full intercourse successfully. The last two sessions clarified and reinforced his resolution to live his own life and enjoy his sexual relationships. A six-month follow-up showed continued successful results. The values of "mother's approval" and "self-sacrifice" gave way to the more adaptive value of "living one's own life," after the hypnotically created pseudoreality instilled an experiential awareness for the destructive impact of the original values.

Causing dissonance: Case examples

Erickson often noted that out of confusion comes enlightenment. Helping a patient discover experientially that a value is not working can cause shock, surprise, and dissonance, sometimes but not necessarily, an unpleasant internal state that precedes the abandonment of the old value in favor of the new. Erickson demonstrated the therapeutic use of surprise with a patient named "Big Louise" (Zeig, 1980b). Big Louise was an unusually strong woman hospitalized for her violent attacks on policemen. Once in the hospital, she routinely threw tantrums in which she destroyed hospital property, and often necessitated physical restraint. Erickson interviewed her, established a rapport with her by providing assurance that he would not encourage the hospital staff to overpower her, and by talking about neutral things.

One day Erickson was called by a nurse and was told that Louise wanted to see him. He found her pacing back and forth, obviously agitated. On a prearranged signal from Erickson, the door flew open and in rushed a number of student nurses who proceeded to destroy methodically the furnishings in the room. Big Louise was shocked at the sight, jumped up and begged them to stop their destruction. That was, according to Erickson, the last time she did any damage, for once she saw how her behavior looked she could no longer engage in it. The value of "personal gratification" came into conflict with the more adaptive value of "social responsibility" through a shocking demonstration, and as a result the more adaptive value came to dominate.

Another example of this pattern is one in which the author and a male co-therapist provided a dissonance-causing intervention to a woman in her mid-forties who complained that "everyone treats me so badly and dumps all their personal junk on me and I can't stand it anymore." The woman presented as a self-effacing placater who was victimized in her marriage by an aggressive, intimidating man. She had few friends and no career outside the home.

In the first session, after a brief history was taken confirming her poor self-image and apparent inability to set limits on others, discussion turned to the general observation that some people will "get away with murder if you let them." Suddenly, my co-therapist untied his shoes, took them off and tossed them into the patient's lap, startling her, but generating no immediate comment. Soon, her lap was filled with shoes, socks, paper clips, notepads, ties, and a wide variety of assorted junk handy in my desk. The patient's anger began to rise with each item tossed her way, but she quickly squashed it as she passively accepted the "dumping," only meekly asking, "Why are you doing this?" With no explanation offered to satisfy her escalating confusion and her demand to know what we were doing, she finally stood up and threw off all the junk she had accumulated. She squarely faced both of us and harshly stated, "I came here for help and all you've done is throw junk at me, and unless you two take me seriously right now and respect my needs I will not come back." She looked and sounded like she meant it, and after a period of silence during which she angrily waited for a response, I quietly said to her, "You did great here, and now I wonder in how many other places you need to do the same thing?" The patient began to cry and lament that she knew that she let people get away with far too much, and that she would need to become more skilled at setting limits. She then accepted that she was no one's victim and that in order to develop healthy, positive relationships with others, she would have to establish some limits as to how far others could go. She was shocked to have two male therapists "dump" on her when she came to get help, and the subsequent experience of confusion allowed her to confront the value of "going along to maintain peace and stability" with the more adaptive value of "maintaining personal integrity." Through subsequent therapy sessions, the more adaptive value became integrated into her lifestyle.

SUMMARY

Milton Erickson had a clearly defined value system. Evident in his work are: the strength of his convictions about the inherent integrity of each human being; the importance of the family; the necessity of strong and close relationships with others; and the positive internal potentials of each person. Accepting and utilizing a patient's value system is a paradoxically simple yet highly sophisticated means for "hooking" effective therapy onto a patient's preexisting framework for living. Each person has many values, some congruent and some seemingly incongruent with life's choices. Therefore, clinicians have many choices of patient value "hooks" to use in therapy. By identifying the significant values in the patient's world, clinicians can choose whether to address a particular value itself or the behavior stemming from the value, just as clinicians can choose whether to address the cause of the symptom or the symptom itself. The treatment deemed appropriate is a matter of professional judgment. As clinicians, we must examine our own value systems, for like the patients we work with, they determine what we can and cannot do as clinicians in particular and as people in general.

REFERENCES

Bandler, R., & Grinder, J. (1975). *Patterns of the hypnotic techniques of Milton H. Erickson, M.D.* (Vol. 1). Cupertino, CA: Meta Publications.

Erickson, M., & Rossi, E. (1981). *Experiencing hypnosis: Therapeutic approaches to altered states.* New York: Irvington.

Festinger, L. (1957). *A theory of cognitive dissonance.* Stanford, CA: Stanford University Press.

Haley, J. (1973). *Uncommon therapy: The psychiatric techniques of Milton H. Erickson, M.D.* New York: Norton.

Massey, M. (1979). *The people puzzle: Understanding yourself and others.* Reston, VA: Reston Publishing.

Rokeach, M. (1973). *The nature of human values.* New York: The Free Press.

Rosen, S. (1982a). The values and philosophy of Milton H. Erickson. In J. Zeig, (Ed.), *Ericksonian approaches to hypnosis and psychotherapy.* New York: Brunner/Mazel.

Rosen, S. (Ed.). (1982b). *My voice will go with you: The teaching tales of Milton H. Erickson.* New York: Norton.

Rossi, E. (1973). Psychological shocks and creative moments in psychotherapy. *American Journal of Clinical Hypnosis, 16,* 9-22.

Simon, S., Howe, L., & Kirschenbaum, H. (1972). *Values clarification: A handbook of practical strategies for teachers and students.* New York: Hart Publishing.

Smith, M. (1977). *A practical guide to value clarification.* La Jolla, CA: University Associates.

Watzlawick, P., Weakland, J., & Fisch, R. (1974). *Change: Principles of problem formation and problem resolution.* New York: Norton.

Yapko, M. (1983). A comparative analysis of direct and indirect hypnotic communication styles. *American Journal of Clinical Hypnosis, 25,* 270-276.

Yapko, M. (1984). *Trancework: An introduction to clinical hypnosis.* New York: Irvington.

Yapko, M. (in press). The implications of the Ericksonian and Neuro-Linguistic Programming approaches for responsibility of therapeutic outcomes. *American Journal of Clinical Hypnosis.*

Zeig, J. (1980a). Symptom prescription techniques: Clinical applications using elements of communication. *American Journal of Clinical Hypnosis, 23,* 23-32.

Zeig, J. (Ed.). (1980b). *A teaching seminar with Milton H. Erickson.* New York: Brunner/Mazel.

Zeig, J. (1982). Ericksonian approaches to promote abstinence from cigarette smoking. In J. Zeig (Ed.), *Ericksonian approaches to hypnosis and psychotherapy.* New York: Brunner/Mazel.

Chapter 16

The Pervasion of the Resolution-Seeking Set

Dan C. Overlade

DESCRIPTION OF THE RESOLUTION-SEEKING SET

It was fashionable among members of one school of learning theorists in the 1950s and 60s to view anxiety as the primary source of drive (Mowrer, 1960; Spence, 1956). Others emphasized that anxiety is a disorganizer of effective action (Sarasan, 1965; Whiting & Child, 1953). In the psychoanalytic view, anxiety was seen as the central problem in neurosis, which led to the erroneous assumption that neurosis and anxiety were essentially synonymous. People with high levels of anxiety are treated by some as though they are neurotic (Cattell, 1965, pp. 245-246).

Clearly, anxiety can be adaptive or maladaptive. It is adaptive when it prompts the organism to remove itself from danger or to defend itself against attack, and when it generates learning or improved and novel responses. It is maladaptive when it functions to disorganize behavior or when it continues to stress the organism in the absence of danger. Mediated like the other emotions at the evolutionarily primitive midbrain, anxiety represents a departure from the homeostatic norm; and it is within that primitive center that the mechanisms to appreciate the reduction of anxiety reside. It is not anxiety, as such, which is the primary source of drive for the organism. Rather, it is the organism's need to reduce anxiety, to return to a more neutral state, which drives much mammalian behavior.

It is the purpose of this theoretical chapter to discuss a particular kind of anxiety—a kind of intellectual and emotional disequilibrium—which has far-ranging influence on human behavior, even when the disequilibrium is slight. Notably, there is a pervasive need to solve, resolve, discover, understand, comprehend, educe and deduce, to remove uncertainties and unknowns. I call this protean collection of pleasure-producing, anxiety-reducing mental activities (partly conscious, partly unconscious) "the resolution-seeking set." Without this sometimes eager readiness to resolve uncertainties or reduce mental disequilibrium, there would be no such event as a pun, a joke, metaphor, bind, non sequitur, shock, surprise, implication, analogy, interspersal or paradox. Approaches such as questioning, cognitive overloading, open-ended suggestions, and shifts in the frame of reference would lead nowhere.

Erickson had a keen "awareness that the patient's unconscious mind was listening and understanding much better than was possible for his or her conscious mind" (Haley, 1967, p. 522). But without a resolution-seeking set, what would drive the patient's unconscious mind to understand or even listen? The resolution-seeking set is the force responsible for the fact that many of Erickson's "approaches . . . initiate a search for new combinations of associations and mental processes that can present consciousness with useful results in everyday life as well as in hypnosis" (Erickson, Rossi & Rossi, 1976, p. 228).

The resolution-seeking set, as a construct, has kinship to the notion of cognitive dissonance (Festinger, 1957), which holds that the individual will strive to avoid or reduce dissonance and to achieve consonance in a *cognitive* system because dissonance is *uncomfortable*. The theory suggests that the responses to cognitive dissonance are also at a cognitive level. The concept of the resolution-seeking set includes responses that may be beyond the realm of cognition and acknowledges that, rather than avoiding the stress of a disequilibrium, the individual often seeks it out in order to experience the joy of resolution.

F. J. Shaw authored what he termed "reconciliation theory," which postulated "that the organism suffers a type of deprivation in the absence of contradictions, but seeks relief from irreconcilable contradictions" (Jourard & Overlade, 1966, p. 14). The impetus to reconcile contradictions which Shaw addressed is a form of the resolution-seeking set. What I have called "the joy of resolution" is not limited to the human animal. Shaw (Jourard & Overlade, 1966, pp. 14-15) cites a study by Hebb and Mahut in which animals persisted in preferring a long path over a short one when the long path provided new problems to be resolved.

Within classical Gestalt theory, the resolution-seeking set would include something akin to the principles of closure and organization. It also includes the Zeigarnik effect. Originally this term was applied to the experimental finding that names of interrupted tasks were better recalled than names of tasks which had been completed; later it came to be loosely applied to many forms of *unfinished business*. The resolution-seeking set includes *insight* of the sudden energizing type such as the *eureka* experience of Archimedes in his bath or of Köhler's chimpanzee, Sultan, when he solved the two-stick problem and retrieved the banana (Köhler, 1925). It also subsumes the gentler, more gradual and seemingly intuitive arrival at a new point of view. The resolution-seeking set is often a striving for enlightenment—not only for the satori of Zen, but also for lesser enlightenment.

EXAMPLES OF THE RESOLUTION-SEEKING SET

Often the resolution-seeking set can be satisfied through abstraction or generalization. A proverb readily can generate the resolution-seeking set and deciphering the proverb produces a "success" feeling that may be ego-enhancing, even when clear translation from the indirect form does not occur. For example, if one were to say, "A stitch in time saves nine," a listener may nod in knowing agreement. But if we ask the listener to explain the meaning of the proverb, more often than not he or she will remain oblique and give another proverb such as, "It's like, 'An ounce of prevention is worth a pound of cure.' " The definition that early attention to a task is more efficient than delaying seems to be made at some level of the mind, but the pleasure is in the *grasping* of the meaning, not in its articulation.

The grasping need not be verbal. The discovery of a designated geo-metrical form embedded within a more complex configuration can pro-vide a similar satisfaction. Moreover, there seems to be a factor common to both verbal and spatial grasping.

I conducted research on the ability to abstract meaning from proverbs and the ability to find embedded figures in the Gottschaldt Embedded Figures Test (Gottschaldt, 1926). Both significantly correlated with sense of humor, r (63) = .451 and .491, $p < .01$ (Overlade, 1954, p. 90). This effect was predicted from a theoretical position that whatever other factors might play a part in the humor experience, the *sine qua non* was the opportunity for success at ferreting out the *only-alluded-to meaning*.

In his analysis of the Gottschaldt task, Thurstone (1944) identified the principal factor involved as representing an "ability to form a perceptual closure against some distraction . . . [and to] hold a closure against dis-traction" (p. 101). A second important factor was "concerned with the manipulation of two configurations simultaneously or in succession" (p. 110).

The similarity of the humor-abstraction task to this figure abstraction problem is apparent. It is possible to consider the humor discovery task as the separation of an item from its field; in a verbal rather than configurational sense, it represents the formation of a closure (the allusion) against the distraction of the total field. It also may be observed that the individual who solves the riddle of a humor situation is manipulating two "pictures" simultaneously or in succession; one picture being the total joke field and the other the abstracted closure of the alluded-to meaning:

> There is the story about a culturally oriented woman who was exasperated because her husband was so obsessed with baseball, especially with his favorite team, the Chicago White Sox. "Baseball, baseball—I hear nothing but baseball all the time. We're going to get a little culture around here and I think the way we'll start is to learn a second language." She purchased a language training course and they listened to the tapes and did the drills and, as she insisted, each Saturday they spoke only German. They had been into this program for a few weeks when she came home from shopping on a Saturday afternoon, walked into their apartment and asked, *"Was sagst du?"* Without looking up from the TV, her husband responded, "They lost seven to three!"

As an example of the importance of *getting* the meaning, this joke serves us especially well, for it requires special information or knowledge. If one lacks that knowledge, she or he is robbed of the opportunity to abstract the humor. If it is necessary to explain that *"Was sagst du?"* is a German translation of the English idiom, "What do you say?" there will be no "discovery" of meaning. Similarly, if a lack of baseball information causes the listener to miss the implication that to the husband the question sounded like, "What'd the Sox do?" then there still is no opportunity for discovering meaning and the story is an incompletely understood narrative, not a joke. This particular joke also demonstrates that it is the *meaning* behind the words, not the words themselves which are important. This pun put solely into English goes—"What do you say?" "They lost seven to three," is not humorous; it is now nonsense.

Thus arises a curious question. Why is nonsense sometimes funny? Would it be a contradiction to say that discovering the meaning in something which has no meaning is responsible for the humor? There is no contradiction when we remember that we are not talking about the meaning of words as such, but to a hidden, alluded-to meaning. Nonsense poetry is a case in point. Consider the refrain from Carroll's *Jab-berwocky* (1971, p. 134):

> *'Twas brillig, and the slithy toves*
> *Did gyre and gimble in the wabe:*
> *All mimsy were the borogoves,*
> *And the mome raths outgrabe.*

Perhaps the best way to describe the important allusion for discovery here is to say: "This may sound like poetry or look like poetry, but it is really nonsense." Surely the words themselves have no humorous meaning. The discovery that it is constructed to parallel meaningful material without being meaningful resolves the search.

Closely related to nonsense is another form which may help to see why nonsense can be funny. I like the verse of W. S. Gilbert (of Gilbert and Sullivan fame):

> *There was an old man of St. Bees,*
> *Who was stung in the arm by a wasp.*
> *When asked, "Does it hurt?"*
> *He replied, "No, it doesn't,*
> *I'm so glad that it wasn't a hornet!"*

(quoted in Wright, 1939, p. 69)

Here there is meaning enough in the words, but the humor is not so much in the words as it is in the allusion to the limerick form. We "see" that it does not fit; we recognize that it is a blunder so far as a limerick is concerned. The person who never heard a limerick before or who failed to note that this starts off in that poetic pattern would not think it funny in the least.

Sudden turns in the content of a verbalization can prompt a search for the unconscious meaning and understanding—for example, "A bird in the hand isn't worth much if you want to blow your nose!" Any attempt to explain why that is funny would be accompanied by feelings far removed from humor. But the insight or discovery that there has been a harmless departure from an expected proverbial direction can resolve the brief sense of puzzlement.

A kind of *puzzlement* was and is practiced by Zen masters in teaching their students. Often a student was presented with a question for pon-dering, such as: What would be the sound of one hand clapping?—and the student might meditate on that koan for years as a means for seeking enlightenment. That one can retain motivation for contemplating an unanswerable question for so long a time is itself puzzling, but such is the drive of the resolution-seeking set when, in this instance, it represents both the means and the objective (enlightenment).

Zen masters, like other master teachers, also employed metaphors and anecdotes. One such story is entitled "Obedience:"

> The master Bankei's talks were attended not only by Zen students but by persons of all ranks and sects. He never quoted sutras (scriptures) nor indulged in scholastic dissertations. Instead, his words were spoken directly from his heart to the hearts of his listeners.
>
> His large audiences angered a priest of the Nichiren sect because the adherents had left to hear about Zen. The self-centered Nichiren priest came to the temple, determined to debate with Bankei.
>
> "Hey, Zen teacher!" he called out. "Wait a minute. Whoever respects you will obey what you say, but a man like myself does not respect you. Can you make me obey you?"
>
> "Come up beside me and I will show you," said Bankei.
>
> Proudly the priest pushed his way through the crowd to the teacher.
>
> Bankei smiled. "Come over to my left side."
>
> The priest obeyed.
>
> "No," said Bankei, "we may talk better if you are on the right side. Step over here."
>
> The priest proudly stepped over to the right.
>
> "You see," observed Bankei, "you are obeying me and I think you are a very gentle person. Now sit down and listen."
>
> (Reps, undated, pp. 8-9)

We can note a similarity to one of Erickson's utilization techniques which he used particularly with clients who were resistive or even defiant. Erickson (Haley, 1967, p. 42) described his utilization of the technique during a lecture and demonstration before a group of medical students when a heckler denounced Erickson as a charlatan, and hypnosis as a fraud. In a rapid series of utterances, Erickson elicited one contradiction after another from the heckler until he was ultimately up on the platform and in a somnambulistic trance. This technique (like that of the Zen master) capitalizes upon the ambivalence of clients, allowing them successfully to achieve contradictory goals "with the feeling that these derived out of the unexpected but adequate use of their own behavior" (Haley, 1967, p. 42).

Ambivalence and contradiction are powerful prompters of the reso-

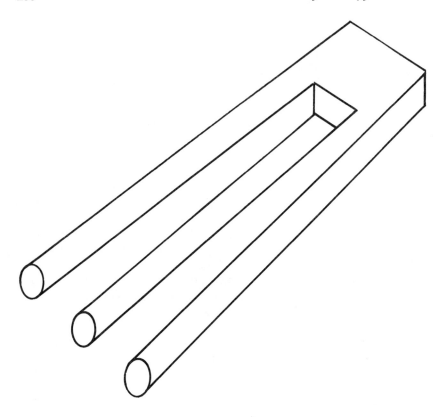

Figure 1. A resolution-resisting illusion

lution-seeking set. Many persons will be able to gain some feelings for the impelling force of the resolution-seeking set by consideration of Figure 1. The force of the resolution-seeking set results from a bilateral reasoning which is competing, and not complementary. This figure also helps distinguish the resolution-seeking set from Erickson's concept of unconscious search. Here visual perception competes with cognition and even though one can seek relief from the compelling alternation by a rational emphasis, what relief is obtained is short-lived and one can only turn away from the visual input to bring an end to increasing discomfort. One's *search* brings an understanding of the contradiction but one's *set* is to go on seeking a resolution.

CLINICAL APPLICATIONS OF THE RESOLUTION-SEEKING SET

Thinking of the client as strongly impelled by the resolution-seeking set can generate in the therapist novel interventions and new ways to approach the client; this same consideration can also make more understandable the client's innovations and potential innovations. Erickson often used digression to enhance the drive to resolution:

> I do certain things when I interview a family group, or a husband and wife, or a mother and son. People come for help, but they also come to be substantiated in their attitudes and they come to have face saved. I pay attention to this, and I'm likely to speak in a fashion that makes them think I'm on their side. Then I digress on a tangent that they can accept, but it leaves them teetering on the edge of expectation. They have to admit that my digression is all right, it's perfectly correct, but they didn't expect me to do it that way. It's an uncomfortable position to be teetering, and they want some solution of the matter that I had just brought to the edge of settlement. Since they want that solution, they are more likely to accept what I say. They are very eager for a decisive statement. If you gave the directive right away, they could take issue with it. But if you digress, they hope you will get back, and they welcome a decisive statement from you. (Haley, 1973, p. 206)

The "teetering" and its discomfort potentiate the resolution-seeking set.

Erickson acknowledged that in almost all of his techniques there was an element of confusion. In describing his handshake induction of Dr. S (Erickson, Rossi, & Rossi, 1976, p. 84), he said: "Her disconcerted feeling is a mixture of her imperfect touch with reality. It is her intellectual awareness that something has happened and her puzzlement about what did happen. She is not really comfortable about it; she is trying to resolve it and is experiencing difficulty in resolving it."

Lankton and Lankton (1983, p. 67) observed that not all confusion is unpleasant and cited the mild and temporary confusion of the joke that precedes its understanding. They reported (p. xiv) that "Erickson was well-known for his wit. His creative wit blossomed everywhere—in his treatment, his teaching, his child-rearing, in the frontispieces of books he signed, in his greetings and even in a wedding 'ceremony' he conducted" for the Lanktons. Erickson's wit often included a strong element of surprise. Immediately after their wedding celebration, Carol Lankton was startled when Erickson hurled what appeared to be a very heavy piece of granite toward her—only to discover that it was a weightless foam rock. She deduced that his action was meant to teach her not to take anything for "granite," but the meaning deduced by others could have differed. Anyone having the experience, however, would have been impelled to search for *some* explanation: The question, "*Why?*" is a popular western meditation and a powerful adjunct to the resolution-seeking set.

CLINICAL APPLICATIONS: CASE EXAMPLES

Once I develop an appreciation of the potentiating capacity of the resolution-seeking set, my unconscious mind is able to generate inno-vative interventions. A college music student was distressed because at her voice recitals (at which time her progress and capability were eval-uated) she consistently encountered an unintentional quavering of her voice. In practice sessions she experienced only a desirable vibrato, but when she knew she was being evaluated she inevitably produced what she referred to as "that damned quaver." In a trance she was told that while my musical training was only that of a percussionist, I enjoyed and found particularly appealing in music the encountering of a hemi-demi-semiquaver and I thought she might learn to enjoy encountering a hemi-demi-semiquaver as well. Her musical training provided her with the knowledge that a hemi-demi-semiquaver is a sixty-fourth note (a half of a half of a half of a *quaver*, or eighth note) and I avoided elaborating or explaining my comment. Just why I might find a sixty-fourth note appealing, or why I would suggest that she learn to enjoy their encounter more than, say, an eighth or a quarter note, presented to her unconscious mind a dual puzzle which she felt pressed to solve. The inference avail-able to her unconscious mind was that her own quaver might be halved successively again and again. She soon reported that the problem of the undesirable voice tremor "just seemed to go away."

An age regression in a 22-year-old obese woman provided the infor-mation that the genesis of her weight problem occurred at age five when she encountered a life-threatening illness. Well-intentioned caretakers repeatedly gave the suggestion that she needed to eat to live; as a result, being overweight had become an artificial assurance of longevity. For many years she resigned herself to being obese despite her halfhearted participation in a variety of weight-control programs. In one trance ses-sion she was told that there was a way in which she could eat more by eating less. Then she was allowed to puzzle over the implied conun-drum. The assertion that one could somehow eat both more and less prompts mental activity toward reconciliation of the apparent contradiction. The set to seek resolution pushes reasoning to the discovery that one might live longer (and thus have opportunity to do more eating) by eating less. I kept her waiting for nearly 20 minutes before saying, "Perhaps you have *weighted* long enough." Indirect suggestions for amnesia followed and, after the trance, she commented that she felt somehow "different"; she soon left the plateau on which she had been stuck and resumed weight reduction.

CONCLUSION

Puns, truisms, indirect, open-ended and embedded suggestions, metaphors and anecdotes directly capitalize upon the resolution-seeking set; the individual at either a conscious or unconscious level enjoys—without distress—the grasping, recognizing, interpreting, understanding, succeeding resolution.

Many of Erickson's techniques, on the other hand, served to disrupt the conscious set or usual frames of reference in a manner which created either a quandary or an intolerable confusion, e.g., confusion, binds, non sequiturs, illogic, contradictions, shock and surprise. In order to extricate themselves, subjects would either accept a suggestion offered that would resolve the perplexity or creatively utilize their own unconscious resources to restructure their understanding.

Erickson urged "a ready and full respect for [the ability of] the patient's unconscious mind to perceive fully the intentionally obscured meaningful therapeutic instructions offered them" (Haley, 1967, p. 522). Comprehension of those instructions requires a resolution of the obscurity.

Erickson demonstrated experimentally "the fact that consciously chosen words, thoughts, and acts can mean more than one thing at a time: their conscious or manifest content on the one hand, and a latent, unconscious content on the other" (Rossi, 1980, Vol. 3, p. 156). The same holds true for words less consciously chosen by the therapist: "Respectful awareness of the capacity of the patient's unconscious mind to perceive meaningfulness of the therapist's own unconscious behavior is a governing principle in psychotherapy" (Haley, 1967, p. 522). An appreciation of the pervasiveness of the resolution-seeking set in influencing consciously and unconsciously determined behavior in both patient and therapist can foster innovative interventions.

REFERENCES

Carroll, L. (1971). *Alice's adventures in wonderland* and *Through the looking glass*. London: Oxford University Press.
Cattell, R. B. (1965). The nature and measurement of anxiety. In R. S. Daniel (Ed.), *Contemporary readings in general psychology* (2nd ed.). (pp. 245-254). Boston: Houghton Mifflin.
Erickson, M. H., Rossi, E. L., & Rossi, S. I. (1976). *Hypnotic realities*. New York: Irvington.
Festinger, L. (1957). *A theory of cognitive dissonance*. New York: Harper & Row.
Gottschaldt, K. (1926). Über den Einfluss der Erfahrung auf die Wahrnehmung von Figuren. I. Über den Einfluss gehäufter Einprägung von Figuren auf ihre Sichtbarkeit in umfassenden Konfigurationen. *Psychologische Forschung, 8*, 261-317.
Haley, J. (Ed.). (1967). *Advanced techniques of hypnosis and therapy: Selected papers of Milton H. Erickson, M.D.* New York: Grune & Stratton.
Haley, J. (1973). *Uncommon therapy*. New York: Norton.
Jourard, S. M., & Overlade, D. C. (Eds.). (1966). *Reconciliation: A theory of man transcending*. Princeton, NJ: D. Van Nostrand.
Köhler, W. (1925). *The mentality of apes*. New York: Harcourt, Brace & World.
Lankton, S. R., & Lankton, C. H. (1983). *The answer within: A clinical framework of Ericksonian hypnotherapy*. New York: Brunner/Mazel.
Mowrer, O. H. (1960). *Learning theory and behavior*. New York: Wiley.
Overlade, D. C. (1954). *Humor perception as abstraction ability*. Unpublished doctoral dissertation, Purdue University, West Lafayette, IN.
Reps, P. (Ed.) (Undated). *Zen flesh, Zen bones: A collection of Zen and pre-Zen writings*. Garden City, NY: Doubleday.
Rossi, E. L. (Ed.). (1980). *The collected papers of Milton H. Erickson on hypnosis* (Vol. 3). New York: Irvington.
Sarasan, I. (1965). *Psychoanalysis and the study of behavior*. Princeton, NJ: Van Nostrand.
Spence, K. W. (1956). *Behavior theory and conditioning*. New Haven: Yale University Press.
Thurstone, L. L. (1944). *A factorial study of perception*. Chicago: University of Chicago Press.
Whiting, J. M., & Child, I. L. (1953). *Child training and personality*. New Haven: Yale University Press.
Wright, M. (1939). *What's funny and why*. New York: McGraw-Hill.

Chapter 17

Permissive vs. Authoritarian Approaches in Clinical and Experimental Settings

Harry E. Stanton

WHAT IS HYPNOSIS?—THEORIES VS. OUTCOMES

Much confusion exists in the professional literature about the nature of hypnosis. Is it some form of disassociation? Perhaps it is simply role playing? Maybe it is no more than heightened suggestibility? Is it creative use of the imagination? We simply do not know.

For some time, I was content to use an operational definition which embraced three elements. If my experimental and therapeutic work included 1) formal induction designed to produce relaxation, 2) verbal suggestion, and 3) imagery, I labeled it "hypnosis." However, this approach is really just as unhelpful as the various theoretical formulations. After all, Barber et al. (1974) demonstrated that a formal induction is unnecessary to the production of a trance state; Meares (1971) found no need for verbal suggestion; my own experience confirmed repeatedly that patients unable to visualize the scenes I suggest still achieve their desired changes.

The theories and explanations are figments of the imagination which often become more important to us than the actual results produced by "hypnotic" interventions. It is outcomes which count rather than theoretical explanations. Although it is nice to have theories to explain the emergence of a particular outcome, the lack of theory should not influence our practice of specific techniques. If something does not work, no matter how many "experts" tell us how good it is on theoretical grounds, we need to try something else. It is, for example, easy to subscribe to

293

the "resistance" theory, that if a technique does not work, it is because of the patient's refusal to cooperate. Maybe. More likely, though, is that this particular approach is not appropriate to this patient, in this situation. Therefore, it becomes necessary to try something else.

We become blinded by our rigid belief systems, interpreting everything in terms of our particular theory, and refusing to accept the facts as spelled out by results. After all, Maier's (1963) law is: "If the facts don't fit the theory, get rid of the facts," and as Bandler and Grinder (1979) put it:

> Every psychotherapy I know has an acute mental illness within it. Each one thinks that their theory, their map, *is* the territory. They don't think you can make up something totally arbitrary and instill it in someone and change them. They don't realize that what they believe is also made up and totally arbitrary . . . they believe their prescriptions are a description of what reality actually is. There is a way out of that . . . not to believe what you're doing . . . if you simply change your belief system you will have a new set of resources and a new set of limitations . . . once you realize that the world in which you are living right now is completely made up, you can make new worlds. (pp. 178-9) (cf. Watzlawick, Chapter 1)

There are so many different ways to go about therapy and hypnosis that it seems a pity to be limited by restricted "maps." Our cognitive maps are not reality, they are only representations of reality. Each of us has created our own particular way of looking at things, a specific map of the way the world is. Sometimes groups of people share a belief in a particular view of the world, experimentalists for example, while other groups, such as clinicians, share a different view.

EXPERIMENTALISTS AND CLINICIANS—THEIR "MAPS" OF REALITY

The typical hypnosis experimentalist and the typical hypnotherapist possess rather different cognitive maps, this probably being the reason for the gulf between the two. To illustrate, consider their rather divergent views of hypnotic induction. The experimentalist normally uses a simplistic ritualized induction involving eye fixation, heaviness of limbs, and relaxation. Little attempt is made to establish rapport with the recipients of hypnosis or to match individually their cognitive maps. In fact, taped inductions are often used to increase experimental purity, a method designed to ensure individual pacing will not take place.

Clinicians often attempt to meet patients where they are, and to fashion an induction personally applicable. That is, the effort is made, in clinical trance induction work, to be sensitive to the patients' perception of the world. This sensitivity makes it possible to pace patients so that the therapist's words are accepted as an accurate description of their experience. Should the initial induction attempt fail to produce the desired outcome, then the therapist uses a different procedure, based on further information elicited.

The contrast between experimentalist and clinician in terms of induction techniques used is oversimplified but it does capture an essential difference. In the laboratory, the experimentalist attempts to eliminate skill factors such as therapist-patient rapport and individual tailoring of induction techniques, yet these are the essence of successful clinical practice.

The actual situation in which the induction of "hypnosis" takes place also reveals important differences. In particular, as Pearson (1979) pointed out, the subject in the laboratory is there for the benefit of the experimenter, and is likely to be imposed upon in some way to meet the needs of this person. However, patients visiting the clinician's office are there for personal benefit, seeking to have their own needs met. Take for example clinical and experimental situations involving pain control: A patient suffering pain brings this pain to the therapist seeking help for its relief. The experimental subject, on the other hand, arrives free from pain, is exposed to painful procedures, and then to pain-reducing procedures. Such an important situational difference suggests considerable caution in generalizing from the laboratory to the clinician's office.

Individual differences, too, make such generalization hazardous. People vary in their level of motivation and in other personal attributes affecting their willingness to enter the hypnotic state. As Wadden and Anderton (1982) have pointed out in their review of the clinical use of hypnosis:

> . . . highly expectant and motivated subjects achieve the greatest benefit from hypnotic techniques for obesity and cigarette smoking. This finding may explain the discrepancy in treatment success rate reported by private practitioners and research investigators. Individuals who pay high fees for a therapist's services are likely to be

more motivated to succeed than are persons participating free of charge in a research study. Similarly, private practitioners are able to provide very positive expectancy, whereas researchers are increasingly obligated to admonish subjects that therapeutic benefits cannot be guaranteed. (p. 237)

Expectancy, i.e., belief in a cure, a factor often considered influential in a healing situation (e.g., Torrey, 1972), is used extensively by clinicians, yet eliminated by experimentalists. No wonder it is difficult to transfer laboratory findings to the consulting room.

Concepts of depth differ, too. The phenomena labeled by research investigators as deep hypnosis, such as amnesia, hallucination, and pain suppression, may occur in individual subjects, in a state of light hypnosis or vice versa, depending upon the individual's personality and his psychological need at the time (Erickson et al., 1976). There appears to be no necessary relation between depth of hypnosis as ordinarily understood and enshrined in the mythology of susceptibility scales, and depth of hypnosis in the sense of the extent to which an individual's personality is really involved. One person manifesting "deep trance" phenomena may be little involved in the "hypnotic" state while another person in a lighter state may be deeply involved.

MODELS OF HYPNOSIS

The key issue between experimentalists and clinicians seems to be the model of hypnosis used. In the laboratory situation, the experimenter tends to control the subjects, "forcing" them to enter trance. The clinician, on the other hand, uses a permissive rather than an authoritarian model, encouraging patients to allow themselves to enter trance under the therapist's guidance. Traditional experimental wisdom suggests the responsiveness of patients to such "hypnotic" treatment will vary as a function of their hypnotizability as assessed by standardized hypnotic susceptibility scales.

However, Barber (1980) has provided evidence which suggests that the use of a naturalistic, nonauthoritarian technique promotes responsiveness to hypnotic treatment in so-called unsusceptible, unhypnotizable subjects. According to Barber, susceptibility, as measured by standardized scales, is not necessarily correlated with hypnotic ability if the hypnotic suggestions are indirect and the total approach is a naturalistic one adapted to the individual rather than direct and authoritarian. Therefore, it would appear that susceptibility is not critical to success. Yet, if we really believe an "unsusceptible" subject cannot benefit from hypnosis, our behavior will tend to ensure this outcome.

Perry et al. (1979) confirmed that susceptibility is not a relevant factor in helping people cease smoking. Patient motivation is the critical element, a finding supported by my own experience. We need to remember that a susceptibility score is simply an index of an individual's response to a particular set of suggestions in a particular standardized situation. Therefore, lack of response to those suggestions cannot be logically construed as inability to be hypnotized in general. Thus, we do not have to accept the experimentalists' view that nonsusceptible subjects, identified by means of standardized susceptibility scales, cannot benefit from hypnotic treatment in the clinical situation where that treatment is permissive and matched to the individual patient. Experimentalists are constrained by their particular "map of the territory"; clinicians do not have to accept such restriction.

SOME GUIDING PRINCIPLES

If the permissive "map" is accepted, four important principles can be used to guide the clinician's behavior. The first of these is to *match the induction to the individual*. Should a patient insist that one becomes hypnotized by gazing at a swinging watch, so be it. Use a swinging watch. Should a patient talk of yoga or meditation practice, use the feelings associated with this experience as a guide into trance. If the patient likes daydreaming, suggest drifting into a favorite daydream and then lead into others likely to promote the desired change.

Patients can usually tell a therapist what is wrong and what they need to do to solve their problem. They can be helped to do so through answering questions such as: What do you want? How will you know when you have it? What will you have to do to get what you want? How can you do this? What prevents you doing this? (Bandler and Grinder, 1975) Thus, a second guiding principle is to *allow patients considerable freedom to direct their own therapy*.

A third principle involves the "theory" behind my own application of permissive therapy. Frank (1972) suggested that people who seek therapy do so not because of specific symptoms but because they are unable to cope with a life situation which they, and those about them, expect them to be able to handle. That is, such patients are demoralized. "Healing" them is a process of morale building so that they come to believe in their own ability to cope with the previous overwhelming situation. In fact, on many occasions, patients will indicate in what areas they lack confidence and what is necessary if morale is to be restored.

Implicit in this third principle, that *therapy is a process of confidence building,* is Erickson's view that *we all have within us the ability to solve our problems and to change in beneficial ways* (Erickson, Rossi, & Rossi, 1976). This may be seen as a fourth guiding principle, for Erickson believed that many abilities are not used consciously. If patients could solve their problems at the conscious level, they would have already done so. As they have not accomplished this, the therapist's role is to help them utilize unconscious potentials, inner resources, to achieve the required changes.

PUTTING THE PRINCIPLES INTO PRACTICE

Let us now consider how these ideas can be put into practice. The steps involved might be diagrammed in this way:

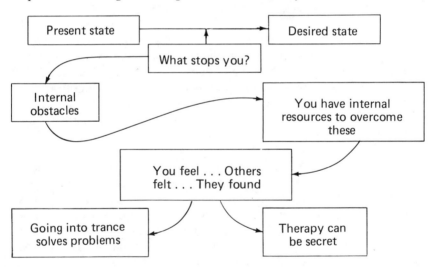

The first step involves *clarification of the problem.* An effective way of doing so has been formulated by Grinder and McMaster (1980). It involves having patients describe their Present state, (i.e., what they have) and then identifying what they want (the Desired state). The gap between these two states is the problem. Once patients have clarified their difficulty in this way, they are asked the key question: What stops you from achieving your Desired state?

Initially, most patients have no answer. They do not know what prevents them from getting what they want. However, as they think further, they conclude that it is some inner obstacle which seems to be blocking them, usually a lack of confidence in their own ability to achieve the Desired state. Doubt, fear, anxiety and guilt often figure prominently as inner obstacles, so too does "lack of will power."

Guided by Frank's (1972) demoralization conceptualization, the therapist encourages patients to believe they have the internal resources to overcome these obstacles. This may be done by reviving memories of past changes or of past learnings. A patient desiring, for example, weight loss can be reminded of a previous occasion when he or she was successful in losing weight, or in stopping smoking, or in coping with a family trauma.

Stories and metaphors can be useful at this stage. One I have found particularly valuable is that of the pyramid (Gibbons, 1979). Patients visualize themselves in ancient Egypt, standing before a huge pyramid, gazing at the entrance. This becomes increasingly difficult to see in the darkness of a desert sand storm. Several senses can be invoked, e.g., "seeing" the images, "hearing" the sound of the whistling wind, and "feeling" the sand stinging their cheeks. As they enter the pyramid they follow a well-lit passageway leading ever downward. The patients feel safe and secure, yet there is a sense of excitement, of expectancy that something of great value will happen.

As patients continue to go deeper into the pyramid, the therapist draws the parallel between this journey and that of going down into the unconscious mind, leaving behind the world of everyday awareness. At the end of the passage is a vast treasure-house, this being an analogy for the many inner resources of the patient. The treasure has not been used. In fact, a huge statue, powered by a brilliant jewel in its forehead, serves as a guardian. This statue is the personification of all the negative forces of failure, and prevents use of the patients' inner potential.

Patients are thus provided with a means of overcoming the negative forces, perhaps by striking the jewel from the statue's forehead and watching it crumble away to ineffective dust, and are then free to gather up as much treasure as can be carried. This is brought back to the world outside the pyramid. The sun is now shining and patients can walk away with confidence.

The analogy with a journey into the mind to retrieve unused resources and potentials for growth is continued, the suggestion being given that as patients return to everyday life, their unconscious will ensure that the treasure will show itself in new habits and new ideas, in changes of great benefit. Further, it is pointed out that the storehouse of potential is never empty; patients can return over and over again, always bringing back some new resource to enhance their lives.

Another helpful story relates to cessation of smoking. I tell of a patient who stopped smoking after our session, remained a nonsmoker for several months, attended a party and started feeling very ill, nauseous, bilious. Suddenly she realized she had a cigarette in her mouth. Quickly she removed it. The unpleasant physical state passed. Finding this difficult to believe, she again picked up the cigarette only to experience a recurrence of the nausea. I point out that I did not tell this patient that smoking cigarettes would make her ill. However, the patient had made a decision to become a nonsmoker and her own body was helping her maintain this resolve. Again, the emphasis is upon the patient's own resources.

A pacing and leading technique borrowed from the repertoire of successful salespeople comes next. The patient's own experience is matched with a "you feel . . ." statement. If patients are concerned with the pain of migraine headaches, their experience is reflected by the therapist. "Maybe you can feel an initial sense of unreality, of vagueness . . . this is followed by a sensation of flashing light in your head . . . distortion of vision . . . considerable pain over your left eye . . . a nauseous feeling in your stomach . . ." Then follows "others feel" statements in which the patients' experience is placed in a broader context. "Many other people feel like this, too, but they found relief through the particular methods you are now going to learn." Stories are again used to illustrate how other patients used hypnotic methods to become free of their migraine symptoms. Thus, the particular technique the therapist chooses to use is "sold" to the patient through accurate pacing.

SPECIFIC PERMISSIVE TECHNIQUES

Erickson's emphasis on people's unconscious potentials for achieving change provides the basis of an effective approach to permissive therapy. The therapist discusses with the patient how the unconscious mind appears to run our lives, controlling our breathing, digestion and movement, and solving problems for us during periods when we are not consciously engaged in the matter in question. Patients usually have no trouble in recalling many instances from their own lives in which the unconscious mind acted in these ways. Of course, the whole concept of such a mind existing may be a myth. However, because it seems to provide an acceptable explanation for how change takes place, it is a myth which can become a truth for many people for it actually works for them.

Once the idea of unconscious potentials is accepted by patients, they can then be encouraged to believe that by simply drifting into a trance state, they can permit their unconscious mind to effect the desired changes. The actual procedure of entering the trance state is compared to daydreaming, absorption in a book or film, and/or the hypnogogic state experienced just before one falls asleep. That is, patients are reassured that it does not really matter if they doubt their ability to enter the trance state for their unconscious mind already knows how to create that state.

The therapist can make entry into the trance state easier by guiding patients to concentrate on breathing, achieve eye closure through fixation on an object, and/or turn inward and enjoy a pleasant visualization. However, once patients accept that the unconscious mind will create the trance state, little assistance is needed and they usually allow themselves to drift into trance quite effortlessly.

They might then be guided into a sanctuary, a place of peace and quiet where no one or no thing can harm them. In this place they can visualize themselves effecting an exchange of things unwanted for things wanted. There are numerous ways of achieving such an exchange (e.g., Stanton, 1982). Inner obstacles such as fears, doubts, worries and guilt, along with physical ailments and unwanted people are "disposed" of, perhaps through sending them into space in a basket, burying them, or burning them. Desired attributes of calmness, relaxation, confidence and happiness are then achieved through success visualization. Patients are encouraged to frame their own success visualizations, "seeing" themselves behaving effectively in situations they have previously mishandled.

Another way of permitting patients to assume responsibility for their own change stems from the work of Erickson (1964). After patients had told him about their problems, Erickson would ask them to close their eyes and to repeat the story slowly and carefully from beginning to end. Once this was done, they were to specify what was wanted from the therapist.

As the patients talked, Erickson suggested that the sound of their own voice would induce in them a satisfactory trance. While in this trance state, they would be able to continue to talk, listen, answer questions, and do anything asked by the therapist. In fact, they would find themselves under a most powerful compulsion to do exactly what was indicated.

Encouraged by Erickson, patients would repeat several times the therapy they thought was necessary for a cure. Then Erickson would point out that he had offered no advice or corrective suggestions, that every item in that regard had come from the patients *themselves*, and that they would find themselves under a powerful compulsion, arising from within, to do everything that they had indicated as necessary to effect a cure.

There are similarities in this approach and one used by Schneck (1975) with patients who feared air travel. He told them that he would offer certain helpful suggestions, after which hypnosis would be induced. This was described as a procedure emphasizing comfort and relaxation, initiated by a simple count of letters of the alphabet, and terminated by a count of numbers.

Schneck's prehypnotic suggestions were that, prior to the induction, patients would think about how they wished to feel, physically and psychologically, throughout all aspects of their travel from preembarkation to safe arrival. They were not to verbalize these thoughts, speaking only to tell the therapist when they were finished. Once they had done so, hypnosis was induced, patients being told that the induction and hypnotic relaxation would themselves automatically reinforce the silent instructions regarding how they wanted to feel during the trip. After several minutes of silence, the trance was terminated. The entire process was then repeated.

On occasion I have combined these two permissive techniques, beginning by asking patients to tell their stories and outline the things they would need to do to achieve their desired goals. They were then asked to close their eyes and slowly retell their stories, allowing the unconscious mind to take control, guiding them into a deeper and deeper trance as they spoke and ensuring that everything necessary to accomplish the change they wanted would be accomplished. After emerging, in their own time, from this self-imposed trance state, patients would discuss their experiences with me, and then use the Schneck technique. This would involve thinking how they wished to be, and drifting back into a trance state to promote such change.

These techniques are all based on the concept that the trance state itself enables a patient to tap unconscious potential for change. The specific change or changes desired are specified by the patient and the therapist's suggestions are oriented towards their achievement. However, another line of permissive therapy works on the assumption that the therapist has no need to know what changes are desired by the patient. In other words, therapy can be conducted in secret.

SECRET THERAPY

This approach focuses on process rather than on content. After assisting the patient to enter trance, restate the concept of the unconscious mind as a storehouse of all experience. Suggest that the patient's unconscious can rapidly review every one of his or her life experiences which resulted in beneficial change, selecting one of particular importance. The unconscious is now asked to review this experience, reliving it, reviewing and rehearing everything that happened so thoroughly that it will be able to learn something new, to gain fresh understanding. This new learning, this additional understanding will then be used by the unconscious to facilitate desired change within the patient.

This is a process instruction in which the patient is given a content-free set of instructions which says "learn something," "change now." Such instructions tell the patient specifically what process to go through to solve personal problems but are unspecific about the content (Grinder & Bandler, 1981). The therapist suggests that the patient search through personal history at the unconscious level, taking time to identify a particular resource that could be of use now in dealing with the present difficulty. It is not necessary to specify what the resource is, only that one will be found. The problem or difficulty is not stated, and the therapist does not have to know what it is.

Another way of using the resource concept is to change a patient's personal history (Bandler and Grinder, 1979). The patient identifies a response to be changed; finds a resource such as more confidence, more trust, more assertiveness, now possessed, which, if available at the time of the unwanted response, would have provided a more acceptable outcome. The patient goes back to the unpleasant experience this time using the resource to provoke a different response; and generalizes this new response to future situations. Again, the therapist need know nothing of the content. He or she simply shows the patient how to go about promoting change at the unconscious level.

CONCLUSION

Permissive therapy assumes that patients can draw on their own inner resources at the unconscious level to effect desired change. The therapist's role is primarily that of guidance and encouragement, helping patients feel confident that they can achieve their therapeutic goals. To this end, inductions are individualized, suggestion is often subtle and indirect, and the therapist reveals a willingness to be flexible when desired outcomes are not forthcoming. Working in this way, therapists are usually able to facilitate change in their patients, if not in one way, then in another.

This situation is far different from that of the experimental laboratory which purports to provide the empirical basis for clinical practice. As pointed out earlier, the two situations are so different that one is inclined to feel that never the twain shall meet. Whether this be true or not, the experimental findings based on standardized inductions, direct suggestions and an authoritarian approach have not been helpful to the clinician. The model of the hypnotic process provided by the laboratory is misleading, causing many patients to be rejected as "unsuitable for hypnotic treatment." The alternative model of permissive therapy outlined in this chapter encourages clinicians in their belief that virtually all patients can benefit from hypnotherapy.

REFERENCES

Bandler, R., & Grinder, J. (1975). *The structure of magic I.* Palo Alto, CA: Science & Behavior Books.

Bandler, R., & Grinder, J. (1979). *Frogs into princes.* Moab, UT: Real People Press.

Barber, J. (1980). Hypnosis and the unhypnotizable. *American Journal of Clinical Hypnosis, 23,* 4-9.

Barber, T. X., Spanos, N. P., & Chaves, J. F. (1974). *Hypnosis, imagination and human potentialities.* Elmsford, NY: Pergamon Press.

Erickson, M. H. (1964). The burden of responsibility in effective therapy. *American Journal of Clinical Hypnosis, 6,* 269-271.

Erickson, M. H., Rossi, E. L., & Rossi, S. (1976). *Hypnotic realities.* NY: Irvington.

Frank, J. D. (1972). The bewildering world of psychotherapy. *Journal of Social Issues, 28,* 27-43.

Gibbons, D. E. (1979). *Applied hypnosis and hyperempiria.* NY: Plenum Press.

Grinder, J., & Bandler, R. (1981). *Trance-formations.* Moab, UT: Real People Press.

Grinder, J., & McMaster, M. (1980). *Precision.* Beverly Hills: Precision Models.

Maier, N. R. F. (1963). Maier's law. In R. A. Baker (Ed.), *Psychology in the wry.* NY: Van Nostrand.

Meares, A. (1971). Group relaxing hypnosis. *Medical Journal of Australia, 2,* 675-6.

Pearson, R. E. (1979). Clinical and experimental trance: What's the difference? *American Journal of Clinical Hypnosis, 13,* 1-3.

Perry, C., Giffard, R., & Marcovitch, P. (1979). The relevance of hypnotic susceptibility in the clinical context. *Journal of Abnormal Psychology, 88,* 592-603.

Schneck, J. M. (1975). Prehypnotic suggestion in psychotherapy. *American Journal of Clinical Hypnosis, 17,* 158-9.

Stanton, H. E. (1982). Hypnotherapy and the inner game. *Australian Journal of Clinical and Experimental Hypnosis, 10,* 67-71.

Torrey, E. F. (1972). *The mind game: Witchdoctors and psychiatrists.* NY: Emerson Hall.

Wadden, T. A., & Anderton, C. H. (1982). The clinical use of hypnosis. *Psychological Bulletin, 19,* 215-243.

Watzlawick, P. (This volume). Hypnotherapy without trance.

Chapter 18

The Hypnotic Lifestyle: Integrating Hypnosis into Everyday Life

Norman W. Katz

This chapter reviews findings from experimental and clinical hypnosis that help us understand how to use hypnosis in more flexible, creative and efficient ways. It combines investigations in experimental hypnosis with Ericksonian clinical inquiry.

DEFINING HYPNOSIS

What does it mean to use hypnosis? The word "hypnosis" has been used so freely that it is hard to define clearly. Recently, Project Enlightenment was developed by the American Psychological Association to explain to the public what hypnosis is. The first step was to ask psychologists to define hypnosis. No two definitions were alike; some 30 different ones were submitted.

The best definition I can find in the literature is by Sarbin and Coe (1972) who define hypnosis as "The Social Psychology of Believed-in Imaginings." That's a useful definition and will help put the rest of this chapter in context.

Erickson's definition of trance was actually very simple. Trance is what happens when one has an inner focus of attention (Erickson, 1980b). Getting someone to have and utilize that inner focus of attention can be done in complex, elegant and sophisticated ways. However, a review of experimental literature on hypnosis sheds light on simpler ways to use hypnosis.

CLINICAL VS. EXPERIMENTAL HYPNOSIS

There are a lot of differences between experimental hypnosis and clinical hypnosis. In the laboratory, hypnosis is defined as an episodic experience. When we hypnotize subjects in the laboratory and let them go back to their introductory psychology classes, we do not want them to be changed.

Nevertheless, what has been discovered in the experimental labs has interesting implications for how we go about teaching hypnosis to clients and using it ourselves. Traditionally, in the laboratory we present subjects with some type of verbal monologue which attempts to promote relaxation and change their attention. This is followed by suggestions for 10 or 12 bizarre behaviors which have come to be the standard in laboratory research. The things we ask in the laboratory scales of hypnosis usually are absurd, trifling behaviors which prove to subjects that they are out of control. They are typically challenge suggestions such as, "Hold up your arm; you can't keep it up; it's going down." "You cannot open your eyes." "You can't bend your arm." We also suggest cognitive items, e.g., "There is a fly landing on your nose; it's bothering you," and we watch to see if the subject brushes the imaginary fly away. We count how many suggestions a person passes and we say that the more they pass, the better the subject he or she is.

One of the things I discovered was that there had not been any effort to train people to do these things through the systematic use of imagery and the development of "hypnotic thinking" as a tool. So through a series of studies (Katz, 1979), we asked the questions, "Can you train people to do these kinds of bizarre behaviors and learn the principles behind how they work, and therefore increase their ability to use hypnosis not only in the lab, but also in personal clinical situations?" The answer over a series of 8 studies was affirmative (Barber, 1983). In fact, this is one of the most replicable series of studies done in experimental hypnosis.

It was found that by learning the *principles* of how hypnosis works, and *self-control techniques,* subjects could learn to *think hypnotically* and generate a wide variety of hypnotic behaviors that could happen at the unconscious level. Also, this could develop spontaneous behaviors which were therapeutic.

There are numerous techniques for modifying hypnotic ability. Techniques are applied during the induction and suggestion phases of the work. In the induction period, the first thing we want is fixation of attention. We want subjects to narrow their attention, to focus on something. We then want that focus to go from outside to inside. Typically, with someone who has a lot of experience with an inner focus of attention, all we have to do is say, "Please close your eyes and go to an inner place and attend to a memory or a dream." With people who have less experience, we need to be a little more sophisticated or explain things a little more carefully.

Once they go to that inner focus of attention, we want them to use imagery. Typically, imagery is not just visual, but kinesthetic, auditory, or any combination of modalities that works best for the person. The use of memories is often effective in accessing powerful inner images. We then take people's inner imagery and combine it with new suggestions, new images that will produce changes in their behavior that will then convince them that something special is happening called "trance" or "hypnotic behavior." So we might say things like, "As your arm is extended you begin to feel a heavy feeling, like the last time you were in the library and you picked up three heavy books. Remember that?" The imagery often causes microscopic muscular movements and sensations of heaviness. The arm might move down and the subject might then say, "I must have been in a trance because that is a very unusual thing to happen." Moreover, we can have the other hand stay levitated. Thus, one hand serves as a control, the other serves as the experimental hand. We could even suggest an imaginary helium balloon on the other wrist to increase the difference between the hands. Most people respond to these simple instructions.

TRAINING HYPNOTIC RESPONSIVENESS

In taking a look at the processes involved in experimental hypnosis, we found that it worked better if we explained and taught people how to use these processes rather than merely suggesting them (Katz, 1978, 1979). Traditionally, the principles by which a person is asked to use imagery are never explained. Therefore, we would say, "Now if your arm goes out, and you want to make it heavy, how would you do that? Well, what you might do is consider the possibility of your hand really having books on it." Now if the person can easily imagine, there is no need for further suggestions. Otherwise, we do a shaping procedure. We take five heavy books and put them on the person's hand. Then we take one off and say, "Pretend there are still five." Then take off two books, then three books, then take off four books, and finally there are no books, but the subject can still match the perception in his or her body with the image. Using similar procedures, we can teach hypnotic behaviors such as arm heaviness, arm lightness, and arm catalepsy. Almost every hypnotic behavior can be taught as a way of thinking, as a way of using imagery, as a way of using mental skills. Incidentally, the one skill that seems most difficult to teach is amnesia. Erickson used to say, "You can pretend anything and believe it and experience it and accomplish it" (Erickson, 1980a).

What happens when you teach people to do these hypnotic behaviors? About 95 percent of experimental subjects easily learn to do typical hypnotic behaviors (Barber, 1972). Then they start applying hypnotic behaviors to other areas of their lives.

For example, we found that joggers would start using images while they were jogging. They would imagine things like large hands pushing them around the jogging course or a magnet pulling them towards objects. It was interesting that a number of our clinical subjects did not apply new hypnotic skills to the presenting problems. But they applied them to other things that were evidently more important and interesting to them. For example, subjects applied them to their sex lives, to control their tempers, and to increase their effectiveness at school work.

Now let's take a look at everyday life and see how hypnotic skills can be useful. In my opinion most of us are in a trance most of the time. In fact, it is difficult to stay out of trance. To stay out of a trance is more work than going into a trance. By trance, I refer to Erickson's simple definition of an "inner state of absorption."

Most of the time our trances are quick and fleeting. You read my words and they remind you of something. Subsequently, you are not reading my words because you are absorbed in reverie. Then you come back to what you are reading.

Attention waivers. It moves from outer stimuli to the inner world. In sustained hypnotic experiences, we deliberately focus our attention outside and then inside to contact our unconscious or transform our conscious experience through inner focus of attention. The use of hypnosis in everyday life is not a question of developing hypnotic interventions which are profound or dramatic, but rather learning to utilize the spontaneous flow of attention, imagery and conscious concern. Let me give you some examples of how this works. Let's say you wanted to pick up a pot on a stove that was very hot, but not hot enough to actually burn your hand, just hot enough to be uncomfortable. The pot holder is across the room and you didn't want the peas to burn. You would not have time to say, "I think what I'll do is sit down and go into a deep trance, count from a hundred to one and find the right imagery." If you were well trained, you could use posthypnotic cues to instantly put yourself into a trance and suggest anesthesia in your hand. A much more effective way is to use *cognitive strategies* of producing anesthesia or protective barriers on your hand. You might imagine a protective sheet of ice on your hand, or *imagine* you have a large glove or the actual pot holder in your hand. In doing so, you will change your perception of the heat of the pan to a tolerable level of warmth that will not injure or make it too uncomfortable to pick up the pan. Of course, if the pot is red hot, you would *not* want to use such strategies as the heat could actually harm your hand. We have to be careful that we do not use hypnotic strategies where they might force the body to go beyond normal limits for endurance or physical safety. But most people can quickly and effectively use this kind of thinking to transform sensory experience and do things that would formerly seem impossible. Imagining or pretending can allow you to do things you did not think you could do. Examples like that can be extended to many areas of daily life. Where things are difficult, annoying or uncomfortable, we can change the "reality of our perceptions" by changing our imagery and thought processes about those perceptions.

NEGATIVE HYPNOSIS

Symptoms are the result of and are maintained by negative self-hypnosis (Araoz, 1982). Aaron Beck's research in cognitive therapy (1976) indicates that almost every person who suffers from depression is indulging in reveries of disaster and self-defeat. People who are anxious constantly indulge in reveries of doom and fear. It is not just arguing with yourself, as Albert Ellis (1977) would believe. Rather it is a complex inner drama of thinking and imagining and believing to the point of making it come true.

How do you undo a hypnotic suggestion? By working with the person to show that what he or she is doing is already hypnosis. Then the subject can learn to use imagery skills in positive directions rather than negative directions.

BIG HYPNOSIS/LITTLE HYPNOSIS

I would like to make the distinction between "big" hypnosis and "little" hypnosis. Most clients come looking for a hypnotic miracle. They expect us to do what Charcot did in the 19th century, what Milton Erickson did, what our own fantasies would have us believe we can do. Big hypnosis is the sudden cure, the instant change in behavior. Now these cures do occur, and Erickson produced many of them. However, the big lasting cure, the instant cure, is really unlikely (Katz, 1978). And clients, even though we explain this to them, consciously don't believe us. You can explain it three or four times, but they still think that they are going to be unconscious and that the "big cure" is not only possible but likely.

I prefer to emphasize little hypnosis which entails learning to do the kind of hypnotic thinking exercises that Erickson taught people to do. Little hypnosis is learning to play with symptoms, to transform them through changes in frames of references, through humor, and through learning to use fantasy. Little hypnosis is the process of teaching clients to transform reality in small, effective ways through direct and indirect training. Some people are virtuosos at doing this.

Barber recently completed a study of the 20 most hypnotizable women he could find in Boston (Wilson & Barber, 1983); some 15 of these women could have orgasms just by thinking about sex. That is how powerful their imaginations and hypnotic abilities were. It is interesting that these people spontaneously learned to develop their imagination without paying psychologists. Some learned it through being punished as children and escaping to a world of fantasy. As adults, abused children are usually good hypnotic subjects (Hilgard, 1965); unfortunately, they had to go through that pain to get to that place.

CASE EXAMPLE

One client, an agoraphobic, especially panicked at food markets. As she went into line at the store, she would begin to worry that her heart would begin to race even though she was on medication for that problem. Then she would run out of the store. I worked with her using relaxation therapy, but that did not do the trick. Then she learned some of these hypnotic thinking exercises, and I asked her to do the following assignment: The next time she began to be afraid in a grocery store, she was to go to the frozen fish counter and imagine that she could actually get in with the frozen fish and lie down and be a perch. She could hide there as a perch for an hour. If she was really good at this, nobody would notice that she was a perch. Further, she could decide at the last minute if she wanted to be a perch or haddock. That was her choice.

She laughed at me and said, "I'm paying you money to tell me these things?" I told her that was right and if she did not do it, she would pay me more money. That was good leverage.

I went with her to the store and we practiced being a perch lying down in the frozen food section. As you might imagine, she came back and said that she did not want to do that stupid thing. She started laughing to herself. Then, she really imagined the fish and played with the idea of whether to be a filet or a whole fish. As a result, she was never forced to leave a grocery store again.

That kind of hypnotic thinking, the transformation of situations by playing with them, is very powerful. You do not have to be one of Barber's subjects to do this. We have done similar things as children. Michel's studies at Stanford University (Meichenbaum & Goodman, 1977) show that when children delay gratification they use hypnotic processes. For example, children who are asked to wait to get a larger toy use hypnosis. They imagine the smaller toy is a broken, lousy toy. They play with the image and transform it. Children are our best subjects, and one of the ways I work with people is to teach adults to become kids again, to remember what it was like as a child and learn to play again. By learning to experience the world through play, one learns to play with fear, to play with anxiety, and to transform experience so that it becomes more positive.

How do you teach adults to play again? Well, you can actually take toys and play with them. Another way to do it is to transform simple experiences. For example, I give Life Savers to people and ask them to change the flavors. Can you learn to change a lime Life Saver to a cherry Life Saver? Can you turn water into wine? If you are an alcoholic, though, it might be a good thing to turn water into wine!

"DEHYPNOSIS"

Of course, this raises an interesting practical question. When is it good not to do this? If life is just a series of imagery transformations and distortions, when is it a good idea to stay out of a trance? For example, if you are eating a gourmet dinner, you might want to appreciate the culinary skills of the chef and pay attention to what is right in front of you and to your taste buds. Now most of us do not do this. As I said earlier, it is harder to stay out of a trance than in a trance. Even when we are eating a gourmet dinner, we are often thinking about how big the bill is going to be, or if only they served a little more, etc., and thus we miss out on much of the enjoyment.

Learning to stay out of trance is an *essential* thing to teach clients. In fact, many of our clients need to be taught how to be *unhypnotized*. Fritz

312 *Ericksonian Psychotherapy I: Structures*

Perls said that one of the goals of therapy is to "come to our senses" (Polster & Polster, 1973). When we are not in a trance, we come to our senses.

We can teach people to experience hypnotic behaviors in a wide variety of settings, to transform reality through imagery patterns and to actually learn to stay out of a trance and pay more attention to sensory experience. If people can do that, even 10 percent of the time, the quality of their lives can change dramatically. They will find that hypnosis becomes not a "big hypnosis" experience of waiting for the next therapy session but rather that in brief moments they can transform experiences to make them more useful and effective.

In conclusion, I should note that this process is not all conscious. When I talk about these things to Ericksonians, sometimes they think, "Isn't this just conscious effort? What about the unconscious?"

These processes have a life of their own. For example, once we begin to imagine while jogging that a hand is pushing us along, that hand takes on a certain reality and develops and changes as we learn to go with the imagery. The imagery changes. It becomes unconscious and we are surprised by what happens. Learn to surprise yourself by seriously playing with your imagination!

REFERENCES

Araoz, D.L. (1982). *Hypnosis and sex therapy*. New York: Brunner/Mazel.
Barber, T.X. (1972). Suggested ("hypnotic") behavior: The trance paradigm vs. an alternative paradigm. In E. Fromm & R. E. Shor (Eds.), *Hypnosis: Research developments and perspectives* (pp. 115-182). Hawthorne, NY: Aldine.
Barber, T.X. (1983). Hypnosis, deep relaxation and active relaxation: Data, theory and clinical applications. In P. Lehrer & R. Woolfolk (Eds.), *Clinical guide to stress management*. New York: Guilford Press.
Beck, A.T. (1976). *Cognitive therapy and the emotional disorders*. New York: International Universities Press.
Ellis, A. (1977). The basic clinical theory of rational-emotive therapy. In A. Ellis, & R. Griger (Eds.), *Handbook of rational-emotive therapy*. New York: Springer.
Erickson, M.H. (1980a). *The artistry of Milton H. Erickson, M.D.* [Videotape]. New York: Irvington.
Erickson, M.H. (1980b). Trance induction and commentary. In E.L. Rossi (Ed.), *The collected papers of Milton H. Erickson, Vol. 1: The nature of hypnosis and suggestion*. New York: Irvington.
Greenberg, D., & Jacobs, M. (1966). *How to make yourself miserable*. New York: Random House.
Hilgard, E.R. (1965). *Hypnotic susceptibility*. New York: Harcourt Brace Jovanovich.
Katz, N.W. (1978). Hypnotic inductions as training in cognitive self-control. *Cognitive Therapy in Research, 2*, 4.
Katz, N.W. (1979). Comparative efficacy of behavioral training plus relaxation, and asleep trance hypnotic induction in increasing hypnotic susceptibility. *Journal of Consulting Clinical Psychology, 47*, 119-127.

Meichenbaum, D.H., & Goodman, J. (1977). Training impulsive children to talk to themselves: A means of developing self-control. In A. Ellis, & R. Griger (Eds.), *Handbook of rational-emotive therapy* (pp. 379-397). New York: Springer.

Polster, E., & Polster, M. (1973). *Gestalt therapy integrated: Contours of theory and practice.* New York: Brunner/Mazel.

Sarbin, T.R., & Coe, W.C. (1972). *Hypnosis: A social psychological analysis of influence communication.* New York: Holt, Rinehart & Winston.

Wilson, C., & Barber, T.X. (1983). The fantasy-prone personality: Implications for understanding imagery, hypnosis and parapsychological phenomena. In A.A. Sheikh (Ed.), *Imagery: Current theory* (pp. 340-387). New York: John Wiley.

PART VI

Hypnotherapeutic Techniques

There are a number of techniques that traditionally are used in conjunction with formal hypnosis. The techniques discussed in this section include amnesia, abreaction, and hypnotic identification. As will be seen, these techniques are not always used while the person is in a formal trance. Rather, as the authors demonstrate, these techniques can also be used naturalistically (i.e., without formal induction).

Jeffrey K. Zeig, Ph.D., discusses how amnesia is a cornerstone of the indirect approach. Amnesia occurs when a patient responds without full awareness of the response or of the stimuli that effected it. Differentiation is made between this kind of "clinical amnesia" and the amnesia that is commonly investigated in the laboratory.
Previously unpublished case examples conducted by Milton Erickson are presented. Seven techniques for creating amnesia are discussed.

Steven H. Feldman, M.A., (clinical psychology, Antioch University) conducts his private practice of individual, group, and family therapy in Seattle, Washington, where he is active in training professionals. Feldman has special interests in multiple personality disorder and in patients who have suffered physical and sexual abuse.
Abreaction is defined in terms of classic hypnotic phenomena (e.g., dissociation, age regression, hallucination, and amnesia). It is suggested that abreaction has limited therapeutic value and that its efficacy is more a function of intrapersonal factors than intrapsychic ones. Case examples demonstrate the effective use of abreaction technique.

315

Marc Lehrer earned his Ph.D. in clinical psychology at Adelphi University. He has a private practice of clinical psychology in San Francisco, and regularly conducts workshops on hypnosis in both the United States and Europe. He formerly served as a clinical psychologist at the Child Study Unit of the University of California Medical School in San Francisco.

Lehrer defines hypnosis in terms of activation of the unconscious mind and presents interesting points about the efficacy of autonomous activity. He discusses the technique of hypnotic identification whereby a patient identifies with another person in order to learn a skill that the other person has mastered. Case examples elucidate the use of this technique.

Moris Kleinhauz, M.D., was born in Chile where he received his education. He has been living in Israel since 1952 where he has practiced psychiatry in a number of hospitals. Currently, he is the director of the Community Mental Health Center of Yaffo and director of the Department of Behavioral Sciences of the School of Dentistry at Tel Aviv University. Kleinhauz is founding chairman of the Israeli Society for Clinical and Experimental Hypnosis and is an International Fellow of the American Society of Clinical Hypnosis.

Hypnosis is not a separate discipline; rather it is one tool that therapists use within an integrated treatment approach. Hypnotic procedures are surveyed. Five major groups of interventions are discussed.

Chapter 19

The Clinical Use of Amnesia: Ericksonian Methods

Jeffrey K. Zeig

PROLOGUE

Hypnosis is a certain state of focused awareness in which you respond to what is immediately relevant and, therefore, use awareness selectively. For example, as you have been reading this, part of you could resist noticing the subtle changes of illumination in the room, or how you refocus to deal with perspective, or the process of integrating the view you knew into the view you now know and the view you will instill.

In hypnosis, you utilize previously unrecognized physiological and psychological resources. Note, for example, how you have already developed anesthesia because you have been oblivious to the feeling of being wrapped up in your clothing or to the pressure of your body being supported by the chair and how you trust and willingly accept it.

Hypnosis is a natural response similar to being lost in reverie. What is here fades and the tone decreases when, for a brief moment, for example, you are daydreaming and foremost in your mind is a phrase from *Alice:* "The horror of that moment," the King went on, "I shall never *never* forget!" "You will, though," the Queen said, "if you don't make a memorandum of it."

As far as my own responses are concerned, it was not unnatural to be hypnotized by Erickson and leave after a trance remembering only a few physical sensations, only to have material filter back to consciousness at a later time. It was just like waking from a dream with a feeling, but without remembering the actual content.

Therefore, one can state, the relevant use of hypnosis is to immediately select, focus and entertain a certain awareness.

INTRODUCTION

Sholem Asch (1939) stated, "Not the power to remember, but its very opposite, the power to forget, is a necessary condition for existence." Forgetting allows learned processes to be affected on unconscious (automatic) levels; people can be influenced not only by what they remember, but by the things outside of conscious awareness.

Milton Erickson certainly was not the first to recognize that people can be influenced by events forgotten. The psychoanalytic tradition is rooted in this idea; it is the repression of past conflicts that leads to psychopathology. In this sense, "amnesia" is negative.

In contradistinction to psychoanalysis, the Ericksonian tradition is one of appreciating the flowers rather than speculating about the seeds. Influence can be applied constructively as well as destructively. Any method patients use to remain ineffective in living can be used by therapists to promote effective living. If amnesia can be negative, it can also be positive.

For example, Erickson was fond of telling a story about how he personally used amnesia in a constructive, positive manner. He unconsciously misplaced a manuscript that he was about to submit for publication. Trusting his unconscious mind, he did not search for the missing manuscript. Sometime later he was rereading an article and found some material that he knew he should have included in the "lost" manuscript. Then, he immediately found the paper and submitted it for publication.

Therapeutic amnesia was often used by Erickson. In his keynote address at the 1980 International Congress on Ericksonian Approaches to Hypnosis and Psychotherapy, Jay Haley (1982) pointed out that, "Erickson was a master in the control of amnesia and he worked with it in hypnosis as well as in ordinary social relations" (p. 14). In fact, the invitation to experience amnesia was present in almost all of the formal inductions Erickson administered.

However, amnesia was not merely a technique that Erickson used in hypnotherapy; it was a cornerstone of his approach and a central component of his indirect technique. Indirect methods are used to set up situations in which patients will "spontaneously" utilize their own power to change. Amnesia is often a concomitant to the effective use of indirect technique.

Haley (1963) indicated that confusion is a part of every induction of hypnosis, whether or not the operator is aware of it. Similarly, amnesia is a part both of the induction and utilization of hypnosis and of the effective use of indirect "multiple-level communication," whether or not the therapist is aware of it. In fact, one way of defining indirect technique (and hypnosis) is the methods whereby responses to communication are effected without full awareness on the part of the respondent. Amnesia is the essence of hypnosis!

The purpose of this chapter is to explain the importance of amnesia in Ericksonian methodology, and to list some of the techniques that Erickson used to accomplish its induction.

WHY USE AMNESIA?

Erickson and Rossi (1974) indicated that amnesia and indirect suggestion are used so that suggestions are not recognized by consciousness, and thus are able to "enter into the patient's preconscious or unconscious and are there utilized in an optimum manner for the patient's overall development" (p. 239). The suggestions are sealed away from the potentially negating effects of the patient's conscious attitude. Erickson used amnesia so the material would "settle" in the unconscious without conscious disruption.

Erickson also used amnesia as a way of demonstrating to the subject that he or she could be influenced hypnotically. Actually, my first experience with Erickson was marked by amnesia (Zeig, 1980). At that time, I doubted that I was a good hypnotic subject. When I returned home and played the tape of my conversation with Erickson and realized that he had effected amnesia in me, I knew I could experience trance and deep trance phenomena.

Amnesia also has a diagnostic purpose. In doing effective psychotherapy, one must understand the patient's memory style. Each person remembers and forgets in an idiosyncratic manner. In traditional psychiatry, this aspect of diagnosis is often overlooked. In Ericksonian methodology, when one diagnoses a person's responsiveness, one can diagnose the patient's style of remembering, forgetting and responding to suggestion without full conscious awareness of doing so. Knowing this information about the patient is important to effective therapeutic communication.

Amnesia makes it possible for the patient to have an "AHA!" experience that emotionally charges a rather simple insight. Part of the charm of indirect technique is that it makes simple ideas come alive (Zeig,

1980). For example, once I watched Erickson conduct a group session around the concept of feeling comfortable with mistakes. This session will be detailed later. It would have been futile for Erickson to directly suggest to the group that they could think about mistakes with a different attitude. By using a complex amnesia technique, Erickson presented a simple idea so that, to their own credit, the members of the group could come to self-determined understandings and have "new associations" about making mistakes. Because of amnesia, the response can occur without conscious knowledge of the source of suggestion and to the credit of the individual patient.

AMNESIA DEFINED AND REDEFINED

A number of interrelated phenomena have been named above—amnesia, forgetting, and responses that can be effected without full conscious awareness. But what are they and how are they different from each other?

Researchers have defined hypnotic amnesia as "forgetting" associated with hypnotic experience which can be recovered upon suggestion (Cooper, 1979, p. 306). Reversibility in response to a cue is a key aspect of this definition because experimental work attempts to illuminate the nature of amnesia per se. Only by including reversibility can one clearly distinguish amnesia from simple forgetting. While the above operational definition has value in the experimental situation, it has limited value in the clinical situation where the primary goal is effecting change. Reversibility is only important in some clinical situations; amnesia can be used without reversibility to promote therapeutic goals.

A clinical definition should center on the response of the subject to the therapeutic communication, not on whether full or partial recall can occur at a later time. Reversibility is not of primary importance and is unnecessarily limiting in the clinical conception of amnesia.

In clinical amnesia, a subject responds without full awareness of the response or of the stimuli that effected it. This technique is used by communicators everywhere, including the advertising industry. Reversibility is unimportant, and possibly detrimental, to responsive behavior. This definition is difficult to use in the laboratory because it is not easy to operationalize.

In the clinical sense, amnesia is part of every induction. When Erickson defined hypnosis as focused awareness, it followed that amnesia was a product of that attention (Haley, 1982, p. 23). While attention is selective, things outside immediate attention also will elicit responses. For example, one cough in a room will automatically set off other coughs. If one person stretches, other people will stretch. This is a naturalistic response. It is "hypnotic" and uses amnesia, yet no induction has been offered.

Amnesia is a part of every induction because, in promoting hypnotic responsiveness, the operator works to get the subject to respond to increasingly minimal cues. The operator works to blur and even make unrecognizable the stimuli that lead to the subject's responses. For example, if you tell hypnotic subjects to raise their arm and they do so in a normal fashion, that is not a hypnotic response. But if it is suggested, "You can, in a way that's *handy*, find that hypnosis is really an *uplifting* feeling in a way that's *right* for you," and the right arm then levitates, that response is considered hypnotic. The essence of hypnosis (and good therapeutic influence) is that the patient responds in an automatic/dissociative manner without fully identifying or comprehending the stimuli that caused the response. In traditional hypnosis, direct suggestions of amnesia often follow the trance work. However, indirect methods are more desirable because they work better.

In a clinical setting, therapists usually do not give depressed patients direct suggestions to become more active. However, if the suggestions for activation are given indirectly (outside of conscious awareness) and associations to the concept are sufficiently established, there is a better chance for autonomous change. Such autonomous change is a desirable goal. Change should come about by the patient's own efforts and because he or she takes responsibility; the patient should get the credit.

It is important to realize that psychotherapy must be conducted at the level of experience at which the problem is generated. Since most problems are generated at the level of associations, that is where they must be changed. In order for this to occur, the patient's associations are therapeutically guided until spontaneous recombinations and activation occur. Amnesia is an integral part of this process.

For example, the interspersal technique (Erickson, 1966) can facilitate pain control by building associations to the concept of comfort to some extent outside of the awareness of the patient. A similar technique has been applied successfully with anorectics (Zeig, 1980). In this conception, some degree of amnesia is an indispensable part of indirect technique.

Amnesia is not only a phenomenon that can be induced through hypnosis—it is a fact of life. There is, for example, that unconscious plagiarism where a writer comes up with a "new" idea without recognizing it as something read at an earlier time. In psychotherapy, patients often have "spontaneous" amnesias that resemble naturalistically induced amnesias. For example, most practitioners can remember a situation in which a patient came to a session reporting newly discovered insight which, in fact, the therapist had mentioned in casual conversation in a previous session.

In summary, it is possible that there are two different types of amnesia—"experimental amnesia" (as defined and used in the laboratory) and "clinical amnesia" (as used by therapists). The former is based on a capacity for temporary forgetting and the latter is based on interactional responsiveness outside of conscious awareness; it entails a response without full awareness of the responsive behavior or the stimuli that effected it. Moreover, experimental amnesia invariably involves formal hypnosis while clinical amnesia may or may not use formal hypnosis.

To illustrate the constructive naturalistic use of amnesia (i.e., amnesia that is effected without the formal use of trance) in psychotherapy, I will discuss two previously unpublished cases conducted by Milton Erickson, in one of which I was an integral part. I also discuss a case in which I successfully used Erickson's naturalistic amnesia technique.

THE NATURALISTIC USE OF AMNESIA

Case One

During one of my early training sessions, I asked Erickson if I might sit in on one of his sessions while he was conducting psychotherapy.

I made my request in the morning and Erickson denied it, explaining that it would probably be inappropriate for me to sit in with his private practice patients. That afternoon, while he was seeing patients, I rested in the bedroom next door to Erickson's office. A knock roused me from a nap. When I opened the door, a very attractive woman explained that Erickson wanted to see me.

I oriented myself and went into Erickson's office. The woman was seated in the patient's chair. Erickson indicated that I was to stand in the doorway. He introduced me: "Kathy, this is Jeff Zeig, a therapist from California." Then he looked at me and said, "Kathy told me that she wears sunglasses to protect herself from the hostile world, but I told her that she didn't need those sunglasses in *here* with me." In fact, at the time, Kathy was not wearing sunglasses; they were lying on the end table next to her chair.

Suddenly, Erickson changed contexts and asked me, "Isn't she pretty?" I looked at Kathy and said, "Yes." Erickson continued, "Doesn't she have beautiful features?" I looked at Kathy and said, "Yes." "Doesn't she have beautiful eyes?" I looked at Kathy and said, "Yes," although I remember being a bit tentative in my response. Erickson continued to question me: "Doesn't she have beautiful lips?" I looked at Kathy, gulped, and said, "Yes." Erickson's next question was, "Aren't her lips kissable?" I started to sweat. Erickson became more animated. He moved from side to side in his chair, speaking rapidly, one question following immediately after the next: "Doesn't she have lovely legs?" "Isn't she dressed well?" "Wouldn't she make a good wife?" "Don't you think she's marriageable?"

I was atwitter. I remember thinking, "Is she in a trance?" "Am I in a trance?" "Is she the patient?" "Am I the patient?" "What's the purpose of this?" "Is he trying to get me married . . . again?" (Erickson had previously tried to interest me in dating one of his other female patients.)

After what seemed an endless number of questions, suddenly Mrs. Erickson appeared and wheeled Erickson out of the office. I was left with Kathy.

I said goodbye to Kathy and locked up Erickson's office. Fifteen minutes later, there was a knock on the door. It was Kathy. In an embarrassed manner, she blurted, "I forgot my sunglasses." Sure enough, the sunglasses were still on the end table where she had left them.

After Kathy left with her sunglasses, I went to the main house to tell Erickson about this "serendipitous" occurrence, thinking how much it would amuse him. But he indicated that he expected her response and in fact had set it up. Kathy had come into his office wearing sunglasses and when he suggested she did not need the sunglasses in the room with *him*, she laid them on the table. Then he talked with her about other matters. During that discussion, he interspersed a suggestion by casually looking at the sunglasses and explaining to Kathy, "You know how easy it is to leave something behind. For example, you've had times in which you forgot your purse." Then he went back to the previous topic of conversation. The result of Erickson's naturalistic technique was that Kathy forgot the sunglasses.

Erickson was obviously pleased with Kathy's response. He explained, "Her unconscious mind is starting to believe in me."

Erickson stated that he used me in the session to reach Kathy because she had an almost delusional belief that something was wrong with her after growing up in a family where she was severely criticized. Through his work, Erickson hoped that Kathy could learn to accept a compliment. I learned something about my ability to endure pressure.

As far as I know, Kathy was not told that, in forgetting her sunglasses, she was responding through a naturalistic amnesia to a suggestion

Erickson indirectly presented. I am also certain that Erickson did not interpret Kathy's responsive behavior back to her.

Case Two

Intrigued by Erickson's technique with Kathy, I looked for an opportunity to apply it in my own practice. As Jay Haley explained at the 1980 Congress, it takes one kind of creativity to invent technique and another kind to know when to apply it effectively.

A professional man contacted me for weight control. Actually, he had more extensive knowledge of dieting and weight control techniques than I did. He "ran" the practice of a local bariatrics physician. This was a highly successful businessman who was insightful and self-assured and had excellent control of his behavior in all areas of his life except for his weight which fluctuated wildly.

In the first session, I was concerned with establishing a responsive set. In the middle of the interview, I engaged John in a discussion about men's purses because it was something that we had in common. Both of us often carried them and, in fact, he brought one with him into my office. We discussed the fact that it was popular for men in other countries to carry purses, but that it was not very popular in the United States.

Subsequently, I looked at John's pipe, which he had placed on the table. I explained that during a recent workshop, I left my purse in a restaurant and had to drive back 20 minutes to reclaim it. Then I continued my initial interview.

At the end of the session, I walked John to the door and said to him, "I'm going to save you a 20-minute drive." (The patient's home was located 20 minutes from my office.) He quickly replied, "I forgot my pipe!" He flushed and said, "That's why you told me that story," and he quickly added, "That doesn't mean anything. I often forget my pipe." I replied, "Your unconscious mind has its own way of responding."

In the second session, the patient reported that, quite to his surprise, he had a rather easy time avoiding taboo foods. The impact of my intervention was that it served to confirm the fact that John could respond to my indirect suggestions. During the session John recognized that I had been presenting indirect suggestions to help him with his problem. My demonstration with the pipe indicated that he could respond to suggestions I presented. Even though he at first denied that his behavior was responsive to my suggestions, he would still have to have some doubt. Moreover, John's overt response is typical of how some patients react to posthypnotic suggestions; it is often the case that a patient will supply a rationalization for carrying out a posthypnotic suggestion.

Case Three

On another occasion, I watched Erickson conduct family therapy with a mother and an adolescent daughter. After the session, Erickson described to me an intervention that he had accomplished during a previous session. He said that while he was interviewing the mother and daughter, he suddenly looked up at the daughter and said, "Your mother *was* a dumb bunny too," referring to the poster on the file cabinet near his desk, and indicating that he knew that the mother had been a smoker. Then he continued the interview.

The poster to which Erickson referred was published by the American Cancer Society. It was a picture (with a purple background, of course) of a rabbit simultaneously smoking a number of cigarettes. The caption at the bottom stated, "THIS IS A DUMB BUNNY."

At the next session, the teenager triumphantly reported that she had quit smoking the night before. She believed this decision to be hers alone, not behavior primed by Erickson's earlier reference. Erickson dismissed the mother from the session and teased the girl about the fact that she might have cheated. In fact, the girl indicated that she had smoked part of a cigarette after she "stopped." However, when Erickson teased her, she definitely stated, "Now I've decided to stop."

Naturalistic amnesia is only one part of responsiveness to indirect communication. Established rapport, and the setup and follow-through, determine the effectiveness of any intervention. Erickson's sensitivity to the issue and his style of setting up the situation so the teenager would take an independent stand showed his sensitivity in responding to the dynamics of the situation.

The techniques for inducing amnesia in the above cases happen to be similar, based on interspersed indirect suggestions and response to multiple-level communication without full conscious awareness. Actually, there are a number of other techniques that can be used to induce amnesia. Before discussing techniques for inducing amnesia, a more general perspective on hypnotic phenomena will be presented which will further distinguish amnesia with reversibility from naturalistic clinical amnesia.

AMNESIA AS A HYPNOTIC PHENOMENON

Hypnotic phenomena are found in everyday life. When you ask a patient to experience hypnotic phenomena, you are not asking for anything new. In hypnosis, these phenomena are consolidated and organized to serve a purpose.

The phenomena of hypnosis are predicated on the ability of the human organism to be plastic in behavior and perception. Our ability to create, distort and delete sensory percepts, emotions, actions, the experience of time, memory, etc., are the building blocks of hypnotic phenomena. Therefore, hypnotic phenomena can be divided into three groups:

I. Group One
   a) Positive hallucinations (visual, auditory, gustatory and olfactory)
   b) Age regression
   c) Posthypnotic suggestion
   d) Automatic writing and drawing

II. Group Two
   a) Negative hallucinations (visual, auditory, gustatory and olfactory)
   b) Amnesia
   c) Anesthesia

III. Group Three
   a) Time distortion
   b) Analgesia
   c) Hypermnesia

In general, phenomena in Group One concern creating human experience; phenomena in Group Two deal with deleting experience;* and phenomena in Group Three have more to do with distorting experience. Hypnotically created experiences such as positive hallucination, age regression and posthypnotic suggestions substantially differ from experiences that are hypnotically deleted as, for example, amnesia, negative hallucination, and anesthesia. The latter entail a capacity for becoming "unaware" and are facets of selective perception. Amnesia is

---

*It is possible to distort experiences in Group One or Two. For example, one could distort memory rather than simply create an "all or none" amnesia; one could distort vision rather than simply create an "all or none" positive hallucination.

selective perception regarding memory; negative hallucination is selective perception regarding sensory experience in the visual, auditory, gustatory and olfactory channels; and anesthesia is selective perception in the tactile and internal sensory aspects of the kinesthetic channel. Most likely, the three phenomena in Group Two involving selective perception have similar neurological bases and those adept at one would be equally adept at the other two.

The technique and mechanisms for hypnotically creating or distorting experience differ substantially from the technique and mechanisms for ablating aspects of experience. Unfortunately, in both laboratory and traditional hypnosis, the methodology for creating experience has been applied to deleting experience, whether appropriate or not.

For example, to create the experiences of positive hallucination, the therapist could use more direct forms of communication and suggest, "When the eyes defocus, you can discover patterns moving and changing shape before your eyes."

However, direct suggestion is not as effective in deleting experience. For example, if the therapist suggests that, "You notice that the chair in front of you has disappeared," the patient must recognize an object in the foreground and then try to forget it, an experience tantamount to forgetting a purple elephant.

There is a problem with directly suggesting the deletion of experience (for example, with amnesia, negative hallucination or anesthesia) because the subject must process the suggestion, recognize the reality and then immediately forget that recognition. Not many people possess this talent, and that is probably why a low percentage of the population experience these phenomena on the standardized scales of hypnotizability.

In the experimental situation, direct suggestion is used to promote amnesia. On the Harvard group scale, subjects are told, "You will have no desire to try to recall," "It will be much easier to simply forget," "You will have difficulty remembering all the things I told you and all the things you did or felt," and "You will remember nothing of what has happened until I say to you, 'Now remember everything'" (Shor & Orne, 1962, p. 11). Traditional hypnotists sometimes use even more direct challenges by suggesting to subjects that they will no longer be able to remember their name, a particular number, etc.

On the scales of hypnotizability, amnesia has been considered to be a difficult item to pass and a characteristic of deep trance subjects (Kilstrom & Evans, 1979, p. 185). Research on amnesia has attempted to separate the nature of amnesia per se from other factors such as demand, characteristics, subject expectations, compliance and role playing (Cooper, 1979, p. 349).

However, it may be that amnesia has been difficult to induce because of the restrictive definition and because of problems inherent in trying to induce amnesia through direct suggestion.

Upon closer examination, it is not difficult to induce amnesia, especially when amnesia is defined naturalistically. Actually, as far as therapy (or life) is concerned, it is more difficult to make an event memorable than it is to make an event forgettable. There is nothing extraordinary about amnesia. People forget and are influenced by what they forget every day. Part of the difficulty in inducing amnesia with reversibility is that it is difficult (and rare) to have the talent to temporarily forget and subsequently remember on demand.*

The preferred method for deleting experience is to use indirection. It is not difficult to delete experience. It is only difficult when one tries to do it directly. Erickson worked on subtle levels to foster the experience of deletion. He was fond of pointing out that people did not notice traffic noise outside his office while listening to him. In fact, he encouraged this effect by keeping his voice modulated as the traffic passed by. Most speakers raise their voice to compensate for the additional noise and thereby can cue their listener to the traffic sounds.

Actually, there is some indication that using different techniques to induce amnesia can cause differential effects. Authoritarian suggestions can produce different effects from permissive suggestions (Barber & Calverley, 1966). However, this phenomenon has not been fully researched.

INDIRECT TECHNIQUES FOR CREATING AMNESIA

Seven techniques were commonly used by Erickson to create amnesia. These techniques can be used separately or in unison, naturalistically or in conjunction with formal hypnosis, and to induce amnesia with or without reversibility. Of course, to be effective, any technique must be tailored to the unique qualities of the individual.

---

*In this conception, laboratory amnesia entails selective perception and subsequent response and reversibility on demand while clinical amnesia uses selective attention and naturalistic responsiveness.

1) Indirect Suggestions

Indirect suggestions are relatively simple forms of multiple-level influence communication. One message is communicated on the social level while it is implied that the response will be to the second message that is subtly provided on the psychological level.

One of the common forms of indirect suggestion used to foster deletion of experience is to get the patient to concentrate on a particular subject while implying that everything in the background can be ignored. For example, "You can pay attention to me, can you not? You just can really attend to me." Alternately, the operator could suggest selective attention to any particular category of experience such as vision or hearing, e.g., "When you come out of trance, you can really remember the feeling of pressure from your body being supported by the chair. You just can really remember that." Thus the patient can forget the trance material without focusing on forgetting. Other examples of such indirect suggestions are: "You can't possibly remember everything in your conscious mind," and "You don't know exactly how your conscious mind remembers one particular detail of your experience."

Multiple-level communication techniques such as the one used in Case Three are more subtle variations of this method. Again, with this form of suggestion, the idea is to bring something into the foreground, implying that things now defined as being in the background will be forgotten.

2) Distraction and Quickly Shifting Contexts

Erickson often used distraction after a hypnotic induction by discussing an unrelated subject when the patient was aroused from the trance. For example, he asked one subject, immediately after rousing him from hypnosis, "What did you do last night?" In keeping with Erickson's style, the distractions often had symbolic and/or psychodynamic significance and were not merely non sequiturs. A variation on this technique was used by Erickson when working with demonstration subjects. Toward the end of the trance, he might ask the subject his name—a question that distracted and also subtly effected an orientation to the beginning of a relationship which is when one commonly asks that question (cf. the "as if" technique below).

Erickson also would use the distraction technique during formal and naturalistic hypnotherapy. For example, Erickson would tell an anecdote with one theme and then switch to an anecdote with an unrelated theme. Thereby, there could be amnesia for one of the anecdotes.

A variation on the theme of distraction involves the presentation of shock—a stimulus that provides an emotional reaction. If done properly, the irrelevant stimuli would be remembered because emotion "fixes" the memory. Thus, the stimuli preceding the distraction and perhaps the stimuli following the distraction would be forgotten.

For example, early in my training with Erickson, I had doubts about my ability to go into hypnosis. Erickson did an induction with me and had me open my eyes, at which time he slapped my hand with a fly swatter. I did not move. In addition to ratifying the trance, there was some amnesia. I did not remember what happened before or after the slap. However, I cannot forget the fly swatter.

3) "As If" Technique

In presenting suggestions to create, distort, or delete an experience, Erickson would often pretend and act "as if" the suggested phenomena were already in effect. For example, in doing age regression, Erickson might speak in a paternal voice, "as if" he were talking with a child. With a negative hallucination, Erickson might act "as if" no one else in the room was present except him.

The "as if" technique plays on and enhances the demand character-istics of the relationship. Demand characteristics are not just artifacts; they are powerful social cues for compliance which can lead to the subject actually having the suggested experience.

Applying the "as if" technique to amnesia, the therapist could act as if the previous segment of trance had never happened. For example, after the trance was terminated, the therapist could say, "When do you want me to begin the hypnosis?" Or, "Do you think you can be hyp-notized?" or "How do you think that you can go into a trance?" Alter-nately, the operator could act as if the event for which amnesia is suggested had never happened.

4) Structured Amnesia

One of the most original techniques that Erickson devised for effecting amnesia was the technique of structured amnesia (Erickson, Haley, & Weakland, 1959; Erickson & Rossi, 1974). "Structured amnesia is effected by awakening the subject in a manner that reorients him to the exact place, time and associative content of consciousness as when he entered trance. The total situation is so structured that the trance period falls into a lacuna between two events structured to be so identical that consciousness does not recognize them as two and is thus amnesiac for the period that has occurred between them" (Erickson & Rossi, 1974, p. 235). Erickson (1964) discussed this technique as being more effective for developing posthypnotic amnesia than direct suggestions.

Stephen and Carol Lankton (1983) have advanced this structured amnesia with their work on multiple-embedded metaphor. In its simplest form, a story is begun and then abruptly terminated before the ending. Another story is told, then the operator picks up the first story where he left off and completes it. There is overlap with the "as if" technique because the first story is completed as if the second story had never been told.

Erickson also used the structured amnesia technique when he took telephone calls. In my early years of study with Erickson, I was often alone with him in the office. It was not uncommon for him to answer the telephone during our sessions. When he did, he often stopped his communication to me abruptly, sometimes even in mid-sentence, to answer the telephone. Subsequently, he continued exactly where he left off, as if the telephone had never rung. Needless to say, I do not remember any of the telephone calls.

Erickson's variations on the structured amnesia technique were endless. Sometimes Erickson would tell a story, continue with a number of other stories, then go back to the first story he had told and add a completing thought. Sometimes Erickson would use a particular phrase in initiating an induction and then come back to the phrase as he terminated the trance. Erickson also used this technique nonverbally as, for example, with his famous handshake induction.

In the handshake induction, Erickson would begin shaking a person's hand, then use verbal and/or nonverbal confusion to elicit catalepsy. After doing additional trance work, he would take the cataleptic hand, shake it again and continue from the point at which he had created disruption. He told me once that some of his colleagues refused to shake hands with him.

5) Confusion

The confusion technique (Erickson, 1964) was one of the most important contributions that Erickson made to hypnosis. Confusion can be used to promote amnesia. Three hypothetical examples follow:

a) It's just as easy to remember as it is to forget. You can do both things consciously and you can do both things unconsciously. You can remember to forget unconsciously or you can forget to remember unconsciously or you can unconsciously forget to unconsciously remember. Or you can consciously remember what you forgot or you can unconsciously remember what you forgot. And the things that you forgot to forget unconsciously are different from the things that you will remember to remember consciously.

b) The important thing about trance is that you can go in and you can go out. The mind that goes in is conscious but when it is out it is unconscious. But when the unconscious is in, it tries to keep the conscious mind coming in, out. What is out of mind is in as far as the unconscious is concerned, and what is out of the conscious mind isn't really what's important now.

c) Dissociation statements (cf. Lankton & Lankton, 1983) provide confusion and can be used to suggest amnesia: Your conscious mind can remember the support of your body by the chair while your unconscious mind can recognize the changes in tone, or your conscious mind can recognize the changes in tone while your unconscious mind recognizes the support by the chair. You can recognize that either consciously, or unconsciously realize that.

In one method of using confusion, the therapist makes concrete suggestions following the confusion when the subject is most receptive and, disliking the uncertainty, is searching for something to do that "makes sense." Therefore, indirect statements could be used subsequent to the induction of confusion in promoting amnesia. However, the disruption and overload created by the confusion technique itself often are enough to disrupt memory of the preceding suggestion.

There are numerous ways to use confusion technique. For instance, distraction itself creates confusion. However, to delve into this area, it would be best to discuss the nature of the confusion technique, which is beyond the scope of the present chapter.

6) Key Words

Erickson was acutely aware of the multiple meanings of words and of the fact that words could be used to guide associations. For example, to create amnesia, Erickson might use the word "forget" in a context not associated with the idea of amnesia for the particular trance period or trance event, as he did in Case One. Another example was that after bringing a person out of trance, Erickson might mention that the patient had "forgotten" that Erickson was sitting in a wheelchair. Alternatively, one could talk about flowers and the beauty of the forget-me-not.

Once the patient associates to the idea of forgetting, that "momentum" can be attached to an aspect of the previous trance experience. Any of the synonyms of "forget" could be used to guide associations, e.g., "lapse," "lose sight of," "think no more of," "out of mind," etc.

Words that suggest the process of amnesia can be similarly used. For example, in my first interaction with Erickson, he fostered an amnesia in me by creating an association to the word "select" (Zeig, 1980). Synonyms of "select" that could be used, include "choose," "pick," "single out," "separate out," etc. This process makes use of the "figure/ground" issue wherein one makes one item foreground, allowing the items that now become background to be overlooked.

Usually, key words are not solely used to induce amnesia. They also can be used to "seed" an amnesic response.

7) Seeding

Seeding was one of the most important and least understood techniques that Erickson used. He was acutely attuned to the process of communication. He would not just present an intervention, but would seed the idea well in advance. In this way, he would build a responsive set, and thereby build response potential by creating sufficient associations to the intended suggestion or behavior so that it would be carried out once it was offered. The importance of this type of priming cannot be overemphasized. Erickson would not only seed specific interventions, he would also seed his stories before presenting them. It should be noted that one of the reasons the effectiveness of direct technique is limited is because seeding/priming is not used.

"Common everyday examples" is one method to seed or build association to the idea of amnesia. Once sufficient associations have been built, the amnesia can "fall into place" without the necessity of further suggestions. For example, in an induction, Erickson might talk about the fact that a person can be introduced to someone and then a few seconds later say to himself, "Now what was that person's name?" Alternately, he would talk about how he would give students in his class information about the date and location of an upcoming exam only to find that after the class the students were asking each other, "What was the room? What was the date?" Other examples include stories about misplaced car keys and humming a song without realizing it had just been heard on the radio. The anecdotes could be told contiguously or they could be interspersed in other communication.

There are multiple purposes for using amnesia, and the technique selected may depend on the intended effect. To illustrate the complexity Erickson used in his therapy, a transcript which features complex use of amnesia techniques is present and discussed.

USING TECHNIQUES IN UNISON

What follows is a transcript of a complex use of a number of amnesia techniques. The interaction took place in one of Erickson's teaching seminars in 1979. At the time, Erickson was midway through an induction with a woman subject. He had already established a responsive set in the central patient and in other members of the seminar. Then he worked with two men, demonstrating responsiveness to locus of voice. He induced arm catalepsy in each of the males while they had their eyes closed and demonstrated that catalepsy was removed only when he directed his voice to each man separately and suggested the removal of catalepsy. The transcript continues from that point:

E: Then I pointed my voice to him and I intentionally directed it to him (Erickson indicates he is talking about Man Number One.), then you will see that I had to direct it to him (Indicating Man Number Two) because unconsciously (Erickson directs his voice to the floor.) you are aware of much more than you are consciously. (Erickson sits back in his chair.) You recognize intonations, inflection, emphasis, changes of tense, repetitions, hesitations, a cessation of thought. And ordinarily you'd consciously follow along. (Erickson looks up.) Now my wife has had a lot of experience in proofreading. She has all that experience in proofreading. She finds, to her amusement, that she finds all of the typographical mistakes in TV, in every book she reads, in every advertisement. (Erickson shifts in his chair.) But the entire question of hypnosis is really getting the patient's attention and holding it. Now I can be talking to you and she's doing two things . . . (Erickson indicates that he is talking to the group about the woman subject.)

This is a rather remarkable sequence of communication. Erickson initiates by talking about the fact that the unconscious mind is more aware than the conscious mind. He is not only referring to the response of the men. He is also making the suggestion to effect responses in group members. His tautology seeds the idea of selective attention and dissociation. Subsequently, Erickson methodically presents a list of output channels of communication—intonations, inflection, emphasis, changes of tense, repetitions, and hesitations. The effect of this sequence on many listeners is boredom and/or "spacing out." This effect is enhanced by the fact that Erickson directs his voice to the floor rather than at specific people. Subsequently, the list stops with the phrase "a cessation of thought," which is a different category of operation than the ones previously mentioned. It is not really an output operation, it is really an effect. Literally, it is the effect that Erickson is attempting to induce; he wants the subjects in the room to experience a cessation in thought (amnesia). Although it is not emphasized by changes in voice tone, the suggestion stands out because it is not in the same category as the earlier items on the list. Erickson continues with an indirect suggestion for amnesia, namely, "And ordinarily you'd consciously follow along. . . ," thereby implying that now there is no need to follow along consciously. Rather, it is the unconscious that can follow along.

Erickson then distracts and quickly changes contexts by telling an anecdote about proofreading and his wife's delight in finding mistakes. (One of the themes that Erickson seemed to be discussing with this group was how to feel comfortable with mistakes.) The crux of the therapy seems to be one of subtly changing associations to and attitudes about making mistakes.

Next, Erickson returned to the idea of selective awareness with the phrase, "But the entire question of hypnosis is really getting the patient's attention and holding it."

"Attention" and "holding it" are key words that can be an imperative and (re)orient the listener to the immediate moment. These words were marked out by Erickson who changed his intonation when he said them.

To end the sequence, Erickson reorients the listeners to the woman in the room. He started the sequence by talking about people in the room. By changing contexts to talk again about participants, he recreates the associative context that was in effect when the sequence began. Hence, we effectively have a structured amnesia.

There are other techniques of creating amnesia. For example, one could use metaphor, nonverbal technique, overload, or even boredom. Alternately, one could divide amnesia into component parts, e.g., the feeling of knowing, knowing just the auditory component, knowing the source but not the content, etc. Subsequently, full amnesia could be created by establishing each part and "joining" parts together. The seven techniques listed represent the methods Erickson used most often, but they often were used in combination. It goes without saying that Erickson's focus was not on using technique per se but on the responsive effect of his communication on the subject.

CONCLUSIONS

Erickson's use of amnesia demonstrates that he dramatically departed from the traditional understanding of human memory as concerns the ways in which people are influenced. In this chapter, amnesia has been defined as a process by which a response can be effected in a subject without full awareness by the person of the response and/or the stimuli that effected the response. It would be beneficial if future research into amnesia could focus more on the response of the subject. In fact, in light of recent research on subliminal suggestion (J. Feldman, Chapter 26), it may be that the subject's response would vary depending on whether or not awareness of the source of suggestion is present.

EPILOGUE

And, as far as this chapter is concerned, the unconscious mind can consign to itself the task of being oblivious to many things and realize how the words go in one ear and the unconscious mind can pick and choose from a select source of association because there is no need to forget benefits or to forget one's self in the process. And you don't know what you consciously wish to remember, or that you could use hypnosis to remember exactly what posture you assumed when you first started reading the introduction.

REFERENCES

Asch, S. (1939). *The Nazarene.* New York: Putnam.
Barber, T.X., & Calverly, D.S. (1966). Toward a theory of "hypnotic" behavior: Experimental analyses of suggested amnesia. *Journal of Abnormal Psychology, 71,* 95-107.
Cooper, L.M. (1979). Hypnotic amnesia. In E. Fromm, & R. Shor (Eds.), *Hypnosis: Developments in research and new perspectives* (pp. 305-351). New York: Aldine.
Erickson, M.H. (1964). The "surprise" and "my-friend-John" techniques of hypnosis: Minimal cues and natural field experimentation. *American Journal of Clinical Hypnosis, 4,* 293-307.
Erickson, M.H. (1966). The interspersal technique for symptom correction and pain control. *American Journal of Clinical Hypnosis, 3,* 198-209.
Erickson, M.H., Haley, J., & Weakland, J. (1959). A transcript of a trance induction and commentary. *American Journal of Clinical Hypnosis, 2,* 49-84.

Erickson, M.H., & Rossi, E. (1974). Varieties of hypnotic amnesia. *American Journal of Clinical Hypnosis, 4*, 225-239.

Feldman, J. (This volume). Subliminal perception and information processing theory: Empirical and conceptual validation of Erickson's notion of the unconscious.

Haley, J. (1963). *Strategies of psychotherapy*. New York: Grune & Stratton.

Haley, J. (1982). The contribution to therapy of Milton H. Erickson, M.D. In J. K. Zeig (Ed.), *Ericksonian approaches to hypnosis and psychotherapy*. New York: Brunner/Mazel.

Kilstrom, J.F., & Evans, F.J. (Eds.). (1979). Memory retrieval process during post-hypnotic amnesia. *Functional disorders of memory* (pp. 179-218). Hillsdale, NJ: Lawrence Erlbaum Associates.

Lankton, C., & Lankton, S. (1983). *The answer within: A clinical framework of Ericksonian hypnotherapy*. New York: Brunner/Mazel.

Shor, R.E., & Orne, E.C. (1962). *The Harvard group scale of hypnotic susceptibility, form A*. Palo Alto, CA: Consulting Psychologists Press.

Zeig, J.K. (Ed.). (1980). *A teaching seminar with Milton H. Erickson*. New York: Brunner/Mazel.

Chapter 20

Abreaction Revisited: A Strategic and Interpersonal Perspective

Steven H. Feldman

INTRODUCTION

Since the publication of Breuer and Freud's landmark *Studies on Hysteria* (1955), abreaction has been viewed in dynamic psychotherapy and hypnosis as an important and valuable tool. This chapter represents a significant departure in theory and practice from the generally accepted view of abreaction. The central notion that an abreaction facilitates insight and that the acquisition of this type of insight is therapeutically valuable is explored and challenged. It is suggested that abreaction should be used only in limited cases.

Abreaction is discussed in terms of its essentially hypnotic nature and the social psychological factors operating within the therapy context. The productive use of abreaction is illustrated through case example and the inherent dangers in abreactive therapy are elaborated.

DEFINITION AND BACKGROUND

Abreaction is defined by Hinsie and Campbell (1977) as

> the process of bringing to consciousness and thus, to adequate expression, material which has been unconscious (usually because of repression). Abreaction refers to the two aspects of a "complex"—the intellectual representation and the accompanying affect—and includes not only the recollection of forgotten memories

and experiences but also their reliving with appropriate emotional display and discharge of affect. (p. 4)

The therapeutic purpose of abreaction is to help the patient understand the link between previously undischarged emotion and symptoms. "The patient is thereby enabled to modify his anachronistic, immature, incongruous and unreal emotional demands in favor of adequate and appropriate behavior" (Hinsie & Campbell, 1977, p. 4).

According to Strachey (Breur & Freud, 1955), abreaction was introduced into the literature by Freud in 1893. The anecdotal descriptions of symptom resolution achieved through hypnotically induced abreaction in such famous cases by Breuer and Freud as those of Anna O., Frau Emmy Von N., and Miss Lucy R. are regarded as paradigmatic examples of the use of abreaction in the treatment of neurosis in general and especially in hysterical disorders. Although Freud eventually abandoned hypnosis in favor of psychoanalysis, the theoretical assumption that neurotic disorders (particularly hysterical and dissociative illnesses) were the direct result of the repression of consciously unacceptable thoughts and of feelings or memories of traumatic events remained a cornerstone of psychoanalytic theory (Ellenberger, 1970).

Freud conceptualized a linear causal model of neurotic psychopathology where psychic functioning was represented as a dynamic, hydraulic process; repressed affects and memories cause a blockage in the flow of psychic energy, the discharge of which (through abreaction) results in the restoration of a proper dynamic balance.

Ironically it was shortly after the publication of the controversial *Studies on Hysteria* that Freud discontinued his use of hypnotic therapy. His disillusionment with hypnosis, widely discussed elsewhere (Ellenberger, 1970; Kline, 1950; Kroger, 1977), was less an indictment of its efficacy than a testimony of Freud's personal discomfort with the hypnotherapeutic methods of his day.

Despite pretentions to innovation, many current affectively based psychotherapies bear a remarkable theoretical resemblance to the early suppositions of Breuer and Freud. The assumption that emotional release fosters insight and leads to therapeutic change underlies a number of ostensibly dissimilar schools (gestalt, primal, rebirthing, redecision therapy, etc.). In actuality it is the specialized techniques for addressing a client's defenses and evoking emotional discharge that distinguishes these psychotherapies from each other.

For example, Janov (1970, 1971, 1972), the developer of Primal Therapy, suggests that neuroses result from the repression of childhood affect associated with the realization that basic needs for love and acceptance will never be met adequately. Accordingly, the objective of this highly confrontive therapy is the elicitation of a series of intense abreactions during which patients are completely overwhelmed by their pain, often to the point of incoherence, and sometimes even to incontinence. The results of this ordeal are said to be insight, attentuation of fear surrounding abreactive experiences, and ultimately the abandonment of the neurotic patterns that previously blocked the emergence of the "real person."

In Gestalt therapy the model of psychopathology posed by Perls (1969; Perls, Hefferline, & Goodman, 1965) is also repression-based; unmet psychological needs blocked from conscious expression are transmuted into neurotic symptoms. Gestalt therapists utilize a variety of creative and confrontive maneuvers to evoke unrecognized affect. Catharsis and abreaction are encouraged, although the content of therapy is the here and now. The goal is the integration of affect and experience (both past and present) resulting in an enhanced awareness of the multiplicity of influences faced by the individual and the capacity to deal with them more effectively.

Rebirthing therapy (Freedman, Kaplan, & Sadock, 1975), loosely based on the "birth trauma" model of Otto Rank (1952), one of Freud's original psychoanalytic collaborators, hardly differs in form and practice from Primal Therapy (if support and encouragement are substituted for a head-on assault of the patient's defenses). Essentially, however, the therapy equation is identical: affective discharge plus insight equals change. In regard to these techniques, the departure from Freud is in the area of technique while basic assumptions about etiology and therapeutic transformation have undergone only cosmetic revision.

ABREACTION DEFINED IN TERMS OF HYPNOSIS

Obviously, at the content level each person's experience of an abreaction will be unique. However, what all such experiences share is the special set of psychological mechanisms necessary to produce them. For purposes of clarification these processes will be described in terms of hypnotic phenomena, namely, dissociation, age regression, hallucinations, and amnesia. Abreactions are a complex of these ordinary hypnotic phenomena.

For an abreaction to occur an individual must be dissociated or detached from the immediate environment. When experiencing an abreaction the patient loses much contact with ongoing reality. Dissociative phenomena occur on a continuum ranging from mild depersonalization to a total alienation of the self from the self. Additionally, such elements as affect and cognition can become dissociated from one another such that any event could be experienced only partially (i.e., without affect or intellectual understanding, but with vivid imagery of the event). An abreaction is, therefore, a dissociation at the extreme end of the continuum.

In hypnotic terms an abreaction is also composed of an age regression. The individual is transported back in time to the traumatic event without recognition of life experiences occurring thereafter. Age regressions too are experienced on a continuum ranging from the actual reliving of an event, to a revivification, where the incident is recalled only in detail, a phenomenon usually referred to as "hypermnesia."

For any event to be relived, various sensory alterations are required. In an abreaction there can be hallucinations in all sensory modalities which conform to the realities of the specific event being reexperienced. These visual, auditory, tactile, gustatory, and olfactory hallucinations can be experienced to various extents; therapeutically they can be separated from one another, amplified, decreased, or eliminated from an experience altogether.

The last hypnotic phenomenon associated with abreaction is amnesia. In the vast majority of abreactions conscious memories of traumatic events are either incomplete or absent altogether. It is not uncommon for individuals to relive a trauma while in hypnotic or nonhypnotic psychotherapy and later have no conscious recollection of the experience. This phenomenon is similar to nightmares and flashback experiences where upon awakening all of the physiological concomitants of terror are evident but there is no conscious memory of the precipitating events.

THERAPEUTIC EFFECTIVENESS

Although both patients and therapists corroborate that abreactions evoke tremendous emotional discharge combined with the return to consciousness of repressed memories, that an abreaction actually causes spontaneous, curative insights has not been established. In fact, Horowitz (1970), in a comparison of three methods for reducing snake phobia, found that fear arousal during recall of snake-related events was no more effective in reducing phobic responses than either posthypnotic suggestion for fear reduction or relaxation suggestions during recall of previously fear-arousing situations.

If reexperiencing a past trauma is inherently valuable, then it is difficult to explain why the nightmares of rape victims or flashbacks of Vietnam veterans do not result in spontaneous curative insights. Although they are phenomenologically identical to abreactions, nightmares and flashbacks usually are perceived by the patients experiencing them as evidence of a serious psychological problem. Often such events lead the client into treatment.

Even when an abreaction occurs in a therapy session there is no guarantee that it will prove therapeutic. In several cases clients with extensive histories of physical and sexual abuse have lapsed into spontaneous regressions to past traumatic episodes, making it difficult to establish rapport, much less foster insight or resolve any underlying issues.

One client, Bernie, a successful stage actor and businessman in his late forties who had undergone intensive Primal Therapy for treatment of depression, reported that he had "become addicted" to his abreactions and compulsively provoked them in an unsuccessful effort to release himself from his psychic pain. After four years of enduring between 20 and 100 abreactions a month, Bernie reported no significant improvement in his depressive symptoms; however, he feared that he would become overwhelmed by anxiety if he did not submit to a "primal" at least every few days.

In the foregoing examples the reexperiencing of past traumas did engender affective discharge, but no appreciable symptom amelioration resulted. To understand why abreactions are or are not therapeutic, the assumption that they are exclusively intrapsychic events needs to be reexamined; the therapeutic basis of abreaction may not be due to emotional release from within the patient.

ABREACTIONS: INTRAPSYCHIC OR INTRAPERSONAL

Although abreaction is hardly a neglected subject in the clinical literature, little attention is paid to it from interpersonal, social psychological, or phenomenological perspectives. Instead, clinical investigators have focused on the content of material revealed and the technology for inducing abreactions.

The role of the therapist in defining the meaning and significance of an abreaction should not be separated from its occurrence in psychotherapy. It is not surprising that there are few reports of spontaneous abreactions in the literature of non-insight-oriented therapies (i.e., strategic therapy, behavioral approaches, Ericksonian approaches), whereas such reports are not uncommon in the literature of psychodynamically based approaches. This is not to suggest that the therapist alone is responsible for a client's having or not having an abreaction. Certainly the individual makeup of the patient is as important in the case of abreaction as it is in the occurrence of any hypnotic phenomenon.

The experience of discovering that the content revealed has not caused the therapist to reject or criticize them may be a therapeutic element in an abreaction for many clients. Therapists who utilize abreaction generally convey the message to their patients that they have accomplished a monumental task and in fact have risen in the therapist's estimation by going through the experience. This serves to amplify the significance of the recovered material and provides a positive framework for organizing the very real trauma of having relived the original trauma.

Most patients are confused and exhausted following an abreaction. In a state of acute confusion or shock the patient is especially receptive to any clear direction provided by the therapist (Erickson, 1980a and b; Erickson, Rossi, & Rossi, 1976). What often passes for spontaneous insight may be more the result of well-timed and executed direct and indirect suggestion. Thus the clients' understanding of their own internal experience is mediated significantly by the therapist's reaction to and interpretation of the abreactive experience.

Therefore, the significance or therapeutic value of an abreaction perhaps is more a function of the therapy context (including both the patient and therapist) than of the content of the memories recovered or the discharge of affect. The efficacy of an abreaction seems directly linked to the therapeutic relationship. The patient's attributions about his/her own internal experience are influenced heavily by the therapist's reception and interpretation of such material.

SUGGESTED USE OF ABREACTION

As mentioned earlier, although the therapy context may favor an abreaction being defined as therapeutic, there is no guarantee that the experience will yield any meaningful, permanent changes in the symptom complex. Even when abreactive therapists have been successful, questions have been raised about the durability and reliability of symptom amelioration. Breuer & Freud (1955), Ochoberg (1978), Wolberg (1945), and Zilborg (1952) all cautioned against the use of abreaction in the treatment of neurotic disorders because they felt the clinical benefits were evanescent and incomplete.

However, there are numerous case examples of abreaction being used successfully to permanently treat a variety of neurotic and characterological conditions (Alexander, 1967; Fisher, 1945; Leahy & Martin, 1980; Rosen & Myers, 1947; Wilkins & Field, 1968). It may well be that the discrepancy results when there is a confusion about whether an abreaction is a therapy or a therapeutic maneuver. Breuer and Freud viewed abreaction as the mechanism by which therapeutic change occurred. Other clinicians have downplayed the psychic significance of abreaction (Brende & Benedict, 1980; Caldwell & Stewart, 1981; Spiegel, 1981) and focused instead on the relationship implications and directions for further investigation highlighted by its use in ongoing treatment.

I conceptualize abreaction as a psychotherapeutic tool with applicability in certain types of clinical problems (e.g., Vietnam veterans, trauma victims, multiple personality). Clearly the experience of an abreaction in and of itself is not curative. When rapid, permanent symptom resolution does occur then the abreaction has operated the same way as any other successfully implemented hypnotic intervention.

HOW TO USE ABREACTION

The experience of an abreaction is its most powerful element. The intensity and shock associated with it makes an abreaction an ideal vehicle for the acceptance of a variety of contingent suggestions. Analogously, abreactions often operate as profound conviction phenomena. The patient who has come to expect a powerful, emotionally loaded experience scarcely could be disappointed by the average abreaction.

When an abreaction is effectively utilized in hypnosis and psychotherapy (whether its occurrence is spontaneous or induced), the experience itself must be directly linked to the acquisition of some discernible skill or competency. The abreaction, in effect, becomes a demonstration that a significant obstacle has been overcome. Ideally it should serve as an enactment of novel behavior, attitudes, beliefs, affect, etc. (Minuchin & Fishman, 1981).

Unfortunately, in many cases the occurrence of an abreaction does not provide an opportunity to enact new learnings or confirm a patient's inner strength. In fact, subsequent to an abreaction some clients experience a reification of their sense of helplessness and concomitant erosion of confidence. In those situations where the abreaction itself does not produce an enactment of psychological competency it is necessary to provide an additional experience of client action resulting in positive change. Unless a patient can experience some degree of psychological mastery over the past in the present, the abreaction is likely to amplify any manifest feelings of helplessness and despair.

Following are two case examples illustrating the efficacious use of abreaction in psychotherapy to achieve specific goals that the experience of an abreaction itself helps to validate. The enactment of higher order functioning and how to attain it when the abreactive experience itself does not automatically provide it are also discussed.

Case Example One

Abreaction to demonstrate that negative affect can be constructive and that strong emotional responses will not result in identity diffusion.
A 32-year-old man, Karl, sought psychotherapy for anxiety attacks, headaches, gastrointestinal distress, and dermatitis. He was an extremely controlled and emotionally modulated individual. Karl had been married for six months at age 21 and had had only intermittent romantic connections since then. He reported being uncomfortable whenever he got close to people (men and women) and he avoided intimacy whenever possible despite constant feelings of loneliness and dissatisfaction with his isolated lifestyle. He was college educated and worked for a computer firm. He had no hobbies to speak of and spent his free time playing computer games and cleaning his apartment.

Hypnosis was employed and the patient was responsive and cooperative. After four sessions his symptoms ameliorated significantly; however, ideomotor questioning revealed significant gaps in the patient's memories of his childhood that were clinically related to the current symptom complex. The patient reported in the waking state that he had no recollection of his childhood prior to age 11½ when he and his younger sister went to live with their maternal grandparents.

He was "curious" about his lack of childhood memories and speculated about a connection between his social inadequacy and his early upbringing. When queried about his willingness to explore that connection in a trance he simultaneously was eager and apprehensive. Previous ideomotor questioning had revealed that the patient had survived several severe traumas of which he had no conscious recollection. Because of this and the following factors it was determined that an abreaction might be a useful approach in Karl's case: his high degree of motivation, his curiosity, his high level of trust in the therapist and therapy, and his manifest need to experience strong emotions, survive them, and utilize them to expand his affective and interpersonal repertoire.

A modified version of Watkins's (1971) affect bridge technique was employed where the patient was instructed to inventory his interpersonal and affective capacities, identifying those particular feeling states that were most troublesome for him. He rather quickly isolated love and anger as equally conflictual and inextricably linked.

Karl then was instructed to feel these feelings as thoroughly as possible while his unconscious mind prepared him to suddenly return to the experience or experiences most responsible for his failure to successfully integrate those emotions. He abruptly age-regressed to a scene when he was 11 years old.

His father, a chronic alcoholic, had just beaten his mother (also an alcoholic) into unconsciousness, when Karl returned home from football practice. He was carrying his football helmet in his hand when he happened on the scene. His father had just grabbed his two-year-old sister, who was awakened by the clamor and wandered into the room. He was about to pound her head against the hardwood floor, when Karl instinctively ran to her aid and slammed his helmet against his father's face with enough force to knock him out. He then hit him repeatedly with the helmet, breaking his nose, jaw, and most of his teeth.

His mother revived, saw what Karl was doing, and proceeded to slap him around the room cursing at him, blaming him for the entire incident, and threatening to kill both him and his sister. Karl did not defend himself (although he still held the helmet in his hand), for fear that if he were to take any action, he would "explode" and "totally destroy" his mother. The incident was terminated when a neighbor, having overheard the commotion and knowing the parents' penchant for violence, entered the house, restrained the mother, and subsequently called the police.

Following the abreaction, the patient broke into heaving sobs and cried for 20 minutes as he recalled at least 15 other instances of child abuse. He then collapsed in his chair and began laughing uproariously for another 15 or 20 minutes. At the conclusion of this he leapt out of his seat, hugged the therapist, and began composing himself gradually while discussing the events he had reexperienced.

At the end of the session he reported having a sense of "emotional freedom" unlike anything he could remember having felt previously. He also was complimentary about his own capacity to endure the experience and was extremely curious about the immediate and long-term effects it would have on him.

In the week following the abreaction the patient arranged for his first date in two years, signed up for a karate class, and bought a sports car. During the next few months he changed his style of dress and haircut, began dating frequently, and developed some solid friendships with other men at the office. He also developed an interest in his physical health. He started jogging and swimming and joined the office touch football team (a game he had not played since he was 11 years old).

Case Example Two

The use of abreaction to challenge feelings of helplessness and demonstrate psychological durability.

Chris was a 26-year-old woman diagnosed multiple personality disorder. She had an extensive history of physical, sexual, and psychological abuse. One of her personalities was an extremely bright, but hostile and withdrawn 14-year-old girl.

Chris had been brutally raped by a gang of boys and then beaten and tortured in a high school bathroom. Her psychosexual development was effectively truncated at prepubescence and she would routinely starve herself for periods of as long as a month to reduce her bust size and interrupt her menstrual cycle. She was morbidly fearful of all males, especially adolescent boys, and could not tolerate discussion of any sexual material whatsoever. Chris also reported a profound sense of worthlessness and despair. She felt hopeless and defiled—unworthy of help, love, or even human kindness. Historically she was uncooperative with treatment and had unilaterally terminated therapy on several occasions with previous therapists.

The patient had only sketchy conscious memories of the bathroom incident and refused to discuss them. She claimed that to remember what had happened to her would be "totally devastating"; it already had caused "permanent irreversible damage," and there was no sense "adding insult to injury."

Chris's assertion that she was weak and powerless never was challenged directly. Given the tenacity with which she adhered to her description of herself as fragile, it was determined that above all else she needed to discover that she was not as helpless as she believed herself to be. It was felt that an abreaction would be useful in reconnecting Chris's abundant anger and hostility with an even more appropriate target than the therapist (whom she routinely lambasted with criticism and provocation) and would also serve to demonstrate to her that her fundamental ability to defend herself had not been permanently destroyed in the attack.

To further increase the patient's confidence and understanding of herself as powerful and competent (nonfragile) a double bind strategy for eliciting the abreaction was employed. The patient was told that unless she was capable of productively reliving the incident in the bathroom she would not be able to resist the therapist's orders to "shut up, go into a trance and return there immediately."

At that point she steadfastly refused to go into a trance or to allow the therapist access to any other personality. This was defined as proof of her inner strength and an indication that she was truly ready to encounter and psychologically defeat her tormentors. She was then told that she faced yet another choice: Either she could go into a trance immediately and confront whatever she might find, having just proven to herself that she was far more capable than she believed, or the therapist would be pleased to provide her with an experience even more appalling and terrifying in the waking state that would accomplish exactly the same ends.

Chris chose the former option and promptly went into a trance and returned to the bathroom scene. She relived the event in complete detail. The most impressive material revealed was the valiant, relentless, albeit futile struggle she engaged in despite the animalistic barbarity and degradation doing so engendered. (After raping her the gang urinated and defecated on her and flushed her head in a dirty toilet.)

At the completion of the abreaction Chris was drained and devastated. She was overwhelmed with a sense of futility and embarrassment. In order to prevent this experience from reifying, Chris was immediately instructed to return to the scene. She was told that this time each of her original acts of defiance would infuse her with a progressively increasing sense of strength and power. She was to realize that she had survived the original incident and the abreaction, both of which were evidence of her tremendous inner resources and capacity to endure.

Chris was further instructed in an authoritative tone that the sole purpose of the second visit was to secure justice for herself in any way her unconscious saw fit. She was to attain that justice by utilizing all of her previously unrecognized potentials and newly acquired skills. She then returned to the bathroom scene and began to relive the incident again, but in a highly revised form.

She reported herself to become immensely powerful with each defensive action she took. Ultimately, Chris hallucinated that the boy who had been the ringleader of the gang and her chief tormentor had shrunk to midget size while she had become an enormous giant. At that point she picked him up in her hand, threw him into a glass jar, and shook it up violently until she was sure that he had been severely injured. Over the next few days she often returned him to the jar for an additional dose of punishment.

During the subsequent month the patient became increasingly comfortable discussing sexual issues. Additionally, Chris relinquished all sense of herself being responsible for the assault and reported a general increase in self-esteem. There was a marked decrease in her fear of males and, most surprisingly, a significant increase in bust size although her body weight and eating habits reportedly remained constant.

Discussion

In the preceding cases abreaction was chosen as an intervention because it both offered patients an experience that immediately and profoundly challenged their prior negative self-assumptions and demonstrated their access to specific emotional competencies. It was the unique personality characteristics and concomitant psychological needs of each patient that led to selection of the technique. In both cases the value of the experience was not in the discharge of psychic energy or the recollection of repressed material; rather it was in the elegant and forceful manner in which the patients' experience of themselves was interrupted and effectively reformulated in a positive direction.

In Case Two abreaction alone was not enough to provoke the kind of comprehensive psychological readjustment that occurred in Case One. It did lay the groundwork for an effective reworking of the traumatic incident, but it is almost certain that without the addition of an experience of the client herself taking action resulting in positive change, the abreaction would have resulted only in an entrenchment of her assumptions of powerlessness and diminished self-worth.

Because the stakes are high when abreaction is employed it makes sense to evaluate the applicability of alternative approaches that might accomplish the same objectives without the associated risks. When abreaction is understood to be a complex hypnotic phenomenon comprised of specific identifiable components (i.e., dissociation, age-regression, amnesia, hallucinations), then the same principles governing the application of any other hypnotic phenomenon apply equally to abreaction.

Thus the fundamental components of an abreaction are available to strategic alteration. Hypnotic phenomena can be experienced variably and their elements also can be divided into separate and variable subcomponents (e.g., the events of a traumatic incident could be recalled without any affect, in black and white and with all olfactory stimuli deleted). This capability to alter the structure of an experience provides a wide variety of options for reexperiencing traumatic events in a manner that is more controlled, more predictable, less overwhelming, and which in many cases offers a more direct pathway to an enactment of psychological, behavioral, and affective competency.

The writings of Milton H. Erickson (1980c) pertaining to the use of uncovering techniques such as abreaction emphasize the singular importance of evoking within the client an experience of self-initiated action that serves as a symbolic and actual demonstration of adaptability and competence. Specific events uncovered and the affect associated with them form the backdrop or proving ground for the patient to appreciate and practice utilizing newly acquired or recognized skills and assets.

Erickson employed abreaction in the classical manner only rarely (Erickson & Rossi, 1979). When he did use uncovering techniques he did so in a climate of emotional support and safety exerting the minimal force necessary to achieve his goals. Psychological and emotional upheaval were kept to a minimum unless there was some compelling therapeutic benefit to be achieved thereby.

In those cases where Erickson felt that uncovering techniques were appropriate, he demonstrated remarkable dexterity—restructuring, juxtaposing, deleting, adding, and otherwise manifestly altering the various subcomponents of the patient's experience. Following are several case examples illustrating a variety of alternatives to classical abreaction. These approaches represent an integration of the essential hypnotic nature of an abreaction with the unique multilevel needs and hypnotic capacities of the individual patient.

Case Example Three

The use of time distortion, dissociation, and amnesia to resolve an iatrogenic addiction to abreaction and to promote alternative approaches for managing anxiety and depression.

The patient Bernie, described earlier, initially requested therapy for depression. He was extremely demanding, critical, and at times openly hostile. He was actually seeing a Primal Therapist but could not find a "competent" practitioner in the area. He was referred for hypnotherapy by his physician but held out little hope that his symptoms were treatable by any method other than Primal.

The first four sessions of the therapy were spent securing conscious rapport, introducing the patient to hypnosis, and providing instruction in self-hypnosis. Bernie proved to be a moderately good subject with a special facility for time distortion; he could experience both time expansion and time condensation readily. Upon completion of the fourth session Bernie was asked if he would be willing to have his next scheduled "primal"—he was still engaging in four to six self-induced abreactions per week—in the office so that the therapist could develop a more thorough understanding of the process.

Bernie agreed that this was a good idea and began the next session curled up on the floor in the fetal position. He swayed and rocked for several minutes and then began to undulate rhythmically. He started to moan in syncopated bursts, eventually crying out louder and longer until he became hoarse. After 35 minutes of wailing and writhing the patient appeared to have a massive convulsion. He then began whimpering softly; drenched in sweat he exhaustedly dragged himself onto a chair.

I immediately began a conversational induction during which Bernie was complimented on his openness, intensity, and perseverance. Suggestions for him to become impatient about the amount of time and energy his primals required were interspersed along with characterizations of the trance state as being a place to learn new things, gradually, thoroughly, and many times unexpectedly. The patient was also instructed to await his next session eagerly but cautiously and to prepare himself for it by practicing self-hypnosis daily.

At the next session Bernie was formally induced and trained to produce a variety of phenomena (e.g., hand levitation, physical relaxation, age regression, and revivification). In the trance the patient recounted (without affect) a history of sexual molestation by his uncle from ages 6 to 10 and a chronicle of 15 years of parental physical abuse alternating with abject neglect. These scenes had previously been abreacted hundreds of times but only temporary symptom relief had ensued.

The patient persisted in his assertion that his primals were essential for releasing psychic pain and he steadfastly refused any suggestion that he might eventually give them up. Rather than argue this point I initiated a strategy for altering Bernie's experience of his abreactions in a way that would make them less obtrusive in his life.

Bernie's facility with time distortion was tapped. He was trained to compress one hour's worth of perceived time into less than five minutes. He also age-regressed to some of the scenes he routinely abreacted and was instructed to go through each scene at 10 times the usual rate. He then was instructed to experience the emotional upheaval engendered by each scene 10 times more intensely than usual.

Bernie was able to accomplish these tasks and then was taught to combine them so that he would experience an incredibly intense abreaction for no more than three minutes. The abreaction was to be so thoroughly overpowering that he would be completely "paralyzed with pain and terror" for the duration of the experience. He then was told to repeat this procedure as needed during the next few weeks, as an adjunct to his usual primals.

Additionally, Bernie was given suggestions that his unconscious mind would automatically produce a trance state subsequent to each mini-abreaction during which time a variety of images, thoughts, ideas, and feelings which represented a more satisfactory approach to meeting his real needs would occur.

For a period of several months Bernie continued to have several mini-abreactions per week. By the end of six months he had begun to involve himself in a great variety of activities and was down to three to five abreactions a month. After one year the patient still occasionally indulged in mini-abreactions but was far more socially active, physically fit, happy, and emotionally stable.

Case Example Four

The use of dissociation, negative hallucinations, positive hallucinations, and hypnotically induced dreams to rechannel negative affect, reduce anxiety, and increase the capacity for intimacy.

Ralph was a 39-year-old man who had undergone many years of affectively based psychotherapy. His symptoms included anxiety, depression, inability to form and maintain attachments, and low self-esteem. The patient reported an unhappy childhood which he felt he had dealt with adequately in previous psychotherapy.

The initial focus of his treatment was helping Ralph develop the confidence required to make some major career decisions. Hypnosis was employed and he also was taught autohypnotic techniques. Ralph was able to sort out a variety of issues relating to past failures in school and employment and also was beginning to evaluate his interpersonal experiences in a similar light.

For a year Ralph made steady progress, gradually reducing his therapy contacts to once every 6 to 8 weeks. He then began experiencing some unusual psychophysiological symptoms. He reported dramatic alterations in heart rhythm, muscle spasms, and waves of intense anxiety, followed by a morbid fear of death.

The experiences always were terminated by a crying jag of up to several hours duration. He was unable to definitively trace any behavioral or affective antecedents to these attacks, nor could he attach any imagery to them.

A number of techniques were attempted but proved unsuccessful. Subsequently, I decided to use formal hypnosis. Ralph agreed to go into a trance for the purpose of "allowing his unconscious mind to properly determine the focus of therapy." Ideomotor signaling and trance verbalizations confirmed my suspicion that he had been abused as a child. Upon awakening, Ralph had a partial amnesia for the session but did recall confirming that he had suffered extensive childhood abuse.

Ralph was wary of the possibility of going through an abreaction. His experiences in previous psychotherapy left him dubious of the value of such methods, as he had endured numerous abreactions with no appreciable long-term benefit. Given his conscious apprehension and ideomotor confirmation that he was in no way prepared to relive the abuse, an alternative strategy was initiated.

In Erickson's treatment of a patient with an airplane phobia he systematically isolated various aspects of the patient's experience and had her reexamine them sequentially (Erickson & Rossi, 1979). By utilizing a similar approach Ralph's past experiences were subdivided into components. The affect associated with each incident was experienced first. Once he was able to handle the emotional content, physical sensations were added. Then followed an intellectual appreciation of each incident in combination with a visual hallucination. Ultimately, the entire experience was recovered but not necessarily relived, unless ideomotor responses indicated that it was necessary to do so.

Posthypnotically induced dreams were utilized extensively to help Ralph appreciate the extent to which he was changing. A variety of his difficulties adjusting to the revelations of past abuse were addressed in these dreams.

The final incident Ralph reexperienced was especially illustrative of the efficiency of this approach for promoting an integration of severely abusive experiences in a manageable fashion. Ralph's dreams began to change dramatically following the recollection of several abusive incidents. He dreamed that he was approaching a dangerous situation involving himself both as a little boy and as an adult. Although he could not see the danger he definitely felt it. In the session ideomotor responses indicated that a tremendous amount of affect surrounded the events referred to in the dreams.

A trance was induced and Ralph was instructed to experience the dream affect—first as he had as a child, next as an adolescent, and finally as an adult. It took nearly an hour and a half for this to be accomplished. Once completed, Ralph began to experience spontaneously the associated physical sensations. He felt himself alternately being beaten and suffocated. He experienced his head being pounded on a concrete floor. He could smell a foul odor; he felt his hair was pulled and his arms were pinned down so that he was prostrate and immobile.

Once he was able to thoroughly appreciate these sensations as an adult, Ralph was instructed to observe himself as a child going through the events associated with these experiences. At first he watched himself as a little boy age 2½ or 3 being dragged by his grandmother into a back room. His grandmother was a paranoid, rigid, and abusive woman. Ralph's parents had left him with her without adequate explanation and he believed that he had been abandoned. Each time he asked his grandmother about his mother, she went into a frenzy, railed at him, told him that his mother hated him, that she was dead, and that she (his grandmother) was his real mother.

The image Ralph recalled was every bit as gruesome as the dreams predicted. In the incident, Ralph's grandmother responded to his questions about his mother's whereabouts by throwing him on the floor and pinning his arms down. She then lifted up her skirts and lowered herself on his face and told him to lick her or she would suffocate him. He then remembered being dragged to the back of the house where he was locked in a dark fruit cellar for several days. His grandmother had killed his pet dog and thrown it in the cellar with him as punishment. She told him that he could not come out until he called her mommy, and if he did not do so he would end up like the dog.

As with all of the incidents of abuse revealed in this mosaic fashion, upon achieving an intellectual appreciation of the events Ralph was instructed to return to each scene as an adult and to correct the experience for himself as a child, adolescent, and adult. In the incident just described, Ralph saw himself pulling the grandmother off the little boy before she could really hurt him. He then threatened her life and chased her away. He picked up the child, hugged him, wiped away his tears, and began reassuring him that everything would be all right.

Ralph made remarkable improvement during the therapy. He quit a dissatisfying job and found adequate part-time work. He enrolled at a university after a nine-year hiatus and reported making excellent grades. He has become increasingly self-assured. No further psychophysiological manifestations have occurred and Ralph no longer reports any serious difficulties with depression.

Discussion

In each of the two cases described above no protocol or formula dictated either the selection of specific techniques or the method of application. The therapy was in essence naturally selected by the therapeutic context in accordance with the patients' manifest psychoemotional needs, hypnotic capacities, and the ongoing relationship between the therapist and the client.

The segmentation of the patient's traumatic past experiences into small, more manageable elements increases the degree of therapeutic control available to the clinician. Similarly, the process of restructuring negative experiences is made easier when the emotional intensity of the therapy does not exceed the patient's capacity for integrating it.

No analogous level of control exists when a classical abreaction occurs. The short- and long-term effects of material abruptly revealed in an abreaction are far less discernible or remediable than when alternative uncovering strategies are employed. The interpersonal and social psychological dynamics of the therapeutic relationship are also significantly more predictable when the revelation of highly charged material is approached systematically.

CONCLUSION

Abreaction has a long tradition in the psychotherapeutic and hypnotic treatment of various psychiatric disorders. It has been defined as a process by which repressed memories of a traumatic event are relived intellectually and affectively. Breuer and Freud conceptualized abreaction as the primary mechanism for releasing bound-up psychic energy blocked from conscious expression as a defense against the overwhelming affect associated with the trauma (Breuer & Freud, 1955). Once the traumatic scene was abreacted the patient supposedly was free to discontinue symptomatic behavioral, psychological, and affective patterns.

Viewed from a hypnotic perspective an abreaction represents a complex of associated and ubiquitous hypnotic phenomena, including dissociation, age regression, hallucinations, and amnesia. An abreaction has the same properties of expression as other hypnotic phenomena. It can be experienced variably along a continuum of perceptual realism and affective intensity.

This chapter expands the notion that an abreaction is an exclusively intrapsychic phenomenon and identifies the specific components of the therapeutic relationship which largely determine the efficacy of the intervention. The role of the therapist in eliciting and defining an abreaction is discussed in light of the tremendous impact that communication occurring in the midst of an extremely shocking and confusing experience is likely to have.

The affective intensity of an abreaction is its most potent feature. It operates both as a vehicle for the acceptance of contingent suggestions and as a profound conviction phenomenon. For an abreaction to be therapeutic, the experience itself must be directly tied to the acquisition of some discernible skill or competency. If a demonstration of psychological mastery is not contained in the experience it will serve only to reify the patient's presumptions of helplessness and debilitation.

The two cases cited to illustrate the effective use of abreactions emphasize its selection as a means of challenging the patients' negative self-assumptions and proving their inherent emotional competencies, within the framework of their unique personality characteristics and psychological needs. In Case Two where abreaction itself was not sufficient to provoke a comprehensive psychological readjustment, additional hypnotic intervention was required to ensure an enactment of higher order functioning.

Erickson employed classical abreaction sparingly. He chose instead to segment the essential elements of the patient's past traumatic experience and recombine them in a manner that allowed for a more thorough and systematic integration of conflicted material.

It was not within the scope of this chapter to develop a diagnostic typology of cases or situations where uncovering techniques in general and abreaction specifically would be the appropriate therapeutic approach. My experience with such techniques has been primarily in the treatment of multiply traumatized abuse victims, Vietnam veterans, and trauma-related amnesias.

Such individuals tend to possess a highly refined capacity to dissociate large components of their intellectual and affective experiences from consciousness. It may well be that uncovering techniques are naturally selected in cases where dissociation is the principal psychological maneuver for coping with intrapsychic or external stress.

However, I advise caution in the use of all uncovering techniques and strongly recommend that classical abreaction be selected only when there is a preponderance of compelling multilevel reasons for its use. In my practice (which is largely comprised of victims of severe sexual, physical, and psychological abuse) classical abreaction is employed only rarely.

There appears to be no discernible difference in the degree of psychoemotional integration obtained when alternative hypnotic uncovering techniques are substituted for abreaction. In fact, such strategies usually have expedited the process of working through and resolving conflicts associated with past traumatic experiences. I strongly suggest that abreaction be used cautiously and judiciously and perhaps only as a therapeutic intervention of last resort.

REFERENCES

Alexander, L. (1967). Clinical experiences with hypnosis in psychiatric treatment. *International Journal of Neuropsychiatry*, 118–124.

Bandler, R., Grinder, J., & Delozier, J. (1975). *Patterns of the hypnotic techniques of M. H. Erickson.* Cupertino, CA: Meta Publications.

Brende, J., & Benedict, B. (1980). The Vietnam combat delayed stress syndrome: Hypnotherapy of dissociative symptoms. *American Journal of Clinical Hypnosis, 4*, 565.

Breuer, J., & Freud, S. (1955). Studies on hysteria. *Standard Edition*, 2:1-19. London: Hogarth Press. (Original work published in 1895)

Caldwell, T. A., & Stewart, R. S. (1981). Hysterical seizures and hypnotherapy. *American Journal of Clinical Hypnosis, 23*, 194–198.

Ellenberger, H. F. (1970). *The discovery of the unconscious.* New York: Basic Books.

Erickson, M. H. (1980a). The confusion technique in hypnosis. In M. H. Erickson & E. L. Rossi (Eds.), *The collected papers of M. H. Erickson* (Vol. 1). New York: Irvington.

Erickson, M. H. (1980b). The "surprise" and "my-friend-John," techniques of hypnosis: Minimal cues and natural field experimentation. In M. H. Erickson & E. L. Rossi (Eds.), *The collected papers of M. H. Erickson* (Vol. 1). New York: Irvington.

Erickson, M. H. (1980c). A study of an experimental neurosis hypnotically induced in a case of ejaculation praecox. In M. H. Erickson & E. L. Rossi (Eds.), *The collected papers of M. H. Erickson* (Vol. 3). New York: Irvington.

Erickson, M. H. (1980d). The method employed to formulate a complex story for the induction of an experimental neurosis in a hypnotic subject. In M. H. Erickson & E. L. Rossi (Eds.), *The collected papers of M. H. Erickson* (Vol. 3). New York: Irvington.

Erickson, M. H. (1980e). The February man: Facilitating new identity in hypnotherapy. In M. H. Erickson & E. L. Rossi (Eds.), *The collected papers of M. H. Erickson* (Vol. 4). New York: Irvington.

Erickson, M. H., & Rossi, E. L. (1979). *Hypnotherapy: An exploratory casebook.* New York: Irvington.

Erickson, M. H., Rossi, E. L., & Rossi, S. I. (1976). *Hypnotic realities.* New York: Irvington.

Fisher, C. (1945). Hypnosis in treatment of neurosis due to war and other causes. *War Medicine, 4*, 565.

Freedman, A. M., Kaplan, H. I., & Sadock, B. (1975). *Comprehensive textbook of psychiatry* (Vols. 1 & 2). Baltimore: Williams & Wilkins.

Hinsie, L. E., & Campbell, R. J. (1977). *Psychiatric dictionary.* New York: Oxford University Press.

Horowitz, S. L. (1970). Strategies within hypnosis for reducing phobic behavior. *Journal of Abnormal Psychology, 75* (1), 104–112.

Janov, A. (1970). *The primal scream: Primal therapy, the cure for neurosis.* New York: Putnam.

Janov, A. (1971). *The anatomy of mental illness: The scientific basis of primal therapy.* New York: Putnam.

Janov, A. (1972). *The primal revolution toward a real world.* New York: Simon & Schuster.

Kline, M. V. (1950). *Freud and hypnosis.* New York: Julian Press.

Kroger, W. S. (1977). *Clinical and experimental hypnosis,* (2nd ed.). New York: Lippincott.

Leahy, M. R., & Martin, I. C. A. (1967). Successful hypnotic abreaction after twenty years. *British Journal of Psychiatry, 113*, 383.

Minuchin, S., & Fishman, C. H. (1981). *Family therapy techniques.* Cambridge: Harvard University Press.

Ochoberg, F. M. (1978). The victim of terrorism. *The Practitioner, 220*, 293.

Perls, F. S. (1969). *Ego, hunger and aggression.* New York: Random House.

Perls, F. S., Hefferline, R., & Goodman, P. (1965). *Gestalt therapy.* New York: Bell Publishing.

Rank, O. (1952). *The trauma of birth.* New York: Brunner.

Rosen, H., & Meyers, H. J. (1947). Abreaction in the military setting. *Archives of Neurology and Psychiatry, 57*, 161.

Spiegel, D. (1981). Vietnam grief work using hypnosis. *American Journal of Clinical Hypnosis,* *24,* 33–40.

Spiegel, H., & Spiegel, D. (1978). *Trance and treatment.* New York: Basic Books.

Watkins, J. (1971). The affect bridge: A hypnoanalytic technique. *International Journal of Clinical and Experimental Hypnosis, 19* (1), 21–27.

Wilkins, L. G., & Field, P. B. (1968). Helpless under attack: Hypnotic abreaction in hysterical loss of vision. *American Journal of Clinical Hypnosis, 10*(4), 271–275.

Wolberg, L. R., (1945). *Medical hypnosis* (2 vols.). New York: Grune & Stratton.

Zilborg, G. (1952). The emotional problem and the therapeutic role of insight. *Psychiatric Quarterly, 21,* 1945.

Chapter 21

Hypnotic Identification: Metaphors for Personal Change

Marc Lehrer

This chapter has two parts. The first involves metaphors that are useful in developing a relationship between the conscious and the unconscious mind to enable a person to use hypnotic identification states. The second involves practical techniques to develop hypnotic identifications with others, or, in some therapeutic instances, toward undoing previously established hypnotic identification states which have outlived their purposes.

I will first present some of my perspectives on the nature of hypnosis and the unconscious mind. These ideas have been helpful in allowing both professionals and patients to develop deeper states of hypnosis within themselves. The ability to use deeper states of hypnosis is often a prerequisite to being able to hypnotically identify with another person.

HYPNOSIS CAN BE DIFFERENT FOR DIFFERENT PEOPLE AND MAY CHANGE FOR THE INDIVIDUAL OVER TIME

There have been many attempts to define the hypnotic process in a way that makes the same definition applicable to all persons, e.g., attempting to define hypnosis as a "deep relaxation state," a state of "highly focused attention," a state where the "unconscious mind is dominant"; or using hypnotic induction profiles or scales to define the degree of hypnosis that is present (Udolf, 1981). I think of states of hypnosis in a different way. *They are those times in which a person relates to aspects of personality, cognition and memories which are not usually brought*

359

to conscious awareness. Thus, what we call hypnosis can be different for different people and may change for individuals as they progress in learning to use what is discovered in hypnosis. The central issue in self-hypnotic exploration then becomes learning to monitor communications from those other parts of the self, i.e., from the unconscious mind.

This is, in many cases, a freeing notion of what it means to go into hypnosis, because it allows people to learn to go deeper into hypnosis in their own way. Positive results of using hypnosis with athletes support this position. Reports by Lars-Eric Unestahl (1981), by Norman Katz (1979) on skill training methods of hypnosis, and Charlie Garfield's (personal communication, 1981) work with optimum performers have demonstrated that when individuals attempt to better their own performance, rather than compete against an externally established guideline (such as a world record), they are more likely to go beyond their previously best accomplishments.

ONE PERSON'S TRANCE CAN BE ANOTHER PERSON'S PLEASURE

Jack Schwarz (1978), as observed at the Menninger Clinic and UC Medical School in San Francisco, has been able to control his bleeding at will and to vary his brain wave states as we might shift gears while driving a car. He states that he does not enter a hypnotic state; rather, he learned this control by years of practice when he was a youngster, after having read about the similar achievements of Indian yogis. Many other persons also have shown remarkable abilities to enhance or reduce sensory experience or control physiological functions without seeming to enter hypnosis or any other unusual state; they simply want to do what they do. If you or I, however, attempted right at this moment to stick an unsterilized knitting needle through an arm, as Jack Schwarz has done, our preparation process would be very interesting. Just like Eisdale's (Bramwell, 1906) patients in the rural areas of India who were given a simple choice—either have surgery with no anesthetic, or use hypnosis first to go into a trance, and then have the surgery—we would probably choose the latter, something we usually do not do. We would then be relating to an unusual part of ourselves, characterized by an ability to control bleeding, reduce surgical shock, and to speed post-operative recovery. This would be a deep state of hypnosis.*

I think that the lesson is that whenever we go beyond our typical

---

*I recently experienced this preparation process myself before walking over a fifteen-foot bed of burning coals.

conscious actions, thoughts, and patterns of behavior, we reveal additional abilities which are often underutilized in daily actions. An unfortunate consequence of much of the "scientific" investigation of hypnotic states has been the creation of a bind, i.e., the more that we know of others' experiences in hypnosis, the more we are likely to become intimidated about the adequacy of our own experiences. We all have worked with patients and colleagues who devalue their ability to use hypnosis because they do not believe they can duplicate other people's achievements which they have observed.

In contrast, Milton Erickson's investigations of hypnotic phenomena demonstrates an almost relentless search for frontiers of hypnotic experiencing both in his patients and in himself. This is one reason why people attend the Erickson Congresses. There is an implied promise that the achievements of this master of trance will inspire his students to develop their own style of hypnotic technique and self-hypnosis expertise. I believe that this is our shared hypnotic potential.

DEVELOPING A RELATIONSHIP WITH YOUR UNCONSCIOUS MIND

Developing a relationship with your unconscious mind does not depend upon demonstrating remarkable trance abilities. The majority of people can go further in hypnosis if they initially accept and observe the naturalistic trance states that occur all the time. Erickson called these "common everyday trance." For example, someone catches our attention while we are in the midst of a motor action and our arm remains suspended in space (I train my students to watch for likely arm catalepsy subjects by observing the way coffee cups are held in large gatherings of intense conversational activity); a friend mentions an extraordinarily tasteful meal at a new restaurant and we immediately enjoy the bouquet of the wine; or, as I am typing a presentation, suddenly a brief daydream makes the time midnight, when the stars are out and the view of Phoenix from the top of Squaw Peak is quite beautiful.

It is my contention that the more one attends to the possible meaning and/or information inherent in any trancelike experience, the more a relationship with the unconscious develops.

RESPECTING SIGNALS FROM THE UNCONSCIOUS

I have used the idea of developing a relationship with one's unconscious mind with many patients. One patient, with a history of five lumbar surgeries and intense back pain from scarring, was taught to get a signal from himself *before* his back started to hurt. He felt so good about his experiences with self-hypnosis that he went on a walk. After a mile or so he got his signal. He later told me that previously he would have continued on, ignoring that message since his back still felt all right. However, he turned around and found, much to his surprise, that he enjoyed the return twice as much, partly as a result of knowing that he would be free of pain and partly from realizing what it would have been like if he had been twice as far down the road and had to return in intense pain. His subsequent experiences with obtaining signals from himself and respecting them point to ongoing elaboration of better and more useful information from himself to himself and better relief from pain.

On a more humorous note, I have successfully treated a number of women and several men who have complained of back and shoulder spasms. I noticed that many carried heavy shoulder bags. All were taught to respect the signal from their unconscious mind when to shift their bags from one shoulder to the other. Of note, the problem seemed more pronounced on trips they took. They were, for the most part, unaware of the toll that two extra pounds or so of cameras and guide-books in their shoulder bags made (especially when walking around attending externally to sightseeing for five or six days).

THE UNCONSCIOUS AS A SEPARATE ENTITY

Milton Erickson popularized the idea of the "unconscious mind" as benign or positive, in marked contrast to the Freudian view of the unconscious as a mass of unacceptable impulses. Paraphrasing some of Erickson's statements about the unconscious reveals a pattern of personification of the unconscious mind: "I knew that I was intelligent but my unconscious mind is a great deal more intelligent than I am"; "Just drop into a trance and let your unconscious do it for you"; and "As soon as you know what you know but don't know that you know, then you'll solve the problem."

There is a boundary within ourselves. On one side of this boundary is what we usually consider to be our self, or our conscious mind; on the other side of that boundary is that which is unfamiliar to us, or our unconscious mind. Within this distinction it becomes apparent that no matter what I consciously think of my personal limitations, no matter what I think I can or cannot do, there is a place in myself where more alternatives exist. The nature and limits of the boundary between our conscious and unconscious mind are ever in transition.

Milton Erickson, in the Ocean Monarch lecture fondly stated,

> I like to regard my patients as having a conscious mind and an unconscious, or subconscious mind. I expect the two of them to be together in the same person, and I expect both of them to be in the office with me. When I am talking to a person at the conscious level, I expect him to be listening to me at the unconscious level. (Erickson & Rossi, 1981, p. 29)

Many of Erickson's hypnotic utilizations demonstrate this conceptualization of the unconscious as a separate identity. For example, he would explain a point to the patient in hypnosis and then explain the same point to the patient once he had emerged from hypnosis. He observed a person's unconscious compliance and agreement with an issue which could have been and frequently was totally in disagreement with the patient's conscious opinions or beliefs. In work with patients and in presenting self-hypnosis to persons in training groups, I have used and elaborated upon the idea that the unconscious can be thought of as a separate entity within the person.

I have had excellent clinical success with the metaphor of the unconscious as a separate entity. In teaching individuals to prepare to go into hypnosis, I ask them to find a comfortable position and then to ask a part of themselves "what would allow them to become just a little more comfortable." I direct the patient to "pay attention to any thoughts, feelings, visual images or words which may occur." In almost every instance there is a further shifting of body position or internal emotional shifting which can be observed in facial expressions and in minimal bodily changes after these instructions are given. These reactions are reinforced by simple acceptance of their usefulness, such as by saying, "That's right" or "That's good." The result from relating to the patients as if they had an internal regulator of comfort and relaxation in their unconscious minds is often rapid, and produces hypnotic states with little or no resistance to the idea that patients can help develop the use of hypnosis within themselves.

MAKING FRIENDS WITH THE UNCONSCIOUS

Consider the metaphorical process of making friends with your unconscious. How would you go about making friends with a person whom you had just met? You would discuss ideas and interests, and decide if there was a degree of compatibility in attitudes and beliefs, in ways of doing things, in priorities, in a sense of humor, and in life circumstances. You would be learning to appreciate and enjoy the other person in many different ways. Essential to developing this relationship is your desire to do so, and your willingness to treat the other on equal terms.

Think of patients whom you are working with. Often they are not at peace with themselves in this way. For example, what type of relationship between the conscious and unconscious mind does an obese person have. At the unconscious level the sensory cues related to hunger and satiation are perceivable. These same cues characteristically are ignored by individuals who are grossly overweight. To make the illustration more graphic, what type of relationship would you expect to develop with a person who you were feeding, who you fed on a schedule which rarely depended upon his or her level of hunger? You might continue to feed the person way past the time he or she was interested in food. You might also select foods which did not satisfy the basic physiological needs and would, instead, tend to continually overload the person's internal regulating mechanisms. What kind of relationship would you be developing with that person? A highly antagonistic relationship? I believe so.

Isn't it strange that we are often more easily able to represent the concept of taking good care of our objects, pets, and patients than we are able to develop a deeply caring relationship with the one lasting relationship that we have, with ourselves.

HYPNOTIC IDENTIFICATION FOR PERSONAL CHANGE

In order to use hypnotic identification states to take on another person's perceived identity, I think it is important to have done the preliminary work in developing a positive relationship with one's unconscious mind, to make one's own learnings about identification available as a resource. The process of hypnotic identification mimics the naturalistic conscious and unconscious identification states which occur in childhood, adolescence and adulthood.

An infant mimics parental affects, motoric behaviors and facial expressions in an effort to become proficient in actions, speech and emotional expression. In this sense he or she becomes those aspects of the parents and modifies them according to need. We are all familiar with typical childhood expressions of wanting to grow up to be a fireman, ballerina, nurse, or baseball player. At these times, the child intensely fantasizes who he or she wishes to become. Several years ago it seemed almost impossible to walk down a busy street that had youngsters playing without seeing one of them doing Kung Fu kicks and making the warbling sound that was Bruce Lee's personal trademark. In adolescence, emotional intensity and growing behavioral sophistication allow for even more accurate modeling of important and contemporary figures toward the goal of accomplishing tasks. In early adulthood, effort is placed in identification with social and job roles. Having children often presents a conflictual identification paradox upon the parents: They become aware of some of the parental patterns they unconsciously have incorporated as they relate to issues of discipline and child rearing.

TECHNIQUES OF HYPNOTIC IDENTIFICATION

First, I have subjects prepare to identify with a person who has abilities they wish to learn to use. I have my patients and members of self-hypnosis identification groups prepare by reading about their subjects or observing them in movies, or in life if possible. For example, Margaret Mead's autobiography, *Blackberry Winter*, is a good reference for people who want to develop a sense of individuality. I also have sent patients and therapists-in-training to view movies such as "Popeye," with Robin Williams, and "Coal Miner's Daughter," with Sissy Spacek. Both these actors do an excellent job of (hypnotically) identifying with their characters. I also recommend seeing the Academy Awards speech Sissy Spacek gave where there seemed some back and forth confusion as to which person she really was. Bette Midler's movie, "The Devine Miss M," also demonstrates the seemingly effortless changes of personality of Miss Midler's different screen portrayals.

Once people become familiar with the subject with whom they wish to identify, I have them do preparatory hypnosis work. As I mentioned, the central issue for learning to go deeper into hypnotic experiencing is being able to develop a good relationship of acceptance between conscious and unconscious processes. I have the subjects go into hypnosis with the goal of first accepting their personality exactly as it is at present. Sometimes I will have them create a specific room or area in which to do this; sometimes I let them choose the way in which to accomplish this process. After the subjects indicate security in accepting their own identity, I initiate trance experiences to review the personality with which they plan to identify.

Then, suggestions are given to allow for maximum selectivity to occur so that identification can include the aspects of the identified person which will be most useful for both the conscious and unconscious goals of the individual. This period can last for several sessions or can be accomplished during one session, especially in self-hypnosis group sessions. After this preparation time I create a formal symbolic experience in hypnosis to serve as an anchoring for transition to the identified personality. For example, I have had people in self-hypnosis classes create a room in which they take off the cloak of personality that symbolizes themselves and place it securely where they can return to it when they are ready. Then, depending upon their personal preferences, they are directed, kinesthetically and/or visually, to join with the identified personality. They spend a period of time in trance exploring situations as the identified personality. I also have used a method similar to that used by Steve Gilligan in having groups of subjects in identification states open their eyes and then relate as their identified personalities while still in hypnosis (unpublished manuscript, Gilligan & Lehrer, 1980). After a period of interaction, the subjects review what they have experienced and learned while still in hypnosis.

Surprising results can accompany the process of hypnotic identification. One young man, in a group session, came out of the hypnotic induction, leapt high in the air, after tearing off his shirt and pants, revealing himself to be wearing a pair of boxing shorts, and then screamed, "I am the greatest." Soon thereafter, he was promoted in his job and received a substantial raise.

During the review period, I instruct subjects to recall the identification state as if in a dream and then to experience a series of additional hypnotic dreams. Subjects are then directed to start to awaken as if from a dream but in the same place where they symbolically had removed their personal identity. Then they are led through a formal reacquaintance with their self while still in hypnosis. Next, they are directed to understand that all of their previous self-identities as well as any new learnings they may have acquired will be available to them in the future when they come out of hypnosis.

I personally find it more interesting to use hypnotic identification states with persons whose talents are outside my own areas of expertise. I assume that I am receiving as much information as is necessary at the unconscious level to incorporate naturalistically those identifications that are useful for me in my frequent exposure to others in my field. Also, I have been using these methods in areas outside psychology, such as in working on a project with theatrical groups and in learning a foreign language. Charles Schmidt's (1980) adaptation of the Lazanof method of language learning involves adopting a foreign identity complete with name, address and occupation, and is consistent with the hypnotic identification process.

I will now discuss some cases in which previously suggested identifications interfered with the patient's adjustment patterns. In these cases the therapy included both methods to undo the effects of unwanted or no longer useful identification states that had been incorporated into the person's identity at an unconscious level, and methods to create specific alternative identifications which were incompatible with the individual's problem state.

1) Removing a symbolic identification

The psychodynamics of a patient who was overweight were such that she wished to defend and protect her mother from an alcoholic and abusive father. The following hypnotic identification strategy was presented in trance. The patient was told that she was overweight by the exact amount of her mother's weight, a fact arrived at through observation and induction (Lehrer, 1984). She was directed to recognize this and to bring in several pictures of her mother to the next session. During that session, the pictures were reviewed by the patient to determine which was most characteristic of her mother. After the target picture was selected, the patient was directed to tear out the mother's part of the photograph and to place it somewhere in her wallet. No direct mention was made that she would now be carrying around her mother in a symbolic way. She was directed, however, to notice the first instance of her thin self that would emerge in a trance or in a dream. The next session she reported a dream in which three separate persons seemed to be different parts of herself; two parts were familiar and the third was a new part—that of a thin woman.

The woman reported progress in her relationship with her mother following this intervention. Her weight also has steadily reduced.

2) Identification with an animal

A patient who held a responsible job in media was working on self-concept development and stress management. His flow of thoughts and ideas stopped frequently—in his words, "froze"—and he could not express himself adequately at these times. At a physical level, his facial expressions also were somewhat frozen, even when he discussed an event involving emotion. I had him use a deep trance identification with an animal which had a fluidity of movement. The patient was led to a mirror and told to remain in hypnosis with his eyes closed while he would proceed to feel his body take on the physical fluidity of a panther. His arms were directed to move up and down in a slight rhythm similar to the pawing motion of a great cat. He was directed to experience his whiskers out in space feeling all the subtle currents of (e)motion (said as "emotion," while in context it would seem to be "motion"). These subtle currents would stimulate all the muscles of his face and he would appreciate the feeling. He then was directed to open his eyes just enough to let in the light, and he and I then walked outside for a period of time. His instructions were to maintain the fluidity of actions as he walked. In subsequent contacts, his facial muscles were more mobile and he was confident when discussing issues with his boss.

3) Identifications with parental emotional states

The patient was a young woman with a problem of stuttering. She felt she had to do what she was told to do. If she attempted to express her concerns, the stuttering increased. In age regression, she recalled that when she was six (around the time that the stuttering first appeared), her grandfather died. She had been forced to kiss him in the open coffin, her father telling her it would be "the last time she could say goodbye to him."

She was told to return to her adult age, to remain in hypnosis, and to let her unconscious mind explain to her to whom her father was really talking. Her nonverbal reactions were monitored and, when she showed signs of understanding, she was again questioned. She then said that she understood that her father was talking to himself. She was told that sometimes parents place emotions, which they cannot easily express, onto their children to express for them. Now that she understood, she could start to express more clearly her thoughts and feelings. Her stuttering was improved markedly as she came out of trance.

CONCLUSION

I will end this chapter with some thoughts about using hypnotic identification with Milton Erickson. Most of the people reading this never met Milton Erickson. Of those who knew him, the vast majority knew him only in his later years, when he primarily was accessible for personal involvements at the level of a wise mentor and teacher, and rarely as a therapist. Much interest has centered upon Erickson's use of therapeutic metaphor, which he presented chiefly during his later years and which make up the content of most of the available video recordings of his work. This is the Erickson with whom many persons will identify.

However, a fair perspective on Milton Erickson would show him to have a remarkable power in being able to influence others irrespective of technique. Erickson used direct and indirect methods; he talked plainly with his patients; he used metaphor with them. Therapists who wish to identify strongly with Erickson, either by using trance work or by imitating what they observe in video presentations of his work, should take into account Erickson's willingness to influence powerfully others toward natural and realistic goals. The zoom perspective of modern technology has treated Erickson unkindly by overemphasizing some of the necessary modifications of his methods brought upon by aging, loss of mobility, voice and energy.

Erickson's trust in relating to the powers of the unconscious mind was ever-present, even in the last years of his life. That is the part of him that we all can carry with us.

REFERENCES

Bramwell, J. (1906). *Hypnotism, its history, practice, and theory* (pp. 14–16). London: Alex Moring.

Erickson, M. H., & Rossi, E. L. (1981). *Experiencing hypnosis.* New York: Irvington.

Gilligan, S., & Lehrer, M. (1979). Untitled manuscript in clinical hypnotherapy. Unpublished.

Katz, N. (1979). Comparative efficacy of behavioral training plus relaxation and the sleep trance hypnotic induction in increasing hypnotic susceptibility. *Journal of Consulting and Clinical Psychology, 47,* 119–127.

Lehrer, M. (1984). *Conversational hypnotherapy: Observational manual.* San Francisco, CA: Medical Hypnosis Seminars.

Schmidt, C. (1980). *Learning in new dimensions handbook.* P.O. Box 14487, San Francisco, CA 94114.

Schwarz, J. (1978). *Voluntary controls.* New York: E. P. Dutton.

Udolf, R. (1981). *Handbook of hypnosis for professionals* (p. 10). New York: Van Nostrand Reinhold.

Unestahl, L-E. (1981, December). *Workshop presentation.* First International Congress on Ericksonian Psychotherapy, Phoenix, Arizona.

Chapter 22

Techniques in Hypnotherapy

Moris Kleinhauz

Owing to the entire preceding life of the
human adult a word is connected with all the
external and internal stimuli coming to the
cerebral hemispheres, signals all of them,
replaces all of them and can, therefore,
evoke all the actions and reactions of the
organism which these stimuli produce.—Pavlov

The definition and theoretical understanding of the concept of
hypnosis continues to be controversial. Nevertheless, there seems to be
consensus concerning its basic phenomenology and practical therapeutic
applications. I hope that there is also a consensus in viewing hypnosis
neither as a kind of therapy nor as a treatment modality in itself, but as
a vehicle for the application of different therapeutic modalities.

Hypnosis is not a discipline or a therapeutic specialization but a tool
in the armamentarium of the therapist. It is a unique interpersonal relationship through which (and given a background of unconscious motivations and inner beliefs) some latent phenomena may be elicited.
These latent phenomena, such as deep relaxation, dissociation, analgesia, hallucinations, or age regression, then can be applied in various
therapeutic settings. Hypnotherapy can be defined as a therapeutic process in which treatment techniques are utilized while the patient is in
an intentional hypnotic relationship with the therapist.

Hypnosis can serve as a catalyst and can be regarded as the "common
denominator" for the construction and application of a flexible, multidimensional and integrative approach to therapeutic intervention through
adaptation of the therapist's armamentarium to the patient's changing
needs. Such an approach has its roots in viewing any symptom as mul-

tifactorial in etiology. Any therapeutic plan should consider the need for different therapeutic techniques in coping with a patient's distress. Hypnosis is a most efficient tool for the application of therapeutic techniques—techniques that have been developed mostly according to the different theoretical understandings of disease.

Accordingly, a possible model could be elaborated by viewing any symptom as developing out of a number of interrelated factors. This model would apply to etiology as well as to any stage of illness.

- Constitutional and biological agents
- Defense mechanisms, unconscious conflicts, fixation and primary gain
- Secondary gain
- Learning processes (mainly reward-punishment)
- Existential and situational experiences
- Cultural, social and familial interactions and expectations
- Anxiety
- Habit ("Habit becomes a kind of second nature which acts as a motive for many of our actions."—Cicero)

The above model can be illustrated by considering a typical asthmatic patient. The biological component is a strong family constitutional tendency to allergic reaction. The psychodynamic evaluation, during the psychotherapeutic process, revealed long-lasting dependent/independent and separation/anxiety conflicts in an aggressive/passive type of personality with extreme and unexpressed hostility. In childhood, the family paid much attention to symptomatology, converting it into an "attention seeking" device which came to act as a "secondary gain" trigger mechanism that reinforced his behavior. Consequently, the patient got "habituated" to his symptomatic reaction whenever he felt anxious. The reaction was conditioned also by existing stimuli of places and circumstances, and the patient accepted his disease in an ego-syntonic way of life.

Accepting this multifactorial model implies that any treatment plan necessarily should involve different degrees of different therapeutic techniques in order to meet the changing specific needs of the individual patient at any stage of treatment. Of course, such a pluralistic, multidimensional approach demands considerable versatility and flexibility in the theoretical framework and technological armamentarium of the therapist.

The rationale for the use of hypnosis as the vehicle for such a therapeutic approach lies in the presumptions that:

1) The qualitative dimensions of the hypnotic relationship facilitate, enhance and shorten the therapeutic process.
2) The hypnotic response lessens the rigidity of thought patterns and emotional resistances, thus enabling the patient to reframe his experiences.
3) In the hypnotic response, the principles of ideomotor, ideosensorial, ideophysiological and ideoemotional reactions are strengthened and intensified, thereby facilitating their utilization.
4) The potential reinforcement of dissociative phenomena enables the therapist to better manipulate processes which interfere with the therapeutic course.
5) Some therapeutic techniques are best, and sometimes almost exclusively, applied during the hypnotic relationship, e.g., age regression, hallucinations, analgesia, etc.

In a general overview of hypnotherapeutic procedures, we find that there are five main groups of interventions, namely,

1) suggestive techniques;
2) relaxation techniques;
3) behaviorally oriented techniques;
4) abreactive techniques;
5) dynamic analytically oriented techniques.

SUGGESTIVE TECHNIQUES

> And the Lord God caused a deep sleep to fall upon Adam and he slept and He took one of his ribs and He closed the flesh in its place.—Genesis, 2:21

"Suggestion" is the noncritical acceptance of an idea. Throughout history, suggestive ritual procedures and ceremonies were, and are, in use in every culture for some specific purpose. Nonverbal suggestive procedures find their most potent expression in the "magic" results obtained exclusively through the prestige of the operator, faith in the operator's curative "powers" and the subject's high motivations and unconscious belief system. Examples of this attitude are found throughout history. Some of the well-known procedures for the intentional or unconscious application of the principles involved include "royal touch," "laying on of hands," "magnetic," "electric," "passes" and to some extent, alternative and conventional medicine.

Liebault, Bernheim and Coué emphasized verbalized suggestive procedures and paved the way for more sophisticated and subtle, verbal and nonverbal, specific and nonspecific, suggestions.

Although suggestive procedures are inherent in the hypnotic process, it is worthwhile to emphasize the unfortunate identification of the striking dramatic effects of suggestive interventions with "magic" that is sometimes made by the lay public and unfortunately by some professionals. These professionals, and many members of the public, tend to expect the hypnotist to have an immediate magic, an omnipotent influence on patients and their symptoms. This approach, enhanced by the use of hypnosis for entertainment purposes, causes fear and reluctance on one hand, disappointment and frustration on the other.

RELAXATION TECHNIQUES

Relaxation, by way of its emotional and physiological concomitants, is in itself a useful and potent therapeutic tool. Techniques such as progressive relaxation, autogenic training, transcendental meditation, yoga, biofeedback, guided imagery, and hypnosis are only some of the means by which the relaxation response may be achieved. The relaxation response is a useful technique for coping with distress in general and more particularly in the comprehensive treatment of so-called psychosomatic or stress disorders where it is used to achieve a new homeostasis of the disturbed patient's processes.

In the present framework, the effects of relaxation procedures are most efficient. Through relaxation, the relaxation response with its concomitants are achieved, and also gained is the value of indirect, nonspecific suggestion. The patient consciously and unconsciously "knows" that this procedure is being applied in order to alleviate suffering or change behavior.

In the contemporary use, the formal induction of hypnosis usually is accompanied by the achievement of the relaxation response. The relaxation response is the background for the administration of different combinations of therapeutic techniques. Nowadays, the relaxation response, in conjunction with guided imagery and suggestion, is a common procedure. (In using the term guided imagery, I refer to the systematic use of the imagination in the visualization of realistic situations [e.g., in desensitization procedures] or in a symbolic metaphoric situation [e.g., wish fulfillment thinking procedures] for the purpose of achieving regulated change in the psychological, emotional, physiological, immunological and behavioral areas.)

The concomitant use of relaxation response, guided imagery and suggestive procedures (that includes hypnotic and posthypnotic suggestions and self-hypnosis training) is demonstrated by reports on the use of hypnotherapy in art, in sports, and in all branches of medicine including the potential regulation of the neurophysiological and immunological systems. This approach is widespread in the comprehensive treatment of psychosomatic or stress disorders (duodenal ulcer, essential hypertension, etc.), allergic reactions (urticaria, asthma), some neurological disorders (muscular spasms, tics, Menière's syndrome), in gynecology (functional menstrual disorders, habitual abortion, hyperemesis gravida, psychogenic sterility, sexual dysfunctions—impotence, frigidity and vaginismus), and in dermatology (verrucosis, pruritus, eczema, lichen planus, penfigo, psoriasis, alopecia areata). This triad has been reported effective also in the management of hemophilia and diabetes. It is frequently reported as facilitating the symptomatic control of habit disorders such as nail biting, trichotillomania, smoking, overweight and anorexia nervosa. Relaxation, guided imagery and hypnotic/posthypnotic suggested hypoalgesia and analgesia are of value in pain control management. Hence, their growing application, not only in obstetrics, anesthesiology and surgery, but in the management of such disorders as trigeminal neuralgia, migrainotic syndrome and phantom pain, and in more chronic, intractable pain, including the pain of terminal disease. Of most theoretical and pragmatic interest are the latest reports of the use of this approach in the comprehensive treatment of cancer, and the control of side effects of chemotherapy.

It should be taken into consideration that the inhibition of anxiety, in conjunction with the lowering of the critical faculties inherent in the relaxation response may, intentionally or unintentionally, bring about a flow of suppressed/repressed material, sometimes with the intensity of an abreactive process.

BEHAVIORALLY ORIENTED TECHNIQUES

The concept of ideoreaction (ideomotor, ideophysiologic, ideoemotional, ideosensory) finds its most effective application in the framework of behavior therapy. It is needless to point to the prerequisite of relaxation response for the application of desensitization procedures in phobic reactions, e.g., claustrophobia, fear of flight and other common and uncommon fear-provoking situations. In desensitization, as well as in other behavioral modification techniques, such as implosion, aversion, and assertive procedures, the value of hypnosis lies in its easy applicability for the enhancement of both the relaxation process and the imaginative processes (including the potential elucidation of hallucinations), and the increased receptiveness to suggestive factors that may be recruited for the facilitation of the therapeutic process in the achievement of the expected behavioral goals, (e.g., symptom management of anorexia nervosa).

ABREACTIVE TECHNIQUES

The abreactive technique is directed towards the overt and direct expression of repressed, encapsulated and frozen emotions concurrent with past traumatic experiences. It has its origin in the early reports of Breuer and Freud and led Freud to his discovery and formulation of the psychoanalytic model.

Although seldom used as the sole technique, abreaction is of indisputable value in dynamic psychotherapy and in the integration of a multidimensional approach to therapy. Its dramatic manifestations sometimes produce an awesome feeling in the observer. In some circumstances, precautions should be taken before attempting such a procedure in order to avoid physical injury to the therapist or to the patient himself. It finds its greatest effectiveness in the treatment of acute conversion reactions, since it allows the therapist to cope with the symptoms before the secondary-gain phase enters into the picture.

In catastrophes like earthquake and war, acute conversion reactions, brief reactive psychoses and other acute psychopathological manifestations are common. I have used abreaction in a very large number of these cases and found it effective when applied as the first step in the therapeutic plan. However, the abreactive process should be followed by an attempt to cope with the problems involved as soon as the acute symptomatology recedes. Obviously, in the course of any psychotherapy, abreaction can be carefully planned in order to elicit and release unconscious material and concomitant emotions whenever such need arises.

The potential utilization of hypnotic phenomena such as relaxation and posthypnotic suggestion, visualization and hallucinations, hypermnesia, age regression and revivification makes hypnosis a potent tool in the implementation of the abreactive procedures and in the postabreactive therapeutic plan.

DYNAMIC ANALYTICALLY ORIENTED TECHNIQUES

Hypnotic procedures are of immense value in uncovering repressed material through relaxation or through "bypass" procedures, using projective techniques such as hypnogenic free associations, theater and TV visualization, blackboard, crystal gazing, keyhole, and other dissociative techniques such as finger response, automatic writing, painting and sculpting.

Introspection and techniques such as dream induction (with or without predetermined context), intensification of emotions, body automatization, time distortion, emotional detachment and displacement, affect bridge, posthypnotic suggestions, and other techniques are widely used by the dynamic-oriented hypnotherapist. Also used are the more dramatic hypnotic phenomena such as experimental conflict, hypermnesis, age regression and revivification. All of these techniques are directed towards the facilitation of psychodynamic diagnostic formulation and the psychotherapeutic process. This is accomplished by:

1) the uncovering of repressed traumatic experiences and their abreaction;
2) the working-through process and cognitive understanding of such elucidated material;
3) the potential use of suggestions aimed towards a reorientation of the attitudes underlying the symptomatological manifestations;
4) the utilization of hypnotherapeutic techniques as agents for the facilitation of the mutual understanding of resistance and transference.

Of course, this rough classification of hypnotherapeutic techniques is only for didactic purposes. In any given treatment a flexible, ever changing combination of procedures should be used. I firmly believe that the effectiveness of any specific treatment will be enhanced by the plastic intentional coordination and integration of therapeutic techniques. Hypnosis serves as the main highway for the transportation and delivery of such techniques.

A NOTE OF CAUTION

Consequent to the processes involved therapists should be aware of the extreme, though often covert and subtle transference/countertransference processes inherent in the hypnotic interpersonal relationship. One should be aware, as well, of personal motives for the use of hypnosis, including inner fantasies, drives and wishes for power and omnipotence. In themselves, these are legitimate as long as one is aware of their existence and as long as they do not blur one's perceptions, judgment and sensitivity to patients and their emotional needs.

CLOSING REMARK

"Common sense is not so common."—Voltaire

PART VII

Comparisons

The chapters in this section describe a number of interesting parallels. There are similarities between hypnotic induction and cult induction. The values in Ericksonian therapy are similar to the basic values in pastoral counseling. Also, the psychological approach of Milton Erickson has structural similarities with the physical methods developed by Moshe Feldenkrais.

Hillel Zeitlin received his M.S.W. from Syracuse University. He is the codirector and cofounder of Options for Personal Transition Counseling Services in Berkeley, California, which is an agency providing counseling services especially for those involved in cultic groups.
Cult inductions are structured to generate specific responses. Hypnotic-like techniques such as confusion and truisms are used to create receptivity and foster dissociated states. Hypnotic models can be used to describe the process of cult induction and conversion.

Henry T. Close, Th.M., earned his degree at Columbia Theological Seminary in Decatur, Georgia. Currently, he is a pastoral counselor and psychotherapist at the Center for Pastoral Counseling and Human Development in Fort Lauderdale, Florida. He is a Diplomate of the American Association of Pastoral Counselors and has authored 25 articles in professional publications.
Ericksonian approaches are amenable to pastoral counseling. Basic philosophies are similar in both approaches. The concepts of "authenticity" and "manipulation" are discussed.

Mark Reese earned his M.A. in psychology from Sonoma State University. He is an instructor and practitioner of the Feldenkrais method and has been working with this modality for more than seven years.

Information is presented on Moshe Feldenkrais and his methods, and comparisons to Erickson are provided. Both Feldenkrais and Erickson were atheoretical, and both stressed the generative capacity of the unconscious. Moreover, some of the techniques that Erickson used were developed in parallel by Feldenkrais who applied them to altering physical structure. Effective techniques of change draw from the same source regardless of whether they are directed to promoting structural or psychological well-being.

Chapter 23

Cult Induction: Hypnotic Communication Patterns in Contemporary Cults

Hillel Zeitlin

Cults have been a part of every society, representing alternative lifestyles, ideologies, faiths, and social forms. As such they traditionally have served a social function of being reformers and change agents (Appel, 1983). Usually they have begun as fringe elements that eventually are either incorporated into the broader society or die out. Modern cults are distinguished from many of their historical predecessors by a near universal emphasis on consciousness and consciousness-altering practices. This emphasis, as well as deceitful and antisocial actions in the recruitment and maintenance of members, has generated much controversy.

Due to many influences, our society has access to an unprecedented variety of traditional and modern methods for altering consciousness (Conway & Siegelman, 1978). Developments in group dynamics, mass communications, advertising, humanistic and other psychological movements, as well as the availability of traditional meditation and ritual practices, serve to redefine the nature of subjectivity in contemporary life. Many cultural observers refer to a veritable "consciousness explosion" that affects virtually every strata of modern life (Roszak, 1978; Schur, 1977). Particularly affected are those institutions that traditionally deal with the subjective dimensions of life, namely, psychology and religion. And cults represent the extreme aspects of this trend.

There is much debate on what constitutes a cult, and the word "cult" has even come to connote a destructive and duplicitous movement. For present purposes, however, it is not necessary to define explicitly what constitutes a cult. Rather, we are concerned with the effects of a "cultic relationship," i.e., the relationship between individuals and group where the individuals surrender personal decision-making strategies in favor of an externally imposed or suggested ideology. Though this type of relationship may occur in various social affiliations, cults are organized to induce systematically such changes.

The material for this paper has been taken from personal interviews, research, and counseling with members of such groups as the Unification Church, Divine Light Mission, the Local Church, Scientology, Rajneesh, est, the Way, and the Children of God. These groups differ widely in their beliefs, practices, social structures, modes of authority, and demand for commitment. Yet they are alike in four distinct ways: 1) they claim to offer a unique experiential means for accessing a transformed consciousness; 2) they sever themselves from traditional religious or psychological authorities; 3) they use formalized consciousness-altering practices to buttress their social order and belief system; and 4) they each have generated journalistic or narrative accusations of cultic abuses.

THE STRUCTURE OF CULT INDUCTION

Cult induction is the means used to induce a cultic relationship. It is generally initiated by a recruiter who presumes to know the ideal behavioral and attitudinal outcomes that his potential recruit should assimilate. Cult induction then proceeds to take the form of structured encounters which are intended to generate certain prescribed sequences of experiences within the recruit. Though the philosophy, language and behaviors of various groups are different, there are nonetheless characteristic stages of induction, the structures of which have significant parallels and differences from those of therapeutic hypnosis.

For the cultic organization or recruiter, their first encounter with potential recruits must affirm their right to some authority within those individuals' lives. The simplest and most effective way of accomplishing this is to convey that they have something to offer. The cult's task, then, is to arrange the encounter so that individuals become reflective on their own status and welfare.

A classic example of this approach occurs in street recruiting. Recruiters often travel anonymously, looking for transient or unattached individuals, particularly of the opposite sex. They initiate a friendly discussion, eliciting information about the individual's status, and appear intensely interested and engaging. This beginning of the recruitment encounter is meant to establish rapport, leading to eventual unconscious receptivity. Recruiters are trained to "love-bomb" potential recruits, to make them feel special and important. One recruit for the Children of God described her response to her recruiter:

> More than anything else I wanted to get away. "No, no, I must go," I pleaded. His intense gaze was hard to break. I could see he wasn't playing games. He was intent on getting me to come and sit on the bench with him and his companion. Why was it so important that I come and talk with him? (McManus & Cooper, 1980, p. 16)

An encounter of this unusual sort can be compelling, particularly for young, explorative people. Additionally, there is no prescribed social format or response for this type of encounter. Though it may be flattering or frightening, it is generally confusing, and as will be seen, confusion is an integral part of hypnosis.

The first encounter leads to heightened arousal and response attentiveness. Recruiters are even taught specialized techniques for promoting this effect. Margaret Singer, a prominent authority on cults, frequently refers to a technique used by one group, where recruiters are taught that the edges of the pupils of the eye are indicative of spiritual openness—jagged pupils indicate that people are spiritually attuned; if the edges are smooth, they are not yet spiritually open. Naturally, looking closely enough in any eye will reveal that the pupil edges are jagged. Moreover, the functional result of this gazing is a prolonged and intensified eye contact and concomitant arousal. Subsequently, the recruiter could promote receptivity. For example, a former Divine Light Mission member reported, "Our meditation technique involved an ongoing breath meditation. When I would get around other individuals I would find that if I practiced the technique they would soon be breathing at a similar pace. And the more our breath would be synched, the more receptive they would seem to become" (Zeitlin, personal communication, 1981). A similar pattern is employed in the sankirtan witnessing and fundraising of the Hare Krishna movement. Female recruiters often approach males in such transient locales as airports and bus stations. Walking directly up to the man, they unhesitantly pin a flower or button on their lapel, while establishing eye contact. Then they ask the individual if he would be interested in their books, or in making a donation.

What these methods have in common is that they all intentionally transgress the unspoken barriers which govern nonverbal interaction in our culture. Just as the hypnotist provides confusion, arousal, and expectation in the subject (Haley, 1963), the cult recruiter creates a disorienting and arousing experience which heightens attention, and then deliberately attempts to develop unconscious receptivity. The effects of a typical encounter are described by a former female recruit:

> I was standing outside the public library when this guy who was about six feet came over to me. He seemed to be very happy, like he had a lot of answers to things. . . . He seemed to be in a different place than most people. At the time, he seemed kind of spiritual. He asked me to this dinner they had, and I had to lean against the wall. He seemed to be a very powerful person. (Conway & Siegelman, 1978, p. 30)

The significant element in this description is the obvious intensity in the process of the interaction, although a minimal amount of actual content is shared by the recruiter. By the time this woman and her husband accepted the invitation, they only knew that they were invited to a "group called the New Age Fellowship, just a group of people who come together, and sit around and talk about different things." Nonetheless, they thought the initial encounter had some significance due to its remarkable intensity. Yet, they lacked a conceptual framework to understand how they had come to be influenced the way they did. Upon meeting the cult members, this recruit later said, "My initial reaction to these people was, I don't know what they have but I want it."

In order to begin the process of influencing individuals to change fundamental attitudes, unconscious rapport must be established. This is an axiom of the hypnotherapeutic process, and is present in cult induction as well. The influencer must be sensitive to whatever cues of manner, dress, speech, and behavior indicate about an individual's world view, and must evidence to the subject that he is able to address and include their reality. In cult induction, recruiters have an ideological understanding of the significance of the encounter. Thus, they know that whatever it is, the individuals' "model," doesn't work. Therefore, as a pacing procedure, recruiters often elicit the individuals' life goals, extrapolating the intent behind the aspiration. For instance, in one encounter the author had with a recruiter, she began, "Oh you're a social worker, it must be very important for you to help people." In response to my affirmative reply she continued, "Do you really feel that the ways you have been taught help people in the best or most important ways?" The pattern present in this interaction is comparable to the hypnotic process of pacing and leading. By initially extrapolating the best possible motivation for my work she attempted to create rapport. Once the rapport was established, she could proceed to engage my motivation by appealing to a broader expression of it. Most truly thoughtful and idealistic individuals will be aware of the flaws or limitations of their methods, and are likely to be interested in finding ways to improve. A former cult member reported, "If you're into rock music, they have a band; into health food, they have an organic farm. . . . They'll say anything to make you stay" (Freed, 1980, p. 70).

A subsequent feature of cult induction is comparable to "cultural rapport" in Erickson's approach (Gordon & Meyers-Anderson, 1981). "Part of everyone's world model is a cultural milieu. . . . Erickson is sensitive to the importance of the clients' cultural backgrounds and gracefully utilizes his knowledge of cultures and subcultures to help create the rapport necessary for impactful communication" (p. 51). Recruiters are often given explicit instructions on whom to approach, and how to conduct the encounter. Utilizing individuals' interests, and extracting the motivations present, recruiters can then expand those aspirations to their more universal expressions. For example, after engaging me in conversation about the crises in mental health delivery and budget cuts in social services, the recruiter said to me, "Could you imagine a world where everyone was like a social worker, helping everyone else?" Thus she attempted to lead out of the framework in which I operated into abstract realms, the dimensions of which I could not possibly evaluate, and the validity of which I could not argue.

The outcome of a recruitment encounter must include some behavioral response on the part of the recruit. In order for the process to lead further, it must influence the individual to change some plans or behavior. Usually this simply includes accepting an invitation to a dinner or some unthreatening introductory lecture, course, etc. But the behavioral response must follow the arousal of interest. Somehow, the suggestion must be made that this group or recruiter has something to offer. In order to conceive this, recruits must first have become aware of some personal lack or limitation that could change. Thus, the recruits come to the first meeting as seekers, psychologically primed to respond, whether the sense of lack was native to them or had been induced.

CREATING PSYCHOLOGICAL RECEPTIVITY

Following the initial arousal of interest and behavioral response on the part of the inductee, cult recruitment must enhance and develop a broader and deeper psychological response. A variety of patterns are used to enhance unconscious receptivity. While recruiters continue to develop rapport and interest, they also prime recruits for a series of new attitudes and experiences.

The next stage of cult induction requires that the cult convey a sense of continuity between recruits' prior existence, and that which the cult is offering. The continuity can either be that of completing or enhancing the existing personal direction, or that the individuals' path has failed, and they need something entirely new to fulfill themselves. These approaches may have differing psychological consequences, but both serve to draw potential recruits into the cult's process.

In this phase of creating psychological receptivity, the cult must find ways of convincing the recruit that what they have to offer is worth committed exploration. They frequently begin with a process akin to the hypnotic induction pattern of evoking universal experiences. Note the typical opening of one discourse: "Who among us has not stood on a hillside, looking out over a valley . . . and felt some mysterious emotion welling up in our heart?" (Cameron, 1973, p. 43). By evoking a universal moment listeners are directed to their own internal processes. "In search of this brief instant, men climb mountains, soar on the winds . . . and attempt impossible feats of bravado. We search for that affinity with nature in which we can glimpse within us something as perfect as the sun. . . . A glimpse of unity, a oneness with all things only faintly hinted at from around the edges of the mind" (Cameron, 1973, p. 43). Again the pattern of communication directs outward attention to internal process with the suggestion that at "the edge of the mind," outside of ordinary awareness, is unity and perfection. Another structural element is the embedded presupposition that behind all human activities the goal is a "brief instant" of experience. Thus listeners are primed to accept later the premise that ". . . our experiences of nature recall some distant memory of the soul to us. . ." and "The purpose for which this human body was created is just this. . . ." Thus, the direction or momentum of any human activity is established, leading to the possible conclusion that listeners have always been desiring what the cult offers.

By sequencing ideas in this manner, cult recruiters create a situation where the listeners (potential recruits) cannot say "no." The process asks them to say "yes" to universal premises about the human condition in ways that proceed from the general to the specific. This is analogous to the Ericksonian technique known as "yes-sets (Erickson, Rossi, & Rossi, 1976). By accepting premises about society at large, or the broader "human condition," in a milieu which is progressively directing them towards an internal absorption or preoccupation, recruits become increasingly receptive to the cult's suggestions, and conclusions.

This induction pattern establishes truisms about the human situation, and then builds upon them, evoking strong emotions and associations in the process. A former lecturer in the Unification Church describes a ploy that he included in his introductory lectures. Following a moving speech on the plight and suffering of the world he would say, "Can anyone name one good reason why people should hate each other. Yet we do, don't we?" (Zeitlin, personal communication with G. Scharff 1982). This creates a kind of unarguable logic, as it builds upon universal truisms towards the process of agreeing. And the cult milieu often is constructed to promote and value agreement. In most situations, the ostensible end product being promoted is greater personal well-being, usually represented by expressions of happiness. Thus if interest has been aroused, it is likely that potential recruits have been affected by the personal qualities manifested in the cult recruiters, and they either aspire to, or respect those qualities. The cult further defines the meaning of communication such that the process of agreeing is evidence of "openness" or "positivity," and is inherently evidence of the recruits' virtue. The behavior of agreement is reinforced, and disagreement becomes associated with "negativity."

An ultimate goal of the cult induction process is internally directed attention whereby recruits begin to question themselves. The language of early phases of cult induction induces in recruits a receptive feeling state. The first maneuver is the direction of attention, creating absorption on internal processes. As in hypnosis, the most effective way to do this is to make the internal state as enticing and absorbing as possible. The discourse mentioned above continues: "All of the power and beauty that has gone into this creation lies in seed form at the center of our being" (Cameron, 1973, p. 44). This phase is characterized by the evocation of the individual potential for feeling. Words like "love," "inner peace," "happiness," "transcendence," or even the ambiguous "it," are nominalizations characteristic of early cult induction procedures. These words tend to evoke strong internal associations and reactions while providing minimal explicit content. Because they are words which represent experiential states, they force listeners to go within themselves and access those states in order to make sense of the language being used. Often this is sufficient to induce a light trance state. At the same time the credibility of the cult is reinforced by its promotion of such virtuous goals. The capacity for critical evaluation is numbed and the desire to trust is induced. If potential recruits have disquieting feelings or responses, they frequently find little they can criticize. A visitor who was later recruited described this very experience:

> Everyone else at the house seemed a bit weird and superficial too. There was this "Hello, how are you?" routine, and everyone kept telling me, "Oh you're Ron's cousin, he's such a great guy." I must have heard that line a dozen times. . . . It was corny, definitely not my kind of thing but in other ways it was impressive—the businesses, health clinics. . . . I couldn't figure it all out. (Freed, 1980, p. 136)

The use of vagaries and uncertainty can have the immediate result of making individuals more compliant and suggestible.

Erickson referred quite extensively to the role of confusion and uncertainty in the induction of hypnotic states. He viewed confusion as a means of disrupting the continuity in a person's self-awareness. "When confused you suddenly become concerned about who you are and the other person seems to be fading" (Erickson, Rossi, & Rossi, 1976, p. 106). Uncertainty in and of itself tends to orient individuals inwardly, making them increasingly susceptible to outside suggestion. "If the surrounding reality becomes unclear, they (the hypnotic subject) want it cleared up by being told something" (p. 106). The disruption or blurring of outer reality leads to the experience of confusion, which leads to an increased receptivity to suggestions which are definite and provide clarification. "If you add to that the suggestion of a pleasant inner reality, they'd rather go to it" (p. 107). Erickson suggested that confusion was an integral element in any trance induction, as it resulted in a disruption of the normal means by which an individual organizes his reality (cf. Haley, 1963).

Many cults construct their initiation procedures by inducing confusion to promote increased responsiveness and suggestibility. In addition, they use the situational confusion which may characterize the initial stages of induction to create a more existential life uncertainty. A former DLM member reported that in street recruiting he would approach individuals, extending a leaflet, establish eye contact, and ask, "Do you know the purpose of your life?" (Zeitlin, personal communication, 1981). Confusion and shock methods form a theme that runs through the early stages of cult induction, from the uncertainty created by an initial encounter, to an existential confusion concerning the meaning of existence.

Confusion is then accompanied by the suggestion of the inner alternative which the cult inevitably offers.

DISSOCIATIVE STATES

The induction of dissociative states is a distinguishing characteristic of contemporary cults. Uniformly emphasizing that understanding their message must involve more than routine conscious evaluation, cults often punctuate their presentations of doctrine with meditations, chanting, dancing, guided fantasies, prayers, etc. "This neutralizes critical thinking while giving the lectures, rituals, and even social activities a spurious sense of importance." (Clark et al., 1981, p. 51).

Dissociation emerges from a universal psychological uncertainty. While most individuals have a coherent sense of what constitutes their identity, the very existence of unconscious processes indicates that there is more going on than an individual can be cognizant of or can fully control. Therefore, one can never know exactly who they are! In the book *Unity and Multiplicity,* John Beahrs (1982) points out that the boundaries that divide that which is conscious from that which is unconscious are never distinct; rather they form a continuum. What is conscious and available to the individual at one moment may be unconscious at another. Thus any mental mechanism may, at one time or another, be more or less under conscious control. Beahrs further suggests that there are times when it is more accurate to view an individual as a collection of part-selves, than as a static identity. He defines dissociation as "the mechanism or combination of mechanisms by which two or more collections of mental units can be kept separate from one another" (p. 61); dissociation is central to the coherence and continuity of the individual.

Hypnotic communication often is characterized as "multidimensional." Thus it simultaneously provides multiple meanings and multiple opportunities for response. This stems from the premise that there is an organizing mental mechanism that maintains the normal bounds of awareness, and that communication can influence those bounds. Numerous researchers and practitioners have thus proposed that dissociation underlies the essence of hypnotic process (cf. Beahrs, 1982).

Cults develop dissociative experience when they purport to provide answers to existential quandaries. They extend an invitation to an orchestrated inward self-examination. Meanwhile, the entire social system of the cult is set up to provide a continuous demonstration that it offers a valid and coherent means to divide and organize inner awareness and thought, resulting in a better life. Individuals come to call into question their own inner makeup, and whether it accurately can speak to the reality of their life situation. This process takes place in a cultic milieu, where individuals are exposed to a tremendous input of new information and experiences. The result can be a dissociated state in which "the usual connections between mental components are severed or at least severely attenuated" (Clark et al., 1981, p. 51). The dissociative experience tends to be inexplicable, for it emerges as a state of consciousness which is novel, often overwhelming, and usually experienced as avolitional. The cultic milieu characteristically discredits traditional sources of knowledge, and ways of knowing. Hence, individuals are left with the experience that something of importance and profundity has emerged in awareness, but nothing in their previous life has provided the faculties to understand, grasp, or utilize it.

This quandary constitutes a kind of double bind; there is something important to understand, but recruits are not capable of understanding it. The only way to come to understand it is to give up (often termed "surrender" in cultic language) familiar ways of knowing, for they are what prevent true understanding. Some cults term this as giving up the "mind" or the "ego." Individuals are bound by the fact that they have been invited to evaluate and comprehend something of tremendous potential value to their lives. However, in the process of evaluation, they have been led to the insight that there is something within them that limits their potential for understanding. Thus, if the recruits do not understand or agree, it is because they have not yet developed the necessary faculty. Consequently, recruits, on a psychological level, have no choice but to accept the cult's definition of their own inadequacy, and consequent need. They thereby accept the cult's authority, not on the basis of evaluating the cult, but on the basis of accepting their own incapacity to evaluate.

Erickson referred to the "conscious-unconscious double bind" as essential to many hypnotic interventions. In this situation "conscious intentionality and one's usual mental sets are placed in a bind that tends to depotentiate their activity; unconscious potentials now have an opportunity to intrude" (Erickson, Rossi, & Rossi, 1976, p. 61). Erickson further views this liberation as "an opportunity for growth" (p. 61) on a level that is "outside the person's usual range of self-direction and control" (p. 61). Thus it forms a "mild quandary" that "can lead one to experience those altered states we characterize as trance so that previously unrealized potentials may become manifest" (p. 61). In contrast, this phase of cult induction creates an inherent power imbalance, for recruits do not possess the means to access the necessary consciousness to comprehend and experience the depth of the cult. In response to the untenable discomfort of such existential uncertainty, and having been primed that the cult offers an inward alternative, recruits can easily enter a trance state. And the very fact of entering into trance becomes confirming of the cult's veracity and authority because such an experience had been predicted. When the hypnotic experiences and releasing of unconscious potential begin to manifest, they come as confirmations and property of the cult. Thus the evocation of these hypnotic potentials creates a dependency, which can lead recruits to ascribe the cult authority over their hypnotic potential, in other words, to those portions of awareness that are outside of individual conscious voluntary control.

PSYCHOLOGICAL FEATURES OF THE RECEPTIVITY STAGE

Following the recruitment phase of cult induction is the mode of creating enduring psychological receptivity. Inductees have come into interaction with the cultic milieu, and are now susceptible to the influences present in that situation. For many recruits this particular phase of cult induction is characterized by a pervasive discomfort and uncertainty. The social intensity of the interactions within the cult have aroused response potential, while simultaneously forcing them into a social environment whose rules are unclear. At the same time, they are being exposed to new ideas about the nature of reality, spirituality, and their own psychology. While this tends to foster introspection, it can also induce uncertainty about the very apparatus of self-examination. Meanwhile, though, self-examination can be very exciting, particularly in a milieu which extends promises of a new community, more expansive states of consciousness, and answers to existential uncertainties.

The continued induction is characterized by an ongoing psychological tension. The recruits' existing faculties for monitoring and testing reality have been altered and called into question. At the same time that they have been invited to suspend previous identity, the cult members around them are modeling new ways of responding, and consciousness-altering practices are inducing both inward absorption, and heightened suggestibility. One might deem this stage a form of "personality fractionation," comparable to the stage of hypnotic induction where a person goes in and out of trance, until finally attaining a stable trance state. Cult inductees go in and out of the cult mentality, providing an ongoing and immediate contrast with their previous lives. One recruit described his reaction: "My whole life seemed in crisis. Who was I? Where would

I go next? What could I do to change my life? Everything seemed muddled up. I knew I agreed with lots of things in Booneville—the community, the togetherness, honesty and idealism. . . . I needed perspective
badly" (Freed, 1980, pp. 145-146). He continued, describing the effects
of this inward tension: "My head felt like it was splitting open from
pressure, as though something inside me were swollen and about to
burst. . . . My head was stuffed with conflicting ideas and emotion;
thoughts were racing through my mind and then stopping short. My
mood was changing wildly from happy to miserable."

Not all recruits experience the intensity described above. However,
it is illustrative. Like a hypnotist who uses his communication to cover
all classes of possible responses, the cult creates a milieu where every
behavior of the recruit is both anticipated and interpreted. When the
above recruit confided this crisis to his cult confidant, expressing his
desire to leave and sort things out, "she turned the statement on its
head to induce more guilt at my desire to leave. . . . The way she put
it, it seemed to be a part of my pattern of noncommitment, looking for
another excuse to leave something or someone behind . . . searching for
a flaw so I could avoid committing myself again" (Freed, 1980, pp. 146-
147). Thus, an assumption in the environment is that the cult member
has the right to comment on and interpret the internal process of the
recruit. The recruit is in a position much like the "illusion of alternatives"
described by Erickson (Erickson, Rossi, & Rossi, 1976). His range of
responses has been anticipated by the cult, so that the only real choice
is to comply and ultimately understand compliance as an intensely personal decision. For the recruit above, that "was a really key point. Something changed drastically, as though a very powerful force were gripping
me. . . . I lost my resistance. The intensity of my desire to go just seemed
to surrender. . . . I had bought out all my problems, and now I felt as
though I had thrown them away. . . . They weren't my problems anymore" (p. 148). That night he awoke to see a "brilliant white light"
which he felt to be "warming and soothing me, draining the tension
from my body . . ." This "seemed terribly important to him. He had
never before believed in revelations, but it seemed as though he had
been sent a signal 'telling me I was through the impasse, and my decision
to stay longer at Booneville had been right' " (pp. 148-149). From the
hypnotic point of view it would appear that this tension resolved itself
in a dissociated state. Indeed the recruit described this experience as
"though I were watching a film" (p. 149). He came to identify the experience, not as resulting from social process, but as emerging from his
internal process. Thus, in a manner comparable to the way a hypnotist
weaves communications so that they ultimately are experienced by the

subject as arising spontaneously from within, this recruit lost the capacity to differentiate his own native internal process from that introduced by the cult.

REFRAMING THE RECRUITS' UNDERSTANDING OF THEIR CONDITION

The hypnotic pattern known as reframing is based on the relativity of meaning of a given event. Hypnotic subjects will have a habitual frame of reference through which to interpret their own life situations as well as the behavior of others. This "model of the world" may be more or less applicable, but it nonetheless tends to be limited and predictable. The hypnotist or therapist often can make dramatic differences simply by offering new ways to understand and interpret a life situation.

The human need for meaning and a sense of personal continuity creates a vulnerability to the ploys of cult induction. For in an intrapsychic sense, meaning is reinforced by the ongoing capacity to make sense of external circumstance (including interpersonal communication), and internal process. When one's meaning-making apparatus is interrupted or discredited, psychological crisis will follow. In cult induction, the cult must reframe recruits' understanding of prior life so that they can then come to comprehend the significance of what the cult offers. Therefore, the traditional means by which recruits evaluate themselves and others must be replaced.

Cults often begin their indoctrination with a critique on the effects of modern life on the inner life of the individual. Most individuals will tend to use relative measures to evaluate their status and place. Cultic process contrasts the social compromises of modern life with absolute values, eventually substituting an abstract ideal for the standard of personal behavior. The ideal, in the cult environment, is the devotee who transcends inner restraints to serve the cause. This transcendence is generally seen as evidence of spiritual growth and progress. For potential recruits, the values by which they can test the validity of the cult are the very restraints which inhibit spiritual or psychological development, and is the very inhibition that the cult labels as evidence of the psychologically crippling effects of ordinary life. Thus, to the degree individuals hold back commitment to the totalist cult, they are evidencing the very problems which need healing.

DEEPENING ABSORPTION

Once individuals come to accept the basic premise that their lives are possibly in need of radical changes and evaluation, most cults arrange their social system to escalate involvement. Rather than allowing individuals time for solitary reflection and contemplation, they will deepen their absorption in group processes. Many of these deepening methods are comparable to the techniques used in creating hypnotic absorption.

For example, a characteristic of cultic communication is the use of metaphor. Most of the cults under consideration posit that understanding of essential "truth" lies outside the "mind," or normal awareness. To grasp it requires an act of absorption rather than an act of comprehension. Metaphoric communication includes the understanding that no communication can ever entirely represent the experience of an individual. Thus "by understanding that all communication is metaphorical and based on unique experience we alert ourselves to the fact that it is therefore also incomplete and that it is the listener who fills in the holes" (Gordon, 1978, p. 11).

A metaphor reportedly used in several cults, illustrates the effect of directed ambiguity. The story describes the attempt of five blind men to describe an elephant. One touches its trunk, another its tail, a third its body, the fourth its ears, and the last its leg. So the first blind man describes the elephant as a tree trunk, the second as a rope, the third as a large rock, etc. The meta-message of this metaphor is that each of our perceptions is limited, and that we tend to believe that our limited perceptions are accurate representations of the whole. The metaphor goes on to describe the disagreement and conflict that ensued because of the conviction held by each blind man, until someone intervened who could see the whole elephant. The metaphor thus infers that limitations in perception cause human conflict, and require the intervention of someone who is beyond subjective limitations. Thus listeners are primed to accept the possibility of some insight, technique or enlightened master that will enable them to go beyond subjective limitation and see reality as it really is.

The use of metaphor is a deliberate way to depotentiate the conscious mind, and activate unconscious and symbolic resources. The effectiveness of a given metaphor depends on how completely there is an "experience of similarity between the subject's own situation and that portrayed by the metaphor" (Gordon, 1978, p. 21). As we have seen, cults tend to manipulate the symbols of the human quandary in ways that heighten the difference between the life available to the individual outside, and that which the cult offers. Furthermore, metaphors consolidate a given world view by delineating those behaviors within the natural world which confirm subjective impression. So metaphors become a means of conveying a total world view that could not be as completely communicated by linear, logical expression.

Thus, metaphoric communication allows a tremendous amount of information to be conveyed in a relatively simple, condensed, and often apparently innocent format. For instance, one former disciple commented:

> Around the time of our big festivals, or whenever there were difficult things going on, we would hear a lot of stories from the Bhagavad-Gita and other scriptures. In this one, the main character and disciple, Arjuna, is freaking out because he's arrayed to battle his own family. He is on the battlefield with Krishna, his Guru and charioteer, and Krishna says to him, "Go ahead and do your duty because to me they're already dead anyway." The implication was that our master, who could see the past and the future, knew everybody's destiny. So if he said to do the service of killing them, it was simply helping them to fulfill their destiny. I never thought of myself as a violent person, but because I believed I was cultivating the virtuous quality of detachment, this didn't seem like anything violent. But looking back, I wonder if I could have changed the meaning of killing enough to do it, even to my parents? (Zeitlin, personal communication, 1981)

The nature of metaphor is that it turns everyday events into symbolic occurrences and thus bypasses the normal conscious ethical evaluation of behavior. It is an axiom in the hypnotic world, that in a hypnotic state, individuals cannot be influenced to perform antisocial actions that they would normally find ethical violations. However, numerous cult members report that the metaphorical and symbolic ways that behavior is described and explained can serve to depotentiate even deep-seated philosophical or moral premises. The state of mind described by the followers of Charles Manson (Conway & Siegelman, 1978, pp. 194-206, 231-245), as well as those of the followers of Rev. Jim Jones underscore how deeply the cultic reality can come to replace individual sensibilities.

In the therapeutic application of hypnosis, metaphor is helpful in providing an unconscious message that reality is subjective, and that an individual need not be limited to habitual or self-defeating ways of responding to a problem. In contrast, metaphors in cults, while initially providing a similar message that habitual ways are limited, then replace those understandings with a prescribed and total world view. The ther-

apeutic application can be viewed as integrative in that it activates unconscious resources which presumably will become available in ways
that can eventually dovetail with conscious, self-directed mental activity
and behavior. The cultic application initiates a similar process of de-
potentiation, but then uses the responsivity of the subject to substitute
the abstract and symbolic world view of the cult for the existing one of
the individual.

Another feature of metaphoric communication in cults is that of discrepancy and contradiction, reframed as "paradox" and a "higher order
of reality." For instance, one popular spiritual leader teaches, "I deny
being a guru, but I do not deny your being a disciple. One should never
be a guru, but discipleship is something without which nothing is possible" (Rajneesh, 1975, p. 45). This same guru initiates disciples by giving
them a new name, a uniformly colored code of dress and a necklace
bearing the guru's picture. He explains:

> First, the picture is not mine. The picture only appears to be mine.
> No picture of me is really possible. The moment one knows oneself,
> one knows something that cannot be depicted, described, framed.
> I exist as an emptiness that cannot be pictured, that cannot be
> photographed. That is why I could put the picture there. . . . The
> more you know the picture—the more you concentrate on it, the
> more you come in tune with it—the more you will feel what I am
> saying. The more you concentrate on it, the more there will not
> be any picture there. (pp. 45-46)

The above communication constitutes a double bind: Things are not
as they appear. They only appear that way because of limitations on
one's awareness. In order to expand awareness one has to accept that
things are not as they appear. Thus a spiritual hierarchy becomes embedded. The disciple accepts that they do not have the requisite awareness
to truly see reality. This is evidenced by perceiving an apparent duality
or contradiction. To see consistency or unity within reality is evidence
of a "higher consciousness." Moreover, the presence of a response to
the contradiction becomes a signal that one's consciousness is in need
of improvement.

AGE REGRESSION

Whether an individual is seduced or comes voluntarily into a cultic
milieu, they enter an environment which is intrinsically educational.
They are there to learn something, regardless of whether or not they

know what there is to be learned. The nature of the learning environment provides a kind of vertical hierarchy between those who already know, and those who have yet to know. This creates a kind of embedded authority, which can evoke the expectation of learning. This "learning set" can evoke earlier learning situations, and thus can stimulate age regression. This is a hypnotic state whereby a subject revivifies an earlier life phase and experiences it as if he were that younger self.

Much of the cultic milieu can be understood as inducing age regression and dependency. In addition to the ubiquitous scriptural references (which are practically universal in modern cults, regardless of philosophical orientation) such as, "You must be like a little child in order to enter the kingdom of God," many cults tend to recreate a family. Many of the male cult leaders are referred to as "Father" by their followers, several women leaders are "Ma," and the relationships between followers are those of "brother and sister."

The induction of age regression is further illustrated by groups that use a retreat or camp milieu for their indoctrination. In the process of securing rapport, potential recruits are engaged in a sincere and energetic style. They are love-bombed by such means as physical affection, hand-holding, back rubs (all strictly nonsexual, but implicitly seductive) and continuous flattering. Subsequently, there are group activities such as singing, dancing, playing games, doing exercises, chanting, etc., thereby often inducing altered and suggestible states. Additionally, with its implicitly well-defined social structure and its similarity to a camp, those suggestible states can have the additional feature of harkening back to earlier life stages and struggles. This process becomes especially significant in the aftermath of conversion, where the cult is set up to provide an alternative personal history to explain the relationship between the former life and cultic identity.

CONVERSION: INDUCING THE SUBLIME MOMENT

The study of the nature of conversion is a subject broad in scope and implication that has preoccupied theorists and researchers from a variety of disciplines. Conversion is important in this study because of the implications of *induced* conversion, the active manipulation of a social environment to precipitate and maintain the psychological momentum of conversion. Robert Lifton, writing on the Chinese use of thought reform describes the implications of this difference:

> Such imposed peak experiences—as contrasted with those more freely and privately arrived at by great religious leaders and mys-

tics—are essentially experiences of personal closure. Rather than stimulating a greater receptivity and "openness to the world," they encourage a backward step into some form of "embeddedness"—a retreat into doctrinal and organizational exclusiveness, and into all or nothing emotional patterns more characteristic of the child than of the individuated adult. (Lifton, 1963, p. 436)

The moment of conversion usually is recalled as pivotal, after which one's self-definition changes. A characteristic feature is the discontinuity; it is usually characterized by an intense entrance into an altered state of consciousness. To capture the discontinuous nature of this moment, researchers Conway and Siegelman refer to it as "snapping" (1978). Devotees or followers are more likely to describe it as the "inflowing of the spirit," "opening up of God's heart," "getting it," "becoming clear," etc. The experience generally has two differing characteristic descriptions; some refer to it as if something (a grace or a spirit) entered them. However, more frequently, it is described as emerging from within. In both of these orientations, however, the experience is basically passive. Something happens to individuals at a level beyond normal awareness.

On the individual psychological level, this experience presents a cognitive dilemma. How does one make sense of a massive, overriding experience that one never had before (at least to such depth and intensity)? Furthermore, throughout the relationship with the cult, recruits have been primed to anticipate just such an experience. This can induce a crisis. Individuals have no frame of reference for understanding what has happened, and the intensity of experience demands explanation and clarification. Accompanying the new experience can be a feeling of disorientation. If other steps along the path of induction have rendered recruits suggestible, this experience makes them more completely in need of direction—their models of reality have been dismantled. And in the midst of this overwhelming experience, the need for psychological order forces the converts to search for an explanation of the experience.

What is it that stimulates the momentum of induced conversion? From a hypnotic view, the individuals have been operating in a milieu that continually has expressed certain assumptions about life, spirituality, the nature of internal process, etc., until something finally triggers a whole series of associations and experiences, eventually understood as conversion. Erickson and Rossi use the term "psychological implication" to describe an analogous process in the hypnotic context:

Psychological implication is a key that automatically turns the tumblers of a patient's associative processes into predictable patterns without awareness of how it happened. The implied thought or response seems to come up autonomously within patients, as if it were their own inner response rather than a suggestion initiated by the therapist. Psychological implication is thus a way of structuring and directing patients' associative processes when they cannot do it for themselves. (Erickson, Rossi, & Rossi, 1976, p. 59)

Perhaps one of the most inexplicable phenomena in the whole process of cult induction is how a process which has been operating outside recruits, comes to be identified and experienced, as originating within themselves. Somewhere in the technology of influence that is employed must be some process which engages a psychological transfer through which individuals undergo a major redefinition of the direction of their experience, and interpret those impulses which tie them to the group or ideology as genuinely emanating from within. From this point on they identify themselves as agents of the cultic ideology in converting their own internal processes to conform to the expectations established by the cult. Henceforth, every aspect of personal identity must be restructured as the conversion event becomes the central and defining element of the recruits' identity.

CONSTRUCTING BELIEF AND IDENTITY

Following the conversion experience and existential crisis, new members undergo a fundamental overhauling of identity, and must learn the behaviors and responses appropriate to their new identity. Cults are generally characterized by their own language, morality, and styles of interpersonal relating. New members must relearn how to negotiate the basic transactions of life from within their new identity. The cultic metaphor often used to describe this process is as "spiritual childhood." As new initiates, young in the experience, they must learn from spiritual elders. This encourages a kind of ongoing and conscious modeling of appropriate behavior. It is also likely to deepen the qualities of age regression, while it strengthens the dependency relationship. Many new members report extreme disorientation and confusion during these periods, and can be grateful for the older cult members who "protect them from difficult situations."

The exact moment when recruitment becomes membership is variable. However, what is significant is that the experience has, at that point, altered the recruits' self-definition, and as they learn the new behaviors

appropriate to the role of membership, individual personal history becomes reinterpreted to conform with the ideology or cosmology of the
group.

The utilization of personal history is often essential to the hypnotherapeutic process. However, Erickson also demonstrated that the context of the hypnotic relationship was one in which identity could be
created (see the "February Man" case, Rossi, 1980). Erickson goes beyond the simple utilization of existing memories and associations to
hypnotically create experiences that were otherwise not a part of the
individual's history. Thus the inductees' whole understanding of their
past is reintegrated with the hypnotically induced experiences, providing new resources for behavior.

As we have discussed, the "sublime moment" and "existential crisis"
of cult induction become the most significant event in the life of the
member. The ideology of the cult then reframes the recruits' prior lives
as leading them up to and preparing them for this consummate moment.
All the prior happinesses become pale prefigurings of this transcendent
experience, and all prior sufferings become evidence of the human condition prior to conversion. Much of the cult language emphasizes that
without this transcendence, life is meaningless. Conversely, it is this
experience from which the revelation on how to live and the authority
of the cult rests. Having now had this experience, recruits become witness to the authority of the cult over their lives and the lives of others.
The cult will often use this phase to emphasize how important it is for
new recruits to mobilize inner resources to commit themselves. In the
service of this commitment, using the lens of cultic ideology to reevaluate
personal history, intensive self-scrutiny is encouraged:

> Benji was encouraged to talk of his past relationships with women
> and work, focusing on the egocentrism and lack of commitment
> he was now convinced they demonstrated. The more he exagger-
> ated negative aspects of his life, the more enthusiastically he was
> received. Day by day, his stories grew grimmer and more incrim-
> inating, as "I started to believe what I was saying and experience
> a growing sense of relief at the life I had escaped. The more I talked
> about my life, the more I felt separated from it, until
> eventually . . . my old life seemed almost never to have existed."
> (Freed, 1980, p. 157)

Cult induction becomes complete when recruits have so thoroughly
redefined prior history that it is no longer recognizable. Many cults have

elaborate rituals for describing this transformation, including the giving of new names. Recruits have now committed, not only the present and future to the cult, but the past as well.

MAINTENANCE OF ALLEGIANCE

As new members become integrated into the lifestyle of the cult, every aspect of inner life comes to revolve around a basic polarity; those experiences which confirm the world view of the cult are valued, those which do not are the ones from which one seeks refuge and healing. Every aspect of the individuals' inner lives reflect this polarity; thoughts, feelings, fantasies, desires, illness, even dreams, must all be subject to inner regulation. To accomplish this, most of the cults teach some ongoing practice of inner thought stopping, thereby teaching the cultist to maintain an ongoing state of partial absorption via a self-hypnotic technique. These methods range from breath meditation, to speaking in tongues, and incessant chanting of mantras, prayers, or affirmations. The state cultivated by these disciplines becomes identified as the recruits' "center," and any other inner thoughts or feelings are understood to be attempting to distract or remove the individual from this center. Thus, the rest of the individuals' selves are usually relabeled as an inner enemy, and the trancelike state cultivated by the practice, as the sole inner refuge from these turbulent distractions.

In contrast to hypnotherapeutic applications cultic techniques are often continuously applied. As anthropologist Willa Appel writes, "What is unusual about many of our contemporary cults is that they do not allow the individual to return to normalcy, but rather attempt to maintain the dissociated state" (1983, p. 89). These states are relabeled as evidence of the healing power at work, thus they are interpreted as evidence of "higher consciousness." Eventually an automaticity develops which researchers have called the "sustained altered state" (Conway & Siegelman, 1978, p. 155). A former member reported:

> The whole point in the cult was to stay in the Kingdom of God, which basically meant staying in the Spirit of God. You kept on repeating "Thank you Jesus, thank you Lord. . . ." It could be done out loud or internally. After a while I could snap into that state of mind after only a word like "Hallelujah" or "Praise be." I didn't need to go through the whole chanting. (Appel, 1983, p. 89)

CONCLUSIONS

Explicitly hypnotic techniques are certainly only one dimension of the nature of cultic conversion and control. For these operate in a complete and totalistic social system. But the primacy of hypnotic experiences and states are central to the authority and social structure of a cult, and constitute a veritable hypnotically organized social system.

Yet, the abuses of cults mask a broad social interest, namely the search for legitimate means of self-development, for learning in altered states, to improve functioning, enhance sensitivity, and explore existential concerns. Consequently, it becomes essential that practitioners of therapeutic hypnosis also become educators, in order that altered states of awareness and trance phenomena be demystified, and less available for exploitation. As practitioners, we must ensure that every induction is a journey from which an individual has the opportunity to return.

REFERENCES

Appel, W. (1983). *Cults in America.* New York: Holt, Rinehart & Winston.

Beahrs, J.O. (1982). *Unity and multiplicity: Multilevel consciousness of self in hypnosis, psychiatric disorder, and mental health.* New York: Brunner/Mazel.

Cameron, C. (1973). *Who is Guru Maharaj ji?* New York: Bantam.

Clark, J.G., Langone, M.D., Schechter, R.E., & Daly, R.C.B. (1981). *Destructive cult conversion: Theory, research, and treatment.* Weston, MA: Monograph of the American Family Foundation.

Conway, F., & Siegelman, J. (1978). *Snapping: America's epidemic of sudden personality change.* New York: Dell.

Erickson, M.H., Rossi, E.L., & Rossi, S.L. (1976). *Hypnotic realities.* New York: Irvington.

Freed, J. (1980). *Moonwebs: Journey into the mind of a cult.* Toronto, Canada: Dorset.

Gordon, D. (1978). *Therapeutic metaphors.* Cupertino, CA: Meta Publications.

Gordon, D., & Meyers-Anderson, M. (1981). *Phoenix: Therapeutic patterns of Milton Erickson.* Cupertino, CA: Meta Publications.

Haley, J. (1963). *Strategies of Psychotherapy.* New York: Grune & Stratton.

Lifton, R.J. (1963). *Thought reform and the psychology of totalism.* New York: Norton.

McManus, U., & Cooper, J.C. (1980). *Not for a million dollars.* Nashville, TN: Impact Books.

Rajneesh, B.S. (1975). *I am the gate.* New York: Harper & Row.

Rossi, E.L. (Ed.). (1980). *The collected papers of Milton H. Erickson. Vol. I, Innovative hypnotherapy.* New York: Irvington.

Roszak, T. (1978). *Person/planet.* Garden City, NY: Anchor Press/Doubleday.

Schur, E. (1977). *The awareness trap.* New York: McGraw-Hill.

Chapter 24

Erickson's Contributions from the Perspective of a Pastoral Therapist

Henry T. Close

I seem to have stumbled into the position of being the primary spokesperson for Ericksonian approaches for the profession of pastoral counseling. In various articles and seminars, my purpose has been to intrigue people, to expose them to Erickson's work, and then let nature take its course. Today I want to take a different approach. I want to talk about Erickson's approach from the *perspective* of a pastoral therapist.

Some of you may not be familiar with the field of pastoral counseling, so I would like to start with a kind of overview of the profession, so you will know where I am coming from.

Pastoral counseling as a professional subspecialty of ministry began back in the 1920s when a young Congregational minister, Anton Boisen, suffered a series of psychotic episodes, and was hospitalized on three different occasions. By a kind of personal reframing, Boisen came to regard these psychotic episodes as a kind of religious experience that in fact helped him with his own sense of inner integration. So he started a program for bringing theological students into mental hospitals as part of their theological training. This was really the beginning of pastoral counseling as a separate profession.

An interesting note is that during Boisen's last hospitalization, he was Erickson's patient. Dr. Erickson told me this with an obvious sense of pride, and he knew something of Boisen's work. Basically, he reaffirmed and amplified the kind of reframing that Boisen had been telling his own students, and applied it to Boisen. He told him that some people had a special kind of sensitivity and insight into life, and he should not be disturbed if other people did not really understand him when he spoke of his somewhat peculiar ideas, or even if he couldn't understand them himself sometimes. How much influence Erickson had on Boisen I don't know. Apparently, Boisen never spoke of Erickson afterward, although he did speak of others who had influenced him and helped him (Note 1). But it is interesting to me to realize that Erickson did have some input at the very beginning of the pastoral counseling movement.

The process by which people become pastoral counselors is rather interesting and in some ways different from the ways people become therapists in other professions. The pastoral counselor starts off as a pastor. In his basic graduate training in a theological seminary, he is taught to be a kind of general practitioner in the area of ministering to people's psychological and spiritual needs. He is told to visit people in their homes and businesses; to utilize stories and parables and metaphors as a basic way to communicate. He is taught how to reframe situations—how to put people's issues of living in a religious perspective. He is taught to utilize rituals, and sometimes to instruct people to do certain things that will have a symbolic significance for them, such as the practices of penance.

When he graduates from theology school and decides to specialize in pastoral counseling, he enrolls in a postgraduate training program. Traditionally, up until the last five years or so, these have been heavily oriented toward a psychoanalytic point of view, where its unique emphases are integrated with the earlier pastoral and theological training. Although family systems approaches are now becoming more popular, there is still a strong psychoanalytic bent to many pastoral training programs. In the typical training program, the trainee is taught a new kind of reframing, where things are described in psychoanalytic concepts as well as in religious concepts. But many of the things that were an important part of his original training to be a pastor are minimized or even discouraged by his new training to be a therapist. He is taught *not* to visit people in their homes and businesses, and not to be the one who initiates conversation about sensitive issues. The use of metaphor and ritual are not encouraged. And he is told not to instruct people to do things, since this is seen as manipulative.

Some of us, like myself, have been fortunate enough to encounter Milton Erickson. This has been a real breath of fresh air for me and for others of us who take our original pastoral training seriously. Erickson visited people in their homes and businesses, told metaphors, utilized still another kind of reframing, and was unembarrassed about manipulating people. He would make house calls, where he might deliberately stomp on a girl's foot to help her get over being so self-conscious (Haley, 1973). Or he would take someone to dinner and use that setting for therapeutic purposes (Zeig, 1980). He would play games with people—even to the point of engaging a depressed girl in a bicycle race (Erickson, 1959b). He would see people who could not afford to pay. On at least one occasion, he let someone sleep in his backyard for a few days, to have time to "think things over" (Zeig, 1980). Perhaps more than anyone else, he has given initiative and responsibility back to the therapist. He has brought to the field of psychotherapy some of the important things that pastors have always been taught to do, before these were minimized by training programs in pastoral counseling. He has given us a renewed sense of what it means to be a caring person/therapist.

Another of Erickson's emphases that has a kind of religious flavor is his emphasis on the creative moment—the miraculous. When we look at the important religious leaders of the past—people like Jesus for those of us in the Christian tradition—we see very little of their long-term work with people. What we see is the creative moment. But in traditional psychotherapy, the significance of this has been eclipsed by the emphasis on long-term work and the slow, gradual changes that this implies. On the other hand, much of Erickson's work centered around the creative moment and has brought a new respect for the validity of the transforming moment.

But there is a problem with it also. Erickson did not often write about his own uncanny diagnostic skill that helped formulate his interventions, nor about the long, hard groundwork that often preceded and prepared the way for the creative moment. A superficial reading of Erickson can miss this, and can lead to a serious misunderstanding of his work. It can be tempting to try to imitate his creativity without subjecting oneself to the hard work of diagnosis and preparation.

Pastoral counseling is a rather diverse profession, like the other mental health professions. The one theme that seems to be paramount in pastoral counseling is that of *respecting the patient*. This emphasis is taken very seriously and I think that when a new approach or perspective to psychotherapy appears, it is evaluated primarily by this criterion: "Does this approach truly respect the patient in depth?" There are a couple of other criteria that grow out of this emphasis. One is the essential equality of the therapist and patient. Another is the importance of the therapist being truly authentic and involved in his or her dealings with the patient. If these principles are embodied in the therapist's approach, then he or she is most likely to facilitate growth in his or her patient's life. These three emphases, as they are generally understood in pastoral counseling, are especially incompatible with anything that looks like manipulation.

This has been a major hindrance to the acceptance of Erickson's approach by pastoral counselors. Manipulation as it is commonly understood seems to violate the essential respect for the patient, to deny or negate something of his or her dignity and personhood. To manipulate someone knowingly seems to be putting oneself in a kind of one-up position in which the therapist is detached and uninvolved—unauthentic—and these things preclude any real growth for the patient.

Let me give an illustration. You will recall the Erickson case study about the girl with the eighth-inch gap between her front teeth (Erickson, 1955). She regarded this as such a terrible deformity that life was no longer worth living. When she consulted Erickson, she had already decided that therapy would be useless and was planning to kill herself after the final session. A major part of Erickson's therapy was to have her learn to squirt water between her front teeth and then play a practical joke on a young man at work that she was attracted to by squirting him with water! Mrs. Erickson told me that this was one of Dr. Erickson's favorite case studies. The first time I read it, I was deeply touched by his sensitivity to this girl and his ability to tap into her growing edge. So I told it to a friend who is one of the foremost leaders in the field of pastoral counseling. His response was to ask me how I could justify manipulating somebody like that.

Another of Erickson's really beautiful case studies is of an engaged couple who came to ask him to use hypnosis to tranquilize the girl so she could have an abortion (Rossi, 1980). He sensed that it was the parents of the couple who were pressuring them to have the abortion, and he tried to discourage them. They became very upset at this, so he then told them that if they were to be able to get the abortion they said they wanted, there was one thing they would have to avoid. They would have to avoid thinking of a name for the baby. Of course, being told not to think of a name made them think of many names and made them realize how important the baby was to them. They came back a few days later—married—to apologize for having "made such damn fools of themselves." When I quoted this in a seminar at our national conference, I said that this raised the question of manipulation and I heard a large chorus of agreement.

Let me give another example. Erickson wrote of a young woman, Cathy, who was in a hospital dying of cancer (Erickson, 1959a). He worked with her for 12 straight hours, 6 P.M. to 6 A.M., doing a hypnotic induction for her pain, so she could live her last days in full conscious contact with her family instead of being half-conscious with morphine. He told her that she could stay awake from the neck up, implying that the lower half of her body could go to sleep and be free from pain.

There is certainly manipulation in these cases. But there is also a deep quality of authenticity, both in Erickson's participation and in the results for the patients. There is no sense that Erickson's patients *felt* manipulated in the sense that something sneaky had been done to them; or that they had been "had"; or had lost something of their essential human dignity. I know that when I have utilized Erickson's approaches, I have never felt that I was compromising my own integrity or authenticity, or that of my patients. Instead, to work with someone more effectively adds to my sense of self-respect. I remember a mental health worker whom I saw for only four sessions to help her with her depression. At the end of the last session, she told me, with tears in her eyes, "You have been *so* important to me. You simply let me be," and then quoted one of my Ericksonian interventions as an example of letting her be.

From my perspective, one of Erickson's significant contributions to psychotherapy is that he has helped transcend the apparent dichotomy between authenticity and manipulation. He has helped to bring an end to the encounter group mentality, where expressing feelings was an end in itself and where people would take it on themselves to evaluate each others' authenticity, oblivious to how manipulative that was. Erickson has done this *experientially* rather than intellectually. Instead of giving us an explanation about how authenticity and manipulation can mesh, he has given us countless demonstrations. He has *shown* us that a very authentic, caring person can do manipulative things with people, and that the outcome *increases* the patient's sense of wholeness and authenticity. In that sense he stands near the heart of my own religious tradition where there are many examples of Jesus manipulating people openly, wisely, lovingly, and effectively.

Erickson had a remarkable sense of playfulness, through which much of his authenticity was expressed. I referred to him once as the patron saint of the psychotherapy of play (Close, 1981). It's true that he didn't do the things we traditionally associate with authenticity. He didn't talk about his own pathology; he didn't share his own feelings with patients; he didn't explore transference issues. Instead, he shared his commitment, his creativity, his toying with new ideas and options, his flirting with new ways of living and feeling and relating. He shared his playfulness and his enthusiasm for living. All of this was based on his incredible sense of what creates change. To me there is a profound kind of authenticity in the kind of playfulness that Erickson exhibited—such as when he prescribed a mouthwash of raw cod liver oil for an anorectic girl (Zeig, 1980).

Erickson has also helped heal this schism between authenticity and manipulation indirectly, through his influence on the communication theorists such as Haley, Watzlawick, Weakland and others. These theorists have pointed out some of the complexities of communication, such as the fact that all communication influences, usually at several levels, most of which are probably outside of our awareness. Whenever we are involved with others, we are influencing them. You cannot *not* influence people. By being maximally *thoughtful* about how I influence people—that is, by manipulating them—I can hopefully influence them more intelligently and beneficially. But just because I don't influence someone intelligently—consciously, deliberately—it doesn't mean that I am not influencing him or her. I dislike the point of view that says, "If you influence people deliberately, you are showing a lack of respect, but if you influence them accidentally, you are thereby affirming and augmenting their inherent human dignity."

If I were to summarize my point of view, I would say that Erickson has helped to humanize psychotherapy. In another sense, he has also helped to "religionize" psychotherapy. This is a kind of paradox, because he was not a religious person in any traditional sense of the word. But he has brought to the field of psychotherapy many emphases that parallel emphases in religious thinking and experience.

It has been pointed out that there are two great traditions from our past that have influenced the thinking of Western man: the Greek tradition, with its emphasis on reason, and the Judeo-Christian tradition, with its emphasis on faith. The Greek tradition as it is generally understood is the tradition of the philosopher, emphasizing the preeminence of reason, the rules and principles of logic, the importance of reflecting on the ultimate nature of things. It is also the tradition of the democratic society, and there are some who have suggested a connection. The logic that says, "A is obvious, and from A we can logically proceed to B and then to C," is a logic that is meant to persuade rather than to teach or to inspire. It is designed to reach an unambiguous decision, rather than to encourage growth. It is the kind of logic one would expect of an orator who is campaigning for election in a democracy. It is also the kind of activity that is oriented primarily to the left brain.

The Judeo-Christian tradition, on the other hand, is the world of faith and the things that are associated with faith: the world of mystery, rituals, symbolism, metaphors, miracles, the importance of relationships and behavior, and the value of a world view that is related to these things. It is very much a right-brain orientation.

Traditional psychotherapy—especially psychoanalysis—has owed much more to the Greek tradition than to the Judeo-Christian. So it is pleasing to me to hear of Milton Erickson, who utilized primarily right-brain phenomena—such as telling a depressed young woman to squirt water between her front teeth at a potential boyfriend. He is affirming categories and perspectives that are important to a religiously oriented therapist. He is telling her to *do* something that has symbolic significance, that is a kind of ordeal, that is designed to modify her world view and, with that, her feelings, her attitudes about herself, her relationships, her ways of living.

Let me tell you about one of my patients with whom many of Erickson's emphases expressed themselves very naturally. This was a woman in her early forties who was already near death from cancer. The family had been referred by their pastor who described Mary as an energetic, charming, playful woman who was the backbone of their small church. Mary's father, who lived with them, had been surrounded by death. Within the past year, he had lost another daughter and a sister, and another sister was in the hospital with serious physical problems. Now he was faced with a daughter who was dying. This was more than he could accept. He insisted that Mary was not dying, that there was hope, and that Mary *was* trying and *would not* give up—even though it seemed fairly obvious that Mary was ready to die and get it all over with.

I saw Mary in her home for six sessions. The first two times she was barely ambulatory and very disoriented. Her panic expressed itself in an insatiable thirst. She would alternately drink a glass of something and then go urinate—several times an hour. Her husband and her father tried to stop her from doing this because they thought it was bad for her. I was able to reframe it as her way of coping, and of gaining some sense of control over her body. I said that this was necessary for her to do if she were to keep on trying. With this explanation, they stopped bothering her about the drinking. The next four sessions, she was bedridden and breathing laboriously. In each of the sessions, she would begin by saying in a gasping voice, "I don't want to talk today. You talk." So I would say, "I'll be glad to talk today, but let me first ask you how you are." She would tell me she was tired, or that she was worried about her family, or that she wanted to give up. So I would use a metaphor or a guided imagery as I talked for the entire hour. I talked a lot about comfort and some of the things people can do to be more comfortable. When she said she was tired of trying and wanted to give up, I told her that I could understand that. I thought that sometimes people felt they ought to keep on trying because somebody else wanted them to, even though the person's own body was ready to stop trying. I said that she had the right to give up, just like she had the right to keep on trying. As a human being, she had many rights, and she could exercise those rights as she saw fit. Then I told her that if she were ready to stop trying, one of the things she could do was, in her imagination, to visit some of the places and people that had been important to her and say goodbye to them. If there were a tree, for instance, that she had planted and watered and watched grow (she enjoyed working with plants in her yard), she might visualize visiting the tree, touching it and saying goodbye to it. She could extend this to other things and people that had been important to her. Finally, I told her that I was going to say goodbye now, and that she could keep on doing whatever she needed to do inwardly with her thoughts and feelings, and I slipped out of the room. Two days later, she died quietly.

I think most sensitive pastors would recognize this as a pastoral ministry. I also think that most Ericksonians would recognize this as an example of Ericksonian hypnotherapy. And as I see it, the possibility of this dual perspective is one of Erickson's great contributions to the field of psychotherapy.

In addition to helping transcend the dichotomy between manipulation and authenticity, and to his stress on right-brain phenomena, Erickson has also left us a kind of tradition of his own, complete with genealogy, childhood experiences, an ordeal in the "wilderness," a "conversion" (when he studied with Clark Hull), parables, miracles, sacred writings, and an organization with apostles and disciples. I'm glad to be one of the disciples, and I confess to a degree of evangelistic zeal in helping acquaint my colleagues with this remarkable man and his work.

REFERENCE NOTE

1. I wrote in an article ("A Visit with Milton H. Erickson: The Grandfather of CPE," *The Journal of Pastoral Care*, March, 1981) that on the basis of Erickson's work with Boisen, I thought of Erickson as the grandfather of Clinical Pastoral Education—an educational program that is the background of pastoral counseling. This article elicited a response from one of Boisen's students, Carroll Wise, who was working with Boisen at Worcester State Hospital at that time. He said that Boisen never spoke of Erickson afterward. He also said that Erickson was rather outspokenly antagonistic to religion at that time, and he doubted that Erickson had any influence on Boisen or his work ("The Grandfather of CPE?", *The Journal of Pastoral Care*, Dec. 1981).

REFERENCES

Close, H. T. (1981, December). Play in CPE. *The Journal of Pastoral Care.*

Erickson, M. H. (1955). Hypnotherapy of two psychosomatic dental problems. *The Journal of the American Society of Psychosomatic Dentistry, 6,* 6–10. (Reprinted in J. Haley (Ed.), *Advanced techniques of hypnosis and therapy: Selected papers of Milton H. Erickson, M.D.* New York: Grune & Stratton, 1967.)

Erickson, M. H. (1959a). Hypnosis in painful terminal illness. *American Journal of Clinical Hypnosis, 1,* 117–121. (Reprinted in J. Haley (Ed.), *Advanced techniques of hypnosis and therapy: Selected papers of Milton H. Erickson, M.D.* New York: Grune & Stratton, 1967.)

Erickson, M. H. (1959b). Further clinical techniques of hypnosis: Utilization techniques. *American Journal of Clinical Hypnosis, 2,* 3–21. (Reprinted in E. Rossi (Ed.), *The nature of hypnosis and suggestion.* New York: Irvington, 1980.)

Haley, J. (1973). *Uncommon therapy: The psychiatric approach of Milton H. Erickson, M.D.* New York: Norton.

Rossi, E. L. (Ed.). (1980). *Innovative hypnotherapy.* New York: Irvington.

Zeig, J. (Ed.). (1980). *A teaching seminar with Milton H. Erickson.* New York: Brunner/Mazel.

Chapter 25

Moshe Feldenkrais's Work with Movement: A Parallel Approach to Milton Erickson's Hypnotherapy

Mark Reese

The work of Moshe Feldenkrais and Milton Erickson epitomizes mastery of the facilitation of human learning. On the surface their approaches are dissimilar: Feldenkrais works primarily in the physical domain of touch and movement, while Erickson worked primarily in the symbolic domain of image and language. Nevertheless, there are striking parallels in their philosophical emphases on human individuality, the importance of learning, and the role of unconscious processes. Even more remarkable are the similar innovations of utilization, indirect techniques, and pattern interruptions that each employs with a subtlety which defies verbal description and strains the powers of observation.

Those who are familiar with Erickson's work can discern many similar patterns of communication in the following Feldenkrais excerpt. In this workshop session, Feldenkrais had participants lie on the floor on their stomachs and do various slow, gentle movements related to childhood crawling. After a while, Feldenkrais asked the group to begin bending the fingers of the right hand "as if you're going to make a fist," and then to:

> Undo it, as if you stopped thinking of the fist. . . . That is the easiest movement we can do. It's almost like moving the eyelid. . . . Close and open, as slowly, as comfortably, and as little as is necessary for you to feel that you're actually flexing and stretching

[pause]. . . . We can do everything to our own comfort. . . . You'll find that in order to be able to do a thing comfortably, elegantly, and aesthetically right . . . we must do it with a minimum of exertion, with the feeling of lightness, the feeling, the sensation of lightness, of lightness of the movement [pause]. . . . You will see that the lightness exists only when you flex it a little bit more and open it, but not completely. In order to make the hand completely flexed and completely open, you have to make a real effort, enough effort, but to flex it a little bit more and flex it a little bit less . . . gives you a sensation that is easy, light [pause]. . . . Now, being easy, light, will you please continue that movement . . . easy, light . . . so that the feeling of easy, light, is actually connected . . . it will be . . . whether you want it or not . . . you can't do it otherwise. . . . Your entire motor cortex, the entire nervous system is now pervaded with that feeling, light, and you should know that in our motor cortex the hand occupies, next to the lips, the largest area . . . so very slowly there will be a feeling of lightness permeating the entire musculature, . . . the entire self, making it . . . keep on doing it . . . and while you do that, while you feel it's really light, you'll find out the whole arm gets light and slowly you will feel the neck and the shoulder blade . . . over that . . . getting soft and nice and actually prepared to act without preparing itself. In other words, it's getting ready for action and you will see when we get that, how quickly, how nicely, we will all be moving, doing the same thing independently, whether you have arthritis, whether you had an operation or not, you will still move infinitely better than you started [pause]. . . . Don't stop moving the right hand, flexing and . . . slowly, slowly see a remarkable sort of thing. . . . If you keep on doing that movement, it will actually teach you . . . slowly, keep on moving the fingers gently and on top of that movement, lift your right shoulder and you will see that the gentleness of the movement, the skill of the movement permeates our entire being and therefore you will see that other things we do improve without doing them. You don't have to exercise in order to improve. You only have to be your own self. (Feldenkrais, 1981b)

In this example, Feldenkrais utilizes a hand-grasping movement—an infantile reflex and embryological "growth action" (Blechschmidt, 1977)—in order to induce hypnoticlike learning. His students are placed in a situation where they learn *from their own movements* the means to achieve "comfort, elegance, and aesthetic satisfaction." During the past 40 years Feldenkrais developed a somatopsychic discipline incorporating numerous effective techniques that in many essential respects complement and parallel the work of Erickson.

Many of us in the Feldenkrais community are drawn to Erickson's work because he so well conveyed certain implicit but unstated insights of Feldenkrais's approach. Similarly, some Ericksonians have discovered in Feldenkrais's work a subtle intelligence about nonverbal behavior, learning, and communication which makes Ericksonian skills more accessible. In this chapter I hope to stimulate reciprocal study and collaboration between practitioners of the two methods—a collaboration which has, in fact, already begun. Furthermore, by understanding certain common principles that are instantiated but differentially applied in the two methods, I hope to promote the emergence of more integrated and effective somatopsychic theory and methods.

I begin with an overview of the life and work of Feldenkrais, followed by a discussion of the awareness of movement Feldenkrais and Erickson both learned through personal physical traumas. Then I describe their parallel philosophies of learning and their parallel techniques. The chapter concludes with a reflection on the artistry and experimentalism of Feldenkrais and Erickson.

MOSHE FELDENKRAIS: HIS LIFE AND WORK

Moshe Feldenkrais was born in Russia in 1904 and emigrated to Palestine at the age of 13. Like many innovators, he came to his field by a circuitous route, weaving together numerous influences. As a young man, he was an excellent athlete, a soccer player, and self-taught in jujitsu. He did construction work and tutored problem students while attending night school preparing to study physics. He had an early interest in hypnosis and translated Emile Coué's book on autosuggestion into Hebrew.

In Paris, Feldenkrais earned his doctorate in physics at the Sorbonne and assisted Joliot-Curie. During his university years he met Kano, the originator of judo, and trained with Kano's students to become a high ranking black belt and well-known judo teacher.

Evading the Nazis, Feldenkrais fled to England where he worked in antisubmarine research during the war, wrote scientific papers, trained paratroopers in self-defense techniques, and authored books on judo. On slippery submarine decks he aggravated an old soccer injury to his knees, and began the extended work on himself which led to his discoveries about movement reeducation. After he publicly presented his ideas, people sought his help with their problems. For several years he was an amateur somatic practitioner, first in England and later in Israel where he had returned to work as a research scientist. In the mid-1950s Feldenkrais gave up his career in physics and devoted himself fully to his work with people. By the late 1960s he was training his first Tel Aviv group to become practitioners of his method, and he trained two subsequent groups in the United States. He wrote four books on his method, and his teaching is preserved in thousands of hours of audio- and videotapes.

Moshe Feldenkrais originated two interrelated, somatically based educational methods. The first method, Awareness through Movement, is a verbally directed technique designed for group work. The second method, Functional Integration, is a nonverbal contact technique designed for people desiring or requiring more individualized attention.

As exemplified in the quote above, Feldenkrais's Awareness through Movement lessons incorporate active movements, imagery, cues for sensory attention, and various informative and suggestive material. A typical lesson lasts about an hour and combines a few dozen thematically linked movements. Lesson themes may include developmental movements such as rolling, crawling, and standing up; functions such as posture and breathing; systematic explorations of the kinetic possibilities of the joint and muscle groups; and experiments in somatically based imagery and visualization.

These lessons are not "physical exercises" such as calisthenics; they are *somatopsychic explorations* which foster improvement by accessing inherent neurological competencies, increasing self-awareness, and facilitating new learning. The initial movements are usually very small with an emphasis on ease, comfort, and learning so that gradually one becomes aware of how the musculature, skeleton, and entire personality are involved in every movement. From seedlike beginnings, small movements grow into movements of greater complexity, magnitude and speed. The result is learning to move with greater efficiency and satisfaction.

Awareness through Movement lessons often evoke a trancelike state. Unlike a typical exercise class, one is not told where the movements are leading or shown what they look like; thus, what one learns arises organically and as a surprise. Often only one side of the body is physically worked at a time but the other side is worked mentally; that is, in the imagination. This mental practice refines kinesthetic sensitivity to the point where muscular impulses and patterns are clearly felt and differentiated with minimal mobilization. Throughout the lesson, one is guided to integrate and apply one's newly discovered skills by means of verbal suggestions or stories.

The individual lessons of Functional Integration are based upon the same logic as Awareness through Movement. They are used with a broad spectrum of people, from those with physical limitations and discomfort, including neurological and musculoskeletal problems, to athletes and performing artists. The method of Functional Integration is neither a medical nor a therapeutic practice; it is learning-based, primarily nonverbal, and directed at enhancing the efficiency, coordination, grace, and self-possession of a person's movement. Lessons are done with the student lying on a soft but firm work table, or standing, or sitting. The practitioner gently touches or moves the student in a variety of ways to facilitate the student's awareness and stimulate organic learning and vitality. Each move in the lesson is part of a communication Feldenkrais has likened to dancing. Through touch, the practitioner partially discloses or hints at a functional motor pattern, and the student's nervous system responds with altered muscular responses. Gradually, with repetitions and variations, the student assembles or synthesizes—mostly at an unconscious level—a new neuromuscular image of movement which can later be translated into active performance. At the end of a session the practitioner helps the student to integrate the learning in everyday life through alternative movements based upon the lesson's functional theme and through verbal suggestions.

In recent years Feldenkrais has become well-known for his work with brain-injured children and adults, but he is equally respected in the theater and dance worlds for performance training. Many people have sought his aid for muscular and joint problems, and others for personal growth. By working with the whole person, Feldenkrais's techniques promote self-esteem and learning skills.

Within this broad educational context Feldenkrais focused especially on the unconscious sensory-motor experience that lies beneath the surface of human behavior. This includes but is not limited to: (a) sensations of the muscles and joints; (b) the sense of gravity, balance, space, and time; (c) kinesthetic associations; (d) motor skills and competencies; and (e) self-image. Feldenkrais spent a lifetime exploring and revealing the inexhaustably rich, multidimensional world of human movement (Note 1).

A PARALLEL AWARENESS OF MOVEMENT

One of the most striking parallels between Feldenkrais and Erickson is that the origin of their awareness of movement was grounded in their personal discoveries while overcoming physical traumas that impaired their movement abilities. Erickson said:

> I had a polio attack when 17 years old and I lay in bed without a sense of body awareness. I couldn't even tell the position of my arms or legs in bed. So I spent hours trying to locate my hand or my foot or my toes by sense of feeling, and I became acutely aware of what movements were. Later, when I went into medicine, I learned the nature of muscles. I used that knowledge to develop adequate use of the muscles polio had left me and to limp with the least possible strain; this took me ten years. I also became extremely aware of physical movements and this has been exceedingly useful. People use those telltale movements, those adjustive movements that are so revealing if one can notice them. (Haley, 1967, p. 2)

For many years Feldenkrais's knee injuries were a major problem in his life, sometimes confining him to bed for weeks at a time. He knew that certain movements aggravated his condition, but only intermittently. Therefore, he felt that there must be some unconscious aspects of his movements which contributed to reinjury and which he could correct if he developed sufficient awareness. He lay in bed experimenting with tiny movements for hours on end, refining his kinesthetic awareness so that he could feel the subtle subconscious connections between all parts of himself. He studied biology and the neurosciences which supplemented what he had learned from physics and from his training in judo. In this way Feldenkrais reeducated his own movement habits and learned to walk efficiently and painlessly. In the process he learned a great deal about learning itself.

Thus, both Feldenkrais and Erickson had the intense motivation and curiosity to undertake the extraordinary project of becoming precisely aware of their own muscular efforts and movement. They learned to sensitize their feelings to that twilight reality at the boundary of intention and muscular action, emotion and sensation, conscious and unconscious experience and expression. Through a subjective, inner process of discovery they each acquired the perceptiveness to observe the subtle reflections of life in the visible and palpable body. Their experience of discovering and utilizing their personal resources prompted the vision that now awakens these resources in others.

A PARALLEL PHILOSOPHY OF LEARNING

While neither Feldenkrais nor Erickson espoused a "theory" per se, a working philosophy of learning is discernible throughout their writings. This philosophy is essentially positive and growth-oriented, and goes beyond the therapeutic dichotomy of sickness and health. In fact, the work of Feldenkrais and Erickson is as much transformational as it is remedial.

Learning entails going beyond one's limitations. One senses in Feldenkrais's and Erickson's work a tremendous enthusiasm and confidence in people's ability to learn. Yet, they lament, people limit themselves instead of using their potential. Erickson noted, "When we were very young, we were willing to learn. And the older we grow, the more restrictions we put on ourselves" (Zeig, 1980, p. 75). Similarly, Feldenkrais remarked that as people get older "movements or actions are gradually excluded from their repertory" (1981a, p. xii). In order to convince people of their potential, Feldenkrais and Erickson often reminded them of the learning they did as children: learning to stand up, to talk, learning the alphabet, learning about the body and sex (Feldenkrais, 1981a; Zeig, 1980). These learning parables are woven into Erickson's inductions and Feldenkrais's lessons as affirmations of the fact that people can learn.

Both men attached importance to the therapeutic and self-actualizing value of human learning; they demonstrated how learning new abilities can lead to such positive transformations that symptoms spontaneously disappear. The key is that learning builds self-confidence. Erickson said, "Most neurotic ills come from people feeling inadequate, incompetent" (Zeig, 1980, p. 222). And according to Feldenkrais, what makes therapies effective is that "your acts and responses must contain, even in your expectations or imagination, feelings of satisfaction and pleasurable achievement or outcome" (1981a, p. 37). They carefully and masterfully created learning situations which established a foundation of success so that feelings of accomplishment could generalize to other situations (Feldenkrais, 1981a, p. 92; Zeig, 1980, p. 314).

For Feldenkrais and Erickson, learning is not fundamentally an intellectual process; learning is a sensory-motor process involving the entire self, and results from *doing*. Feldenkrais quotes an old Chinese saying: "I hear and forget. I see and remember. I do and understand" (1981a,

p. 89). Erickson said, "The thing to do is get your patient, any way you wish, any way you can, to do something" (Zeig, 1980, p. 143). Both Feldenkrais and Erickson were men of action who enjoyed the life of the body. Erickson's polio, despite the physical restrictions it caused, seemed only to heighten his appreciation for physical experience. Telling a client to climb Squaw Peak was an example of one of Erickson's prescriptions, parallel to Feldenkrais's more general emphasis on physical activity.

The concern for experiential learning is reflected in the way Feldenkrais and Erickson trained students to practice their methods. Erickson taught that learning hypnosis was like learning to swim: You have to get in the water (personal communication, November, 1979). Most people spent their time in an Erickson seminar "in the water." Likewise, Feldenkrais's training programs bear little resemblance to academia where objective knowledge is often dissociated from subjective experience. Instead, Feldenkrais creates a personal learning context where students have the opportunity to discover in themselves the kinesthetic sensitivity he learned through the work he did with himself.

Underlying these methods of experiential learning is the assumption of somatopsychic unity which has profound implications for everyone in the helping professions. This unity is the basis for psychic complaints "surfacing" in the body and for neurotic complaints disappearing as a result of physical improvements. Out of the experience of their own integrity, both Erickson and Feldenkrais transcended the traditional mind/body dichotomy and saw human beings as fundamentally whole. Thus, Feldenkrais emphasizes that he does not touch *bodies* but rather *persons*. And when Erickson spoke to a person's unconscious *mind*, he was likewise relating to a whole person.

Learning and the Unconscious

Erickson described the unconscious as "made up of all your learnings over a lifetime, many of which you have completely forgotten, but which serve you in your automatic functioning" (Zeig, 1980, p. 173). Feldenkrais said, "Immense activity goes on in . . . us, far greater than we appreciate or are aware of. This activity is related to what we have *learned* during our whole life from inception to this moment" (Feldenkrais, 1981a, p. 6).

There is a special, other kind of "learning": phylogenetic knowledge, learning acquired and passed on through evolution over countless generations. When Erickson taught the little bedwetting girl to control her

urination by imagining being frightened, he used a reflexive, phylogenetic potentiality that with awareness she could learn to utilize (Zeig,
1980, p. 82). Similarly, many Feldenkrais techniques are based upon
utilization of latent, neuromuscular phenomena, including tonic and
righting reflexes, grasping and sucking, protective reactions, and muscular synergy. Thus, for Feldenkrais and Erickson "the unconscious" is
not the reservoir of difficult-to-manage instinctual impulses depicted by
Freud, but a life-sustaining activity which supports our thinking, feeling,
sensing, and acting. Accordingly, many of their techniques are designed
to reduce the interference of overly conscious controls in favor of facilitating healthy, subconscious autoregulative processes which are older
and more reliable than our conscious direction and will.

Curiously, in light of the foregoing discussion, Feldenkrais rarely if
ever uses the term "unconscious"; he refers instead to the biologically
specifiable entity, the nervous system. However, he speaks of the nervous system in a way that is comparable to Erickson's use of "the unconscious." When giving lessons, Feldenkrais will say, "Don't *you* decide
how to do the movement; let your *nervous system* decide. It has had
millions of years of experience and therefore it knows more than you
do" (Note 2). This injunction parallels Erickson's characteristic induction: "You don't know what all your possibilities are yet. Your unconscious can work on them all by itself" (Erickson & Rossi, 1979, p. 46).

Organic and Hypnotherapeutic Learning

Feldenkrais's philosophy of learning is perhaps best expressed by
what he calls organic learning. Organic learning is related to the physical
development of the body and nervous system in codependent interaction
with the outer world. The first few years of life display the most intense
expression of this learning which is linked with organic growth. However, for human beings, there is no limit to potential growth since neurological growth is concomitant with new learning and is, in effect, the
direct continuation of our embryological and infantile ontogenesis. Unfortunately, the social norm is for organic learning to stop at puberty
except in the social sphere. The personal somatic functions usually become arrested in their development or gradually deteriorate, causing a
host of preventable somatopsychic difficulties from ulcers to backache.

The parallel between organic learning and Erickson's hypnotherapeutic learning is that each represents an inner-directed, highly personal
learning process which unfolds the individual's potential. This process
lies at the heart of how the person experiences and regards him or

herself. Both of Feldenkrais's methods (Awareness through Movement and Functional Integration) are intended to reinstate the self-perpetuating movement of organic learning. They lead the student through primal sensory-motor pathways and forests of discovery where the nervous system has retained the memory of, and thus the competency for free and natural movement. Analogous to Erickson's hypnotherapeutic learning, this process of reconnection with the inner, intelligent, sensory-motor self reinforces the impulse of growth, individuation, and creativity.

The essence of both organic learning and Ericksonian learning is that they are *self-directed*. As Erickson relates:

> I didn't know what her problem was. She didn't know what her problem was. I didn't know what kind of psychotherapy I was doing. All I was was a source of weather or a garden in which her thoughts could grow and mature and do so without her knowledge. The therapist is really unimportant. It is his ability to get his patients to do their own thinking, their own understanding. (Zeig, 1980, p. 157)

Similarly, Feldenkrais has called himself "a funny sort of teacher who doesn't teach, yet the students learn" (Note 2). The two methods thus create the conditions that nurture the flowering of individuality and self-realization.

PARALLEL TECHNIQUES

Creating a Learning Context

Analogous to some of Erickson's "reframing" procedures, Feldenkrais often resituates his students' problems in a learning context. For example, a woman approached Feldenkrais to be treated for her scoliosis. Feldenkrais told her that he would not deal with her "scoliosis" since many therapists had already tried unsuccessfully to "correct" her spine. She could, of course, go to a surgeon; but if he straightened her spine surgically, she would surely lose mobility. Feldenkrais explained that he could help her to learn how to move without pain and with ease in all cardinal directions. Furthermore, by learning how to perform functionally symmetrical movements, she would learn to appreciate in herself an improved skeletal organization and, in effect, learn to "straighten" herself.

Feldenkrais's learning orientation is atypical of most somatic approaches which (a) diagnose and isolate specific structural or physical problems; and (b) attempt to cure or correct these problems; by (c) administering authoritarian, directive forms of manipulation and behavioral prescriptions. In contrast, Feldenkrais (a) situates the problem in terms of the availability or unavailability of choices and options open to the person; (b) engages in a mutual search for new options of behavior and experience which can lead to more favorable outcomes; and (c) utilizes already present competencies and works indirectly to support the person's ability to discover solutions through awareness and learning. In the following sections I describe how this general approach is embodied in Feldenkrais's techniques which parallel those of Erickson.

Utilization

The "utilization principle" (Erickson & Rossi, 1979) is recognized as central to Erickson's work, and it is likewise important in understanding Feldenkrais. Feldenkrais and Erickson often match the student-client's ongoing experience and behavior in order to facilitate learning and change. In one dramatic example, Erickson joined in with the agonized chant of a terminally ill cancer patient in order to induce hypnotic anaesthesia (Zeig, 1980, p. 185). Once I saw Feldenkrais work, rather grossly I thought, with a small boy with an athetoid form of cerebral palsy until I realized he was matching the child's rhythm and quality of movement; the boy was able to learn far more easily from this resonant pattern than from very smooth movements which lay outside his range of experience. Bandler and Grinder (1975) have discussed utilization in terms of "pacing and leading" and say that in pacing, "the hypnotist is making himself into a sophisticated biofeedback mechanism" (p. 16). Feldenkrais's methods indeed exemplify a sophisticated biofeedback mechanism. Functional Integration creates a direct kinesthetic linkage whereby the practitioner and student become "a new entity," joined by the hands of the practitioner (Feldenkrais, 1981a, pp. 3-4). Feldenkrais kinesthetically "paces and leads" the student's breathing, muscular tonus, rhythm, and other subtle qualities and styles of minimal neuromuscular behavior.

Feldenkrais's movements often accentuate the student's way of holding the body; his hands shape themselves to the musculoskeletal contours, supporting and exaggerating what is already being enacted and taking over the student's own muscular effort. For example, Feldenkrais might lift and support a pupil's hunched shoulders or tightened lumbar arch. Once, while working under Feldenkrais's supervision, I was attempting to release a muscle spasm in an elderly woman's pelvic muscles. He came over to me, put his hands on mine, and I felt his hands and my hands merge with the woman until the three of us were moving as one "ensemble." As her spasm released and her pelvis began to softly move, Feldenkrais rhythmically intoned, "Don't contradict her nervous system. It is very intelligent. It has been making life feasible for this woman for 76 years. Help it to do its job" (personal communication, April, 1979). For Feldenkrais, muscular tensions are intelligent, useful behaviors that serve some purpose to the person.

Utilization means cooperating with these unconscious patterns and adjusting to the individual so that "we can all do our own learning in our own way" (Zeig, 1980, p. 224). Thus it may be helpful to lengthen further the side of the body which is longer, or twist the student in the habitual direction of musculoskeletal torque; this establishes rapport with, and enables reorganization of those individual-specific patterns which are often called "symptomatic." Paradoxically, when a person is pushed sufficiently in his or her *own* extreme, it begins to feel right for the person to spontaneously correct his or her posture. For example, if a man habitually carries his head to the right, by gently increasing his natural "bent," his own "biofeedback" will redirect him toward more symmetrical functioning. However, if the man were corrected directly, he would perceive it in his self-image as an unnatural movement to the left and his unconscious bias might undermine the correction. In another instance, Feldenkrais taught a student to open an eye which could not open properly by exaggerating the eye's closure, thus rendering the movement of opening, however slight, more perceptible. Even as a young man, Feldenkrais was predisposed to this general orientation. For example, he once tutored the son of a high-school principal who had a mathematical learning block and a love for football. To the irritation of the boy's father, Feldenkrais only played football with him until one day the boy insisted, on his own, that they do some math homework together. In this case, utilization of the boy's rebellious feelings toward his father and his positive feeling for sports were the means to carry him beyond his learning block (Note 3).

Indirect and Paradoxical Techniques

Erickson was well-known for employing indirect and often paradoxical techniques in hypnosis and psychotherapy. As in some of the examples already discussed, Feldenkrais, too, avoids direct and obvious approaches and believes that an indirect solution is often the most effective and elegant one.

For example, in Functional Integration Feldenkrais often works only with the "good" side and not the injured or restricted side of the body. A person with an injured leg depends heavily upon the "good" leg which, therefore, often becomes strained from doing the work of two legs. Working on the "good" leg helps the person to move easier and gives the "bad" leg a chance to rest and heal. In addition, passively lengthening and shortening the "good" leg effects an isomorphic, reciprocal movement on the opposite side of the pelvis and spine; thus, the "bad" leg undergoes the same movement but *indirectly*. Indirect movements can bypass protective reactions which may be considerable in cases of pain and trauma and help teach the person how to move in a healthful manner.

Feldenkrais's "artificial floor" technique illustrates how he can elicit the learning of whole functions through partial cues conveyed through any part or parts of the body (Feldenkrais, 1981a, pp. 139-142). With a pupil lying supine on the work table, Feldenkrais applies subtle pressures to the sole of the foot with a flat board or book in order to "simulate walking on even ground" through proprioceptive cues. While on the table, the person probably has no conscious inkling of what is being learned; he or she is simply absorbed in pleasant kinesthetic sensations. However, upon getting up and walking, the pupil will appreciate that his or her nervous system has undergone a substantial reorganization in its "image" of walking. In this manner Feldenkrais teaches "sensory-motor excellence" to normal individuals and to individuals with problems such as cerebral palsy.

Feldenkrais's indirect techniques are made possible by what neurophysiologist Karl Pribram (1971) has called the "hologramic" nature of the nervous system whereby each part expresses an image of the whole. This idea also helps explain Erickson's ability to "mind read" from minimal cues. Feldenkrais's and Erickson's techniques represent a refinement of what we all observe in nonverbal communication: the signaling of intentions through partial and initiatory actions. We follow a person's attention through eye movements and posture; the readiness to speak—or even its content—is conveyed by changes in a person's mouth or breathing; and so forth. By extension we can conceive how, by delicately moving a cellist's scapula, one could not only "relax" the musician, but much more precisely, convey the means to bow the instrument in a new way. Every motor skill is inscribed in a global pattern of organization in the person's body and nervous system. Erickson pointed out, for example, that writing is an action of the entire body (Zeig, 1980, p. 319). Accordingly, our wealth of lifelong motoric learning has created a kinesthetic matrix of associations as individualized as "our own linguistic patterns, our own personal understandings" (Zeig, 1980, p. 78). The efficacy of these indirect learning techniques is therefore dependent on a Feldenkrais practitioner's ability to "speak" with the hands in a way that the individual student kinesthetically understands.

Pattern Interruptions

"Differentiated" and "nonhabitual" movements form a group of Feldenkrais techniques which can be understood as analogous to Erickson's pattern interruptions. Just as Erickson often prescribed out of the ordinary behaviors and even engineered situations in order to shake people out of their patterns, Feldenkrais often creates sufficiently novel and unfamiliar learning situations to do the same. "Differentiated" movements may refer to moving the eyes, head, shoulders, and pelvis in separate directions; "nonhabitual" movements may consist in simply reversing one's habitual way of interlacing the fingers or being asked to perform unfamiliar and familiar movements in novel positions. The situation of learning something radically new produces a major shift in the brain and often induces a trancelike state reminiscent of Erickson's "confusion technique." Feldenkrais's differentiated and nonhabitual movements are modeled on the organic, experimental learning of children.

Normal motor development follows a rhythmical course of increasing differentiation and synergistic integration. For example, discrete movements of the extremities are differentiated from global actions involving the entire trunk; discrete finger movements are differentiated from undifferentiated hand movements such as grasping, with each succeeding differentiation supported by integrated activity of the whole body. In cases of abnormal development such as cerebral palsy, Feldenkrais may initially go with, and pace a person's spastic, undifferentiated patterns. Gradually he induces the differentiated functioning that displays the action of "higher" neurological inhibition. In cases of stroke or even stress-related muscular tension, people regress to less differentiated functional states; and differentiation must be reacquired. Again, Feldenkrais's approach is to "pace and lead," shifting between undifferentiated and increasingly differentiated patterns.

Nonhabitual and highly differentiated movements displace a person from his or her customary mind and body "set." The person who, for example, has back trouble or is depressed is transported to a novel situation where he or she has not already learned how to have this problem (Baniel, personal communication, July, 1983). The new way of acting is therefore not tainted with recollections of inability and discomfort. When learning, we disengage from customary patterns and awaken to discover ourselves capable of doing things formerly believed impossible.

Hypnotic Communication

Functional Integration as described by Feldenkrais certainly evokes the image of trance experience:

> Functional Integration turns to the oldest elements of our sensory system—touch, the feelings of pull and pressure, the warmth of the hand, its caressing stroke. The person becomes absorbed in sensing the diminishing muscular tonus, the deepening and the regularity of breathing, abdominal ease, and improved circulation in the expanding skin. The person senses his most primitive, consciously forgotten patterns and recalls the well-being of a growing young child. (1981a, p. 121)

Similarly, the Awareness through Movement extract at the beginning of the chapter calls to mind many Ericksonian patterns of hypnotic communication, including embedded and indirect suggestions. And, the effect of the lesson is certainly "hypnotic."

Yet, interestingly, Feldenkrais does not refer to "hypnosis" or "trance" either in practice or theory. His language is situated in the context of human movement learning, and it is sensory-based. "States of consciousness" are invoked primarily insofar as they are embodied in sensible qualities of activity. In actual practice this is not as restricting as it may sound since movement is an expression of the self.

Feldenkrais's parallel "hypnotic" approaches may be summarized as follows: (a) the induction of a positive, subjective state which is conducive to learning, including feelings of ease, comfort, reduced muscular tonus; (b) the sensitivity to and validation of self-experience; (c) the training of somatopsychic skills including imagery, memory, attention, physiological and neuromuscular control; (d) the utilization of life-experiential and species-experiential knowledge; (e) indirect approaches; (f) pattern interrupting techniques; and (g) emphasis upon mutual respect, codependent interaction and communication where practitioner and student reciprocally learn from each other.

An Illustration

Once Feldenkrais worked with a middle-aged man who had been in a wheelchair for 16 years after an automobile accident and subsequent spinal operation. His legs were spastic and he sat quite stooped with a depressed look on his face. Feldenkrais began by seemingly attempting to straighten the back directly, gently pushing with his hands into the middle of the kyphotic curve. As long as Feldenkrais supported him, the man sat erectly; but as soon as he took his hands away, he slouched into his original position. Clearly, the man's nervous system would reject any willful attempt, on his own part or anyone else's, to straighten his back.

Then Feldenkrais asked him to stick out his tongue and do the movement animals do to lap water (which involves a wavelike movement of thrusting the head forward). He was asked to repeat the movement slowly, reducing his effort, and making each movement more comfortable than the last. After resting, he was asked to repeat the movement with his face turned to the right, then to the left, and finally while moving his head slowly from one side to the other. As his movements gradually involved more of his spine and entire self, minute by minute he sat more erectly in his chair; and after about 15 minutes, he sat with his head held high and an alert, pleasant look on his face. Feldenkrais then pointed out that his legs were relaxed and no longer spastic. Next, Feldenkrais had the man lie down on the table on his back; and in the process his legs became spastic once again. Feldenkrais asked the man to think of what he had been doing with his tongue. As the man imagined the movement of lapping water, his legs again relaxed. After working nonverbally with the man for about 15 minutes, Feldenkrais had him move back to his wheelchair. But as he started the effort of lifting himself, his legs again became spastic. After Feldenkrais reminded him of the tongue movement, he was then able to manage himself much more easily without his legs becoming stiff.

In order to understand the movement of lapping water, experience the movement yourself and observe what your head and neck do. You will discover that if you perform the movement slowly, gently, and repeatedly, your entire body will become involved in the act. Notice that although the active, intentional, and conscious movement is to thrust the head forward as the tongue reaches for "water," the relatively passive, unintentional, and unconscious phase requires straightening the cervical arch and taking the head into its most erect position. Thus, in light of what has been said, we can see that this movement is an indirect technique of learning improved posture and spinal organization; a utilization of the man's forward stoop in a pleasant-feeling movement; a pattern interruption of his usual manner of seeing himself and holding himself; a "naturalistic trance induction" involving repetitious movements and sensory-based suggestions for increasing ease, comfort, and satisfaction; and a utilization of latent phylogenetic and ontogenetic neuromotor patterns involving movements of the mouth and jaw in organic relation to the first cervical vertebra, the tongue, swallowing, breathing, and locomotion. Finally, we can see how the new movement quality can be used as a kinesthetic reminder—and a form of "posthypnotic suggestion"—for the possibility of increased ease and lightness of movement.

THE ARTISTRY OF FELDENKRAIS AND ERICKSON

Feldenkrais and Erickson are artists as well as therapists and teachers. As artist-scientists, they continually go beyond themselves and never abandon an experimental attitude. With their students they consistently attempt to provoke creativity, individuality, and originality of thinking. For example, when Erickson said that the practice of psychotherapy should be "charming and interesting," he was going beyond a solely practical, therapeutic frame of reference. He was challenging himself as an artist to be inventive as well as effective. Analogously, Feldenkrais directly compared his lessons to "procedures . . . in learning to paint, to play an instrument, or solve a mathematical problem. . . . Pianists of genius when practicing . . . always . . . discover an alternative to the habitual" (1981, p. 95). Thus, over the years Feldenkrais developed literally thousands of different Awareness through Movement and Functional Integration lessons, and Erickson displayed a similar virtuosity of styles and techniques.

A Teaching Seminar demonstrates how Erickson was able to find unexpected ways to humor and stimulate his students to "think in all directions" (Zeig, 1980, p. 128); and Feldenkrais, like Erickson, tells stories to teach flexible thinking as well as moving. He relates that he once was seated opposite a man on a train who was reading from a book held upside down. After a few moments of bewilderment, wondering if the man were crazy, joking, or only pretending to be literate, Feldenkrais asked him why his book was upside down. "Upside down?" the man replied. "How can a book be upside down?" The man had gone to a school in a small Yemenite village where there was only one book to a class. The children sat each day in a small circle reading their book from "all directions" (personal communication, March 1979).

REFERENCE NOTES

1. For information concerning Feldenkrais's work and trained practitioners, contact the Feldenkrais Guild Office, P.O. Box 11145, San Francisco, California 94101.
2. Feldenkrais, M. Professional Training Program, June, 1975.
3. Feldenkrais, M. Unpublished autobiography, undated.

REFERENCES

Bandler, R., & Grinder, J. (1975). *Patterns of the hypnotic techniques of Milton H. Erickson, M.D.* (Vol. 1). Cupertino, CA: Meta Publications.

Blechschmidt, E. (1977). *The beginnings of human life.* New York: Springer-Verlag.

Erickson, M., & Rossi, E. (1979). *Hypnotherapy.* New York: Irvington.

Feldenkrais, M. (1949). *Body and mature behavior.* New York: International Universities Press.

Feldenkrais, M. (1967). *The case of Nora.* New York: Harper & Row. (Out of print, but available from the Feldenkrais Guild Office.)

Feldenkrais, M. (1972). *Awareness through movement.* New York: Harper & Row.

Feldenkrais, M. (1981a). *The elusive obvious.* Cupertino, CA: Meta Publications.

Feldenkrais, M. (1981b, May). San Francisco "Quest" Workshop. Washington, DC: ATM Recordings.

Haley, J. (1967). *Advanced techniques of hypnosis and therapy.* New York: Grune & Stratton.

Pribram, K. (1971). *Languages of the brain.* Englewood Cliffs, NJ: Prentice-Hall.

Zeig, J. K. (Ed.). (1980). *A teaching seminar with Milton H. Erickson, M.D.* New York: Brunner/Mazel.

Zeig, J. K. (1982). *Ericksonian approaches to hypnosis and psychotherapy.* New York: Brunner/Mazel.

PART VIII

Conceptual Issues

Two of the three chapters presented in this section concern neurophysiology; one deals with the idea of subliminal perception and the other addresses hemisphere lateralization. The third chapter presents suggestions for the ethical practice of Ericksonian hypnotherapy.

Jeffrey B. Feldman, Ph.D., earned his clinical psychology degree at Case Western Reserve University. He is founding vice-president of the New York Society for Ericksonian Psychotherapy and Hypnosis.

Feldman conducts a private practice in New York City and works as a staff psychologist in a pain management center in Brooklyn. He is an adjunct associate professor in psychology at the Department of Continuing Education of the Long Island University. Because of the original ideas presented in his chapter, Feldman was co-recipient (along with Lawrence Gindhart) of the Award for Most Scholarly Accepted Paper at the 1983 Erickson Congress.

Comparisons between Erickson's notion of unconscious processing and the scientific concept of subliminal perception are presented. It is important to note that information processed consciously can lead to a different response than information that is processed subliminally (unconsciously).

Lynn D. Johnson, Ph.D., earned his degree in counseling psychology in the Department of Educational Psychology at the University of Utah. He conducts a private practice in psychology in Salt Lake City, is an instructor in the Department of Educational Psychology at the University of Utah, and has served as president of the Utah Society of Clinical Hypnosis.

Johnson describes hemisphere specialization and reviews the theory that hypnosis involves activation of the right hemisphere. Johnson points to the limitations of this concept for the clinician, and stresses the importance of cooperative interaction between the right and left hemispheres.

Due to a speaker cancellation, Jeffrey K. Zeig, Ph.D., gave a second presentation on the topic of ethical dilemmas facing practitioners of Ericksonian hypnotherapy. Discussion centers on two issues, namely, informed consent and qualifications for receiving training in hypnosis.

To illustrate problems with informed consent as defined in the ethical guidelines of the American Psychological Association, one of Milton Erickson's famous cases is discussed from the point of view of ethics. A previously unpublished letter by Erickson about the ethics of this particular case is also presented.

Training standards are in a state of flux in professional hypnosis organizations. The Erickson Foundation's position on training standards is presented and the underlying philosophy is described.

It is interesting to note that just before the volume went to press, the American Society of Clinical Hypnosis initiated the process of altering their ethical guidelines to allow training of previously disqualified professionals, including licensed marriage, family and child counselors, nurse anesthetists and podiatrists.

Chapter 26

Subliminal Perception and Information Processing Theory: Empirical and Conceptual Validation of Erickson's Notion of the Unconscious

Jeffrey B. Feldman

Two central and revolutionary principles in Milton Erickson's therapeutic legacy involve his conceptualization of trance and the unconscious. Erickson viewed trance as an active process of unconscious learning. Through hypnosis, he helped patients utilize their own unique life experience and associations to create and restructure themselves from within, bypassing the mediation of consciously directed thinking (Erickson, Rossi, & Rossi, 1976, p. 298). Thus, where other therapists worked to construct interpretations that would create insight in their patients, Erickson usually avoided interpretation, pioneering hypnotic techniques for preventing conscious interference of his interventions. Such work was based on a positive view of the unconscious.

Rather than distrusting the hostile, aggressive, or sexual impulses of the unconscious, Erickson encouraged individuals to trust the unconscious as a positive force that contained more wisdom than the conscious mind (Haley, 1982, p. 20). Erickson's notion of the unconscious is compatible with what the cognitive psychologist George Miller referred to when he said, "Most of what the mind does best it does unconsciously, whether the behavior product is talking, walking or juggling" (quoted by Ferrell, 1982). In other words, the Ericksonian unconscious encompasses functions of the brain outside of an individual's awareness and includes the vast array of information processing, storage and retrieval processes, learned neuromuscular responses, and physiological self-regulatory mechanisms.

Nevertheless, one might justifiably question the utility of this notion of the unconscious as well as the validity of the principle that insight not only is unnecessary for change but may indeed prevent it. Beyond Erickson's case reports, what, if any, empirical validation exists for the processing of information without conscious awareness leading to subsequent behavioral change? Further, how is the Ericksonian view compatible with existing knowledge and models of psychological functioning?

Fortuitously, the rich experimental literature in the area of subliminal perception provides a fascinating parallel to Erickson's clinical work in hypnosis. This literature provides evidence that under certain circumstances information can be processed without conscious awareness, and that responses contingent on subliminal stimulation can be qualitatively different from those elicited by the same stimulus when presented above the awareness threshold. In other words, *the same stimulus can have different effects if the individual is consciously aware of it or not.*

It is the primary purpose of this chapter to explore parallels between subliminal perception and hypnosis and to examine how they can be understood within the information processing models of cognitive psychology. Empirical and conceptual validation of Erickson's notions of trance and the unconscious are delineated, and, reciprocally, Erickson's work in hypnosis and the literature in subliminal perception are used to expand existing psychological models of information processing.

SUBLIMINAL PERCEPTION

Subliminal perception generally refers to the perception and processing of information the individual is not consciously aware of because the presentation of the stimulus is either too brief or too low in intensity (i.e., below an awareness limen). Contemporary investigation of subliminal perception owes an intellectual debt to Norman F. Dixon for his two books (1971, 1981) that comprehensively review the literature devoted to this phenomenon, its implications, and the controversy surrounding it. In an effort to clarify the concept, Dixon (1971) specified three criteria which, if satisfied in a given situation, justify the phenomenon's inclusion as an example of subliminal perception:

> 1) The eliciting of contingent responses by stimulation below the absolute awareness threshold, where this threshold is itself defined

as the lowest level of stimulus energy at which the subject *ever* reports hearing (or seeing) anything of the stimulus. 2) The retrospective reporting by the subject that he neither saw nor heard anything of the stimulus. 3) The occurrence of contingent responses, without reported awareness of the stimulus, that differ qualitatively from those elicited by the same stimulus when presented *above* the awareness threshold. (p. 18).

These criteria can be clarified and the development and refinement of the subliminal perception paradigm can be traced by considering a few studies. The first criterion was established in response to the development of signal detection theory (Green & Swets, 1966) and its criticism of the classical psychophysical measure of the limen (awareness threshold). Swets (1964) justifiably criticized early studies in subliminal perception which utilized as evidence for the phenomenon the observation that subjects who initially report seeing no stimulus could identify the stimulus with greater than chance accuracy in a forced-choice situation. He pointed out that in the forced-choice situation, individuals simply have a lower response threshold than in the yes/no procedure because of less stringent response criteria. Signal detection theory pointed out the necessity for viewing individuals as having a range of limens depending on conditions that affect their response criteria. It is for this reason that Dixon specified that stimulation be below an "absolute awareness threshold," meaning that it is below the lowest point in the range of possible limens for the individual.

The second criterion mentioned by Dixon (the individual reports neither seeing nor hearing the stimulus) is implicit in what traditionally has been termed subliminal perception and is neither as interesting nor as important to this discussion as the third criterion. It is the last criterion—responses contingent on subliminal stimulation are qualitatively different from those elicited by the same stimulus when presented above the awareness threshold—that makes this a fascinating area of inquiry and provides a link to Erickson's hypnotic work.

The importance of the third criterion for establishing the phenomenon of subliminal perception can be illustrated by experiments which in retrospect did not meet the test. One experiment initially conducted in 1900 by Dunlap (Dixon, 1971, pp. 38–44) examined whether the subliminal presentation of arrows upon the supraliminal horizontal lines of the Muller-Lyer figure ( ) would result in the discrepant judgment of line length predicted by the illusion. Dunlap postulated that it would, and although problems in replication and controversy concerning this effect ensued, the weight of evidence according to Dixon appears to be on Dunlap's side. A somewhat similar experimental paradigm was utilized by Murch (1969, 1973).

In Murch's experiments (see Figure 1), during supraliminal viewing of the incomplete letters in the first field, subjects were given subliminal presentations of their correct completion in the second field. They then were required to select a pair of letters from the third supraliminal display. Murch found that subjects selected those letter pairs for which they had received subliminal cues. The problem with the Dunlap and Murch studies is that they did not provide evidence (according to criterion 3) to indicate a qualitatively different effect due to subliminal stimulation from the effect one would expect from supraliminal stimulation. This leaves the results of such experiments open to explanations other than one involving subliminal perception. For example, Murch felt that his results could be explained parsimoniously in terms of retinal summation. Similarly, one side in a long-standing dispute (Kleespies & Wiener, 1972; Wiener & Kleespies, 1968) argued that results in a number of supposedly subliminal perception experiments (Silverman, 1968; Silverman & Spiro, 1967) could be explained best in terms of partial cues available. In other words, Wiener and Kleespies argued that some partial information of stimulus characteristics of the display were received by subjects and caused the effects attributed to subliminal perception. While it is difficult to conceive how a partial cues explanation would explain the results of a study by Somekh and Wilding (1973) in which subliminal presentations of words affected judgments of facial expressions of a neutral face, it is not the most damaging evidence against the partial cues hypothesis. The two most convincing arguments against such an explanation and for a qualitatively different parallel processing of information below an awareness threshold are studies which suggest that subliminal stimulation is less effective as it ap-

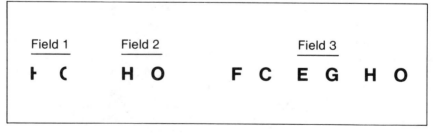

Figure 1. Murch's experimental procedure. (From Murch, 1969. Reprinted with permission from *Perception and Psychophysics.*)

proaches the individual's perceptual threshold (Dixon, 1971, p. 240; Silverman, 1966) and studies best exemplified by Silverman and his associates' work (summarized in Silverman, 1976; Silverman et al., 1976) which demonstrate a qualitative difference between individuals' response to a stimulus when it is subliminal as opposed to supraliminal.

Since the work of Silverman and his associates originated in efforts to utilize an empirical methodology to verify psychoanalytic postulates, I will summarize the psychodynamically oriented line of research in subliminal perception from which it stems. This research originated in the finding of Poetzl in 1917 that a subliminal stimulus received during normal waking consciousness can affect subsequent dream experience (Dixon, 1971, pp. 103–126; Fisher & Paul, 1959). This phenomenon was investigated further by Shevrin (1973) and his associates in a series of studies which utilized the psychoanalytic distinction between primary and secondary process thinking. In the Shevrin experimental paradigm a picture of a pen with its point touching a knee was presented subliminally to night nursing students prior to sleep. Following awakening from REM sleep (dreaming) associations were more "penny"-related (primary process clang associations), while awakening from non-REM (nondreaming) sleep yielded "pen" and/or "knee" associations (secondary process conceptual associations). Previous research indicated that supraliminal presentation yielded only secondary-process associates, and a lesser total number of associates. This phenomenon was termed by Spence and Holland (1962) the "restricting effects of awareness." The implication of this work is that the same material subliminally received is processed in different ways at different times by the same individual at different stages of consciousness.

Also substantiating the fact that meaning can be processed without conscious awareness, Shevrin and Fritzler (1968) found that the primary wave amplitude of a visual-evoked response was significantly greater for meaningful than for meaningless subliminal stimuli flashed for 0.001 sec (Shevrin, 1975).

Despite the importance of this work, the most impressive clinically oriented work utilizing subliminal perception was conducted by Silverman and his associates. This extensive body of work not only clearly meets all three criteria posited by Dixon, including the differential effect of subliminal and supraliminal presentations, but also established the existence of differential effects for discrete stimuli on dissimilar individual types. In a series of 16 studies (summarized in Silverman et al., 1976), a subliminal presentation (4 msec) of a stimulus designed to elicit conflictual aggressive wishes ("Destroy Mother") increased "primary process ego pathology" in schizophrenics relative to a control neutral stimulus.

Other experiments along psychoanalytic lines indicated that stimuli designed to increase aggressive wishes led to an intensification of depressive feelings in three groups of depressed individuals; stimuli designed to increase conflict over "incestuous wishes" led to an increase in homosexual feelings and a decrease in heterosexual feelings in two groups of homosexuals; and stimuli designed to increase conflict over "anal wishes" led to an increase in stuttering in two groups of stutterers. In each case, the presentation of the stimuli supraliminally had no effect, and neither did an irrelevant wish-related stimulus (e.g., the stimulus used effectively subliminally on homosexuals had no effect on stutterers). Furthermore, Silverman and his associates have been able to reverse the process and utilize subliminal stimulation for therapeutic goals. Through the subliminal presentation of the message "Mommy and I are one" (intended to activate the fantasy of symbiotic gratification) Silverman and his associates were able to reduce primary process ego pathology in schizophrenics (1976), decrease ratings of anxiety and overt phobic behavior in a group of 20 female insect phobics (Silverman, Frank, & Dachinger, 1974), and help obese women lose weight (Silverman, Martin, Ungaro, & Mendelsohn, 1978). If one is skeptical of dependent measures such as Silverman's Rorschach indices of "primary process ego pathology" and/or the therapeutic rationale of his "Mommy and I are one" message, a subsequent study is more straightforward. In this study Silverman, Ross, Adler, and Lustig (1978) subliminally presented subjects either the oedipal conflict message "beating father is bad" or the message "beating father is good," and they found significantly higher scores in a subsequent dart throwing contest (scored as in archery according to proximity to the center) for the latter group. Once again, supraliminal presentations of the same message had no effect. It is difficult to conceptualize a more objective measure, and in these latter studies experimenters were blind as to the subliminal stimulation condition of the subjects. Silverman's work clearly indicates that information presented at a speed of 4 msec—too brief a presentation to reach conscious awareness—can have a contingent effect on behavior and that the effect is lost if the individual becomes aware of it.

PARALLELS BETWEEN ERICKSONIAN HYPNOSIS AND SUBLIMINAL PERCEPTION

I next delineate some of the parallels between Ericksonian hypnotherapy and the findings in subliminal perception just discussed. Erickson utilized hypnosis to bypass the learned limitations and rigid sets of conscious awareness. Similarly, subliminal stimulation bypasses consciousness with material presented too briefly or faintly to reach an awareness threshold. Erickson's view that the unconscious can work autonomously and generate behavioral change without conscious awareness is supported by Silverman's work on subliminal psychodynamic activation. Moreover, the painstaking work Erickson did utilizing such techniques as posthypnotic amnesia to prevent conscious interference with hypnotic suggestions can be supported by the findings that if an individual becomes aware of a subliminal message it loses the effect it would have had if it had remained subliminal. Erickson believed that when freed from the common sets, biases and inhibitions of consciousness, an individual can utilize a wider range of potentialities and learnings (Erickson, Rossi, & Rossi, 1976, p. 298). The findings in subliminal perception which indicate the restricting effects of awareness substantiate this view. For instance, the research in subliminal perception indicates that a verbal stimulus of which an individual is unaware elicits a far wider range of associations than does a stimulus of which the individual is consciously aware (Dixon, 1981, p. 24). A further parallel can be seen between the Poetzl effect, in which stimulus material the subject is unaware of emerges in a subsequent dream, and the therapeutic work of Erickson and Sacerdote utilizing hypnotically induced dreams (Sacerdote, 1982). The similarities between a posthypnotic suggestion and a subliminal stimulus were not lost on Dixon, who summarized them as follows: "Both evade scrutiny by normal waking consciousness. Both may be retained in unconscious secondary memory, and both may influence subsequent behavior without the subject being aware of what is determining his responses" (Dixon, 1981, p. 112).

Before uncritically embracing the findings of the subliminal perception paradigm, the reader should be cautioned that this is a controversial area within psychology, in which experiments have not often been replicated. In attempting to explain the consistent positive findings which "some experiments, some academic departments and even some countries" invariably find for the subliminal perception phenomenon, while others "with equal monotony" do not, Dixon utilized two explanatory concepts (Dixon, 1971, p. 242). The first is an experimenter effect in which the belief system of the experimenter is in some way communicated to the subject. Dixon also emphasized the repeated experimental finding that subliminal perception effects are facilitated by the subject being in a passive, relaxed, nonselectively attentive state (Dixon, 1981, pp. 34, 94, 197). Dixon argued that it is likely that either this relaxed state or an opposing state may be inculcated unintentionally by experimenters with divergent belief systems.

Whether or not Dixon is correct in these explanations, even clearer parallels between hypnotic therapy and the experimental work in subliminal perception can be surmised. Translated into the jargon of hypnosis, Dixon's review of the research states that subliminal perception effects are enhanced by the subject being in at least a light state of trance. Furthermore, that consciously and unconsciously communicated expectations are important in trance induction and utilization is a clinically well-known effect. The dependence of hypnotic suggestion and subliminal perception on similar factors points to a similar underlying process in human functioning. To examine this process and to help demystify both hypnosis and subliminal perception it is necessary to examine established models of human information processing.

INFORMATION PROCESSING THEORY

Information processing theory developed as a means by which cognitive psychologists organize existing knowledge concerning how people perceive, process, store, and retrieve information. A model typical of such efforts to schematize information processing is illustrated in Figure 2 (Haber & Hershenson, 1973). This model illustrates how stimulation that impinges both on eyes and on ears first reaches a stage of brief storage (iconic for visual; echoic for auditory) before becoming a conscious image. This image then is processed through a stage of short-term memory where, based on its relevance to the individual, it is thought to be either rehearsed and consolidated into long-term memory or forgotten. Also, it is at this stage that the incoming information is thought to be analyzed, utilizing prior learned information stored in long-term memory, to decide upon an appropriate response to the incoming stimulation. The dashed arrows in Haber and Hershenson's model illustrate how long-term memory helps to organize the percept, based upon prior experience, into meaningful units to be processed efficiently (e.g., organizing a trunk, branches, and green leaves into the percept "tree"). Of greater interest to this discussion are the arrows in the model from iconic and echoic storage to short-term memory, indicating a possible pathway for information reaching memory and being processed without first becoming a conscious image. A problem with this model from a purely information processing perspective is its failure to explain how the wide range of channel capacity at the peripheral receptor sites is narrowed down to the relatively limited channel capacity of short-term memory: 7 ± 2 (Miller, 1956). In other words, what is the

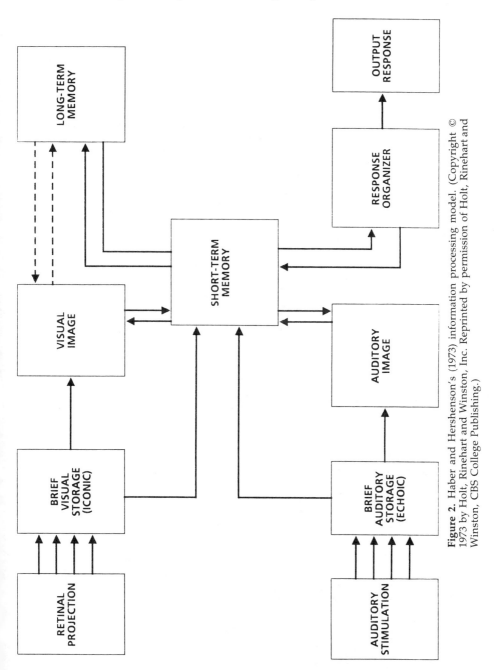

Figure 2. Haber and Hershenson's (1973) information processing model. (Copyright © 1973 by Holt, Rinehart and Winston, Inc. Reprinted by permission of Holt, Rinehart and Winston, CBS College Publishing.)

process by which an individual selects a stimulus for attention from the vast array of possibilities?

Figure 3 is a model proposed by Erdelyi (1974) that might answer this question. While Erdelyi equates short-term storage (memory) with conscious awareness and has a few other steps delineated in this information processing flow diagram, what is most relevant to this discussion are his proposed cognitive control processes. These hypothesized cognitive control processes (stemming from long-term memory or storage) point to multiple stages of possible selectivity in the information processing continuum.

Erdelyi's model was designed to explain how information processing theory could account for the phenomenon of perceptual defense and vigilance in which emotionally laden stimuli have different recognition thresholds from nonemotional stimuli. One of the long-standing criticisms of the perceptual defense paradigm is that it is a logical paradox. It is argued that in order to perceptually defend against some information, one would first have to perceive it. The work in subliminal perception erases this objection by indicating that material can be processed meaningfully without awareness.

Similarly, and more to the heart of the issue, one must provide some mechanism of processing information before it reaches awareness to account for the process by which an organism selects a stimulus for attention and conscious perception. This notion of discrimination without awareness or preconscious processing is viewed by Dixon (1981) as being essential to a notion of selective attention. Hilgard (1977) stated, "Selectivity is the mark of attentive focusing" (p. 221) and, "It is important for a modern form of dissociation theory to explain the nature of the executive control and the monitoring systems that permit information processing and behavior management to proceed without conscious representation" (p. 216). Dixon (1981) further argued that it is highly adaptive for an individual to have a high-capacity system for scanning incoming information while having an interrelated but separate system which allows for more focused conscious analysis of selected material.

In returning to Erdelyi's model to reevaluate the cognitive control processes that provide possible mechanisms for selectivity (both Erdelyi and Dixon view iconic storage as the most likely site for such a mechanism), it is apparent that his model is incomplete. The arrows that extend down from long-term memory indicating higher order storage influencing what reaches conscious awareness should point in *both* directions. For long-term storage or central ("executive") control processes

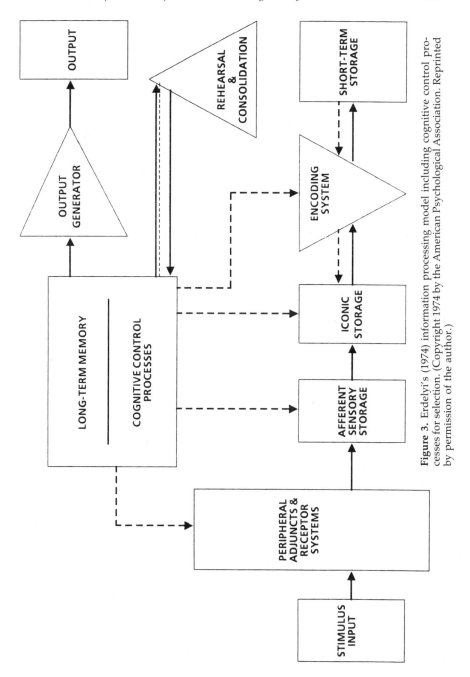

Figure 3. Erdelyi's (1974) information processing model including cognitive control processes for selection. (Copyright 1974 by the American Psychological Association. Reprinted by permission of the author.)

to exert any influence upon what becomes consciously perceived, information must reach it and be analyzed at some level. In other words, in the normal perceptual process, information must be preconsciously processed before it reaches conscious awareness; otherwise there can be no basis for selectivity. Further, though one purpose of this process is to determine what is to reach the limited capacity of conscious awareness, a great deal more information must be processed by the nervous system than reaches an individual's conscious awareness. Evidently in normal states of functioning there is a parallel processing of information with some of the products of preconscious processing reaching awareness, while the rest are processed on some nonconscious level.

The further implication of the evidence that material can enter long-term storage directly, without being consciously processed through short-term storage, is that there is a lot more to memory than traditionally has been thought. In addition to what typically is considered as residing in long-term memory—information that has reached conscious awareness, been processed through short-term memory, consolidated into long-term memory, and is retrievable through what colloquially is termed "memory"—one must postulate a parallel process (or processes). In such a process, material that bypasses awareness also reaches some kind of storage which probably is not governed by the rules of conscious processing. The results of such processing may affect subsequent behavior in a manner qualitatively different from consciously perceived material. One might view material stored through both processes, which is not readily accessible, as comprising the "unconscious" mind.

Furthermore, the parallel processing normally occurring in all perception provides an explanation for the phenomena of processing without awareness characteristic of both subliminal perception and certain hypnotic states. In the subliminal perception paradigm, information evidently is processed preconsciously, but is not able to reach conscious awareness either because it is too low in intensity or too brief in duration to be processed beyond the level of iconic storage. It nevertheless must reach some form of central storage prior to affecting behavior. Similarly, one can view hypnosis as a state of consciousness in which there is minimization of the focally attentive processes by which information enters short-term storage and is consciously evaluated, consolidated, and stored. In minimizing or disrupting this process, normally occurring preconscious processing can be freed from its role of subserving conscious awareness, thus allowing for independent processing within long-term storage (i.e., on an unconscious level) without conscious interference. This can be clarified by the simplified information processing diagram found in Figure 4.

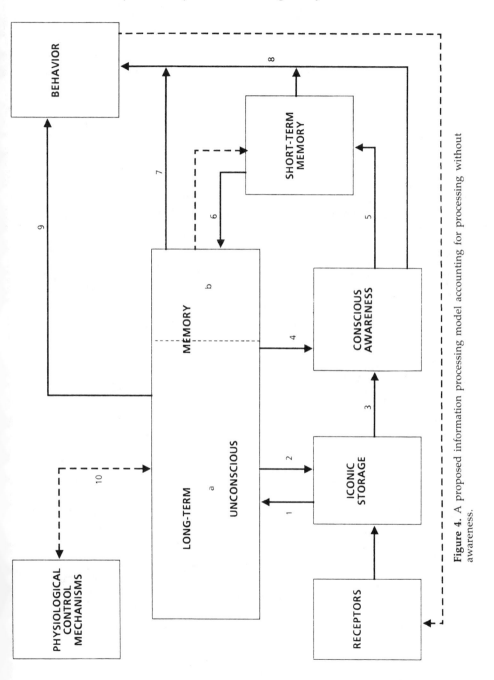

Figure 4. A proposed information processing model accounting for processing without awareness.

Trance, then, can be viewed as an organismic state in which the normally occurring processes subserving conscious awareness or short-term memory (channel 3) are diminished. This allows a utilization of the normally occurring channel (1) subserving preconscious processing to be utilized maximally for communication to long-term storage (unconscious) without conscious interference. Material then can be processed and reorganization can occur within long-term memory (Erickson's "unconscious search") without having to subserve conscious awareness (channel 2). Furthermore, through limiting the ordinary information processing channel underlying conscious awareness (3), retrieval of long-forgotten memories or unconsciously generated imagery or dreams characteristic of trance can be facilitated (channel 4). Finally, by bypassing conscious awareness (STM) behavioral change can be generated (9) without the limitations of habitual frames of reference.

This expanded model has numerous advantages. It explains the paradox of trance as a naturalistic state within the realm of normally occurring cognitive processes, yet being a qualitatively different state of consciousness than focally attentive awareness. An explanation is provided for the phenomenon of processing without awareness that is characteristic of subliminal perception and deeper levels of trance. This model also is consistent with available evidence that relaxation facilitates both subliminal perception and hypnotic suggestion, and that awareness has a restricting effect on subliminal or hypnotic messages.

This model's acceptance of the human capacity for parallel processing of information on multiple levels simultaneously is consistent with the phenomenon of the "hidden observer" described by Hilgard (1977). Hilgard found certain subjects who while deeply in trance verbally report experiencing no pain even though samples of their automatic handwriting describe a painful experience.

It is important to be aware that in this model for purposes of simplification I have delineated only one source of information processed within the nervous system—the visual. As stated by Thompson, "The organization of the brain implies parallel processing; there are many different routes for information to pass from input to output structures in the brain" (as quoted by Hilgard, 1977, p. 224). The information processing model of Haber and Hershenson was cited in part to illustrate the processing of both auditory and visual stimulation. However, there are countless sources of stimulation that the brain handles. These include the remaining primary senses, cognitively generated thought, and information generated from within the body. An interesting study by

Spence and his associates indicated that information generated within the body and centrally processed without awareness had an effect upon individuals' choice of words. In an interview prior to receiving biopsy results, women who eventually had a malignant diagnosis used the words "death" and "cancer" more frequently than those for whom the diagnosis was benign. While the word "death" was most often used in a metaphorical sense, (e.g., "I was tickled to death" and "He'll be the death of me") it provides fascinating evidence that there are pathways of communication below the awareness level from within the body to the brain (Dixon, 1981, pp. 76–78; Spence et al., 1978). Might not hypnotic suggestion exert some of its effects upon physiological processes by utilizing such pathways in the reverse direction (Figure 4, channel 10)? If physiological processes are governing lexical choice without awareness, can words similarly affect physiological processes?

This expanded model of information processing provides conceptual validation of Erickson's notion of the unconscious, the nature of trance, and even ways to facilitate it. The notion of the parallel processing of information provides an understanding of how Erickson spoke to the unconscious mind through the interspersal technique, stories, and metaphors, with or without formal induction procedures. He was a master of utilizing and maximizing channel 1 in the proposed model (Figure 4). Whether or not the individual was in trance, Erickson knew how to send information along this route to facilitate unconscious processing.

The model also clarifies the means by which the techniques Erickson utilized for depotentiating conscious processes (boredom, confusion, distraction) worked. Such techniques interfere with the normal processes subserving conscious awareness (channels 2 and 3), thus providing increased communication to and autonomous processing within the unconscious mind. This is a clearer way of understanding what Hilgard was referring to when he wrote that "hypnotic procedures are designed to produce a readiness for dissociative experiences by disrupting the ordinary continuities of memories and by distorting or concealing reality orientation through the power that words exert by direct suggestion, through selective attention and inattention, and through stimulating the imagination appropriately" (1977, p. 226).

Finally, this expanded notion of the unconscious mind as containing all the information processed and stored with or without initial conscious awareness (Figure 4, a and b of long-term memory) is compatible with Erickson's view of the unconscious mind as being far wiser than the conscious mind. A greater understanding is therefore possible of the idea he frequently stated in a number of ways and left to all of us: You know far more than you know you know (Erickson et al., 1976, p. 247; Rossi, 1980, Vol. 4, p. 98).

REFERENCES

Dixon, N. F. (1971). *Subliminal perception: The nature of a controversy.* London: McGraw-Hill.
Dixon, N. F. (1981). *Preconscious processing.* New York: Wiley.
Erdelyi, M. H. (1974). A new look at the "new look": Perceptual defense and vigilance. *Psychological Review, 81,* 1–25.
Erickson, M. H., Rossi, E. L., & Rossi, I. (1976). *Hypnotic realities: The induction of clinical hypnosis and forms of indirect suggestion.* New York: Irvington.
Ferrell, J. (1982, October 12). Pioneering cognitive psychologist has everyone's mind on his. *The New York Times,* p. C-1.
Fisher, C., & Paul, I. H. (1959). The effect of subliminal visual stimuli on imagery and dreams: A validation study. *Journal of the American Psychoanalytic Association, 7,* 35–83.
Green, D. M., & Swets, J. A. (1966). *Signal detection theory and psychophysics.* New York: Wiley.
Haber, R. N., & Hershenson, M. (1973). *The psychology of visual perception.* New York: Holt, Rinehart & Winston.
Haley, J. (1982). The contribution to therapy of Milton H. Erickson, M.D. In J. Zeig (Ed.), *Ericksonian approaches to hypnosis and psychotherapy* (pp. 5–26). New York: Brunner/Mazel.
Hilgard, E. R. (1977). *Divided consciousness.* New York: Wiley.
Kleespies, P., & Wiener, M. (1972). The "orienting reflex" as an input indicator in "subliminal" perception. *Perceptual and Motor Skills, 35,* 103–110.
Miller, G. A. (1956). The magical number seven, plus or minus two: Some limits on our capacity for processing information. *Psychology Review, 63,* 81–97.
Murch, G. M. (1969). Responses to incidental stimuli as a function of feedback contingency. *Perception and Psychophysics, 5,* 10–12.
Murch, G. M. (1973). *Visual and auditory perception.* Indianapolis: Bobbs-Merrill.
Rossi, E. (Ed.). (1980). *The collected papers of Milton H. Erickson* (Vol. 4, p. 98). New York: Irvington.
Sacerdote, P. (1982). Hypnotically induced dreams: Theory and practice. In J. Zeig (Ed.), *Ericksonian approaches to hypnosis and psychotherapy* (pp. 228–238). New York: Brunner/Mazel.
Shevrin, H. (1973). Brain wave correlates of subliminal stimuli, unconscious attention, primary and secondary process thinking, and repressiveness. *Psychological Issues, 8* (2, Monograph 30), 56–87.
Shevrin, H. (1975). Does the averaged evoked response encode subliminal perception? Yes, a reply to Schwartz and Rem. *Psychophysiology, 12,* 395–398.
Shevrin, H., & Fritzler, D. E. (1968). Visual evoked response correlates of unconscious mental processes. *Science, 161,* 295.
Silverman, L. H. (1966). The effects of subliminally presented aggressive stimuli on the production of pathological thinking in a schizophrenic population. *Journal of Consulting Psychology, 30,* 103–111.
Silverman, L. H. (1968). Further comments on matters relevant to investigations of subliminal phenomena: A reply. *Perceptual and Motor Skills, 27,* 1343–1350.
Silverman, L. H. (1976). Psychoanalytic theory: The reports of my death are greatly exaggerated. *American Psychologist, 31,* 621–637.
Silverman, L. H., Bronstein, A., & Mendelsohn, E. (1976). The further use of the subliminal psychodynamic activation method for the experimental study of the clinical theory of psychoanalysis: On the specificity of relationships between manifest psycho-

pathology and unconscious conflict. *Psychotherapy: Theory, Research and Practice, 13,* 2–16.

Silverman, L. H., Frank, S., & Dachinger, P. (1974). A psychoanalytic interpretation of the effectiveness of systematic desensitization: Experimental data bearing on the role of merging fantasies. *Journal of Abnormal Psychology, 83,* 313–81.

Silverman, L. H., Martin, A., Ungaro, R., & Mendelsohn, E. (1978). Effect of subliminal stimulation on symbiotic fantasies on behavior modification treatment of obesity. *Journal of Consulting and Clinical Psychology, 46* (3), 432–441.

Silverman, L. H., Ross, D. L., Adler, J. M., & Lustig, D. A. (1978). A simple research paradigm for demonstrating subliminal psychodynamic activation: The effect of oedipal-related stimuli on dart throwing accuracy in college males. *Journal of Abnormal Psychology, 87,* 341–357.

Silverman. L. H., & Spiro, R. H. (1967). Some comments and data on the partial cue controversy and other matters relevant to investigations of subliminal phenomena. *Perceptual and Motor Skills, 25,* 325–338.

Somekh, D. E., & Wilding, J. M. (1973). Perception without awareness in a dichoptic viewing situation. *British Journal of Psychology, 64,* 339–349.

Spence, D. P., & Holland, B. (1962). The restricting effects of awareness: A paradox and an explanation. *Journal of Abnormal and Social Psychology, 64,* 163–174.

Spence, D. P., Scarborough, H. S., & Ginsberg, E. H. (1978). Lexical correlates of cervical cancer. *Social Science and Medicine, 12,* 141–145.

Swets, J. A. (1964). Is there a sensory threshold? In J. A. Swets (Ed.), *Signal detection and recognition by human observers.* New York: Wiley.

Wiener, M., & Kleespies, P. (1968). Some comments and data on the partial cue controversy and other matters relevant to investigations of subliminal phenomena: A rejoinder. *Perceptual and Motor Skills, 27,* 847–861.

Chapter 27

"I Am Now Talking with Your Right Hemisphere": A Critical Evaluation of the Lateralization Hypothesis

Lynn D. Johnson

In the past few years, several investigators (Bandler & Grinder, 1975; Carter, Elkins, & Kraft, 1982; Graham & Pernicano, 1979; Wall, 1982) have suggested that trance behavior is isomorphic with, and therefore presumably originates with, the abilities and behaviors of the right hemisphere of the brain. These investigators suggest that during hypnosis the right hemisphere is more dominant than the left, while in waking states the left is more dominant.

While there is some evidence, which I will review, that hemispheric activity patterns change in some states of hypnosis, other evidence suggests that this view is oversimplified. I propose instead a more complex neuropsychological model of hypnotic behavior, using recent reviews and hypotheses about the functions of the brain.

In 1969, Bogen reported on work he and colleagues had done with patients with intractable epilepsy. In an attempt to stop the seizures, they severed the corpus callosum, the thickly innervated structure that connects the two hemispheres. As a result, experimenters such as Gazzaniga (1983) were able to psychologically evaluate and report on the

I would like to thank Jeffrey K. Zeig for his encouragement, support, and above all friendship during the writing of this chapter. Stephen Gilligan provided generous editorial comments which were scholarly and helpful, and I thank him for them, as well as his warmth and caring. David Blair and Tom Schenkenburg provided helpful neuropsychological comments.

differences between the two hemispheres. With the commissurotomy (the severing of the corpus callosum) the patient could be given stimuli to only one hemisphere, whereas in a person with a normal corpus callosum, the two hemispheres continually exchange information.

Gazzaniga (1983) reviewed some of the commissurotomy work. In a patient with a commissurotomy, visual stimuli can be presented to the right occipital area only. When one patient was shown the word "laugh" in the left eye (and therefore perceived only in the right hemisphere), she began to laugh. When asked why she laughed, she replied, "Oh, you guys are really something." Similarly, when shown the word "scratch," her left hand (controlled by the right hemisphere) scratched her right hand. She was asked what word she had been shown, and she replied, "Oh, . . . itch." These and other examples have been cited by clinicians as parallels between the dissociative and "incongruent" behavior of patients. The behaviors also obviously resemble the rationalizations given by hypnotic subjects when asked why they performed a posthypnotic suggestion. The subject performs the task but confabulates an explanation for it.

Ornstein (1972) in *The Psychology of Consciousness* combined the information from split-brain work with oriental and mystical ideas about the duality of human nature. He characterized the left hemisphere as the logical, rational side of our experience and the right hemisphere, with a more holistic, diffuse, intuitive style of information processing. Ornstein equated the right hemisphere with the mystical, and the left with the rational, behavioristic approach to psychology. The left hemisphere (right side of the body) was analogous with light, daytime, time-oriented, linear thinking, focused attention, rationality, and, to use the oriental term, *yang*. The right hemisphere was analogous with night, dark, sensuality, intuition, holistic processes, timelessness, diffuse attention, and *yin*. Ornstein suggested that we in the West had become alienated from the *yin* side of our beings and suggested a renascence of the mystic to create a more balanced existence.

Many of the early findings about the hemispheres have held up well, while others have been modified. Investigation of hemispheric differences has mushroomed and currently new reports appear almost weekly in the professional literature. A summary of commonly reported differences in the two hemispheres is found on Table 1.

Bandler and Grinder (1975) presumably were influenced by Ornstein's arguments (although he is not cited) in their analysis of Milton Erickson's verbal patterns. In Part II of their work, they dichotomize suggestions into "pacing the dominant hemisphere" and "accessing the nondomi-

Table 1
Cerebral Hemispheric Specialization*

*Left Hemisphere***

Expressive Language, Receptive Language
Symbolic Classification
  (classification by usage)
Propositional Thought
  (proposes, analyzes, uses)
Motor Control of Language Apparatus
  (tongue, lips, etc.)
One-at-a-Time Processing (Serial)
Focused Attention Style
Time-Focused
  (able to accurately judge passage of time)
Executive, Planning, Decision-Making Style

*Right Hemisphere***

Limited Receptive Language
Visuospatial, Map-Making
Classifies by Shape
Appositional Thought
  (receives, compares in global ways, divergent thought)
Manipulospatial Behavior
  (touching, drawing, making, exploring through touch)
Recognition, Production of Music, Melody, etc.
Processing by "Chunks" (Parallel in the sense of receiving
  large chunks of information at a time)
Diffuse Attention Style
Timeless

*summarized from Allen, 1983, & Corballis, 1980.
**Some abilities are exclusive, such as language in the left hemisphere, while some can be performed by either hemisphere but one seems more adept at it than the other.

nant hemisphere." They postulated that *sometimes* when Erickson used the term "unconscious," he meant the "nondominant" hemisphere.

Watzlawick (1978) also utilized this idea, suggesting the right hemisphere "hears" language in a different way than the left, and is more influenced by allusion, pun, metaphor and indirection. He suggested that the two hemispheres figuratively form two separate brains, and therapeutic suggestions must be directed to the right hemisphere if they are to have an effect on the essentially alogical behavior of symptoms.

Carter, Elkins, & Kraft (1982) reviewed the laterality model and also suggested that hypnosis be conceptualized as a process of accessing the right hemisphere. They cited the techniques of Erickson, for example, in asking musically oriented patients to imagine a melody or pieces of one, to hear it more clearly, to feel a desire to beat time, to hear it more and more clearly, becoming stronger, and so on. They argued that these melody-oriented techniques constituted accessing of the "nondominant" hemisphere. The general use of imagery in inducing a trance, such as Erickson's approach of suggesting visualizing the letters of the alphabet, was posited as being "aimed" at the left hemisphere. Similarly, according to Carter et al. the use of indirect suggestions was supportive of their hypothesis. They agreed with Watzlawick that the right hemisphere responds to "special classes of language, such as puns, allusions . . ."; to language which is *more* symbolic than usual, that is, where the symbols are ambiguous and multilevel.

Wall (1982) reviewed the evidence for the right hemisphere being more active during hypnosis. He suggested that imagination is a right hemisphere activity and then cited Hilgard (1977) that imaginative involvement is highly correlated with hypnotizability. Erickson's confusion techniques were seen by Wall as overloading the dominant, verbal hemisphere and promoting a shift to the right hemisphere.

Other evidence of the hemisphere activation in hypnosis, cited by Wall, includes Zeig's (1977) study of variations in the temperature of the eardrum. Zeig found that highly susceptible subjects showed less blood flow to the right eardrum during hypnosis, and subjects with low hypnotizability showed reduction in the tympanic temperature in the left ear. This statistically significant interaction was interpreted as suppression of the left hemisphere for highly susceptible subjects during hypnotic induction. Similarly, Chen, Dworkin, & Bloomquist (1981) studied evoked potentials in patients having oral surgery with hypnotic anesthesia. They found a reduction of total cortical power during hypnosis, but found that the power output of the right hemisphere was higher than the left. After surgery, the left showed greater power output. They concluded that this indicates a dominance of the right hemisphere during hypnosis.

Graham and Pernicano (1979) used the autokinetic effect to test the laterality hypothesis. They assume that the shifting *direction* of the light as perceived by the subject (either to the left or the right) implies a relative dominance of the contralateral hemisphere. Graham and Pernicano found that in right-handers, 28% of the movements were to the left in the waking state, while 53% were to the left during hypnosis.

In summary, the evidence for laterality shift in hypnosis comes from the parallels between trance or posttrance behaviors and the behaviors of commissurotomy patients, from parallels between trance behavior and right hemisphere cognitive styles, and from the physiological studies including evoked potentials, eardrum temperature and autokinetic effects.

However, there are a number of flaws in the above arguments. First, there is good reason to think that the responsiveness to puns, allusions and indirect suggestions is not the right hemisphere hearing the meaning implied. Rather, it is probably cooperative interaction between the right and the left hemispheres. Second, much of the investigation into laterality in hypnosis does not specify the level of trance being experienced. In light to medium trance states, the subject often describes a pleasant, dreamlike experience with much visualization present. If the psychophysiological studies are basically using light or medium trance states then we would expect to see more activity in the right hemisphere, not because of the nature of hypnosis but because of the nature of the experience, namely, that it is one of visualization. Any tasks involving extensive visualization would tend to activate the right hemisphere. Third, much of the phenomena of deep trance is both right- and left-hemispheric behavior, and the deeper the trance, the more likely the subject is to show complex behaviors of both hemispheres. Finally, in regard to the "musical" inductions (i.e., asking the client to imagine strains of music), my impression is that Erickson used such induction procedures with skilled musicians, and I will cite evidence that for professional musicians, music is a predominantly *left*-hemispheric activity.

In my personal experience with trance, one of the first systems to experience alteration is body sense. I am not sure where my arms and legs are or what they are doing. This is a common experience and, in fact, may be a marker of trance (Hilgard, 1977). Erickson, Rossi, and Rossi (1976) pointed out the similarity between the experience of a deeply hypnotized person believing he can be in two places at once and the experience of persons with right-hemispheric deficits being unable to tell where their arms or legs were, or believing also they could be in two places at once (Luria, 1973). In regard to this common trance experience, it appears that the *right*-hemispheric abilities are impaired, or suppressed, rather than the left.

As far as language abilities of the right hemisphere are concerned, evidence indicates that extensive language comprehension in the right hemisphere is a rare phenomenon; most researchers suggest only rudimentary right-hemispheric linguistic comprehension (Gazzaniga, 1983; Levy, 1983). Levy uses the analogy of domestic animals' comprehension to the right hemisphere's manner of comprehension of language, although she adds that the right hemisphere is more intelligent than, say, a dog's brain. Now if we can apply that to the use of hypnotic language, it may be that what Watzlawick (1978) calls the language of the right hemisphere is actually a combination of right- and left-hemispheric processing. The hypnotic induction is presented verbally, accessing the left hemisphere. If the words do not make immediate sense to the left hemisphere in its usual method of understanding, it would begin to search for symbolic meanings at various levels, including representations through visualization at conscious and unconscious levels in the right hemisphere. Along with such visualizations, the limbic system and the emotions could also make changes in state to search for meaning.

Actually, it is possible that symbolic representations may take place in the left rather than the right hemisphere. The left is particularly suited for symbolism, since it contains language and math functions, which are, of course, symbolic in nature. Does the left hemisphere "take to" symbols because of some innate ability, or does it develop symbolic abilities because that is the nature of the task which is necessary to understand language? The left hemisphere may be suited uniquely for symbolic representation, thus making language acquisition easier. In any case, Levy and Trevarthen (1976) reported a study which suggests that the left hemisphere represents symbolically while the right hemisphere represents in a more isomorphic way. In other words, the left hemisphere can classify things according to use, while the right classifies according to shape.

It may be, then, that symbolic psychotherapy, which Erickson utilized extensively, is effective because of unique right-left cooperation fostered by the symbolic operations. The concept that the left hemisphere tries out permutations of meanings by enacting visualizations through the right hemisphere seems a more accurate representation than the idea that the right hemisphere somehow "hears" the language directly. In a recent workshop I heard Watzlawick emphasize that he is aware of the right hemisphere's inability to comprehend language, and he suggests he is using the concept of the "language of the right hemisphere" in a somewhat metaphoric way (Watzlawick, personal communication, 1983).

Earlier I mentioned that imaginative involvement was taken by some theorists to suggest right-hemispheric involvement. I am not aware of studies that suggest imagination is *right*-hemispheric. Bogen and Bogen (1969) suggested the corpus callosum is a major contributor to creativity, or that it is the cooperation which makes for creation. It may be that in thinking of creativity as right-hemispheric, we have been overly affected by Ornstein (1972) in which he forced right-left distinctions which have only limited validity (Corballis, 1980).

In terms of creativity in music, there is indirect evidence that the left hemisphere may be preeminent. Gordon (1970) found that musically naive persons mainly listen to music with the right hemisphere, while professional musicians mainly activate the left while listening. Similarly, Davidson and Schwartz (1977) found that musically naive persons show greater right hemisphere activity while composing and whistling a tune, while accomplished musicians show more left-hemispheric activity. It may be that lack of imaginative involvement as an impediment to hypnosis reflects watchfulness but not necessarily hemispheric differences. People with a habit of examining everything carefully are not necessarily deficient in right-hemispheric behaviors.

We can perform right-hemispheric tasks without being in hypnosis. We can enjoy melody, imagine shapes and pictures, change tires, assemble objects, etc. While being in certain hypnotic states, probably ones involving visualization, increases right-hemispheric activity, so can reading stories which facilitate visualization, in which case the right hemisphere probably supplies pictures in response to the left interpreting the meaning. Current thinking suggests that ". . . modern researchers now generally agree that the relationship between the hemispheres is not 'dominant versus minor' but rather that of equals, each with its own functional specialities" (Allen, 1983).

Models of behavior can be both a help and a hindrance. The idea that *eliciting the right hemisphere* will produce trance can be a valuable guide but also limits one to do what one thinks the right hemisphere is capable of doing. Some of Erickson's most interesting and powerful experiments involved left-hemispheric tasks performed either in trance or as posthypnotic responses. For example, in investigating posthypnotic responses, Erickson (1980d) gave a posthypnotic suggestion to a secretary to change pencils during dictation on the 320th, 550th, and 725th word. Notes were made when she changed pencils, and she was found to be accurate within 10 words and usually within three. This complex counting task seems to be a left-hemispheric function, and yet somehow she did not show any interference with taking written dictation.

In another article, Erickson (1980b) reported on a subject in a deep trance who was instructed to *appear* awake. His deep trance was evident when an unexpected visitor arrived. The subject was completely out of rapport with the new visitor and could not perceive him even when he lifted the subject's arm. This ability to be completely unaware of something is more like the focal style of the left hemisphere than the global, inclusive style of the right.

Erickson also enjoyed exploring automatic writing, and writing is certainly a left-hemispheric activity. In one example (1980a), a subject was asked to estimate the time it took for something to happen. She consciously estimated two to three minutes. Then through automatic writing, she wrote "thirty sec." with the "y" on thirty forming an unusual shape, like the numeral 8. Erickson suggested that her unconscious demonstrate that things could have more than one meaning, and it complied by writing a message which could be read either as "30" or as "38." It seems likely that in this situation, conscious awareness is dissociated from writing/language abilities of the left side of the brain, since her conscious estimate was two to three minutes. The clever hiding of meaning within meaning may be a right-hemispheric function, perhaps suggesting the ability of right and left hemispheres to cooperate outside of conscious awareness.

A similar example was a story Erickson told me about trusting the unconscious mind. It seems he wanted to find out if he was a good writer, so he wrote editorials for the school paper in college, but wrote them in a trance state. He had amnesia for what he had written, so he was able to critically evaluate them without knowing whether they were his own or not.

Time distortion is probably right-hemispheric, but Erickson and Cooper (1980) demonstrated time distortion through ingenious counting and visualizing tasks, combining right- and left-hemispheric activities.

Erickson and Hill (1980) reported on two cases of women who were unable to decide whether to marry. One subject reported on the hypnotic process she used to settle the problem. She hallucinated two lists with various words and attributes written down, one list representing marriage and the other the option of remaining single. She went through those lists in a logical, systematic way, balancing, weighing, and judging, and thus was able to decide. Immediately after the decision, she had amnesia for the whole trance and only much later was able to report what had gone on.

I have taken a stand against the lateralization hypothesis not because I judge it has *no* utility but because I assume that having such expectations as the lateralization hypothesis fosters, tends to inhibit what the clinician expects from the patient. The evidence I have cited suggests that all behaviors can be successfully dissociated, whether we classify them as "right-hemispheric" or "left-hemispheric." In fact, I have used those terms with great reservation in this chapter. I am not at all convinced they are useful paradigmatically in clinical work.

Erickson, Rossi, and Rossi (1976) say, ". . . in the typical trance right-hemispheric functions can be depressed just as well as those of the left. In fact, because of the more global and diffuse character of the right-hemispheric functioning, the right hemisphere may be more easily altered than the left. . . . It may be too simple to view the trance as a function of the right hemisphere. The way a trance is usually induced with suggestion for relaxation and comfort tends to alter the functioning of both left and right hemispheres" (pp. 278-9).

To summarize, I would like to remind the reader that years ago hypnosis theory was influenced by psychoanalytic thought. Trance was viewed as a type of age regression, caused by the hypnotist manipulating the transference aspects of the relationship. Erickson addressed that idea in the following way:

> Hypnosis, by permitting the individual to call upon and utilize singly or collectively the great multitude of bodily learnings accumulated in a fragmentary fashion over the years, offers endless opportunity . . . to single out . . . individual manifestations. In this way, hypnosis offers a means of reaching an eventual understanding of the processes entering into the development of various behavioral phenomena. This will not be achieved, however, if scientists formulate a hypothesis of what things should be and look for those items that fit into the hypothesis and discard those that do not, as in the case with those who say that hypnosis is role-playing and consider any contrary hypnotic phenomena as invalid, or those who say that hypnosis is a regressive phenomenon and ignore the great wealth of obviously nonregressive phenomena. (1980b, p. 348)

REFERENCES

Allen, M. (1983). Models of hemispheric specialization. *Psychological Bulletin, 93*, 73–104.

Bandler, R., & Grinder, J. (1975). *Patterns of the hypnotic techniques of Milton H. Erickson, M.D.* (Vol. 1). Cupertino, CA: Meta Publications.

Barber, T. X. (1969). *Hypnosis: A scientific approach.* New York: Van Nostrand Reinhold.

Bogen, J. E., & Bogen, G. M. (1969). The other side of the brain III: The corpus callosum and creativity. *Bulletin of the Los Angeles Neurological Society, 34*, 191–200.

Carter, B. D., Elkins, G. R., & Kraft, S. P. (1982). Hemispheric asymmetry as a model for hypnotic phenomena: A review and analysis. *The American Journal of Clinical Hypnosis, 24*, 204–210.

Carter, R. L., Hohenegger, M., & Satz, P. (1980). Handedness and aphasia: An inferential method for determining the mode of cerebral speech specialization. *Neuropsychologia, 18*, 569–574.

Chen, A., Dworkin, S., & Bloomquist, D. S. (1981). Cortical power spectrum analysis of hypnotic pain control in surgery. *International Journal of Neuroscience, 13*, 127–134.

Cohen, G. Hemispheric differences in serial versus parallel processing. *Journal of Experimental Psychology, 97*, 349–356.

Corballis, M. C. (1980). Laterality and myth. *American Psychologist, 35*, 284–295.

Davidson, R. J., & Schwartz, G. E. (1977). The influence of musical training on patterns of musical self-generation tasks. *Psychophysiology, 14*, 58–63.

Elithorn, A., & Barnett, T. J. (1967). Apparent individual differences in channel capacity. *Acta Psychologica, 27*, 75–83.

Erickson, M. H. (1980a). An experimental demonstration of unconscious mentation by automatic writing. In E. L. Rossi (Ed.), *The collected papers of Milton H. Erickson,* (Vol. 3, pp. 145–157). New York: Irvington.

Erickson, M. H. (1980b). An experimental investigation of the hypnotic subject's apparent ability to become unaware of stimuli. In E. L. Rossi (Ed.), *The collected papers of Milton H. Erickson,* (Vol. 2, pp. 33–50). New York: Irvington.

Erickson, M. H. (1980c). Basic psychological problems in hypnotic research. In E. L. Rossi (Ed.). *The collected papers of Milton H. Erickson,* (Vol. 2, pp. 340–350). New York: Irvington.

Erickson, M. H. (1980d). Concerning the nature and character of posthypnotic behavior. In E. L. Rossi (Ed.), *The collected papers of Milton H. Erickson,* (Vol. 1, pp. 381–411). New York: Irvington.

Erickson, M. H. (1980e). Historical note on the hand levitation and other ideomotor techniques. In E. L. Rossi (Ed.), *The collected papers of Milton H. Erickson,* (Vol. 1, pp. 135–138). New York: Irvington.

Erickson, M. H. (1980f). Initial experiments investigating the nature of hypnosis. In E. L. Rossi (Ed.), *The collected papers of Milton H. Erickson,* (Vol. 1, pp. 3–17). New York: Irvington.

Erickson, M. H. (1980g). Investigation of specific amnesia. In E. L. Rossi (Ed.), *The collected papers of Milton H. Erickson,* (Vol. 3, pp. 38–44). New York: Irvington.

Erickson, M. H., & Cooper, L. F. (1980). Time distortion in hypnosis. In E. L. Rossi (Ed.), *The collected papers of Milton H. Erickson,* (Vol. 2, pp. 221–265). New York: Irvington.

Erickson, M. H., & Hill, L. B. (1980). Unconscious mental activity in hypnosis—Psychoanalytic implications. In E. L. Rossi (Ed.), *The collected papers of Milton H. Erickson,* (Vol. 3, pp. 207–220). New York: Irvington.

Erickson, M. H., Rossi, E. L., & Rossi, S. I. (1976). *Hypnotic realities.* New York: John Wiley & Sons.

Gazzaniga, M. S. (1983). Right hemisphere language following bisection. *American Psychologist, 38*, 525–541.

Ericksonian Psychotherapy I: Structures

Gordon, H. W. (1970). Hemispheric asymmetries in the perception of musical chords. *Cortex, 6,* 387–398.

Graham, K. R., & Pernicano, K. (1979). Laterality, hypnosis, and the autokinetic effect. *The American Journal of Clinical Hypnosis, 22,* 79–84.

Hilgard, E. R. (1977). *Divided consciousness.* New York: John Wiley & Sons.

Kinsbourne, M. (1970). The cerebral basis of lateral asymmetries in attention. *Acta Psychologica, 33,* 293–201.

Levy, J. (1983). Language, cognition and the right hemisphere: A response to Gazzaniga. *American Psychologist, 38,* 538–541.

Levy, J., & Trevarthen, C. (1976). Meta-control of hemispheric function in human split-brain patients. *Journal of Experimental Psychology, 2,* 229–312.

Luria, A. (1973). *The Working Brain.* New York: Basic Books.

Ornstein, R. E. (1972). *The psychology of consciousness.* New York: Viking.

Semmes, J. (1968). Hemispheric specialization: A possible clue to mechanism. *Neuropsychologia, 6,* 11–26.

Wall, T. W. (1982, August). *Laterality and hypnosis.* Paper presented at Scientific Meeting of the American Society of Clinical Hypnosis, Denver, CO.

Watzlawick, P. (1978). *The language of change.* New York: Basic Books.

Zeig, J. K. (1977). *Tympanic temperature, hypnosis, and laterality.* (Doctoral dissertation, Georgia State University).

Chapter 28

Ethical Issues in Hypnosis: Informed Consent and Training Standards

Jeffrey K. Zeig

The field of hypnosis has been subject to more sensationalism and mystification than any other therapeutic methodology in the history of psychotherapy. This is due in part to both the fact that hypnosis has been associated with the loss of self-control (cf. Gravitz, Mallet, Munyon, & Gerton, 1982), and the fact that hypnotic methodology often provides an opportunity for patients to change without conscious insight or rational understanding.

Sensationalism and mystification have not been confined to the lay public; hypnotherapy has been subject to special scrutiny in the professional arena. Historically, special guidelines have been constructed for the ethical use of hypnosis. Ostensibly, special protections are needed for the consumer. For example, around the turn of the century, the British Medical Association Commission on Hypnotism made the recommendation that a practitioner should only hypnotize a female client if a relative or another female was present (Ambrose & Newbold, 1980).

Traditional therapies are based on rational linear approaches and/or insight, and ethical codes reflect that bias. More than these methodol-

Portions of this paper were also presented at the August 1983 meeting of the American Psychological Association in Anaheim, California.

The author is grateful to Melvin Gravitz, Ph.D., for providing editorial assistance.

ogies, hypnotic approaches and strategic psychotherapies utilize concealed techniques including indirect suggestion, paradoxical techniques and metaphor. The modern hypnotic psychotherapy techniques espoused by Milton H. Erickson and his followers are especially based on covertly eliciting unconscious processes. Change is effected spontaneously; therapeutic situations are composed in which patients, perhaps outside of their conscious recognition, discover previously unrecognized potentials for change.

If traditional ethical codes are based on linear methodology and/or conscious insight, are they incompatible with modern approaches based on indirect techniques? Moreover, does the use of direct or indirect techniques in hypnosis warrant specialized ethical codes? The purpose of this chapter is to examine the aforementioned questions centering on the issue of informed consent as described in the American Psychological Association Code of Ethics (1981). Ethical considerations of a case conducted by Erickson are discussed and a letter to the author from Erickson about his view of the ethics of this particular case is presented. An additional purpose of this chapter is to present a position on the issue of training standards for the use of hypnotic techniques. It will be maintained that in ethical codes, definitions of both "informed consent" and "training standards" must change to reflect changes in morality and advances in therapeutic technique and theory.

THE NEED FOR SPECIAL ETHICAL GUIDELINES

In general, the ethical issues involved in hypnosis are not different from the ethical issues involved in using any symptomatically based technique. However, this is not to say that hypnosis does not provide some special ethical problems.

The ethical codes of the multidisciplinary professional hypnosis societies stress two issues which may not be clearly covered by the ethical standards of their members' professional societies. These two issues are training standards and the use of hypnosis for entertainment purposes. The International Society of Hypnosis (1979), the American Society of Clinical Hypnosis (1981), and the Society for Clinical and Experimental Hypnosis (1978) all have ethical codes addressing training standards (i.e., the qualifications of those professionals who will be trained by members of their respective organization). Also, the codes of these organizations address the fact that hypnosis should not be used as a form of entertainment. For other ethical issues, members of these multidisciplinary organizations are referred to the ethical codes of their respective professions (e.g., the American Medical Association, the American Dental Association, the American Psychological Association).

INFORMED CONSENT

None of the three hypnosis societies mentions the issue of informed consent in their code of ethics. Additionally, the American Medical Association Principles of Medical Ethics, which consists of a preamble and seven one-sentence sections, does not mention the idea of informed consent. (In the medical arena, it seems that the issue of informed consent is in the domain of law rather than in the ethics of the professional association.) However, the ideas of "informed consent" and "freedom of choice" with regard to participation are both mentioned in the American Psychological Association (APA) Code of Ethics (1981). This next section provides background and speaks to the intersection of Ericksonian hypnotherapy and informed consent.

Like laws, ethical codes are based on ever-changing morality. As morality changes, ethical codes must change. The APA Code of Ethics has been revised a number of times reflecting changes in morality. For example, at one time it was considered unethical to be a media psychologist or to engage in advertising.

The issues of informed consent and freedom of choice as they appear in the current APA Code of Ethics are also based on a particular morality. These issues need to be examined before proceeding. The issue of informed consent is confused and muddled in current APA ethical principles and standards. The term "informed consent" seems to apply only to research (Principle 9) and confidentiality (Principle 5), as the actual term is only used in these two sections of the code.

Informed consent may not apply to the actual practice of psychotherapy. In Principle 6 (Welfare of the Consumer), it is noted that "psychologists fully inform consumers as to the purpose and nature of an evaluation, treatment, educational or training procedure and they freely acknowledge that clients, students or participants in research have freedom of choice with regard to participation" (p. 5). Therefore, it seems that according to the APA Code of Ethics, consumers do not have to explicitly *consent* to treatment. This is not true for research subjects or for patients relinquishing confidentiality; in addition to being *informed* in the case of research and confidentiality, participants/consumers must overtly *consent*.

There is, however, confusion in APA literature as to whether informed *consent* applies to the clinical situation. In practice, it seems that clinicians are expected to actually get consent. For example, in the January 1977 version of the Standards for Providers of Psychological Services, the interpretation provided for Principle 2.3.2, which concerns establishing a treatment plan, states: "Whenever appropriate or mandated in the setting, this plan shall be in written form as a means of providing a basis for establishing accountability, obtaining *informed consent* (my italics) and providing a mechanism for subsequent peer review" (p. 8). The standards seem to make a significant departure and extend the idea of informed consent directly to the treatment situation, a position seemingly in conflict with the actual wording in APA ethical guidelines.

Perhaps there is a purposeful underlying morality implicit in the APA ethical position of allowing freedom of choice rather than demanding overt consent. It can be assumed that, by virtue of their position, clinicians have more of the interests of their patients at heart than researchers. Moreover, it would seem that clinicians are afforded more freedom, ostensibly due to the specific demands of the clinical situation.

However, some experts argue that informed consent should operate in both the clinical arena and the research arena (Veatch, 1981, p. 200). The argument here stems from the fact that people have a right to autonomous choice and that the classification of the contract between the professional and the subject/consumer is irrelevant; there is no real reason for the therapeutic situation to have a lower standard of consent. According to Veatch, the terms of the relationship should be spelled out and agreed to overtly.

In addressing the issue of consent, two problems arise: a) As previously mentioned, the distinction between "being informed, with freedom of choice," and "informed consent" is not clearly stated in the APA ethical literature; and b) more importantly, it may not be wise to "fully inform" consumers in the first place. To examine and illuminate the practical issues involved let us examine a case conducted by Milton Erickson.

The Case of Joe

Erickson (1966) reported the use of the interspersal technique, namely, a hypnotic technique that does not involve formal trance induction. In this particular instance, it was used for pain control.

The case is one of a florist named Joe who suffered from terminal cancer. At the time of Erickson's visit, Joe was hospitalized and seemed to have toxic effects from heavy doses of pain medication. As medication reportedly had little positive effect, Erickson was asked by a relative to see Joe in order to use hypnosis for pain relief. Erickson reported that shortly before being introduced to Joe, he was informed that Joe "disliked even the mention of the word hypnosis." Moreover, one of Joe's children, a resident in psychiatry who did not believe in hypnosis, was also present at the time that Erickson met Joe.

When Erickson was introduced to Joe he thought that it was doubtful if Joe really knew why Erickson was there. Joe could not talk to Erickson because of a tracheotomy. He communicated by writing.

Erickson began his therapy by stating,

> Joe, I would like to talk with you. I know that you are a florist, that you grow flowers, and I grew up on a farm in Wisconsin and I liked growing flowers. I still do. So, I would like to have you take a seat in that easy chair as I talk to you. I'm going to say a lot of things to you but it won't be about flowers because you know more than I do about flowers. *That isn't what you want.* (The reader will note that italics are used to denote interspersal of hypnotic suggestions which may be syllables, words, sentences or phrases uttered with a slightly different intonation.) Now as I talk and I can do so *comfortably*, I wish that you will listen to me *comfortably* as I talk about tomato plants. That is an odd thing to talk about. It makes one *curious. Why talk about a tomato plant?* One puts a tomato seed in the ground and he *will hope* that it will grow into a tomato plant that *will bring satisfaction* by the fruit it has. The seed soaks up water, *with not very much difficulty.* In doing that, because of the rains that *bring peace and comfort.* . . . (p. 203)

Joe responded well to the monologue about tomato plants which continued with more interspersed suggestions. Erickson stated that Joe was in a hypnotic trance and that the induction of subsequent trances was done by indirect interspersal of suggestions. Erickson saw Joe for a full day and was invited to see Joe one month later. During this month, Joe left the hospital and began living at home. He gained weight and strength and used little medication for pain. During his second visit with Joe, Erickson continued to use his indirect technique reporting that his use of disguise might not have been necessary at that point due to good rapport, but that he continued to use his interspersal technique because "he preferred to take no risks."

Erickson's summary of the case was as follows:

> The symptom amelioration, abatement and actual abolishment ef-

fected by hypnosis, and the freedom of Joe's body from potent medications, *conducive only of unawareness* (my italics), unquestionably increased his span of life, while at the same time permitting an actual brief physical betterment in general. . . . Joe undertook to live the remainder of his life as enjoyably as possible, a vigor expressive of the manner in which he had lived his life and built his business. (p. 207)

Ethical Issues in the Case of Joe

In this case, Erickson's behavior seems to conflict with Principle 6 of the APA Code of Ethics. Erickson neither informed Joe of the purpose and nature of his treatment nor ensured that Joe had freedom of choice in regard to participation. Erickson did not inform Joe that he would be using hypnosis but he provided Joe with a hypnotic trance. Also, in the hospital setting, the patient's freedom of choice is different than in the office setting, where there is more freedom to leave. Consent and freedom to leave might have been interfered with in another way. As Erickson pointed out, it is possible that the patient was initially unaware of why Erickson was present.

Obviously, it seems that Erickson departed from APA ethical guidelines about the need of the consumer to be informed and afforded freedom of choice. However, it is equally obvious that he supplied effective treatment—treatment which he indicated was facilitated by Joe's lack of awareness.

Erickson's Viewpoint

I wrote to Erickson and asked him what he thought the ethical issues were in the case of Joe. At the time, I informed him that I thought that the important thing was being "relevant" to the patient. Erickson's handwritten response did not take current ethical guidelines into consideration; however, it is important in understanding the underlying morality of his method and thinking. Moreover, his reply provides interesting insight into his approach:

> [Regarding the] ethics involved in tomato plants and dying of cancer, I think that only an academician could implant them where they would not belong.
>
> Joe, with tracheotomy hence speechless, knew he was without

hope, in severe pain, that doctors could do nothing and that they knew that they were helpless. I didn't agree with them in toto but I didn't tell him and I didn't think it a matter of relevance or ethics to tell him so.

I was willing to talk to him and willing to walk away if he didn't want to hear me. Simple social courtesy—not ethics.

Ah, but here's the rub. [Someone might think] that I forced on him a discourse on a tomato plant and that would involve ethics.

Oh, but I didn't talk to him about a tomato plant. The undiscerning might think so. I only spoke words of his experiential learning and I could only guess at those and only the words of his own language that I spoke would he understand. Those words of his inner understanding would be heard—the rest of what I said was interlarded noises.

Joe's wife, daughter, brother-in-law all listened and finally his wife intruded to ask me to start hypnosis—she was startled to discover that it had been done. What I had been saying to Joe they all thought to be nonsense.

But to Joe I had been saying words that he could understand in his own inner recorded experiential learnings.

Now why did I talk about a tomato plant? Well, Joe came up from great poverty, worked on a garden truck farm, liked tomatoes, peddled flowers for pennies on the street, got more flowers to peddle, acquired land carefully, grew flowers in rows, with vegetables in between rows—an Asiatic practice carried out in Europe, in South America, Mexico, Canada and the U.S.A.

Joe loved living plants in essentially this order: beauty, nourishment, ornamentation and utility.

When you examine an abdomen for possible appendicitis, you begin the examination at that part of the abdomen most removed from the appendical area, slowly approaching the critical area.

When I saw Joe it was a cognitive assumption not involving ethics that he would like freedom from pain, some kind of hope, enjoyment of life, of sleep, of hunger, social life—go ahead, name the rest.

Well, I started as far away from Joe's cancer as I could, without trying to identify it. Indeed, I said a lot of words that Joe translated into the experiential learnings that he thought he had lost forever until he had built up a sufficient supply of his good associations to replace the things he didn't want.

Ever sit in a hard chair and listen to a boring lecturer while your bottom protests about its agony? Then listen twice as long to a fascinating lecturer and be surprised that your bottom likes that hard chair.

No ethics involved! (M. H. Erickson, personal communication, March 4, 1976)

Discussion

In regard to modern theories of psychotherapy, the issue of informed consent is especially problematic. Modern theories are not based in the same morality as traditional approaches. As applied to clinical situations, APA ethical principles are based on a model where overt understanding on the part of the patient is a primary part of the treatment. This position is based on a morality that favors direct approaches over indirect influence.

In traditional insight-oriented therapy the therapist works to interpret back to the patient what the patient "really means." The patient's psychological level message differs from what is said on the social level, and the therapist interprets what is happening on the psychological level based on the therapist's theoretical orientation. Strategic and Ericksonian therapists as a rule do not interpret; an interpretation is a limited (and limiting) evaluation that oversimplifies a complex interaction (cf. Haley, 1982).

Communications are not merely reports of information on multiple levels; they are also attempts to interpersonally influence. Rather than basing treatment on insight and understanding, strategic and Ericksonian methods are based on effecting change; therapeutic communication is directed to have specific influence.

An unstated moral presupposition of psychotherapy is that therapeutic communication should be direct and concrete. However, besides being impossible, direct concrete communication may be antithetical to constructive influence. Those familiar with Ericksonian methods use alogical communication, confusion, allusions, and metaphors to elicit therapeutic responses.

Modern strategic and Ericksonian approaches elevate the idea of influencing change and downplay rational logical understanding. The purpose of (therapeutic) communication is to influence behavior. Most influence is done unconsciously. Ericksonian psychotherapists will not follow Principle 6 and *fully* inform consumers of the nature of the treatment. Moreover, they may not require overt consent. This position reflects a different underlying morality about the nature of human beings and how they change.

Clinical experience indicates that patients do not necessarily communicate clearly, rationally, concretely, and on one level. For example, a patient may present psychosomatic complaints rather than talking about depression. The patient has a right to communicate indirectly. Why should the therapist infringe on that right? It seems more polite and may be more effective for a therapist to continue to talk (at least initially) about somatic complaints rather than confronting a patient about his or her depression and informing him or her fully of what the treatment for depression will entail. However, in talking about somatic complaints the therapist can speak on multiple levels and intersperse therapeutic directives. The Erickson case cited above provides one possible example of such an approach.

Many clinical situations are not logical. Informed consent is based on the morality of logical, conscious self-control. However, symptoms by their very definition happen autonomously. It does not make sense to initially demand of the patient that they take logical, conscious responsibility for their symptoms when that is diametrically opposed to what they describe in their presentation.

A patient often has to be "prevented from intruding unhelpfully into a situation which he cannot understand" (Erickson, 1966, p. 198). There is tyranny in providing too much information; providing too much information may inhibit change. For example, providing Joe with awareness could have given him issues around which to organize resistance. Joe was skeptical about hypnosis and about his ability to receive help. A discussion of even general aspects of the therapeutic relationship could have mitigated against effective treatment. It is a particular quirk of consciousness that awareness can be both a benefit and a hindrance.

Moreover, it is really impossible to "fully" inform; the idea of providing "full information" may defy operational definition. For example, in providing information, should a therapist say to a patient that he or she will be using the social-psychological principles of conformity and compliance and outline this area of research before agreeing to provide treatment? Similarly, when using paradoxical techniques, is the clinical situation served by having the therapist inform the patient that he or she is giving the patient a directive to continue having the symptom, and a facetious rationale in the hope that the patient will defy the directive and thereby become asymptomatic? In using multiple-level communication, does the therapist inform the patient that since all communication is multiple level he or she will be communicating on multiple levels to influence the patient to "spontaneously" get in touch with his or her unrecognized capabilities? Clearly, it would not be therapeutic to provide such information in these situations.

Some experts have tackled the problem of operationalizing the concept of providing full information. According to Veatch (1981), "the proper standard is what the reasonable lay person would want to know (unless the individual lay person has signaled otherwise)" (p. 202).

The proper standard can be determined by surveying a group of lay people. Veatch believes that the consumer should be involved in the process of determining ethical standards: "Information should be transmitted unless fewer than 5% of reasonable people would have desired that information" (p. 203). Ethical codes are proprietary and generated by professionals. Professional ethical codes are not generated by the population that is affected by their contents. Codes become ways of legitimizing professional roles. A patient should not be blindly bound by the consensus of a professional group (Veatch, 1981).

In the case of Joe, I maintain that Joe adequately signaled his cooperation and consent with both his behavior and his positive response. However, Veatch would disagree because he states that the person must directly signal that he does not want information, or directly indicate that he will waive the normal requirements of consent; indirect indication is not enough. Veatch takes a conservative position pointing out that "the overinformed person is inconvenienced; the underinformed has his or her autonomy violated" (p. 203). While this position may have merit in medical situations, it would not be used in many situations by those practicing strategic and Ericksonian approaches.

Recommendations

Ethical codes must be clearly conceived and be able to change flexibly in response to changing morality and technical advances. The crux of the issue in clinical work is that therapeutic techniques should be used responsibly and effectively. The patient has a right to successful treatment. Psychotherapy cannot be tailored to the Procrustean bed of antiquated ethical strictures that are impossible to follow.

It is ill-advised to require psychologists to fully inform consumers and/or to require overt consent. Requiring overt consent does not have sufficient scope to cover modern strategic and Ericksonian approaches. Providing full information and demanding direct consent can intrude into the clinical situation.

However, the patient's right to self-determination cannot be compro-

mised. Patients must be afforded freedom of choice. While fully informing patients of the nature of treatment is impossible and based on an
antiquated linear conception of human functioning, patients should generally be informed of inherent risks of treatment.

In the courts, the primary purpose of the doctrine of informed consent
is to maintain the patient's right to self-determination by providing information about inherent risks of procedures (King, 1977). To reflect that
philosophy, the APA Code of Ethics could be amended to state, "Psychologists *inform consumers as to the inherent risks* of an evaluation, treatment, educational or training procedure. . . ." This wording provides
a concept that can be operationalized, researched and applied.

The doctrine of informing the patient of risks cannot be applied in-
discriminately, because a therapist will not be merely providing information; he or she will also be influencing the patient. As Watzlawick
(Chapter 1) has mentioned, communication is simultaneously both indicative and injunctive.

For example, if the therapist tells the patient that the potential risk of
treatment is divorce, not only is a fact being stated, a suggestion is also
being made. As experts in communication, therapists should be sensitive
to the multilevel structure of communication and responsible for its effect
in all aspects of the therapy, including those involving ethics.

TRAINING STANDARDS

In the United States, there are two membership organizations that
provide training for professionals interested in learning hypnosis,
namely, the American Society of Clinical Hypnosis (ASCH) and the
Society for Clinical and Experimental Hypnosis (SCEH). These organizations have slightly different training standards. According to the
ASCH Code of Ethics (1981),

> A member of ASCH shall not support the practice of hypnosis by
> lay persons. A lay person is defined here as one who is not a
> member in good standing of a therapeutic or scientific profession;
> that is, he is not a physician, dentist, psychologist, or a member
> of another recognized therapeutic or scientific profession with cre-
> dentials in addition to competence as a hypnotic practitioner. (p.
> 1)

In practice, the ASCH provides training only to doctoral level practitioners or doctoral level graduate students. Its ethical constraints are

such that members of the organization should provide training in hypnosis only to practitioners whose academic qualifications are sufficient for eligibility for ASCH membership.

The Society for Clinical and Experimental Hypnosis has different training standards from the American Society of Clinical Hypnosis in that the former admits certain categories of psychiatric social workers. As far as training standards are concerned, it is

> unethical for a member of the Society to teach hypnosis to anyone other than SCEH members or doctoral level psychologists, physicians (M.D.'s or D.O.'s), dentists (D.D.S.'s or D.M.D.'s), psychiatric social workers, or social workers listed in the national register with the exception of paramedical groups (i.e., nurses, technicians, or students) directly involved with patient care or research and working under direct supervision of a physician, dentist, or doctoral level psychologist competent in the use of hypnosis. (p. 82)

Obviously, the standards of these two societies restrict a large group of mental health professionals from receiving training in hypnosis. This group consists of master's level counselors and some master's level psychiatric social workers. The Milton H. Erickson Foundation, however, provides training to these professionals.

The Erickson Foundation uses the same guidelines for training that were used by Milton H. Erickson, M.D., for attendance at his teaching seminars. Besides having a personal loyalty to these guidelines, the Foundation believes that its standards are logically consistent and that they reflect modern directions in health care delivery. Master's level practitioners are increasingly trained to work independently. As such, they should have access to modern therapeutic techniques.

Rationale

Training standards for the mental health professionals should be decided by the governing board of the respective profession, in conjunction with accredited graduate level training programs and governmental legislation. For example, the American Psychological Association should dictate admission and training standards for the profession of psychology; the National Association of Social Workers should dictate admission and training standards for social work, and so forth. Subsequently, these organizations cooperate with graduate schools and local legislators to establish standards for independent practice.

It does not seem proper for a multidisciplinary specialty agency (e.g., ASCH or SCEH) to judge the admission and training standards of a mental health profession (e.g., social workers and other master's level mental health practitioners), and then state that, according to the pre-selected standards of the specialty organization, the standards for the profession in question are not up to the level of competence for practitioners in that particular discipline to use a specific technique (viz. hypnosis). If practitioners are able to practice independently according to their education, local legislation, and the governing body of their profession, they should be able to use any technique at their disposal.

If a specialty organization hypothesizes that its treatment techniques should be restricted only to specific groups of trained professionals, that decision should be made on the basis of scientifically gathered data, rather than opinion. If the data support the theory that training and admission standards are not acceptable for professionals from a particular field to be competent in the use of a particular therapy technique (e.g., hypnosis), then the multidisciplinary specialty organization should enter into dialogue and provide counsel to the governing board of the profession, graduate schools, and legislatures regarding the standards of admission and training that would be minimally proper and acceptable for use of the technique in question in independent practice.

The Erickson Foundation is of the opinion that master's level mental health professionals do have the necessary training to competently use hypnosis in private practice. The training in master's level programs has substantially improved in quality in recent years. Moreover, it seems that a professional with a master's degree would be more qualified to use hypnosis than a nonpsychiatric physician or dentist simply by virtue of a broader background in psychology, since hypnosis is a psychological technique that so obviously requires an understanding of psychodynamics and psychological systems.

The underlying morality of the professional societies' position on training standards is unclear. Training standards are in a state of flux. Not long ago it was "unethical" for a nurse to take a patient's blood pressure. Now nurses perform complicated medical procedures in high technology settings.

The training standards of the professional societies are also changing. It was only recently that the SCEH modified its admissions criteria to accept certain types of social workers. Actually, it seems inconsistent that SCEH would accept only specified social workers. These professionals may not be any more well trained than other professionals with master's degrees in mental health fields who have commensurate postgraduate experience.

Taking the respective ethical guidelines of the professional societies to the logical conclusion, a member could be labeled "unethical" for providing training to master's level mental health practitioners. The determination in this scenario would be made on the definition of the concept of what is entailed in being a "professional." It would not be made on the basis of ethics per se. Considering the weight that censure by a professional organization carries, such action should be carefully examined. Moreover, in a number of states an ethical violation is tantamount to a felony since ethical guidelines have been written into state law (Elgan Baker, personal communication, September 6, 1984)

In summary, the position of the Erickson Foundation is to provide training to master's level mental health practitioners. Our eligibility requirements are as follows:

> The Erickson Foundation provides training to professionals in health-related fields including physicians, doctoral level psychologists, and dentists who are qualified for membership in, or are members of, their respective professional organizations (e.g., AMA, APA, ADA). The Foundation will also provide training to professionals with mental-health-related graduate degrees (e.g., M.S.W., M.S.N., M.A. or M.S.) from accredited institutions. Applications will be accepted from full-time graduate students in accredited programs in the above fields who supply a letter from their department certifying their student status.

The Foundation believes that these training standards reflect current morality and are logically consistent. Today's trend allows master's level mental health practitioners to be independent practitioners. Therefore, they should be afforded the ability to use the most modern techniques available to provide assistance to their patients.

CONCLUSIONS

Ethical codes in the medical fields may carry the weight of law. The power of ethical standards should not be underestimated. As previously mentioned, the effects of professional censure for violating the ethical code of an independent professional organization is great. Also, ethical codes can be used as legal standards since courts often defer to professional standards in their determinations of negligence (King, 1977). For example, in the case of informed consent, to determine the extent of a practitioner's duty to disclose, the court could use the established ethical guidelines of the profession in question.

Ethical codes must be worded as clearly and unambiguously as possible. Terms such as "informed consent" and "professional" must be spelled out. In defining these terms, technical advances and changes in morality must be considered. Important terms (viz. "informed consent" and "professional") cannot be included solely because of opinion or precedent, but must be defined and researched carefully. Similar to laws, proprietary ethical codes frequently must be evaluated and changed to keep abreast of developments in society.

REFERENCES

Ambrose, G., & Newbold, G. (1980). *A handbook of medical hypnosis.* London: Balliere-Tindall.

American Psychiatric Association (1981). *Principles of medical ethics with annotations especially applicable to psychiatry.* Washington, D.C.

American Psychological Association (1977). *Standards for providers of psychological services.* Washington, D.C.

American Psychological Association (1981). *Ethical standards of psychologists* (rev. ed.). Washington, D.C.

American Society of Clinical Hypnosis (November 1981). *Code of ethics.* Des Plaines, IL.

Erickson, M.H. (1966). The interspersal technique for symptom correction and pain control. *American Journal of Clinical Hypnosis, 3,* 198-209.

Gravitz, M.A., Mallet, J.E., Munyon, P.T., & Gerton, M.I. (1982). Ethical considerations in the professional applications of hypnosis. In M. Rosenbaum (Ed.), *Ethics and values in psychotherapy: A guidebook.* New York: Free Press.

Haley, J. (1982). The contribution to therapy of Milton H. Erickson, M.D. In J.K. Zeig (Ed.), *Ericksonian approaches to hypnosis and psychotherapy* (pp. 5-25). New York: Brunner/Mazel.

International Society of Hypnosis (August 1979). *Code of ethics.* Philadelphia, PA.

King, J.H. (1977). *The law of medical malpractice in a nutshell.* St. Paul, MN: West Publishing.

Society for Clinical and Experimental Hypnosis (October 1978). *Code of ethics.* Liverpool, NY.

Veatch, R. (1981). *A theory of medical ethics.* New York: Basic Books.

Watzlawick, P. (This volume). Hypnotherapy without trance.

PART IX

Research

Unfortunately, there is a paucity of research on Ericksonian methodology. Perhaps the work of Whiteside, and of Freeman and Kessler will stimulate more research into Ericksonian approaches.

James W. Whiteside III is currently working on his doctorate in counseling psychology at the University of North Carolina at Chapel Hill. He describes a model for delineating different approaches to hypnosis and uses studies of obesity to compare approaches. Additionally, he describes a process through which practitioners can research therapy effectiveness within their own practice.

William B. Freeman, Jr., is currently working on his Ph.D. in clinical psychology at the University of Vermont in Burlington.

Marc Z. Kessler, Ph.D., is an associate professor in psychology at the University of Vermont. He earned his degree in clinical psychology at the University of Nebraska in Lincoln. He has authored a number of papers on alcohol dependency and neuropsychology.
Freeman and Kessler's study compares a social learning method of modifying hypnotizability to an Ericksonian utilization method based on indirect suggestions. Results point to the fact that the subject's internal experiences can be best altered by an Ericksonian utilization approach.

Chapter 29

The Four Schools of Hypnosis: Who's Best?

James W. Whiteside, III

The goal of this chapter is to demonstrate how to bring the tools of science to bear on questions of comparative hypnosis. The first step is standardization of the terms. To this end, I will describe four schools of hypnosis. Subsequently, I illustrate how this system can be applied retrospectively to analyze existing research. Finally, I will describe a model which will enable hypnotherapists to use their own practice for much needed, scientific research.

STANDARDIZATION OF HYPNOSIS

In research, practice, and theory, hypnosis is increasingly being differentiated along two dimensions—approach and basis—depending on whether the writer is a state or nonstate theorist. The state theorists, like Joseph Barber (1980) and Ernest Rossi (1980), are principally interested in differences between the direct and indirect approach to hypnosis. Nonstate theorists, like Nicholas Spanos and T. X. Barber (1974), emphasize the difference between suggestion- and imagination-based hypnosis. Along these two dimensions, four schools of hypnosis can be identified:

Type of Hypnosis	Approach to Hypnosis	Basis for Hypnosis
1) Traditional	Direct	Suggestion
2) Permissive	Direct	Imagination
3) Indirect	Indirect	Suggestion
4) Metaphorical	Indirect	Imagination

History

Traditional hypnosis, as practiced today, dates from Abbe Faria who developed the fixed-gaze method in 1819 and James Braid who added the suggestion method around 1842 (Teitelbaum, 1965). Permissive hypnosis dates back at least to Emile Coué who believed trance was unnecessary and taught self-hypnosis (Teitelbaum, 1965). However, it was the widespread clinical use of hypnosis after World War II that really led to the development of more permissive methods of hypnosis (Matheson & Grehan, 1979). The very existence of trance was later challenged by Spanos and T. X. Barber (1974) who proposed a skill-building model which emphasized the use of imagination.

Traditional hypnosis faced a challenge from the state theorists who split hypnosis along a second dimension. Indirect hypnosis dates back at least to Moll in the 1890s, but Milton Erickson was its major practitioner and proponent (Erickson & Rossi, 1980). At the juncture of the indirect approach and imagination-based hypnosis lies metaphorical hypnosis. Examples are found in the 1800s (Sidis, 1924, p. 19), but it has been recognized as a major approach to hypnosis only in the last decade. Erickson was not only its major practitioner, but his 1944 explanation of a story he created in 1935 is still the most penetrating analysis of this technique.

I will turn now to the content of the four schools. In each case, I will provide a one-line excerpt followed by a list of the techniques that characterize that school.

Traditional Hypnosis

You will follow all of my commands. (Teitelbaum, 1965, p. 70)

How does one attain such power? The answer is that the power of the hypnotist is probably limited to what is in the best interest of the client (Erickson, 1939) and even then is possible only after groundwork has been laid. The standard techniques used in traditional hypnosis to induce this level of control are listed at the top of the next page.

The technique used in the quotation is "external control"; the many techniques above external control represent the preliminary preparation. Hypnotic catalysts include things like eye fixation which, unknown to the S, create fatigue and facilitate suggestions for eye closure. An example of prophetic suggestion is "You will find it easier to learn if you

STAGE SETTING
  Prestige enhancement
INDUCTION
  Fixation of attention

Hypnotic catalysts
  Threshold phenomena
  Ambiguous control

SUGGESTION TECHNOLOGY
  Traditional motivation
  Authoritarian suggestion
    Prophetic suggestion
    Factual suggestion
    Imperative demand
  Repetition
CONDITIONING
  Undisclosed hypnotic condition-
    ing
DEHYPNOSIS
  Traditional dehypnosis

Suggest and test
Challenge
Failure transformation
Dramatic effects
External control

relax." A factual suggestion is "Your breath is beginning to slow and even out." Examples of imperative demand are "Relax now. Enjoy. Enjoy. Enjoy." Like repetition, challenge suggestions and dramatic effects are also characteristic of traditional hypnosis.

Permissive Hypnosis

> At all times you will be in complete control just as you are right now. (Stein, 1969, p. 131)

In a sense, permissive hypnosis is the exact opposite of traditional hypnosis. If the quote is true, however, how can anything hypnotic happen—since the essence of hypnosis is nonvolitional response. In other words, if the subject simply raises a hand, it is no longer hand levitation. The resolution of this dilemma lies in the remoteness of control. The experience of control must be so remote from consciousness that the activity becomes automatic. For example, when we drive home from work we often put ourselves on remote control while we enter a naturalistic trance in order to replay something that happened at work that day. Standard techniques used in permissive hypnosis to help induce similar experiences are listed below:

PRELIMINARY INSTRUCTION
   Attitude maximization   Task-motivational instructions
   Expectation enhancement   Think-with instructions
INDUCTION AND MAINTE-
NANCE
   Attention-control development   Relaxation training
SUGGESTION FRAMEWORK
   Permissive motivation   Permissive suggestion
   Remote control   Instrumental suggestion
                            Potential suggestion

IMAGINATION ACTIVATION
   Nonmetaphorical goal-directed
      fantasy
   Imagination cues   Role-absorption cues
DEHYPNOSIS
   Permissive dehypnosis

The primary method for producing removal from the experience of control involves imagination. For example, when you become deeply involved with the image of a large helium balloon tied to your finger, you may be surprised to suddenly feel your finger rising up into the air. Yet you retain ultimate control because the whole process is disclosed in the form of "If . . . then . . ." statements (labeled instrumental and potential suggestions above). The balloon is a goal-directed fantasy and is usually supplemented with other techniques for imagination activation, relaxation, and attention-control. This model is ascribed primarily to T. X. Barber, Spanos, and Chaves (1974).

Indirect Hypnosis

   It's your ears I'm talking to. (Erickson, 1964, p. 10)

This quote is an example of the dissociation patter that is so bewildering and so characteristic of Erickson's inductions. It accomplishes several things. It fascinates the mind and dissociates it from the environment, but it also dissociates the ears from assumed conscious possession and begins construction of an unconscious complex in the Jungian sense. When Erickson (Erickson & Rossi, 1980, p. 460) adds, "If your unconscious wants you to enter trance, your right hand will lift. Otherwise your left will lift," he dissociates the hands as well and increases the probability that they will form a unit with the ears which will respond automatically to his suggestions. These techniques, astonishing as they are, still belong to a standard repertoire and can be catalogued under the following headings:

INDUCTION AND MAINTE-
NANCE
    Indirect utilization   Dissociation patter
SUGGESTION TECHNOLOGY
    Indirect suggestion   Indirect motivation
        Suggestion induction   Pace and lead
        Suggestion deduction   Unconscious control
        Suggestion assumption   General indirect suggestion
CONDITIONING
    Indirect hypnotic conditioning
DEHYPNOSIS
    Indirect dehypnosis

The second example presented above is what Erickson and Rossi call a double bind, one of a larger class of indirect suggestions labeled suggestion assumption. This is one of three categories into which all indirect suggestions can be classified. The other two are suggestion induction, an example of which is the interspersal technique (Erickson, 1966), and suggestion deduction which, like symptom prescription, initiates a response sequence which culminates in the desired behavior, often in a roundabout way. In any case, the locus of control is neither the subject per se nor the operator, but the unconscious.

Metaphorical Hypnosis

> In that little seed there does *sleep* . . . a beautiful plant. (Erickson, 1966, p. 204)

This quote is an example of a vicarious suggestion: it invites the listener to identify with the seed and out of that identification to rediscover hope. It comes from Erickson's interspersal technique (1966) in which his whole focus, paradoxically, is on indirect rather than metaphorical hypnosis. The techniques which distinguish metaphorical hypnosis are listed below:

INDUCTION AND MAINTE-
NANCE
  Metaphor utilization
SUGGESTION TECHNOLOGY
  Metaphorical suggestion   Metaphorical motivation
    Metaphorical directive   Metaphorical collaboration
    Vicarious suggestion   Metaphor in vivo
    Interspersed metaphor   General metaphorical suggestion
CONDITIONING
  Metaphorical conditioning
DEHYPNOSIS
  Metaphorical dehypnosis

In the article cited above, Erickson utilizes an object from the patient's fondest activity, gardening. It is, therefore, already imbued with rich, symbolic meaning for the patient. Erickson further motivates the patient by attributing to the plant what the patient most wants, freedom from pain. Through a combination of vicarious suggestion and interspersal, he shows the patient how to regain peace of mind. An example of metaphor in vivo is found in Erickson's article on complex induction (1935).

The Stages of Hypnosis

With the exception of preliminary activity, the four schools emphasize the stages of hypnosis about equally. When hypnotherapists talk with patients about myths that surround hypnosis, they are approaching the subject from the point of view of permissive hypnosis. Traditional prac-titioners like Teitelbaum (1965) claim that this may actually do more harm than good and one rarely found Erickson broaching such subjects.

LITERATURE REVIEW

In this section, I review the research on the comparative efficacy of the four schools, and illustrate how to review other studies in order to shed light on the question of efficacy. I begin by reviewing the challenges which initially sparked controversy.

Research on the Basis for Hypnosis

Subjects respond overtly and experientially to suggestions when

they become involved in imaginings that are consistent with the
aims of the suggestions. . . . It was unnecessary and misleading
to posit a special or qualitatively different state in order to explain
the experiences of the good hypnotic subject. (Spanos & T. X.
Barber, 1974, p. 508)

This quote comes from an article proposing the replacement of the
concept of trance with that of imagination. However, the evidence for
this proposal consisted primarily of 16 correlational studies from which
causation cannot be inferred. More germane are the results of nine analog studies which controlled the degree of imaginative involvement on
the part of the Ss. Unlike the correlational studies, only three of the nine
studies, one-third, favored the nonstate hypothesis (Chaves & T. X.
Barber, 1974; Spanos, Horton, & Chaves, 1975; Spanos, Spillane, &
McPeake, 1976). All three of these involved the use of goal-directed
fantasies, but three other such studies found no significant differences
(Buckner & Coe, 1977; Spanos & T.X. Barber, 1972; Spanos & McPeake,
1977). Two studies even found suggestion to be more influential than
imagination (T. X. Barber & Glass, 1962; Hilgard & Tart, 1966). The ninth
study (Spanos & Ham, 1973) also found no significant difference. All of
these studies employed a direct approach to hypnosis. Combined with
the correlational research, they suggest that the connection between
imagination and hypnosis may be unpredictable and resistant to external
influence. They provide little evidence for the superiority of permissive
hypnosis.

Research on Hypnotic Approach

Susceptibility is not critical to clinical success if indirect hypnotic
suggestions are used. (Barber, 1980, p. 6)

Barber proposes, in effect, the demise of traditional hypnosis because
of its ineffectiveness with low-susceptible subjects. The debate over the
relative efficacy of direct and indirect hypnosis had been around for a
long time (Erickson & Rossi, 1980), but it did not really become heated
until J. Barber (1977; J. Barber & Mayer, 1977) demonstrated that indirect
hypnosis could be nearly 100% effective in reducing dental pain. In
controlled comparisons of the two approaches, however, two (Angelos,
1978; Reyher & Wilson, 1973) out of three (Alman & Carney, 1980) failed
to support the laboratory analog of J. Barber's hypothesis. Angelos even
found that susceptibility correlated with success in indirect hypnosis.

484 Ericksonian Psychotherapy I: Structures

At present, however, the studies are too few to draw any conclusions about the superiority of direct vs. indirect hypnosis. These findings are also based on analog studies and do not test the target of J. Barber's original critique, clinical hypnosis.

One quick way to multiply our knowledge about the relative effects of the four schools, within a clinical or analog context, is to classify the hypnotic protocols in existing research and compare the results. This type of analysis must be performed one dependent variable at a time.

Research on Hypnotic Treatment of Obesity

The clinical variable chosen here was weight loss. Because of the large number of studies involved, references and details of the analysis will be published in a separate article. Out of 55 studies on hypnotic treatment for weight loss, 21 were found which reported enough information to compute the weekly weight loss during treatment. Of these, only six provided sufficient information to classify them along both dimensions of hypnotic technique. A breakdown of the results by school is listed below:

Type of Hypnosis	Weight Loss per Week	Number of Studies
Traditional	.6	2
Permissive	.5	1
Indirect	2-3	2
Metaphorical	2-5	1

In the case of indirect and metaphorical hypnosis, a range is listed because exact figures were not reported. The figures seem to indicate the superiority of the indirect approach. However, when the degree of experimental control is considered, the following results are obtained:

Approach	Type of Study	Weight Loss per Week	Number of Studies
Direct			
	Randomized studies	.9	5
	Single group studies	1.7	1
	Case studies	2.5	4

Approach	Type of Study	Weight Loss per Week	Number of Studies
Indirect			
	Randomized studies	——	——
	Single group studies	2-3	1
	Case studies	2.3-3.3	3

Eight additional studies which could be classified by approach, but not by basis have been included here. The original difference between the two approaches practically disappears when the level of experimentation is controlled. Combined with differences in specificity in reporting results, these tables also provide no hard evidence for the superiority of any school of hypnosis.

A second criterion for comparison is weight loss at follow-up. To place this variable in perspective, consider this finding by Brownell in a review of behavioral approaches (1982, p. 220): "If 'recovery' from obesity is defined as reduction to ideal weight, and maintenance of that weight for five years, a person is more likely to recover from almost any form of cancer than from obesity." In 17 behavioral studies with one year follow-ups, Brownell (1982) found an average weight loss at posttreatment of 10.4 pounds which regressed to 10 pounds after one year.

The combined hypnotic results, by comparison, demonstrate continuing weight loss from 10.8 pounds at posttreatment to 16 pounds at follow-up. This finding is based on the seven hypnotic studies which reported both posttreatment and follow-up results. Treatment averaged eight weeks in length with an average follow-up eight months and three weeks later. When data points from 17 additional studies are included, the weight loss trend is confirmed: weight loss in pounds = 1.379 × time since beginning of treatment in months + 9.600. The strength of this relationship is suggested by the correlation coefficient of 0.57. More importantly, the significance of the regression F ratio falls at the 0.0007 level. However, if only the ten randomized studies are included, the results are no longer significant (Pr = 0.11). In this case, the slope actually increases to 2.283 (y–intercept = 2.004), but the variability of the results also increases (correlation coefficient = 0.45). Nevertheless, if the trend toward increasing weight loss continues to find support in controlled long-term research, hypnosis will become the treatment of choice for obesity.

Which type of hypnosis should be used? Unfortunately, not even roughly comparable data is available to answer this question. Even if only case studies are included, those for the direct approach involve as many as six to 10 Ss per study while the two reports on the indirect approach involve a total of four Ss. It is perhaps not surprising, therefore, that the follow-up results favor the indirect approach. What is surprising, however, is the magnitude of those results, particularly in a study by Milton Erickson (1960). He reported an average weight loss for three Ss of 85.7 pounds over an average of ten months with indirect hypnosis. This outcome is 62 pounds, almost four standard errors of estimate, over what the above regression equation predicts. The only other follow-up report on the indirect approach was 12 pounds, 0.75 standard errors, above prediction. Even in this case, however, only one direct study did better. While these results are tantalizing, they are methodologically insufficient to draw conclusions about the superiority of a single school of hypnosis.

RESEARCH DESIGN

In this section, I will illustrate how to build an experimental framework around a clinical practice in order to encourage more hypnotherapists to contribute to the scientific debate currently raging in hypnosis over which approach is best.

Standardization vs. Individualization?

Suppose, for instance, that you are working with overweight clients whom you typically see for a month with a follow-up booster session about a month later. You can standardize the treatment by putting the hypnotic inductions on tape and outlining the content of the sessions in a manual. Individualization is included through multiple choice-points which enable you to respond flexibly *within* a standardized con-text. You do not even need to use tape recordings, but if you plan the treatment as if it were to be automated, you will come far closer to producing research that can be replicated, i.e., that actually is research.

Dependent Variables

Next choose the dependent variables. Besides weight, variables that have been found in past studies to suggest symptom substitution may also be included. Increased anxiety and depression are two such variables in obesity research. Also include variables of interest to researchers in other areas. In this case, blood pressure and self-image are suggested by a literature review.

Independent Variables

What are the independent variables? Ideally, they include a treatment variable, a subject variable, and a time variable. Besides the hypnotic treatments you are currently using, I encourage you to team up with another therapist who uses a different form of hypnosis. Another way to do this is to use the audiotapes of others. In addition, add a control group for such nonspecific factors as self-monitoring and interpersonal attention and support. In some cases, a no-treatment control group may suffice.

The most logical subject variable in hypnotic research is susceptibility. However, if as in this case only 4 of 14 studies support a relationship between susceptibility and weight loss, look for other predictor variables. Locus of control, for instance, is significant in 18 out of 27 studies checked. The inclusion of such variables is particularly important when, as here, the dependent variable is traditionally associated with wide fluctuations within every treatment. Time is included as an independent variable for a similar reason. When short-term improvements have proven temporary in the past, long-term assessment points are a necessity.

Process Variables

Few hypnotherapists realize that the clinical use of hypnosis is being systematically challenged by behavioral scientists who are demonstrating in study after study that the effective agents in hypnotic treatments may be behavioral, rather than hypnotic phenomena (Wadden & Anderton, 1982). It has, therefore, recently become important to demonstrate that the outcome is at least correlated with hypnotic experiences in treatment. Such experiences include trance depth, imagery involvement, role absorption, trance phenomena, and the experience of non-volitional change. Wadden and Anderton also argue that if the results on the dependent variables do not correlate with susceptibility, hypnotic processes are probably not responsible for the change. Therefore, susceptibility should probably always be included—as a process variable, if not an independent variable.

Multivariate Analysis

Another recent development is the increasingly standard use of multivariate statistics. Hilgard, in his 1965 book on susceptibility, repeatedly asserts his frustration with chasing illusory variables which correlate with hypnotic effects in one study only to prove irrelevant in the next. The agent of his torture was multiple, but not multivariate *t* tests, correlations, and even analyses of variance. Because the nature of human phenomena is inherently multivariate and because it is a nonexistent experimenter who can resist running that extra correlation, every study should probably use multivariate analysis. If you know what you want to test, a statistical consultant can tell you how to do it and even do it for you. This is a small price to pay for the difference between wasted energy and a lasting scientific contribution.

DISCUSSION

In review, I have presented three topics: number one, a framework for standardizing the divisions of hypnosis; two, a review of the comparative research suggested by these divisions; and three, a research model with which you can use your own practice.

I described a four-way division of the schools of hypnosis. In this framework, the word *permissive* is reserved for the work of T. X. Barber, rather than Milton Erickson. While both indirect and metaphorical hypnosis are indeed worded permissively, they are based on subtle misdirection of attention which circumvents rather than educates the conscious mind. Their permissiveness, therefore, is more apparent than real. Nevertheless, since these techniques probably work only if they are in the best interest of the client (Erickson, 1939), they may be considered permissive in an indirect way. For the more formal purposes of classification, however, the term will be reserved for the more congruently permissive approach of T. X. Barber. The term *naturalistic hypnosis* is also encountered occasionally and may be considered a synonym for the indirect approach. In other words, it subsumes both indirect and metaphorical hypnosis. The same definition applies to the term *Ericksonian hypnosis*.

In its evolution, hypnosis may have now entered a phase less of invention than of scientific standardization and verification. In this process, traditional and permissive hypnosis are far in advance of indirect and metaphorical hypnosis. In Ericksonian hypnosis, even the definition of terms remains intuitive for the most part. As a result, the number of theoretical models explicating Ericksonian hypnosis have proliferated in the last few years (O'Hanlon, this volume), and it will still be some time before a professional consensus develops on the operational character- istics of indirect and metaphorical hypnosis.

Research on the relative efficacy of the four schools provides little hard evidence for the superiority of any of them. The results of analog studies are evenly balanced. Even the weekly weight-loss differences favoring indirect hypnosis are suspect because they are based on case studies rather than controlled group studies. Only Erickson's exceptional results (1960), even compared to other case studies, stand out. Combined with Joseph Barber's findings (1977; J. Barber & Mayer, 1977) of nearly 100% effectiveness in reducing dental pain, a case can still be made for the superiority of indirect hypnosis. Given that their results have yet to be replicated by other researchers, however, perhaps a better case can be made for the superiority of these two hypnotherapists. A more pro- ductive line of research may, therefore, ask the question, "Which sub- jects with which hypnotists?" rather than, "Which school of hypnosis?" These are questions which you can help answer.

With appropriate changes, those of you who are practicing hypno- therapists can use your clinical population to answer multivariate ques- tions which were statistically impractical a decade ago. Or you may review the research literature in a single problem area as I have done here for the treatment of obesity. As it stands, there has been only this one comparative review of the literature, about 12 analog studies, and no comparative clinical research.

What we may find is that there are not four schools of hypnosis after all, that in fact there are not even two dimensions in hypnosis, that instead there is only one general factor which underlies and explains the efficacy of every hypnotic treatment. Only you who understand the necessity of scientific validation can say for sure.

REFERENCES

Alman, B.M., & Carney, R.E. (1980). Consequences of direct and indirect suggestions on success of posthypnotic behavior. *American Journal of Clinical Hypnosis, 23*(2), 112- 118.

Angelos, J.S. (1978). A comparison of the effects of direct and indirect methods of hypnotic induction on the perception of pain. *Dissertation Abstracts International, 39*(6), 2972B- 2973B.

Barber, J. (1977). Rapid induction analgesia: A clinical report. *American Journal of Clinical Hypnosis, 19*(3), 138-147.

Barber, J. (1980). Hypnosis and the unhypnotizable. *American Journal of Clinical Hypnosis, 23*(1), 4-9.

Barber, J., & Mayer, D. (1977). Evaluation of the efficacy and neural mechanism of a hypnotic analgesia procedure in experimental and clinical dental pain. *Pain, 4,* 41-48.

Barber, T.X., & Glass, L.B. (1962). Significant factors in hypnotic behavior. *Journal of Abnormal and Social Psychology, 64*(3), 222-228.

Barber, T.X., Spanos, N.P., & Chaves, J.F. (1974). *Hypnotism: Imagination and human potentialities.* Elmsford, NY: Pergamon.

Brownell, K.D. (1982). The addictive disorders. In C.M. Franks, G.T. Wilson, P.C. Kendall, & K.D. Brownell (Eds.), *Annual review of behavior therapy: Theory and practice* (Vol. 8). New York: Guilford.

Buckner, L.G., & Coe, W.C. (1977). Imaginative skill, wording of suggestions and hypnotic susceptibility. *International Journal of Clinical and Experimental Hypnosis, 25*(1), 27-36.

Chaves, J.F., & Barber, T.X. (1974). Cognitive strategies, experimenter modeling, and expectation in the attenuation of pain. *Journal of Abnormal Psychology, 83*(4), 356-363.

Erickson, M.H. (1935). A study of an experimental neurosis hypnotically induced in a case of ejaculatio praecox. *British Journal of Medical Psychology, 15,* 34-50. (Also in E.L. Rossi (Ed.). *Collected papers,* 1980, *3,* 320-335.)

Erickson, M.H. (1939). An experimental investigation of the possible anti-social use of hypnosis. *Psychiatry, 2*(3), 391-414. (Also in E.L. Rossi (Ed.). *Collected papers,* 1980, *1,* 498-530.)

Erickson, M.H. (1944). The method employed to formulate a complex story for the induction of an experimental neurosis in a hypnotic subject. *Journal of General Psychology, 31*(1), 67-84. (Also in E.L. Rossi (Ed.). *Collected papers,* 1980, *3,* 336-355.)

Erickson, M.H. (1960). The utilization of patient behavior in the hypnotherapy of obesity: Three case reports. *American Journal of Clinical Hypnosis, 3,* 112-116. (Also in E.L. Rossi (Ed.). *Collected papers,* 1980, *4,* 181-187.)

Erickson, M.H. (1964). An hypnotic technique for resistant patients: The patient, the technique and its rationale and field experiments. *American Journal of Clinical Hypnosis, 7*(1), 8-32. (Also in E.L. Rossi (Ed.). *Collected papers,* 1980, *1,* 299-330.)

Erickson, M.H. (1966). The interspersal hypnotic technique for symptom correction and pain control. *American Journal of Clinical Hypnosis, 8*(3), 198-209. (Also in E.L. Rossi (Ed.). *Collected papers,* 1980, *4,* 262-278.)

Erickson, M.H., & Rossi, E.L. (1980). The indirect forms of suggestion. In E.L. Rossi (Ed.). *The collected papers of Milton H. Erickson on hypnosis* (Vol. 1, pp. 452-477). New York: Irvington.

Hilgard, E.R. (1965). *Hypnotic susceptibility.* New York: Harcourt, Brace & World.

Hilgard, E.R., & Tart, C.T. (1966). Responsiveness to suggestions following waking and imagination instructions and following induction of hypnosis. *Journal of Abnormal Psychology, 71*(3), 196-208.

Matheson, G., & Grehan, J.F. (1979). A rapid induction technique. *American Journal of Clinical Hypnosis, 21*(4), 297-299.

Reyher, J., & Wilson, J.G. (1973). The induction of hypnosis: Indirect vs. direct methods and the role of anxiety. *American Journal of Clinical Hypnosis, 15*(4), 229-233.

Rossi, E.L. (Ed.). (1980). *The collected papers of Milton H. Erickson on hypnosis* (Vols. 1-4). New York: Irvington.

Sidis, B. (1924). *The psychology of suggestion: A research into the subconscious nature of man and society.* New York: Appleton. (Original work published 1898.)

Spanos, N.P., & Barber, T.X. (1972). Cognitive activity during "hypnotic" suggestibility: Goal-directed fantasy and the experience of nonvolition. *Journal of Personality, 40*(4), 510-524.

Spanos, N.P., & Barber, T.X. (1974). Toward a convergence in hypnosis research. *American Psychologist, 29*(7), 500-511.

Spanos, N.P., & Ham, M.L. (1973). Cognitive activity in response to hypnotic suggestion: Goal-directed fantasy and selective amnesia. *American Journal of Clinical Hypnosis, 15*(3), 191-198.

Spanos, N.P., Horton, C., & Chaves, J.F. (1975). The effects of two cognitive strategies on pain threshold. *Journal of Abnormal Psychology, 84*(6), 677-681.

Spanos, N.P., & McPeake, J.D. (1977). Cognitive strategies, reported goal-directed fantasy, and response to suggestion in hypnotic subjects. *American Journal of Clinical Hypnosis, 20*(2), 114-123.

Spanos, N.P., Spillane, J., & McPeake, J.D. (1976). Cognitive strategies and response to suggestion in hypnotic and task-motivated subjects. *American Journal of Clinical Hypnosis, 18*(4), 254-262.

Stein, C. (1969). *Practical psychotherapy in nonpsychiatric specialties.* Springfield, IL: Charles C Thomas.

Teitelbaum, M. (1965). *Hypnosis induction technics.* Springfield, IL: Charles C Thomas.

Wadden, T.A., & Anderton, C.H. (1982). The clinical use of hypnosis. *Psychological Bulletin, 91*(2), 215-243.

Chapter 30

A Comparison of a Utilization
and a Social Learning-Based
Approach to the Modification
of Hypnotizability

William B. Freeman, Jr.,
and Marc Kessler

Given that there are differences in peoples' response to hypnosis, the locus of the difference has been described as being in the person, in the hypnotist's suggestions, or in an interaction of the two. The most common concept of hypnotizability is that the ability is located in the individual, that it varies among people, and that it is more or less stable over time. Based on this conception, hypnotizability has been operationally defined by Weitzenhoffer and Hilgard (1959, 1963) and others (Morgan & Hilgard, 1978; Shor & Orne, 1962) as the number of "hypnotic items" an individual behaviorally carries out following a standardized induction. The induction procedures are lengthy, repetitive, emphasize relaxation and drowsiness, and present direct suggestions and challenges.

Using these scales Hilgard (1975) and others (Cooper & London, 1971; Morgan, 1973; Morgan, Johnson, & Hilgard, 1974) concluded that hypnotizability is a trait. Diamond (1974, 1977a, 1977b, 1982) and Katz (1978,

The authors would like to acknowledge and thank the following people who participated in this research: hypnotists—S. A. Bastien IV, S. Bregman, G. Hoff, and L. W. Yost; research assistants—E. Greenwald, J. Vigne, and J. Bean. Special thanks are also due to the following people who contributed their advice and/or materials in support of this research: Andre M. Weitzenhoffer, Ph.D.; Martin T. Orne, M.D., Ph.D.; Frederick J. Evans, Ph.D.; and Michael J. Diamond, Ph.D.

1979a) suggested that hypnotizability is a learnable set of skills which can be modified with behavioral methods, while Erickson (1980a, b) and others (e.g., Barber, 1980; Gilligan, 1982) state the ability to experience trance is roughly equal in all people although varying in how the state may be manifested, accessed and utilized.

A number of studies found that subjects given behaviorally based skill training increased their scores on hypnotizability measures more than subjects given traditional sleep trance inductions or placebos (Diamond, 1977a, 1977b, 1982). The implication was that subjects so treated would be more susceptible to hypnotherapeutic procedures. However, Frischolz, Spiegel and Blumstein (1982) pointed out that Katz (1979a) merely exposed subjects to a ritualized sleep trance procedure, while other studies found that "traditional" clinical procedures produced similar gains in hypnotic susceptibility scores.* Perry (1977) criticized the methodology used in studies of the modification of hypnotizability, contending that training subjects on items from the dependent measures or similar measures mitigated the results. In addition, social learning procedures provide subjects with a clear and conscious idea of the desired "hypnotic behavior"; give example strategies of how to achieve it; and include modeling, direct suggestion, and self-paced successive approximation with practice. Praise is provided in such shaping. Praise tends to increase a targeted behavior but inhibits generalization to other classes of behavior (Brink, 1981). Neither depth nor non-volition were assessed in these studies. Social learning procedures may essentially train subjects to produce hypnotic behavior due to reinforcement of the expected response, and have no effect on the experiences of depth and nonvolition.

Erickson's method differs from the social learning method in several respects. For example, in contrast to reinforcement a "yes-set" can be established (Erickson & Rossi, 1979). Further, indirect suggestion and metaphor are used. Erickson and Rossi (1979) observe that these procedures evoke an associative process which deepens the level of trance and increases nonconscious involvement and automaticity, all experiences classically associated with trance (Weitzenhoffer, 1980; Bernheim, 1889). Through the use of the Ericksonian approach subjects should show more of the classical suggestion effects and produce greater scores

---

*The term hypnotic "susceptibility" is used here to refer to performance on standardized tests of hypnotic ability to clarify the distinction between performance on these from other measures of hypnotic performance and experience. Although it can be said that the term "susceptibility" carries with it certain possibly negative connotations regarding hypnosis (e.g., surrender of will, helplessness, gullibility) the scales have not been renamed and we choose to refer to them here by name for the sake of clarity.

on scales of hypnotizability than subjects exposed to a social learning-based skill training approach.

This study compared changes in measured susceptibility and in the experienced levels of depth and nonvolition in subjects exposed to: 1) a utilization approach; 2) a social learning/cognitive skills approach based on the procedures of Katz (1978, 1979a) and Diamond, Steadman, Harada and Rosenthal (1975); 3) a combination of these approaches; and 4) a placebo. We used simulators (Orne, 1971, 1973, 1979)—subjects who score poorly on standardized tests of hypnotizability—to control for demand characteristics and to clarify the distinction between *performance* on these tests and the levels of nonconscious involvement *experienced*. Our hypothesis was that subjects in the utilization condition would show changes on susceptibility scores and report greater depth and nonvolition than those in the other conditions. The subjects in the social learning condition would show changes in susceptibility scores but their scores on the subjective indices would be similar to simulators and placebos. The combined group would fall between the utilization and social learning groups on subjective measures. Hypnotists would be able to detect simulation only in the utilization condition and simulators would experience trance only in this condition.

METHOD

Subjects

Volunteers were solicited for participation in hypnosis research using radio advertisements and posters in the Burlington, Vermont area. Fifty-four subjects (25 males, 29 females, ranging in age from 18 to 47 years, with a mean age of 24.8) were selected from an initial sample of 153 subjects who were screened using the Harvard Group Scale of Hypnotic Susceptibility (HGSHS; Shor & Orne, 1962). One-third of this sample were undergraduate students, and the remainder were nonstudents from various occupations. Selection criteria were: (a) score of seven or less on the HGSHS, and three or less on the Stanford Hypnotic Clinical Scale for Adults (SHCS; Morgan & Hilgard, 1978); (b) at least 18 years of age; (c) little or no previous experience with formal hypnosis; (d) seeking no therapeutic benefits and not in treatment with hypnosis; and (e) no negative emotional reactions to hypnosis at pretest. Simulating subjects had to meet additional criteria of a score of three or less on the HGSHS and a score of two or less on the SHCS. The ratio of real subjects to simulators was 2:1 in each group.

Hypnotists

Four hypnotists of varying skill levels were used. The senior author administered pretests, all SHCSs, and the first battery of posttests. The four moderately experienced hypnotists were trained in a four-month program using 53 volunteers for practice. The second author, blind to experimental conditions, administered the second battery of posttests and debriefed subjects. Three undergraduate assistants also administered HGSHSs at the first pretest.

Measures

Prior experience with hypnosis questionnaire. A questionnaire inquiring about prior experience and involvement with hypnosis was given at the subject selection phase.

Crowne Marlowe Social Desirability Scale (C-M) (Crowne & Marlowe, 1964). The C-M is a 33-item forced choice questionnaire which assesses "need for approval" and was used to control for the tendency to give socially desirable responses to the other questionnaires and tests.

Harvard Group Scale of Hypnotic Susceptibility (Shor & Orne, 1962). The HGSHS consists of ratings of hypnotic responsivity of eleven behaviors which subjects are requested to perform after undergoing a standardized hypnotic induction. A twelfth item, "amnesia," is based on timed recall of certain items and is scored later by the experimenter. The induction and test suggestions were administered via audiotape at both pre- and posttest.

Stanford Hypnotic Clinical Scale. The SHCS is a five-point standardized scale of hypnotic susceptibility which was administered and scored live by the senior author at the second pretest. This is a shorter form of the Stanford Scale of Hypnotic Susceptibility-Form C (SSHS-C; Weitzenhoffer & Hilgard, 1963). Criteria for scoring are similar to those on the HGSHS.

Percentage of successful suggestions. Training hypnotists met with the senior author after each training session and listed hypnotic phenomena attempted by the subjects. The hypnotists rated each suggested phenomenon based on their clinical judgment of whether the subjects "successfully experienced" the item. Percentages were used because the number of attempted items varied from subject to subject.

Nonvolition scales. A questionnaire previously employed by Bowers (1981a, 1981b) asked subjects to rate their own responses to the posttest HGSHS as voluntary or involuntary using a five-point scale. Subjects were also asked to rate their experience "as a whole" for the post-HGSHS on this scale.

LeCron Ruler. The LeCron Ruler Subjective Depth Scale (LeCron, 1953), which asks subjects to estimate their depth of trance on a 100-point scale, was administered at the second posttest. Subjects were first asked to rate their deepest trance during the experiment. Then, after an induction, subjects estimated their depth both immediately after this induction and again five minutes later, following a deepening procedure. Subjects were brought out of trance and asked to rerate their experience during the experiment.

Nonconscious involvement rating. A six-point scale of non-volition (Shor, 1979) was rated in an unstructured interview by the second author at the second posttest.

Simulator detection. At the end of the second training session the hypnotists and the second author were asked to guess the identity of simulators. No feedback was given so as to avoid "training" in simulator identification.

Procedure

Following pretests, real subjects and simulators were randomly assigned to groups. Using guidelines provided by Orne (1979; personal communication, March 3, 1982) simulators were told that they were essentially nonhypnotizable and that we had a special job for them to perform. They were asked simply to simulate hypnosis for the training sessions and during the second posttest, with no explicit instructions given on how to do so. They were further told that they would be dismissed and sent for debriefing if detected as simulators. Hypnotists were not told to dismiss subjects. This strategy was designed to heighten motivation and effort in *both* simulators and hypnotists. The groups were run in cohorts of twos and threes in order to maximize individual attention. Two training sessions of two hours each were completed. In all, four hours of testing and inquiry were done with each subject.

Subjects in all groups except the placebo were trained on items not included in the dependent measure. (A description of the pool of training items is available from the authors on request.) Social learning subjects were also trained on the first three items from the SSHS-C as in Katz (1979a). Subjects in all groups except the placebo were provided with written information designed to dispel common misconceptions about hypnosis (adapted from Gregory & Diamond, 1973).

Social learning approach. In the first session subjects engaged in a question-and-answer period about hypnosis and then completed a programmed learning booklet from Diamond et al. (1975). They read paragraphs of disinhibitory information and cognitive strategies for achieving hypnotic phenomena, turned the page to multiple choice questions on the paragraphs with instructions to "think with and answer," and then turned the page for immediate feedback. Next a videotaped model demonstrated four hypnotic phenomena from the SSHS-C (Weitzenhoffer & Hilgard, 1963). An hour was then devoted to shaped practice following a standard eye fixation-closure, progressive relaxation induction. In the second session the videotaped model described cognitive strategies used to achieve the phenomena modeled earlier. A text provided by Katz (1979b) was used for this purpose. The final hour and a half was spent in practice, and the hypnotist used the shaping procedures. Only direct suggestion was used.

Utilization approach. Following a question-and-answer period, trance was induced with the same standardized procedure described above. A guided fantasy followed, and the next hour and a half were spent in experiencing hypnosis with the hypnotist using various individualized inductions (Erickson, 1964, 1968), direct and indirect suggestion, trance ratification (Erickson & Rossi, 1979) and "pacing and leading" (Bandler & Grinder, 1975). In session two, the full two hours were devoted to again experiencing hypnosis and various phenomena.

Combined approach. In this group subjects were offered the same training as that provided in the social learning group, and utilization procedures were employed during the hour-and-a-half practice period.

Placebo. In the first session subjects viewed the film *Trance and Ritual in Bali* (Attenborough, 1972) in which people from a different culture perform various acts, such as spirit possession. A 45-minute nondirective group discussion about the film and hypnosis followed. Subjects next stared at a spiral after-image effect producer, viewed three-dimensional pictures and color wheels, and experienced the Chevreul pendulum effect (Easton & Shor, 1977). In session two, subjects viewed more spirals, practiced the pendulum effect, did a postural sway exercise, engaged in an interpersonal trust exercise (being blindfolded and led around), and "experienced" rocks, acorns, and fruit. Hypnotists gently redirected subjects' attention if in their clinical judgment any signs of spontaneous trance developed.

RESULTS

The basic statistical procedure used was a 2 × 4 factorial analysis of variance (ANOVA) followed by linear contrasts of planned comparisons using a one-way analysis of variance. (The argument for the case of using ad hoc linear comparisons or post hoc multiple comparisons in the face of nonsignificant interactions can be found in Howell, D. C., 1982, *Statistical Methods for Psychology*, Boston: Duxbury Press.) All planned comparisons were run with pooled variances.

Pretests

While there was a significant main effect for group on need for approval (Crowne Marlowe Scale, $p < .03$), post hoc Student Neuman Keuls comparisons ($\alpha = .05$) showed no differences between groups. On both pretest hypnotic susceptibility tests (SHCS, HGSHS) there were no significant differences between groups, and the group by subject type interactions were nonsignificant.

Hypnotic Susceptibility

To assess changes in hypnotic susceptibility on the HGSHS a repeated measures ANOVA was performed. Table 1 shows that the effects for group, subject type, and pre- to postchanges were significant. The subject type by pre- to postchange interaction approached significance. These findings indicate that real subjects were higher in rated susceptibility than simulators at both pre- and posttest, and that real subjects changed more than simulators. There is a suggestion that both real subjects and simulators changed. The placebo group was not compared due to an imbalance in the design (i.e., there were no simulators in the placebo group). To compare the other groups to the placebo subjects an ANOVA was performed on the change scores which yielded a significant effect for group, ($p < .01$), and an effect approaching significance ($p < .08$) for subject type. Post hoc Student Neuman Keuls comparisons indicated that real subjects in the utilization condition were higher than the placebo subjects, but the other groups did not differ either from the placebo subjects or the utilization real subjects. Interestingly, the change score difference between real subjects and simulators in the social learning condition was only one tenth of a point, whereas there was a 2.2-point difference between real subjects and simulators in the utilization condition. The group means on hypnotic susceptibility are presented in Table 2.

Table 1
Repeated Measures ANOVA on HGSHS Scores

Source	DF	SS	MS	F	ρ
Group	2	15.857	7.928	3.15	.05
Subject Type	1	206.134	206.134	81.96	.001
Group x Subject Type	2	2.248	1.124	.45	ns
Error	42	105.63	2.515		
HGSHS Pre/Post	1	102.96	102.96	51.67	.001
Group x Pre/Post	2	1.542	.77	.39	ns
Subj. Type x Pre/Post	1	6.885	6.885	3.46	.07
Group x Subj/Type × Pre/Post	2	3.814	1.907	.96	ns
Error	42	83.691	1.99		

Table 2
Group Means on Hypnotic Susceptibility

Group		SHCS	HGSHS-1	HGSHS-2	HGSHS-Change
Utilization			Hypnotic Susceptibility		
Reals	11	1.55	4.55	7.73	3.18
Simulators	5	.2	2.6	3.6	1.0
Social Learning					
Reals	11	1.91	5.36	8.0	2.6
Simulators	6	.67	2.67	5.17	2.5
Combined					
Reals	10	1.7	4.8	7.3	2.5
Simulators	5	.2	1.8	3.2	1.4
Placebo Ss	6	1.33	4.83	4.5	− .33

Nonconscious Involvement Measures

Nonvolition. An ANOVA was used to determine if there were differences in ratings of subjective experience of nonvolition on *passed* items of the posttest HGSHS. Significant effects were found for treatment group, ($p < .001$), and for subject type, ($p < .001$). Planned linear comparisons showed that utilization real subjects were higher in nonvolition than social learning real subjects, ($p < .006$). Combined real subjects were higher than social learning real subjects, ($p < .05$); and social learning real subjects were higher than placebo subjects, ($p < .005$). In addition, utilization real subjects were higher than their simulators, ($p < .03$); combined real subjects were higher than their simulators, ($p < .04$); social learning real subjects were higher than their simulators, ($p < .03$); and utilization simulators were significantly higher than social learning simulators, ($p < .04$).

The ANOVA for the ratings of nonvolition on *failed* items at posttest HGSHS produced a significant effect only for subject type, ($p < .01$). However, planned linear contrasts did not show any differences between the real subjects and simulators. The ANOVA for the ratings of nonvolition on all items, regardless of passing or failing, yielded a significant effect for group, ($p < .001$) and subject type, ($p < .001$). Planned linear contrasts showed that utilization real subjects were higher than social learning real subjects, ($p < .03$), and social learning real subjects were higher than placebo subjects, ($p < .02$). Utilization real subjects were higher than their simulators, ($p < .001$); combined real subjects were higher than their simulators, ($p < .001$); and social learning real subjects were higher than their simulators, ($p < .004$). In this case the social learning real subjects were higher than the utilization simulators, ($p < .04$).

The ANOVA for ratings of *overall nonvolition* showed a significant effect for group ($p < .003$) and subject type, ($p < .001$). The planned linear contrasts indicated that utilization real subjects were higher than social learning real subjects, ($p < .01$). Utilization real subjects were significantly higher than their simulators, ($p < .02$), and combined real subjects were higher than their simulators, ($p < .001$).

The ANOVA on the second author's ratings of nonvolition made during the phenomenological inquiry yielded only a significant effect for subject type, ($p < .005$). The planned linear contrasts showed that utilization real subjects were higher than their simulators, ($p < .004$). Insufficient data were collected for placebo subjects on this measure to allow a comparison of placebo to social learning real subjects. The group means on nonvolition measures can be found in Table 3.

Hypnotic depth. The second measure of subjective experience was depth (i.e., the degree to which subjects feel they are distant from their general reality orientation following an induction). Although four depth ratings were made, results are only reported here on the last two due to the high intercorrelations between the ratings (see Table 4). The means fell in the predicted direction in virtually every case (see Table 3). The ANOVA on the second depth rating made during trance yielded significant effects for group ($p < .03$) and for group by subject type interaction ($p < .03$). The planned linear contrasts showed that utilization real subjects were higher than the social learning real subjects, ($p < .01$). The comparison of social learning real subjects to placebo subjects was not done due to insufficient data on the latter. As the simulating subjects were under instructions to simulate again at this point in the experiment, it is impossible to tell how much of their responses are due to simulation and how much might be due to genuine hypnotic depth. However, it is interesting to note that utilization simulators were lower than utilization real subjects, ($p < .05$). The ANOVA on the rating of the deepest trance during the experiment showed a significant effect for group, ($p < .001$) and group by subject type interaction, ($p < .05$). The planned linear contrasts showed that utilization real subjects were superior to

Table 3
Group Means on Nonconscious Involvement Measures

| Group | n | Self Rated Nonvolition at Post HGSHS | | | | 2nd Author's ratings of nonvolition | Hypnotic Depth Ratings | | | | Hypnotists' Ratings of Success on Suggested Phenomena |
		"on the whole"	passed items	failed items	total items		pre trance	trance 1	trance 2	post trance	
Utilization											
Reals	11	3.55	3.99	2.07	3.27	2.73	71.1	49.1	64.1	77	85%
Simulators	5	2.6	3.26	1.49	2.08	1.0	61.3	36.25	42.5	57.5	76%
Social Learning											
Reals	11	2.72	3.21	1.88	2.72	2.2	45.5	34.1	43.1	50	65%
Simulators	6	2.0	2.48	1.4	1.85	1.25	35	28.8	37.5	40	78%
Combined											
Reals	10	3.3	3.75	1.94	3.04	2.4	56.1	30.9	45.5	56.6	84%
Simulators	5	1.8	3.04	1.43	1.85	1.8	64.6	46	61.6	66.6	77%
Placebo Ss	6	2.17	2.26	1.63	2.02	—	—	—	—	—	—

social learning real subjects ($p < .001$), and utilization real subjects were superior to utilization simulators ($p < .03$).

Hypnotists' ratings of subjects' trance experiences. To increase the reliability of this measure, the ratings for the two treatment sessions were collapsed into one analysis. The ANOVA on the hypnotists' ratings of how successfully the subjects experienced the suggested practice phenomena yielded significant effects for group, ($p < .01$) and group by subject type interaction ($p < .05$). The planned comparisons showed that the utilization real subjects were superior to the social learning real subjects ($p < .001$).

Simulator Detection

Four out of five simulators were detected by hypnotists in the utilization group compared to two out of six in the social learning group and three out of five in the combined group. This difference was not significant nor was the second author able to significantly differentiate simulators in the different groups.

Relationships Between Measures

A correlation matrix was done to examine the degree of relationship between the traditional measures of hypnotizability (the HGSHS and SHCS) and the measures of nonvolition and depth. The results are presented in Table 4. It can be seen that, although there are often significant correlations between the HGSHS, SHCS, and the other measures of hypnotic responsivity, the magnitude of the effects are not overwhelmingly high.

DISCUSSION

We set out to determine if the social learning-based skills approach to the modification of hypnotizability neglected the subjects' internal experiences. In addition, we sought to determine if a utilization approach could produce changes on the measures usually given in modification experiments and if it would have a greater effect on the subjects' subjective experiences than the social learning approach.

Our findings, though not conclusive, suggest that we were heading in the right direction. Both the social learning-based skills approach and the Ericksonian utilization approach produced changes on the test of hypnotic susceptibility, and the utilization subjects were found superior

Table 4
Intercorrelations Between Measures

	Hypnotic Susceptibility[a]					Nonvolition		Hypnotic Depth[b]			
	SHCS	HGS-1	HGS-2	Passed Items	Total Items	Overall	2nd Author's Rating[b]	1	2	3	4
SHCS	1.00	.74***	.66***	.26*	.48***	.42***	.38**	-.09	-.05	-.8	.03
HGS-1		1.00	.48***	.29**	.51***	.44***	.18	-.20	-.11	-.01	-.06
HGS-2			1.00	.36**	.65***	.56***	.54***	.17	.16	.22	.26
Passed items				1.00	.82***	.78***	.44***	.41**	.11	.26*	.43**
Total Items					1.00	.86***	.48***	.29*	.07	.19	.34**
Overall						1.00	.49***	.33**	.13	.17	.38**
2nd Author							1.00	.29*	.15	.26*	.37**
1								1.00	.51***	.63***	.92***
2									1.00	.85***	.66***
3										1.00	.72***
4											1.00

*$p < .05$
**$p < .01$
***$p < .001$

[a] $n = 54$
[b] based on n's varying from 48 to 42

to the placebo subjects. In addition, subjects in the utilization approach scored higher on all of the ratings of nonvolition except for items not passed in the HGSHS. The utilization approach was also found to alter general reality orientation more than the social learning approach as reflected in the measures of hypnotic depth. These findings are strengthened when we examine the results for the simulators. There were clear differences in the results between the real and simulating subjects in the utilization and combined groups, especially on the subjective measures. By contrast, in the social learning group the simulators performed like the real subjects. A further finding supporting the greater efficacy of the utilization approach was that the simulators in this group reported greater effects on the subjective measures than any of the other simulators. Such an effect is consistent with a hypothesis offered by Erickson (1980c) based on his own informal experiments with simulation. Overall, these findings suggest that the expectations and demand characteristics were more potent and discernible in the social learning group than in the utilization group, thus influencing behavioral responses while minimally influencing subjects' internal experiences.

The strength of these conclusions must be tempered by the fact that some of these findings, though all in the expected direction, were not statistically significant. Hypnotists were not statistically better at detecting simulators in the utilization group though they detected proportionally more. During the phenomenological inquiry the ratings of nonvolition made by the second author did not discriminate between the groups.

It could be argued that in the utilization group the expectations of the experimenters and hypnotists might have been communicated to the subjects inadvertently (while the expectations were more overt in the social learning group). We controlled for the tendency to give expected responses (e.g., by the use of the C-M, and simulators), and we would have expected far greater effects in the ratings of nonvolition made by the second author if it were the case that we had not sufficiently controlled for expectancy.

A sidelight to the study was that the subjects in the social learning-based group and some in the combined group complained about the inflexibility of the hypnotists and the repetitiveness of the procedures. This was not the case in the utilization group and suggests that the utilization approach is a more comfortable approach for the subject than the behavioral approach.

These findings also support our concern about the dependent measures used in previous studies of the modification of hypnotizability.

We found only moderate correlations between the susceptibility tests and the subjective measures, accounting for between 0.06% and 42% of the variance in the scores. These correlations were lower than those reported by Bowers (1981a, 1981b) and by Farthing, Brown, and Venturino (1983). These studies were more directly approaching the question of the correlation between the objective and subjective measures but erred, we believe, in creating unwanted expectancy effects. To tell subjects, as did Farthing et al. (1983), that *faking* a response is part of hypnotic performance might suggest to the subjects some urge to report experiences as real. Further, in finding a relationship between passing items and nonvolition on items passed, they seemed to assume that subjects would forget their performance. By contrast, one of the most consistent chance observations in our study and in Bastien's (1983) was that subjects reported that their performance on the second administration of the HGSHS was influenced by their clear memory of the first. Our results were similar to those of Council, Kirsch, Vickery, and Carlson (1983) who found reports of hypnotic depth unrelated to increases in measured susceptibility when social learning procedures were used.

What is the clinical significance of modifying hypnotic susceptibility scores? None has yet been determined, although Diamond (1977a,b, 1982) and Katz (1978, 1979a,b) might have us believe that there is one. The question of the external validity of the measured changes is still open. While both prior studies and the present one found changes in susceptibility scores, no study has yet attempted to relate such changes to performance in other situations, clinical or experimental. For example, are such changes related to performance on a cold pressor test (i.e., clinical sensitivity to pain)? Touching on this issue is the finding that, on the whole, increases in hypnotic susceptibility scores produced tend not to be maintained at follow-up (Perry, 1977). At this juncture any attempt to suggest that increases in susceptibility test scores are either stable or related to clinical procedures or outcome is highly premature.

Finally, most studies on modification of hypnotizability suffer from obviousness of their procedures, both in the measurement of hypnotizability and the performance expected during training. Erickson and Erickson (1941) suggested that, to demonstrate genuine effects in hypnotic studies, it is *essential* to ensure that the subject does not know the expected or desired response. In studies of the modification of hypnotizability we still have a way to go before reaching this goal. Perhaps the way can be lighted if we pay more attention in the future to Milton Erickson's clinical and experimental methods and to his ideas about the nature of hypnotizability.

REFERENCES

Attenborough, D. (Producer, Director). (1972). *Trance and ritual in Bali* [Film]. Lexington, MA: Xerox.

Bandler, R., & Grinder, J. (1975). *Patterns of the hypnotic techniques of Milton H. Erickson, M.D.* (Vol. 1). Cupertino, CA: Meta Publications.

Barber, J. (1980). Hypnosis and the unhypnotizable. *American Journal of Clinical Hypnosis, 23*, 4-9.

Bastien, S. A. (1983, August). *Hypnotic treatment of smoking.* Paper presented at the annual meeting of the American Psychological Association, Anaheim, CA.

Bernheim, H. (1889). *Suggestive therapeutics: A treatise on the nature and uses of hypnotism.* (2nd ed.) (C. A. Herter, Trans.). New York: Putnam.

Bowers, K. (1981a). Do the Stanford scales tap the "classic suggestion effect"? *International Journal of Clinical and Experimental Hypnosis, 24*, 42-53.

Bowers, K. (1981b). Has the sun set on the Stanford scales? *American Journal of Clinical Hypnosis, 24*, 79-88.

Brink, N. E. (1981). Hypnosis and control. *American Journal of Clinical Hypnosis, 24*, 109-116.

Cooper, L. M., & London, P. (1971). The development of hypnotic susceptibility: A longitudinal (convergence) study. *Child Development, 42*, 487-503.

Council, J. R., Kirsch, I., Vickery, A. R., & Carlson, D. (1983). "Trance" versus skill hypnotic inductions: The effects of credibility, expectancy, and experimenter modeling. *Journal of Consulting and Clinical Psychology, 51*, 432-440.

Crowne, D. P., & Marlowe, D. (1964). *The approval motive: Studies in evaluative dependence.* New York: Wiley.

Diamond, M. J. (1974). Modification of hypnotizability: A review. *Psychological Bulletin, 81*, 180-198.

Diamond, M. J. (1977a). Hypnotizability is modifiable: An alternative approach. *International Journal of Clinical and Experimental Hypnosis, 25*, 147-166.

Diamond, M. J. (1977b). Issues and methods for modifying responsivity to hypnosis. *Annals of the New York Academy of Sciences, 269*, 119-128.

Diamond, M. J. (1982). Modifying hypnotic experience by means of indirect hypnosis and hypnotic skill training: An update (1981). *Research Communications in Psychiatry, 7*, 233-239.

Diamond, M. J., Steadman, C., Harada, D., & Rosenthal, J. (1975). The use of direct instructions to modify hypnotic performance: The effects of programmed learning procedures. *Journal of Abnormal Psychology, 84*, 109-113.

Easton, R. D., & Shor, R. E. (1977). Augmented and delayed feedback in the Chevreul pendulum illusion. *Journal of General Psychology, 97*, 167-177.

Erickson, M. H. (1964). The "surprise" and "my-friend-John" techniques of hypnosis: Minimal cues and natural field experimentation. *American Journal of Clinical Hypnosis, 6*, 293-307.

Erickson, M. H. (1968). An hypnotic technique for resistant patients: The technique, its rationale, and field experiments. *American Journal of Clinical Hypnosis, 7*, 8-32.

Erickson, M. H. (1980a). A brief survey of hypnotism. In E. L. Rossi, (Ed.), *The collected papers of Milton H. Erickson on hypnosis* (Vol. 3). New York: Irvington.

Erickson, M. H. (1980b). Hypnotism. In E. L. Rossi (Ed.), *The collected papers of Milton H. Erickson on hypnosis* (Vol. 3). New York: Irvington.

Erickson, M. H. (1980c). Further experimental investigation of hypnosis: Hypnotic and nonhypnotic realities. In E. L. Rossi, (Ed.), *The collected papers of Milton H. Erickson on hypnosis* (Vol. 1). New York: Irvington.

Erickson, M. H., & Erickson, E. (1941). Concerning the nature and character of posthypnotic behavior. *Journal of General Psychology, 24*, 95-133.

Erickson, M. H., & Rossi, E. L. (1979). *Hypnotherapy: An exploratory casebook.* New York: Irvington.

Farthing, G. W., Brown, S. W., & Venturino, M. (1983). Involuntariness of response on the Harvard Group Scale of Hypnotic Susceptibility. *International Journal of Clinical and Experimental Hypnosis, 31,* 170-181.

Frischolz, E. J., Spiegel, D., & Blumstein, R. (1982). Comparative efficacy of hypnotic behavioral training and sleep trance hypnotic induction: Comment on Katz. *Journal of Consulting and Clinical Psychology, 50,* 766-769.

Gilligan, S. G. (1982). Ericksonian approaches to clinical hypnosis. In J. K. Zeig (Ed.), *Ericksonian approaches to hypnosis and psychotherapy.* New York: Brunner/Mazel.

Gregory, J., & Diamond, M. J. (1973). Increasing hypnotic susceptibility by means of positive expectancies and written instructions. *Journal of Abnormal Psychology, 82,* 363-367.

Hilgard, E. R. (1975). Hypnosis. *Annual Review of Psychology, 26,* 19-44.

Katz, N. W. (1978). Hypnotic inductions as training in cognitive control. *Cognitive Therapy and Research, 2,* 365-369.

Katz, N. W. (1979a). Comparative efficacy of behavioral training, training plus relaxation, and a sleep trance hypnotic induction in increasing hypnotic susceptibility. *Journal of Consulting and Clinical Psychology, 47,* 119-127.

Katz, N. W. (1979b). *Increasing hypnotic responsiveness: Behavioral training vs. trance induction.* Unpublished manuscript, University of New Mexico, Dept. of Psychology.

LeCron, L. M. (1953). A method of measuring the depth of hypnosis. *Journal of Clinical and Experimental Hypnosis, 1,* 19-30.

Morgan, A. H. (1973). The heritability of hypnotic susceptibility in twins. *Journal of Abnormal Psychology, 82,* 55-61.

Morgan, A. H., & Hilgard, J. R. (1978). The Stanford Hypnotic Clinical Scale for Adults. *American Journal of Clinical Hypnosis, 21,* 134-147.

Morgan, A. H., Johnson, D. L., & Hilgard, E. R. (1974). The stability of hypnotic susceptibility: A longitudinal study. *International Journal of Clinical and Experimental Hypnosis, 22,* 249-257.

Orne, M. T. (1971). The simulation of hypnosis: Why, how, and what it means. *International Journal of Clinical and Experimental Hypnosis, 14,* 183-210.

Orne, M. T. (1973). Communication by the total experimental situation: Why it is important, how it is evaluated, and its significance for the ecological validity of findings. In P. Pliner, L. Krames, & T. Alloway (Eds.), *Communication and affect* (pp. 157-191). New York: Academic Press.

Orne, M. T. (1979). On the simulating subject as a quasi-control group in hypnosis research: What, why, and how. In E. Fromm, & R. E. Shor (Eds.), *Hypnosis: Research developments and perspectives* (pp. 399-443). Chicago, IL: Aldine-Atherton.

Perry, C. (1977). Is hypnotizability modifiable? *International Journal of Clinical and Experimental Hypnosis, 25,* 125–146.

Shor, R. E. (1979). A phenomenological method for the measurement of variables important to an understanding of the nature of hypnosis. In E. Fromm, & R. E. Shor (Eds.), *Hypnosis: Developments in research and new perspectives* (pp. 212-215). Hawthorne, NY: Aldine.

Shor, R. E., & Orne, E. C. (1962). *Harvard Group Scale of Hypnotic Susceptibility—Form A.* Palo Alto, CA: Consulting Psychologists Press.

Weitzenhoffer, A. M. (1980). Hypnotic susceptibility revisited. *American Journal of Clinical Hypnosis, 22,* 130-146.

Weitzenhoffer, A. M., & Hilgard, E. R. (1959). *Stanford Hypnotic Susceptibility Scale—Forms A & B.* Palo Alto, CA: Consulting Psychologists Press.

Weitzenhoffer, A. M., & Hilgard, E. R. (1963). *Stanford Hypnotic Susceptibility Scale—Form C.* Palo Alto, CA: Consulting Psychologists Press.

PART X
Forensic Issues

There has been considerable controversy in recent years about the use of hypnosis to "refresh" the memories of victims and witnesses of crimes. A number of experts theorize that hypnosis should not be used in court because it can alter a witness' testimony. However, the authors of the chapters in this section are in agreement with Erickson's position that hypnosis has a place in the courtroom.

Martin Reiser, Ed.D., earned his degree from Temple University. Currently, he serves as Director of Behavioral Science Services for the Los Angeles Police Department. Reiser is author of the Handbook of Investigative Hypnosis *(Lehi Press, 1980),* Practical Psychology for Police Officers *(Thomas Press, 1973), and the* Police Department Psychologist *(Thomas Press, 1972). He received the 1980 Milton Erickson Award for Excellence in Scientific Writing from the* American Journal of Clinical Hypnosis.

Reiser is a strong supporter of the forensic use of hypnosis, a position to which Milton Erickson subscribed. In fact, Erickson supplied training to Reiser and some of his investigative team of police officers.

A number of courts have ruled that hypnotically refreshed testimony is inadmissible because of the possibility of confabulation on the part of the subject. According to Reiser, hypnotic recall can be effectively used in forensic work.

Leo Alexander, M.D., earned his degree at the University of Vienna in 1929. He has an impressive list of contributions to the fields of neurology, psychotherapy, forensic psychology, and

509

hypnosis. Alexander was a long-time colleague of Milton Erickson; they worked together at Worchester State Hospital in the 1930s.

Patrick J. Brady is a full-time member of the Boston Police Department and is director of its Hypnosis Unit. Brady has been active in lecturing on hypnosis for major universities and professional organizations and has brought the subject of forensic hypnosis to the public's attention through television and newspaper interviews.

In their chapter, Alexander and Brady describe aspects of hypnosis that make it a valuable forensic tool. They present the background needed by the forensic hypnotist and outline an approach that the hypnotist should use. Cases demonstrate the efficacy of investigative hypnosis; guidelines are presented for its use.

Chapter 31

Investigative Hypnosis: Scientism, Memory Tricks and Power Plays

Martin Reiser

Janet Buell watched her husband die in an exchange of gunfire with an intruder at their rural Arizona home. Her two small children were also present. Traumatized, and in shock, neither wife nor children could clearly describe the killer. Subsequently, during a hypnotic interview, Mrs. Buell was able to recall the assailant and assist an artist in constructing a composite likeness. The suspect was recognized from the drawing and located. He was identified by the widow; a fresh bullet wound as previously described by her was found on the man, and other key descriptors were validated. However, the Arizona court disqualified Mrs. Buell from testifying because of the hypnotic interview and the case was dismissed. The suspect was released and quickly disappeared.

In another case in California (*People* v. *Bamberg*, 1982), a woman was viciously raped and traumatized. The defendant was identified the day after the rape and charged. Suffering from symptoms of posttraumatic stress syndrome, the victim underwent hypnotherapy from a psychologist. Two years later, she was declared incompetent to testify because of the therapeutic use of hypnosis, and the case was dismissed (Relinger, 1983).

In other major crime cases in the states of Maryland (*Collins* v. *State*, 1982), Michigan (*People* v. *Gonzales*, 1982), Minnesota (*State* v. *Mack*, 1980), Nebraska (*State* v. *Palmer*, 1981), and Pennsylvania (*Com.* v. *Nazarovitch*, 1981), witnesses and victims are also being kept off the witness stand if they had their recall enhanced by hypnosis interviewing. Ironically, the California Supreme Court has ruled that a previously hypnotized *defendant* may testify because of his right to a defense (*People* v. *Shirley*, 1982).

The majority of state appellate courts have ruled that hypnotically refreshed testimony is generally admissible, the main question being how much weight should be given it by the trier of fact. These jurisdictions include Georgia (*Creamer* v. *State*, 1974), Illinois (*People* v. *Gibson*, 1983; *People* v. *Smrekar*, 1979), Indiana (*Morgan* v. *State*, 1983), Louisiana (*State* v. *Wren*, 1983), Missouri (*State* v. *Greer*, 1980), North Carolina (*State* v. *McQueen*, 1978), Oregon (*State* v. *Brom*, 1972), Tennessee (*State* v. *Glebock*, 1981), Wyoming (*Chapman* v. *State*, 1982), and North Dakota (*State* v. *Brown*, 1983). The federal courts have also adopted this rule (*United States* v. *Waksal*, 1982).

A few courts have allowed hypnotically aided testimony subject to certain procedural "safeguards," supposedly to ensure reliability. These include Florida (*Brown* v. *State*, 1983), New Jersey (*State* v. *Hurd*, 1981), New Mexico (*State* v. *Beachum*, 1981), and Washington (*State* v. *Martin*, 1982). However, ensuring reliability of any eyewitness testimony is problematic in any case, with or without hypnosis.

A number of states have modified their original *per se* rulings against any testimony by hypnotized witnesses and now allow their prehypnosis recall. These jurisdictions include Arizona (*State* v. *Collins*, 1982), Colorado (*People* v. *Quintana*, 1982), Michigan (*People* v. *Jackson*, 1981), Minnesota (*State* v. *Blanchard*, 1982), Nebraska (*State* v. *Patterson*, 1983), New York (*People* v. *Hughes*, 1982), and Pennsylvania (*Com.* v. *Taylor*, 1982).

The interest in the plight of the *victims* of crime has been growing as exemplified by the burgeoning of the field of victimology. Recently, the President's Commission on Crime and Violence issued its final report which contained recommendations designed to aid the victims of crime (President's Commission Report, 1983). The American Psychological Association also convened a Task Force on Victims of Crime and Violence to review research and practices and to recommend appropriate action for psychologists and others having input into the criminal justice system (APA Task Force Report, 1983).

Clearly the swing of the pendulum, in terms of public concerns about crime and the vagaries of the criminal justice process, is toward more awareness and consideration of the problems and rights of victims. This is exemplified in California by the passage of Proposition 8, the so-called Victim's Bill of Rights. One aspect of this new law reaffirms the jury's right to hear all of the evidence as provided by the state evidence code.

The clear inference is that for expert witnesses to be allowed to preempt the hearing of testimony by a jury is dangerous and tantamount to ignoring critical evidence.

This is precisely what has happened in the area of investigative hypnosis. It has led to several negative court decisions and consequently to bad law. A few hypnosis "authorities" with impressive credentials have been on an avowed crusade to "shoot down" the police use of investigative hypnosis. In the process, they have misinformed the courts, colleagues and the public on many key hypnotic and psychological issues. Using assertion and fiat, without the required relevant data, these individuals, claiming to represent the "scientific community," have engaged in scientism in the guise of science and injected proprietary guild interests under the cover of ethical concerns.

An underlying territorial motive can be seen in the identical resolution passed by two separate clinical hypnosis societies declaring it unethical for members to teach, supervise or consult with police who use investigative hypnosis in criminal cases (ISH Resolution, 1979; SCEH Resolution, 1979). Attempts are also being made to extend the power play, still in the guise of an ethics problem, to other psychological and hypnosis associations. Toch (1981) discussed the use of ethics as a weapon by researchers who have vested interests and desire to cause conflict within the research community. Lederer and Singer (1983) also focus on this issue:

> Gullible students and the public are being told falsehoods by our colleagues. Belief in these falsehoods is no doubt being facilitated by public trust that, if these ideas were outright nonsense or fraud, the university would not permit their teaching. We are lending public forums and academic authority to pseudoscience or nonsense, and have acted as if we had no responsibility in the matter. (p. 59)

ISSUES

Several unsubstantiated and patently incorrect assertions have been made in the name of "the scientific community" by opponents of the police use of investigative hypnosis. The assertions serve mainly to perpetuate myths and misinformation about hypnosis that conscientious professionals have been trying to dispel for many years.

Issue: Hypersuggestibility

The assertions that hypnosis always involves hypersuggestibility and that hypnotic recall is essentially unreliable (Diamond, 1980; Orne, 1979) are linked to the old Svengali myth of mind control which Conn (1982) lucidly addressed.

Charcot (1877) and Hull (1933) popularized the notion that hypnosis and suggestibility are synonymous. This has remained an all too common belief among some professionals and much of the public despite a current scientific consensus that suggestibility per se plays a relatively small part in hypnosis processes (Bowers, 1977; Frankel, 1976; Hilgard, 1965; Hilgard, 1981; Sheehan & Perry, 1976). Long ago, Bernheim (1890) recognized that hypnosis and suggestibility existed independently of each other. More recently, Erickson, Rossi, and Rossi (1976) pointed out that hypersuggestibility is not necessary in trance states:

> This is a major misconception that has frustrated and discouraged many workers in the past and has impeded the development of hypnosis as a science. Trance is a special state that intensifies the therapeutic relationships and focuses patients' attention on inner realities. Trance does not insure the acceptance of suggestions. (p. 312)

Kroger (1977) discussed the pervasiveness of suggestion in everyday life and pointed, as an example, to the success of the multibillion dollar advertising industry which relies mainly on suggestion and persuasion. Other ordinary examples of suggestibility are the placebo effect, religious conversions, faith healing, confidence games, and love relationships. It is apparent from studies of voodoo, communications and systems theory, attitudes, beliefs and values that suggestibility and the potential to be influenced are a part of normal waking life and do not require a state of hypnosis to operate (Barber, 1961; Rokeach, 1968; Von Bertalanffy, 1968; Watzlawick, 1978). The conclusion to be drawn is that with or without hypnosis, people are suggestible to varying degrees.

Implied in the concept of suggestibility is the image of the hypnotist utilizing a magical state of power and control over the subject. Hypnotic potential is actually a capability residing within each individual. All the hypnotist does is guide or teach the motivated subject to tap into these latent abilities. The Spiegels have stated it simply: "All hypnosis is really self-hypnosis, and the patient is taught from the beginning to master his own trance capacity (Spiegel & Spiegel, 1978). In this regard, Hilgard

(1977) and Barber (1980) have pointed out the need to differentiate among three related but distinct variables: hypnotic ability, hypnotic susceptibility and hypnotic suggestibility. The three factors frequently are lumped together and confused by those unfamiliar with current research.

Issue: Confabulation

The main spokespersons opposing the police use of investigative hypnosis assert that confabulation and fantasy are invariable consequences of the procedure (Diamond, 1980; Orne, 1979). Their support for this position consists mainly of laboratory-derived *theory* and anecdotes from hypnotherapy and psychotherapy literature involving therapists treating "patients" to elicit unconscious conflicts, material from childhood, and dreams and fantasies. In the therapy arena, the truthfulness of material recalled by the patient is secondary to the emotional significance it has for the overall therapeutic process. In this context, screen memories may be as useful as historically accurate ones (Freud, 1953).

Aside from an occasional instance of abuse or misuse, no valid data have been presented to justify claims of the certainty of confabulation in actual crime cases where investigative hypnosis is properly used. The scientific literature on confabulation in general is sparse and there are virtually no relevant data to show that hypnotized subjects invariably confabulate more than nonhypnotized persons or produce more incorrect information.

Our data in over 600 major crime cases at the Los Angeles Police Department show that hypnosis interviews with cooperative, traumatized witnesses enhanced investigatively useful recall in approximately three-fourths of the cases, using original police reports as the criterion measure. Adequate follow-up was possible in only 50% of these cases, and accuracy levels of the hypnotically elicited information was found to be around 90% (LAPD Report, 1982). Reports by law enforcement practitioners of investigative hypnosis consistently have been similar (Ault, 1980; Reiser, 1976; Stratton, 1977).

It is certainly possible for a witness, hypnotized or not, to lie, confabulate or fantasize if motivated to do so. However, my experience over a 12-year period with witnesses and victims who cooperated in an investigative hypnosis interview suggests that confabulation does not routinely or invariably occur. The legal-psychological literature on eyewitness problems and the misidentifications of suspects by nonhypnotized witnesses clearly indicate that this is a generic problem involving individual cognitive processes, sensory perceptual mechanisms, apperceptive mass, attitudes, values and belief systems (Buckhout, 1974; Loftus, 1979; Yarmey, 1979). These human cognitive variables have been labeled incorrectly as a hypnosis problem, leading to confusion, misunderstanding and negative legal consequences (Diamond, 1980; Orne, 1979).

Related to the confabulation issue is the question of the truthfulness and accuracy of witness recall and testimony. In an interesting "Catch-22" situation, critics falsely accuse police practitioners of believing that hypnosis is a truth-detecting device (Diamond, 1980; Orne, 1979). They then turn around and assert that because hypnosis does not guarantee truthfulness, previously hypnotized witnesses should not be permitted to testify. This apparently stems from an attempt to force inapropos psychological definitions into a dissimilar legal framework.

Relinger (1983) recently reviewed the literature assessing the reliability of hypnotically enhanced recall and found that meaningful material measured in a free-narrative response format is consistently enhanced. Nonsense material is generally not recalled well. He cited two recent studies that revealed no difference in the number of inaccurate responses between hypnotized and nonhypnotized subjects if deliberately misleading manipulations were avoided (Timm, 1981, 1982).

In the legal domain, what is required is not absolute accuracy but information having probative value. No eyewitness testimony has to be proven entirely correct to be admissible. Spector and Foster (1977) elucidate this important point in their law review article:

> Unfortunately, hypnosis has become linked in the minds of courts and commentators with the polygraph and narco-analysis as a technique for mechanically ascertaining the truth of the witnesses' testimony. Requiring hypnosis to perform a truth determinant function, however, distorts the scientific process and aborts its potential benefit for litigation. The value of hypnosis lies in its scientifically established reliability as a device for retrieving relevant testimony previously forgotten or psychologically suppressed, regardless of the factual truth or falsity of that testimony. (p. 567)

Issue: Memory Distortion

Assertions have been made in articles and in numerous court cases that a previously hypnotized witness automatically has tainted memory, is unable to discriminate among temporal events, becomes more certain about his recall and is impervious to cross-examination (Diamond, 1980).

The evidence to support these statements consist of a few "horror sto-ries" where hypnosis was misused or abused, most often by improperly trained health professionals.

In a recent study, confidence and accuracy of witness recall were positively related only when the original context was reinstated and when the "suspect" photograph was actually included in the array (Krafka & Penrod, 1982). Another new study on eyewitness recall found that a cognitive interview based on verbal learning experiments did not lead to increases in the amount of incorrect information or in the subject's confidence (Geiselman et al., 1983).

My own experience in numerous investigative hypnosis cases and in reviewing tapes and transcripts of other practitioners involved in the legal process, consistently reveals that previously hypnotized witnesses retain their prior mental abilities and are not significantly changed cog-nitively because of the hypnotic interview. They usually remain able to discriminate among events before, during and after hypnosis if indeed they had that capacity to start with.

One critic claims that police trainees of investigative hypnosis naively hold a tape recorder model of memory and are ignorant of how memory *really* works (Orne, 1979). The fact is that *no one* yet knows how memory really works despite a hundred years of laboratory research (Baddeley, 1976; Bahrick, 1979; Neisser, 1978; Nilsson, 1979). There are dozens of theories and models of memory. These include: the two-stage theory which says that recall involves both search and decision (Anderson & Bower, 1972); levels of processing theory which considers depth of pro-cessing questions and recall (Craik & Lockhart, 1972); the repression-blockade model (Freud, 1899); the cybernetic communication theory (Miller, Galanter & Pribram, 1960); the tape recorder model (Penfield, 1969); the two-system theory of episodic and semantic memories (Tul-ving, 1972); neodissociation and parallel processing theory (Hilgard, 1977); the holographic model (Pribram, 1969); the RNA molecule storage model (Hydén & Tange, 1965); the two-component theory of long-term and short-term memory (Baddeley, 1976); associative interference theory and trace decay theory (Postman & Underwood, 1973); the theory of context-bound recall (Hilgard & Bower, 1975); the uniqueness increases depth of processing theory (Moscovitch & Craik, 1976); the selective amnesia theory (Rackover, 1975); state-dependent learning theory (Overton, 1974); multiaccess and multichecking modes of retrieval theory (Mandler, 1979); encoding specificity theory (Tulving & Thomson, 1973); and the superiority of cued recall over uncued recall theory (Roediger, 1975; Stalnaker & Riddle, 1932; Tulving & Pearlstone, 1966).

Memory processes and research questions include the areas of perception, encoding, storage and retrieval of information. Recently, attention has been paid to the fact that acquisition of memory may involve subconscious as well as conscious processes (Cheek, 1959; Hilgard, 1977; Raikov, 1974; Reiser, 1980). This is a significant issue since a witness himself may not know consciously what has been registered in memory (Key, 1972).

Whether memory is deeply stored or permanently acquired, whether it can be retained in its originally perceived form or whether it is always reconstructed are some questions being asked in current memory research (Estes, 1970; Lachman et al., 1979; McGaugh, 1980; Spear, 1978; Tulving, 1972).

What is known is that episodic memory and visual images seem to be more deeply and permanently processed (Craik & Lockhart, 1972; Paivio, 1969, 1971). It appears that recognition memory for pictures is better than memory for words (Shepard, 1967; Standing, 1973) and that this memory tends to get better over time (Erdelyi & Kleinbard, 1978). Memory for faces seems to be remarkably resistant to forgetting (Watkins, Ho, & Tulving, 1976).

Kihlstrom (1981) concludes that it is difficult to attribute memory to a solely reconstructive process in light of the studies of eidetic images, screen and flashbulb memories. Dorcus (1956) found that the likelihood of accurate witness recall was correlated with the emotional involvement of the person. In the investigative hypnosis literature, there are numerous examples of the occurrence of a hypermnesia effect leading to increased recall of crime details and subsequent corroboration (Hibbard & Worring, 1981; Kroger, 1977; Reiser, 1980). In sum, it appears that misleading statements about complex memory theories and assertions about how memory *really* works (Orne, 1979), are out of keeping with the memory research literature and serve primarily to malign police investigative hypnosis practitioners and to negatively influence the courts.

CONCLUSION

Thus far, the state of the art of investigative hypnosis allows some pragmatic inferences: 1) hypnosis does not always result in hypersuggestibility; 2) investigative hypnosis is a specialty within the police science arena rather than the therapy domain; 3) the witness is not changed into a different person by hypnosis and retains his or her prior cognitive abilities to discriminate among events; 4) memory is not automatically tainted by hypnosis and confabulation is not an invariable consequence regarding recent crime situations; and 5) the model of memory favored by the hypnotist is irrelevant compared to properly cued recall (Tulving & Osler, 1968).

While there are obviously legitimate questions in any court case involving witness credibility, it is improper for so-called experts to manipulate courts into letting them limit what is admissible at trial. The evidence code of every jurisdiction in the country indicates that the trier of fact has a right to hear all of the relevant testimony, including cross-examination, and decide how much weight it deserves.

When many issues are misrepresented in court, where assertion replaces valid data, then scientism and not science is operative and our criminal justice process is infected by pseudoscientific censorship. Justice Gardner of the Fourth Appellate District in California addresses this issue in an opinion pointing out the illogic of the earlier *Shirley* decision (*People* v. *Williams*, 1982):

> I am firmly of the belief that jurors are quite capable of seeing through flaky testimony and pseudoscientific clap-trap. I quite agree that we should not waste our valuable court time watching witch doctors, voo-doo practitioners or *brujas* go through the entrails of dead chickens in a fruitless search for the truth. However, this is only because the practice is too time-consuming and its probative value is zilch. I like the rule established in *Frye* v. *United States*, 293 F.2d 1013 (D.C. Cir. 1923), on the basis that it is a good pragmatic tool to keep out unnecessary, time-consuming and nonproductive evidence. In other words I am a great believer in Evidence Code 352. However, the idea that an eyeball witness to a transaction be denied the opportunity to tell a jury his recollections of what he saw is disturbing to me whether that recollection has been refreshed by hypnosis, truth serum, drugs, intimidation, coercion, coaching, brainwashing or impaired by the plain old passage of time.
>
> Another aspect of *Shirley* disturbs me even more. In its modification *Shirley* determined that a defendant who submits to pretrial hypnosis may nevertheless testify. The idea that the predator may testify and yet his victim may not offends my sense of justice. It appears to me that the scales of justice are tilted—dangerously. (p. 4)

Milton Erickson approved of the use of investigative hypnosis by police to help solve crimes. He clearly distinguished it as a field removed from hypnotherapy, as one requiring its own training and expertise. His own early experience as a psychologist for the Wisconsin Correctional and Penal Institute (Gordon & Meyers-Anderson, 1981) provided him insight and helped reinforce a lifelong interest in criminal behavior, rehabilitation and justice.

Erickson was the first honorary member of the International Society for Investigative and Forensic Hypnosis; he also provided important adjunctive training to members of the Los Angeles Police Department and the Law Enforcement Hypnosis Institute, contributing significantly to the skills and professionalism of these trainers and practitioners. His support was extremely valuable and his open-mindedness and genius are greatly missed.

REFERENCES

American Psychological Association Task Force Report on Victims of Crime and Violence. (1983). Presented at the American Psychological Association Annual Conference, Anaheim, CA, August 29, 1983.
Anderson, J.R., & Bower, G.H. (1972). Recognition & retrieval processes in free recall. *Psychological Review, 79,* 97-123.
Ault, R.L., Jr. (1980). Hypnosis—the FBI's team approach. *FBI Law Enforcement Bulletin,* January, 5-8.
Baddeley, A.D. (1976). *The psychology of memory.* New York: Basic Books.
Bahrick, H.P. (1979). Broader methods and narrower theories for memory research: Comments on the papers by Eysenck and Cermak. In L.A. Cermak and F.I.M. Craik, (Eds.), *Levels of processing in human memory* (p. 142). Hillsdale, NJ: Erlbaum.
Barber, J. (1980, July). Hypnosis and the unhypnotizable. *The American Journal of Clinical Hypnosis,* 4-9.
Barber, T.X. (1961). Death by suggestions. *Psychosomatic Medicine, 23,* 153-156.
Bernheim, A.M. (1980). *New studies in hypnotism.* New York: International Universities Press. (Original work published 1890)
Bowers, K.S. (1977). *Hypnosis for the seriously curious.* New York: Aronson.
Brown v. State, 426 So. 2d 76 (Fla. Dist. Ct. App. 1983).
Buckhout, R. (1974). Eyewitness testimony. *Scientific American, 231,* 23-31.
Chapman v. State, 638 P. 2d 1280 (Wyo. 1982).
Charcot, J.M. (1877). *Lectures on the diseases of the nervous system.* London: New Sydenham Society.
Cheek, D.B. (1959). Unconscious perception of meaningful sounds during surgical anesthesia as revealed under hypnosis. *American Journal of Clinical Hypnosis, 1,* 101-113.
Collins v. State, 52 Md. App. 186, 447 A. 2d 1272 (1982).
Com. v. Nazarovitch, 496 PA. 97, 436 A.2d 170 (1981).
Com. v. Taylor, 294 PA. Super. 171, 439 A.2d 805 (1982).
Conn, J.H. (1982). The myth of coercion under hypnosis. In J. Zeig (Ed.), *Ericksonian approaches to hypnosis and psychotherapy* (pp. 357-367). New York: Brunner/Mazel.
Craik, F.I.M., & Lockhart, R.S. (1972). Levels of processing: A framework for memory research. *Journal of Verbal Learning and Verbal Behavior, 4,* 671-684.
Creamer v. State, 232 GA. 136, 205 S.E. 2d 240 (1974).

Diamond, B.L. (1980). Inherent problems in the use of pretrial hypnosis on a prospective witness. *California Law Review, 68,* 313-349.

Dorcus, R.M. (1956). *Hypnosis and its therapeutic applications.* New York: McGraw-Hill.

Erdelyi, M.H., & Kleinbard, J. (1978). Has Ebbinghaus decayed with time? The growth of recall (hypermnesia) over days. *Journal of Experimental Psychology: Human Learning & Memory, 4,* 275-289.

Erickson, M.H., Rossi, E.L., & Rossi, S.I. (1976). *Hypnotic realities.* New York: Irvington.

Estes, W.K. (1970). *Learning theory and mental development.* New York: Academic Press.

Frankel, F. (1976). *Hypnosis: Trance as a coping mechanism.* New York: Plenum Medical Books.

Freud, S. (1953). Screen memories. *Collected papers, Vol. 5* (pp. 47-69). London: The Hogarth Press. (Originally published in 1899)

Geiselman, E., Fisher, R.P., & MacKinnon, D.P. (1983). *Enhancement of eyewitness memory: An empirical evaluation of the cognitive interview.* Unpublished report, UCLA Psychology Department.

Gordon, D., & Meyers-Anderson, M. (1981). *Phoenix: Therapeutic patterns of Milton H. Erickson.* Cupertino, CA: Meta Publications.

Hibbard, W.S., & Worring, R.W. (1981). *Forensic hypnosis.* Springfield, IL: Charles C Thomas.

Hilgard, E.R. (1965). *The experience of hypnosis.* New York: Harcourt, Brace & World.

Hilgard, E.R. (1977). *Divided consciousness: Multiple controls in human thought and action.* New York: Wiley-Interscience.

Hilgard, E.R. (1981, January). Hypnotic susceptibility scales under attack: An examination of Weitzenhoffer's criticisms. *The International Journal of Clinical and Experimental Hypnosis, XXIX,* 24-41.

Hilgard, E.R., & Bower, G. (1975). *Theories of learning* (4th ed.). Englewood Cliffs, NJ: Prentice-Hall.

Hull, C.L. (1933). *Hypnosis and suggestibility.* New York: Appleton-Century-Crofts.

Hydén, H., & Tange, P.W. (1965). A differentiation in RNA response in neurons early & late during learning. *Proceedings of the National Academy of Sciences, 53,* 946-952.

International Society of Hypnosis Resolution. (1979). *The International Journal of Clinical and Experimental Hypnosis, 27,* 453.

Key, W.B. (1972). *Subliminal seduction.* Englewood Cliffs, NJ: Prentice-Hall.

Kihlstrom, J.F. (1981). Puzzles of imagery. *Journal of Mental Imagery, 5,* 43.

Krafka, C., & Penrod, S. (1982, August). *Reinstatement of context in a field experiment on eyewitness identification.* Paper presented at the American Psychological Association Annual Meeting, Washington, D.C.

Kroger, W.S. (1977). *Clinical and experimental hypnosis* (2nd ed.). Philadelphia: Lippincott.

Lachman, R., Lachman, J.L., & Butterfield, E.C. (1979). *Cognitive psychology and information processing.* Hillsdale, NJ: Erlbaum.

Lederer, R.J., & Singer, B. (1983, Spring). Pseudoscience in the name of the university. *The Skeptical Inquirer, VIII*(1), 59.

Loftus, E.F. (1979). *Eyewitness testimony.* Cambridge, MA.: Harvard University Press.

Los Angeles Police Department Report. (1982, March). *Hypnosis survey.* Unpublished.

Mandler, G. (1979). Organization and repetition: Organizational principles with special reference to rote learning. In L.G. Nilsson (Ed.), *Perspectives on memory research* (pp. 293-327). Hillsdale, NJ: Erlbaum.

McGaugh, J.L. (1980, December). Adrenaline: A secret agent in memory. *Psychology Today,* 132.

Miller, G.A., Galanter, E., & Pribram, K.H. (1960). *Plans and the structure of behavior.* New York: Holt.

Morgan v. State, 445 N.E. 2d 585. Ind App. (1983).

Moscovitch, M., & Craik, F.I.M. (1976). Depth of processing, retrieval cues, and uniqueness of encoding as factors in recall. *Journal of Verbal Learning and Verbal Behavior, 15,* 447-458.

Neisser, U. (1978). Memory: What are the important questions? In M.M. Greenberg (Ed.), *Practical aspects of memory* (pp. 27-34). New York: Academic Press.

Nilsson, L.G. (1979). *Perspectives on memory research.* Hillsdale, NJ: Erlbaum.

Orne, M.T. (1979, October). The use and abuse of hypnosis in court. *International Journal of Clinical and Experimental Hypnosis, 27,* 311-339.

Overton, D.A. (1974). Experimental methods for the study of state-dependent learning. *Federation Proceedings, 33,* 1800-1813.

Paivio, A. (1969). Mental imagery in associative learning and memory. *Psychological Review, 76,* 241-263.

Paivio, A. (1971). *Imagery and verbal processes.* New York: Holt, Rinehart & Winston.

Penfield, W. (1969). Consciousness, memory and man's conditioned reflexes. In K. Pribram (Ed.), *On the biology of learning.* New York: Harcourt, Brace & World.

People v. Bamberg, #H2196 (CA, 1982).

People v. Gibson, No. 4-82 0415 Ill. App. 4th District (1983).

People v. Gonzales, 415 Mich. 615, 329 N.W. 2d 743 (1982).

People v. Hughes, 88 A.D. 2d 17, 452 N.Y.S. 2d 929 (1982).

People v. Jackson, 114 Mich. App. 37, 312 N.W. 2d 387 (1981).

People v. Quintana, Colo. App. 535, P. 2d 525 (1982).

People v. Shirley, 31 Cal. 3d. 18, 181 Cal. Rptr. 243,641 P. 2d 775 (1982).

People v. Smrekar, 68 Ill. App. 3d 379, 385 N.E. 2d 848 (1979).

People v. Williams, 4 Crim. No. 12526, 4 Cal. App. 2d (1982).

Postman, I., & Underwood, B.J. (1973). Critical issues in interference theory. *Memory and Cognition, 1,* 19-40.

President's Commission on Victims of Violent Crime Report. (1983, January). Washington, D.C.: U.S. Department of Justice.

Pribram, K.H. (1969). The amnestic syndromes: Disturbances in coding? In G.A. Talland & N.C. Waugh (Eds.). *The pathology of memory.* New York: Academic Press.

Rackover, S.S. (1975). Voluntary forgetting before and after learning has been accomplished. *Memory and Cognition, 3,* 24-28.

Raikov, V.L. (1974, October). Hypnotic age regression to the neonatal period: Comparisons with role playing. *International Journal of Clinical and Experimental Hypnosis,* 84-87.

Reiser, M. (1974, October). Hypnosis as an aid in a homicide investigation. *The American Journal of Clinical Hypnosis, 17*(2), 84-87.

Reiser, M. (1976, November). Hypnosis as a tool in criminal investigation. *The Police Chief,* XLIII(11), 36-40.

Reiser, M. (1980). *Handbook of investigative hypnosis.* Los Angeles: LEHI Publishing Co.

Relinger, H. (1983, September). *Are courts restricting hypnotherapy? Current status of forensic hypnosis.* Paper presented at the American Psychological Association Convention, Anaheim, CA.

Roediger, H.L. (1975). Current status of research on retrieval processes in memory. *Polygraph, 4,* 304-310.

Rokeach, M. (1968). *Beliefs, attitudes and values.* San Francisco, CA: Jossey-Bass.

Sheehan, P.W., & Perry, C.W. (1976). *Methodologies of hypnosis: A critical appraisal of contemporary paradigms of hypnosis.* Hillsdale, NJ: Erlbaum.

Shepard, R.M. (1967). Recognition memory for words, sentences and pictures. *Journal of Verbal Learning and Verbal Behavior, 6,* 156-163.

Society for Clinical and Experimental Hypnosis Resolution. (1979). *International Journal of Clinical and Experimental Hypnosis, 27,* 452.

Spear, N.E. (1978). *The Processing of memories: Forgetting and retention.* Hillsdale, NJ: Erlbaum.

Spector, R.G., & Foster, T.E. (1977). Admissibility of hypnotic statements: Is the law of evidence susceptible? *Ohio State University Law Journal, 38,* 567.

Spiegel, H., & Spiegel, D. (1978). *Trance and treatment.* New York: Basic Books.

Stalnaker, J.M., & Riddle, E.E. (1932). The effect of hypnosis on long-delayed recall. *Journal of General Psychology, 6,* 429-440.
Standing, L. (1973). Learning 10,000 pictures. *Quarterly Journal of Experimental Psychology, 25,* 207-222.
State v. Beachum, 97 N.M. 682,643 P. 2d 246 (Ct. App. 1981).
State v. Blanchard, 315 N.W. 2d 427 (Minn. 1982).
State v. Brom, 8 Or. App. 598,494 P. 2d 434 (1972).
State v. Brown, Crim. No. 906, (N. Dak. Supreme Court, 1983).
State v. Collins, 132 Ariz. 180,644 P. 2d 1266 (1982).
State v. Glebock, 616 S.W. 2d 897 (Tenn. Crim. App. 1981).
State v. Greer, 609 S.W. 2d 423 (MO. Ct. App. 1980).
State v. Hurd, 86 N.J. 525,432 A. 2d 86 (1981).
State v. Mack, 292 N.W. 2d 764 (Minn. 1980).
State v. Martin, 33 Wash. App. 486,656 P. 2d 526 (1982).
State v. McQueen, 295 N.C. 96,244 S.E. 2d (1978).
State v. Palmer, 210 Neb. 206,313 N.W. 2d 648 (1981).
State v. Patterson, 213 Neb. 686, 331 N.W. 2d 500 (1983).
State v. Wren, 425 So. 2d 756 (La. 1983).
Stratton, J.G. (1977, April). The use of hypnosis in law enforcement criminal investigations. A pilot program. *Journal of Police Science and Administration, 5,* 399-406.
Timm, H.W. (1981). The effect of forensic hypnosis techniques on eyewitness recall and recognition. *Journal of Police Science and Administration, 9,* 188-194.
Timm, H.W. (1982). *An empirical examination of the effects of forensic hypnosis.* Paper presented at the meetings of the International Congress of Hypnosis and Psychosomatic Medicine, Glasgow, Scotland.
Toch, H. (1981). Cast the first stone? Ethics as a weapon. *Criminology, 19,* 185-194.
Tulving, E. (1972). Episodic and semantic memory. In E. Tulving & W. Donaldson (Eds.), *Organization of memory.* New York: Academic Press.
Tulving, E., & Osler, S. (1968). Effectiveness of retrieval cues in memory for words. *Journal of Experimental Psychology, 77,* 593-601.
Tulving, E., & Pearlstone, Z. (1966). Availability versus accessibility of information in memory for words. *Journal of Verbal Learning and Verbal Behavior, 5,* 381-391.
Tulving, E., & Thomson, D.M. (1973). Encoding specificity & retrieval processes in episodic memory. *Psychological Review, 80,* 352-373.
United States v. Waksal, 539 F. Supp. 834 (S.D. Fla. 1982).
Von Bertalanffy, L. (1968). *General systems theory.* New York: Braziller.
Watkins, M.J., Ho, E., & Tulving, E. (1976). Context effects in recognition memory for faces. *Journal of Verbal Learning and Verbal Behavior, 15,* 505-517.
Watzlawick, P. (1978). *The language of change.* New York: Basic Books.
Yarmey, D.A. (1979). *The psychology of eyewitness testimony.* New York: The Free Press.

Chapter 32

Forensic Hypnosis

Leo Alexander and Patrick J. Brady

DEFINITION

Definition: Hypnosis is an inward turning of the mind, with an enhanced concentration on one subject at a time. It was given the name "monoideism" by one of the founders of hypnosis, James Braid. It was he who coined the word "hypnosis," derived from the Greek word *hypnos* meaning sleep. However, after a number of years he recognized that hypnosis was not a state of sleep, but a state of enhanced concentration on one subject at a time, hence, the name "monoideism."

The Cognitive and Conative Aspects of Hypnosis

Hypnosis has a cognitive aspect as well as a conative aspect. The cognitive aspect is the basis for the phenomenon of hypermnesia, or enhanced memory function which enables a person to revivify memories of early childhood. In the waking state these experiences may be remembered dimly or not at all because of repression. Hypnosis may effect revivification of memory in which apparently unnoticed details of a stressful situation, such as details of the appearance of an assailant or the license number of a getaway car, can be brought back to conscious memory with surprising clarity.

The conative aspect is the capacity of persons under hypnosis to initiate actions and make decisions suppressing pain, fear or depression, or even carry out feats of endurance and strength by intense concentration on the desired result. The capacity is mobilized by response to suggestion provided by the hypnotist.

It is important to realize, however, that the hypnotist can suggest only those feats of accomplishment that the subject wishes and is physically able to perform. If a suggestion goes against the grain of the subject, the subject may become distressed or troubled and emerge from the hypnotic state spontaneously.

It is very important to keep the cognitive and conative areas separate. If enhancement of recall is desired but an emotional block is present, the subject should be directed to recall only the events of the day as if they were seen on a TV or movie screen, and to exclude his own emotions. Suggestions to recall specific data should be avoided.

As stated above, the key to hypnosis is concentration upon a single event, idea, intent or action. In its cognitive aspect it may be compared with a searchlight or magnifying glass; in its conative aspect, with an electric stimulus for motivating or directing action.

Interference with the Cognitive and Conative Functions of Hypnosis

The cognitive purpose of hypnosis may be interfered with by a counterwish to obscure, rather than to reveal information. Personal defensive reasons may motivate the subject to cover up by means of a fabricated memory. Thereby facts may be obscured and the conative effects of hypnosis may be inhibited by a counterwish to prevent decisive action, rather than to facilitate it. But because of the intense concentration on the subject in question, such counterwishes make these contrary efforts on the part of the hypnotized subject more obvious than in the waking state. Hence, the cover memories in such situations are more elaborate and uniform than in the waking state, and the fictitious nature of the defensive effort is recognizable.

For example, when hypnotized subjects make an effort to deny guilt, they exaggerate the denial by making themselves look like paragons of virtue in interpersonal relations. There is an "all or none aspect" to such a response in the hypnotic state. When people are able to find fault with their own behavior during the recital of past events, it is a point in favor of truthfulness; those presenting themselves as paragons of virtue in all their actions reinforce the suspicion of culpability.

METHODOLOGY

One of the most important aspects of conducting a forensic hypnotic session is that the witness's recollection should not be contaminated by suggestions given by the hypnotist. To ensure this, the questions asked by the hypnotist of the witness of a crime should be neutral and non-leading. This can be accomplished by ensuring that the investigative hypnotist receives from any case investigator or police officer only enough information that will allow the hypnotist to know what crime has been committed and the approximate time and place of the event. This will lessen the possibility of contamination since suggestive questions will be greatly reduced.

The investigative hypnotist should be familiar with all the techniques of a criminal investigation, to enable him or her to prepare the proper line of questioning. However, there should be no personal involvement with the ongoing investigation; the hypnotist should remain independent of all preconceived notions. Some experts have suggested that independence can be achieved only when the hypnotist is not a salaried employee of the police department (*State* v. *Hurd,* 1981, affidavit, p. 25). Such a mechanistic requirement would exclude police officers as a class of persons competent to perform investigative hypnosis. But it is clear that a police officer properly trained and qualified in the use of forensic hypnosis is in a better position than many other individuals to undertake hypnosis in the forensic context. Excluding qualified police officers from such responsibilities will not assure the main objective of "ethical independence" (Alexander, 1981). The ethical independence and sense of professionalism of the individual hypnotist is the appropriate field of inquiry. The senior author pointed out many years ago (Alexander, 1965) that hypnosis is not an independent specialty, but rather a "super-charging system."

Hypnosis can be done effectively only by people competent to deal with the problem at hand without hypnosis. For example, the psychotherapist using hypnosis should not provide dental treatment. Expertise does not come with hypnosis itself, but from the field in which people are trained, whether they be psychiatrists, psychologists, dentists, surgeons, or criminal investigators. It is foolhardy for anyone, within or without the healing arts, to think they are omniscient. Many, however, are unaware of their own limitations and become defensive about them. They feel that as a professional psychiatric or psychological hypnologist they should be able to do everything with hypnosis, but this is simply not so.

It became very clear to the senior author when he carried out hypnotic criminal investigations in the case of the Boston strangler (Frank, 1966) that the psychiatric and psychological aspects of the work were not sufficient to supply the ability to follow up leads that the hypnotic subject provided. The one surviving victim of the strangler recalled under Alexander's hypnosis, as well as under ether and pentothal narcosis administered by Dr. William Sargant of London, England, her tremendous fright and disturbance when "all that green jumped on me." This did not mean anything to either of us, but Detective Mellon of the Metropolitan District Police Commission in Boston, who stood by during this investigation at Alexander's suggestion, made a very important connection. He said immediately after this session: "Gee, Doctor, we better take a look at the green man." The "green man" was a rapist known to police under that name because he always carried out his crimes dressed in green overalls. At that time he was under observation at Bridgewater State Hospital. Detective Mellon went to see him that same day, and the "green man," Albert De Salvo, immediately confessed to all his stranglings. He not only knew his victims' names, but also numerous details about his crimes which, at Alexander's suggestion, had been kept out of the newspapers so that these details would be known only to the murderer and not to any of the self-appointed clairvoyants who had previously become misleading prime suspects. This case illuminated an outstanding difference between hypnotherapy and investigative hypnosis. In investigative hypnosis we want to become acquainted with new leads and new information, rather than with the emotional aspects of the witness, the victim or the perpetrator. It so happened that Albert De Salvo was greatly relieved when he was able to confess. He also expressed gratitude for having been prevented from continuing his compulsive murderous rampage. He was then treated by another psychiatrist during his imprisonment; hence, Alexander could never find out whether he was a true multiple personality or not.

Since the Boston strangler case in 1962-64, investigative hypnosis techniques have advanced to meet the demands of the courts. The following discussion presents our suggested guidelines to ensure that the hypnotic interview will be acceptable in the court system and helpful for further investigation of the crime. Subjects should be given the correct demand characteristics so that they know what is expected and are not placed in a position where they feel obligated to give information they do not have. We have found that if subjects are properly instructed in the pre-induction phase, their critical judgment is not impaired nor will they feel the need to please the hypnotist. It is also important that a complete and detailed report of the subject's recollection of the event be recorded prior to the investigative hypnosis session. We further feel that all interaction between the hypnotist and the subject should be recorded on video- as well as audiotape, one system backing up the other in case of a malfunction. The taping should include the preinduction, the induction and the postinduction phases.

During the preinduction phase of the interview, it should be fully explained to the subject that this procedure is strictly voluntary. We feel that it is important that the subject show an interest and trust in hypnosis as a possible means of assisting the police in their investigation. It is also important that the subject have no "hidden agenda" or "axe to grind" that would motivate the subject to lie or distort. For example, the testimony of a hypnotized spouse of a criminal defendant, who may have strong desire to exonerate or incriminate the defendant, should be received with more caution than that of a hypnotized eyewitness to an event who has no known connection to the case. The subject should understand exactly what will take place during the hypnotic sessions and he or she should be made aware of the area of the inquiry.

Several tests are commonly used during the preinduction phase to assess susceptibility (the subject's degree of responsiveness to the administered hypnotic suggestion): the "postural sway" test, the "hand levitation" test, the "hand clasping" test (Crasilneck & Hall, 1975). Spiegel's "eye roll" test (1972) can also be used. (A negative response to susceptibility tests would not disqualify for hypnosis; it would mean that more time would have to be spent with the subject to help relieve any fears that had made the person resistant to the tests.)

After it has been determined that the subject is suitable for the hypnotic induction, the procedure to be used should be fully explained, e.g., eye fixation, progressive relaxation, deepening techniques and the method to be used to enhance or refresh memory. The Boston Police Hypnosis Unit has excellent results in improving memory using the TV method whereby subjects are asked to visualize a television set on which will appear the perception of the particular event of interest. The TV is used because it is commonplace and because it allows the subject to dissociate from the actual experience and thereby depict accurately and vividly the things of importance. Even though the experience was traumatic, the subject will be able to reduce emotion and remain calm and in control. It is like watching the event on a special documentary. The subject will be observing it as a reporter, seeing the event as he or she originally perceived it.

The results of this method were proven effective in the case of *Commonwealth* v. *A. Juvenile* (Brady, 1980). There, the junior author used this method on a young lady who had been kidnapped and brutally and repeatedly raped while she was held captive for a three-hour period. The victim was able to give the police only a general description of her attacker and could not make a composite because it was dark during the attack and the victim did not really know if she got a good look at him. She was placed under hypnosis and as she described what was happening she stated that the car she was in became stuck in the snow and the attacker got out to push it. Brady realized that when a car door is open an inside light goes on. Therefore, he asked the victim whether the inside light was on or off when the attacker got out of the car. She responded that the light was on. She was then asked if she could see her attacker and she stated she could. She said she could see him clearly and was asked just to concentrate on his face as she was perceiving him and was told that she would recall this after hypnosis.

She was taken out of hypnosis and led to another room where she was turned over to a composite artist who made a composite of the attacker. She was asked on a scale of one to ten—one being the worst, ten being the best—where she would place that composite. She stated she didn't know anything about a scale, but that she was absolutely sure that the composite depicted the man who had attacked her.

After intensive investigation with the aid of the composite, identification was made and the culprit located, tried and found guilty of kidnapping, assault with intent to murder, rape, and assault and battery. There was a remarkable likeness between the composite and the person who was found guilty of the attacks. On the request of the Commonwealth, the senior author examined the victim, testified that she was able to distinguish between what she knew before, during and after the hypnosis, and recommended to the court that the victim be allowed to testify.

Another case involving the Boston Police Hypnosis Unit was an assault that occurred on Valentine's Day in 1980. A 35-year-old man was working in a liquor store when two unknown white males entered. One pulled out a pistol and, pointing it at the clerk, told him to lie on the floor. The two culprits then rifled the cash register and took a six-pack of beer. As they were leaving, one of the assailants noticed the store clerk was sitting and told him to lie down. He lay down face up looking at the ceiling. As the culprits started to leave the store, the older culprit said to the younger, "You better give him a hit." The younger man went over and shot him in the face. They started out again and the older culprit suggested, "You better give him another." He was shot again. One bullet entered the cheek, the other is still lodged in the victim's head. Sometime after the victim's recuperation, he told the investigating police officer that he knew what his assailants looked like but that he was unable to get a perception of them. He tried unsuccessfully to make composites. He was taken to the Boston Police Hypnosis Unit, where the junior author used hypnosis. He was then able to make composites that he was satisfied with. The culprits eventually were apprehended and were seen to bear a striking likeness to the composites. They were both found guilty of attempted murder and armed robbery.

Diamond (1980) suggests that a person who has been the subject of hypnosis should be disqualified from testifying in court as to events that were the subject of the hypnotic experience. This blanket exclusion of testimony from a hypnotized witness on the grounds of incompetence is contrary to what is known about hypnosis and human memory and to the law of witness competency. However, the California Supreme Court, among others, has adopted Diamond's position, albeit with an anomalous exception for previously hypnotized defendants who wish to take the stand (*People* v. *Shirley*, 1982).

Diamond (1980) maintains that a previously hypnotized witness is incompetent to testify because: (1) he will confound, or mix up, his hypnotic memory of events with his pre- and posthypnotic waking memories and, indeed, will be convinced that his hypnotic memory is an accurate and true account of events; (2) he will fantasize, or confabulate, while hypnotized and, after hypnosis, not be able to separate his fabrications from true recall; and (3) he will, after hypnosis, be subjectively certain of the accuracy and truth of his hypnotic memory whereas before hypnosis he was willing to express some uncertainty. However, while such problems can occur, they are not inevitable and can in fact be safeguarded against by appropriate procedures.

Hypnotic recall is subject to the same weaknesses as nonhypnotic recall, including distortion due to suggestion, confabulation, i.e., a tendency to fill gaps, and increased subjective certainty. Contrary to Diamond's claim, experimental psychologists recognize that hypnotic subjects can discriminate between hypnotic and nonhypnotic memories if properly cued by the hypnotist (Reiser, 1983). The experience of forensic hypnotists strongly indicates that with proper demand characteristics established and proper questioning by the hypnotist, hypnotic subjects can remember and differentiate their original memory from the memories subsequently revivified by hypnotism. Diamond's article (1980) uses many equivocal words such as "may" and "often" and presents examples of abuses in the hypnotic process that are obvious and avoidable. The literature in the field of hypnosis establishes convincingly that hypnosis per se does not render a witness incompetent to testify. Whether a particular hypnotic session has rendered a witness incompetent to testify depends upon the degree of impropriety of the procedures used. Even an improperly conducted hypnotic session may have no effect upon the hypnotic subject's ability to separate memories, recall accurately what he initially perceived, or express varying degrees of certainty (Orne, 1979).

The competency rule adopted by the California Supreme Court is particularly egregious in that victims of crime who undergo hypnosis are barred from testifying about any aspect of their ordeal while those accused of committing the crimes may testify no matter how improperly suggestive the hypnotic procedures which they have undergone may be (*People* v. *Shirley*, 1982). Such a rule is unsound logic and policy. It is a cruel irony that the very experts who oppose the admission of posthypnotic testimony in the courtroom would employ it in a therapeutic context. Thus, rape victims seeking psychiatric counseling may have to choose between treatment—using hypnosis, which would render them incompetent to testify—and trial—testifying about the rape by foregoing hypnosis even though in a given case it may be the best course of treatment for the traumatic disorders that can ensue from rape. ". . . justice, though due to the accused, is due to the accuser also. The concept of fairness must not be strained till it is narrowed to a filament" (*Snyder* v. *Mass.*, 1934, p. 41).

A majority of the courts that have considered the question of whether the testimony of a witness who has undergone hypnosis to revivify his memory is admissible in a criminal trial have held that such hypnotically induced testimony is admissible (*State* v. *Hurd*, 1981).

These cases generally have reasoned that testimony of a witness whose memory has been revived through hypnosis should be treated like any other refreshed recollection. That the witness's memory may have been impaired by hypnosis or that suggestive material may have been used to refresh his recollection is considered to be a matter affecting credibility, not admissibility. It is assumed that skillful cross-examination will enable the jury to evaluate the effect of hypnosis on the witness and the credibility of his testimony. The purpose of using hypnosis is not to obtain truth, as a polygraph or "truth serum" is supposed to do. Instead, hypnosis is employed as a means of overcoming amnesia and restoring the memory of a witness (Spector & Foster, 1977). In light of this purpose, hypnosis can be considered reasonably reliable if it is able to yield recollections as accurate as those of an ordinary witness, which likewise often are historically inaccurate. If it is conducted properly and used only in appropriate cases, hypnosis is generally accepted as a reasonably reliable method of restoring a person's memory. Consequently, hypnotically induced testimony may be admissible if the proponent of the testimony can demonstrate that the use of hypnosis in the particular case was a reasonably reliable means of restoring memory comparable to normal recall in its accuracy.

The Massachusetts Supreme Judicial Court (*Commonwealth* v. *Kater,* 1983) recently decided the issue of the admissibility of testimony of a witness who had been hypnotized. This court conclusion did not bar the use of hypnosis in future cases, but did establish stringent guidelines for its use. The court said:

1) A record must be established of what the witness knew prior to the use or attempted use of hypnosis.
2) A witness will be allowed to testify to his or her present memory of events prior to hypnosis only if that record has been made.
3) The court defines "hypnotically aided testimony" as testimony by a witness to a fact that became available following hypnosis.
4) Hypnotically aided testimony not remembered before hypnosis will not be admissible unless corroborated by tangible evidence and a case for independent reliability can be made.
5) The party that uses hypnosis must make disclosure that hypnosis or its attempted use was employed.
6) The court also said there may be occasions in which the hypnotist need not be a licensed psychiatrist or psychologist. The important points are that he be qualified in the use of hypnosis, and independent of the investigation of the crime. There may also be situations in which a person in addition to the subject and the hypnotist (such as the parent of a child) could be present before, during and after the hypnosis.

Watson (*Commonwealth* v. *Watson,* 1983) was involved in the murder of a cab driver. A witness who saw the suspects getting into the cab made a prehypnotic photograph identification of two of the three suspects. He was 100 percent sure about the photograph of suspect #1 and 88 percent sure of suspect #2. He could not identify suspect #3. After the junior author hypnotized the witness, he was again 100 percent certain as to suspect #1, but this time he was 100 percent certain as to suspect #2. Suspect #3 remained unidentifiable. Thus, hypnosis enhanced the witness's confidence in his identification of suspect #2 but the hypnosis produced no new evidence against either defendant. Therefore, the court held that the defendants were not prejudiced by the admission of the witness's testimony concerning the posthypnotic positive identifications.

It is interesting to note that the witness did not identify the third suspect. It is our belief that the witness's critical judgment was not interfered with by the hypnosis, nor did he try to please the hypnotist as some of the opposition has suggested. Certainly if he wanted to please the hypnotist he would have identified all three. This was not the case; he identified only two of them.

The junior author assisted in the formulation of safeguards approved by the International Society for Investigative and Forensic Hypnosis at their 1982 convention in San Diego, California. We strongly suggest that these safeguards be followed in those states presently using or anticipating the use of investigative hypnosis for memory revivification of the victim and/or witness:

1) There shall be an audio and/or video recording made of the entire investigative hypnosis session.
2) The investigative hypnosis session shall be performed only by a person who is qualified as an investigative hypnotist. (Qualified means proper educational and investigative experience.)
3) The investigative hypnosis interview shall not be performed by the primary case inspector.
4) A detailed description of the victim's/witness's recall shall be taken prior to the investigative hypnosis session.
5) Only those persons deemed necessary to properly conduct the investigative hypnosis sessions shall be present during any phase of the investigative hypnosis session. This includes both pre- and post-hypnosis interviews.
6) All recorded materials of the investigative hypnosis session, including but not limited to audio and/or video recordings, transcripts and notes, shall be kept secure according to that state's rules of evidence.

REFERENCES

Alexander, L. (1965, January). Clinical experiences with hypnosis in psychiatric therapy. *American Journal of Clinical Hypnosis, 7,* 190-206.
Alexander, L. (1981). In *Commonwealth* v. *Scott Colihan,* Suffolk Superior Court Department of the Trial Court, No. 030302.
Brady, P. *Commonwealth* v. *A. Juvenile,* 381 Mass. 727 (1980).
Brady, P. (1982). International Society for Investigative and Forensic Hypnosis annual conference, San Diego, California.
Commonwealth v. Kater, 388 Mass. 519 (1983).
Commonwealth v. Watson, 388 Mass. 536 (1983).
Crasilneck, H.B., & Hall, J.A. (1975). *Clinical hypnosis; Principles and applications.* New York: Grune & Stratton.
Diamond, B. (1980). Inherent problems in the use of pretrial hypnosis on prospective witnesses. *California Law Review, 68,* 313-349.

Frank, G. (1966). *The Boston strangler.* New York: The New American Library, 1-X, 1-364.

Orne, M.T. (1979). The use and misuse of hypnosis in court. *International Journal of Clinical & Experimental Hypnosis,* 311-341.

People v. Shirley, 31 Cal. 3rd 18, 181 Cal, Rptr. 243 641 P. 2d 775, *as modified,* 31 Cal. 3d 18 (1982).

Reiser, M. (1983). Director of Behavioral Science Services Los Angeles P.D., *Commonwealth v. Watson,* 388 Mass. 536.

Snyder v. Massachusetts, 291 U.S. 97, 122, 54 S. Ct. 330, 338 (1934).

Spector & Foster (1977). *Admissibility of hypnotic statements: Is the law of evidence susceptible?,* 38 Ohio St. L.J. 567, 584.

Spiegel, H. (1972). An age-old test for hypnotizability. *American Journal of Clinical Hypnosis, 25, 41.*

State v. Hurd, 86 N.J. 525 (1981).

PART XI

Cross-Cultural Perspectives

As was demonstrated in a number of preceding chapters, Erickson modified his approach according to the values of the patient. Understanding cultural background is important in tailoring treatment to the unique qualities of the individual.

Another issue presented in this section is how methods of influence draw from common sources. Effective communicators use strategic principles and many strategic techniques have been used across cultural groups.

Madeleine Richeport, Ph.D., earned her degree in anthropology from New York University. She has served as a visiting professor of anthropology at the Federal University of Rio Grande de Norte in Natal, Brazil. Investigating spiritism and cultural trance had been a major part of her research endeavors.

Richeport studied extensively with Milton Erickson. Erickson thought that it was important for psychologists to study anthropology and for anthropologists to study psychology.

There is an anthropological basis to Erickson's world view. Richeport describes cases where Erickson used cultural models to promote change. Additionally, she presents a case of a Brazilian psychiatrist, David Akstein, who used concepts from spiritism in conjunction with traditional therapeutic methodology.

James R. Allen, M.D., is a psychiatrist who earned his degree at the University of Toronto. He is professor and chair of the Department of Psychiatry and Behavioral Sciences for the University of Oklahoma, Tulsa Medical College, and is medical director of the Tulsa Psychiatric Center. Allen is eclectic in his approach; he trains students in psychoanalysis, family therapy, Transactional Analysis, gestalt therapy, and hypnosis.

The techniques used by effective communicators are similar and often incorporate the strategic use of multilevel communication, symbolism, metaphor, and tasks. Similarities between Milton Erickson and Mahatma Gandhi are described.

Sung C. Kim, Ph.D., earned his degree in clinical psychology from Bowling Green State University and is director of training at the National Asian American Training Center in San Francisco.

Just as effective communicators use similar techniques, effective psychotherapies have similarities. Kim introduces us to Morita and Naikan as currently practiced in Japan, and examines these methods from an Ericksonian perspective.

Chapter 33

The Importance of Anthropology in Psychotherapy: World View of Milton H. Erickson, M.D.

Madeleine Richeport

The United States is not really a melting pot. We still find enclaves of Jews, Italians, Poles, Arabs, Puerto Ricans, Haitians, Japanese, and other ethnic groups. Even third generation immigrants still may show profound cultural influences in family and social relationships: e.g., the way they communicate with others; their perception and reaction to stress; their definitions of health and illness; their source of help when they are ill; their expectations of healers and treatments; preferred treatment techniques; and to whom they credit with the cure. Similarly, people within the same culture can vary greatly according to social class and religious ideology. For example, if a patient is Pentecostal or in the punk movement, active in high society or a poor farmer, therapy must be adapted accordingly.

Milton H. Erickson was profoundly aware of the importance of a patient's culture in psychotherapy. He often said, "Now I am going to give you a case record and it shows you the importance of knowledge of anthropology." Erickson viewed trance as a normal phenomenon, an extension of everyday behavior. He worked with clients as individuals through careful observation of them, and in this respect he acted like an anthropologist recording and processing naturally occurring behavior from which he developed his therapeutic interventions. Most behavior is culturally conditioned, and the knowledge recorded by anthropolo-

The author wishes to express her sincere appreciation to Hilton L. Lopez, M.D., and Harriet Lefley, Ph.D., for their comments on this chapter.

gists provided materials for Erickson's understanding of patients from different ethnic groups, for the universality of unconscious processes, for his illustrations and metaphors, and for his own world view. From the anthropological perspective "world view deals with the sum of ideas which an individual within a group and/or that group have of the universe. It attempts to define those ideas outside, emphasizing cognitive aspects of ideas, beliefs, and attitudes" (Mendelson, 1968, p. 576). I will describe Erickson's world view which is an anthropological view of humanity. In addition to its application in therapy, this view provided many who knew him with new ways of being, thinking and feeling.

ERICKSON'S WORLD VIEW

Cultural Relativism

Cultural relativism assumes that the observers can transcend their own cultural conditioning and view phenomena from the perspective of the participants. Using imagination and empathy observers must see others as they see themselves (Bidney, 1968, p. 543). Erickson put it this way:

> Cultures vary so greatly. Some other culture isn't all wrong because it isn't our culture. The rich American tourist eats beefsteak. They don't know any better. The French peasant eats horse meat. If you are in Korea and you want to give someone a Sunday dinner, roast dog is very nice. In Hong Kong you serve snake stew. It's nutritious. It's tasty. In World War II, half the natives enjoyed themselves tangling with the American GI's, tearing open rotten logs, collecting grubs, and swallowing them the way we would swallow an oyster, and the GI's would get sick to the stomach, vomit, when they saw the natives swallowing live grubs. But you know, the American soldiers had their revenge. I have forgotten what year it was the ship of eggs reached Africa. American GI's had a picnic eating eggs and making the natives sick to their stomach. (Note 1)

In this example, Erickson takes an exotic unfamiliar custom from another culture and relates it to a custom familiar in our culture. The familiar is the habitual frame of reference. Relating it to the foreign is a learning experience, a new relationship, which may then be used as a metaphor for the personal resolution of a problem, thereby having an integrative effect. Turning the exotic familiar, and the familiar exotic, lets us think in all directions about options for behavior, and enhances our perspective. Sometimes it is even easier to understand the exotic, the foreign, something removed from oneself, because less emotion is attached. The familiar may be more difficult to grasp. Erickson integrated the exotic and familiar, facilitating at one level an interest in the behavior in other cultures, on another level, the capacity to think of behavior in new ways. Erickson expressed his use of anthropological illustration in the following way: "When I talk about my life and my family, you translate it into your life and your family; when I talk about a foreign society, we translate it together into our terms."

Participant Observation

> When a patient tells you something, listen to their language. I gave you this illustration previously: Where there are no points to the compass, where there are six points and where there are only two points (Note 2). You can answer that question only by recognizing what kind of life situation would give you no points to the compass. I showed you that Du-gongs carved by Australian aborigines with straight lines. The artistry of the carving is crude but the straight lines are very straight. Straight lines are very important in the arctic and on the Australian desert. Someday you may read the story of a white man's crossing of Australia, a white man's crossing of the desert with death, starvation and hardships, while the aborigines can hunt in the desert with the greatest of ease.

For Erickson, observation of verbal and nonverbal behavior was vital in performing psychotherapy. He often used anthropological illustrations to emphasize behavioral differences, which are often easier to see than behaviors we see every day. For example, he would talk about Margaret Mead's work in the South Seas where nonverbal cues are subtler than our own. Bateson and Mead's (1942) photographic study of childrearing practices in Bali recorded how mothers nonverbally teased and tantalized babies; they incited them to emotion which invariably was undercut before it reached a climax. They based an argument for passive Balinese character on these nonverbal cues in child rearing.

The standard anthropological technique of participant observation is particularly useful in learning hypnotherapy. Erickson said, "You can't really learn about any form of trance without experiencing it." Just as he emphasized delving into new experiences, he taught hypnosis in the same way, through experiential learning. Hypnosis allows one to be a participant and an observer through the utilization of different levels of consciousness simultaneously. See Rossi (1976, p. 16) for exercises in observation.

Erickson was

> born with several congenital sensory-perceptual problems that led him to experience the world in ways so different that his acute mind could survive only by realizing at a very early age the relativity of our human frames of reference. To these early problems was added the rare medical tragedy of being stricken by two different strains of polio at the age of 17 and 51. His efforts to rehabilitate himself led to a personal rediscovery of many classical hypnotic phenomena and how they could be utilized therapeutically. (Rossi, 1980, p. xi)

Rossi (1977, pp. 36-54) emphasized Erickson's development of hypnosis through his exploratory observations, re-educating himself to move his own muscles. In addition to these experiential learnings, Erickson studied anthropological material from ancient civilizations to trance patterns in other cultures. He wrote,

> Down through the ages, priests and priestesses rendered their services to the ailing and troubled in Temples of Sleep, built upon the ruins of other Temples of Sleep belonging to previous civilizations. The Chinese, Hindus, Greeks, Egyptians—all had temples where suggestion and hypnosis were administered to lessen hurt and suffering. Undoubtedly, there are ancient civilizations yet-to-be-discovered that used hypnosis expressed in magical sleep, rites, and incantations. For men forever remain men with needs in common. (Erickson, 1970, p. 71)

Also vital to Erickson's development of hypnosis was his observation of trance in their naturally occurring context in other cultures. In comments on the fieldwork in ritual trance of several anthropologists including Bateson and Mead in Bali (1942); Belo in Bali (1960); Deren in Haiti (1970); and Richeport in Puerto Rico and Brazil (1975, 1978, 1979, 1980a, 1980b, 1981, 1982) he personally communicated that he viewed the ritual trances as essentially the same psychophysiological phenomena as hypnosis.

Using the Patient's Emic for Cultural Congruence

Erickson described the arrogance of the Castilian elite, male chauvinism in mid-eastern cultures, the rigidity of Asians, and the overprotectiveness and meddling of the Jewish mother and mother-in-law. His cultural understandings led to developing therapeutic strategies in working with patients from different ethnic groups. "Emics" refers to a variety of theoretical field approaches concerned with the inside view of a culture as opposed to "etics" or the outsiders view of the culture. These terms were coined by the missionary linguist Kenneth Pike as an analogy with the "emic" in phonemic and the "etic" in phonetic. An "emic" viewpoint requires the observer to identify the cognitive categories, values, meanings and attitudes of people (Harris, 1968, pp. 568-604). The cases described below illustrate how Erickson utilized the patients' emic and particular subcultural features in therapy.

Rick (Note 3)

"Now I am going to give you a case record and it shows you the importance of knowledge of anthropology.

"Referred by a Massachusetts psychologist, Rick was a 17-year-old, very intelligent boy, who just graduated from the third year of high school. He had stuttered since he first began to speak. His father was a wealthy businessman who hired many professionals to teach his son how to talk without any success.

"A few days later Rick arrived with his mother. When they walked into the office, I recognized the mother's ethnic group. Rick couldn't talk. I took the history from her. She came from a remote mid-eastern village. The culture is very, very rigid and her husband came from a similar village. Both had grown up, emigrated to Massachusetts when adult, met in Massachusetts, got married, and became naturalized citizens. Now, their culture I already know. One in which man is much much higher than God. American women speak of chauvinistic cultures!

"A man will take your daughter off your hands and the first baby has to be a boy. If it's a girl, the father, the husband says, 'I divorce thee, I divorce thee, I divorce thee,' and his wife with the clothes on her back takes her girl baby out into the world to make a living any way she can. She may have brought her husband a million dollars in dowry. That's his. She's failed her duty as a woman to have her first child a boy. So, she is unfit to live with. Rick's parents' first child was a girl. Massachusetts divorce law doesn't permit anything like a summary divorce, and they were law-abiding citizens. The father swallowed his pride. The second baby was a girl, that compounded the insult, a deadly insult. That father had to take it. Rick was the third child, a boy. Instead of doing the very least thing he could, which was to look like his father, have a physique like his father, Rick didn't resemble his father. He was broad shouldered, built strongly, but not slender and willowy like his father. He was a living insult to his father. His father was a very rich merchant, and in that culture, the father owns the wife and all the children. The children grow up and the daughters are sent out to work because there's a lot of dirty work to be done and that's what the women are fit for. And their wages belong to the father. The son can work for his father and the father, in a generous mood can give him a penny, maybe a nickel, rarely a dime. The son is working for his father and not until the son marries is the father willing to give the son anything. After I confirmed all my understanding in mid-eastern culture, I told the mother, 'Your son interests me. I'll keep him a few more days under two conditions. The first condition is: you may rent a car and see all the sights in Phoenix but do not speak to another mid-eastern person. Avoid them. ([Explaining to the students to whom he was speaking:] This culture is very clannish and there is a large colony in Phoenix.) The second condition: I have a friend who has a flower shop, a nursery. I'm going to call her up. I want you to listen. You will know exactly the terms of my second condition for continuing to see Rick.' Now, no mid-eastern man would work for a woman. It's absolutely wrong. They won't work for nothing. That's wrong too. And he won't do dirty work. That's for women. I called my friend, Minnie, and made certain they heard my friend is a *her*. 'Minnie, I've got a 17-year-old boy in my office. I want him to work in your shop, or your nursery. You'll recognize him immediately, Minnie. He won't have to say hello or good-bye. Just point to the dirtiest, dirtiest work you can. He'll work two hours a day without pay. And you're his boss.' Minnie is of the same ethnic origin. I had had two of her brothers in therapy, so Minnie understood what I meant.

"And mother agreed to that. I knew she was very troubled by it. I checked up with Minnie and Rick was putting in his two hours a day. He couldn't even take a wilted flower as payment. He got dirty work, mixing manure with soil.

"During that time, I saw Rick from time to time. I questioned mother about him very carefully, about the sisters, where they lived in Worcester and so on, just to be sure of my general background. And after I had seen Rick on rare occasions, for an hour each time, I told mother,

'Mother, I want you to rent a temporary apartment for Rick. I want you to give him a checking account. And then you get the first plane back to Worcester.' And mother said, 'I do not think his father will approve!' I said, 'Woman, I never allow anybody to interfere with my patients. Now go and do as I say.' So she knew she was speaking to a man. She rented an apartment, gave him a checking account and left for Massachusetts that same day."

(In the therapy sessions, Erickson asked Rick to communicate in writing.) "My communication to him was: Write the numbers from one to ten. And he communicated back what? 'Nine, eight, seven, six, five, four, three, two, one, zero.' Those are numerical symbols. They are not the numbers from one to ten. He didn't get my communication and didn't communicate back that which I asked. I asked him to write the alphabet. He wrote all the letters, but not the alphabet. So again, he didn't get my communication and didn't communicate back. Then in the composition every other (*other* is the important word) word is misspelled. How is it misspelled? The last two letters are reversed.

"He came from mid-eastern parentage. That is the first part of the family, and they are all right. And he had two sisters who were born before he was and there should be two reversals in that family. But you can't reverse them.

"I explained that to Rick and then said, 'Now your therapy is this, Rick. I want you to get hold of any book you wish and read it aloud backwards from the last word to the first word. That will give you practice at saying words without communicating. . . . So read the book backwards, word by word, the last word to the first word. You'll have practice in saying words.

" 'Now the next thing, Rick, you come from a home where the dominant culture is mid-eastern. There is nothing wrong or bad about mid-eastern culture. It is all right for mid-eastern people. But you and your sisters are native-born Americans. Your culture is American. You are first-class citizens of America; your parents are second-class. This is not to disparage them because they did the best they could. So you can respect the mid-eastern culture, but it isn't your culture. Your culture is American.

" 'You are a 17-year-old American boy. You work in your father's store. He gives you a penny, a nickel, maybe a dime once in a while. Mid-eastern children work for nothing, and they do everything as their father says. But you are not a mid-eastern boy, *you* are an American boy. Your sisters are American girls. In American culture, you are a big boy, a big 17-year-old American boy. You know your father's store better than any of his clerks. You tell your father you'll be glad to work in his store but you expect an American worker's salary.

" 'And, your parents have the right to ask you to live at home, and you have the right to pay for your room rent, pay for your board and pay for your laundry. That is what an American does. I want you to explain it to your sisters.

" 'Now your parents from the mid-eastern culture think that the American law says that you don't have to go to school after the age of 16. And every young American girl has the right, if her parents have the money, to go on and finish high school, and go to college if she wants to. That is their American right, their cultural right. You explain this very carefully to your sisters and make them understand *they are* American citizens, native American citizens, in a native American culture.

" 'Now, Rick, living in a mid-eastern home, you've been taught how to think, when to think, and in what direction to think. But you are an American. Americans can think any way they please. Now I want you to get a good book, a good novel. I want you to read the last chapter first and then you sit down and try to think, wonder and speculate on what was in the preceding chapter. Think in all directions, and read that second to last chapter and see in how many ways you were wrong; and you will be wrong in a lot of ways. Then you read that second to the last chapter and wonder about the preceding chapter and by the time you read a good book from the last chapter to the first chapter, wondering and speculating, imagining, and figuring out, you'll learn to think freely in all directions.'

"A year ago last Christmas, Rick came to me. His speech was clear, easy, comfortable. His father had wanted him to go to Yale or Harvard, but he chose a different college, as any American boy would do. The father wanted him to study business administration. Rick said, 'I know a business administrator wouldn't hire me. I took it for one semester and didn't like it so I dropped it. I am more interested in chemistry or psychology.'

"After going to college for three years, he got to thinking, 'Any good American boy ought to earn at least a part of his way through college. The employment in Massachusetts is very poor, I am going to take a regular job with my father's store. I know that store better than the other employees do and I am going to get an American salary. I am going to pay my board and rent and laundry. I am going to buy my own clothes and I am going to save money and help for my fourth year in college.

Then maybe I will drop out and earn money to go to graduate school.'

"I said, 'All right, Rick, what about your sisters?' He said, 'I talked things over with my sisters and they agreed with me that they were native-born Americans and they were going to live like Americans. So my sisters didn't drop out of school at the age of 16. One sister has graduated from the university and she is living alone and teaching school. I know that the mid-eastern way is for unmarried children to live with their parents. My sister is an American girl and she is living alone and she likes teaching. My other sister went through the university, was dissatisfied with her university education, so she entered law school. She is practicing law.'

"I don't know what the parents think about me, but I do know that they have three children to be proud of. You might call it family therapy.

"The therapy for the mother was: 'Woman, you heard what I said. Now do it.' Now, I knew mid-eastern culture. There are various cultures in Lebanon, various groups, Christians, Muslims, Zoroastrians, and so on.

"But the important thing is: Deal with your patient and don't substitute your ideas.

"And the mid-eastern may write from right to left, but Rick was born in the United States. In the United States you write from left to right. And in America, you speak your own mind; you do your own thinking. And that is the important thing . . . to recognize everything there is about the patient.

"Of course, having Minnie's two brothers as patients taught me an awful lot more about the mid-eastern culture. Her two mid-eastern brothers now respect their sister, Minnie. They regard her as a competent businesswoman and their equal as an American citizen."

Margaret Mead expressed the stress between opposing cultures in the following way: It is the discontinuity between the world view which "emphasizes a sense of timeless continuity with the past" and which excludes the possibility of alternative life styles and the more open universal world view of the heterogeneous rapidly changing postindustrial society (Danna, 1980). For example, the difference in thinking and independent judgment encouraged in urban schools as opposed to the dependent following of the old ways causes psychological stress and mental illness to some members of migrant groups. In Rick's case, traditional childhood socialization practices were incompatible with the demands of urban American society. Because Erickson had patients from a similar ethnic background, he understood mid-eastern cultural norms and utilized these cultural knowledges in his therapy. Just as Erickson considered each patient as a unique individual, he did not stereotype ethnic groups. He was aware of intraethnic variations. Erickson mirrored Rick's culture through verbal and behavioral authoritarianism to establish ethnic rapport. Then he introduced changes more adaptive to mainstream American culture (i.e., freedom of choice, right to an education and to earn a living, male-female equality). Erickson used the emic of the family subculture when appropriate and useful to develop cultural congruence. (Gordon & Meyers-Anderson, 1981, pp. 53-54).

SPIRITS IN THERAPY

An Indian couple

In a teaching seminar, a student cited a case related to occult and spirit forces. The patient, a school teacher, was hypnotized to lose weight. She brought in a ouija board and said she was talking to it in the evening and she said there were spirits around her bed at night. Erickson replied: "I can see far enough in advance. I am very careful to develop additional spirits to control this and to control that. And finally all of the spirits are under my control." Erickson then related the following case:

"An Indian couple, man and wife, became obsessed with the idea they could tip tables. In the hospital they demonstrated it to me. They could tip tables and bad spirits would take over; they assured me that a bad spirit followed them around and took control of them. So I helped them tip a table. I know more about tipping a table than they did. I know how you do table-tipping, even with heavy tables. Pretty soon the table-tipping disclosed that there was a weak good spirit there *also*, and another weak good spirit and I started adding all the weak good spirits. Their total strength exceeded the strength of the evil spirit.

"Do you know how to tip a table? Keep your face straight. If it's a great big table, you'll need several allies. I called in my residents who did not know how to tip a table. I coached them. They learned to breathe in unison. And you breathe in unison with the believer. . . . You keep your hands on the surface of the table and as you breathe in you tip back, you exhale, you lean forward, now the pressure. . . . Keep your hands clasped. That flatness prevents evaporation of the normal perspiration and soon your hand gets slightly moist. You are all breathing in unison, you are all exerting a certain friction or force; you can tune your breathing to their breathing, they are on one side, you are on the other side. Pretty soon the table starts to move. As soon as it starts moving, they get less critical. You have your thumbs on the edge of the table and you can really move it."

This case is a good example of mirroring the cultural model to create rapport, and then utilizing that cultural model to make the appropriate changes. Erickson responded to the Indian couple within their own model "spiritdom." The mirroring took place at many levels including the cultural level. Mirroring the Indian couple's belief in spirits did not mean that Erickson believed in spirits, only that he was able to acknowledge and/or utilize features of that belief system when required (Gordon & Meyers-Anderson, 1981, pp. 51-54). In Erickson's view, where change is impossible, you channel behavior into socially acceptable areas (Richeport, 1982, p. 382). You may not be able to change the belief in spirits, only the meaning, in this case, from evil to good.

Strong religious affiliations often present difficulties for therapists to handle. In many cultures, therapists have difficulty differentiating between pathoplastic and pathogenic syndromes because spirit causation of illness is an acceptable explanation in all social classes. To illustrate this point we may ask why the New York Puerto Rican has a relatively higher mental hospitalization rate than other ethnic groups. Often the transitory syndrome *ataque* with supernatural overtones is not recognized as a transient culturally conditioned response to stress, not requiring hospitalization. A Spiritist healer with a few prayers and hand passes could resolve the situation rapidly.

Elsewhere, I presented cases of Puerto Rican and Brazilian patients who were treated by Puerto Rican psychiatrist, Hilton Lopez (Richeport, 1982, pp. 385-387), and Brazilian psychiatrist, David Akstein (1972), friends and colleagues of Erickson. They combine their cultural knowledge and knowledge of hypnosis to work with patients who accept Spiritist ideology (Richeport, 1978, 1979, 1980a, 1980b, 1981). More recently I have seen the importance of therapists knowing how to work with cases involving spirit possession at the University of Miami School of Medicine. Jackson Memorial Hospital treats patients from many ethnic groups (Southern Blacks, Bahamians, Puerto Ricans, Cubans and Haitians who are often recent rural migrants) (Weidman, 1978, 1979).

In many Latin American and Caribbean cultural heritages which combine African, Catholic, and indigenous belief systems, spirits manifest in the therapy session. The way these spirits can be utilized as part of therapy is well illustrated in one of the cases of Brazilian psychiatrist, David Akstein,* who I observed over a two-year period in Rio de Janeiro. It is the case of Gladis, an Umbanda medium (Note 4).

Gladis was an attractive 39-year-old married woman who presented

*The author wishes to express her sincere appreciation to Dr. David Akstein for providing the opportunity, patience, and knowledge in making this study possible.

symptoms of dizziness, nausea, and fear of going outside of her apartment alone. Thus, she was always accompanied by her husband, Fernando, or her 12-year-old daughter, Sonia. After consulting many specialists, she reluctantly agreed to see a psychiatrist; she did not believe that her symptoms were psychologically caused. It was obvious that Gladis was an *Umbandista* medium. She displayed 21 silver bracelets on her arm and talked about the rituals she performed daily to protect herself and her family. However, when she entered therapy, she said that her Indian guide advised her to give up her full-time mediumship practice performed in her own home. She attended a large clientele all night long which caused fatigue. Besides dizziness, the only other problem which she expressed was her hostility toward her mother who lived directly across the street, and from her window supervised Gladis' life. She behaved timidly, subordinating herself to her husband, and showed little discipline to her daughter, a spoiled, hyperactive child, who continuously disrupted the therapy sessions.

Akstein treated her with medication, psychotherapy, relaxation and desensitization techniques. She improved but the dizziness and street phobia did not disappear. He began to encourage her to return to mediumship. During one appointment, as he jokingly gyrated her, a typical trance induction technique employed in Umbanda, Gladis entered mediumship trance, which she had never done during other hypnotic inductions. During the 13 taped sessions which followed, Gladis was possessed by 11 of the 27 spiritual entities who incorporated her. Akstein conversed with her strong, aggressive *Caboclo* (Indian) guides, and asked them to aid him to help her. He asked the entities to protect her when she went out in the street. Akstein graciously accepted the guides' ritual prescriptions, and had a cigar available so the *Caboclo* could use smoke to cleanse himself, Fernando, and Sonia. The *Caboclo* told Fernando, who acted as auxiliary, how to behave toward Gladis and even hit him on the forehead reprimanding him for his lack of attention to her. *Caboclo* told Sonia to study in school and to be obedient. Sonia showed respect for and accepted discipline from the guide. Gladis then received one of her Exu guides. She cursed, drank rum, enticed the doctor, and expressed her sexual desire to him. She had also received a child entity permitting her to skip, eat candy, talk baby talk, and be treated like a child.

Akstein (1972) utilized mediumship trance to reinforce suggestions, to learn more information about his patient, and to mobilize all facets of his patient's personality.

Elsewhere, I analyzed this process as a "mazeway resynthesis" (Richeport [Michtom], 1975) where in trance individuals function on multiple levels of awareness, bypassing conscious learning sets and habitual patterns of association, the process resulting in a new form of learning. Playing alternate roles is an opportunity to practice solving problems on a symbolic level where the form and material that transpires between the medium and guides is the creative process by which the unconscious creates its own solutions. These solutions are symbolic enactments which become translated into the real world. Analysis of the tapes of Gladis supported this interpretation.

It was found that many of the behaviors which Gladis first expressed in mediumship trance—strength, aggressiveness, feminine liberation, freedom of expression, also were expressed in the nontrance sessions, and then were translated into her everyday life. She was able to feel strong enough to go outside alone, to express her dissatisfactions to her husband, to discipline her daughter, and to recognize that her dizziness was related to her phobia. Encouraging mediumship trance in the clinical setting permitted Akstein to utilize an important experience in his patient's life and permitted him to dialogue with her alternate selves and thereby promote behavior change.

Similarly, hypnotherapists utilize active imagination, directed fantasy, hypnosynthesis, re-dreaming, rehearsal, and other techniques to cultivate personality change and psychosynthesis. Hypnotically induced hallucinations are analogous to mediumship trance behavior, although the latter provides a set of ritual actions which includes the possibility of achieving a prestigious role in the society. Therefore, hypnosis provides a referential bridge for Spiritist patients to communicate in a therapeutic encounter. An astute hypnotherapist like Akstein arranges circumstances to facilitate patients' receptivity to the inner associations and mental skills often expressed in ritual trance.

APPRECIATION OF CROSS-CULTURAL DATA AS A BASIS FOR THE UNIVERSALITY OF UNCONSCIOUS PROCESSES

Anthropology focuses on transcultural studies of interest to psychotherapists. Anthropologists have investigated dreams, symbols, trance states, automatic drawing and writing and other unconscious products in disparate cultures. Erickson investigated cross-cultural differences in the dream content of American and Hindu mentally ill patients. Pictures drawn by newly admitted mentally ill American patients were compared to those collected of mentally ill Germans. The similarities in the dream content and pictures of mentally ill patients from different cultures illustrated for Erickson "that the dreams and the pictures come from essentially similar human minds even though from different mental states and cultures" (Rossi, 1980, p. 338).

PSYCHOTHERAPISTS AS CULTURE BROKERS

The culture broker, a popular term used in anthropology, refers to individuals who mediate and translate between different institutions or traditions. Weidman (1973) used the term to designate a bridging role between community and health systems. In psychotherapy culture brokers are people who are scientifically trained to do therapy and also have an understanding of the ethnic backgrounds of their clients, to allow mediation and translation between their frame of reference and the treatment orientation. Erickson was a culture broker, who effected behavioral changes by motivating and encouraging an acceptance set for resolving problems by using the patient's own behavior. He said, "Whatever your patient has, make use of it. If she has a chant, you chant too. If she is a Mormon, even though you aren't, you should know enough about Mormonism so that you can make use of the Mormon religion."

Culture is one important aspect of "what the patient brings to you." Erickson utilized the following strategies in communicating with patients of other cultural backgrounds:

Acculturation. Where factors of migration affect mental illness, Erickson utilized the basic values and attitudes of the patients' culture to bring them into the urban American fold. For example, in the mid-eastern patient, Erickson constructed his communication in terms of strongly chauvinistic male authoritarian statements as one therapeutic strategy to initiate the therapy. He used the patient's emic to construct cultural congruence.

Channeling behavior into a socially acceptable area. When change is impossible, Erickson utilized clients' behavior but limited it. For example, in the case of "table-tipping" cited above, Erickson did not change the belief, or inhibit the practice regardless of his own belief that table-tipping is a delusion. Rather, he changed the meaning of the belief, channeling it into a socially acceptable area.

Provide the patient with a world view. All societies have local (folk) medical systems which usually are closely tied to religion. Therapy not only cures the symptoms but provides a religious ideology, a moral code that gives structure and meaning to experience. Group support reinforces beliefs and practices. Like healers in other societies, Erickson was not satisfied with improving only emotional capacities. He communicated plans and values for living which replaced rigid, ethnocentric and limited lifestyles. Erickson's world view was an anthropological view, seeing people in the widest context possible—their behavior in the archeological past, and in different cultural environments. Erickson marveled over the migration patterns of arctic tern, sea turtles, and whales, the growing patterns of desert flowers, the way kangaroos nurse, and horses sleep, how space is patterned, and how time is perceived. His knowledge of behavioral diversity provided an important base for constructing meaningful therapy.

REFERENCE NOTES

1. The case material for this chapter was transcribed from tapes recorded during teaching seminars with Erickson attended by the writer (undated).
2. Mrs. Elizabeth Erickson clarified this material. She reported how interested Erickson was in the way different cultures use space. Island cultures have only two directions to the compass—landward and seaward. Indians living on plateaus have six directions–north, south, east, west, oriented from the sun and up and down. She thought that Eskimos have no directions on the compass as they do not see the daily pattern of sunrise and sunset.
3. For a complete case report, see Zeig, 1980, pp. 121-132.
4. Umbanda has been called the national Brazilian religion. It syncretizes African, Catholic, and Amerindian beliefs and practices. Mediums are possessed by prescribed supernatural entities including strong Indians, wise and patient old slaves, ingratiating children, sensual pranksters *Exus*, and Yoruban gods and goddesses (Pressel, 1973).

REFERENCES

Akstein, D. (1972). *Hypnologia* (Vol. 1). Rio de Janeiro: Hypnos.
Bateson, G., & Mead, J. (1942). *Balinese character*. New York: New York Academy of Sciences.
Belo, J. (1960). *Trance in Bali*. New York: Ballantine Books.
Bergantino, L. (1981). *Psychotherapy, insight and style: The existential moment*. Boston: Allyn & Bacon.
Bidney, D. (1968). Cultural relativism. *International Encyclopedia of the Social Sciences* (Vol. 3, pp. 543-547). New York: Macmillan.
Danna, J. (1980). Migration and mental illness: What role do traditional childhood socialization practices play? *Culture, Medicine and Psychiatry, 4*, 25-42.
Deren, M. (1970). *Divine horsemen, the voodoo gods of Haiti*. New York: Chelsea.
Erickson, M.H. (1970). Hypnosis: Its renascence as a treatment modality. *American Journal of Clinical Hypnosis, 13*, 71-89.
Erickson, M.H. (1980). Pantomime techniques in hypnosis and the implications. In E. Rossi, (Ed.), *The collected papers of Milton H. Erickson on hypnosis: Vol. I. The nature of hypnosis and suggestion* (pp. 331-339). New York: Irvington.
Erickson, M.H., Rossi, E., & Rossi, S. (1976). *Hypnotic realities: The induction of clinical hypnosis and forms of indirect suggestion*. New York: Irvington.
Gordon, D., & Meyers-Anderson, M. (1981). *Phoenix: Therapeutic patterns of Milton H. Erickson*. Cupertino, CA: Meta Publications.
Harris, M. (1968). *The rise of anthropological theory*. New York: Thomas Crowell.

Mendelson, E. (1968). World view. *International Encyclopedia of the Social Sciences* (Vol. 16 pp. 576-579). New York: Macmillan.

Pressel, E. (1973). Umbanda in São Paulo: Religious innovation in a developing society. In E. Bourguignon (Ed.), *Religion, altered states of consciousness and social change.* Columbus, OH: State University Press.

Richeport (Michtom), M. (1975). *Becoming a medium: The role of trance in Puerto Rican spiritism as an avenue to mazeway resynthesis.* Ann Arbor: University of Michigan Press.

Richeport, M. (1978). Una investigación personal de trance y mediumidad desarrollada a través de la terpsicoretranceterapia (T.T.T.). *Revista Ibero Americana de Sofrología y Medicina Psicosomática, 7*(4), 208-210.

Richeport, M. (1979). The psychiatrist as a culture broker: The hypnotic techniques of Dr. Hilton L. Lopez, M.D. *Svensk Tidskrift for Hypnos, 5,* 16-19.

Richeport, M. (1980a). El trance ritual como hipnoterapia clinica (Tres casos de psiquiatria transcultural), *Revista Ibero Americana de Sofrología y Medicina Psicosomática, 8*(4), 261-266.

Richeport, M. (1980b). O uso do transe ritual na clinica hipnoterapica: Estudo de casos em psiquiatria transcultural. *Revista Brasileira de Hipnologia, 1,* 39-46.

Richeport, M. (Director), & PAHO-WHO (Producer). (1981). *Alternative curing systems in Brazil.* [Videotape]. Rio de Janeiro; Washington.

Richeport, M. (1982). Erickson's contribution to anthropology. In J. Zeig (Ed.), *Ericksonian approaches to hypnosis and psychotherapy.* New York: Brunner/Mazel.

Rossi, E. (1977). Autohypnotic experiences of Milton H. Erickson. *American Journal of Clinical Hypnosis, 20,* 36-54.

Rossi, E. (Ed.). (1980). *The collected papers of Milton H. Erickson on hypnosis: Vol. 1. The nature of hypnosis and suggestion.* New York: Irvington.

Weidman, H.H. (1973, March). *Implications of the culture broker concept for the delivery of health care.* Paper presented at the annual meeting of the Southern Anthropological Society, Wrightsville Beach, NC.

Weidman, H.H. (1978). *Miami health ecology project report: A statement on ethnicity and health,* (Vol. 1). Miami: University of Miami.

Weidman, H.H. (Ed.). (1979). The transcultural perspective in health and illness. *Social Science & Medicine, 13B* (2), 85-167.

Zeig, J. (Ed.). (1980). *A teaching seminar with Milton H. Erickson.* New York: Brunner/Mazel.

Chapter 34

The "Uncommon Therapy" of Mohandas K. Gandhi

James R. Allen

On the morning of February 28, 1948, the men of the Somerset Light Infantry marched under the once triumphal arch of the British Empire, Bombay's Gate of India. As they stepped into their waiting barges, the strange and sadly moving sounds of "Auld Lang Syne" arose. Suddenly aware of the significance of that moment, people all along the waterfront and across the great esplanade joined the chorus. One era was ending, another beginning, one that Mohandas K. Gandhi had opened for three quarters of the inhabitants of the earth—the era of decolonization.

To examine certain aspects of interpersonal influence, I wish to point out similarities between Gandhi and Milton Erickson, in regard to their underlying philosophies. Then, I will emphasize some techniques both found useful: multilevel communication, symbolism, the metaphoric use of the charismatic life and the use of strategic behavioral tasks.

It is not my intention merely to apply to Gandhi what we have learned from Erickson, or vice versa. Rather, I wish to emphasize a few of the techniques both found useful in initiating change, Erickson as a therapist and Gandhi as a politician and guru to a nation. A host of commentators have elucidated some of the complexities of Erickson's methods. It is instructive, however, to look at similar techniques as applied by another master in another culture, in another arena of human endeavor. It is my hope that this will lead to a closer study of the use of these and related methods by other charismatic and creative individuals, an area which, with the exception of Haley's *The Power Tactics of Jesus Christ* (1969), has been largely neglected.

These techniques are not new. They are the tools of every great communicator, every great manipulator, every great demagogue. With the power of our current mass media greatly amplifying their effects, however, it is important that we, both as behavioral scientists and as citizens, look more closely at them. Because of his exceptional skills, his efforts to explain what he was doing, and the vast documentation of his work, Erickson offers a unique lens through which to study interpersonal influence. Although requirements of the printed page make it necessary to discuss these techniques one by one, both Erickson and Gandhi used them in combination and within an ongoing process.

SIMILARITIES BETWEEN GANDHI AND ERICKSON

Erickson and Gandhi had many similarities. They both recognized the importance of pacing. Erickson met his patients in their frame of reference. Gandhi utilized traditional Indian concepts in a way that changed them and the world forever. Both had an attitude of positive expectancy, both emphasized creating new experiences for others, and both were willing to take full responsibility for what happened. Both were pragmatic and largely atheoretical. Like Erickson, Gandhi had no handy guidelines. Conceptualizing himself as conducting experiments, he even subtitled his autobiography, *My Experiments with Truth* (1927). In a similar sense, Erickson's therapeutic stance was also "experimental."

Gandhi believed that individual dysfunction arose from social causes and it was this belief that led him into the political arena. His attitude and behavior towards his adversaries were striking. His goal was essentially therapeutic—nothing less than their transformation. He believed his adversaries had within them the potential for change. They knew things they did not know they knew.

SATYAGRAHA

Gandhi has served as a model for a number of activist movements in Africa and the West, including our own civil rights movement in the United States. Many of the techniques he developed have been widely employed—the burning of registration cards, organized tax refusal, sit-down strikes, and the deliberate violation of regulations limiting free speech. Yet, he has been followed only superficially. The religious and political theory behind these techniques, unifying them into *Satyagraha* or "truth-force," is much less familiar. Indeed, Gandhi's concept of politics contrasts strongly with most other views. However, the basic principles of *Satyagraha* are strikingly similar to Erickson's philosophy.

Satyagraha has meant many different things to different people. Gandhi coined the word from his native Gujarati. *Satya* means that which is, that which never changes; it can be translated as truth or love. *Agraha* means firmness, a potent and viable source of energy that belongs to all. In practice, *Satyagraha* is a method for conflict resolution and an attitude of nonviolent love which frames relationships, as well as an obstinate firmness in clinging to truth. There are five main aspects of the concept:

First, Gandhi did not advocate peace for its own sake, nor did he refuse to take sides. Like Erickson, he was a pragmatist who used specific techniques (in his case, nonviolence) under specific conditions, conditions where they could be expected to be effective, and against a specific adversary, an adversary who could be counted on to respond. Some of his followers, especially in the West, have advocated nonviolence for its own sake—a phenomenon similar, perhaps, to using paradox for its own sake. Indeed, he stated, "Where there is only a choice between cowardice and violence, I would advise violence" (Pontara, 1965). This is not advocacy of turning the other cheek. It is the advocacy of non-violent, but active and provocative resistance.

Second, Gandhi preceded *Satyagraha* with careful study. Only then did he make his interventions. Erickson also was known to prepare diligently before conducting treatment. However, while Erickson emphasized individuals, Gandhi worked with groups. His planning included the development of a disciplined and well-trained core group of activists to spearhead simultaneous action in different areas of the country. Finally, the masses were stirred to join in the struggle.

Yet he gave great trust to his unconscious and listened to his own inner voice. In describing his decision to fast during the strike of the Ahmedabad millhands, for example, he wrote: "Unbidden and all by themselves, the words came to my lips: Unless the strikers rally, I will not touch food" (Fischer, 1950, p. 431).

It was perhaps this combination of logical analysis and trust in unconscious processes which most confounded his opponents. He pressed forward when they would have withdrawn, and withdrew when they would have capitalized on the weaknesses of their adversaries. Similarly, if one reads Erickson's accounts of "The Method Used to Formulate a Complex Story for the Induction of the Experimental Neurosis" (Haley, 1973) or "The Permanent Relief of an Obsessional Phobia Through Communication with an Unsuspected Dual Personality" (Erickson & Rossi, 1979), one is struck by his careful planning and his extraordinary awareness of the subtleties of interpersonal encounter. Yet, at other times, he trusted the work at hand to his unconscious.

Third, *Satyagraha* assumes a potential openness of one's opponents to change and to the claims of justice, truth and love. This is a stance similar to that of Erickson. For many of us who sat long hours in his tiny office in Phoenix, perhaps our most lasting impression of him is that of a man of great decency, a man who cared about those he met and who seemed sure they could change if they so wished. Indeed, Erickson's therapeutic wizardry seems to be a function of this model of the world.

It is difficult to resist a movement which has the benevolent purpose of saving one—the more so when it seems to represent some next step in the development of man, one which has to be discovered through the mysterious working out of "Truth Force." In the March 17, 1927, edition of his newspaper, *Young India*, Gandhi wrote: "It is a matter of perennial satisfaction that I retain generally the affection and trust of those whose principles and policies I oppose. . . . I have always attempted to regard those who differ from me with the same affection as I have for my nearest and dearest." Indeed, Gandhi refused to submit to injustice not only because it destroyed him, the victim, but also because it destroyed its perpetrators themselves.

Fourth, *Satyagraha* proceeds from a search for the manner in which a conflict can be solved so as to satisfy both antagonist and protagonist, again a position similar to that of Erickson. When all attempts to reason have been made and one's adversaries remains unmoved, there are two alternatives: To force them to renounce their claim, or to find a way to change their hearts. Traditional political strategies generally have attempted the former. The *Satyagrahi* (the person who participates in *Satyagraha*), in contrast, does not know the correct answer, but searches and creates. The feelings and needs of both sides are acknowledged, and attempts are made to modify, change or satisfy wishes which initially were in conflict. Means are treated as inseparable from ends. Approaches which do violence to basic values are rejected.

Much of Erickson's fame rests on his ability to find ways to change people's hearts. In a famous case, he tells of treating a woman who was set on killing herself. She told him she was unlikeable and did not interact with men she was attracted to, although there was one in her office. He suggested that she ought to have at least one good memory before she killed herself and urged her to play a prank. Noting that she had a gap between her teeth, he instructed her to go to the water cooler in her office, take a mouthful of water and, when the young man approached, to squirt him. She did. The young man chased her and kissed her—initiating a series of events which led to relief from her depression and to her marriage (Haley, 1973).

Erickson frequently addressed simultaneously both his patients' hopes that he could help them and their predisposition to reject his suggestions. By pacing such resistance, he assured that his patients would experience him as someone who understood them and their complex motivations.

Fifth, Gandhi's key religious concept was Truth, and it is this concept which underlies his politics. The working out of Gandhi's "Truth Force" has much in common with Erickson's understanding of the unconscious—unclear and mysterious, but real, powerful and potentially positive. Unlike our traditional western concept of truth as some external objective actuality which is divorced from the particular persons involved, Gandhi's concept of Truth was that of a style of active behavior which expressed wholehearted commitment. "God," he said, "never appears to you in person, but always in action" (Bondurant, 1965).

When we look at Erickson's work, it is clear that he also valued wholehearted action—preferably, it seems, as expressed in getting on in the life cycle, marrying and having many children. Ericksonian therapy was based on effect rather than understanding (Zeig, personal communication, 1982). No matter how cleverly veiled, the message ultimately was: "Do something."

GANDHI'S STRATEGIC INTERVENTIONS AND USE OF SYMBOLS

Despite his failures and his personal quirks, Gandhi was a brilliant strategic therapist, good at judging the potentialities of the situation, highly creative in the invention of tactics, and acutely aware of the symbolic value of his acts—all qualities which characterized Erickson. Appropriately enough for the political arena, he was also good at arousing the masses, a good organizer and a superb publicist.

Like a good Ericksonian clinician, Gandhi was flexible in his tactics. Like the practitioners of the MRI Brief Therapy Project in Palo Alto, and Erickson himself, he settled for the smallest acceptable gain—a reasonable technique when one is dealing with positive feedback loops. It is noteworthy that even a minor change in a behavior pattern alters the feedback and feedforward loops between a person's external behavior, internal experience, and the world. A pattern of behavior is a calibrated homeostatic system and if one part of it is changed, the entire system must change to accommodate that change. New patterns of behavior can be caused by the environmental feedback created by the new behavior itself. Thus, a thing can become its own cause. Erickson called this process "snowballing."

As the final struggle came into being, however, Gandhi took a position of no compromise: Only the end of the British raj was acceptable. Yet, even then, he was not willing to press for the advantage at any cost. At the stroke of midnight, on the first of January, 1930, the Indian Congress party raised the flag of a new nation to usher in the struggle for complete independence. People looked to Gandhi to signal the next move, but he did nothing.

Suddenly, after weeks of deliberation, the answer came to him in a dream. He decided to lead a small band of marchers to the Indian Ocean to make salt in defiance of the law taxing salt. This was a brilliant choice of cause. The whole British Empire was indicted for preventing the Indian masses from taking a cheap and necessary substance from the shores of their own land. The manufacture and sale of salt was the exclusive monopoly of the state, which built a tax into its price. It was a small tax, but for the poor, it represented weeks of work.

Salt itself has many symbolic meanings. It comes from the sea, the mythical giver of life. It is used for the ceremonial affirmation of mutual bonds. In a hot country it is necessary for survival. In his classic paper of 1928, "The Symbolic Significance of Salt in Folklore and Superstition," Ernest Jones suggested its equivalence with semen. Consequently, it has been suggested that Gandhi's taking salt from the British can be seen as reclaiming for the Indian masses the potency properly theirs.

On March 12, 1930, Gandhi set forth leading 78 disciples whose names he had previously published in *Young India* for the benefit of the police. Villagers gathered along their route and sprinkled water before them to settle the dust. Day after day, the strange image of a little old man marching down to the sea to challenge the British raj dominated the presses of the world. The procession grew in numbers. It became a triumphal march. It was as if Gandhi was saying, "I am about to give a signal to the nation and to the world."

On April 5, after a slow, but newsworthy trip, the party reached the banks of the Indian Ocean. Western readers probably did not appreciate the fact that the marchers were scheduled to arrive at the ocean on the anniversary of a massacre of Indians. They could, however, understand that Gandhi was marching in the name of God. Some began to compare the march to the journey of Jesus to Jerusalem. His followers even found a donkey to follow behind him.

Gandhi had trapped the British in a clever bind. Although he wrote the Viceroy of his intentions beforehand, neither the English nor his own associates such as Nehru understood the power and meaning of what he intended. Now, the English could no longer ignore him and the widespread civil disobedience he had set in motion without giving him incredible power. On the other hand, they could not repress him and his movement without conferring on him the mantle of martyrdom and placing themselves in the role of outrageous oppressors. In either case, they increased his power.

The British reacted with the greatest police round-up in the history of India. Gandhi was imprisoned, but never again could British control of India be framed in terms of the "white man's burden" or "the civilizing mission" of a beneficent Britain.

Just before his arrest, Gandhi had drafted a letter to the Viceroy informing him of his intentions to raid the Dharsana Salt Works. In his place, Mrs. Naidu, the poet, led some 2,500 volunteers to the site. Row after row of workers walked up to the police who clubbed them and kicked them in the genitals. Women carried their bloodied bodies off until they themselves dropped from exhaustion. Still, the men came forward, row after row, Moslem and Hindu alike, with heads held high. The United Press correspondent Webb Miller was present, and his description of the event was dispatched to over a thousand newspapers.

By prescribing the symptom, by going with and even increasing British resistance, Gandhi set up a deviation amplification loop of such power that whatever moral ascendancy the West imagined they held was lost. Rabindranath Tagore summed it up in the *Manchester Guardian* of May 17, 1930: "Europe has completely lost her formal moral prestige in Asia. She is no longer regarded as the champion throughout the world of fair dealing, and the exponent of high principles, but as the upholder of western race supremacy and the exploiter of those outside her borders."

Gandhi, the prophet of nonviolence, had defeated the greatest military power in the world! As a psychotherapist influences the associations his patient makes, Gandhi changed the associations of millions. Britain now had to leave India. The only questions were when it would leave and how.

Traditional schools of psychotherapy elucidate the symbolic productions and communications of patients. However, Erickson, like Gandhi, used symbols as a therapeutic tool to effect change. Generally, we are not fully aware of how much we respond to symbols—the process is unconscious. Because of this, we tend to be less defended against symbolic aspects of communication (Zeig, personal communication, 1982). Consequently, there is much power to be gained through manipulating the symbolic aspects of symptoms and in using symbols in a direct manner.

In *A Teaching Seminar* (Zeig, 1980), we read of the case of a woman who was suicidally depressed at the death of her infant daughter. First, Erickson chided her for daring to destroy her memories of the child, her nine months of pregnancy and the months of the child's life. Then he suggested she plant a eucalyptus, a fast-growing tree, in her backyard, and that she name it Cynthia in memory of the child. He then promised to come to visit in a year, so that they could sit together in her garden and enjoy Cynthia's shade.

THE CHARISMATIC LIFE AS METAPHOR

A metaphor accesses in the listener some intended content although the content is not explicitly identified. Erickson was a master in this use of anecdotes and tales, and in the giving of metaphoric tasks. Less attention has been given to how Erickson lived his life as a metaphor, although, as Zeig has pointed out, he created in it a work of art, overcoming incredible deficits, pain and disease (Zeig, 1980).

As a master symbolist, Gandhi also used his life to enhance and extend his charisma. The identity he projected was that of a Hindu holy man and guru. As Nehru put it, "Indian mythology is full of great ascetics who by the rigor of their sacrifices build up a mountain of merit which threatens the domain of some of the lesser gods and upsets the established order" (Nehru, 1936). With such a metaphor so readily available to the masses, it was easy for them to interpret the confrontation between Gandhi and the British Empire as the struggle between good and evil. For members of the western world, he stirred up memories of the early saints, even of Christ himself. He adopted symbols that reinforced such an identity—e.g., the loincloth, fasting and the darshan.

The Indian custom of the darshan at first baffles the western observer. The collective glow of happiness that comes from being in the presence of a great man has been codified in India into a ritual. Gandhi's mere presence was enough to stir the hearts and hopes of thousands. We generally are squeamish about recognizing this process in the West. Yet, this is what happened, I believe, for many of the pilgrims who trekked across the country to spend even a few hours with the Wise Old Man of Phoenix, just as it always has with healers of power or fame.

From a therapeutic point of view, we can conceptualize a patient's symptoms as existing in a web of patterns of thinking, feeling, and behaving, a web of attitudes, relationships and contexts. Even a small change in any of these—the small change Erickson so often seemed to seek—makes a change in the pattern and may "snowball," leading to an ever-growing number of changes. A relationship, attitudinal and contextual change of this type is made, it seems, by the mere presence of a charismatic figure.

Gandhi adopted the loincloth for a number of reasons. It struck a blow against British economic imperialism, setting an example for others to boycott imported cloth. It suggested self-sacrifice and a lack of concern for the vanities of this world. In a country where few could afford adequate clothing, it established a bond with the masses. When he wore it to meet the King at Buckingham Palace, he defied the customs of the British Court. Winston Churchill may have been more accurate than he knew when he remarked that he was revolted by the nauseating and humiliating spectacle of "this one-time Inner Temple lawyer, now a seditious fakir, striding half-naked up the steps of the Viceroy's palace, there to negotiate on equal terms with the representative of the King-Emperor" (Fischer, 1950).

Since he wore cloth he made himself, Gandhi made spinning digni-fied. Through this humblest of chores, he linked the members of his political party, the Congress party, with a common daily rite. Its product, cotton khaddi, wrapped the humble and the small in a common swath. His little wooden spinning wheel became the symbol of his revolution, a peaceful challenge to Western imperialism. Thus, Gandhi projected himself as a saint, even while decrying the burden of Mahatmaship—but a saint who identified with the masses just as the masses could identify with him and his purpose.

Gandhi's use of the prayer meeting was masterful. He read from the scriptures of all the religious groups in India—Hindu, Christian, Bud-dhist, Sikh and Zoroastrian—suggesting unity and integration. How-ever, an even more important strategy may lie behind this: He was not so much deviating from established Hinduism, always an accepting re-ligion, as giving voice to a truer expression of religion. He was presenting himself as both an orthodox Hindu and a religious revisionist.

Such a prayer meeting would, of course, also provide a broth rich in metaphors, stories and anecdotes, a broth sure to be filled with analogies which related to the problems of his followers in some way, even though not always perceived consciously. It would also permit Gandhi to talk about one thing while simultaneously communicating about quite dif-ferent matters.

GANDHI'S STRATEGIC USES OF FASTING AND STRATEGIC BEHAVIORAL TASKS

Gandhi employed two kinds of fasts. The first was a fast until death in which he vowed to achieve some specific object or die. The second kind was for a fixed period. Although it was usually framed as a form of personal penance, often a public atonement for the errors of his followers, it was compelling also in bringing them back into his fold.

Fasting has long been regarded as a kind of prayer—more so if undertaken under divine guidance—and as a way to allow the spirit to dominate the flesh. Strategically, Gandhi used it to give a problem an added dimension of significance and urgency—especially so if he had declared a fast unto death. This forced people's thinking out of old ruts. To be effective, it also had to be accompanied by great publicity. Above all, it had to be taken against an opponent on whose care and conscience he could make claim. As he wrote in *Young India,* September 30, 1926: "Fasting cannot be undertaken against any opponent. Fasting can be resorted to only against one's nearest and dearest, and that solely for his or her good."

Gandhi's 1947 fast to restore order in Calcutta is instructive. As he lay dying, his followers sought out the Hindu extremists. By the second day, rioters paused to consider his blood pressure, his heart rate, and the constituents of his urine. As his life seemed in danger, mixed groups of Hindus and Moslems invaded the slums where the worst rioting had taken place. On the third evening, a group of *goondas* appeared, surrendering their weapons, confessing their crimes, and offering to submit to any punishment he deemed suitable. In a move of strategic brilliance, he announced their punishment: They were to go into the Moslem neighborhoods and pledge themselves to be the protectors of the very people they had victimized.

Those who saw the movie *Gandhi* will likely recall a compelling scene. A Hindu whose son had been killed by Moslems came, covered with Moslem blood, to ask Gandhi's forgiveness. He promised Gandhi he would do anything to escape damnation because he had murdered a child. Gandhi gave his prescription: He was to adopt a Moslem boy and to raise him as a Moslem! To what degree this scene is historically accurate I do not know. In any case, it was strategically brilliant: The replacement of the lost object, the change of affect, the changing of behavior patterns to new ones more likely to lead to new and potentially satisfying feedback loops, and the moving of the man forward into the next stage of his life cycle. Gandhi's goal, like Erickson's, was to change symptomatic behavior to something more functional in the person's developing life.

Gandhi's 1948 New Delhi fast at Birla House galvanized the world. This, his last fast, he undertook on January 13 to encourage the Indian payment of 550 million rupees to Pakistan. It was typical of him that he broke the fast by receiving a drink from the hands of Mauland Azad, a Moslem, and Jawaharlal Nehru, a Hindu, along with the Indian promise of payment.

SYMBOLIC IMMORTALITY

Becoming part of nature is a time-honored mode of gaining immortality symbolically. Erickson was cremated and his ashes scattered on Squaw Peak, the mountain whose ascent so many of us had been urged to undertake just before sunrise. Gandhi's ashes were delivered to all the separate provinces of India. Such bones as were not consumed in the funeral pyre were carried by a special train of five third-class carriages to Allahabad, where the clear waters of the Jumna join the muddy turbulence of the Ganges and, the faithful believe, the invisible waters of a celestial river. There, they were cast into the water, making Gandhi, as far as possible, a part of all India.

It seems fitting to end this chapter by recounting one event which encapsulates much of the therapeutic talent of Gandhi: his use of symbolism, multilevel communication and indirect suggestion, his ability to express almost unlimited implications in a simple gesture, his gentle, teasing affability and his respect for his opponents, whom he worked to transform.

While in prison after the Great Salt March, he was invited to the Viceroy's palace to negotiate with Lord Irwin, the representative of the King-Emperor. When asked to take tea, he refused, but he did accept a cup of hot water. Taking a small packet of illegal salt from the folds of his shawl, he put a pinch into the water, with the simple remark, "To remind us of the famous Boston Tea Party" (Nanda, 1958).

REFERENCES

Bondurant, J. (1965). *Conquest of violence—The Gandhian philosophy of conflict*. Berkeley: University of California Press.

Erickson, E. (1969). *Gandhi's truth*. New York: Norton.

Erickson, M. H., & Rossi, E. L. (1979). *Hypnotherapy: An exploratory case book*. New York: John Wiley.

Fischer, L. (1950). *The life of Mahatma Gandhi*. New York: Collier Books.

Gandhi, M. K. (1927). *An autobiography or the story of my experiments with truth* (M. Desai, Trans.). Ahmedabad: Navajivan.

Gay, V. P. (1982). Repression and sublimation in religious personalities. *Journal of Religion and Health, 21*(2), 152-170.

Haley, J. (1969). *The power tactics of Jesus Christ and other essays*. New York: Discus Books.

Haley, J. (1973). *Uncommon therapy: The psychiatric techniques of Milton H. Erickson*. New York: Norton.

Mayer, P. (Ed.). (1966). The doctrine of the sword. In P. Mayer (Ed.), *The pacifist conscience*. New York: Holt, Rinehart & Winston.

Nanda, B. R. (1958). *Mahatma Gandhi, a biography*. Boston: Beacon Press.
Nehru, J. (1936). *An autobiography*. London: Oxford University Press.
Pontara, G. (1965). The rejection of violence in Gandhian ethics of conflict resolution. *Journal of Peace Research, 31*, 197-214.
Rosen, S. (1983). *My voice will go with you*. New York: Norton.
Zeig, J. (Ed.). (1980). *A teaching seminar with Milton H. Erickson*. New York: Brunner/Mazel.

Chapter 35

Ericksonian Hypnotic Properties of Japanese Psychotherapies: Morita and Naikan

Sung C. Kim

Morita and Naikan are Japanese forms of psychotherapy that are relatively unknown in the West. They have gained little acceptance, in part due to the difficulty in understanding them from the viewpoint of traditional Western therapies. The Ericksonian framework shares many features (principles and pragmatics) with Morita and Naikan and offers much in the way of elucidating the nature of psychotherapeutic processes in these Japanese therapies. A comparative study of both Japanese and Ericksonian therapies can point to certain fundamental therapeutic elements which intuitively may have been grasped and utilized by their founders. The overlap is intriguing, especially in view of Erickson's relative unfamiliarity with these Asian therapies. Conversely, the study of Morita and Naikan from the Ericksonian perspective can further an understanding of Erickson's work and can become an opportunity to validate his hypnotically based psychotherapeutic framework cross-culturally.

Following the description of Morita and Naikan, the philosophical premises and strategic aspects of each therapeutic design will be examined from an Ericksonian perspective. Essential features (principles, processes, and techniques) shared among Ericksonian, Morita, and Naikan therapies are then discussed.

Preparation of this paper was supported by the Richmond Area Multi-Services, National Asian-American Psychology Training Center.

MORITA THERAPY

She had come to the point where she could only lie in bed. Any time she raised her head, even slightly, she became extremely dizzy. She couldn't raise her body at all. She arrived for examination in an ambulance and was carried into the examination room on a stretcher. I told her, "In order to diagnose your illness I must see you in your most distressed state, so as much as possible try to produce the greatest dizziness you can." With those instructions I took her head in my hands and raised it. However, the patient didn't complain of any unpleasantness. "That's too bad; how about this?" and I lifted her into a sitting position. Still nothing happened. The patient was surprised. I explained, "Because of your fear and anxiety over your symptoms, they occurred. Now you tried to make the dizziness appear so you weren't afraid or anxious about it and nothing happened, no dizziness. From now on, while encouraging your dizziness to come forth live an active life." (Kora, 1968, p. 320)

The therapist was not Erickson but Kora. What he did illustrates Morita therapy in action, his grasp of its principles, and his flexibility in applying them to a case.

Morita therapy was developed in Japan by Dr. Shoma Morita (1874-1938) and is discussed by various writers (e.g., Murase & Johnson, 1974; Reynolds, 1976). The condition for which Morita therapy was originally designed is *shinkeishitsu*, which literally means nervous temperament. In Western terminology, this condition is comparable to states of obsessional psychoneurosis featuring perfectionism, ambivalence, rumination, and social withdrawal. It also includes the presence of neurasthenia and hypochondriacal symptoms.

Morita believed that a major factor contributing to the development of shinkeishitsu was the "psychic interaction of attention and sensation." It is a process by which sensation (e.g., blushing) intensifies when attention is directed to it by chance. Attention is directed to it all the more when the sensation intensifies thereby creating a vicious cycle, eventually fixing the symptom (e.g., erythrophobia: morbid fear of blushing). For the Moritist, the pattern inherent in shinkeishitsu symptoms is seen to be fundamentally a misdirection of attention inward. This internal focusing involves the painful awareness of the patient's faults and limitations to the degree that spontaneous behavior is inhibited by (self-)

consciousness. Instead of focusing attention outward on tasks/behaviors, the patient focuses inward on feelings and sensations.

Therapy is aimed at breaking the cycle of hypersensitivity and social failure by training patients 1) to accept themselves as they are and 2) to immerse themselves in constructive activity. Because Morita viewed the patient's difficulties as the result of self-limiting habit patterns, his therapeutic task/aim was to redirect the patient's energy in a therapeutically desirable direction. In this effort the therapist takes an active, directive role in a highly structured strategic environment. Reynolds (1976) stated the same point: "For Morita, neurosis was misdirected attention, and cure was directing attention. The whole of Morita therapy may be viewed as efforts to guide patients by setting up a situation in which they learn to refocus attention on more productive and constructive topics" (p. 230).

The notion of the psychic interaction of attention/sensation and the goal of directing patients to refocus their attention is analogous to the Ericksonian orientation referred to as "displacement of cathexis" (Beahrs, 1971), one of Erickson's most important and frequently used major therapeutic approaches. This orientation enables patients to shift or displace large amounts of emotional cathexis from their original problems to some constructive outlets. Rather than attempting to uncover underlying conflicts with whys and interpretations, patients simply are helped to redirect their psychic energy into new channels, be they objects or relationships. Consonant with the displacement of cathexis orientation, Moritists believe there is a third option other than suppressing or discharging emotions. It is a retraining of attention, as when patients become so immersed in a task or a pleasure that they forget their pain and problems.

Both Erickson and Morita viewed the unconscious as source of a powerful, constructive force for life and growth which needs to be worked with, not against. Morita postulated the existence of a "life creative force" as the basic source of development and growth in the human being and he believed this life force was largely untapped by his patients.

> The goal can be achieved if the patient's hypochondriacal tendency is destroyed so that the desire to live, which is the underlying vital force creating this personality tendency, can be properly utilized in a more constructive way. . . . In Morita therapy it is not an increase of conscious control over the unconscious by the ego. It is, rather, an integration of the unconscious and conscious pre-

paratory to the type of living, thinking and acting that in Zen is called "mushin," a state where acts and decisions are handed over to the same unconscious process that organized the ingenious structure of the body. (Kondo, 1975, p. 257)

Similarly, Erickson held the most positive faith in life and reality. He viewed the unconscious as "a powerful constructive (life) force which held more wisdom than the conscious" (Haley, 1982). The essence of both therapies lies in the creation of a powerful therapeutic situation (trance) in which patients can experience this life force (the unconscious resources).

To achieve therapeutic goals, Morita devised "personal-experience therapy" (Kondo, 1975), which later was renamed as Morita therapy by his followers. Like Erickson, Morita believed that it is only through personal experience that the patient can overcome symptoms, gain insight, and realize one's true self. What is important is the transformation of experience itself. While Morita was not against words, he used a different method of persuasion, which is indirect and strategic. Thus, in Morita, as in Zen, there is minimal use of abstract, rationalistic discourse and maximal use of concrete illustrations and metaphorical communication (Haley, 1977), designed to induce "experiential" (trance) learning.

Both Erickson and Morita emphasized doing (i.e., getting the patient to do something) and experiencing. Both believed that one can get a new feeling by having a new experience, and that as the constructive force is strengthened and mobilized freely, the pathological aspects will fade away. Erickson would have been in agreement with Reynolds and Kiefer (1977) who, in describing Morita, stated,

> It isn't necessary for the patient to understand intellectually; he needs simply to do as he is told, and will come to understand through experience . . . the patient's own experience should soon confirm or disconfirm the usefulness of what he is told to do. (p. 405)

Reframing is also an integral part of both therapies. According to Morita, it is an excess of positive tendencies that results in misdirected attention and ultimately, neurosis. A strong energy source, a desire for perfection, a need to be thought well of by others—all these can be reoriented into creating a "superior" person. Moritists see the hunger for activity (stemming from the absolute bed rest to be discussed later) as an expression of the life force, which is the dynamic, unself-conscious "self," which in Ericksonian terminology corresponds to the "unconscious." As discussed by Reynolds (1976), "cure," once defined as "removal of symptoms," is redefined/reframed as "living actively with symptoms"; "hospitalization" is redefined as "a period devoted to the learning of how to live fully"; "living fully," once defined as "symptom-free living," is reframed as "purposeful living for others." Watzlawick sees one major aspect of Ericksonian therapy to be reframing in trance; Morita's therapy appears to be a fine example of the type of therapy that is predicated on "the gentle art of reframing" (Watzlawick et al., 1974, p. 92).

STAGES OF MORITA THERAPY

Morita therapy consists of four stages conducted in an inpatient setting. To provide an overview, the first period (about a week) is called "absolute bed rest" during which patients are placed in a highly structured therapeutic environment and instructed to "stop doing everything" and to place themselves at rest. During the remaining three stages patients gradually are guided to take on increasingly demanding activities in the direction of becoming a socially productive person. The second period (about a week) begins with them being allowed to do a few simple activities under the guidance of the Moritist. During this time, they are still socially restricted. "Resting" continues to be an important part of their routine. They are asked to keep diaries and the therapist makes comments on selected entries. In the third period (about a week) they are gradually allowed to begin hard physical work. The therapist meets briefly with them individually and makes suggestions on how they may correct both their thinking and behavior. The work is calculated to give an opportunity to experience satisfaction and confidence in the accomplishment of simple, physical tasks, which patients typically disdain. Finally, in the fourth stage (one to two weeks) they are encouraged to resume real-life activities in the outside world.

There is a parallel between Ericksonian and Morita therapies from the perspectives of design, strategy, and therapeutic elements. The stages of Morita (i.e., periods of 1) absolute bed rest, 2) light work, and 3) heavier work) correspond to the threefold stages of an Ericksonian approach (Beahrs, 1971): 1) pacing: meeting the patient at the patient's level and gaining rapport; 2) modifying the patient's productions and gaining control; and 3) using this control to help the patient change in a desirable direction.

The First Stage: A Period of Absolute Bed Rest

The first stage is distinct from the others in that patients are bedridden during the entire period (except to take their meals and use the toilet), whereas they are engaged in physical activity during the other stages. The therapist may make brief visits daily to check the patients' progress. For the remainder of the time, patients are instructed to accept their thoughts and feelings as they are. The Moritists may instruct patients in the following way:

> You can think of anything you want to think of. As a matter of fact, it is better that you ruminate as much as possible. If you are worried about your symptoms and conditions, go ahead and worry. If you are suffering from them, suffer to your heart's content. During the course of bed rest, you might get bored and feel the strong urge to get up . . . wonder if you would be cured by just lying in bed like this. . . . Whatever mood might grip you, lie in bed as you are told and keep it to be your duty. (Kora, 1964, p. 28)

It should be noted that the neurotic personality of Morita's time, the shinkeishitsu personality, was characterized first, by its introversive and hypochondriacal tendencies, lacking the ability to meet and converse with people, or carry out everyday activities. What the Moritist may be doing, is pacing the patient in a powerful, strategic sense. The pacing has several functions: 1) It encourages patients' symptomatic behaviors (avoidance of interpersonal contacts and internal preoccupation) in a highly structured and dramatic way; 2) it heightens patients' confusion over knowing what to do about their symptoms (thereby preparing them to rely on the Moritist for guidance later); 3) absolute bed rest encourages an experiential/behavioral insight (as opposed to intellectual/motivational insight). It sets an experiential limit, a benchmark of distress and inactivity and withdrawal and boredom against which they can measure later productivity. Patients know with a fundamental gut-level knowledge that extreme inactivity is unnatural for them and that such a life would not be satisfying. As a Morita patient remarked, "The work wasn't much fun, but when I think about bed rest, moving my body is pleasant" (Reynolds, 1976, p. 29). From the Ericksonian viewpoint, the absolute bed rest strategically creates a deep, experiential anchor compared to which any activity other than the absolute bed rest becomes more desirable. In this sense it is a benevolent ordeal. Toward the end of the bed-rest week, the confusion (with the associated loss of the patient's usual frame of reference) mounts, self-preoccupation declines, and ordinary sensations, like washing, going to the toilet, and seeing the therapist, even briefly, are experienced with pleasure. One patient, for example, wrote at the end of the bed rest: "I have nothing more to think about. I have no way of passing the long day doing nothing. I'm now at my wits' end: I don't care what would happen now . . ." (Kora, 1964, p. 18). Another patient wrote: "The ennui is so unbearable that even going to the toilet is now a great pleasure. I have never experienced such a great joy in my life" (Kora, 1964, p. 18).

Morita, like Erickson, took an approach in which the therapist

> . . . is constantly looking for and looking at health in his client and considering how to redirect the patient toward a more satisfactory implementation of his health concerns. Just as in judo or karate one uses an opponent's force, redirecting it slightly to accomplish one's own goals, so the sensitive therapist refrains from disaffirming his client's basic concerns. Rather, he identifies them, supports them, and utilizes them to meet the self-defined needs of the clients. (Reynolds, 1976, p. 3)

The absolute bed rest is constructed to create a trance experience. The patients' attention is bound/absorbed in the task of accepting all thoughts and feelings as they come and as they are. Conscious resistance is framed as a part of the process of Morita therapy (thereby depotentiating the patients' conscious resistance). Patients are given the *koan*-like nonrational task of accepting what one has not been able to, which eventually forces them to experience "deeper" levels of mental functioning and which ultimately frees them from their symptoms (Reynolds, 1976; Watts, 1961). The loss of the patients' "generalized frame of reference" thus induced by the bed rest brings patients to a level other than that of their conscious, symptom-ridden level. This process of going into the trance state can be gleaned from a patient's diary writing, who upon rising from his bed rest experience remarked:

> I got up at 5:30 . . . What a beautiful day! I wandered around in a dream. It was wonderful feeling my body move. First I swept up the fallen leaves and trash with a broom. Until the breakfast chimes I worked as if in a dream . . . I simply wasn't aware of the passage of time. (Reynolds, 1976, p. 29)

Moritists use both indirect and direct forms of suggestions throughout all stages of therapy. Indirect suggestions are primarily used in earlier stages, similarly to the way Erickson worked. Predictions of success (based on the Moritists' clinical experience) are made, beginning as early as the absolute bed-rest phase of treatment, promoting credulity and increased suggestibility in patients. This is similar to the Ericksonian use of truism and open-ended suggestions covering all possibilities, all designed to pace patients and gain their rapport. Other examples of indirect suggestions are the Moritists' use of diary writing and citing cases of successful cure. Direct suggestions occur in interviews, during *kowa* (Morita lectures), and as written comments on the diaries.

The Second Stage: A Period of Light Work

During this stage patients are allowed to go outdoors and do some light work (e.g., sweeping and raking leaves); however, they are prohibited from social relationships and activities like reading. They are advised to keep daily diaries. Advice and interpretation are given at the scene of their work and careful comments are made on their diaries. During this period, patients begin the formal instruction in Morita's theory and his world view through the diary, kowa lectures, meetings, and discussions.

The essence of this period is to consolidate the patients' learning that when their attention is directed outward they do not notice their symptoms as much. This period is to be regarded as a transitory period, in which the constructive forces are striving for normality and need to be carefully and vigilantly guided toward later stages.

This period of light work corresponds to the second Ericksonian stage, i.e., modifying the patients' production and gaining therapeutic control. It is designed to enhance the patients' spontaneous impulses towards engaging in activities. The choice of work and time are left entirely up to the patients' spontaneous desires, analogous to the permissive approach of Erickson. Indirect suggestions consonant with the therapeutic aims are utilized and can be illustrated by the Moritists' use of diary writing. In diary writing, patients are isolated and told to write all thoughts and feelings. The therapist goes over the diaries and provides comments only on entries that are objective and task-oriented. In the Japanese cultural context, the diary writing is an interaction which utilizes the tendency of the shy, sensitive shinkeishitsu patients who may find it easier to communicate their inner experiences through an indirect means. The diary gives patients the necessary time and distance through which they can communicate with minimum discomfort.

The kowa lectures are another important part of Morita therapy and take place at least once a week during which patients gather to hear a lecture from the Moritist. During the kowa the therapist (in a role analogous to the guru) may read from a book, explain the meaning of various calligraphies, or simply talk on his experience of treating other cases. In addition to case histories, there are also illustrations and parables. The kind of content appropriate for the kowa lectures and the style of delivery (inherent in a monotone, soft-spoken Japanese style of speaking) appear to be similar to the various forms of Erickson's conversational approach to trance induction. In reference to kowa lectures, we may note that 1) Asian communication patterns and style are indirect and utilize anecdotes, parables, stories, proverbs (Kim, 1983), and 2) the authority/therapist/guru-patient/disciple relationship in Morita therapy induces an expectant and responsive set, a listening and accepting attitude, on the part of Morita patients.

To illustrate the conversational approach to trance induction by Moritists, there is an illustrative kowa point used by many Moritists: "Every day your nose is perfectly visible, but you don't notice it. Since I just now pointed it out to you perhaps you have become very much aware of it. But, now, while you are so conscious of your visible nose, you haven't been paying any attention to the headache you came complaining of, have you" . . . (Reynolds, 1976). Similarly, Kora writes:

> . . . One man couldn't stand the sound of rain on the roof, so he woke up his servants in the middle of the night ordering them to put mattresses on the roof to reduce the noise; but there are more poetically minded people who enjoy the sound of rain on the roof . . . Then I ask the patients, "Now did you hear the clock ticking?" "No, we didn't," they answer . . . . (Kora, 1968, p. 223)

The Third and Fourth Stages: The Period of Heavier Work and Life Training

The third stage is designed to develop the patients' self-confidence and self-image by experiencing the joy of accomplishment as they complete some activity or work they choose, moved by their spontaneous, emerging desire for activity and productive work. Patients engage in tasks requiring greater physical output (e.g., gardening and carpentry), often in conjunction with others. They are given permission to read selected books (which have reality orientation, such as history books, as opposed to fantasy or intellectual orientation) and to have more contact with people in their environment. In this period, their constructive force is mobilized and developed by their attainment of an affirmative, accepting attitude of mind. By this time, patients are beginning to develop confidence and joy in their accomplishments. They are more reality-grounded. They do not notice the passing of time because they are fully occupied in their work. Their symptoms have receded.

The fourth stage, the period of life training, may best be construed as an extension of the third stage of Morita. At this time, patients begin to resume some of the work carried on in their usual occupation and living, often resuming part-time work outside the hospital or making visits home. Important and responsible work is allowed to patients. Usually their diaries come to be filled with expressions of self-confidence, joy, and gratitude.

Both the third and fourth stages of Morita correspond to the third stage of Ericksonian psychotherapy: using the therapeutic control to help patients move in a therapeutically desirable direction. In these stages, induction of change via suggestions continue, in order to consolidate patients' learning; however, suggestions are more direct since patients are more receptive to direct suggestions and guidance-giving. A meeting of patients is instituted, in which they hear accounts from ex-patients who have surmounted their problems and returned to normal living. Reading is generally permitted, but only those books directed toward reality. Patients "work through" their realizations 1) by consolidating their newfound understanding of their relationship to nature, life, work, responsibility, and symptoms, and 2) by practicing the Morita path in a systematic and gradual fashion.

NAIKAN THERAPY

Naikan therapy is guided self-reflection aimed at uncovering a new perspective on who we have been, are, and can become. The process of Naikan therapy involves seven days of continuous, intensive meditation based upon a highly structured experience in self-observation. The process of meditation enables clients to recall significant persons and events from the past and ultimately to recognize the love and support upon which all their "imperfect" lives have been built.

Procedurally, the form of Naikan is elegantly straightforward. The content of instructions and themes for meditation or reflection, as well as the way of giving instructions, are of central significance. The Naikan clients are asked to examine themselves in relationship to others from the following three perspectives:

1) Recollect and examine your memories of care and benevolence that

you have received from a particular person during a particular time in your life.
2) Recollect and examine your memories of what you have returned to that person. . . .
3) Recollect and examine the troubles and worries you have given that person.

These three perspectives can be named: "benevolence given," "benevolence returned" and "trouble given to others."

As a rule, one begins with an examination of one's relationship to one's mother on the above three questions and then proceeds to examine, reexperience, and reflect on relationships with other family members and significant others. One at a time, with each person, the sequence is to move from childhood to the present, reflecting on a certain segment of that period in a very methodical, systematic fashion.

The client begins the Naikan recollection and reflections at 5:30 in the morning and continues them until 9:00 in the evening. The client sits in a quiet, confined place enclosed by Japanese screens to reduce distraction and to increase concentration on one's inner world. Since the client is not allowed to leave this very narrow space except to visit the bathroom or go to bed, the place inside the screen constitutes the client's whole environment. Even meals are brought to the client and taken while meditating. Such a fixed environment facilitates concentrated self-reflection.

While meditating, the *sensei* (Naikan therapist) comes to the client for *mensetsu* (Naikan interview) every one to two hours during the day. The sensei bows his or her head to the floor before entering the client's meditation space in appreciation of the hard work in Naikan. He opens the folding screen and then the sensei listens to the client's story. The sensei asks, "What have you been reflecting upon during this period?" The client's response is similarly ritualistic. The client reports the person and time period of the reflection. For example, the client may say, "During this period, I have been reflecting upon my father during my college years." Following this, the client states the recollections made concerning the three questions. The client may soon fall into the pattern of reporting having received a great deal, returning little, and causing a great deal of trouble to the person. This is "proper" Naikan.

The Process of Change in Naikan

The two goals of Naikan therapy (i.e., the rediscovery of personal guilt and the discovery of a positive gratitude toward others) are accomplished through an approach which shares many hypnotic principles and elements utilized by Erickson. Naikan can be viewed as a strategic therapy which utilizes pacing, trance learning, suggestions (particularly indirect and nonverbal), imagery, and reframing.

Pacing

To facilitate the trance induction, the client's initial resistance to the Naikan work is paced in the Ericksonian manner. If the client is not doing proper Naikan, this resistance is accepted as a valid part of Naikan, belonging to an initial phase of the therapy. The client is educated beforehand about this sort of resistance and is told that it will be replaced by more serious Naikan. In the Naikan sense, resistance is used to describe those thoughts and strategies that threaten to disrupt the process or goals of the therapy. Instead of interpreting the resistant behavior, the Naikan therapist utilizes it to redirect the client back to the task of proper Naikan. When the client intellectualizes, the therapist directs the client away from abstract or vague description of past events to more concrete statements about specific personal experiences.

Trance Learning

Naikan produces an intense, focused, emotional learning experience which is hypnotic. After seven successive days, the client has sat for more than 100 hours almost continuously—except for sleeping and toileting. The intensity of the hypnotic Naikan experience is made possible through a number of factors. First of all, Naikan has an exquisitely straightforward structure/form with clear boundaries of roles, clear feedback about what is and is not Naikan attitude and behavior, and clear expectations about goals, processes and obstacles. Such a structure fosters task-orientation on the part of the client by focusing the client's attention. The Naikan experience takes on an almost life-or-death quality for the client. Unless one is willing to take the Naikan experience deadly seriously, one would not willingly submit oneself to the confinement of a four-by-four-foot space and continuous reflection for every waking moment of seven days. Furthermore, the demand characteristics inherent in responding to frequent *mensetsu* with the sensei discourages any unfocused, non-Naikan cognitive activities. Parenthetically, the frequent awakening of the client to report on the client's inner work may also have an effect of deepening the client's trance, analogous to Vogt's fractionation technique (Kroger, 1977).

In essence, Naikan therapy accomplishes its goals hypnotically by holding everything (physical and psychological) in the client's environment constant, except for the focused therapeutic task, i.e., introspection involving the three Naikan questions. The focusing of attention onto the Naikan task facilitates this process of reducing competing responses and increasing trance response potential. When all competing stimuli in the client's environment are made constant or relegated to the background, what surfaces through the work of Naikan can be seen with hypnotic clarity and occurs in a hypnotic reality. The client is powerfully, yet permissively, guided to suspend his or her present, conflict-ridden frame of reference and to hold nothing but the Naikan perspective, which will reframe the past. The reframing occurs unconsciously, since the client's conscious mind is bound to the therapeutic task.

Suggestions and Imagery

In this overall trance state, both direct and indirect suggestions are utilized. The goals and procedures of Naikan are explicitly stated, along with the prediction about the process and obstacles. Periodic public playing of audiotapes of actual Naikan sessions by previous clients at various stages of Naikan reinforces the suggestions and predictions made previously.

There is a heavy reliance on imagery and nonverbal experiencing. *Nai* in Naikan literally means "inner." *Kan* means "observation" but carries a specific meaning in the context of Japanese Buddhism. Kan implies visually imagining an object during meditation with intensively integrated states of mind. Naikan may be likened to "sweeping the dust from the soul" and the task of Naikan is "digging and digging" with a prediction that the client will eventually go into "deeper Naikan," during which the client will experience specific, vivid detailed memories and images.

The therapist-client relationship in Naikan is akin to the Ericksonian hypnotherapist-client relationship. In Naikan the therapist relates to the client in a highly intensive and direct way, providing a clear structure and directives; yet, the therapist respects any of the client's responses as valid as long as it is consistent with the Naikan framework. If it is not, it is ignored. The therapist-client relationship in Naikan is also similar to that of Ericksonian methods since the structure, setting, environment, and therapeutic contract enable the client to view the therapist as the benign authority and guide. As in Morita, transference aspects of the therapeutic relationship are deliberately kept as simple and uncomplicated as possible. The relationship is firmly established on the basis of a positive, dependency relationship which is utilized to allow the client to own the process of change later on.

Strategic Approach

An essential part of Naikan lies in its ability to instill a sense of deep appreciation of others and life within, together with an attitude and feeling of a newfound appreciation for others' part in one's life. From the strategic point of view, the structure of Naikan fosters this sense of appreciation in a powerful way. The strategy is indirect so as to bypass the client's conscious resistance to change.

First, the sensei models a sense of appreciation for the client and as such the sensei-client relationship mirrors the kind of relationship the client is guided to experience while the client is reflecting on his or her relationship to others. For example, the attitude and behavior of appreciation is concretely (yet symbolically) enacted and modeled for the client when the sensei bows to the client, takes on a menial (but benevolent) role of serving food, and totally devotes him- or herself in the act of helping clients come to certain realizations. Appreciation modeled for the client by the sensei may thus set the stage for the client to learn to discover how the client was appreciated and how to appreciate in return.

Second, in order to help the client attribute change internally, the therapist strategically plays a minimal role. As a guide, the therapist's function is to make sure that the client is following instructions and reflecting successfully on the topics assigned for self-reflection. The therapist, in the initial stage, accepts and respects clients as people with the potential will and capability to realize themselves and discourages any non-Naikan attitude and behavior on the part of clients by simply redirecting the clients' attention and intention to the Naikan method proper. The minimization of the therapist's role elevates the client's role and responsibility in the changing process and maximizes the client's internal attribution of therapeutic changes. Within this framework, the client is not a "patient" to be treated and worked on by the therapist; instead, the client is a student whose learning potential is to be realized from within through the method of Naikan reflections—through his or her own effort. Consistent with the Ericksonian emphasis on the learning potential of the client, and the internal locus of change, the Naikan sensei's role is to create a psychological and physical environment which materializes the realization of this learning potential. The devotional and appreciative stance of Erickson toward his clients is well-known. Erickson, Naikan, and Morita therapists embody this devotional (in contrast to professional) stance and role in therapy. The quality of strong devotion thus demonstrated by the therapist obviously creates a strong psychological and emotional climate of trust which allows the client to experience the trance.

Reframing

A restructuring/reframing of the client's view of the past is another key mechanism of change in Naikan. Naikan offers a pragmatic framework and a clear systematic method for reordering the past. In Naikan, past interpersonal events and one's associations to them which hinder present functioning are reconstructed and reinterpreted in a deliberate, strategic, positive way. The client willingly subjects him- or herself to view the past from a unique perspective and is led to discover a cognitive and emotional order in what appeared to have been a chaotic, confused past, marked by conflicts, anger, resentment, blaming, and so on. As DeVos (1980) puts it,

> What occurs in Naikan therapy overall is a reorganization of one's recollections. A framework is created for reordering the past. The past, in effect, is mythologized to release a capacity for gratitude . . . there is a reversal of one's instrumentalization of relationships . . . of using others as tools for satisfying selfish needs. One turns rather toward an attitude of being able to give to others. (p. 130)

Thus, the purpose of Naikan is to develop a positive, adaptive reorientation to personal relationships through the positive cognitive reconstruction of past relationships. Viewed in another way, the ultimate goal of Naikan is to change the basic self-concept. This goal is achieved by directing the client's attention to recollecting the experience of "having been loved and cared for" in earlier days, which in turn gives the client a feeling of inherent continuity and consistency between the client's present self and his or her basic trust of the world. In the end this experience brings about a more integrated ego identity. Again, as DeVos (1980) states,

> What is sought instead (in Naikan) is tranquility—forms of internal manipulation of thought that lead to quietude, not anger. Rather than facing head-on anxieties that block us from experiencing our

primal sense of destructiveness or sexual attachment, so that the
dark unconscious powers within us are laid to rest or at least
brought to heel by conscious control, the Japanese learn to exercise
control over thoughts in a hypnotic way. Rather than exploring the
miasmic marshes of early memory, they reconstruct the past. . . .
(p. 125)

Restructuring the past can best be illustrated by examining the way
Naikan reframes the emotion of anger. Many Western psychotherapeutic
approaches hold the assumption that unless the emotion of anger is
unblocked, other underlying emotions may not surface. While in the
West anger is often treated as an isolated emotion, the Naikan perspective places anger in a much broader context. It juxtaposes anger
with other, equally relevant and potent emotions such as appreciation,
love, and authentic guilt, and allows the client to understand the place
of anger more realistically. Naikan changes the basis of self, which in
turn changes one's response to anger, since it gives a more harmonious
perspective with other people. This perspective in turn reduces the narcissistic part of the anger. When anger is viewed in the context of appreciation and gratitude, the strength and intensity of anger is bound
to lessen. Thus, the Naikan method renders anger ineffective as an
emotion. This maneuver is accomplished by redirecting the client's focus
on an incompatible, and in the long-run more adaptive response, i.e.,
development of a sense of deep gratitude toward the person one has
been angry at. There is liberation of energy in finding within oneself
capacity to appreciate. Anger is no longer as important and becomes
neutralized by other dominant emotions.

CONCLUSION

The external forms of Morita, Naikan, and Ericksonian psychotherapies are quite different from each other. Yet, they are all "uncommon"
therapies sharing many essential assumptions and utilizing hypnotic
properties. To summarize, Erickson's basic strategy in therapy is to structure whatever happens so that the change occurs in a therapeutically
desirable direction (Beahrs, 1971). This basic strategy is also shared by
Morita and Naikan. These Japanese therapies, like Erickson's, are both
accepting of the client's behavior and at the same time powerfully directive. The directing is indirect in order to bypass the client's conscious
limitations and resistances. The structure of the three therapies occurs
while in "therapeutic trance" which is "a period during which the lim-

itations of one's usual frames of reference and beliefs are temporarily altered so one can be receptive to other patterns . . ." (Erickson & Rossi, 1979). All three therapies are oriented toward the present and the future. The past is reframed in therapeutic trance to create new frames of reference and belief systems.

In this chapter, the Ericksonian framework is presented as a parallel in understanding the workings of Morita and Naikan. Conversely, understanding unique therapies such as Morita and Naikan can be an occasion to refine our conceptual understanding and practice of Ericksonian therapy, identifying various hypnotic elements inherent in it, experimenting with alternative ways of utilizing these elements, and validating the Ericksonian framework cross-culturally.

REFERENCES

Beahrs, J. O. (1971). The hypnotic psychotherapy of Milton H. Erickson. *American Journal of Clinical Hypnosis, 14*, 73–90.
DeVos, G. (1980). Afterword. In D. Reynolds, *The quiet therapies: Japanese pathways to personal growth.* Honolulu: The University Press of Hawaii.
Erickson, M. H., & Rossi, E. L. (1979). *Hypnotherapy: An exploratory casebook.* New York: Irvington.
Haley, J. (1977). *Problem-solving therapy.* San Francisco: Jossey-Bass.
Haley, J. (1982). The contribution to therapy of Milton H. Erickson, M.D. In J. K. Zeig (Ed.), *Ericksonian approaches to hypnosis and psychotherapy.* New York: Brunner/Mazel.
Kim, S. C. (1983). Ericksonian hypnotic framework for Asian Americans. *American Journal of Clinical Hypnosis, 25*, 235–241.
Kondo, A. (1975). Morita therapy: Its sociohistorical context. In S. Arieti & G. Chrzanowski (Eds.), *New dimensions in psychiatry: A world view.* New York: John Wiley.
Kora, T. (1964). Morita therapy. In *Memorial lectures to Professor Emeritus Kora.* Tokyo: Jikei University.
Kora, T. (1968). Seishim ryoho ni okeru shido no shitaka (A method of instruction in psychotherapy). Nihi Iji Shimpo Special Publication number 2291, 1968. Trans. D. Reynolds. Repr. In *Jikeikai Medical Journal, 15*(4), 315–325.
Kroger, W. B. (1977). *Clinical and experimental hypnosis.* Philadelphia: J. B. Lippincott.
Murase, T., & Johnson, F. (1974). Naikan, Morita, and Western Psychotherapy. *Archives of General Psychiatry, 31*, 121–128.
Reynolds, D. (1976). *Morita psychotherapy in the west.* Unpublished manuscript.
Reynolds, D., & Kiefer, C. (1977). Cultural adaptability as an attribute of therapies: The case of Morita psychotherapy. *Culture, Medicine, and Psychiatry, 1*, 395–412.
Watts, A. W. (1961). *Psychotherapy: East and west.* New York: Ballantine.
Watzlawick, P., Weakland, J., & Fisch, R. (1974). *Change: Principles of problem formation and problem resolution.* New York: Norton.

PART XII

About Milton H. Erickson

Milton Erickson was a charismatic individual and a great source of personal inspiration to those who knew him.

He often added suspense and drama into his contacts with people, which made his impact memorable. Those who spent time with Erickson have numerous anecdotes about the important effect that he had on their lives.

John H. Weakland has academic training in chemical engineering, anthropology, and sociology. He is a California licensed Marriage, Family and Child Counselor, and a Fellow of both the American Anthropological Association and the Society for Applied Anthropology. Weakland worked on the Bateson Research Project on Communication from 1953-1962 and has been affiliated with the Mental Research Institute since 1959. He received the 1981 Award for Distinguished Achievement in New Directions in Family Therapy from the American Family Therapy Association. Among numerous publication credits, Weakland coauthored Change *(Norton, 1974) and* The Tactics of Change *(Jossey-Bass, 1982).*

A professional description of Jay Haley is contained in Volume II, Clinical Applications, *of* Ericksonian Psychotherapy.

Remembering Erickson is a discussion between Jay Haley and John Weakland about the times that they came to Phoenix to study with Erickson. A number of previously unpublished cases are presented and described. New insights about Erickson's professional contributions are provided.

Haley and Weakland place Erickson's work in historical perspective—Erickson's teachings were singularly unique in the

583

1950s. Although most psychotherapists rely on a historical lineage and build on the clinical and theoretical practices of previous masters, Erickson was an independent explorer who blazed his own trails.

Comments are included on Erickson's style and his disciplined approach to therapy. The discussants reflect on Erickson's remarkable memory, legendary perceptiveness, attention to detail, personal power, and his meticulousness in training himself.

Remembering Erickson *is actually a videotape that was made by Haley and distributed through the Family Therapy Institute of Washington, D.C. The videotape was shown at the Congress media program and donated to the Erickson Foundation.*

Irving I. Secter, D.D.S., M.A., earned his dental and psychology degrees at Loyola University and Roosevelt University, respectively. He is a registered psychologist in the state of Illinois.

Secter is a past president of the American Society of Clinical Hypnosis and is a Fellow of numerous organizations, including the Academy of General Dentistry and the American Psychological Association. He has published 30 articles and book reviews, and is coauthor of Practical Applications of Medical and Dental Hypnosis *with Milton Erickson and Seymour Hershman. Secter is a member of the Editorial Board of the* American Journal of Clinical Hypnosis. *He has been an active teacher of hypnosis. During the mid-1950s he was a member of Erickson's group that traveled throughout the United States and taught hypnosis.*

Secter describes the first time he was hypnotized by Erickson in 1954. Letters from both Secter and Erickson indicate how Secter responded to Erickson's indirect posthypnotic suggestions.

Chapter 36

Remembering Erickson: A Dialogue Between Jay Haley and John Weakland

The following is a transcript of a videotape produced by Jay Haley and donated to the Erickson Foundation. It was shown at the Congress media program.

H: What's your first memory of meeting Milton Erickson?

W: My recollection is that you met him before I did. You went to a workshop and that got the whole thing started. I did not actually meet him until we went to Phoenix for the first time.

H: You met him in Phoenix then?

W: I believe so.

H: I recall that I wanted to take a seminar on hypnosis to study hypnotic communication as part of the Bateson project. I heard that a traveling seminar was coming to San Francisco. So I asked Gregory if I could go up there and learn some hypnosis. He asked who was giving it and I said Milton Erickson. He said, "I will call him," and that way I found out that he knew Milton Erickson; he had had lunch with him and Margaret Mead years before.

W: Somehow Bateson knew almost everybody. But you didn't know he knew Erickson.

H: So he called Milton on the phone and said could an assistant of his come up and take the seminar. Finally, Milton said yes.

The minute that Gregory got off that phone he said to me, "That man is going to manipulate me to come to San Francisco and have dinner with him." Since I was interested in manipulation, I asked, "What did he say to you?" And Gregory said, "He said to me, 'Why don't you come up to San Francisco and have dinner with me.' " I will never forget that. Gregory was so concerned about the power of

585

Erickson and his influence that he was uneasy even about a simple statement from him.

Anyhow, I took that seminar. It was one of those where they lectured and talked, then demonstrated, and then you worked with fellow students to learn how to do it.

Well, one of the things that I remember about that is Erickson talking to the group and then wanting to demonstrate. So he said, "Someone in this group would like to come up and volunteer to be a subject." And the muscle in my thigh just twisted. It was the most curious feeling—an involuntary movement. It almost pulled me up. Then the guy in front of me stood up and went up. So I didn't do anything, but I had never had a feeling like that before.

W: If that guy hadn't stood up reasonably fast, you might have been up on the stage then.

H: That's right. It was a curious feeling. So then I came back and decided to make hypnosis a part of the project. And then we started going to visit Milton and we managed a week a year at least. I think that 1955 was the first visit. My last one was 1971, I believe.

W: You kept going a good deal longer after I stopped.

H: Sixteen or 17 years. Also, whenever he came to Palo Alto, he would call me up and I would go to his seminar.

W: You asked about my memory of my first meeting. I have a memory but I am not sure that it was the first meeting. We went into his house and he was sitting there at his desk and leaning forward and saying, "All right. What is it that you want from me?"

H: I remember once after I went into practice and I went up to talk with him about how to cure people, that was the first line he gave me, "What is it you really want from me?"

I remember his house so well. It was a little brick house, near downtown Phoenix, with three bedrooms and there were six or eight kids in there.

W: Very modest little place.

H: Yes. And people flying in from New York and Mexico and from all over the world. His living room was the waiting room. The little kids were playing in the living room while the patients were waiting.

W: I remember how very striking that seemed to me then. I had been in more or less analytic treatment in New York where you came in and there was never anyone in the waiting room and you went out through a different door so that you never saw any other patients. And to think that his kids were in there playing with his patients, some of whom he described as really rather far-out people. It was a revelation to me.

H: I remember his wife, Betty, saying to me once that a guy said to her, "Well, I never dressed a doll before." It was Kristi or Roxie who had asked him to dress a doll.

He had a living room and a dining room and on the dining room table was all the stuff from the journal that he and his wife were editing. And then he had this little office which was about 8 × 8, or 10 × 10 at the most, with two or three chairs, his desk and some bookcases.

W: I remember that with just the two of us in there, it seemed to me to be rather full.

H: He liked to have people close enough so that he could reach them, is what he said. He could reach out and take a hand and touch them. In those conversations with him, with the air conditioner going, the dog barking outside, and his wife hollering for the children—it made quite a background. And that clock ticked, ticked, ticked over the desk.

W: All of that, in his way, was characteristic. He didn't think that you had to get in a sanitized soundproof environment to do your treatment, for hypnosis or anything else.

H: One of the things about our visits was that we stayed at a hotel downtown and then we would go spend an hour with him between patients. Then we would go back to the hotel, figure out what he had been saying, revise our plans on what we would ask, and then go back and spend another hour with him, and that was how we would spend the week.

W: Well, we were always making plans and always revising the plans because he never exactly followed our plans.

H: He would tend to tell us what he thought was good for us rather than what we had in mind.

W: It usually had some relation to our questions and our plan, but it was not what you would call a direct answer.

H: He had a style of talking so that you could never be quite sure whether he was talking about you personally, whether he was telling you about a case because it interested him, or whether he was educating you about the nature of the event. All three at once, really. He told us some great cases.

Thinking of that, I was listening to a tape of ours a while back and I heard the first mention of an ordeal therapy, I think. We both thought it was funny and apparently had not heard it before. There was a man who panicked when he had to go up to a microphone in a TV studio. He was a TV announcer. He spent about fifteen minutes gasping for breath, and then he had to go up and talk. Erickson gave him a theory about energy, and excess energy, and had him do deep knee bends every time he was anxious. Then he had him get up in the middle of the night and do deep knee bends when he was anxious. We thought that was hilarious. After that, I tried that in practice with a number of cases and it was very effective. But I think that was the first mention of it and he mentioned it so casually—not like this was an old procedure that he had worked up.

W: I don't remember that that was the first ordeal thing that we heard about. I would have thought it was about having an insomniac get up in the middle of the night and clean the house.

I remember when I heard that, like many things I heard from Milton, I did a funny sort of double take. On the one hand, I thought this is highly interesting and there must be something there. It certainly seemed to me that there was, but I couldn't figure out what the devil it was because this was so different from all the treatment that I had ever heard of before.

H: That's the important thing to me—what a contrast he was to everything else that we knew about. At that time we were studying therapy from a number of other people, doing a lot of reading on it, trying to examine the nature of it, and his was so unusual that it was just hard to grasp. It is hard to believe now, because many of these things now seem obvious. But at that time. . . . And to hear those tapes and to hear us laughing every once in a while at something he did that now seems rather routine. . . .

W: I think that there are probably still times when I read about or hear about some of his cases when I get the feeling that there is something that I am grasping that I hadn't grasped before.

H: There were so many things he mentioned that he would expand on if you asked him about them. If you didn't ask, he wouldn't mention it.

I don't know if I ever told you this one. We may not have discussed it. Remember that case of the couple who both wet the bed and found each other and got married, and then wet the bed jointly? He had them kneel on the bed, and deliberately wet the bed, and lie down in that wet bed for about 30 days. One time, for some reason, just in passing, I said, "Why kneel?" And he said, "Well, they are religious people. They knelt by the bed every night and prayed anyhow." Now, even that was planned. He could have had them stand on the bed or it could have been done in a different way.

W: Well, I think similarly about the story of the woman he had sit on her obstreperous kid. It wasn't until I had heard that from him the second or third time that it became clear that the woman also had a weight problem and that the intervention was, in addition to everything else, a way of saying, "Your heavy weight can also be constructive."

H: It would make a positive thing out of the negative.

W: And I had not seen that point in it the first time or two at all.

H: It is so rich the way he worked, each detail becomes so important—if you go into it. If you don't go into it, you don't even know it is important.

At the Bateson project we were interested in the parallels between schizophrenia and hypnosis. Since schizophrenics have many characteristics of hypnotic subjects, we were interested if one could induce hypnosis and schizophrenia in the same way. Were they similar?

We were first investigating hypnosis with him and then we began to realize that he had a whole new school of therapy that we didn't know about and that's when we got into what he was doing in therapy.

I can recall that when I started a private practice as a hypnotherapist, you and I had been attending classes.

W: Yes, and over a long period there, holding meetings to practice hypnosis.

H: I learned quite a bit about how to hypnotize people but when I sat down to cure them, that was a different matter. That was a different kind of hypnosis, and I went to ask him about that.

W: Well, that's when that old difficult question comes up, "Now that you are in a trance, what do you do?"

H: The fact that research hypnosis and clinical hypnosis are not necessarily related at all I hadn't thought through until that moment. He used to have hypnotic evenings in Phoenix every week.

W: Yes. I went to at least one of them.

H: I remember that is where we recorded Ruth.

W: That's right. The one we asked about in detail to make that paper of the trance induction and commentary.

H: I think that was the first paper, certainly on hypnosis, in which somebody is asked step by step what they did all the way through it. Since then, it has been done on therapy too. That was the first though. He kept surprising us with what he was doing. What we thought he was doing was somewhat different.

Do you remember the most unusual case you ever heard him talk about then? I remember one he had who was psychotic. She was a schoolteacher with young men floating over her head. And he had her put those young men in the closet in his office so they wouldn't interfere with her school teaching. And then when she was going to leave the city, she said, "What if I have psychotic episodes in the other city?" And he said, "Why don't you put them in a manila envelope and send them to me." And so she sent him her psychotic episodes in a manila envelope. I think that was one of the most extraordinary cases I ever heard from him.

W: Which he finally filed away in the closet.

H: He filed it away. He knew that she would come back and check if he had them. And he saved all of them. He had a drawer full of them. In fact, I remember him pulling open the drawer and there was a whole bunch of manila envelopes in that drawer.

W: Well, that one would be hard to top.

H: It was an extraordinary case—and the quickness of his thinking, and how he related ideas. Putting the young men in the closet led logically to putting the psychotic episodes into the envelope. It was putting something in something.

W: Just filing it away where it wouldn't get in your way.

H: I think she was also the woman who said there was a giant bear trap in the middle of the floor. And he very carefully walked around that whenever she was in the room. He was so courteous to patients.

I have been teaching his therapy as "courtesy therapy," as a way of accepting and joining people and helping them without making a confrontation out of it.

W: Well, it sure fits with that emphasis which I see more of with every passing year. Accept what your client offers you. Don't get in an argument about it. Accept it.

Do you remember, much later, the time he came to MRI and was doing a hypnotic demonstration with a young woman. Her boyfriend heard about it and arrived outside the door boiling mad.

H: I don't remember.

W: I think that was while you were still there. He did a beautiful piece of accepting and it had one of the most dramatic rapid change effects I ever saw. It was all very simple. As he finished the demonstration, he was told the young man was being kept outside. They weren't going to let him into the demonstration. But he was very mad and he wanted to know what they were doing with his girl in there.

Erickson said, "Open the door." As the young man came rushing in, Erickson turned to him and said, "I am very happy to meet you and to find that there is still at least one young man in the world who is concerned to protect his young lady and be sure that she comes to no harm."

All the anger was dissipated because Erickson made no argument about it. "This is wonderful. So pleased to see it." But, how many would do it that way?

H: He was so quick. I remember a time—I think we were both there—a woman and her mother just came and knocked at the door. It turned out that it was a woman who had been in the state hospital and he helped her get out years before. She came to see him. Just dropped in. So he came out and talked to her a few minutes and asked his wife to get a picture. And he gave the girl a picture. She was a Mexican girl. And she was so happy to get that picture. He knew exactly that he should do that. Then he wrote something on it and gave it to her. She expressed her appreciation for his getting her out of the hospital and all, and then she went away.

Later on, in passing, he said, "Did you notice whether I signed that picture on the front or the back?" We had no idea. He said, "Well, the back, of course. I made that decision very quickly because she is going to frame that picture, and then she will discover at that time that this is a personal message to her that no one else can see because it is on the back of the picture."

Now, something like that happened so fast. He had two or three minutes with that woman, and he made a decision that fast. He knew he should give her a picture, that she would be pleased and it would help sustain her. He knew he should put a message on it and it really should be a personal one, not on the front where everybody could see it.

W: The front was for the world and the back is her private and personal information.

H: And he did that so quickly. He was one of the few psychiatrists around who covered the whole range of patients. He was as comfortable with a raving psychotic as he was with a little kid with whom he was playing jacks. He had a tremendous range.

W: I think part of it was that he had seen so much that he was in danger of "I'm going to get bored if I don't see something further, if I don't see the whole range, if I don't try to handle an old problem in a new way."

H: He would do a home visit, which other people would not do at that time. He would take somebody to a restaurant, as well as work in the office. That isn't so uncommon today, perhaps, but in the 50s it was extraordinary for someone to cover that range and to do work outside the office.

W: Well, I think at that time there were a great many people—in fact, probably almost everybody else in the field—who were bound by a multitude of restrictions that they didn't even recognize as restrictions. And one of the things about Erickson in both his life and his practice was he was always getting rid of other people's limits and going beyond them.

H: Beyond his own.

W: Sure.

H: He had a way of making each case a unique approach. One of the things that he was so quick at was just observing people and diagnosing them. I was listening to a tape recently and finding out that in medical school, while he was getting a masters in psychology, he tested just about every mental patient in Wisconsin and just about every criminal in Wisconsin. He tested hundreds of people. So he covered so many kinds of people. He did this deliberately so he would learn about psychopathology of all kinds and meet a broad spectrum of it, while also making a living.

But a lot of people who are so casual about taking up one of his techniques don't realize what a tremendously disciplined gathering of information about people he did for so many years before he sat down with somebody and then quickly did something.

W: Well, yes, I think that they tend to look on Erickson as a magic worker but this is absolutely antithetical to the way he worked. Because he worked with a great deal of skill, care, and calculation. The magic was only in that the art was concealed.

H: And he was so impatient with students who wanted to do things quickly before they understood the situation. This whole magic hoax stuff around him where he "laid on his hands" and people did things was not really what he had in mind at all about the nature of therapy. You really had to know your business.

W: I have often wondered, and your mention of all this testing brings it up, how he ever found the time to do all the things he did, because he did a lot of things all his life like that.

H: And he spent hours over some automatic writing or something like that.

The thing about him is that in his own life he was as clever as he was with his patients. For example, there was the way he handled the criminal situation. He got interested in medical school or internship —somewhere there—in criminology. He did his first paper on criminology, I believe. And the way he got a job in that was he started to provide, on the desk of the big wheel in the criminal division in Wisconsin, a report of all the crimes committed that week. Something like that. Some statistical report on crime which interested Erickson. And he would put it on the desk of this guy every Monday morning. One Monday morning he didn't do it and the guy sent for him and said, "I want to speak to that man Erickson." He said, "Erickson, you are going to get fired if you don't put this on my desk the way you have been." Erickson said, "Well, you never hired me." And that's how he got the job. It was first making himself valuable and then not doing it so the guy realized that he was valuable and hired him. And that is how he helped pay his way through school. He did so many things like that.

He had such an ability to combine several things at once. Like the fact he mentioned in passing once that a doctor had told him to live in Phoenix for his allergies, but to get out regularly. So he lived in Phoenix but he did traveling seminars regularly. That was part of his professional life and was also for his health.

W: Well, that may be part of the answer to my question of how he did so much. He made combinations so that he was always doing more than one thing at the same time.

H: He also worked very hard. He used to work from seven in the morning to 11 at night, he would see patients and then he left weekends open for people who traveled long distances to spend two or three hours with him.

W: You asked about the most amazing case. This isn't the most amazing but it was one of the most puzzling to me when he first told it to me. I think that I have got some grip on what he was doing now. But when he first told me the case, I kept thinking, what is that about? What is he doing there?

A musician came to him from New York. He said, "I am just so anxious that I can't perform." Milton spent nearly two days of the weekend with him. He spent almost all of the time giving him long dissertations about the need to be flexible, I believe. Long, long stories about how you need to be flexible in various tasks such as typing. I kept thinking, "What is the treatment here?" He had been getting the guy madder and madder at these long boring dissertations. Then, finally, just before he finished, and just before the guy had to catch a plane back to New York, so that he wouldn't have any time to raise any questions, he said, "And if you, with all your experience and training, can't walk up to the platform and play a piece, that wouldn't be very flexible, would it?" And I was flabbergasted. That was another one of those things where . . . there is something very important here, but I can't quite get a hold of it.

H: You know, there was another piece on that one. He first explained to the guy that he himself was tone deaf. Then Milton said, "Let me explain to you how you should play the piano. You should hit the keys with the little finger a little harder than with the forefinger because the little finger is not as strong as the forefinger." And for a concert pianist to listen to Milton who was tone deaf explain how to play the piano. . . .

W: But that was the whole thing, he was building up. . .

H: That guy—by God, had to prove to him that he could. . .

W: That's right. He was building up the motivation of resentment until that guy wouldn't sit still for that final remark.

H: The only way he could prove Erickson wrong was to perform well. Absolutely.

W: But I think part of the difficulty was at that time, like everybody else, I was thinking, "Well, there are good motives and bad motives and therapists work with good motives and therapists themselves are full of good motives—like you understand and sympathize with somebody's difficulties." And in that context, you couldn't understand Erickson's treatment.

H: The guy couldn't disagree with him. Everything he said was true and said benevolently and kindly.

W: With a twist to it.

H: I remember him once saying that you had a much greater chance of success with somebody who flew 3,000 miles to see you because they had so much invested in just coming there that they almost had to get over something, because they had put so much into it.

There was another thing that he told us—and this was typical of the way he put it. He said, "I am waiting for a woman to come into my office who has had a very important premarital affair or is having a very important extramarital affair who doesn't tell me that by the way that she sits down in the chair." And the way that he put it was not that women always told that. Rather, he said, "I am waiting for the exception, because they always tell me by the way they sit down in a chair."

He was always interested in the exception. You remember the time he had us come into the office—we were in the living room and he told us to come into the office—and we came in and this girl was sitting in the chair and we looked at him and he sent us out again.

Then after she left, he sat us down and said, "What did you see?"
Do you remember that?

W: Yes, I remember it, a little vaguely. I don't remember what I saw
and what I didn't see, though.

H: I remember that we said, "Well, she was a woman." And we said
she was in a trance. And he said, "Well, that's true." And finally he
told us that we should have observed that the right side of her face
was a little larger than the left side. That the right hand was a little
larger than the left. She had some neurological problem. It was evident to him and we were expected to see, and we failed the test.

That was part of the way that he set us up, by asking it in such a
general way, "Didn't you see. . . ?" that we didn't know whether he
was talking about the hypnosis, trance, this woman, the nature of
life, or what. But we sure didn't do well.

W: I think in all probability it was rather deliberate that he didn't give
us much hint and it was rather deliberate that he made us fail because
in some way, I am sure, he thought that would be instructive and
useful for us.

H: That we would do better the next time. We would observe the next
time.

I talked to residents whom he had trained and he would give them
hell if they didn't do a proper diagnosis. The next time they would
observe the patient. I remember that. He was great on observation.

One of the interesting things that was hard for us to grasp in those
days, I think, was that he took the way a patient sat down and the
way that a patient moved as a message to him. Not just as an expression about the person; he took it that they were telling him something.

It was Gregory Bateson's old notion that such nonverbal behavior
wasn't just a report about their nature, it was a command of some
kind. And that was hard to see. He was so interpersonal in that sense.
He took whatever they did with him as a message. And we took it
as, "Well, that's an interesting person," or something like that.

W: We were the ones who were supposed to be interactional.

H: That is true.

And we had many arguments with him about whether something
was interpersonal or not. But on that kind of a level he was absolutely
interpersonal.

We used to argue with him about a wife's symptom—whether that
was an adaptation to a husband who had the same or similar problem.
And he often, at least in the early days, in the early 60s, described
it like an independent phenomenon while treating it as if it wasn't.

That was what was also throwing us. His therapy was absolutely interpersonal while his theory was not.

W: He had the capacity to stick very tight to a view of his, if you called it into question or even wanted to discuss it. That was true when we brought down those ideas about similarities between schizophrenic behavior and trance behavior. He stood quite firm, as I remember, as he did in something I brought up with him many years later.

After reading some of Carlos Castaneda's stuff, I wrote to Milton and said, "I am wondering if Castaneda ever met you because there seemed to be some things about the figure Don Juan that are reminiscent." And he sent me back a rather irritated message: "Absolutely no, and there is no such connection."

H: So many people now think of Erickson as a cult figure and a guru, partly because of the bad shape he was in in his old age. When we knew him, he was young and vigorous and placed a big emphasis on how you should control your voice, you should control your speech, control your body movement, and use all of that in therapy. And what was so sad to me was how he lost control of his speech and movement as he got older. It was really a shame.

I remember once saying to him that I would like to film him. I wanted to set up a camera in his office. He said he would rather not, because he didn't want to be remembered as an old man who couldn't speak well and do his therapy well. Then he let himself be videotaped and now what people have is him as an old man, which is a shame.

W: Well, fortunately, there is still a little around from the earlier period.

H: It was also fortunate that he was able to work as well as he did, given all those handicaps. The people who came back said it was extraordinary what he went through.

W: Well, in a sense, it is the epitomization of his whole career. He was always a man who did his thing in spite of so many handicaps.

H: His whole life. And he loved to tell a story by saying, "I had this impossible situation."

W: Yes. After that, you knew what was coming: "Here is how I did the impossible."

H: It was the way that he liked to present a case. He would lay it on as so impossible and then he would have it all solved. The solutions were usually so obvious once he did it.

Remember that case of inhibited Ann that he told us about? She was the one who had the choking and gasping and it came on just before bedtime. So he talked to her about all the things in the bedroom—the dresser and the drapes. And then he said, "Of course, there is a carpet." I said to him, "You haven't mentioned the bed." And he said, "When I said, 'Of course, there is a carpet,' that bed is mentioned. When you say, 'Of course, there is a carpet,' you are mentioning a bed by not mentioning it." That again was so obvious once he said it, but it wasn't obvious at the time.

W: Well, again, if you make too much of a point of something, it is easier to resist it. And as he comes all around, it comes to mind in a way you can't resist because he is not pushing anything on you.

H: He had this way of getting your participation in hypnosis by partially saying something so you had to finish it. When you finished it, you were participating. Or if you do something incomplete, the other person has to complete it.

W: You always pay more attention to what you say yourself than to what somebody says to you. So he gets it started off and you complete the message; therefore, you have told yourself. And you have got to take that seriously.

H: There is a film of him hypnotizing five women in 1964.* There is a piece of that we should look at, because if I am right about what he did—and I talked to him later about it and I believe he agreed—it is the most interpersonal piece of hypnosis that I have seen. He said to this woman, "My name is Milton. My mother gave me that name. It is an easy name to write."

As I watched that film, what seemed evident was that he was acting very young. One of the things that he used to say about regressing somebody was that when he regressed somebody back to childhood, he wasn't there. They would have to make him somebody, like a teacher. I think what he was doing with this woman was that if he were childlike, she actually had to become childlike to join him. The way he got her to regress was by regressing himself. And I don't think you could have anything more interpersonal than that in that style of working.

W: I have often found that some of those things he did that looked most simple were the things that you would have to look at hardest to see what the point was.

H: He must have told us hundreds of cases over the years as a way of educating us to get us to think "as simple" as he did about these things.

---

*Editor's Note: Selections from this film are part of a training videotape on hypnotic induction sold to professionals through The Erickson Foundation. The videotape was transcribed by Barbara Bellamy, Administrative Assistant at The Erickson Foundation.

W: Well, he would have an incredible amount of case material in his head that he could reel off.

H: He would associate to a case as he was talking about it. He had so many cases. The observation and his diagnosis were very complex. It's the interventions that are simple.

W: I think they got more and more so.

H: I think that as he got older, they got more economical. The efficiency with which he worked got better.

I think he got more confronting as he got older and I think that makes people feel he was more a confronting therapist than he really was in our day. I think perhaps he confronted more when he had fewer skills of physical control. Because we really remember him as a very accepting and joining sort of a therapist and I think a lot of people don't think of him in that way.

W: I certainly remember him in the early days as someone who was accepting. Also, at the same time, as someone you could readily be fearful of because it was easy to see he was powerful and penetrating even while being accepting. You could shake a little about it as a client.

H: As a client and as a colleague. I think his colleagues were largely afraid of him.

W: I think a lot of them were.

H: Because he did have such a reputation for indirect influence.

W: It wasn't only Gregory who was worried about, "He's invited me to dinner."

H: They were pleased if he was benevolent but a little uncertain that he was.

I don't know if I ever told you about the guy who came to Palo Alto. A man came to see me and asked if I would treat his daughter. I said, "What's the problem?" He said she wasn't doing well. She was depressed or something. He said, "I have been to see Milton Erickson with my other daughter and she is fine." The guy was a wealthy man. So I said, "Why don't you take this daughter to Milton?" And he said, "I am afraid to." And I said, "Why are you afraid to?" He said, "Well, when I took my other daughter there, Dr. Erickson put me under house arrest in Phoenix for six months." And he said, "I don't want to go down there and spend six months again." So I said, "Well, you might not have to this time." And I persuaded him to take the other daughter down. He did, and Erickson didn't put him under house arrest. That was a family that Erickson stayed with when he visited us in Palo Alto for one of those seminars. He stayed with that family and they were on pretty good terms, but the guy was scared to death of him. The idea of refusing to do what Erickson said—that didn't cross his mind. What power he had!

W: Well, as an explicit patient I saw Milton for only a couple of sessions, but I was scared. And to this day, I cannot tell you exactly what he did with me. I can only tell you that a great many things changed within a year and a half after I saw him. I came home and got out of my analytic treatment forever and decided that I would see what I could do on my own. That was the last time I had any therapy. Within a year, I had gone to the Far East to where my wife's people lived. And I had a major operation.

H: That's right. You had that heart operation that you hadn't decided about yet.

W: That's right. And our first child was conceived. That's a fair amount of things happening in a year. And I don't quite know how.

H: Did he discuss any of those things explicitly with you?

W: Well, it is going to sound a little strange, but I am not too clear about what we did discuss explicitly. I don't think that I was in a trance the whole time.

H: You are a good subject.

W: But something happened.

H: I am sure that there are things you remember.

W: Yeah. But I am not sure that even Milton could take care of the ravages of the next 20 years. I may have had more at one point and lost some of it.

Let's go back a minute to the fact that he could be rather stubborn about some things that were brought up. In a way, I think that is rather nice. Because the last thing that I think we would want to contribute to is the image of someone without flaw. Milton had his limitations and Milton was very human, thank God for that. He was not really the perfect guru sitting on the mountaintop by a long way.

H: Now, on his subject of hypnosis or influencing people, he was exceptional. But in other aspects of his life he was just an ordinary guy. He would only occasionally drop the professional attitude with us. Once or twice after a dinner, he was just a guy. But ordinarily he was in a professional stance with us teaching us something all of the time. But he bragged a lot and he had his flaws, that's true.

W: He was just a man. Except for the bragging, he didn't pretend to be anything else.

H: No. The bragging was part of being just a man in the sense he would consider himself like others and then surmounted that.

W: There was one thing. I don't know if it is a flaw, but we did run into it a couple of times. If you will recall, a couple of times we approached him about his failures. Milton said, "Well, I would be glad to give you an example." And then he would give the example. But at the last moment, the failure would somehow turn into a success. Well, that may be a bit of a weakness but. . .

H: As he said at one point, he didn't see what you learned from talking about a failure unless you knew why it failed, and then you might learn something.

W: He did have, I think, a few highly fixed opinions, some of which I certainly saw differently. I remember him telling about cases where there was no point at all in trying to do something. I really don't see those cases that way now and I am not sure that I saw them that way then. But his opinion was rather heavy then or he just had some fixed ideas about those cases.

H: I think so. In fact, Don Jackson said something that I thought was rather wise. Erickson had mentioned a manic-depressive he didn't think was curable. And Jackson said, "Well, what he must mean is that with his technique he was not curable." And that had never occurred to me. That he couldn't reach him with his technique.

W: Well, people shouldn't put him up on a pedestal, cover him with white paint, and nail a halo up.

H: He would have been the first to object to that, I think.

W: That's correct. I am sure you will remember the demonstration he put on with the hot sauce. Even when we were just in a social situation, and he was just being a guy, he was still showing us that he was an extraordinary guy. We were in a Mexican restaurant and he said, "This isn't very hot. Bring me out something hotter." He did this two or three times, until the chef thought, "This will set him on fire." And he just had a spoonful of it, and licked it down, I presume with an anesthetized mouth done by self-hypnosis.

H: It had to be. Nobody could take that hot sauce with an ordinary tongue. But I think he did self-hypnosis ordinarily as part of his pain control, and then he did it as part of that hot sauce demonstration.

We always said that if he had any time at all, he could control the pain. When it took him by surprise, when the muscles wrenched away from the ligaments by surprise from cramps, he couldn't. But if he had a few minutes, he could do it. He had a lot of strength. I mean, he would take two or three hours to put himself together in the morning so that he could be comfortable. But once he got himself organized, then he would wear us out, hour after hour, talking. When we were ready to go, he was still going strong.

I was listening to a tape of Erickson with a guy (we'll call Dr. G) who was an Erickson disciple. Dr. G went down there to set up practice in Phoenix. He was setting up a beautiful office in a high rise down there, and he wanted to do it properly. He was talking to Milton about this. And Milton said, "Well, when I set up practice, all I had was this little room. I came down here to work in the state hospital and we had a falling out, so I left and I set up a practice sooner than I expected. I didn't have any furniture. All I had in this room was two chairs and a card table." So Dr. G said, "Well, that wasn't very much to set up practice." And Milton said, "Well, I was there." What more was necessary? And he absolutely felt that way. That is why he could work in a train station or an air terminal.

W: I remember stories about his going to Chicago and there was somebody that wanted to see him, so he had him come out to O'Hare Airport. He had half an hour and he talked to him right there in the airport lounge.

H: He used to do that. The only time that I saw him express any reluctance at the burden of being a therapist was once when he came to San Francisco. He worked at the workshop all day and at lunchtime he had to see a patient or two, and then at the end of the day there was a woman waiting to see him. He said something like, "My God. That's a lot." And then went off to see her. It was the only time I heard him object. Ordinarily, he would work all day, see people at lunch, see people before dinner, have dinner with his group, and then see a patient afterwards. And that was on his workshop days. Everywhere he went there were patients and they would take advantage of his visit to talk with him.

The case he was to see last, that day, was interesting to me because I knew the woman. I was trying to get patients of his and talk to them privately about what the therapy was. One of her problems was that she picked at her face and made sores. Also, she didn't like beans. So she had to put a can of beans in her bathroom by the mirror. She always picked her face in front of the mirror and if she picked at her face she had to eat the can of beans.

W: Tying two things together.

H: Milton had a sense of humor. So that most of the talking, that "grim" business of therapy was funny really, what they did, what he did, and the whole bizarre situation.

W: Well, I think we were probably rather important to him. I don't think there were many people he could let on to how humorous he found things or that he would rather spend most of his life sitting there seeing patients, seeing things that he thought were very humorous. He had to keep the lid on it completely and with most of his colleagues. He could begin to let us see.

H: I think that he was really looking forward to our visits. We brought ideas from outside and we were a great audience for him when he was telling about his cases.

I was thinking of that musician with the fat lip who used to come in and yell at him. The guy was angry at his father. And Erickson actually had the guy come in and yell. He couldn't play at home because his lip swelled for psychosomatic reasons. The guy would come in and yell at him session after session. That was the one where he arranged an appointment without ever telling the guy about the appointment.

He said to the guy, "Well, let's see, this is May, isn't it?" And the guy said, "What do you mean, May. My God, this is June. Don't you even know what month it is?" And then Erickson would say, "It must be about the 15th." The guy would say, "What do you mean, the 15th? It is the 10th. I've got a psychiatrist who doesn't even know what day it is." And then Erickson would say, "Well, it must be about four o'clock." "Four o'clock, it's only two o'clock."

At the end of the sessions, Erickson would open his book and say, "I am writing an appointment in and I want you to be on time," and he would close the book. And the guy would show up on June 15th at four o'clock. As long as he said that while the guy was shouting and it was dropped in inappropriately to what the guy was saying, the guy couldn't forget. And he also couldn't refuse to come in, because he never was told to come in. He couldn't be late because he had never been told an exact time where he could be late.

W: I seem to remember that in that case and in some others we would try to bring up something about the parallel between expressing anger at him and anger at his father. And Milton would just brush that aside. It was very curious what he would listen to and what he would just disregard.

H: We were trying to find out how he dealt with couples and families. Sometimes he saw them together and often he saw them separately.

W: That's right. We were looking for a policy, a common line.

H: At one point, he would say that the sexual symptom is absolutely a couple's case. That is the way he would treat it, like a couple.

Another one he would treat individually, like Ann who had tremendous inhibitions; she went to bed and couldn't have sexual relations because she had all that choking and gasping. When he got her over that, we asked him, "What about the husband? Isn't there going to be some adjustment for the husband?" He said, "He'll have no problem adjusting." We said, "What do you mean?" He said, "Well, he rather passively accepted the way the wife was. Now that she has changed, he will accept the way that she is."

The fact that there was a contract between them wasn't what he was thinking in that case. And we were trying to emphasize that, and he was just puzzled by it, really. Whereas with another case, he would assume it was a contract. And we never knew which way he was going to jump.

I think that he partly hesitated to make a simple statement or a theoretical statement because it was too simple. The case was a metaphor; it contained all the ideas that he wanted to communicate. Any reduction of that case, down to a few sentences of description theoretically, would do violence to its complexity.

W: But have less in it than the story.

H: One of the things that was missing in a discussion with him was that he never referred to a teacher. I don't think he ever referred to doing something because some authority said so, or said, "I did this because I learned it from so and so." He presented everything as if it originated with him.

Usually, you draw from a previous authority to support what you say. Erickson absolutely never did that. He would say, "Try it and see if it works." He didn't even use himself as an authority in that sense. He didn't say, "Do it this way. Come back and tell me how you did it." That was why he wasn't a guru in the usual sense.

W: And yet at the same time, he would insist that people do the proper background study as he himself did. Therefore, it came out something like, "Get yourself properly trained and learn all that stuff carefully, and then go your way."

H: The whole thing about him not being a cult leader was that he absolutely was for diversification—everybody working in their own way, in their own style. So he didn't want us to imitate. And he didn't imitate anybody before him.

Gregory Bateson was considered a deviant in his own profession of anthropology. I think it is interesting that Erickson, who was a deviant in psychiatry, was admired by Bateson who was a deviant in his field. Erickson actually admired Bateson very much. Neither one was at all concerned about conforming to the proper way according to his profession. They really were explorers of what they felt was relevant in life.

W: They both thought very similarly in that respect.

H: You know there was a case that sort of describes him. When he worked in that hospital in Eloise or somewhere, they had this violent woman who came in. And she said, "I am going to yell for a while and then I am going to break a few bones." And she yelled, and then she would stop and say, "I'm going to yell for a while and then I am going to break some bones." And they had about six aides who were afraid to take her on. They called for Erickson and he came and she yelled, "You better not touch me, Doctor. I am going to yell and break a few bones." And he said, "I won't touch you. I want you to go on yelling." So she went on yelling. And then he took a syringe. . . .

W: I think there is another step before. He said, "OK, yelling seems to be your job. I am not going to touch you, but is it alright with you if I just do my job?" And she said, "If you don't touch me, you go ahead and do your job." He got permission.

H: He took a syringe and when she had her mouth open yelling, he squirted it in her mouth and she swallowed it. Then she stopped yelling and she said, "Was that sleeping medicine, Doctor?" And he said, "Yes it was, but I didn't touch you, did I?" And she said, "No. You didn't." And then she said, "Now there is a doctor that knows his business."

Chapter 37

A Session with Milton Erickson

Irving I. Secter

My first opportunity to meet Milton Erickson was in August 1954. He was teaching at a workshop I attended in Chicago. By this time I was already using hypnosis clinically and sharing my experiences with others in a variety of teaching situations. While successful in helping others to develop hypnotic states, I was disappointed that, subjectively, I had never experienced the state myself. I discussed this with Milton and requested that he put me in a trance.

Milton received many requests for personal instruction during workshops. One of Milton's ploys was to defer responding to these requests until only five or ten minutes remained. Then it became a situation of, "If you really want to learn, you had better do it quickly." In my case, a whole hour still remained when Milton came to me and asked, "Was there something you wanted from me?"

What transpired is condensed in the following correspondence which (see pp. 606–615) was exchanged. The content of the automatic writing reads:

"Write me something you did posthypnotically."

The *"write me"* is discernible when the paper is turned upside down and read from left to right.

"Something did" can be seen on the second line when the paper is held right side up. There is a pronounced "h" in thing and special "P" where the "g" should be. These of course represent the word "posthypnotically."

Note that the automatic writing was done on September 25, 1954 between 4:40 P.M. and 4:45 P.M. My letter to Milton was written on October 26, 1954.

I still enjoy reading and rereading the letters.

My meeting with Erickson led to our association which endured for more than a quarter of a century. We taught together in more than 100 seminars and workshops. At the same time, I learned from him. He contributed to my progress in both areas. We worked together for the advancement of the American Society of Clinical Hypnosis.

Milton guided research that I conducted, and as a result, he published several of my papers. All of my current clinical interactions are influenced by what he taught me.

I have already described a significant portion of this period in a chapter entitled "Seminars with Erickson: The Early Years" (1982). This present chapter is really a companion piece to the earlier publication. Those whose interest and curiosity have been piqued by this chapter are referred to "The Early Years."

REFERENCE

Secter, I. (1982). Seminars with Erickson: The early years. In J.K. Zeig (Ed.), *Ericksonian approaches to hypnosis and psychotherapy* (pp. 447-454). New York: Brunner/Mazel.

TOP   R

AUTOMATIC WRITING PRODUCED IN SELF INDUCED LIGHT TRANCE. MUCH CONSCIOUS ACTIVITY TOWARDS END OF TRANCE (AWARENESS OF EXTERNAL STIMULI).

BOTTOM.

PHONE NATIONAL 2-7227

IRVING I. SECTER, D. D. S.
7407 WEST IRVING PARK ROAD
CHICAGO 34, ILLINOIS

10/26/54

Dear Dr. Erickson:

I would have written to you more than a month ago, if only to express the pleasure I had in meeting you, to thank you sincerely for the giving of your time and self to me personally, and to acknowledge that listening to you and watching you has augmented my knowledge and stimulated my interest and desire for further study in the psychological field.

However in our experimental session together you indicated that I had performed an act post-hypnotically with a complete amnesia for the act. You said also that I would write to you and in writing I would make reference to the post-hyp' act.

On a conscious level I still seem to have an amnesia

but I feel that I cannot delay
writing you because such delay
seems to violate an inner
sense of propriety

I thought that I would
write rather than type. The
automatic coordination of the
fingers grasping the pen
and the mechanism of ideation
might thus release on paper
that which eludes me.

I enclose a sample
of automatic writing (2) resulting
from a self-induced light
trance. I find levitation very
easy and my hands go thru
all sorts of manoeuvres not
guided by me at a conscious
level.

I said to myself in
this trance, "wouldn't it
be pleasant to know if it
was something you said
or did that was the
p-h act. your subconscious
mind can guide your

PHONE NATIONAL 2-7227

IRVING I. SECTER, D. D. S.
7407 WEST IRVING PARK ROAD
CHICAGO 34, ILLINOIS

fingers and tell you" The
writing towards the end
was on a more conscious
level — that is — I was
consciously aware of what
my fingers were writing
without consciously guiding
them." Apparently the p-h
act was something I did.

(Interruption here by patient).

Dr. Erickson, I would
like to propound some
questions concerning the
trance you induced for me.
I know of the demands
on your time and energy
and will understand if you
cannot take the time to do so.
Furthermore, although I desire to
know, there is no compulsion
to know that must be satisfied.

In going into the trance, I heard your suggestions that it would be pleasurable to experience dissociation. I experienced the feeling of levitation and my hands rose to a position suitable for typing or piano playing. You suggested that my fingers could type and that I might even type a word or words. That my assistant might be horrified to see. I do not type except on a hunt & peck basis and I do not play the piano. I remember thinking on a conscious level — "These suggestions won't help — and that naughty word thing is an invitation to allow subconscious sexual motivations or expressions to come forward — I'll ignore that."

Then my hands engaged in various activities, from what might be interpreted as a cradling motion and then to motions which might be made if I were trying to estimate the size of some large object.

You indicated then that these gestures were very meaningful — that my subconscious understood.

PHONE NATIONAL 2-7227

IRVING I. SECTER, D. D. S.
7407 WEST IRVING PARK ROAD
CHICAGO 34, ILLINOIS

Question — Did you make an interpretation of the significance of these hand motions?

If so would you care to explain them to me?

If not — could a parallel be drawn to similar activity in others and the interpretations which were made there?

Following the trance & after discussing it — you went to the blackboard and drew a series of lines (vertical) like this

| | | | | | | | | |

you handed me the chalk without saying anything. Wordlessly I took the chalk and drew a horizontal line across your lines

⫴⫴⫴⫴⫴⫴ — —

You took the chalk from me and drew another series of vertical lines and

| | | | | | | | | |

and then handed the chalk back to me.

I remember thinking, "he wants me to do something different than the last time. But I don't know what he wants so I'll do what comes naturally"

My line again went thru all your lines.

-| | |·|·| | | | |—

You took the chalk from me & replaced it in the blackboard tray. I sensed that you were either disappointed or displeased with my response. You then said "you want to learn too much — too quick."

PHONE NATIONAL 2-7227

IRVING I. SECTER, D. D. S.
7407 WEST IRVING PARK ROAD
CHICAGO 34, ILLINOIS

Question —
        Would you care
to comment on The
above?

        I feel honored
and privileged for the
opportunity of ever so
brief and casual an
association

            Sincerly
            Irving Secter

MILTON H. ERICKSON, M. D.
32 WEST CYPRESS STREET
PHOENIX, ARIZONA
—
TELEPHONE ALPINE 2-4254

November 5
1 9 5 4

Irving I. Secter, D.D.S.
7407 West Irving Park Road
Chicago 34, Illinois

Dear Dr. Secter:

I am utterly delighted with that letter that you wrote me. In fact,
I am returning it to you, so that you can read it again. Perhaps
after reading this far in my letter, you would like to put it aside
and read your letter, to see if you can understand it. If you do
not succeed, then you can read further in this letter and find out
what it was you did so excellently.

As for the automatic writing that you sent me, I was much intrigued
by it. You have done both right side up, and upside down and backwards writing. In other words, you are decidedly competent in automatic writing and you need now only practice in the matter of the
actual recording of ideas and thoughts.

Incidentally, I should arrive in Chicago on the evening of November 14.
Dr. Hirshman, who was at the seminar, wants me to see a number of his
patients and I hope that I will have an opportunity to see you then.
Therefore, I am suggesting that you keep this letter and return it to
me at that time.

As for my notes on the trance I induced in you, if you will read the
first sentence of your letter, you will note that it is rather incomplete. And it properly should be. You had to write that letter
to me on the 26th of the month. No other day would have been suitable.
It could have been October 26, or November 26, or December 26, but it
nevertheless had to be the 26th. Furthermore, my notes state that you
had to use the word "perform". You will note the use of this word in
the second paragraph of your letter. You will also observe that this
part of the letter is not written in your usual script. It is a
transitional script from your ordinary handwriting to the script that
follows on line 4 of that paragraph, where the spacing of the words
is remarkable and the actual letter formation is most outstanding.
Line 5, which begins "a complete amnesia..." is most emphatically
written, with special spacing. Note the diminishing script in the
terminal two words of that sentence "...the act." Again your handwriting

changed, with particular emphasis upon "you said." In other words,
a post-hypnotic suggestion given to you to carry out was to write
a letter on the 26th, in which you would use the word "perform" and
in which you would express a complete amnesia and, at the same time,
would be so carried out that I would recognize the post-hypnotic
act. I think you will enjoy contrasting your script here and there
throughout the letter and how remarkably it changes and not in relation
to the interruption by the patient.

Concerning the diagrams you will note that you drew a line, putting
half of each line above and half below the line. Isn't that really
what you did in writing your letter? However, we can discuss this
in Chicago.

Sincerely,

MILTON H. ERICKSON, M.D.

MHE:fbc

PART XIII

Keynote Address: Special Panel on Milton Erickson

The Erickson Family Panel was one of the five keynote addresses presented at the Congress. Six of Erickson's eight children comprised the hour and a half panel. They discussed the child-rearing techniques of their father and answered questions on that subject for members of the audience. The Erickson Family Panel, chaired by Betty Alice Erickson Elliott, was filled with warmth and humor.

The panel members in order of both age and presentation were:

Lance Erickson, Ph.D., Erickson's second oldest son, who is an administrator at the University of Michigan in Ann Arbor;

Betty Alice Erickson Elliott, a teacher in Dallas, Texas, who is currently working on her Master's degree;

Allan Erickson has a Master's degree and works as a mathematician in Washington, D.C.;

Robert Erickson, M.A., is a teacher who resides in Phoenix, Arizona;

Roxanna Erickson Klein has a Master's degree in nursing and lives in Dallas, Texas;

Kristina K. Erickson, M.D., earned her degree at the University of Arizona and practices emergency medicine in Columbia, Missouri. Kristina is a member of the Board of Directors of the Milton Erickson Foundation.

Two of the Erickson children were not on the panel. The oldest son, Bert, is a farmer in Fort Smith, Arkansas, and the oldest daughter (third oldest child), Carol, is an M.S.W. who practices in Berkeley, California.

Chapter 38

Erickson Family Panel: The Child-Rearing Techniques of Milton Erickson

BETTY ALICE ERICKSON ELLIOTT

Good afternoon. I am Betty Alice Erickson Elliott, the second oldest of Milton Erickson's daughters, and I am serving as moderator of this panel.

Milton Erickson had eight children. Six of us are here today: Lance, Allan, Robert, Roxanna, Kristina and myself. The oldest brother, Bert, lives in Arkansas. The oldest daughter, Carol, lives in California.

Yesterday, Mama received a letter from Bert and I would like to read one line from it. "It amazes me how often, on this Arkansas hill country farm, mention is made of lessons learned from Dad, both directly and indirectly."

That is why we are here today. To give you an idea or two of some of the techniques used in raising us which we believe were effective and which we have incorporated into our lives. While we are not giving Daddy *sole* credit for originating all of the techniques and tactics used, you have to remember that these are techniques and tactics that he was using 45 and 50 years ago which are still effective today.

We all have children. The ages of the children range from Lance's 25-year-old daughter to Kristi's child, sex unknown, age minus two months. The total number of our children is 17 and two thirds.

Over the years, all of us have been asked, "Didn't your father ever make a mistake?" "Was everything that he did, right and perfect?" Of course not. Daddy wasn't perfect any more than any of the rest of us are. Of course he made mistakes and of course he did things which on second thought he could have handled differently. But we are not here to discuss that. We are here to talk about the techniques and tactics that he taught us that have been beneficial to our lives, careers, and our child-rearing. None of us are professional therapists, as most of you are. But, hopefully, you will be able to gain perhaps a little more insight into some of the workings of the way that he thought.

One other thing I would like to stress is Mama's participation. Our mother, Elizabeth Moore Erickson, was a full partner, in every sense of the word, in our rearing and our education. She was and she continues to be a great influence on us all. Among many other things, she continues to contribute a great deal of tempering and mellowing. Thank you, Mama.

Each of us will give a short presentation and introduce the next speaker. Then there will be a question and answer period. Please address the questions to the person whom you wish to answer it. If you have a question for the panel at large, that is okay too.

The first speaker will be Lance. He is the second oldest son.

LANCE ERICKSON

Thank you, B.A. When Betty Alice talks about 50 years of intervention here, I am not sure I go back long enough to meet her expectations in terms of remembering the interventions that Dad provided for me.

I would like to start by expressing our appreciation to all of you for allowing us this very informal, nonthreatening, unstructured, and relaxed environment in which to give you a little insight into the personal life of the Erickson family.

As the oldest of the children who are speaking today, I will be discussing some instances in which Dad specifically created interventions in order to modify my behavior. He did this very successfully, I might say. I think that you might enjoy these instances.

These examples are from the time that we lived in Eloise, Michigan, at the County Hospital. They occurred between the years that I was around nine to 12 years old. I have vivid recollections of the interactions that I and my brothers and sisters had during those years. Dad would deliberately watch us, evaluate our behavior, and on occasion intervene to effect specific types of responses. He always did this in a very positive way. I would say that we never felt that we were manipulated or in any way received negative vibrations, if you will, from the experiences.

Sometimes at the evening meal, Dad would sit at the table and seem to be preoccupied for a period of time, or after the evening meal he would sit in the living room and we would realize that he was thinking about something in particular. Well, after periods of time like this, he might initiate a conversation with one or another of us, usually indirectly, and do something or effect something that would cause us to behave in a particular manner. I am going to relate to you a couple of instances where I think he affected my behavior in a positive way. Let me give you the background.

Bert and I were ages nine and 11 at the time, living in Eloise, and we would run errands for Dad when he needed something. After the dinner meal, Dad usually liked to sit and read the evening paper before he got around to doing the work that he usually had to do. We had a patient at the hospital who delivered the paper but was not very dependable and would frequently miss the delivery. On those occasions, Dad would ask Bert, or me, or both of us to go down to the hospital store and get a paper. We would do this but often we were not prompt about returning with it.

Now, Dad liked to do things in his time frame—not necessarily in ours. And we might relax and look at the sights on the way home or get into a softball game with some of the other kids at the hospital, or something like that. It might be two hours before we returned with the paper. That didn't sit very well with Dad and he tried to modify our behavior in rather direct ways at first by suggesting that he was displeased with us and hoped that we would do better the next time. That didn't make too much of an impression. We also sat in the chair to help us remember that Dad expected us to do this in his time frame. That didn't do too much good either.

So Dad devised a rather ingenious way of doing something about this. Without telling us, he arranged for the paper not to be delivered for four consecutive days. On the first day Dad asked Bert and me to go down to the store and get it. He told us not to rush; he wasn't in any hurry. Now, that was unusual. We got the paper and got back rather quickly with it. Dad thanked us and said, "But, I didn't want you to hurry. Why did you rush back?" That was all that was said.

The next day, the paper was not delivered and he sent us again and told us, "Don't rush. Take your time." Well, we did take longer because he had indicated to us that he didn't want us to rush. When we got back, he thanked us again for getting the paper and told us, "But you really didn't need to rush. I told you to take your time."

The third day, he again sent us out for the paper and told us to be sure and take all the time we needed to explore everything, to be involved in whatever we wanted to do and not to get back as fast as we had the previous night.

Now, we didn't know what to do with that. We took longer because we were directed to do so. We got back with the paper. He thanked us and said, "You needn't have rushed."

On the fourth day: "Please go get the paper and just bring it back when you are ready." Well, at this point, the only thing that we wanted to do was to get back with the paper. We set a record in getting the paper back. Our behavior was modified. We had more time to do the things we wanted to do and Dad had his paper on time thereafter. I think that it was a paradoxical intervention with some use of misdirection, and it worked.

Another instance involved me alone. Dad grew up on a farm. On a farm you have chores to do. Chores are not a very positive thing to most people. In fact, the word chore gives one the impression of something undesirable. But we had chores when we were young. Dad saw that we had chores to do and he expected us to do them. He valued diligent work. One of my chores was cleaning the basement. We had a basement kitchen in the hospital building, and it collected all kinds of dirt and dust. A lot of people went through that basement and we had trouble keeping it clean. I was to clean it once a week. That was a very undesirable thing to do. Nobody wants to sweep the basement and put things in order every week, but it needed to be done.

I missed doing it. I would forget. I would be preoccupied with other things and Dad would have to get after me for not doing it, or not doing it well. I would have to repeat it. Things of this sort occurred for a while, until one day when Dad came out while I was sweeping the basement and he just stood and watched me for a little while. Now, I should have known that that meant something, but at that time I was oblivious.

After a while Dad initiated a conversation with me. He said, "Lance, have you ever noticed how this concrete floor has expansion cracks in it?" He said, "Did you ever notice the pressure cracks that are caused by the settling of the concrete? Those expansion cracks kind of look like boundaries, like perhaps the boundaries between countries." He said, "These pressure cracks, they look like rivers and tributaries of rivers." I said, "Yes, perhaps they do." He said, "Those rolls of dust and dirt that you are sweeping up, those kind of remind me of armies of soldiers marching toward the boundaries of another country." I said, "Yeah, I can see that. Perhaps they do." He said, "The rivers might be detours or barriers that you would have to move around if these were really armies." I said, "Yeah. That's true." He said one final thing: "Do you suppose if these were looked at as armies and so on, and battles took place between these rows of soldiers, that perhaps it might happen the same way each time?" I said, "Well, I don't know."

He left. I got the idea. Dad knew something at that time, that I didn't consciously realize until many years later, which was that at that point I was very interested in the Civil War. I had been reading a great deal about the various battles that occurred during the war.

Well, I really got into Dad's idea. I had all different kinds of strategies on that basement floor! I swept and I swept. I went into the patients' part of the basement and swept from there. I would go back over and sweep again because I didn't have reinforcements for the rows of soldiers.

I would say that Dad did a very good job of effecting several goals. The basement got cleaned very thoroughly each week and I enjoyed it. So that was a second instance where I think that Dad made a good intervention in my development.

I would like now to introduce my *much* younger sister, Betty Alice, who will provide you with a few insights of her own.

BETTY ALICE ERICKSON ELLIOTT

Thank you, big brother. It has been very interesting to hear the topics that my brothers and sisters have chosen and speculate as to why each of them chose that particular topic.

I know why I chose mine. I have always believed that pure bliss would be to do nothing but sleep and eat and, on a busy day, watch a bit of TV, and that's it. I have never been able to pursue this, however. And I blame it all on Daddy because he taught me to believe that you get out of life just exactly what you put into it. And I do want more out of life than just a peaceful rest.

My first recollection of Daddy instilling this attitude in me was on a trip that he and I and Allan took to Oak Creek Canyon, in the northern part of Arizona. Allan and I walked about a mile to the bottom of a wash and there we got the brilliant idea of leaving our initials. So, even though it was raining and cold, we gathered up huge boulders and we carried them to a flat place that we had swept clean, and laid out our initials on the sand. It was exhausting. In fact, if we had been ordered to walk around in the pouring rain carrying big rocks and lay them in a specific pattern, we would have protested bitterly. But we laid down all our initials and we were very proud when we finished. We climbed back up triumphantly, and showed Daddy. He took his binoculars and looked real carefully, and sure enough, he could see our initials.

On the way home, Allan and I complained about how tired we were. (Allan swears he didn't complain, but I remember him clearly complaining.) Whatever had possessed us to run around in the rain lugging big hunks of rock? Daddy laughed and he said, "Look what you've gained."

Well, what had we gained besides our initials where no one was ever going to see them? "Well," he said, "we will remember this for years. And if you were to compare the amount of effort you had expended with the amount of pleasure and the number of smiles that you would receive over the years in remembering this, you would discover that you had made a pretty wise investment."

I didn't accept this thought at the time. I thought, "Well, that's just Daddy." But it was such a novel idea that I filed it away in my head to wait and see. Well, Daddy was right. That was over 30 years ago. And the sore muscles and the skinned hands have long since faded. But that memory is still bright and clear and I have had a lot of pleasure and a lot of smiles. With that change of perspective from what something meant in the present to what something would mean in the future, I have done things which weren't what I particularly wanted to do right then, but which were things I wanted to have done when I reached the future. As I look back, I see that Daddy had many ways of giving you the idea that you get out of life what you give to life.

Many of you have been told by Daddy to climb Squaw Peak. He would say it for any number of reasons. And usually his reasons for doing so would appeal to you. Because it is there; because at the top things look different; because you have never seen a sunrise from the top of a mountain; because you can't think of a reason not to.

When I was living in Michigan, he was on a lecture tour and I wanted to go to a cocktail party that was being held. Daddy didn't, but he went to please me, and it was not very much fun. So, when we were back at the hotel, I apologized for making him go, and he was astonished. Of course he had a good time. He was very serious. If you have to do something, you might as well enjoy it while you are doing it.

Those words labeled behaviors I had been shown my whole life. Of course, we are going to have a good time. "Lean forward literally as well as figuratively. Be expectant. Be ready to recognize and meet it when it comes." Mama expects a good time and she always has one. She is always ready for it. Whether it is a trip to South America or if it is a trip to the video arcade to play Pac Man—which her grandchildren have taught her to play (she plays better than I do).

Pleasures aren't necessarily great events. A sunrise on Squaw Peak happens 365 times a year. And then there is the recapitulation of the pleasure. When I was little, Daddy always used to ask me, "What part did you like best?" To answer I would have to sort over the event, and I would discover a little more about myself and what I really liked. My own family has always played this game.

We have moved a lot and we always expect a new environment to be great, and it is. And if it has drawbacks—which it always does—when we talk about them, it is in terms of "well, that is not the part that we liked best" (which, by the way, changes the definition of a drawback).

My last example is a time when Daddy was helping me practice driving. We spent three or four days taking one-day car trips. I remember on the last day that Daddy came into my room very early to wake me up and I did not want to get up. "Please let me sleep," I begged. He gave me one of those looks that only Daddy could give and he said, "You will get up, and you will go on this trip, and you will enjoy it. You can sleep forever in 60 or 70 years, but, right now, you are going to get up and you are going to enjoy life." I have never forgotten those words. Sometimes I still say them to make myself get out of bed.

As I reread this when I was writing it, it seemed that I have leaned heavily on the things that Daddy said to me. Well, he had a gift for saying exactly the right thing at exactly the right time. Perhaps it was something that I already knew, but it was nice to have the words for it. Maybe it was a phrase or summary timed just right. He was able to redirect my perspective or to redefine a reality so clearly that I knew that I had no option. At least no option that I wanted. I know that I have used these sentences, these tactics, and ideas that I have talked about. Sometimes I even use the exact words that Daddy used, as I remember them. I have used them in my life. I have used them in my work, and I have used them with my own children. And we have all climbed Squaw Peak; I hope you have. Thank you.

The next speaker is my slightly younger brother, Allan.

ALLAN ERICKSON

I understand that I am here to speak of my childhood experiences and how I used my dad's technique in raising my own children. My own children are three beautiful girls, who are currently 11, eight, and five.

You may notice that I might stray from the subject. If you do, please remember this one item. My dad taught us all to stand up for ourselves and to be independent. Thus, I often view with amusement situations where one Erickson offspring is trying to tell another Erickson offspring what to do.

I have thought long about what I should say in my few minutes here. I have come up with the seemingly simple subject of listening. I know my dad listened well and somehow he imparted at least some of his ability to me. I am trying to impart that ability to my offspring because

I feel it is important. I must admit that I am not perfect at this "simple" skill. My wife is somewhat taken aback that *I* am speaking about listening!

I am not sure how my dad taught me this skill or even when he did. I don't even have a precise definition of what exactly I mean. However, I do remember my dad carefully *listening* and at times I can see myself carefully *listening*.

What do I mean? I mean, among other things, that when you listen to someone, you listen at their level with full attention. You never put yourself above them or belittle their thoughts. I have noticed that I have a particular way of listening to small children. I almost automatically sit on the floor. Some people think it is because I like to sit on the floor all the time. But when I go to talk to a little child, I sit down. Or if that is impractical, I lift the child to my eye level. I never seem to baby talk to them, but I do find myself thinking in a different frame of mind.

I am going to give you a few examples to further illustrate what I mean. However, before I do, I have to give you a little background about myself. My family and I have just spent three wonderful years in Australia. Now, contrary to rumor, they don't speak the same language there. Close, but it is definitely not the same! Long before I knew that I was going to speak here, I was reading one of their uniquely Australian magazines and I came across a little story that reminded me of my dad. I cut it out and saved it. When I was asked to give this talk, I remembered this story and thought it would help illustrate what I mean. I will translate it as I go along.

> "I used to have terrible nightmares everytime I cut out the check," the shearer told his mates. (Loosely translated, that means that whenever the sheep shearer used up his paycheck drinking with his friends, he had terrible nightmares.) "All sorts of horrible animals used to come out from under my bed. I told the bush carpenter about them and he fixed it up for me." "Bush psychiatrist, too, is he?" his mate asked. "Naw. Sawed the legs off the bed."

I have another example that will help illustrate my thoughts in a different way. I have been in the business of creating computer software, the programs that let you use the computer. I find it appalling how bad, and how unnecessarily hard to use, a lot of computer programs are. I was expressing this thought to my dad and said that it was very clear to me that many software developers never talked to the people who have to use their products. In fact, I have even come across program developers who refuse to talk to the user as "it might confuse them." It probably would.

Anyway, I related to my dad how software developers seemed to hold themselves above the software users and often do not want to communicate with them. I guess I expected my dad to give me some words of wisdom on how to make people listen. As he usually did, my dad told me a little story instead. It was something along these lines:

When he first started at Eloise State Hospital in Michigan, there was a man in his office who took on the task of setting up an exercise program for all the patients. He got out maps, charts and books and worked and worked. He was quite proud when he finished. He had a balanced exercise program, interspersing heavy exercise with periods of rest, good for young and old alike. However, what he really had was absolutely worthless. He had the poor souls running through buildings that didn't show on his maps, doing push-ups in swamps, etc.

It was never beneath my dad to ask anyone for advice. When he wanted to know something, he would go to the person most likely to have the information he wanted. Also, he would listen to people for the sheer pleasure of listening. I remember once my dad was talking to the store clerk about something. He was carefully listening to the answers before asking the next question. Even though I was a typical, self-centered 15-year-old, barely aware of external stimuli, it was very obvious to me that the clerk was telling my dad a great deal, much much more than he realized.

I will finish with kind of a flippant remark that I think kind of sums up the way my dad felt about listening: If you want to know how to protect your bank against a robbery, you ask all the bank robbers you can find.

Next, Robert, my younger brother.

ROBERT B. ERICKSON

As a parent I frequently find myself using techniques which I observed my father using. One particular technique which many of you may already be familiar with concerned an incident which involved me as a youngster. This incident was repeatedly used by my father in his teaching tales. I thought it might interest you to hear this teaching tale from the subject's point of view—that is, mine. So I would like to explain how his treatment affected me personally from my vantage point as an adult.

The incident occurred when I was not quite four years old. I had fallen down the back steps of our house, split my lip, and knocked a front tooth into my maxilla. I was bleeding profusely and screaming out of both pain and fright. Both my mother and father responded to my cries. My father's first step to aid me was to establish effective communication with me. As I paused between screams, my father said, "It hurts, Robert, it hurts real bad. It hurts." At that very moment he had established a bond of rapport between us. He was agreeing with me by telling me, "It hurts." My father had convinced me that I could trust his diagnosis. The injury was painful and his acknowledgment of that fact convinced me that he knew. . . . "It hurt!"

Perhaps this step seems obvious, but many parents frequently compound such a crisis by not responding properly to a child's need for comfort and attention. An example comes to mind in which the opposite response was applied. It involved one of my younger sisters as a preschooler. She had suffered a somewhat painful but minor injury and was crying loudly. The adult in charge at that time, in order to console my sister, said something to the effect of, "There, there now—that didn't really hurt, did it?" To which my preschool sister stopped sobbing long enough to interject, "It did too hurt! Stupid!" And then my sister continued crying after having been further traumatized and frustrated by being told, "You're wrong, it doesn't hurt," when, in fact, she knew she was experiencing pain.

As for my own case, when my father agreed with me, I realized that he clearly understood the pain I was experiencing, so I was ready to listen. My father had established credibility with me.

My father then continued speaking to me explaining the reality of which I was becoming aware. "It hurts, and it will keep right on hurting," he said. I was in total agreement with this statement because he was right. It was still hurting. Then between sobs I heard him say, "And you really wish it would stop hurting," and again he was right. After additional sobs my father offered the suggestion, "And maybe it will stop hurting after a little while." The suggestion was clearly made and it was what I desired, so I continued to listen.

I was willing to listen because he understood the pain I was experiencing. And because of his sharing of that knowledge, it seemed to me that we were sharing the pain. That is, the degree of pain was being psychologically reduced. It was at this point that I had my first lesson in how to control pain. In other words, my father was teaching me to concentrate on the end goal of comfort rather than the present state of pain.

The next step my parents took to aid me was to get me into the house in order to examine and fully assess my injury. They wanted me, as well, to fully assess and understand the extent of my injury.

These steps I consider of great importance. I was able to first look at the injury in a mirror. I was then able to touch the wound and understand that it was part of me. And, most importantly, I was able to *realize* or *see the reality*—my injury, which still hurt. But as the moments passed, the pain decreased, because I didn't really want the pain to last. The pain seemed to decrease because I had been provided with all of the information that a child of that age needed in order to cope with the injury.

As my wound was being cleaned, my father further enhanced my knowledge of both my wound and of my situation. He commented on the blood that I had lost on the pavement. He pointed out that there had been "a lot of blood," which I had likewise perceived. He stated that it "was good strong red blood," which then "mixed with water would turn pink," and so it did as the wound was being washed. I was being taught several important concepts. I was examining reality. I was learning that my blood was good and that the swelling of my lip was right and that the bleeding was natural and right. Thus I could see and understand all that was taking place before me.

I was then taken to a doctor for the suturing of the lip. My father had led me to understand that this suturing was an integral part of the healing process and that, more importantly to a youngster, suturing was another step in making what pain remained, subside. In other words, as a child, I was given the impression that suturing would "fix me up." My father, explaining the need for the stitches, told me that my wound was small and that I would not be able to have as many stitches as some of my older siblings had had in their previous injuries. But he told me that I would have more stitches than some of my other older siblings had had in their injuries. That was very important to me. My father had made it possible for me to share with my siblings a common experience. He was also giving me an opportunity to express sibling rivalry in a positive and healthy manner.

My father then suggested that I count the stitches as they were being made. I did this and it made me feel important. Because I knew that I was further involved in the experiencing and the understanding of this initially painful crisis. As I counted the seventh and final suture, I felt that I was an important part of the healing process. My father had allowed me to take charge of the situation.

So, from this experience, my father taught me that it is important for the adult dealing with an injured child to be as truthful as realistically possible. He taught me never to attempt to falsify or to trivialize physical pain—rather, to present a clear and understandable reality to the child so that the child can take charge as soon as possible.

I will now pass the microphone to my younger sister, Roxie.

ROXANNA ERICKSON KLEIN

The topic I have selected is the balance of giving, sharing and receiving.

Due to the broad nature of the topic, I want to begin by emphasizing that Dad and Mom nearly always agreed on concepts of child-rearing. I credit them with being equally responsible for our childhood experiences and the way we each have grown. The memories that I have are not merely interactions with Daddy, but of interactions in which Mama played a significant part.

Every individual must learn the interaction skills of giving, receiving and sharing. The balance of, and the ability to derive pleasure from, each of these experiences is an individual quality that is learned. Parents role-model their values to their children, and create situations so that the offspring will have opportunities to experience these interactions. The balance of giving, sharing, and receiving is stressed differently within different individuals, different cultures, and different situations. Over time, a healthy child learns that all three can be pleasant experiences. Striking a balance that blends with the expectations and opportunities of society is a challenge.

I feel that our parents dealt with this issue by placing an emphasis on sharing, and I have selected three illustrations to demonstrate how the pleasures of sharing were instilled in me.

The first took place in 1954. I was about five years old at the time. On weekends, the family used to take a drive out to the desert. On these excursions, we would all find "pretty rocks" which we would bring home. Each of us kids had our own collection of rocks. That year, my oldest brother, Bert, completed construction of a fish pond in the backyard. He reached the stage where the cement was setting, and we had a triumphant family gathering to admire it. At that time, a decision was made for each of us to donate our most beautiful specimens from our rock collections. We eagerly ran to our collections and selected our most prized specimens. Robert even donated some of his favorite marbles which we pressed into the cement. After all, they deserved to be displayed in a setting where they could be appreciated by everyone.

The second illustration took place in 1967. I had just graduated from high school and was eager to find a summer job. I was disappointed to learn how tight the job market was, but the disappointment didn't last long. Daddy called me into his office to offer his advice. "Wasn't I lucky to have not yet found a job. Mama had just become aware of a position where I was truly needed. Not only would I derive the satisfaction of knowing how much I was really wanted and appreciated, but a summer's work as a volunteer would be an invaluable asset to my resumé. I would have the additional benefits of setting my hours at convenient times, and of taking off a week if I chose to go on vacation."

I snapped up that opportunity to be a volunteer at Head Start, and even recruited Kristi and a girlfriend to join me.

The third illustration is not a memory, but an ongoing experience. It is how I share the values I hold with my children. Because my children are young—the oldest is four years old—the techniques are very basic. However, these few points might illustrate the concepts that I am trying to express:

1) If one of my children draws a "beautiful" picture, we often either give it to someone, or mail it to someone. (This serves the additional purpose of keeping my house clear of some of this excess.)
2) If one receives a treat, I inquire, "Are you going to share that?" expressing my expectation that, of course, they are going to want to share it.
3) For lunch I make one sandwich for the two older children. One gets to cut it in half and the other gets first choice of which half he or she will take.
4) I encourage participation in planning special events for each other. For example, for my daughter's birthday, my son Ethan, who is two years old, helped wrap all of Laurel's birthday gifts.

In conclusion, we all learn the skills of giving, sharing, and receiving. Mom and Dad both seemed to get the most pleasure from sharing. I think we all do too, or else we probably wouldn't be here.

Now I will introduce my youngest sister, Kristi. She is the youngest in the family.

KRISTINA K. ERICKSON

As my brothers and sisters have indicated, a prominent feature of our particular home setting was my parents' support of one another. Without my mother and her warm and loving but strong support of my father and the entire family, I believe that my father would not have achieved the level of success and accomplishment that he did achieve, both professionally and in his family life.

A theory behind the therapeutic techniques of my father's work that I have come to most appreciate was his frequent reduction of therapy to basic and fundamental interventions. The intervention may appear so simple and basic that a patient or, in our case, the children, did not perceive it as therapy. Furthermore, when a problem is solved with this type of straightforward management, a patient often will not give recognition to his or her therapist for the treatment.

It can be disconcerting to some therapists to see their very carefully prescribed but simplistic therapy achieve success and find a patient stating that the therapist is a nice person but really didn't help much and, besides, the problem is all gone and he doesn't need to see him anymore.

Actually, this reaction used to delight my father. He thought that it was funny. I once asked him about it and he said, "Well, once the problem is solved, that's the goal, and who cares who gets the credit." Well, I was young and I cared then, but it's a good philosophy.

The key to simplistic and practical therapy that I came to appreciate is that ultimately and obviously it is extremely complex. It just looks easy when it is well done. My father did it very well. But by the time that I knew him, he had had a lot of practice.

In terms of child management, these simplistic techniques reflect the philosophy of child rearing that I feel is present in my home. I feel this is nonpunitive, constructive and educational.

On the part of therapists and parents, utilizing these techniques requires thought, imagination and versatility. Children can be challenging to manage. My mom used to say that children enjoy stirring up the world because they don't have a lot of other things on their schedule. My mom also used to say that though a child might be intellectually smarter than she was, by virtue of years and experience she was wiser and therefore she would be able to manage the child.

I will briefly present some methods which demonstrate how some of the simplistic therapeutic techniques that I learned from my father may be used in child-rearing and management.

The first technique I have entitled "practicing." I do a lot of this. This can be utilized to manage some of the classic behavior of children which can cause strife in a home, such as carelessness and inattentiveness.

For example, consider when a child leaves toys and games scattered after playing with them. Simplified, the problem is responsibility. Your goal is to have the child assume responsibility for his possessions without imposing on others. In a matter-of-fact way, you explain to young Timmy that you notice he has some difficulty in putting away the Monopoly game. So this morning he will need to devote two hours to *practicing* putting away the Monopoly game. You further clarify that different people require different amounts of practice time to learn skills in different areas. You are confident that he will be able to master the skill, but are uncertain if two hours will be adequate time to practice and really learn to do it well. Dad was always willing to let us practice again if we needed it.

We all experienced *practicing* and my dad was always enthusiastic about it. He always felt that we would catch on; we could take our time. But emphasized in this is a principle that he did teach in child rearing, which is that when you don't care, the struggle is over. Sometimes children don't put away their toys and games, and that is because they forget and that's OK. But sometimes it becomes a power issue and a means of instigating arguments. If you don't care, you end the struggle.

If you really don't care that little Mary is spending three hours learning to hang up her blouses neatly and, on the contrary, you are pleased that she has the opportunity to practice and master the skill, Mary will most likely not involve herself in a power struggle by leaving her blouses on the floor. After all, if she does, she will not anger you; she will only invite some practice time. And if you really don't care, she may as well hang them up right and be done with it.

This "I really don't care" attitude is very hard for many parents to assume. This was not hard for my father to assume. I never felt he minded if I spent a hundred hours *practicing* things. He was always pleased and hoped I was enjoying myself.

You must also sometimes feel that the parent will be sorry for the child who misses softball practice because he is *practicing* making his bed. Again, my dad never felt sorry for us. In fact, he would tell us what a great time they had without you. Such a shame you couldn't come. I think Mom felt sorry for us a little bit now and then. But, too bad, she agreed anyway.

Therapists may consider suggesting to parents that they give this method a trial and try to really not care for a few weeks. Reassure them that practicing making a bed for three hours has never caused illness, death, or permanent disability and that the child will have a choice in these matters. After all, if he does it right, he won't be *practicing*.

I call another quite simplistic and related tactic the "inconvenience" method. Jay Haley clearly made reference to this in his Keynote Address when he talked about ordeal therapy. The most frequently used inconvenience method, for myself and for my sister, who shared my room, was the middle-of-the-night routine. There we would be in bed and since we shared the room, if it involved one, the other would be included.

We would be all warm and cozy in bed. The lights would flip on. There would be Dad. He had just noticed that the wheelbarrow and rake I had used that day were in the middle of the backyard instead of in the garage where they belonged. Such a problem. Looks like I would need to get up and go put them away. So here you would drag yourself out of bed, haul yourself out to the backyard, put away the stuff, drag yourself to bed, while your sister is over there going, "Are you kidding? Again!"

In the future, I did not forget to put tools away after I used them. Who wants to get up at midnight? The other thing was that I wasn't mad at Dad about this. After all, it made sense. I knew I was supposed to put tools away after I used them. I did sometimes offer, "Well, I'll do that tomorrow. First thing, I'll get up and run out there and . . . no problem, Dad." And Dad would say, "No. You see, because that is not a choice." He would say, "You were supposed to put them away then and since you didn't, I guess you will do it now." And I guess we did.

Somebody questioned what to do if there is still continued refusal and argument. Obviously, then you would have a family situation where other interventions and counseling are warranted and these methods may not be applicable or may be applicable only interwoven with other therapy.

Both these techniques require imagination and versatility. If one variation doesn't work, you can think up another. It is amazing how simplistic it is if you look at the problem and reduce it to "what is the goal?" If the goal is to have the child learn to make the bed properly without argument, then you can reduce it to a simplistic way to deal with it without argument.

If you need a little thinking time, it is acceptable to tell the child, "You know, you seem to have trouble remembering to feed the dog. I will think over how to help you manage this responsibility." Sometimes you can add on the phrase, "Perhaps you have some suggestions." Often a child will come up with suggestions. We would come up with suggestions, because sometimes we felt ours would be better than Dad's, because who knew what Dad would come up with. Plus, these statements are a preliminary notice that the issue is diffused, it is no longer a power struggle, and it is going to be managed in a new way.

Some parents raise the question of whether practicing and doing things at an inconvenient time lead a child to developing a dislike of, or an aversion to, the task in question. I really don't think this is a problem and I believe the reason that it is not a problem is that punishment and power are not really the issues. The emphasis is that responsibility and choice revert to the child. It is the child's choice whether he or she has to practice more or less and I don't think that an aversion develops. Plus these methods are self-reinforcing as arguments in families disappear and more time emerges to be spent for pleasant interaction rather than arguing.

In summary, I have discussed methods which emphasize simplicity and practicality in dealing with some of the management problems in child-rearing. Solutions to a problem can be designed in a logical, practical fashion. You can remove anger and frustration and irritation from the issues.

When my father would deal with us, I never really felt he was angry or frustrated. He was problem-solving. There would be a problem and he would help you solve it. Sometimes you would figure this would make a problem for Dad, and you would solve it ahead of time on your own. As you remove some of these arguments and struggles and interactions of a negative nature, then time for positive interaction is provided.

Also intrinsic are the concepts of independence, turning the choice back to children to enhance self-reliance, to make them accept responsibility and dependability. Importantly, self-confidence and pride are preserved and emerge from these concepts. Appreciation and enjoyment of life also can be cultivated into chores and other activities of everyday living. Phrases can be incorporated into your interactions with children to give them awareness of life and its enjoyment as they do their activities.

My father helped me have an awareness and an appreciation of life. He might comment with a type of phrase which was typical of what he would do with us. He would say, "As a child feeds his dog, he can enjoy seeing the dog play, and grow, and be strong because he has food." And he might comment that a child might take pleasure in learning to control a pen so that his writing is smooth and neat and legible. The small things in life can be seen as pleasurable. In addition, as Betty Alice pointed out, one adjusts to enjoying one's surroundings and circumstances.

I feel that my father was, and my mother continues to be, expert at finding enjoyment in any situation or circumstance. Thank you.

BETTY ALICE

I think it is significant that each of us chose, without consulting the others, a different topic and we each had a different way of presenting it. I think it illustrates well a prime premise of Ericksonian thought. Daddy knew that techniques and tactics must be varied for the individual and carefully thought out in order to be effective.

We have a few minutes left for questions from the floor.

Q: Lance, why do you think that the newspaper reversal that he did was effective for you?

Lance: It was a confusion or misdirection kind of technique on his part because we were clearly very used to a situation where he was unhappy when we came back late. When he told us to take more time, we couldn't understand that because he had never said that before. He had always urged us to get the paper back as quickly as possible and when he completely reversed his position on that, it left us up in the air a little bit. We were nine, 10, 11 or 12 at the time, and he did not explain anything to us. He just presented the situation to us. Please go get the paper and take your time about it. Well, we couldn't comprehend what he was trying to do.

Q: What impact did Dr. Erickson have on your professions?

Betty Alice: I worked in special education with children with emotional problems and, of course, the things that I learned growing up were invaluable.

Lance: I would say that he merely allowed me to go in the directions that I seemed to find most appropriate for me. He gave me permission to explore and to go into an area that I wanted. I never got signals from Dad that I should do this or I should do that. It was really left up to me. He encouraged the directions that I seemed to have an interest in, whether it was reading about the Civil War, gardening, geology, or whatever else.

Allan: He influenced me in a couple of ways. First, when I was in grade school and high school, I would say to my friends, like most kids do, "What are you going to be when you grow up?" Each of my friends would have his own thing. My friend would say, "Oh, I'm going to be a carpenter." And I would say, "Why?" "Because my dad's a carpenter." I would come out with my own thing, but I never did say I wanted to be a psychiatrist. I always wanted to do my own thing. My father encouraged that. I am very happy that he did because I don't think that I would have been that good a psychiatrist.

He also influenced me to have the attitude that when you do something, you do it well. It is not worth doing it sloppy; therefore, you have got to do the things that you are good at. So you do the things that you are good at and you do them well, and you'll be happy.

Robert: I am an educator. I feel that he taught me a great deal that I incorporate in my teaching, using some of these very methods that we have been talking about right here. When my peers would ask me, "What are you going to be when you grow up?" I would tell them whatever was popular as an answer. My father was always supportive of allowing me to be myself.

Roxie: Well, I am a registered nurse and I think the most important way that he influenced my thinking in terms of how it affects my work is that he taught me there are multiple ways to approach any problem and there are multiple correct ways. And if one approach doesn't work, you have a lot of others to fall back on and a whole bunch of different routes to follow.

Kristi: I'm a physician and I am in family practice. I can use my father's techniques in my work and I have found them to be incredibly helpful. However, in terms of what he wanted me to be when I grew up, I always felt that what he wanted me to be was to be somebody who was productive, enjoyed her work and did a good job, and it didn't matter what it was. As long as you did a good job and were productive and took care of yourself, it really didn't matter what you chose, so he really didn't influence me to become a doctor. It was more, "Do a good job at something."